THE SVĀTANTRIKA-PRĀSAṄGIKA DISTINCTION

Studies in Indian and Tibetan Buddhism

THIS SERIES WAS CONCEIVED to provide a forum for publishing outstanding new contributions to scholarship on Indian and Tibetan Buddhism and also to make accessible seminal research not widely known outside a narrow specialist audience, including translations of appropriate monographs and collections of articles from other languages. The series strives to shed light on the Indic Buddhist traditions by exposing them to historical-critical inquiry, illuminating through contextualization and analysis these traditions' unique heritage and the significance of their contribution to the world's religious and philosophical achievements.

STUDIES IN INDIAN AND TIBETAN BUDDHISM

THE SVĀTANTRIKA-PRĀSAṄGIKA DISTINCTION

What Difference Does a Difference Make?

Edited by Georges B. J. Dreyfus
and Sara L. McClintock

WISDOM PUBLICATIONS • BOSTON

Wisdom Publications
199 Elm Street
Somerville, Massachusetts 02144 USA
www.wisdompubs.org

Library of Congress Cataloging-in-Publication Data
The Svatantrika-Prasangika distinction : what difference does a difference make? / edited by Georges B.J. Dreyfus, and Sara L. McClintock
p. cm.
Includes bibliographical references and index.
ISBN 0-86171-324-9 (alk. paper)
1. Svātantrika. 2. Prāsaṅgika 3. Mādhyamika (Buddhism)—China—Tibet. I. Dreyfus, Georges II. McClintock, Sara L.
BQ7478. S73 2002
294.3'92—dc21 2002151800

07 06 05 04 03
5 4 3 2 1

Designed by Gopa and Ted2

Wisdom Publications' books are printed on acid-free paper and meet the guidelines for permanence and durability set by the Committee on Production Guidelines for Book Longevity of the Council on Library Resources.

Printed in the United States

Table of Contents

Publisher's Acknowledgment

The Publisher gratefully acknowledges the generous help of the Hershey Family Foundation in sponsoring the publication of this book.

Acknowledgments

The editors of this volume wish gratefully to acknowledge David Kittelstrom and the editorial team at Wisdom Publications for their careful work on this book. We would also like to acknowledge Chris Haskett and Chizuko Yoshimizu for their respective help in checking Tibetan and Japanese terms and names. Finally, we wish to acknowledge with deepest thanks John Dunne for his generous and unflagging assistance during the final stages of the production of this book.

Introduction

An Unusual Doxographical Distinction

ONE OF THE CONTRIBUTING factors to the recent growth of Madhyamaka studies has been the discovery by modern scholars of the rich Tibetan tradition. Contact with contemporary Tibetan scholars and their enormous learning, clarity, and sophistication has provided an invaluable resource in many areas of Buddhist studies, particularly in the study of Madhyamaka philosophy. Such a development is certainly most welcome. It is only fitting that this great scholarly tradition receive due recognition. The appreciation of Tibetan sources and their use in the elucidation of Madhyamaka is not, however, without complication, for it introduces in the study of classical Buddhist texts terms and distinctions not used by the original Indian thinkers.

The Svātantrika-Prāsaṅgika distinction *(thal rang gyi khyad par)* provides one of the clearest examples of such a difficulty. This distinction has become widespread in the secondary literature on Madhyamaka, and on Indian philosophy more generally. It is current nowadays to find references to *Prāsaṅgika philosophy* and *Svātantrika philosophy,* as if these were self-evident and unproblematic categories on a par with other doxographical distinctions. Likewise, one frequently encounters statements to the effect that Candrakīrti (7th c.) and Bhāvaviveka (6th c.) are the respective founders of the Prāsaṅgika and the Svātantrika schools.[1] The present volume, an outgrowth of a panel on the topic at a meeting of the International Association of Buddhist Studies in Lausanne in 1999, is an attempt to scrutinize more critically this doxographical distinction, clarifying and highlighting its problematic nature as well as suggesting arguments that may stand in support of it.

At the start of this project, it is important to recognize the clear limitations of doxographical distinctions in general. Labels such as *Madhyamaka* and *Yogācāra* need to be understood as hermeneutical devices intended to bring order to a wide variety of individual texts and ideas. As such, they cannot be taken as providing anything more than useful but limited guidelines in the interpretation of discrete works. Consider, for example, that it is not possible to infer the contents of a particular text based on its accepted membership in a given doxographical category.[2] Nevertheless, despite their inherent lack of precision, doxographical categories may be helpful when used with caution. Certainly, they have the support of a long lineage of traditional commentators, with roots going back early in the history of the traditions they describe. In the case of Madhyamaka, for example, the main Mādhyamikas, at least after Bhāvaviveka, knew themselves as such, and the term has since been used by a lengthy succession of thinkers, who understood it, for the most part, in relatively similar ways.[3]

As we believe this volume amply attests, the distinction between Prāsaṅgika and Svātantrika is quite different, being much more problematic than other doxographical distinctions used in the study of the classical Indian Buddhist tradition. Put otherwise, the terms *Prāsaṅgika* and *Svātantrika* are not on a par with terms such as *Madhyamaka* or *Yogācāra.* In part, this is simply because, as Tibetan scholars themselves recognize, the Svātantrika-Prāsaṅgika distinction is a Tibetan creation that was retroactively applied in an attempt to bring clarity and order to the study of competing Indian Madhyamaka interpretations. Granted, in creating new doxographical distinctions, Tibetan interpreters were not doing anything particularly unusual. Indeed, they were following a venerable Buddhist tradition going back at least to Bhāvaviveka, who seems to have been the first to use doxographical categories in his systematic presentation of Buddhist philosophy.[4] His successors continued this task, creating further distinctions to capture the differences among Mādhyamikas and other Buddhists.

In India, however, it appears that the most basic division in the study of Madhyamaka interpretations was not a distinction between the views of Bhāvaviveka and those of Candrakīrti. Rather, the basic division was between those—such as Bhāvaviveka and Candrakīrti—who accepted external objects conventionally and those—such as Śāntarakṣita and Kamalaśīla (8th c.)—who argued for an interpretation of conventional reality similar to the Yogācāra in which external objects do not exist. This distinction, which unlike the Svātantrika-Prāsaṅgika distinction places Bhāvaviveka and Candrakīrti in the same camp, may have its root in the famous debate between Dharmapāla and Bhāvaviveka alleged to have taken place at Nālandā,[5] In any case, it was well established in the later Indian Madhyamaka tradition.[6] Even as late an author as Atiśa (11th c.) uses it, classifying on its basis both Candrakīrti and Bhāvaviveka as authoritative interpreters of Nāgārjuna.[7] Other late Indian doxographical divisions of Madhyamaka, such as the distinction between the Māyopamādvayavādins (*sgyu ma lta bur gnyis su med par smra ba,* lit., those who hold the nondual to be like an illusion) and the Sarvadharmāpratiṣṭhānavādins (*chos thams cad rab tu mi gnas par smra ba,* lit., those who hold that all things are unestablished), are connected variously to different thinkers, but there seems to be no conspicuous parallel to the Svātantrika-Prāsaṅgika distinction as it was later applied in Tibet.[8]

As Tibetans like Tsong kha pa (1357–1419) were fully aware, it was only later, during the eleventh or twelfth century, that Tibetan scholars coined the terms *Rang rgyud pa* and *Thal 'gyur ba* on the basis of passages in Candrakīrti's *Prasannapadā* (PPMV) that seem to indicate significant divergences in Madhyamaka interpretations.[9] These terms, which were eventually Sanskritized by modern scholars as *Svātantrika* and *Prāsaṅgika,* may well have been invented by the Tibetan translator Pa tshab nyi ma grags (1055–1145?) in the course of his work as a translator of Candrakīrti's texts.[10] But whoever invented them, we know that it is around this time that the terms first became important categories in Madhyamaka exegesis and that Candrakīrti's interpretation, described with increasing frequency as the Prāsaṅgika view, became established as preeminent in Tibet over what was understood to be Bhāvaviveka's inferior Svātantrika view.[11] It is perhaps surprising that Pa tshab and others chose to single out Candrakīrti as Nāgārjuna's most important interpreter, for available evidence suggests that Candrakīrti's place in the history of Indian Buddhism had been rather limited up to that point. As far as we know, his works have rarely been quoted by other Indian scholars, and it is only in the eleventh century that Jayānanda wrote the first known commentary (apart from Candrakīrti's own) on his *Madhyamakāvatāra* (MAv). It may be that the later period of Indian Buddhism saw an increase in Candrakīrti's popularity among scholars in India. Atiśa seems to have valued him highly, although, as we noted, he did not separate his view from that of Bhāvaviveka. Alternatively, Pa tshab's choice may simply have reflected the historical accident of his association with Jayānanda, one of Candrakīrti's few Indian partisans.

The late and retrospective nature of the Svātantrika-Prāsaṅgika distinction, as well as its apparent non-Indian provenance, together signal its unusual status as a doxographical category that should render us cautious about its use in the interpretation of Indian material. By themselves, however, these qualities do not warrant rejection of the distinction. The mere fact that the

Indian authors themselves were not cognizant of being Svātantrika or Prāsaṅgika and that it is only later Tibetan exegetes who thought of them as such is not enough to disqualify these descriptions. There is no problem in principle in retrospectively applying a description to an author even if he or she never conceived of it. For is this not what interpretation is largely about? As Gadamer puts it, "we understand in a different way if we understand at all."[12]

In our case, the fact that Candrakīrti might not have understood himself to be establishing a new school does not preclude describing his view as Prāsaṅgika, though it does place a heavier burden of proof upon the interpreter who embraces that description. It requires that the use of the term (and its counterpart, Svātantrika) be well grounded in an analysis of the original texts. Such analysis, however, is not easy. As is revealed in this volume, Tibetan scholars, far from being unanimous in their understanding of the distinction, have been and continue to be bitterly divided over the Svātantrika-Prāsaṅgika distinction. If at least there were some degree of unity in their understanding of the terms, it might be possible to examine this understanding, consider the reasons behind the use of the terms, and then decide whether or not they apply to the original Indian sources. Unfortunately, the reality is much more complex. Whereas Tsong kha pa, the founder of what later became known as the dGe lugs pa school and the most ardent proponent of the distinction, argues that the two subschools are separated by crucial philosophical differences, including a different understanding of emptiness and of conventional reality, many other Tibetan commentators have tended to downplay the significance of any differences. Bu ston rin chen grub (1290–1364), for example, goes as far as to claim that this distinction is an artificial Tibetan conceptual creation *(bod kyi rtog bzo)* without much merit.[13] For him, no substantive issue divides the two sides; instead, the difference can be reduced to two particular styles of exegesis in relation to Nāgārjuna's *Mūlamadhyamakakārikā* (MMK), with no implications for philosophical differences whatsoever. Indeed, the Tibetan tradition is so deeply divided over the meaning of the Svātantrika-Prāsaṅgika distinction that there is even dispute about whether the distinction has legitimacy at all.

The highly contested nature of this distinction, like its status as late and retroactively applied, also does not in itself disqualify its use. Many important terms are used despite being contested, and such use is frequently quite legitimate. At the same time, however, the contentious nature of the distinction does require anyone choosing to employ these terms to make a strong effort at clarifying how he or she understands them. One temptation to be resisted at all costs is the use of the terms Prāsaṅgika and Svātantrika as if they referred to well-established and self-evident Indian subschools (avoiding this use is not as easy to achieve as it sounds). In fact, most of the time what are really indicated by these terms are not Indian subschools per se but rather particular Tibetan interpretations of Indian Madhyamaka, interpretations that are often interesting and well-informed but not necessarily accurate and nearly always a matter of great dispute. Thus, far from having any degree of transparency, immediacy, or even clarity, the Svātantrika-Prāsaṅgika distinction is highly problematic and in great need of clarification.

To meet this challenge, we have solicited contributions to this volume along two distinct avenues of inquiry. The first proceeds through an examination of the basic Indian texts that are supposed to be relevant to the Svātantrika-Prāsaṅgika distinction, seeking clues as to whether and in what ways the distinction can be said to apply. This avenue is explored in the first part of the book, where the reader will find articles examining the works of some of the great Indian Madhyamaka commentators such as Bhāvaviveka, Candrakīrti, Śāntarakṣita, Kamalaśīla, and Jñānagarbha in light of the Svātantrika-Prāsaṅgika distinction and some of the issues that it raises. The second avenue of inquiry attempts to clarify a variety of Tibetan views concerning the distinction, seeking to sort out the role that the distinction plays in the thought of various figures in Tibetan Madhyamaka. This avenue is explored in the second part of the book, in which the contributors examine the ideas of such pivotal Tibetan philosophers as Phya pa chos kyi seng ge (1109–1169), Go rams pa bsod nams seng ge (1429–1489), and Tsong kha pa. This second part of the book concludes with a consideration of the views of a recent eclectic Tibetan thinker, 'Ju Mi pham rgya mtsho (1846–1912), whose efforts to reconcile the conflicting Tibetan interpretations help to bring out their complexities.

Although these two endeavors—the analysis of Indian sources and the exploration of Tibetan interpretations—may be conceived as discrete, they are not and cannot be entirely separate. That is, because the Svātantrika-Prāsaṅgika distinction is a Tibetan creation, any investigation of it in relation to the Indian materials necessarily proceeds through questions raised by Tibetan concerns. Hence all of the contributions dealing with Indian sources, to greater or lesser extent, analyze their texts in the light of concepts provided by later Tibetan intellectuals. Likewise, because the distinction was created vis-à-vis Indian sources and as a means to classify Indian thought, any investigation of the distinction in the Tibetan context necessarily requires a degree of direct consideration of the Indian texts. Thus all of the articles on Tibetan thinkers refer to the Indian sources, even when the focus is not on the Indian sources per se but rather on the Tibetan interpretations of those sources. Ultimately the question of the Svātantrika-Prāsaṅgika distinction cannot be adequately addressed without both angles of inquiry, and it is for this reason that a collected volume, with contributions from specialists of the Buddhism on both sides of the Himalayan divide, was conceived as offering the greatest potential for making some headway in understanding this unusual and difficult doxographical distinction.

Part 1: Examining the Distinction in the Indian Tradition

In pursuing the first avenue of inquiry and considering the views of some of the central Indian Mādhyamikas, the first five contributors to this volume lay out the basis for a critical examination of the Svātantrika-Prāsaṅgika distinction and raise the fundamental questions of this work. Does the Svātantrika-Prāsaṅgika distinction apply to the Indian Madhyamaka tradition? Does it help us to understand its complexities? And if it does, how should the distinction be drawn? Is the Svātantrika-Prāsaṅgika distinction based on deep substantive and philosophical issues as Tsong kha pa and others assert, or is it based merely on methodological and pragmatic considerations as asserted by Go rams pa, Shākya mchog ldan, and others? The first contributions examine these questions in relation to the works of Bhāvaviveka, Candrakīrti, Śāntarakṣita, Kamalaśīla, and Jñānagarbha. Although all these essays deal with the same questions, they often come to rather startlingly different conclusions. This disagreement reflects the individual perspectives of the authors, but also signals the highly contested nature of the Svātantrika-Prāsaṅgika distinction itself.

The volume begins with a contribution by William Ames, who turns his attention to the genesis of the controversy in which the differences that later Tibetan scholars consider crucial to the Svātantrika-Prāsaṅgika distinction initially emerge. The controversy gets under way when Bhāvaviveka in his commentary on Nāgārjuna's MMK, the *Prajñāpradīpa* (PrP), criticizes his predecessor Buddhapālita (5th c.) for failing to present formal probative arguments *(prayoga, sbyor ba)* encapsulating Nāgārjuna's arguments. Responding to this critique, Candrakīrti comes to Buddhapālita's defense and strongly rebukes Bhāvaviveka for his insistence on the use of formal probative arguments, known also as *autonomous arguments (svatantraprayoga, rang rgyud kyi sbyor ba).* On Candrakīrti's view, for Mādhyamikas debating about the ultimate with non-Mādhyamikas such arguments are improper, as they require a commitment to natures *(svabhāva, rang bzhin)* that contradicts the core insights of Madhyamaka thought. Instead of formal probative proof statements, Mādhyamikas should restrict themselves to arguments that proceed from the opponent's own premises, either through a consequence *(prasaṅga, thal 'gyur)* or through an inference whose elements are accepted by the opponent alone *(gzhan grags kyi rjes dpag, *paraprasiddhānumāna).*[14] According to later tradition, Bhāvaviveka can thus be seen as the founder of the Svātantrika stream of Madhyamaka, while Candrakīrti should be recognized as the father of the Prāsaṅgika school.

Ames' contribution focuses exclusively on the first element of this debate, namely, Bhāvaviveka's critique of Buddhapālita. In his article, Ames seeks primarily to answer a single question: what is Bhāvaviveka's own view of his criticism of Buddhapālita? As we have seen, some later interpreters have held that the Svātantrika-Prāsaṅgika distinction is not simply a matter of a different mode of presenting Madhyamaka thought but implies a difference in philosophical outlook that is not easily reconciled. Ames seeks to discover whether Bhāvaviveka's criticism of Buddhapālita was intended also to convey a critique of Buddhapālita's understanding of Madhyamaka doctrine, or whether the critique is in fact concerned only with philosophical method. After providing a useful historical and philosophical introduction to Madhyamaka, Ames proceeds through a close examination of a number of passages in which Bhāvaviveka cites and attacks Buddhapālita's commentary. The most significant and recurrent criticism in these passages concerns Buddhapālita's failure to employ Indian syllogisms or formal probative arguments in the exegesis of Nāgārjuna's root text. As Ames amply demonstrates, Bhāvaviveka holds that it is imperative for Mādhyamika commentators to keep up with the new developments in Indian logic and to use the tools of formal probative arguments that had been recently developed by Dignāga, the founder of the Buddhist logico-epistemological tradition.

Although it is not entirely clear what motivates Bhāvaviveka's insistence on the use of autonomous arguments, we discover in Ames' contribution that it may have something to do with Bhāvaviveka's understanding of the role of a commentator in explicating the highly condensed, aphoristic statements of the master Nāgārjuna. That is, Bhāvaviveka appears to hold that, while the master may legitimately avoid expressing his views through autonomous arguments, his pithy statements and *prasaṅga*-style presentations nevertheless do *imply* such arguments, and it is the job of the commentator to draw these out and make them explicit. On this reading, every *prasaṅga* argument implies a formal probative autonomous argument through a process of "reversing the consequence," *(prasaṅgaviparyaya, thal bzlog pa)*[15] and by neglecting to present these autonomous arguments explicitly, Buddhapālita fails to elucidate the master's intention. Since, apart from the exceptionally intelligent, most persons cannot be expected to understand the master's intention through the aphorisms alone, a commentator who fails to draw out the implied autonomous arguments from the *prasaṅgas* in the root verses thereby fails in his duties as a commentator as well, at least on Bhāvaviveka's view.

In his analysis of Bhāvaviveka's criticism of Buddhapālita, Ames observes that the former has probably treated the latter somewhat unfairly. That is, in considering Nāgārjuna's *prasaṅga* arguments, Bhāvaviveka tends to portray them as implying autonomous arguments that demonstrate pure or nonimplicative negations *(prasajyapratiṣedha),* whereas he invariably casts the *prasaṅga* arguments of Buddhapālita as implying autonomous arguments that demonstrate a so-called implicative negation *(paryudāsa),* in which the opposite of the original *prasaṅga* argument is affirmed. Ames finds no grounds on which to support this hermeneutical shift in the interpretation of *prasaṅga,* and remarks as well on the apparent arbitrariness of Bhāvaviveka's stance that commentators must employ autonomous inferences, whereas authors of aphoristic verse treatises need not. After all, as Candrakīrti later points out, Nāgārjuna does not present autonomous arguments when he comments on his own work, the *Vigrahavyāvartanī* (VV).

However inequitable he judges Bhāvaviveka's critique, Ames nonetheless finds no evidence that it contains any attack on Buddhapālita's understanding of specifically Madhyamaka doctrine. Although he does find one doctrinal point for which Buddhapālita draws fire from Bhāvaviveka (on the question of whether *śrāvakas* realize the selflessness of *dharmas* or not), Ames sees no connection between this and the critique concerning autonomous inferences. Thus, for Ames, the issue between Bhāvaviveka and Buddhapālita is rather limited. It concerns only the methodology that Mādhyamikas should follow in establishing and defending their views, not the content of those views or any other deep philosophical issue. Most likely, the attack can be explained by Bhāvaviveka's desire to "modernize" the expression of Madhyamaka thought by casting it in Dignāga's new language of Buddhist epistemology, thus lending it an aura of respectability in a wider intellectual sphere. In this regard, Bhāvaviveka should probably be seen as quite successful: apart from Candrakīrti and Jayānanda, nearly all other Indian Mādhyamikas were to follow in his footsteps and to embrace autonomous arguments as important tools in their endeavors to establish the supremacy of the Madhyamaka view.

Significantly different in both approach and conclusions is the next contribution, that of C. W. Huntington, who examines the subsequent step in the controversy, Candrakīrti's defense of Buddhapālita and attack on Bhāvaviveka in the PPMV. Huntington argues that the difference separating Candrakīrti and Bhāvaviveka runs deep, is substantive, and concerns the very nature of Madhyamaka philosophy. The reason is that, for Huntington, *any* attempt to apply doxographical categories to Buddhist thought and to organize it according to tenets *(siddhānta, grub mtha')* and views *(darśana, lta ba)* is utterly antithetical to Nāgārjuna's original nondogmatic insight. As the progenitor of the Buddhist doxographical tradition, Bhāvaviveka stands guilty of appropriating the term *madhyamaka* as the name of a particular view and a particular school, aligned with particular theses *(pratijñā, dam bca')* and positions *(pakṣa, phyogs)* that can—and, indeed, should—be defended through the autonomous arguments of Buddhist epistemology. In Huntington's estimation, while Bhāvaviveka's misguided feat served to organize the "welter of ideas that were circulating freely about in the Buddhist world of his day," it was done at a cost, and "so far as we know only one individual seems to have had any idea just how steep the price may have been."[16] That individual is Candrakīrti.

Drawing on passages from Candrakīrti's PPMV, Huntington's first argument is that this author is opposed to the transformation of Madhyamaka into a philosophy or view as a betrayal of the skeptical and nondogmatic spirit of Nāgārjuna's original message. Candrakīrti seeks instead to reassert Nāgārjuna's "attitude of non-clinging based on the understanding that there is nothing (no form of ontological reality or epistemological truth) that should be held onto and defended, either conventionally speaking or in any deeper (ultimate) level."[17] Against Bhāvaviveka's high philosophical program, Candrakīrti opposes what Huntington describes as a strict soteriological pragmatism, castigating Bhāvaviveka as having fallen out of the Madhyamaka through his addiction to logic. But, ironically, Candrakīrti's efforts take place in a context already transformed by Bhāvaviveka and others, and hence remain inhabited by a tension. Thus, rather than simply rejecting the whole doxographical approach, Candrakīrti, despite his better instincts, gives in to the temptation to establish a school himself, albeit one based on the idea of shunning any position or doctrinal tenet whatsoever.

This is a highly paradoxical stance, as Candrakīrti himself seems to recognize. But it is a paradoxical stance that is weakened by later doxographical traditions when they unreservedly reduce Candrakīrti's attempt to return to a Nāgārjunian perspective to a set of definable and categorizable doctrinal positions.

This error in the interpretation of Candrakīrti is particularly widespread among later Tibetan doxographers, according to Huntington, who claims that "Candrakīrti would have had very specific and trenchant objections to his being referred to as a 'Prāsaṅgika-Mādhyamika.'"[18] Why is that? In large part, Huntington contends that Candrakīrti would have abhorred the classification because it attempts to fix Madhyamaka as a school, with tenets and subschools. But even more importantly, perhaps, Candrakīrti would have rejected the label Prāsaṅgika-Mādhyamika because of its inherent implication that there is or can be *another kind* of Madhyamaka, namely, that espoused by the Svātantrika-Mādhyamikas and exemplified by Bhāvaviveka and his followers. Such a notion would strike Candrakīrti as impossible, since, as Huntington emphasizes, for Candrakīrti "Bhāvaviveka is not a Mādhyamika at all, he is merely a Logician taking the side of the Madhyamaka school out of a desire to show off his mastery of the canons of logic."[19] Autonomous arguments (and the corresponding theses, tenets, and views) are suspect because they imply an addiction to certainty that is rooted in ignorance and is totally antithetical to Madhyamaka.

Huntington's conclusion poses a serious challenge to the premise of this book, in that it questions the appropriateness of the very doxographical project in which the Prāsaṅgika-Svātantrika distinction is rooted. At the same time, however, much of Huntington's analysis could also be used to *support* the claim that there is indeed a radical division in Indian Madhyamaka between the followers of Bhāvaviveka, on the one hand, and those who oppose his innovations, on the other. While choosing to describe that division in terms of the doxographical categories Svātantrika-Madhyamaka and Prāsaṅgika-Madhyamaka arguably may not be the best way to capture this difference, it may not always have been avoidable. For just as Candrakīrti, as a product of his time, could not refrain from speaking of Madhyamaka as a system or view *(darśana),* later Buddhists (and modern scholars of Buddhism) have been conditioned by a variety of discourses that lead them to employ concepts that may simultaneously clarify *and* occlude aspects of the ideas of earlier thinkers. The trick is to become aware of where our conceptual schemes are serving us well, and where they may be inadvertently leading us astray.

The author of the next contribution, Tom J. F. Tillemans, shares with Huntington a profound appreciation of Candrakīrti as a unique and perhaps even "genuinely extraordinary figure in Indian philosophy."[20] In contrast to Huntington, however, Tillemans offers a far more favorable assessment of the Svātantrika-Prāsaṅgika distinction, especially as it is elaborated in the works of Tsong kha pa. This does not mean that Tillemans holds Tsong kha pa to be justified in all his opinions. For example, Tsong kha pa's attempt to harmonize Candrakīrti's view on the means of valid cognition *(pramāṇa, tshad ma)* with that of the logicians is seen to be thoroughly suspect. But there are other, valuable elements in Tsong kha pa's analysis, which are encapsulated in particular in his "superb insight" that while Svātantrikas accept a degree of "realism" on the conventional level, as is evinced by their endorsement of a nonerroneous perception of unique particulars *(svalakṣaṇa, rang mtshan)* as providing the foundations for empirical knowledge, Prāsaṅgikas (by whom Tillemans means primarily Candrakīrti), in contrast, do away with the need to underpin conventional truth with objective facts, thereby abolishing speculative metaphysics once and for all.

Tillemans begins his argument by sketching out Tsong kha pa's controversial view that the Svātantrikas, while accepting that ultimately all things are devoid of intrinsic nature or true existence, conventionally hold that things retain some kind of intrinsic or objective existence (i.e., they are *tha snyad du rang ngos nas grub pa,* lit., existent from their own side conventionally). As Tillemans explains, this amounts to saying that Svātantrikas accept that there is, on the conventional level, "something that is as it is, independently of, or unaffected by, what we believe, feel, think and say about it."[21] And, since the Svātantrikas, like their logician counterparts, accept that it is *this* independently real thing that grounds ordinary knowledge and practices (albeit only conventionally), whereas Prāsaṅgikas deny that such a real thing is needed to ground ordinary knowledge and practices, it is reasonable to assert that the two camps differ significantly in their metaphysical, hence ontological, commitments. In short, the Svātantrika school allows room for a degree of *realism,* though only conventionally, in the sense that it endorses "deference to the independent and objective facts that make true beliefs true and the self-assurance that we can know these facts,"[22] while the Prāsaṅgika school rejects such deference and self-assurance and is thus thoroughly *anti-realist.*

Of course, as both Tillemans and Tsong kha pa recognize, this description of the Svātantrika is never clearly stated or endorsed by Bhāvaviveka or any other subsequent Mādhyamika. Nonetheless, Tillemans stresses that it is reasonable to emulate Tsong kha pa in teasing out the unacknowledged presuppositions of the Svātantrika authors. While Tsong kha pa does so through the lens of Candrakīrti's attack on Bhāvaviveka's commitment to autonomous arguments, Tillemans turns to an Anglo-American philosophical notion, Wilfrid Sellars' myth of the given,[23] to help evaluate the Indian sources. For Sellars, the given is a kind of impossible entity postulated by some empiricists as the primary ontological support for their foundationalism. It is that fact that, if it were to exist, could be known immediately (i.e., noninferentially) without presupposing any other knowledge, in such a way that knowledge of it would provide an ultimate epistemological court of appeal. But facts that can be known in this fashion do not (and cannot) exist, argues Sellars, and hence they are nothing but a myth. We do not have immediate knowledge of any facts; rather we always come to know all facts through a mixture of sensing and interpretation that allows us to understand them.

In appropriating this analysis in the present context, Tillemans chooses to focus on Richard Rorty's definition of the given as "the sort of entity naturally suited to be immediately present to consciousness."[24] He then argues forcefully that both the Buddhist logicians and the Svātantrikas, particularly Śāntarakṣita and his disciple Kamalaśīla, Indian Mādhyamikas with a "massive and clear debt to the logicians Dignāga and Dharmakīrti,"[25] subscribe to the myth of the given.[26] For, without exception, these philosophers all accept that there *is* an entity that is naturally suited to be immediately present to consciousness, namely the particular *(svalakṣaṇa)*. Although Tillemans acknowledges a difference between the logicians and the Svātantrikas, he says that the only *significant* difference is that for the logicians particulars are fully real, while for the Svātantrikas they are real only conventionally. But putting aside the question of the *level* of reality, for both schools the direct and nonconceptual perception of particulars is what provides the ultimate check on what is and what is not to be accepted as knowledge. Tillemans sees this as evidence in support of Tsong kha pa's claim that Svātantrikas accept a degree of objective existence on the conventional level, with the result that such authors, unwittingly perhaps, embrace a degree of residual realism.

This residual realism comes to the fore in the question of autonomous arguments, in which the terms of the argument must be established similarly by both parties *(mthun snang du grub pa)*. For Tsong kha pa, such a requirement cannot be satisfied in the case of an argument between a

Mādhyamika and a non-Mādhyamika concerning the ultimate. This is so because there is no subject that can be established similarly by both parties: the Mādhyamika holds the subject to be unreal whereas the adversary holds it to be real. A possible Svātantrika rejoinder to this conundrum is that there *is* a subject that is available to both sides, the thing as it appears to ordinary perception. It is precisely this answer that Tsong kha pa finds indicative of a residual Svātantrika realism, for it shows that the Svātantrikas accept that the referents of the argument's terms are "established by their own character" *(rang gi mtshan nyid kyis grub pa)*, a phrase that for Tsong kha pa indicates the very form of objective existence that the Prāsaṅgikas understand to be negated by emptiness.

For Tillemans, all of this is in marked contrast to Candrakīrti, whose distinctive contribution to Madhyamaka thought is probably best understood as his rejection of the generally foundationalist tendencies that inevitably accompany the myth of the given. It is not only that Candrakīrti is free from the realist affinities that the given entails, but he is also free from the entire apparatus of the Buddhist "metaphysico-epistemology" that requires conventional truths to be underpinned by objective "facts." This analysis, if it is correct, paints Candrakīrti as a kind of quietist in the Wittgensteinian sense of advocating a "lucid avoidance of substantive philosophy," or else perhaps as a kind of minimalist for whom "the justificatory undergirdings of our practices do not represent the real conditions of the justification of those practices."[27] With conclusions like these, we are reminded again of the powerful role an interpreter's historical horizons play in shaping the outcome of any investigation—whether that interpreter be situated in the fifteenth or the twenty-first century.

The next contribution, by Sara McClintock, again picks up the theme of the given, and uses the concept to evaluate the classification of Śāntarakṣita and Kamalaśīla as Svātantrikas according to the views of mKhas grub dge legs dpal bzang (1385–1438), one of Tsong kha pa's most influential disciples. McClintock casts mKhas grub's objection to the Svātantrika position as an objection to the use of the given, where the given is understood to be whatever provides a noninferential foundation for empirical knowledge. Acceptance of the given is then seen to imply an ontological commitment, which is revealed by the attendant use of autonomous arguments. As with Tsong kha pa, autonomous arguments are problematic for mKhas grub since they require that the subject and other elements of an inference be established as appearing similarly for both participants in a debate. While so much is standard in Indian Buddhist epistemological and debate theory, McClintock points out that mKhas grub appears to expand the requirement to include the criterion that the elements of the inference be established *in precisely the same way* in the philosophical systems of both parties to the debate. Although mKhas grub allows that there are conventional means of valid awareness *(pramāṇa, tshad ma)* that establish the conventional existence of entities, he rejects that such means gain their validity through reliance on any form of the given, since doing so would imply an acceptance of an objective or unassailable reality that oversteps the Mādhyamika's radical critique of natures on both the ultimate and the conventional levels. Thus, autonomous arguments between Mādhyamikas and non-Mādhyamikas (or those who accept that valid cognitions are justified by the given) are not possible, and the Svātantrika use of them is inappropriate.

Having sketched out mKhas grub's understanding of and objections to the Svātantrika use of autonomous arguments, McClintock then attempts to determine whether his analysis applies to Śāntarakṣita and Kamalaśīla. In this part of her paper, she argues that while it is fair to describe these Indian intellectuals as embracing the given, their use of the given must be seen within the context of their larger philosophical method, wherein conflicting Buddhist views are arranged in a "sliding scale of analysis." At the lowest level of analysis, the authors follow the Sautrāntika model in which causally efficacious external particulars give rise to images *(ākāra)* in awareness; these images then play the role of the given and serve as the foundation for empirical knowledge. At the next level of analysis, that of the Yogācāra, although external particulars are denied, images are still given to awareness; these images also serve as a foundation of knowledge for what is objectively real, which now is understood to be the mind alone. At the highest level of analysis, that of the Madhyamaka, appearances are no longer the given in the technical sense employed by McClintock but are instead *mere* appearances; as such, these images no longer play the role of the given in that they do not yield empirical knowledge of any kind of objective reality.

The question then becomes how these philosophers, as committed Mādhyamikas, can employ inferential reasoning that relies on what *seems* to be given to awareness without (implicitly or explicitly) endorsing the objective reality that mKhas grub asserts is thereby implied. McClintock's analysis here turns on the idea that from the perspective of the Madhyamaka level of analysis, it is possible to see *all* of the apparently autonomous arguments in Śāntarakṣita and Kamalaśīla's works as just provisional. As such, these inferences correspond in important ways to the type of inference that mKhas grub and the dGe lugs pa tradition in general classify as "other-acknowledged inference" *(gzhan grags kyi rjes dpag, *paraprasiddhānumāna)* and which they allow as appropriate even for Prāsaṅgika-Mādhyamikas.

On this reading, Śāntarakṣita and Kamalaśīla differ from those mKhas grub classifies as Prāsaṅgikas not because they accept some inappropriate degree of objective reality on the conventional level, but rather because they insist that *even for Mādhyamikas* images can arise in awareness in a manner similar to how they arise for non-Mādhyamikas. But for Śāntarakṣita and Kamalaśīla this is not the grave philosophical problem that it is for mKhas grub. That is, although images arise similarly, this is not due to acceptance or rejection of epistemological categories like the given, but rather to the fact that both parties participate in a shared form of ignorance that cannot be eliminated through philosophy alone. The fact that Mādhyamikas and non-Mādhyamikas have a different intellectual understanding of the ontological status of these images is irrelevant to the debate; this is why these authors assert that inferential demonstrations on the part of Mādhyamikas must proceed without reference to philosophical positions. If Śāntatakṣita and Kamalaśīla are to be seen as asserting something which "remains" on all levels, it is not the given, but rather reason *(nyāya)*, that, when applied relentlessly to appearances, leads ineluctably to the conclusion that nothing is established objectively at all. Like the Prāsaṅgikas of mKhas grub's system, these thinkers rely on conventional realities to lead to an insight into the ultimate. What else is Madhyamaka about?

Taken together, the articles in the first part of this volume have so far amply demonstrated not only the highly contested nature of the Svātantrika-Prāsaṅgika distinction, but also the hermeneutical complexity that necessarily accompanies any attempt to analyze the distinction in relation to the Indian texts. The next contribution, that of Malcolm David Eckel, pushes this hermeneutical complexity still further, so much so that it becomes difficult to decide into which of the two main avenues of inquiry his piece should fall. Although primarily centering on Tsong kha pa's view in the *Legs bshad snying po*, Eckel's article also examines in some depth a number of the key ideas of two of the most important Indian thinkers usually described as Svātantrika-Mādhyamikas, Bhāvaviveka and Jñānagarbha (7th c.). For this reason, we have placed his article at the end of part 1 of the book, where it may serve as a kind of a bridge between the two avenues of inquiry, and where it may also serve to remind us of the artificiality of any strict separation we may be tempted to see between approaches that focus on Indian sources and those centered on the Tibetan tradition.

Following the insights of Tsong kha pa's masterwork, Eckel describes what is at stake in the Svātantrika-Prāsaṅgika distinction as being less a question of logical method and having more to do with "the elusive and problematic category of conventional truth."[28] In general, while Mādhyamikas agree on the ultimate nature of phenomena, i.e., their emptiness, they seem to diverge more significantly when explaining what it means for phenomena to exist conventionally. For Tsong kha pa, Svātantrikas appear to be just a touch too willing to subject the conventional to analysis and to provide what they claim to be objectively valid arguments to justify their views. This attitude betrays the fact that they are not satisfied with mere ordinary conventional usages and that they seek grounds on which conventional distinctions can be established. Their search for something more objective than mere denominations indicates their assumption that things need some degree of objective reality in order to be conventionally real, that they must exist, to cast the issue in Tsong kha pa's terms, through their own characteristics or through their own intrinsic identity *(rang gi mtshan nyid kyis grub pa).*

But how does this assessment measure up in light of the Indian sources? To get a handle on this, Eckel first examines Tsong kha pa's treatment of Bhāvaviveka. As the Tibetan master himself recognizes, it is far from clear on the basis of Bhāvaviveka's own words that the latter in fact holds that things must exist through their own intrinsic identity. Still, Tsong kha pa is convinced that such is an accurate representation of Bhāvaviveka's position. To find some textual support for his claim, Tsong kha pa resorts to a relatively obscure passage in the twenty-fifth chapter of the *Prajñāpradīpa,* a passage in which Bhāvaviveka is engaged in a critique of the Yogācāra doctrine of the three natures *(trisvabhāva, mtshan nyid gsum).* There Bhāvaviveka takes the Yogācāra to task for denying the reality of the imagined nature *(parikalpita, kun brtags)* and for contrasting that lack of reality to the reality of the other two natures. As Bhāvaviveka argues, why go to this trouble? All three natures are equally unreal from an ultimate standpoint and conventionally all three bear their own characteristics. To deny these characteristics is to fall into the extreme of nihilism. Tsong kha pa reasons that this argument shows that for Bhāvaviveka the imagined nature must have some degree of intrinsic reality if it is to exist at all.

But is this really what Bhāvaviveka meant to say in the passage? After examining Bhāvaviveka's own view, Eckel concludes that there can be no straightforward answer to this question. That is, Tsong kha pa clearly goes beyond the textual evidence and obliges Bhāvaviveka to hold positions that in all likelihood he would have resisted and would not have endorsed. In this respect, Tsong kha pa is like a sculptor, who, following the fault lines of the raw material, fashions that material according to his own vision. But at the same time, Tsong kha pa does not simply impose his own ideas. He may equally be seen as unearthing unacknowledged assumptions in the works of Bhāvaviveka, Jñānagarbha, and others—assumptions that may have been unimportant for these authors or have meant something else, but which are in tension with some of the ideas that these authors were pursuing. In this regard, Tsong kha pa is like a supreme court justice, who makes decisions that go well beyond a literal interpretation of the Constitution but which nonetheless rely on constitutional principles.

Eckel organizes his article around the theme of the "satisfaction of no-analysis," which he maintains is a principle that Tsong kha pa both endorses and finds lacking among the Indian Svātantrikas. But, as Eckel also points out, a problem arises when one takes a close look at some of the Indian sources. Take, for example, the case of Jñānagarbha, who is usually considered one of the foremost Svātantrikas. Jñānagarbha is famous for being one of a number of authors to offer a threefold definition of conventional truth: something is conventional if it can satisfy only when it is not subject to analysis, if it arises dependently, and if it is capable of effective action. Put otherwise, this means that conventional realities exist "as they are seen" *(yathādarśana),* but that they do not withstand logical analysis. All this seems to suggest an attempt to adduce criteria for conventional truth by relying on the ideas of the logicians, specifically on their insistence on the foundational role of causality and on the centrality of perception as providing the privileged means to gain access to reality. But by examining Jñānagarbha's texts, Eckel shows that this interpretation is misguided. While there may be foundationalist elements lurking in Jñānagarbha's texts, many of his ideas lead in a quite different direction. On reflection, it seems that Jñānagarbha is perhaps more similar to Candrakīrti than he is to the logicians, as both Jñānagarbha and Candrakīrti appear to offer a theory that does not limit perception to the nonconceptual and nonerroneous cognitions claimed for perception by the Buddhist logicians. Likewise, both insist that conventional realities are characterized by the fact that they cannot be analyzed,[29] another reason to suspect any easy opposition between these two supposed paragons of Svātantrika and Prāsaṅgika.

Eckel's conclusion supports the idea that while there are certainly significant and revealing disagreements among Candrakīrti, Bhāvaviveka, Śāntarakṣita, Kamalaśīla, Jñānagarbha, and others, these disagreements are probably best not seen as the kinds of sharp distinctions that usually distinguish strict schools of thought and that are characteristic of traditional doxographies. Rather, the disagreements among these authors appear more like fluid and intersecting streams emerging from a common commentarial project of exploration and explication of the foundational texts of the Indian Madhyamaka tradition. Eckel wraps up his investigation of Tsong kha pa's approach to the Svātantrika-Prāsaṅgika distinction with a nuanced analysis. He says,

> It is not necessary to take Tsong kha pa's argument as a distortion of the Indian sources. We also can read it as a plausible and careful study of their implications. But no matter how we read the argument, it is still an interpretation. Tsong kha pa does not reproduce the Indian sources verbatim; he works with them to serve the needs of his own system of classification.[30]

Such might equally well be said of all of the interpretations filling this volume. Each author reveals important and sometimes previously neglected aspects of the Indian and Tibetan sources under investigation, while at the same time also revealing, often through the questions that he or she raises, his or her biases and assumptions in the areas of methodology, philosophical propensities, and Madhyamaka studies. When such is the case, it is no surprise that the collected articles in this volume do not lead to any single resolution of the question of the Svātantrika-Prāsaṅgika distinction.

Part 2: Examining the Distinction in the Tibetan Tradition

As is now abundantly clear, analysis of the Svātantrika-Prāsaṅgika distinction in relation to Indian texts cannot proceed without reference to Tibetan interpretations, since the relevant questions have all been formulated by Tibetans in a Tibetan context. Similarly, as is also perhaps obvious, it is not possible to investigate the Tibetan understanding of the distinction without reference to the Indian texts. Thus, no matter which avenue of inquiry one chooses to take in approaching the Svātantrika-Prāsaṅgika distinction, any absolute separation between original Indian sources and later Tibetan interpretations must remain artificial. The preceding contributions attest to this, as can be seen by the fact that although they deal primarily with Indian sources, they also refer, often extensively, to Tibetan interpretations.

For reasons too various and complex to detail here, but which probably include a tendency in modern scholarship on Tibetan Buddhism until recently to emphasize dGe lugs pa sources, the previous contributors have generally assessed the relevance of the Svātantrika-Prāsaṅgika distinction in light of the views of Tsong kha pa and his dGe lugs pa disciples. This situation has the potential drawback of misleading readers into absolutizing Tsong kha pa's interpretations and assuming that they, or the dGe lugs pa interpretations they inspired, must be representative of the overall Tibetan tradition. The reality, however, is quite different, for Tibetans have been and continue to be profoundly divided on the Svātantrika-Prāsaṅgika distinction, and there is a rich literature on the topic extending well outside the dGe lugs pa fold. While Tsong kha pa has certainly been a pivotal voice in the Tibetan debates on the distinction since the fifteenth century, the power, sophistication, and influence of his arguments should not be allowed to blind us to the underlying historical reality in which Tsong kha pa's perspective is just one within a highly diverse and divided Madhyamaka tradition. Our hope is that the contributions in the second part of the book will go some distance toward dispelling the general impression that the dGe lugs pa perspective on this topic represents, or has ever represented, a single hegemonic Tibetan view.

As stated earlier, the emergence of the Svātantrika-Prāsaṅgika distinction in Tibet is most frequently traced to the twelfth-century translator Pa tshab nyi ma grags and his disciples. Prior to that time in Tibet, the basic doxographical distinction applied to Madhyamaka was that promulgated by the eighth-century author Ye shes sde in his *lTa ba'i khyad par,* namely, the distinction between the Sautrāntika-Madhyamaka of Bhāvaviveka and the Yogācāra-Madhyamaka of Śāntarakṣita and Kamalaśīla.[31] As David Seyfort Ruegg has stated in his recent book on the history of Indian and Tibetan Madhyamaka, the history of Tibetan Madhyamaka from the time of Ye shes sde until the time of Tsong kha pa "is only imperfectly known because few of the relevant sources are accessible to us and several are indeed likely to have been lost."[32] This lack of extant works has been a major obstacle for those who wish to understand the nature of the emergence and the development of the Svātantrika-Prāsaṅgika distinction in Tibet. For example, despite all claims about Pa tshab nyi ma grags being the probable inventor of the distinction, none of his compositions is known to survive.[33]

But the paucity of original sources is not the only difficulty one encounters in investigating early Tibetan philosophical materials. Whereas later texts usually present clear and well-argued standpoints, surviving early texts often appear to contain a bewildering proliferation of views whose relevance is at times far from obvious. This is due in part to our lack of knowledge of this period of the Tibetan tradition, but it may also be attributable in some degree to the fact that the texts themselves are in the process of exploring ideas that only gradually and over time settled into a series of fixed positions. Hence, rather than formulating the often highly insightful and clearly articulated views that we find in the works of later thinkers, the early authors seem more inclined to offer a wide range of opinions, with the result that one is quite often left wondering how to interpret some of their statements.

Such is the case, certainly, for the ideas of one famous twelfth-century author, Phya pa chos kyi seng ge (1109–1169). His views on the issues relevant to the Svātantrika-Prāsaṅgika distinction as preserved in his *dBu ma shar gsum gyi stong thun* are treated by Helmut Tauscher in the first contribution of part 2 of this book. Recognizing the difficulty of analyzing Phya pa's position on the Svātantrika-Prāsaṅgika distinction when Phya pa himself does not explicitly use the terms or invoke the distinction, Tauscher begins with a concise summary of some of the earliest uses of the distinction by a number of Phya pa's near-contemporaries. He starts with the eleventh-century rNying ma pa scholar Rong zom chos kyi bzang po, an author who does not mention the Svātantrika-Prāsaṅgika distinction but who, in addition to invoking the earlier distinction between Sautrāntika-Madhyamaka and Yogācāra-Madhyamaka, divides Madhyamaka into the sGyu ma lta bur 'dod pa (those who maintain that things exist in the manner of an illusion) and the Rab tu mi gnas par 'dod pa (those who maintain that things do not exist in the way that they are designated by words and concepts).[34] Although later discussions in Tibet linked these categories with the Svātantrika and the Prāsaṅgika respectively, Rong zom does not use the terminology.

A Sa skya pa contemporary of Phya pa, Grags pa rgyal mtshan (1147–1216), invokes the Svātantrika-Prāsaṅgika distinction only in a tantric context, while seeming to ignore it when discussing Madhyamaka. Tauscher gives a brief, though fascinating, summation of Grags pa rgyal mtshan's understanding of the terms Prāsaṅgika and Svātantrika in the tantric framework, where the primary distinguishing feature of the two schools is said to be their rejection or acceptance of a "corresponding" or "conceptual" ultimate reality *(paryāyaparamārtha)* in addition to a (seemingly unique) "corresponding" conventional reality *(paryāyasaṃvṛti)*. In the context of Madhyamaka, Grags pa rgyal mtshan invokes a fivefold typology based on the manner of understanding conventional reality: Yogācāra-

Madhyamaka, Sautrāntika-Madhyamaka, sGyu ma pa (proponents of illusoriness), Bye brag smra ba dang tshul mtshungs pa (those who proceed in a manner similar to the Vaibhāṣika), and 'Jig rten grags sde pa (the school [that relies on] what is known in the world).[35] The later Sa skya pa commentator Go rams pa bsod nams seng ge (1429–1489) aligns these divisions with various Indian authors, but introduces the Svātantrika-Prāsaṅgika distinction only at the level of ultimate reality, insisting, however, that the two schools do not differ in their understanding of the ultimate.

The nephew of Grags pa rgyal mtshan, the renowned Sa skya paṇḍita kun dga' rgyal mtshan (1182–1251), or Sa paṇ for short, "divides the Madhyamaka with regard to the interpretation of *paramārtha* into sGyu ma lta bu and Rab tu mi gnas pa, and divides the latter into Svātantrika and Prāsaṅgika exclusively on grounds of the methodological difference of accepting or not accepting the triple characterization *(trairūpya)* of a valid reason for proving the ultimate."[36] As Tauscher points out, these few examples attest not only to the fact that the general contours of the Svātantrika-Prāsaṅgika distinction were still very much in the process of formation during the period in which Phya pa chos kyi seng ge lived and wrote, but also that its importance for the classification of Indian Madhyamaka had not yet reached the proportions that it was to take on in later centuries in Tibet. Thus, in evaluating the question of whether Phya pa should be considered a Svātantrika (as he often was in later times), Tauscher is faced with the vexing problem of what meaning to assign the term. His solution is to introduce the notion of an "old" distinction, one based primarily on the question of whether a Mādhyamika may legitimately be said to maintain a thesis *(pratijñā, dam bca')* or not, and which in many ways bears little resemblance to what Tauscher terms the new dGe lugs pa distinction of later years.

We encountered the question of whether a Mādhyamika should maintain a thesis earlier in the volume in Huntington's contribution, where we saw that the issue stems mainly from the interpretation of Nāgārjuna's famous rejection of a thesis in VV 29. In eleventh-century Tibet, the translator Khu mdo sde 'bar, a student and collaborator of Jayānanda, appears to have interpreted this rejection as meaning that Mādhyamikas should have no thesis at all. Pa tshab is said to have understood Nāgārjuna's statement to rule out only positive theses but not to exclude the use of negative ones. One of Pa tshab's disciples, rMa bya byang chub brtson 'grus (?–1185?), apparently disagreed, arguing that Nāgārjuna's rejection should be understood to apply only to the ultimate; there, no thesis, whether positive or negative, can be entertained, whereas in the conventional domain, both negative and positive theses have legitimate roles. Another of Pa tshab's followers, gTsang nag pa brtson 'grus, who is reported to have first been Phya pa's pupil but then later to have changed sides, similarly argued that the ultimate is beyond any description whatsoever.[37]

It is amid this enormous variety of views that Phya pa should be seen as developing his ideas on the question of the appropriate use of autonomous or *svatantra* reasoning for establishing the ultimate. As Tauscher's article reveals, although Phya pa does not make use of the terms Svātantrika and Prāsaṅgika, he does strongly critique the position (interpreted by later scholars as a reference to Candrakīrti and his followers) that Mādhyamikas should not provide autonomous arguments to establish the ultimate but should limit themselves to consequences *(prasaṅga)*. Entering into the sometimes ambiguous arguments of Phya pa's *Shar gsum stong thun,* Tauscher lays bare the various ways in which this early Tibetan Mādhyamika argues for the position that consequences are insufficient to induce the certainty *(niścaya, nges pa)* necessary to eliminate discursive thoughts *(prapañca, spros pa)*. Autonomous arguments, which are based on the ascertainment of the triple characteristic *(trairūpya, tshul gsum)* of a valid reason and hence can bring certainty, are required. More important, for Phya pa, a consequence necessarily either contains an implied probative argument *(prasaṅgaviparyaya, thal bzlog pa)* such that its use is then tantamount to that of an autonomous argument, or it is based on mere opinion and is thus inconclusive. In other words, to be effective, even arguments that proceed by consequences must be translatable into autonomous arguments. Otherwise, *prasaṅga*s can establish nothing and hence cannot refute inherent existence.

As Tauscher emphasizes, all this presents a relevant contrast for understanding Tsong kha pa's approach. That is, whereas Tsong kha pa's analysis of the Svātantrika-Prāsaṅgika distinction is based on an interpretation of autonomous arguments as implying ontological commitments (i.e., the objective existence of the phenomena to which the terms of the arguments refer), Phya pa instead draws a distinction grounded more fundamentally on a methodological insight into the nature of consequences as necessarily implying autonomous arguments. Hence, in many ways, Phya pa's view of the Svātantrika-Prāsaṅgika distinction—if his arguments can be legitimately cast in such terms—differs significantly from the dGe lugs pa understanding. At the same time, there exist numerous important similarities, which Tauscher takes pains to point out. For example, Phya pa can be seen to be like Tsong kha pa in holding that Mādhyamikas cannot escape asserting theses and should hence engage with the full panoply of Buddhist logic. He also makes a strong separation between the two truths, arguing that Madhyamaka negations should be strictly limited to the ultimate and should not affect the validity of the conventional.

The similarities between Phya pa and Tsong kha pa described by Tauscher highlight another fundamental difficulty in our project, namely, that the meaning of the Svātantrika-Prāsaṅgika distinction tends to subtly shift according to the precise understanding of autonomous reasoning that is embraced. For Tsong kha pa, the Svātantrika and the Prāsaṅgika are rent by an enormous gulf, differing even in their understanding of ultimate reality or emptiness, and this difference comes to the fore in the understanding of autonomous arguments, which are seen to imply an ontological commitment such that an argument is autonomous if, and only if, its terms refer to objectively or intrinsically existent phenomena. For Tsong kha pa, Svātantrikas use and promote such arguments and hence must be committed to the objective existence of phenomena, whereas Prāsaṅgikas reject them and hence are able to hold that phenomena exist merely on the basis of consensual agreement. As many scholars have noticed, Tsong kha pa's view is remarkable not just for the acuity of its insights; it is also both highly original and at times almost paradoxical. That is, while Tsong kha pa sharply marks the Svātantrika-Prāsaṅgika distinction and strongly emphasizes the preeminence of the latter, he also accepts many of the ideas that historically have been the hallmark of those who embrace autonomous arguments, such as the emphasis on the importance of Buddhist logic for Madhyamaka, the existence of only two types of valid cognition, the sharp separation between the two truths, and the insistence on using logical operators to mark this distinction. This paradox has been remarked by many authors, modern and traditional, but few have attempted to further explore its sources.

In stressing the similarities between Phya pa and Tsong kha pa, Tauscher contributes to this task and suggests an intriguing filiation between the two. This filiation is already well known as far as the transmission of Buddhist logic in Tibet is concerned,[38] but has not yet been explored in the realm of Madhyamaka. This is certainly not to say that Tsong kha pa is Phya pa's disciple. If anything, Tsong kha pa should probably be more closely connected to the school that Phya pa appears to oppose, that of Pa tshab and his students. Following his teacher Red mda' ba gzhon nu blo gros (1349–1412), Tsong kha pa loudly proclaims the superiority of the Prāsaṅgika and is thus at odds with Phya pa's apparent emphatic endorsement of the Svātantrika (or, more accurately, of *svatantra* reasoning), and especially with Phya pa's understanding of consequences as implying autonomous arguments. And yet it seems clear that there is a relation between the two, as Tauscher recognizes. On closer examination, Tsong kha pa appears as a follower of Pa tshab who has strong sympathies with Phya pa's views, particularly the latter's insistence on the importance of Buddhist logic in understanding emptiness.

Tsong kha pa's emphasis on the compatibility of Buddhist logic within a Prāsaṅgika system again provides the focus in the next contribution, that of Chizuko Yoshimizu. In her article, Yoshimizu maintains that it is not so helpful to consider Tsong kha pa's presentation of the Svātantrika-Prāsaṅgika distinction as primarily a criticism of Bhāvaviveka's (or "Bhāviveka" in Yoshimizu's article) use of autonomous arguments, as is frequently done; instead, she argues, it is more fruitful to consider the issue from a slightly different perspective, wherein Tsong kha pa's writings on the topic are seen as providing the reasons why Candrakīrti and other Prāsaṅgikas do *not* employ autonomous arguments. This shift in approach to the distinction is subtle, and has the advantage of redirecting the inquiry to the internal dynamics of Tsong kha pa's Madhyamaka system and away from the more overt controversies that his system sometimes provokes. Yoshimizu pursues this line of inquiry to demonstrate that Tsong kha pa has reinterpreted Candrakīrti's arguments in such a manner as to allow him to maintain a place for probative inferential statements while still excluding so-called autonomous inferences.

To accomplish her demonstration, Yoshimizu first revisits a point of interpretation raised by scholars such as Shirō Matsumoto and Kōdō Yotsuya according to which Tsong kha pa, in commenting on certain passages from the PPMV, understands Candrakīrti as taking Bhāvaviveka "*not only* as the proponent of the inferential proof of nonorigination, but also as the opponent who is destined to be refuted by the Prāsaṅgika-Mādhyamika."[39] In other words, on Tsong kha pa's reading, Candrakīrti criticizes Bhāvaviveka not because he offers inferential proof statements per se, but rather more precisely because he does so in a manner similar to a "substantialist" or "realist" *(dngos por smra ba)*, whereby the components of the inference possess natures that are conventionally established as their own real or true characteristics *(rang gi mtshan nyid)*. As Yoshimizu argues, Tsong kha pa's interpretation involves a shift in which the logical form of *svatantrānumāna* comes to imply an ontological commitment that seems not to have been a factor in Candrakīrti's critique of the form in the PPMV.

On Yoshimizu's reading, this ontological shift in the values of autonomous reasoning is Tsong kha pa's most significant innovation. Nearly as important, however, is another crucial shift that Tsong kha pa makes in the values of the Buddhist logical tradition, namely, his reframing of the so-called "rule of common establishment" *(ubhayasiddhatva),* which states that the subject of an inferential statement must be established for both the proponent and the opponent in a debate. The shift that Tsong kha pa makes with regard to this rule is to specify that being established for both parties in the debate necessarily entails that the subject be established by a valid means of cognition *(pramāṇa, tshad ma)* of the same kind for both parties in the debate. Unlike Candrakīrti, Bhāvaviveka and other Svātantrikas are said to hold that the subject of a debate appears similarly to the nonconceptual direct perception of all persons, whether they be Mādhyamikas or not. This direct perception is further held to be "nonerroneous" *(abhrānta),* since it reveals that which is established as a real self-characteristic *(rang gi mtshad nyid kyis grub pa)* conventionally. Thus, even though Bhāvaviveka rejects that the subject of any given debate is established ultimately, this does not prevent him from offering autonomous arguments (with the ontological commitment to self-characteristics that this entails), "for he shares the same appearance of the subject with his substantialist opponent."[40] Candrakīrti, in contrast, maintains that there is no such nonerroneous direct perception in relation to the conventional, and hence an inference in which the subject and so on are established to appear commonly is not possible for a Mādhyamika in a debate with a substantialist.

At bottom, Yoshimizu is arguing that whereas Candrakīrti critiqued Bhāvaviveka as a Mādhyamika who is misguided in his use of probative arguments, Tsong kha pa takes Candrakīrti to be saying that because Bhāvaviveka accepts autonomous arguments, he is closer to the realists *(dngos por smra ba)* than he is to the true Mādhyamikas (i.e., the Prāsaṅgikas). This subtle shift in the understanding of Candrakīrti's arguments supports Tsong kha pa's creation of a gap between Candrakīrti's and Bhāvaviveka's views of Madhyamaka arguments, and reserves Tsong kha pa the space he needs to maintain *another kind* of probative inferential statement for use within the Prāsaṅgika system, namely, an inference whose elements are established solely for others *(paraprasiddha).* As Yoshimizu eloquently shows, this preservation of the tools and apparatus of the Buddhist logical tradition allows Tsong kha pa to reject two key positions widely ascribed to Prāsaṅgika-Madhyamaka in his day in Tibet: 1) the position that autonomous inference is a positive proof that is designed to establish one's own doctrinal thesis and that is wholly opposed to reasoning designed to negate an opponent's position; and 2) the position that a Mādhyamika has no thesis of his own and no valid cognition by which to establish it. Instead, by introducing the issue of the ontological commitment, Tsong kha pa argues that the Prāsaṅgika avoids autonomous inferences because he can find no subject in common with his substantialist proponent, not because he lacks a thesis or means of valid cognition of his own.

By now, we cannot fail to recognize Tsong kha pa's distinctiveness. He offers insightful interpretations, ingenious readings, and a masterful synthesis of two trends of thought that prior to him had tended always to pull apart: the view of emptiness as utterly beyond description *(brjod bral),* which entails the nominalist rejection of conceptuality as unable to even approach this reality, on the one hand, and the more realist trust that thought is able at least partly to understand reality, and hence that the tools of logic can provisionally be used to realize the ultimate, on the other hand. We have seen that Phya pa argues forcefully for the latter approach and logically endorses, at least implicitly, something akin to what most Tibetans would consider the Svātantrika view. Tsong kha pa argues for a similar perspective but presents it as the Prāsaṅgika approach, which had previously been thought to entail the opposing view.

Of course, the extent to which Tsong kha pa's innovations are truly original remains difficult to assess, given that we do not have an adequate understanding of the ideas of some his important predecessors such as Bla ma dam pa bsod nams rgyal mtshan and his student Red mda' ba. Nevertheless, the intensity of the reactions that his theories provoked suggests that Tsong kha pa must have stepped well beyond the orbit of accepted ideas for his time. Starting from Rong ston shākya rgyal mtshan (1367–1449) and the translator sTag tshang (1405–?), and continuing with Go rams pa bsod nams seng ge (1429–1489), gSer mdog paṇ chen shākya mchog ldan (1428–1509), and the Eighth Kar ma pa Mi bskyod rdo rje (1504–1557), a stream of commentators raise strong and vociferous objections against what they consider a fanciful reinterpretation of the true Prāsaṅgika insight. While disagreeing on numerous issues, they uniformly argue, often with considerable vigor, that Tsong kha pa's synthesis of Prāsaṅgika and Buddhist logic is incoherent. sTag tshang, for example, is known for having pointed to eighteen major contradictions within Tsong kha pa's writings. In their critiques, these figures attempt to reassert what they perceive to be the true Prāsaṅgika insight as expressed by Pa tshab and his followers: ultimate reality is utterly beyond conceptuality and hence cannot be reached through the tools of Buddhist logic; it is not by arguing for emptiness but by radically deconstructing logical thinking that one can hope to reach the true Madhyamaka insight. It is this line of attack in response to Tsong kha pa that in one way or the other makes up the subject of the final two presentations.

José Cabezón begins his contribution with some insightful observations concerning the limited but real usefulness of doxographical categorization in general, raising the important issue of the role of socio-political motivations in shaping doxographical commitments. At the same time, Cabezón emphasizes the important point that while "the history of thought cannot be reduced to the history of power,"[41] neither can either domain be adequately studied in complete isolation from the other. In the context of the present volume, Cabezón's argument is particularly significant, since, as he also remarks, our attempts to study Tibetan doxographical traditions are of necessity influenced by "our own penchant to classify the world in distinct ways."[42] Cabezón's contribution focuses upon a distinction that he sees between a "hard" and a "soft" approach to the doxographical categories of Svātantrika and Prāsaṅgika in fourteenth- and fifteenth-century Tibet.

The "hard" doxographical distinction is represented by Tsong kha pa, the later dGe lugs pa tradition that sees him as its founder, and by Tsong kha pa's teacher, Red mda' ba. Such hard doxographers "see what distinguishes one school from another as real, substantive, and irreconcilable differences."[43] Whatever else divides these thinkers, they are united in their commitment to the idea that "Candrakīrti's Prāsaṅgika is the only unequivocally correct interpretation of Nāgārjuna, making the Prāsaṅgika school, and this school alone, the Buddha's true intention."[44] Part of the reason for this emphasis on the irreconcilable differences between the Svātantrika and the Prāsaṅgika, Cabezón argues, has to do with Tsong kha pa's desire to align himself strongly with the Prāsaṅgika position. But another, less overtly political reason can be discerned in his desire to maintain a role for the tools provided by the Buddhist epistemological tradition in his Prāsaṅgika interpretation.

Echoing the arguments in Yoshimizu's article, Cabezón contends that in order for Tsong kha pa's approach to the Svātantrika-Prāsaṅgika distinction to work, he is obliged to reinterpret the meaning of *svatantra* arguments as not only probative but also as entailing a lingering crypto-realism in the form of "the assumption of independent existence."[45] In making this move, Tsong kha pa preserves a place for positive probative arguments such that he can hold that these arguments may play a role even in the context of a discussion of the ultimate. Thus, the Prāsaṅgika interpretation, the only fully correct one, does not exclude probative arguments per se, but only the truly autonomous ones that entail unacceptable ontological commitments.

In contrast to this, Cabezón finds a "soft" doxographical approach to the Svātantrika-Prāsaṅgika distinction in the views of two of the most important critics of Tsong kha pa's Madhyamaka, Rong ston shes bya kun rig and his student Go rams pa bsod nams seng ge. On Cabezón's reading, the first of these figures maintains that there is no substantial difference between the two branches of the Madhyamaka regarding either the object of refutation *(dgag bya)* or the role of formal reasoning in analyzing the conventional. Rong ston pa does see a difference between the two schools in terms of whether they accept or reject the appropriateness of using *svatantra* reasoning when analyzing the ultimate, with the Prāsaṅgika objecting that in such contexts it is not possible to offer a formal reasoning that satisfies the trimodal criteria *(tshul gsum, trairūpya)*, since there can be no common subject on which such a reason could be established. But one should not take this to imply that Prāsaṅgikas are opposed to *svatantra* arguments. The reason is that, for Rong ston pa, arguments in the form of *svatantra* arguments, when they are advanced in the context of Madhyamaka, are in fact *not* ascertained through valid cognitions, but rather should be seen as illusory devices that seek to refute the opponent on his own ground or argue in function of what is commonly accepted. Thus, Cabezón sees a difference between Tsong kha pa and Rong ston pa on the question of the Svātantrika-Prāsaṅgika distinction in that the former asserts that the divergence between the two schools turns on an ontological commitment, whereas the latter understands the divergence to be purely epistemological.

Cabezón next reveals a similar interpretation in Go rams pa, who promotes his own view as standing in contrast with (and in between the extremes of) the views of Dol po pa shes rab rgyal mtshan (1292–1361) on the one hand, and Tsong kha pa on the other. Whereas Tsong kha pa asserts a strong Svātantrika-Prāsaṅgika distinction, Dol po pa rejects the distinction entirely, seeing it as an aberrant invention of later commentators. Such a distinction is entirely without basis in the Indian tradition, argues Dol po pa in a more metaphysical than exegetical mode, since it detracts from the essential oneness of the absolute. In contrast, Go rams pa presents his own opinion as a kind of middle way, arguing that although the Svātantrika-Prāsaṅgika distinction is not without basis in the Indian tradition, it does not amount to an ontological disagreement. Cabezón illustrates the problem that such a soft view must confront, namely, the delicate act of balancing two contradictory imperatives: such a view must provide some account of the differences between thinkers such as Candrakīrti and Bhāvaviveka, but it must be careful that in doing so it does not exaggerate these differences and thereby wrongly suggest a hard distinction *à la* Tsong kha pa.

Like Rong ston pa, Go rams pa's critique of the Svātantrika tradition does not assume that tradition to embrace an inappropriate ontological commitment or to accept independent existence or identity. But unlike Rong ston pa, Cabezón argues, Go rams pa is less perturbed by the supposed consequences of utilizing *svatantra* reasoning in an analysis of the ultimate than he is by the tendency he sees in Svātantrika thought to remain blinded to the reality that "there are contexts in which formal syllogistic reasoning is (a) unnecessary, and (b) actually inappropriate."[46] In other words, the mistake of the Svātantrikas is to believe that logic or syllogistic reasoning is universally applicable in all situations, particularly with respect to the ultimate. It is not that syllogistic reasoning is flawed per se, but rather that the truly skillful Mādhyamika—the Prāsaṅgika—knows when and where to leave it aside as an obstacle to the realization of ultimate reality.

In the concluding essay, Georges Dreyfus presents a similar view in a more recent figure, the rNying ma scholar 'Ju Mi pham rgya mtsho (1846–1912). Although Mi pham shares much with other Tibetans who are critical of Tsong kha pa, in many ways it is inadequate to present him simply as a critic of Tsong kha pa, as Dreyfus reveals. Instead, as a member of the nonsectarian movement *(ris med),* Mi pham provides a synthesis between Tsong kha pa and his critics. At the same time, it is clear that Mi pham is closer to the latter than to the former and that he assents to most of the criticisms raised against the Madhyamaka interpretations of the founder of the dGe lugs pa tradition. For example, Mi pham rejects Tsong kha pa's strong Svātantrika-Prāsaṅgika distinction, arguing in particular that there is no distinction in the view of emptiness between such thinkers as Candrakīrti and Bhāvaviveka. Instead, they are divided only on methodological or epistemological issues, especially concerning the most appropriate way to argue for Madhyamaka and lead others to an insight into emptiness. Dreyfus demonstrates how this disagreement centers on a rejection of Tsong kha pa's claim that Svātantrika-Mādhyamikas do not fully negate the "object of negation" *(dgag bya)* in the manner of the Prāsaṅgikas, with the result that their conception and realization of emptiness remains partial.

Similarly, Mi pham joins the critics of Tsong kha pa in rejecting Tsong kha pa's innovative notion that there are "eight difficult points" *(dka' gnas brgyad)* that distinguish the Prāsaṅgika from other interpretations. After briefly describing these eight points, which for Tsong kha pa show the superiority of the Prāsaṅgika view, Dreyfus explores Mi pham's take on some of them, focusing particularly on his arguments in favor of self-cognition *(rang rig, svasaṃvitti).* The conventional acceptance of this doctrine, which is widely supported by Buddhist logicians, is important for Mi pham, for it allows him to put forth an interpretation that brings traditional Madhyamaka close to the Yogācāra and hence also to the view of the Great Perfection *(rdzogs chen).* This agenda helps to explain Mi pham's strong interest in Śāntarakṣita's philosophy, despite the fact that it is usually classified as Svātantrika and hence is considered as inferior by most of Mi pham's contemporaries, who have been deeply conditioned by a post–Tsong kha pa rhetorical field in which the superiority of the Prāsaṅgika seems to be self-evident. Mi pham minimizes this intuition by devaluing the overall importance of the Svātantrika-Prāsaṅgika distinction, which he restricts to the methodological domain. With the attendant emphasis on self-cognition and the luminosity of the mind that this brings about, Mi pham is then in a position to provide a Madhyamaka synthesis that may be readily integrated into the tantric context of the Great Perfection.

Dreyfus then poses the difficult question of whether and how we should understand Mi pham's own claim to be a Prāsaṅgika when so much of his Madhyamaka thought appears to favor philosophers and ideas that are more frequently associated with Svātantrika-Madhyamaka. This is a truly thorny question, and Dreyfus shows that there is no easy answer. One way to approach the question, however, is to focus on an issue that Mi pham himself makes central to his own interpretation of the Svātantrika-Prāsaṅgika distinction, namely, the question of the role of the figurative *(paryāya)* and the actual *(aparyāya)* ultimate. In brief, as Dreyfus puts it, the figurative ultimate "is the ultimate as it is understood at the conceptual level."[47] Mi pham then defines a Svātantrika as a Mādhyamika who emphasizes *(rtsal du bton)* the role of the figurative ultimate in the larger search for the actual ultimate. The Prāsaṅgika is then one who more readily dispenses with conceptual understandings of the ultimate. This way of drawing the distinction allows Mi pham to maintain the superiority of the Prāsaṅgika without having to concede any philosophical or theoretical defects in the Svātantrika view. As Dreyfus explains, because Mi pham does not see a radical difference between Svātantrika and Prāsaṅgika, he feels free to employ what he understands as Svātantrika techniques of approaching emptiness as long as such techniques are useful. Once a person has a clear grasp of the figurative ultimate, however, it is time to move on to the Prāsaṅgika approach, and to what is perhaps even more effective, the tantric approach of the Great Perfection. Thus, Mi pham's claim to be a Prāsaṅgika can be seen as legitimate, as long as we bear in mind that his version of Prāsaṅgika represents a "*tantric Madhyamaka view,* based on the combination of an extensive investigation of the figurative ultimate with a vision of the luminosity of the mind."[48]

Dreyfus ends his essay with a plea for scholars to reflect on the complexity and fragility of the highly contested Svātantrika-Prāsaṅgika distinction. In exhorting us not to be too hasty to embrace Tibetan formulations of the distinction, Dreyfus reminds us that, much as they differ in their portrayals of Svātantrika and Prāsaṅgika, traditional Tibetan scholars nonetheless share a tendency to "overemphasize the unity of the Indian tradition, presenting it as the recipient of timeless truths rather than as the vehicle for historically situated and hence contingent interpretations."[49] This corresponds to Huntington's point made earlier in the volume, and speaks to a general and pervasive difference in the hermeneutical stance of the scholars writing here as compared to the bygone scholars of Tibet. Thus, even when Tsong kha pa outlines the "eight difficult points" that differentiate Prāsaṅgika from Svātantrika, he does so in a manner that presupposes a far greater unity of thought among the supposed proponents of these two subschools than does the analysis of most, if not all, of the contributors to this collection. For Huntington, the discrepancy between the methods and assumptions of traditional Tibetan doxography and those of modern scholarship stands as a warning to those who wish to penetrate the historical realities of Indian Madhyamaka not to rely on the Tibetan tradition. For Dreyfus, in contrast, the discrepancy suggests only that modern scholars must be scrupulous in attending not only to the historical particularities of the Indian tradition, but also to the (often not immediately apparent) complexities and nuances of the Tibetan doxographical tradition. Thus Dreyfus concludes that while there is nothing self-evident in the Svātantrika-Prāsaṅgika distinction as it is delineated by the variety of traditional scholars in Tibet, this is by no means sufficient to disqualify it; it is, however, enough to oblige the careful interpreter to a greater vigilance in his or her use of the concepts pertaining to this distinction.

In summing up the contributions of this volume, one might point first of all to the presentation of a number of broad historical and descriptive topics important for the larger understanding of Buddhism, including, for instance, aspects of the evolution of Madhyamaka thought and interpretation in India and Tibet. Other benefits are more overtly textual, pertaining to the ways in which particular passages have been interpreted by great

Indian and Tibetan Mādhyamikas. But perhaps the most important substantive issues raised by this volume can be said to be normative, insofar as they bear on the philosophical value of the sometimes sizeable claims made by Mādhyamikas concerning such questions as the limits of philosophical arguments, the implications of logic and inference, and the possibility of truth and objectivity. These topics concern not only Buddhist philosophy but have broader implications in philosophy more generally, as illustrated, for example, by the discussions in this volume on the myth of the given. From its incipience, the Madhyamaka tradition has been defined by, and criticized for, its radical undermining of classical philosophical notions such as truth and objectivity. These notions, however, are not just simple mistakes, but in many ways are foundational to our thinking. Hence, they cannot be dismissed through brute rejection but must rather be dismantled, so to speak, from the inside. This means that in the process of subverting such notions, the Mādhyamika will also be constrained to use them while simultaneously exposing their contradictions. This self-subverting means of proceeding raises an obvious question: how can one use and at the same time undermine philosophical notions? This is one of the fundamental conundrums at the heart of the debates concerning the Svātantrika-Prāsaṅgika distinction; the reader will find that it is explored in a variety of ways and from diverse perspectives in the pages that follow.

The subtitle of this collection of essays takes the form of the question "what difference does a difference make?" The question is inspired by the anthropologist Gregory Bateson's definition of information (and, hence, knowledge) as consisting of "differences that make a difference."[50] A difference that makes *no* difference becomes irrelevant, if it is noticed at all. But what counts as making a difference? In the case of the Svātantrika-Prāsaṅgika distinction, everyone agrees that it is possible to find differences in the ideas of the various Indian Mādhyamika protagonists. But the question remains whether such differences are important or meaningful, or whether they are superficial or perhaps even irrelevant. As the articles in this volume show, differences become more or less meaningful insofar as individuals choose to highlight or downplay them; and the process of highlighting or downplaying differences is always in part directed by an individual's particular interests and goals. Since no two individuals have precisely the same interests and goals, we can expect diverse evaluations of the Svātantrika-Prāsaṅgika distinction inevitably to exhibit divergent contours even when numerous descriptive elements in the evaluations remain the same. In this regard, the differences between traditional and modern scholars—and between those who highlight and those who downplay the Svātantrika-Prāsaṅgika distinction—seem insignificant in light of the greater similarity of our general hermeneutical condition.

NOTES

1 A recent example is found in Donald Mitchell's introductory text on Buddhism (2001): 136: "The 'middle period' of the school [i.e., Madhyamaka] is marked by a disagreement between two philosophers. The first philosopher of this middle period was Buddhapālita (fifth century C.E.). While Buddhapālita employed the logical method of reductio ad absurdum to disprove the views of his opponents, he never attempted to formulate a position of his own. He believed that the ultimate truth cannot be formulated by words, which are always tied to conventional viewpoints. His school of Mādhyamika is called *Prāsaṅgika* after his *prasaṅga* method of logic. The second philosopher of this middle period was Bhāvaviveka (ca. 500–570). He had a more optimistic view of language's ability to bridge the gap between the conventional and ultimate truths. Influenced by the Buddhist logician Dignāga, whom we will introduce later, Bhāvaviveka used logic to present positive expositions of emptiness. His school of Mādhyamika is called *Svātantrika* because it provided a positive position concerning emptiness by 'autonomous' *(svatantra)* logical means." Nowhere does Mitchell remark that the categories Prāsaṅgika and Svātantrika are later Tibetan creations; rather, he uses these terms as if they were indigenous and self-evident.

2 See Cabezón (1990): 18.

3 This is not to say that the category is completely unproblematic. In the early period especially, the categories of Madhyamaka and Yogācāra, which later appear as distinct doxographical classifications, may not apply as neatly as many sources would lead one to believe. For example, Asaṅga, a purported father of the Yogācāra, is credited with writing a commentary on Nāgārjuna's MMK, while Nāgārjuna's student Āryadeva's main work is entitled the *Yogācāracatuḥśataka.*

4 See the contributions by William Ames and C. W. Huntington in the present volume.

5 See Tillemans (1990): 8.

6 Although the early Tibetan author Ye shes sde (8th c.) is usually credited with the first use of the terms *mDo sde spyod pa'i dbu ma* (*Sautrāntika-Madhyamaka) and *rNal 'byor spyod pa'i dbu ma* (*Yogācāra-Madhyamaka), we also find Kamalaśīla in his subcommentary on Śāntarakṣita's MA referring to the "two paths of the Madhyamaka" (MAP, D 128a: *dbu ma'i lam gnyis)* in a context in

which it seems clear that one path upholds external objects conventionally, while the other follows the Yogācāra or Cittamātra tradition of rejecting external objects.

7 Atiśa, *Byang chub lam gyi sgron me dang de'i bka' 'grel,* 182.

8 See, e.g., Ruegg (2000) and Mimaki (1982).

9 Tsong kha pa, *Legs bshad snying po* (Sarnath ed.) 139.

10 Throughout this introduction, we use the conventionally accepted Sanskrit term *Prāsaṅgika* despite its lack of attestation in available Sanskrit sources. In using the term, we do not mean to imply the existence of a school by that name, but rather we use it to refer to certain authors, most often Indian ones, in accordance with the ways in which they are understood by particular Tibetan thinkers. Although the term *Svātantrika* is attested in the Tibetan translation of Jayānanda's MAṬ, its use there is not unambiguous, and we use the term here with similar caution. See Yotsuya (1999): xi.

11 See Lang (1990).

12 Gadamer (1982): 264.

13 Bu ston's opinion is reported by Mi pham in his *Nor bu ke ta ka,* 6.

14 This term appears to have been invented by Tibetan scholars to make sense of the fact that Candrakīrti both criticizes and uses formal arguments; the ones that he uses were then described as being "other-intended" or "other-acknowledged" and thus differentiated from the purely "autonomous" arguments that he rejects. On the concept of *gzhan grags kyi rjes dpag,* see Tillemans (1992).

15 Prior to the flowering of the Buddhist logical tradition in the works of Dignāga and Dharmakīrti, it appears that Buddhist philosophers such as Nāgārjuna understood the *prasaṅga* to be purely a form of reductio, i.e., a way of refuting the adversary on his own ground by drawing out the absurd or unwanted consequences deriving from his positions. With the development of the logical tradition, the scope of the *prasaṅga* was expanded, such that it could now be seen as implying a positive probative argument through the operation of a "reversal of the consequence" *(prasaṅgaviparyaya, thal bzlog pa).* For example, a *prasaṅga* that concludes "it would follow that the subject, a sprout, is not dependently arisen because it is truly existent" can be seen as implying the positive probative argument "the subject, a sprout, is not truly existent because it is dependently arisen." On *prasaṅgaviparyaya,* see Iwata (1993) and Kajiyama (1966): 114ff. For the development of this idea in Tibet, see the contribution by Tauscher in the present volume.

16 See the contribution by Huntington in the present volume, 75.

17 Ibid.: 77.

18 Ibid.: 68.

19 Ibid.: 82.

20 See the contribution by Tillemans in the present volume, 114.

21 Ibid.: 94.

22 Ibid.: 109.

23 Sellars (1997).

24 Rorty (1979): 104.

25 See the contribution by Tillemans in the present volume, 96.

26 [Editor's note:] In arguing for the relevance of Sellars' myth of the given to the analysis of the Svātantrika view, Tillemans deals with at least two major objections to his position. The second objection more or less corresponds to Sara McClintock's analysis in this volume, and her answer can be found in her contribution. The first objection is Georges Dreyfus' contention that Dharmakīrti is not committed to the myth of the given. This is obviously not the place to engage in the detailed arguments that a response would require, but stepping out of my role as a coeditor of this volume, I (Georges Dreyfus) feel compelled to say a few words.

Let me start by saying that I agree that there are many elements of the given in Dharmakīrti's view that bring him close to empiricism: the distinction between conceptual schemes and perceptual objects; the primacy of perception among the two allowable forms of knowledge; the insistence on grounding inference, the other form of knowledge, on perception; the requirement that perception apprehends real particulars; and so on. This is certainly enough to determine that Dharmakīrti is a foundationalist, as I did in my book *Recognizing Reality*. But I would maintain that this is not enough to decide that Dharmakīrti subscribes to the myth of the given in the full Sellarsian sense of the term because a crucial epistemological component is missing: the assertion that real external particulars are known directly and immediately by perception. If I understand Tillemans correctly, he is arguing that Dharmakīrti's perception is cognitive since it apprehends particulars and since particulars appear to it. Moreover, it contributes directly to the epistemic process and is thus different from nonsentient processes such as digestion (this is Tillemans' own example). Hence, perception must be cognitive for Dharmakīrti. These arguments are rather unconvincing. The fact that perception differs from nonsentient processes hardly proves that it is cognitive. Is it not the view of Sellars, the authority Tillemans rightly defers to, that sensing is mental and sentient but neither cognitive nor epistemic? Why couldn't Dharmakīrti's perception be like Sellars' sensing, that is, devoid of content, noncognitive, and nonepistemic, while still being mental, sentient, and making a strong causal contribution to the cognitive process? Moreover, for Dharmakīrti, terms such as "apprehend" and "appear" are little more than conventional designations that refer to causal processes. In reality, perceptions put us in touch with external objects by being directly produced by external objects as bearing their likeness, not by directly cognizing them. Perceptions contribute to the cognitive process by providing sentience (the feeling of pleasant, unpleasant, or neutral experiences) and inducing perceptual judgments. It is only through these judgments, however, that perceptions provide knowledge concerning the external world.

27 See the contribution by Tillemans in the present volume, p. 123, n. 49.

28 See the contribution by Eckel in the present volume, 176.

29 The similarities between Candrakīrti and Jñānagarbha have been noted by the

Tibetan doxographer dBus pa blo gsal (ca. 1300), who describes them both as belonging to the "School [that relies] on what is Renown to the World" *('Jigs rten grags sde)*. See Mimaki (1982): 173. This description, however, has been criticized by sTag tshang and others. See Ruegg (2000): 58.

30 See the contribution by Eckel in the present volume, 194.

31 See Ruegg (2000): 23–25 for further references to Madhyamaka doxographical divisions in the earliest period of the transmission of Buddhism to Tibet.

32 Ruegg (2000): 26.

33 Other authors from the eleventh through early thirteenth centuries whose now lost works may have provided important antecedents to the later debates on the Svātantrika-Prāsaṅgika distinction in Tibet include rNgog blo ldan shes rab (1059–1109), said by later Tibetans to have been a Svātantrika; Phya pa chos kyi seng ge (1109–1169), later considered a Svātantrika and treated in the contribution by Helmut Tauscher in this volume; Phya pa's students, including two who are later renowned as proponents of Prāsaṅgika, namely, gTsang nag pa brtson 'grus and rMa bya rtsod pa'i seng ge; Khu mdo sde 'bar, a disciple of Pa tshab nyi ma grags and a co-translator with Jayānanda of several Madhyamaka treatises; Pa tshab's disciples, including rMa bya byang chub brtson 'grus / rMa bya byang chub ye shes (for whom we do have a Madhyamaka commentary), gTsang pa sar spos, Dar yon tan grags / Dar yul ba rin chen grags, and Zhang thang sag pa ye shes 'byung gnas. On these and other such figures, see Ruegg (2000): 27–55.

34 On the similar doxographical division of the Madhyamaka into the sGyu ma rigs grub and the Rab tu mi gnas pa, and its rejection first by rNgog blo ldan shes rab and later by Tsong kha pa, see Ruegg (2000): 33ff., n. 60. Ruegg also notes here that the distinction is similar to one found in a late Indian text, the *Tattvaratnāvalī* of Advayavajra, where the distinction is drawn between the Mayopamādvayavādin and the Sarvadharmāpratiṣṭhānavādin branches of Madhyamaka. Cf. also Ruegg (1981): 58–59; Mimaki (1982): 31f.; Tauscher (1995): 6f.

35 See Ruegg (2000): 56, n. 122. On the term *'Jig rten grags sde pa*, see ibid.: 58, n. 124.

36 See the contribution by Tauscher in the present volume, 211.

37 The information in this paragraph is based on Ruegg's excellent work *Three Studies in the History of Indian and Tibetan Madhyamaka Philosophy* (2000), which, despite its great merits, is able to present only a tentative account of the history of early Tibetan Madhyamaka, since it is based, of necessity, not on original sources, which are largely lost, but rather on secondary reports provided by such later authors such as Go rams pa bsod nams seng ge, Shākya mchog ldan, 'Jam dbyangs bzhad pa, and so on.

38 See Dreyfus (1997).

39 See the contribution by Yoshimizu in the present volume, 261.

40 Ibid.: 267.

41 See the contribution by Cabezón in the present volume, 291.
42 Ibid.: 291.
43 Ibid.: 298.
44 Ibid.: 298.
45 Ibid.: 303.
46 Ibid.: 305.
47 See the contribution by Dreyfus in the present volume, 335.
48 Ibid.: 339.
49 Ibid.: 342.
50 Bateson (1979): 99.

Part 1: Examining The Distinction in the Indian Tradition

1. Bhāvaviveka's Own View of His Differences with Buddhapālita

WILLIAM L. AMES

Introduction

THE TERMS *Svātantrika* and *Prāsaṅgika* are modern scholars' translations into Sanskrit of the Tibetan terms *Rang rgyud pa* and *Thal 'gyur ba,* respectively, which were used in Tibet from about the eleventh century on to designate two subschools of the Madhyamaka school of Mahāyāna Buddhism.[1] In order to understand why this distinction was made and where Bhāvaviveka and Buddhapālita fit into it, some background is necessary.

The Madhyamaka[2] school is one of the two major philosophical schools of Mahāyāna Buddhism, along with the Yogācāra school. The Madhyamaka is best known for its doctrine of emptiness *(śūnyatā).* The idea of emptiness is found in the "perfection of discernment" *(prajñāpāramitā)* sūtras, some of which are among the earliest Mahāyāna sūtras. While the sūtras expound emptiness in a discursive way, the Mādhyamikas use systematic argument.

Emptiness, for the Madhyamaka school, means that *dharmas*[3] are empty of intrinsic nature *(svabhāva).* All Buddhists hold that conditioned *dharmas* arise in dependence on causes and conditions. For the Mādhyamikas, this fact of dependent origination *(pratītyasamutpāda)* implies that *dharmas* can have no intrinsic, self-sufficient nature of their own. Since *dharmas* appear when the proper conditions occur and cease when those conditions are absent, the way in which *dharmas* exist is similar to the way in which mirages and dreams exist.[4] When one recognizes this, attachment and aversion are undermined, since ultimately they have no substantial objects and lack any self-sufficient status of their own.[5] Moreover, the Mādhyamikas argue that if things existed by their own intrinsic nature, they would be changeless,[6] but that this contradicts our everyday experience.

The Madhyamaka school was founded by Nāgārjuna (active ca. 150–200), the author of the *Mūlamadhyamakakārikā* (MMK). The MMK inspired a number of commentaries that not only expounded the meaning of the work but also often acted as vehicles for the commentators' own views. The *Akutobhayā* seems to be the earliest of the extant commentaries. It is of uncertain authorship, although it is sometimes ascribed to Nāgārjuna himself.[7]

The earliest extant commentary on the MMK by a known author[8] is that of Buddhapālita (ca. 500). Buddhapālita closely followed Nāgārjuna's own method, which utilized mainly *prasaṅga* arguments. These are arguments that show that the opponent's position leads to consequences *(prasaṅga)* unacceptable to the opponent himself, without, however, committing the Mādhyamika to affirming a contrary position.

Bhāvaviveka (ca. 500–570)[9] was the next important Mādhyamika philosopher. Besides his commentary on the MMK, the *Prajñāpradīpa* (PrP), he wrote some notable independent works, such as the *Madhyamakahṛdayakārikā* (MHK) and its autocommentary, the *Tarkajvālā* (TJ). Bhāvaviveka seems to have been the first to use the formal syllogism *(prayogavākya)* of Indian logic[10] in expounding the Madhyamaka. The PrP is the first commentary on the MMK to make use of the formal apparatus of Buddhist logic and the first to discuss non-Buddhist philosophical schools extensively. Bhāvaviveka's accounts, in the PrP and elsewhere, of the positions of other Buddhist and non-Buddhist schools give valuable information on the state of Indian philosophy in his day.

In the PrP, Bhāvaviveka strongly criticized Buddhapālita for failing to use formal syllogisms. He felt that the author of a commentary should state independent inferences *(svatantrānumāna)*[11] rather than simply giving *prasaṅga* arguments. Bhāvaviveka's position was later criticized by Candrakīrti, who defended Buddhapālita in his own commentary on the MMK, the *Prasannapadā* (PPMV).

Bhāvaviveka was retrospectively considered by Tibetan scholars to have founded the Svātantrika subschool and to have initiated the split between the two subschools by his criticism of Buddhapālita. Candrakīrti was retrospectively considered to have founded the Prāsaṅgika subschool through his defense of Buddhapālita and criticism of Bhāvaviveka.[12] Much has been written by both Tibetan and Western authors about the nature of the differences between the two subschools, and in Tibet, views on this subject became subtle and complex.[13] It may, therefore, be illuminating to cast our minds back to Bhāvaviveka's day and consider the debate at its beginnings.

Bhāvaviveka's Criticisms of Buddhapālita

Though Bhāvaviveka never mentions Buddhapālita by name in the PrP, he quotes a number of times from Buddhapālita's commentary on the MMK, the *Buddhapālitamūlamadhyamakavṛtti.* Each quotation is preceded by a phrase like "Others say" and is followed by Bhāvaviveka's refutation of Buddhapālita's position. The quotation is identified as being from Buddhapālita's commentary by Avalokitavrata, the author of a voluminous subcommentary on the PrP called *Prajñāpradīpaṭīkā* (PrPṬ) which is invaluable for understanding Bhāvaviveka's commentary.[14]

Bhāvaviveka criticizes Buddhapālita nineteen times in the nineteen (out of twenty-seven) chapters of the PrP that I have so far examined.[15] As might be expected, many of these criticisms deal with issues specific to the verse being commented on. For example, Bhāvaviveka says that the question that Buddhapālita uses to open chapter 2 of the MMK is inappropriate for the type of person supposed to be asking it,[16] and he charges that Buddhapālita misinterprets a word in MMK 2.2.[17] In his commentary on MMK 9.8d and 16.3cd,[18] Bhāvaviveka claims that Buddhapālita's refutation of an opponent does not apply to that opponent's position. In his commentary following MMK 18.7, Bhāvaviveka argues that Buddhapālita's rejection of an opponent's charge that Mādhyamikas are nihilists is inadequate.[19]

In many cases, however, Bhāvaviveka's criticisms revolve around a particular issue that he states succinctly in his commentary on MMK 6.5ab. Chapter 6 of the MMK is called "Examination of Desire *(rāga)* and the One Who Desires *(rakta).*" Nāgārjuna argues that desire and the one who desires cannot be established, no matter whether they are conceived of as being successive in time or as concomitant, that is, simultaneous in time and proximate in space. (The term that I have translated as "concomitance" is *sahabhāva,* literally, "existence together.") MMK 6.5 is part of a subargument that desire and the one who desires can be concomitant neither if they are identical nor if they are different. Bhāvaviveka first quotes Buddhapālita's commentary and then gives his own critique:[20]

> [*Buddhapālita's commentary:*] Here [Buddhapālita][21] says: To begin with, if desire and the one who desires were concomitant even though they are identical, in that case, there would be concomitance *(sahabhāva)* even without a companion. How? Here "identical" *(gcig, eka,* literally, "one") refers to a single [thing] *(gcig pu).* Then the identity *(ekatva)* of "one cow and one horse" both refers

to the cow and refers to the horse. Therefore it would follow that wherever identity exists, there concomitance [also] exists, and that even without a companion, concomitance would exist in just a single cow or just a single horse. Thus it would be pointless to suppose that [desire and the one who desires] are concomitant.

[*Bhāvaviveka's critique:*] That [explanation] is not right, [1] because an undesired consequence[22] belongs to neither proof *(sādhana)* nor refutation *(dūṣaṇa)* and [2] because, since one wishes to state those [i.e., proof of one's own position and refutation of the opponent's position], just those must be expressed; but they are not expressed [by Buddhapālita].

Here we see that Bhāvaviveka objects to Buddhapālita's use of a *prasaṅga* argument, i.e., an argument that shows that an opponent's position leads to an undesired consequence, and that he insists on the explicit statement of a proof and a refutation. To see what Bhāvaviveka means by a proof, we need to look at his own method of argumentation.

Bhāvaviveka's Syllogistic Method

I have already referred to Bhāvaviveka's use of syllogisms, syllogisms, that is, of the Indian rather than the Aristotelian sort. Bhāvaviveka seems to have been strongly influenced by the work of the great Buddhist logician Dignāga,[23] who was probably his elder contemporary.[24] As far as we know, though, Bhāvaviveka was the first writer to make use of formal syllogisms in expounding the Madhyamaka.

In order to understand Bhāvaviveka's use of syllogisms in the PrP, it is helpful to go back to the MHK, which is probably his earliest work, and its autocommentary, the TJ.[25] Here he introduces the logical method that he will use in the PrP. That is, Bhāvaviveka states formal syllogisms and then refutes any faults in those syllogisms that opponents might allege. The first example of a syllogism is MHK 3.26:

As to that, in ultimate reality *(paramārthataḥ),* earth and so on indeed do not have the intrinsic nature *(svabhāva)* of [material] elements *(bhūta),*

> Because they are contingent *(kṛtaka),* like cognition, or else because they have causes and so on.[26]

This syllogism is typical of the many others that Bhāvaviveka states in the MHK and the PrP. The thesis is a negative statement with the qualification "in ultimate reality." In this case, significantly, it is intrinsic nature that is negated. The TJ on this verse explains that the negation is a pure negation *(prasajyapratiṣedha)*[27] and that the qualification "in ultimate reality" applies to the predicate of the thesis. (If it applied to the subject, "earth and so on," then Bhāvaviveka would be asserting that earth exists in ultimate reality.)

Thus we have a thesis *(pratijñā)* with a subject *(dharmin),* "earth and so on," and a predicate *(sādhya).* This is one member *(avayava)* of the syllogism. The two remaining members are the reason *(hetu),* "because they are contingent," and the example *(dṛṣṭānta),* "like cognition." Here Bhāvaviveka gives an alternative reason, "because they have causes," and implies that there are even more possible reasons by saying, "and so on." Sometimes he gives more than one example as well. Even when a syllogism has multiple reasons or examples, it is still considered to be a three-membered syllogism if it has only three *kinds* of members, i.e., thesis, reason(s), and example(s).[28]

In the PrP, besides three-membered syllogisms, one also finds the five-membered syllogism associated with the Nyāya-Vaiśeṣika school.[29] The two additional members are the application *(upanaya),* which states that the reason is indeed present in the subject of the thesis, and the conclusion *(nigamana),* which consists of the word "therefore" followed by a restatement of the thesis. Five-membered syllogisms seem to occur almost exclusively in the objections that Bhāvaviveka puts into the mouths of opponents,[30] though opponents are also given three-membered syllogisms to utter. Bhāvaviveka himself normally uses three-membered syllogisms in his exposition and answers to opponents' objections.[31]

Bhāvaviveka also answers possible objections to his syllogisms. An opponent objects that ultimate reality *(paramārtha)* is beyond words and concepts and so no thesis, not even a negative one, can hold "in ultimate reality." In response, the TJ distinguishes two kinds of ultimate reality. One is supramundane *(lokottara)* and free from conceptual elaboration *(prapañca).* The other is called "pure worldly cognition" *(śuddhalaukika-jñāna)* and possesses conceptual elaboration. Since the thesis of Bhāvaviveka's syllogism is qualified by "ultimate reality" in the latter sense, there is no difficulty.[32] Another opponent charges that the Mādhyamika's argument is mere caviling *(co 'dri ba)* because he refutes another's position *(pakṣa)* without establishing a position of his own. The TJ replies that the Mādhyamika does have a *pakṣa:* all *dharmas* are empty of intrinsic nature, and that fact is their intrinsic nature.[33]

Bhāvaviveka uses the same syllogistic method in his commentary on the MMK, the PrP, as he does in his independent works. Avalokitavrata's subcommentary analyzes each of the numerous syllogisms, breaking them down into subject *(dharmin)* and predicate (*sādhyadharma,* lit., property to be proved) of the thesis, proving property *(sādhanadharma),*[34] and example *(dṛṣṭānta).* Sometimes the example is characterized as similar *(sādharmya)* or dissimilar *(vaidharmya).* If Bhāvaviveka uses a five-membered syllogism, Avalokitavrata also mentions the application *(upanaya)* and the conclusion *(nigamana).*

Bhāvaviveka's Objections to Buddhapālita's Commentary on MMK 1.1

Buddhapālita's commentary on MMK 1.1 (that is, the first verse of chapter 1 following the two dedicatory verses) is a good example of his argumentation:[35]

> Not from themselves, nor from another, nor from both, nor from
> no cause,
> Do any originated entities *(bhāva)* ever exist anywhere.[36] [MMK 1.1]

> Here if any entity originated, the origination of that entity would have to be either from itself, or from another, or from both itself and another, or from no cause; but upon examination, [origination] is not possible from any [of these].... To begin with, entities do not originate from their own selves, because their origination would be pointless and because there would be no end to origination. For there is no purpose in the origination again of entities which [already] exist by their own selves. If they do originate again even though they exist [already], never would they not be originating;[37] [but] that, too, is not accepted. Therefore, to begin with, entities do not originate from themselves.

> Nor do they originate from another...because it would follow that everything would originate from everything.[38]
>
> Nor do they originate from both themselves and another, because the faults of both [alternatives] would follow.
>
> Nor do they originate from no cause, because it would follow that everything would always be originating from everything[39] and because there would be the fault that all undertakings would be pointless.
>
> Thus because the origination of entities is not possible in any way, therefore the term "origination" is a mere conventional expression *(vyavahāramātra)*, since origination does not exist.

In the PrP, Bhāvaviveka criticizes all of these arguments of Buddhapālita's, except for the third argument concerning origination from both self and other. Regarding the first argument, Bhāvaviveka says,

> That is not right *(ayukta)*, because no reason and example are given and because faults stated by the opponent are not answered. [Also,] because it is *prasaṅga* argument,[40] a [property] to be proved *(sādhya)* and a property *(dharma)* [which proves] that, opposite in meaning [to that intended], [become] manifest by reversing the original meaning. [Specifically, the opponent could say that] entities originate from another, because origination has a result and because origination has an end.[41] Thus [Buddhapālita's own] doctrine *(kṛtānta)* would be contradicted.[42]

Bhāvaviveka criticizes Buddhapālita's second argument in the following way:

> Therefore, because there is a *prasaṅga* argument[43] in that [commentary of yours], [then] having reversed the [meanings of] the [property] to be proved *(sādhya)* and the proving [property] *(sādhana)*, [one could say that] entities originate from themselves or from both or from no cause, because some [particular thing] originates from some [particular thing].[44] Thus [your] previous position

> would be contradicted. Otherwise, [if such an alteration of the property to be proved and the proving property is not allowed,] that [reason], "because it would follow that everything would originate from everything," is neither a proof *(sādhana)* nor a refutation *(dūṣaṇa);* and therefore that [argument of yours] would be incoherent in meaning *(asaṃgatārtha).*[45]

Finally, concerning Buddhapālita's argument against origination from no cause, Bhāvaviveka says,

> Since here also there is a *prasaṅga* argument,[46] if one accepts the meaning of a statement with a manifestation *(vyakti)* of a reversed [property] to be proved and proving [property], [then] that [argument] has stated the following: Entities originate from a cause, [because] some [particular] thing originates from some [particular] thing at some [particular] time and [because] undertakings do have results.[47] Thus that [commentary of yours] is not logically possible, because of the faults which [we] have stated previously. But if it is otherwise, [that is, if the argument is not reversed,] it is incoherent, as before.[48]

Thus Bhāvaviveka thinks that Buddhapālita should have provided reasons and examples, i.e., a formal Indian syllogism *(prayogavākya);* and he thinks that Buddhapālita should have answered possible counterarguments by opponents from other philosophical schools. Moreover, as it is, Buddhapālita's argument against any one of the four alternatives *(catuṣkoṭi)*[49] can be taken by his opponent to mean that one of the remaining three alternatives must be correct; but this is not what Buddhapālita wants to say. Indeed, Bhāvaviveka seems to hold that if a *prasaṅga* argument means anything at all, it has to mean that another alternative is correct.

One might note here that, in the West, reductio ad absurdum arguments are normally used to prove that the second of two possible alternatives is correct.[50] For example, one can prove that the square root of two is an irrational number by first assuming that it is a rational number and then showing that that assumption leads to a contradiction. In India, the use of *tarka* in the Nyāya-Vaiśeṣika tradition is similar,[51] and Bhāvaviveka evidently assumes that Buddhapālita's *prasaṅga* arguments must be understood in the same way.[52]

Bhāvaviveka's Response to the Absence of Syllogisms in Nāgārjuna's MMK

Like Buddhapālita, Nāgārjuna never gives formal syllogisms and often uses *prasaṅga* arguments.[53] How then does Bhāvaviveka avoid applying to Nāgārjuna the same criticisms that he has made against Buddhapālita? Bhāvaviveka's solution to this dilemma was simple and elegant and quite in keeping with the traditional methods of commentators: Nāgārjuna did not state syllogisms explicitly, but they are *implicit* in what he has said. Thus at the very beginning of the PrP, Bhāvaviveka says that Nāgārjuna has shown both the manifestation and the reality of inference and refutation just by means of his MMK. Nevertheless, some have not understood; and so Bhāvaviveka will explain the MMK according to scripture.[54] In his subcommentary, Avalokitavrata adds that those who have not understood the MMK are those who require a full explanation *(vipañcitajña),* as opposed to those who can understand a condensed statement *(udghaṭitajña).*[55]

Thus Bhāvaviveka maintains that syllogisms are implicit in the MMK for those who have the wit to discern them. The rest of us require a commentary to make them explicit. He expands on the first point in his commentary on MMK 6.4ab.[56] Bhāvaviveka has an opponent say,[57]

> *Objection:* The *ācārya* [Nāgārjuna] has not stated the members [of a syllogism] completely; therefore [his argument] has the fault of being an incomplete proof.
>
> *Answer:* That is not good, because the statements of an *ācārya* are [highly] meaningful statements *(arthavākya)*[58] and because [highly] meaningful statements give rise to great meanings *(mahārtha).* Although they have few words, many syllogisms are established [by them].[59] Moreover, the syllogisms [which I have stated as Nāgārjuna's commentator][60] are not defective. Alternatively, [those syllogisms] would not be [defective even if not all the members were explicitly stated], provided that even in that case, something is commonly known to someone from [the context of] the chapter or the doctrine [in question].[61]

Nāgārjuna, as the author of an aphoristic treatise, does not have to formulate syllogistic arguments and can confine himself to terse indications of the intended meaning. Bhāvaviveka evidently felt, on the other hand, that commentators like Buddhapālita are obliged to give formal syllogisms and to refute potential counterarguments by opponents from the various Buddhist and non-Buddhist schools.[62] Thus Bhāvaviveka's own commentary on the MMK, the PrP, has a profusion of syllogisms, as well as opponents' objections with Bhāvaviveka's answers.

How then does Bhāvaviveka draw syllogisms out of Nāgārjuna's verses? A good example of Bhāvaviveka's method is his commentary on MMK 1.1.[63] Nāgārjuna says,

> Not from themselves, nor from another, nor from both, nor from
> no cause,
> Do any originated entities ever exist anywhere. [MMK 1.1]

As it stands, the verse simply makes four negative assertions: entities never originate from themselves; entities never originate from another; entities never originate from both themselves and another; and entities never originate without a cause. Bhāvaviveka, however, supplies a reason and an example for each assertion, thus producing four formal Indian syllogisms. Regarding the first alternative, origination from itself, he says,[64]

> Since the intended meaning of a statement is not established by a mere assertion *(pratijñāmātra),* here the reason[65] is understood to be existence; for "from itself" is designated in [connection with] an existing self.[66] An example [is given] by virtue of the [property] to be proved *(sādhyadharma)* and the proving property *(sādhana-dharma),* because it is an example of a subject *(dharmin)* which possesses a [property] to be proved and a proving property which are common knowledge [to both sides in a debate].[67]

After some further discussion that we will come back to shortly, Bhāvaviveka says,[68]

> Here the syllogism *(prayogavākya)* is:
>
> [Thesis:] In ultimate reality,[69] it is certain that the inner *āyatana*s do not originate from themselves,
>
> [Reason:] because they exist [already],

[Example:] like consciousness *(caitanya).*

The twelve *āyatanas* are the six sense organs (the five physical sense organs and the mind) plus the corresponding six sense objects. The inner *āyatanas* are the six sense organs. Thus the thesis is a more restricted version of Nāgārjuna's assertion that entities do not originate from themselves. It seems clear, however, from Bhāvaviveka's commentary that he thinks that similar syllogisms could be constructed regarding any entity.

In addition to reformulating Nāgārjuna's thesis, Bhāvaviveka has added a reason and an example. In MMK 1.6, Nāgārjuna argues that an already existing effect cannot originate; but in the context of MMK 1.1, the reason is supplied by Bhāvaviveka. The example alludes to the Sāṃkhyas, who are proponents of *satkāryavāda,* the pre-existence of the effect in the cause, a form of "origination from itself." In the Sāṃkhya system, *caitanya* is a synonym of *puruṣa,* the eternal pure consciousness that does not arise or cease and hence, in particular, does not arise from itself.[70]

Bhāvaviveka was, as far as is known, the first Mādhyamika to use the terms *prasajyapratiṣedha* and *paryudāsapratiṣedha* to distinguish two kinds of negation *(pratiṣedha).*[71] Various translations have been proposed for *prasajyapratiṣedha,* such as "pure negation," "simple negation," "absolute negation," and "nonimplicative negation," while *paryudāsapratiṣedha* has been called "relative negation" or "implicative negation." Whatever translation is used, the idea is that in *prasajyapratiṣedha,* one simply negates a proposition without any further implication. In particular, there is no implied affirmation of another proposition. In *paryudāsapratiṣedha,* on the other hand, one does implicitly assert the opposite of what is being negated.

In his commentary on MMK 1.1, Bhāvaviveka says,[72]

> The negation, "not from themselves," *(na svataḥ)* should be regarded as having the meaning of a simple negation *(prasajyapratiṣedha),*[73] because it is predominantly *(gtso che ba,* perhaps *prādhānya)* negation. [This is so] because [Nāgārjuna's] intention is to establish nonconceptual wisdom *(nirvikalpakajñāna),* which is endowed with all cognizable objects *(jñeyaviṣaya),* by negating the net of all conceptual constructions *(kalpanā).*
>
> If it is taken to be an implicative negation *(paryudāsapratiṣedha),* [then] because that is predominantly affirmation *(vidhi),* it would be distinct from [our] doctrine *(kṛtānta).* [This is so] because [that implicative negation] would teach nonorigination by affirming that

> *dharmas* are unoriginated.[74] For it is said in scripture that if one practices *(spyod,* root *car)* the nonorigination of matter *(rūpa),* one does not practice the perfection of discernment *(prajñāpāramitā).*[75]

I am not quite sure what it means to "practice" the nonorigination of matter. I suppose that it means to believe that matter does not originate and to act in accordance with that belief. In any case, Bhāvaviveka is arguing that Nāgārjuna's negations have to be understood as *prasajyapratiṣedha,* in view of what he means to say. According to Bhāvaviveka, Nāgārjuna wishes to establish nonconceptual wisdom. Thus he must be understood as not affirming any conceptual formulations whatsoever, at least as far as ultimate truth is concerned. Hence his negation of origination cannot be taken to imply an affirmation of nonorigination. Nāgārjuna's negations must then be nonimplicative, i.e., *prasajyapratiṣedha.*

Immediately after the passage just quoted, Bhāvaviveka goes on to say,[76]

> Here one should specify that entities do *not* [emphasis represents *eva*] originate from themselves. If one specifies otherwise, one would ascertain, "Entities do not originate from *themselves* [emphasis represents *eva*]; rather they originate from another." Likewise one would ascertain, "Entities do not originate *just (eva)* from themselves; rather they originate from themselves and another." Therefore that also is not accepted, because it is distinct from [our] doctrine.[77]

In other words, Nāgārjuna's negation of one of the four alternatives does not imply an affirmation of one or more of the remaining three alternatives. Again, this is so because of Nāgārjuna's intention, because of what he wants to say.

Clear differences are already evident between Bhāvaviveka's treatment of Nāgārjuna's arguments and the rougher handling he accords to Buddhapālita. Before we discuss this further, however, let us turn to the question of Nāgārjuna's *prasaṅga* arguments.

Bhāvaviveka's Treatment of Nāgārjuna's Prasaṅga Arguments

In his commentary on MMK 2.19 and again in his commentary on MMK 6.1[78] and MMK 10.1–2 and 10.5, Bhāvaviveka explicitly admits that Nāgārjuna gives a *prasaṅga* argument. To quote his commentary on MMK 2.19,[79]

> If a goer were just the same as [his or her] going *(gamana),*
> The identity *(ekībhāva)* of agent and action/object *(karman)*[80]
> would follow.[81] [MMK 2.19]
>
> Thus because here [in MMK 2.19] there is a *prasaṅga-* argument,[82] the original meaning *(prakṛtārtha)* can be negated; and [the verse] has the meaning of a statement in which a reversed meaning is manifest.[83] For example, [it is like the following argument:] If sound were permanent, it would follow that a jar would also be permanent; but it is not maintained that a jar, which is made [and] is impermanent, is permanent. Therefore,
>
> [Thesis:] sound is impermanent,
>
> [Reason:] because it is made,
>
> [Example:] like a jar.
>
> Therefore here, by virtue of the meaning of [that] statement [in which a reversed meaning is manifest], the syllogism is:
>
> [Thesis:] In ultimate reality, goer and going are not just the same,
>
> [Reason:] because they are agent and action/object,
>
> [Example:] like the cutter and the cut *(bcad pa).*
>
> Although [we] have explained that goer and going are not just the same, [we] have not [thereby] shown that they are just different.[84]

Here what Bhāvaviveka calls the "original meaning" is the hypothesis of the *prasaṅga* argument, "If a goer were just the same as [his or her] going." The purpose of the *prasaṅga* argument is to negate that hypothesis that goer and going are the same. Hence it has the "reversed meaning" *(bzlog pa'i don),* i.e., goer and going are not the same; but as Bhāvaviveka reiterates a few lines farther on, "...[we] merely negate sameness;"[85] that is, we do not affirm difference, either.

Thus Bhāvaviveka holds that Nāgārjuna's *prasaṅga* arguments imply syllogisms that simply negate one alternative without affirming another. In this case, because of Nāgārjuna's intention of negating both sameness and difference,[86] his negation of sameness does not commit him to an affirmation of difference.

On the other hand, when he discusses Buddhapālita's *prasaṅga* arguments, Bhāvaviveka takes precisely the opposite view. Now he holds that Buddhapālita's *prasaṅga* arguments imply syllogisms that affirm some position alternative to that negated by the *prasaṅga* argument. (We have already seen this in Bhāvaviveka's criticisms of Buddhapālita's commentary on MMK 1.1.) Here it is difficult to escape the conclusion that Bhāvaviveka is treating Buddhapālita unfairly. It is one thing to insist that commentators must explicitly state syllogisms and refute opponents, while the authors of verse treatises need not do so.[87] It is quite another to change the way in which *prasaṅga* arguments are understood, depending on whether the argument was made by Nāgārjuna or Buddhapālita.

Absence of Self in Dharmas (dharmanairātmya) and the Yānas[88]

Leaving aside issues of logical and commentarial methodology, there was also at least one doctrinal point on which Bhāvaviveka criticized Buddhapālita. That was the question of whether *dharmanairātmya,* the absence of self in *dharma*s, is taught in the sūtras of the Śrāvakayāna. A closely related question is whether the *śrāvaka*s and *pratyekabuddha*s realize the absence of self in *dharma*s. In his commentary on MMK 7.34, Bhāvaviveka first quotes from Buddhapālita's commentary on the same verse and then offers his refutation:[89]

> [*Buddhapālita's commentary:*] [Buddhapālita][90] says: As examples of the absence of self in conditioned factors, the Blessed One pointed out magical illusions, echoes, reflections, mirages, dreams, masses of foam, bubbles in water, and trunks of plantain trees. He also said, "Here there is not any thusness or nonfalsity *(avitathātā).* Rather, these are conceptual proliferation; and these are also false."[91] In the statement, "All *dharma*s are without self," "without self" has the meaning of "without intrinsic nature," because the word "self" is a term for intrinsic nature.
>
> [*Bhāvaviveka's critique:*] As to that, here [in the Śrāvakayāna], the

> appearance of a self is falsity; and also the word "self" is a term for self. Therefore there is no self in those [aggregates] which is different [from them]; nor are [the aggregates] themselves a self, just as *anīśvara* [means both "having no lord different [from oneself]" and "not being a lord"].[92] That [scriptural] source [quoted by Buddhapālita] cannot teach the absence of self in *dharmas* *(dharmanairātmya).* [This is so] because in the Śrāvakayāna, the meaning of the phrase ["absence of self"] must be explained etymologically as "absence of self in persons *(pudgalanairātmya).*" If [Śrāvakayāna scriptures] could [teach the absence of self in *dharmas*], it would be pointless to embrace another vehicle *(yāna)* [i.e., the Mahāyāna].

Avalokitavrata sums up Bhāvaviveka's position as follows:

> Magical illusions, echoes, and so on, which were used by the Blessed One as examples of the absence of self in conditioned factors, were stated as examples of *pudgalanairātmya.* The statement [in Śrāvakayāna scriptures], "All *dharmas* are without self," is also stated in the sense of *pudgalanairātmya,* not in the sense of absence of intrinsic nature in *dharmas*. The word "self" is a term for "person," not "the intrinsic nature of a *dharma.*"[93]

Hence, in Bhāvaviveka's interpretation, the "self" referred to in the phrase, "the absence of a self in persons *(pudgalanairātmya),*" is a person, a personal self. The "self" referred to in the phrase, "absence of a self in *dharmas* *(dharmanairātmya),*" is the intrinsic nature of a *dharma.*

Moreover, given this interpretation, one can speak of *pudgalanairātmya* in relation to all *dharmas*. Thus if one were to translate strictly in accordance with Bhāvaviveka's interpretation, one should translate *pudgalanairātmya* as "absence of a self which is a person" and *dharmanairātmya* as "absence of a self which is [the intrinsic nature of] a *dharma.*"

Similarly, in his commentary[94] on MMK 18.3ab, Bhāvaviveka says that the *śrāvakas* and *pratyekabuddhas* perceive that there is no entity called a "self," but only a collection *(kalāpa)* of *saṃskāras* which arise and cease at each moment. The great bodhisattvas, on the other hand, see that the *saṃskāras* are unoriginated; and they dwell in the practice of discernment free from conceptual construction *(nirvikalpaprajñā).*

In his commentary[95] on MMK 18.4 and 18.5a, Bhāvaviveka explains that the *śrāvakas* and *pratyekabuddhas* see the absence of self in persons *(pudgalanairātmya)* and thus are able to remove the obscuration of the afflictions *(kleśāvaraṇa),* whereas those who follow the Buddhayāna (i.e., the Mahāyāna) are able to abandon both the obscuration of the afflictions and the obscuration of the knowable *(jñeyāvaraṇa),* both of which must be removed in order to attain the omniscience *(sarvajñatā)* of a Buddha. Bhāvaviveka makes the same point in his MHK, when he says,

> [The aggregates, *āyatana*s, and *dhātu*s] were proclaimed to the *śrāvaka*s for the removal of the obscuration of the afflictions.
>
> [The Mahāyāna was taught] to the compassionate for the removal of the stain of the obscurations of afflictions and the knowable. [MHK 3.24][96]

In his commentary[97] on MMK 18.5d, Bhāvaviveka goes on to say that the removal of the obscuration of the knowable—which involves ridding oneself of "unafflicted" ignorance *(akliṣṭājñāna)* as well as the afflictions—is achieved by means of seeing the absence of a self in *dharma*s. Moreover, that is also necessary for uprooting the traces *(vāsanā)* of the afflictions.

Conclusion

Thus we have seen that in Bhāvaviveka's own view, his differences with Buddhapālita were almost entirely methodological rather than substantive. To summarize, Bhāvaviveka finds *prasaṅga* arguments inadequate for showing that things do not exist by intrinsic nature. Instead, he uses formal Indian syllogisms that have a thesis with a negative predicate qualified by the phrase "in ultimate reality" *(paramārthataḥ).* He specifies that the negation is to be understood as a simple, nonimplicative negation *(prasajyapratiṣedha).* He also finds it essential to refute possible objections to his syllogisms that might be offered by opponents from other philosophical schools, both Buddhist and non-Buddhist. While he is willing to find implicit syllogisms in Nāgārjuna's work, he apparently holds that commentators must give syllogisms explicitly and thus finds fault with Buddhapālita for not doing so. Beyond this, he seems to interpret *prasaṅga* arguments differently depending on whether they are found in Nāgārjuna's verses or Buddhapālita's commentary. This shift in interpretation enables him to criticize Buddhapālita without subjecting Nāgārjuna to the same criticism.

As mentioned earlier, the PrP was the first of the extant commentaries on the MMK to deal extensively with non-Buddhist philosophical schools. The MMK itself seems to have been largely directed at Buddhist followers of the Abhidharma schools. The three centuries or so between Nāgārjuna and Bhāvaviveka were a highly creative period in the history of Indian thought, and all philosophical schools underwent major developments. Bhāvaviveka's effort to show that the arguments in the MMK apply to non-Buddhist schools as well can be seen as part of an attempt to make the MMK relevant to the philosophical controversies of his own day, just as his use of syllogisms can be seen as an attempt to "modernize" Nāgārjuna's arguments.

This last point may explain why Bhāvaviveka was at such pains to reject Buddhapālita's methodology of *prasaṅga* arguments. He may have seen it as hopelessly old-fashioned and out of touch with recent achievements in logic and with contemporary intellectual life generally. He may have felt that continued reliance on *prasaṅga* arguments gave the Madhyamaka school an air of quaint irrelevance. One can speculate that it was for these reasons, as much as for any strictly logical considerations, that he felt impelled to introduce the full machinery of Buddhist logic into the Madhyamaka commentarial tradition.

The sole exception to this picture of Bhāvaviveka's differences with Buddhapālita as "methodology, not substance" seems to be the issue discussed in the previous section, of whether *dharmanairātmya* is taught in the sūtras of the Śrāvakayāna. I think that this can fairly be characterized as a secondary issue. Thus there seems to be no evidence that Bhāvaviveka thought that he had significant doctrinal differences with Buddhapālita.

NOTES

1 See Ruegg (1981): 58–59.

2 As a general rule, *Madhyamaka* is the name of the school and its philosophy; a follower of the school is called a *Mādhyamika*. See Ruegg (1981): 1 and n. 3.

3 According to the Abhidharma literature of the various early Buddhist schools, living beings and physical objects are made up of collections of causally interrelated, impersonal, momentary phenomena called *dharmas*. *Dharmas* may be

either mental or physical and are considered to be ultimate in the sense that they cannot be analyzed further.

4 See, e.g., MMK 7.34 and 17.33.

5 See, e.g., MMK chapter 23, which is discussed in Ames (1988).

6 See MMK 15.8.

7 On the *Akutobhayā,* see Huntington (1986).

8 There is also a Chinese translation of a commentary ascribed to Asaṅga that comments directly only on the dedicatory verses of MMK (MMK 1.A–B). See Ruegg (1981): 49, and Keenan (1989).

9 See Kajiyama (1968–69), and Ruegg (1982): 508, 512–513.

10 It has been pointed out that the Indian syllogism contains inductive and cognitive elements that make the term *syllogism* not entirely appropriate. See Potter (1977): 179, 182–183, and Tillemans (1984a). Nevertheless, I shall continue to call it a syllogism for lack of a better word and with the understanding that, in this context, *syllogism* means an Indian formal argument.

11 Bhāvaviveka himself uses the term *svatantrānumāna* near the end of chapter 9 of the PrP. The sentence in question reads, "In that connection, here the meaning of the chapter is that, by means of stating a refutation *(dūṣaṇa)* of the [opponent's] reason for the existence of an appropriator and by means of stating an independent inference *(svatantrānumāna),* it has been shown that the appropriator has no intrinsic nature." The Tibetan text is as follows (from my unpublished edition based on P, D, and C, with notes deleted): {P 158b7, D 129a7, C 129a7} *de la 'dir rab tu byed pa'i don ni nye bar len pa po yod pa'i gtan tshigs sun dbyung ba brjod pa dang / rang dbang gi rjes su dpag pa brjod pas / nye bar len pa po ngo bo nyid med pa nyid* {D 129b} *du bstan pa* {C 129b} *yin no //.* (My translation of chapters 8 and 9 has been submitted for publication.)

12 See Lopez (1987): 231, on why Candrakīrti, rather than Buddhapālita, was considered to be the founder of the Prāsaṅgika subschool.

13 Among many other examples, see Pettit (1999): 109–110, 132–133, and other references to Svātantrika in his index.

14 Like the PrP, the PrPṬ is no longer extant in Sanskrit. Avalokitavrata's subcommentary is the longest work in the bsTan 'gyur. One third of it is devoted to the first two chapters of the PrP, and one-fourth to the first chapter alone. Besides its value as a commentary, it also contains a great deal of interesting information about both Buddhist and non-Buddhist schools. Avalokitavrata at one point criticizes another subcommentary on the PrP, written by Guṇadatta. (See Kajiyama [1963]: 38; Ruegg [1981]: 67, n. 217; and Ames [1993]: 238–239, n. 50.) This work has not survived, and nothing else is known of it or its author, but the fact that at least two subcommentaries were written on the PrP shows that it was highly regarded in some Indian Buddhist circles.

15 I have not examined eight of the twenty-seven chapters: 13, 14, 15, 19, 20, 21, 22, and 27. The criticisms of Buddhapālita that I have found occur in Bhāvaviveka's commentary on the following verses of the MMK: 1.1 (3 times), 1.4a,

1.7, 1.9cd, beginning of chapter 2, 2.2, 2.22c, 2.23cd, 3.2, 3.3, 5.3ab, 6.5ab, 6.5cd, 9.8d, 10.13b, 16.3cd, and between 18.7 and 18.8.

16 See Ames (1995): 300.

17 Ibid.: 304–305.

18 See Ames (1982): 107.

19 See Eckel (1980): 227–229. (I would like to thank David Eckel for very kindly giving me a copy of his dissertation.)

20 Translation from Ames (2000): 17. Tibetan text as follows (from my unpublished edition based on P, D, and C, with notes deleted): {P 119b, D 98b, C 98a} *'di la gzhan dag ni* {C 98b} *gal te re zhig 'dod chags dang chags pa dag gcig pa nyid yin yang lhan cig nyid du 'gyur na ni de lta na grogs med par yang lhan cig nyid du 'gyur ro // ji ltar zhe na / 'di la gcig ni gcig pu la snyegs te / de na ba lang gcig dang / rta gcig ces bya ba'i gcig nyid ni / ba lang la yang snyegs rta la yang bsnyegs pas gang dang gang na gcig pa nyid yod pa de dang de na lhan gcig nyid yod cing / ba lang gcig pu nyid dang rta gcig pu nyid la grogs med par yang lhan cig nyid yod par thal bar 'gyur te / de ltar na lhan cig nyid du brtag pa don med par 'gyur ro zhes zer ro // kha cig na re / de ni rigs pa ma yin te / glags yod pa sgrub pa dang / sun 'byin pa'i khongs su ma gtogs* {P 120a} *pa'i phyir dang / de dag smra bar 'dod pas de dag nyid brjod par bya ba yin na de dag ma brjod pa'i phyir ro zhes zer ro //.*

21 Literally, "others"; identified as Buddhapālita by Avalokitavrata. See PrPṬ P 119b2, D 108a2. Tibetan text of this quotation from Buddhapālita in Saito (1984): 78,14–21.

22 *glags yod pa, prasaṅga.* See n. 40, below, on this Tibetan translation of *prasaṅga.*

23 See Lindtner (1986): 61 and 78–79, n. 24.

24 Frauwallner tentatively assigned dates of approximately 480–540 to Dignāga. See Frauwallner (1961): 137.

25 On the works ascribed to Bhāvaviveka, see Ames (1986): 33–43, and Ruegg (1990). There is some dispute about the authorship of the *Tarkajvālā.*

26 *tatra bhūtasvabhāvaṃ hi norvyādi paramārthataḥ / kṛtakatvād yathā jñānaṃ hetumattvādito 'pi vā //.* Text and translation in Iida (1980): 82; text in Ejima (1980): 274.

27 This term will be explained below, in the context of Bhāvaviveka's remarks in the PrP on MMK 1.1.

28 According to Tillemans (1984a): 74–77, the three-membered syllogism seems to come from the *Nyāyamukha* of Dignāga and the *Nyāyapraveśa* of Śaṅkarasvāmin. In the *Pramāṇasamuccaya,* Dignāga used a two-membered syllogism that was later adopted by Dharmakīrti. A somewhat more complicated picture is presented in Tillemans (1991).

29 The earliest history of the Indian syllogism is obscure. The five-membered syllogism is already present in the *Nyāyasūtra* of Gautama. It seems to have been preceded by various kinds of ten-membered syllogisms. See Ui (1917): 82–84; Randle (1930): 9–18, 161–167; Solomon (1976): 365–422, and esp. 400–405; Potter (1977): 179–189; Tillemans (1984a): 76, n. 9; and Larson and Bhatta-

charya (1987): 94–98. More recently, see Matilal (1998): 2–14, and Walser (1998): 194–204.

30 The first such syllogism occurs in an opponent's objection to Bhāvaviveka's commentary on MMK 1.1; see Ames (1993): 231 for a translation. There are also many other examples.

31 A possible exception occurs in Bhāvaviveka's commentary on MMK 4.1ab, where he seems to have an application and conclusion in one of his own syllogisms. See Ames (1999): 48–49 for a translation.

32 Text and translation in Iida (1980): 86–87. A similar distinction between two kinds of *paramārtha,* namely **aparyāya-* and **saparyāyaparamārtha,* is found in the *Madhyamakārthasaṃgraha.* This work is ascribed to Bhāvaviveka, but it may, in fact, be by another author; see Ruegg (1990): 67. For a translation of most of the *Madhyamakārthasaṃgraha,* see Lindtner (1981): 200–201, n. 14.

33 Text and translation of TJ on MHK 3.26 in Iida (1980): 82–90. Discussions in Eckel (1978): 327–332; Ruegg (1981): 64–65; and Lindtner (1986): 62–63. The question of whether a Mādhyamika does or does not have a *pakṣa* or a *pratijñā* is complex. See Ruegg (1983) and (2000): 105–232.

34 A member of a syllogism that states a proving property is called a "reason" *(hetu).*

35 Tibetan text in Saito (1984): 10,4–11,2; my translation.

36 PPMV (La Vallée Poussin ed.) 12,13–14: *na svato nāpi parato na dvābhyāṃ nāpy ahetutaḥ / utpannā jātu vidyante bhāvāḥ kvacana kecana //.*

37 Quoted by Candrakīrti at PPMV (La Vallée Poussin ed.) 14,1–3: *ācāryabuddhapālitas tv āha / na svata utpadyante bhāvāḥ / tadutpādavaiyarthyāt / atiprasaṅgadoṣāc ca / na hi svātmanā vidyamānānāṃ padārthānāṃ punarutpāde prayojanam asti / atha sann api jāyeta / na kadācin na jāyeta / iti //.* The Tibetan text of Buddhapālita's commentary (which I have translated here) is slightly different, corresponding to *svātmana(ḥ)* for *svata(ḥ), utpādānavasthā* for *atiprasaṅgadoṣa,* and *bhāvānāṃ* for *padārthānāṃ.*

38 Quoted by Candrakīrti at PPMV (La Vallée Poussin ed.) 36,11–12: *ācāryabuddhapālitas tu vyācaṣṭe / na parata utpadyante bhāvāḥ / sarvataḥ sarvasaṃbhavaprasaṅgād iti /.* (For *-prasaṅgād iti* in place of PPMV's *-prasaṅgāt,* see de Jong [1978]: 32.) Again, the Tibetan is slightly different, omitting *bhāvāḥ.*

39 Quoted by Candrakīrti at PPMV (La Vallée Poussin ed.) 38,10–11: *ācāryabuddhapālitas tv āha / ahetuto notpadyante bhāvāḥ sadā ca sarvataś ca sarvasaṃbhavaprasaṅgād iti /.* (For *-prasaṅgād iti* in place of PPMV's *-prasaṅgāt,* see Saito [1984], trans.: 222, n. 5.) Once again, the Tibetan omits *bhāvāḥ.*

40 The Sanskrit, as quoted by Candrakīrti at PPMV (La Vallée Poussin ed.) 15,1, has *prasaṅgavākya;* but the Tibetan translation of the PrP has *glags yod pa'i tshig,* which would usually correspond to *sāvakāśavacana,* "a statement affording an opportunity." This does not necessarily mean that the translators had a different Sanskrit text. They may have translated *prasaṅgavākya* in this way because of the context and because of Avalokitavrata's subcommentary. Avalokitavrata glosses *glags yod pa'i tshig* as *rgol ba gzhan gyi klan ka'i glags yod pa'i tshig,* "a statement affording an opportunity for censure by an opponent" (PrPṬ

P 86a8, D 74a2). See Kajiyama (1963): 50, n. 13, and Ruegg (1981): 64, n. 203. See also PPMV (La Vallée Poussin ed.) 24,1–6, where both *prasaṅga* and *sāvakāśa* are used.

41 Here Bhāvaviveka has "reversed the meaning" of the predicate in Buddhapālita's thesis, "entities do not originate from their own selves," changing the thesis to "entities originate from another." He has also "reversed the meaning" of Buddhapālita's two reasons, "because their origination would be pointless and because there would be no end to origination," so that they become "because origination has a result and because origination has an end." An important point to notice is that Bhāvaviveka has taken the "reverse" of Buddhapālita's thesis to be "entities originate from another," and not just "entities do not originate from themselves." As we will discuss below, Bhāvaviveka interprets Nāgārjuna's *prasaṅga* arguments differently.

In terms of Western logic, reversing a *prasaṅga* argument *(prasaṅgaviparyaya)* is essentially what is called "contraposition." Suppose we have an implication, "P implies Q." The contrapositive of "P implies Q" is "not-Q implies not-P." Note that if "P implies Q" is true, "not-Q implies not-P" must also be true. (The converse of "P implies Q" is "Q implies P." Even if "P implies Q" is true, its converse is not necessarily true, though it may be.) See Tillemans (2000): 21–24. Mimaki (1976): 55–59 places the question of *prasaṅga* and *prasaṅgaviparyaya* in the context of the history of Indian logic. See also Iwata (1993) (not consulted).

42 This translation is essentially that in Ames (1993): 222–223. Sanskrit quoted by Candrakīrti at PPMV (La Vallée Poussin ed.) 14,4–15,2: *atraike dūṣaṇam āhuḥ / tad ayuktaṃ / hetudṛṣṭāntānabhidhānāt / paroktadoṣāparihārāc ca / prasaṅgavākyatvāc ca prakṛtārthaviparyayeṇa viparītārthasādhyataddharmavyaktau parasmād utpannā bhāvā janmasāphalyāt / janmanirodhāc ceti kṛtāntavirodhaḥ syāt //.* The Tibetan (which I have translated) has *skye ba thug pa yod par 'gyur ba'i phyir* (perhaps *janmāvasthāvattvāt)* for *janmanirodhāt.*

43 *glags yod pa'i tshig.* See n. 40.

44 Here Bhāvaviveka has "reversed the meaning" of the predicate in Buddhapālita's thesis, "[entities] do not originate from another," changing the thesis to "entities originate from themselves or from both or from no cause." He has also "reversed the meaning" of Buddhapālita's reason, "because it would follow that everything would originate from everything," so that it becomes "because some [particular thing] originates from some [particular thing]."

45 Translation from Ames (1993): 225–226. Sanskrit quoted by Candrakīrti at PPMV (La Vallée Poussin ed.) 36,13–37,3: *ācāryabhāvaviveko dūṣaṇam āha / tad atra prasaṅgavākyatvāt / sādhyasādhanaviparyayaṃ kṛtvā / svata ubhayato 'hetuto vā utpadyante bhāvāḥ kutaścit kasyacid utpatteḥ / iti prākpakṣavirodhaḥ / anyathā sarvataḥ sarvasaṃbhavaprasaṅgāt / ity asya sādhanadūṣaṇānantaḥpātitvāt / asaṃgatārtham etad iti /.* (For *etad iti* in place of PPMV's *etat,* see de Jong [1978]: 32.) Again, the Tibetan has *glags yod pa'i tshig* for *prasaṅgavākya.* Also, the Tibetan (which I have translated) corresponds to *sādhanadūṣaṇatā-abhāvāt,* rather than *sādhanadūṣaṇa-anantaḥpātitvāt.*

46 *glags yod pa'i tshig.* See n. 40.

47 Here Bhāvaviveka has "reversed the meaning" of the predicate in Buddhapālita's thesis, "nor do they originate from no cause," changing the thesis to "entities originate from a cause." He has also "reversed the meaning" of Buddhapālita's two reasons, "because it would follow that everything would always be originating from everything and because there would be the fault that all undertakings would be pointless," so that they become "because some [particular] thing originates from some [particular] thing at some [particular] time and because undertakings do have results."

48 Translation from Ames (1993): 234. Sanskrit of all but the last sentence quoted by Candrakīrti at PPMV (La Vallée Poussin ed.) 38,12–39,3: *atrāpy ācāryabhāvaviveko dūṣaṇam āha / atrāpi prasaṅgavākyatvāt / yadi viparītasādhyasādhanavyaktivākyārtha iṣyate tadaitad uktaṃ bhavati / hetuta utpadyante bhāvāḥ kadācit kutaścit kasyacid utpatteḥ / ārambhasāphalyāc ceti / seyaṃ vyākhyā na yuktā prāguktadoṣād iti //.* For *atrāpy ācārya*...in place of PPMV's *atrācārya*..., see de Jong (1978): 32. Also, the Tibetan (which I have translated) corresponds to *tena* for *tadā* and omits *vyākhyā.*

49 See Ruegg (1977).

50 See Ruegg (1981): 36.

51 See ibid.: 36–37, n. 93; Sinha (1956): 555–557; and Potter (1977): 203–204, 206–207.

52 Bhāvaviveka likewise points out that an argument given in *Sāṃkhyakārikā* 9 is a *prasaṅga* argument and says that it is intended to be converted into a positive argument for the Sāṃkhyas' thesis that results pre-exist in their causes. The argument in question is the third reason given in *Sāṃkhyakārikā* 9, *sarvasaṃbhavābhāvāt,* "because everything does not arise [from everything]." The idea is that if results did not pre-exist in their causes, anything could arise from anything else. Bhāvaviveka's remarks are contained in a lengthy "appendix" to his commentary on chapter 8 of the MMK.

53 A few examples are given by Candrakīrti, PPMV (La Vallée Poussin ed.) 24,7–25,2.

54 See Ames (1993): 213. Avalokitavrata glosses manifestation *(gsal ba)* as "correct verbal expression" and explains "reality" *(de kho na)* as meaning that the inferences and refutations are not specious. See ibid.: 235, n. 8.

55 Ibid.: 235, n. 9.

56 An identical passage occurs in Bhāvaviveka's commentary on MMK 18.1. See Eckel (1980): 197–198.

57 Translation from Ames (2000): 15–16. Tibetan text as follows (from my unpublished edition based on P, D, and C, with notes deleted): {P 119a, D 98a, C 98a} *gal te slob dpon gyis yan lag rdzogs par ma brjod pa'i phyir / sgrub pa ma tshang ba nyid kyi skyon yod do zhe na / de ni bzang po ma yin te / slob dpon gyi tshig dag ni don gyi tshig dag yin pa'i phyir dang / don gyi tshig dag gis ni don chen po dag skyed par byed de / tshig nyung ngu nyid yin yang sbyor ba'i tshig du ma dag 'grub pa'i phyir ro // sbyor ba'i tshig dag la ni ma tshang ba nyid du yang mi 'gyur ro // yang na mi 'gyur te / de la yang gang gi tshe rab tu byed pa'am / grub pa'i mtha' las cung zad la la la grags pa yin na'o //.*

58 Avalokitavrata says that the *ācārya* is an author of aphorisms *(sūtrakāra)* and that aphorisms are merely [condensed] statements of the meaning *(don smos pa tsam,* perhaps *arthagrahaṇamātra).* See PrPṬ P 117b1–2, D 106a3–4.

59 Candrakīrti seems almost to quote this sentence at PPMV (La Vallée Poussin ed.) 25,3. The Tibetan translation of the PrP has: *...slob dpon gyi tshig dag ni don gyi tshig dag* (P om. *dag) yin pa'i phyir dang / don gyi tshig dag gis ni don chen po dag skyed par byed de / tshig nyung ngu nyid yin yang sbyor ba'i tshig du ma dag 'grub pa'i phyir ro //* (P 119a4–5; D 98a2; C 98a1–2). The Sanskrit of the PPMV reads (PPMV 25,3–4): *athārthavākyatvād ācāryavākyānāṃ mahārthatve saty anekaprayoganiṣpattihetutvaṃ parikalpyate....* See also PPMV 23,1.

60 See PrPṬ P 117b2–6, D 106a4–7.

61 That is, if some member of the syllogism is obvious to both proponent and opponent, either from the context of the discussion or from their knowledge of the doctrine being discussed, it need not be stated explicitly. See PrPṬ P 117b7–118a1, D 106a7–106b1.

62 Compare PPMV (La Vallée Poussin ed.) 25,4–5: *atha syād vṛttikārāṇām eṣa nyāyo yat prayogavākyavistarābhidhānaṃ kartavyam iti //.* I have not seen a parallel passage in Bhāvaviveka's own works.

63 The following translations of MMK 1.1 and Bhāvaviveka's commentary on it in the PrP are taken from Ames (1993): 220–222.

64 Tibetan text as follows (from my unpublished edition based on P, D, C, and N, with notes deleted): {P 58a, N 48a, D 48b, C 48b} *dam bcas pa tsam gyis bsams pa'i tshig gi don mi 'grub pas / 'dir phyogs kyi chos ni yod pa nyid yin par gzung ste / 'di ltar bdag las zhes bya ba ni bdag nyid yod pa la snyad gdags pa'i phyir ro // dpe ni bsgrub par bya ba dang / sgrub pa'i chos kyi dbang gis te bsgrub par bya ba dang / sgrub pa'i chos grags pa dang ldan pa'i chos can gyi dpe yin pa'i phyir ro //.*

65 *phyogs kyi chos, pakṣadharma,* lit., "property of the subject [of the thesis]." The thesis *(pratijñā)* of a syllogism is composed of a subject *(pakṣa* or *dharmin)* plus a property to be proved *(sādhyadharma).* The reason *(hetu)* states a property of the subject *(pakṣadharma),* also called the "proving property" *(sādhanadharma).* The fact that the subject possesses the proving property shows that it also possesses the property to be proved. (One should note that *hetu,* "reason," is sometimes simply synonymous with *pakṣadharma/sādhanadharma.* Also, *pakṣa* is sometimes used to refer to the whole thesis, not simply the subject of the thesis.)

66 In other words, entities do not originate from themselves, because they already exist. They could not be said to originate from themselves unless they already had a "self" from which to originate.

67 The example in a syllogism must possess the proving property and the property to be proved. It must be acknowledged by both sides in a debate *(vādin* and *prativādin).* See PrPṬ P 72b4–73a5, D 62b7–63b4. "Common knowledge" here translates *grags pa dang ldan pa,* probably *prasiddhimat.*

68 Quoted by Candrakīrti at PPMV (La Vallée Poussin ed.) 25,9–26,2: *[atra] prayogavākyaṃ bhavati / na para[m]ārtha[ta] ādhyātmikāny āyatanāni svata utpannāni / vidyamānatvāt / caitanyavad iti /.* The phrase, "it is certain that"

translates the Tibetan word *nges,* which is found in the Tibetan translation of the PrP but has no Sanskrit equivalent in Candrakīrti's quotation.

69 According to Avalokitavrata, the negation here is made with regard to ultimate reality from the standpoint of the truth of superficial reality *(saṃvṛtisatya)*; but in ultimate reality itself, even the conventional designation *(vyavahāra)* of negation does not exist, because there is no verbal expression. See PrPṬ P 77a1–3, D 66b1–2.

70 Avalokitavrata remarks that in the texts of the Sāṃkhyas, etc., consciousness is said to be the intrinsic nature of spirit *(puruṣa)*. See PrPṬ P 78b7–8, D 67b6–7; and compare *Sāṃkhyakārikā* 11. Avalokitavrata also says that the example is common knowledge for both sides, since the Mādhyamikas accept that cognition *(rnam par shes pa nyid, *vijñānatā)* exists in superficial reality. See PrPṬ P 79a5–79b1, D 68a4–7. Bhāvaviveka next considers and refutes two objections to his syllogism, one of which is attributed to "some among the Sāṃkhyas." See Ames (1993): 222. This supports the idea that this syllogism is aimed at the Sāṃkhyas.

71 See Ruegg (1981): 37–38, 65, with 38, n. 94; Kajiyama (1973): 162, 167–175; and Galloway (1989): 1–9.

72 Translation from Ames (1993): 221. Tibetan text as follows (from my unpublished edition based on P, D, C, and N, with notes deleted): {P 58a, N 48a, D 48b, C 48b} *bdag las ma yin zhes bya ba'i dgag pa 'di ni med par dgag pa'i don du blta bar bya ste / dgag pa gtso che ba'i phyir dang / 'di ltar rtog pa ma lus pa'i dra ba dgag pas rnam par mi rtog pa'i ye shes shes bya'i yul ma lus pa dang ldan pa 'grub par dgongs pa'i phyir ro // ma yin par dgag pa yongs su bzung na ni de sgrub pa gtso che ba'i phyir chos rnams ma skyes so zhes sgrub pas skye ba* {D 49a} *med pa ston* {C 49a} *pa'i phyir mdzad pa'i mtha' dang bral bar 'gyur te / lung las gzugs kyi skye ba med pa la spyod na shes rab kyi pha rol tu phyin pa la spyod pa ma yin no zhes 'byung ba'i phyir ro //.*

73 A portion of Avalokitavrata's commentary on this sentence is translated and discussed in Kajiyama (1973): 169–172.

74 That is, it would teach that nonorigination exists or that unoriginated *dharmas* exist. See PrPṬ P 75a4–8, D 65a4–6.

75 Avalokitavrata identifies the sūtra in question only as *Bhagavatī Prajñāpāramitā.* He gives a fuller quotation in which the Buddha also says that one who practices the origination of matter does not practice the perfection of discernment.

76 Translation from Ames (1993): 221. Tibetan text as follows (from my unpublished edition based on P, D, C, and N, with notes deleted): {P 58a, N 48a, D 49a, C 49a} *'dir dngos po rnams bdag las skye ba med pa kho na'o zhes nges par gzung bar bya'o // gzhan du nges par gzung na bdag kho na las skye ba med de / 'o na ci zhe na / gzhan las skye'o zhes bya bar nges par 'gyur ba dang / de bzhin du bdag kho na las skye ba med de / 'o na ci zhe na / bdag dang gzhan las skye'o zhes bya bar nges par 'gyur bas de yang* {P58b} *mi bzhed de / mdzad pa'i mtha' dang bral ba'i phyir ro //.*

77 This paragraph is translated and discussed in Kajiyama (1973): 168–169.

78 Translation in Ames (2000): 10.

79 Translation from Ames (1995): 322–323. Tibetan text as follows (from my unpublished edition based on P, D, C, and N, with notes deleted), omitting Tibetan text of MMK 2.19: {P 85a, N 73b, D 70b, C 70b} *de ltar na 'dir glags yod pa'i tshig yin pa'i phyir / skabs kyi don* {N 74a} *dgag pa nus shing bzlog pa'i don gsal ba'i tshig gi don to // dper na gal te sgra rtag na bum pa yang rtag pa nyid du thal bar 'gyur te / bum pa byas pa mi rtag pa ni rtag pa nyid du mi 'dod de / de'i phyir sgra ni mi rtag ste / byas pa'i phyir dper na bum pa bzhin no zhes bya ba lta bu'o // de'i phyir 'dir tshig gi don gyi dbang gis sbyor ba'i tshig ni don dam par 'gro ba po dang 'gro ba gcig pa nyid ma yin te / byed pa po dang las yin pa'i phyir dper na gcod pa po dang bcad* {D 71a} *pa bzhin no // 'gro ba po* {C 71a} *dang 'gro ba gcig pa nyid ma yin no zhes bshad kyang / de gnyis gzhan pa nyid du bstan pa ma yin no //.*

80 The word *karman* may mean either "action" or "direct object of an action." (In the sense of action, *karman* is synonymous with *kriyā,* "activity.") Here both senses seem appropriate. *Gamana,* "going," is, of course, the name of an action. One can, however, say *gantā gamanaṃ gacchati,* "the goer goes the going." (See, e.g., MMK 2.24–25.) In that case, *gamana* is also the direct object of the verb *gam,* "to go."

81 PPMV (La Vallée Poussin ed.) 104,13–14: *yad eva gamanaṃ gantā sa eva hi bhaved yadi / ekībhāvaḥ prasajyeta kartuḥ karmaṇa eva ca //.*

82 *glags yod pa'i tshig.* See n. 40.

83 According to Avalokitavrata, the explicit hypothesis that goer and going are the same is to be negated. The sense is that goer and going are *not* the same. See PrPṬ P 302b8–303a3, D 260a5–7.

84 According to Avalokitavrata, this is so because the negation is a simple negation, not an implicative negation. See PrPṬ P 303b5–7 and D 261a1–2.

85 See Ames (1995): 323. Tibetan text as follows (from my unpublished edition based on P, D, C, and N, with notes deleted): {P 85a, N 74a, D 71a, C 71a} *...gcig pa nyid tsam dgag pa'i phyir...*

86 See MMK 2.18, ibid.: 322, and "...[we] wish to show that [those two extremes] are not established in ultimate reality...," ibid.: 323.

87 Though even this may be seen as rather arbitrary. As Candrakīrti points out, Nāgārjuna did not state syllogisms in his autocommentary on the VV; see PPMV (La Vallée Poussin ed.) 25,4–7.

88 These issues have been discussed in Lopez (1987): 82–133, and Lopez (1988).

89 Translation from Ames (2000): 63–64. Tibetan text as follows (from my unpublished edition based on P, D, and C, with notes deleted): {P 138b, D 113a, C 113a} *gzhan dag na re / bcom ldan* {P 139a} *'das kyis 'du byed rnams bdag med pa'i dper sgyu ma dang / brag ca dang / gzugs brnyan dang / smig rgyu dang / rmi lam dang / dbu ba rdos pa dang / chu'i chu bur dang / chu shing gi phung po dag bstan te / 'di la de bzhin nyid dam / ma nor ba de bzhin nyid ni 'ga' yang med kyi / 'di dag ni spros pa yang yin / 'di dag ni brdzun* {D 113b} *pa yang yin no zhes kyang* {C 113b} *gsungs so// chos thams cad bdag med do zhes gsungs pa la bdag med*

pa zhes bya ba ni ngo bo nyid med pa'i don te / bdag ces bya ba'i sgra ni ngo bo nyid kyi tshig yin pa'i phyir ro zhes zer ro // gzhan ma yin pa na re de la 'dir bdag tu snang ba ni nor ba'i de bzhin nyid yin pa'i phyir dang / bdag ces bya ba'i sgra yang bdag gi tshig yin pa'i phyir de dag la bdag gzhan yang med la / rang nyid kyang bdag ma yin te / dbang phyug ma yin pa bzhin pas khungs des ni nyan thos kyi theg pa la gang zag bdag med pa'i sgra'i don bye brag tu rtogs par bya ba yin pa'i phyir chos bdag med pa nyid bstan par mi nus so// nus par gyur na ni theg pa gzhan yongs su bzung ba don med pa nyid du 'gyur ro zhes zer ro//.

90 Literally, "others"; identified by Avalokitavrata. See PrPṬ P 174b1, D 154a4. Tibetan text in Saito (1984): 118,20–119,4.

91 A very similar passage is quoted in PPMV (La Vallée Poussin ed.) 41,6–7; see PPMV 41, nn. 5–7. See also PPMV 237,12–238,1.

92 *dbang phyug ma yin pa.* For the gloss in square brackets, see PrPṬ D 154b4; there is an omission in PrPṬ P 175a2. The point is that *anātman* is to be understood as meaning both "not having a self" and "not being a self."

93 Text in PrPṬ P 175a4–6, D 154b5–7: *bcom ldan 'das kyis 'du byed rnams bdag med pa'i dper sgyu ma dang brag ca la sogs pa dag bka' stsal pa yang gang zag bdag med pa'i dper bka' stsal pa yin la / chos thams cad bdag med do zhes gsungs pa yang gang zag bdag med pa'i don du gsung pa yin gyi chos ngo bo nyid med pa'i don du gsungs pa ma yin la / bdag ces bya ba'i sgra yang gang zag ces bya ba'i tshig yin gyi chos kyi ngo bo nyid kyi tshig ma yin pa las...*

94 Sanskrit quoted in PPMV (La Vallée Poussin ed.) 351,15–352,6; trans. in Eckel (1980): 210.

95 Translation in ibid.: 214–215.

96 *kleśāvaraṇahānāya śrāvakāṇāṃ prakāśitāḥ / kleśajñeyāvṛtimalaprahāṇāya kṛpātmanām //.* Text and trans. in Iida (1980): 79–80; text in Ejima (1980): 274.

97 Trans. in Eckel (1980): 216–217.

2. Was Candrakīrti a Prāsaṅgika?

C. W. HUNTINGTON, JR.

MADHYAMAKA—understood as a philosophical system or "school" *(darśana)* founded by Nāgārjuna—is the central preoccupation of virtually all doxographic literature written in Tibet.[1] Tibetan authors were passionately interested in defining the fundamental tenets of this school and establishing, within it, dependable and true subdivisions of doctrine.[2] Whether or not the *grub mtha'* literature may be studied as an accurate portrayal of Indian Buddhism is a matter of one's perspective. David Seyfort Ruegg refers to Tibetan scholars as "Indologists avant la lettre,"[3] while Katsumi Mimaki walks a more circumspect line in pointing out that *grub mtha'* is itself not Indian, since it was written by Tibetans, but neither is it wholly Tibetan, because they are Indian schools that are described.[4] The distinction may be moot, but two relevant facts are not: first, a sizeable majority of the terminology used to classify subschools of Indian Madhyamaka is now recognized to have been an invention of the Tibetans;[5] and second, many of the terms coined by Tibetan writers are routinely adopted—via Sanskrit forms not attested in any classical source—by modern scholars involved in the historical analysis of Indian Buddhist texts. This practice is so common that most contemporary Buddhologists not only use these unattested Sanskrit forms routinely, but many scholars in the field would probably not immediately recognize the actual Tibetan terms without mentally "translating" them into Sanskrit. The two words that serve as the focus for this volume—Prāsaṅgika and Svātantrika—are no doubt the most widespread examples of such neologisms, and they have exerted a profound and subtle influence on our understanding of early Indian Madhyamaka.[6]

It is likely to remain a matter of conjecture as to who first used the original Tibetan terms. What is certain, however, is that the philosophical justification for the distinction embodied in this vocabulary finds its locus classicus in the first chapter of Candrakīrti's *Prasannapadā* (PPMV).[7] It was there that Candrakīrti criticized Bhāvaviveka's use of a form of "autonomous reasoning" *(svatantraprayoga, rang rgyud kyi sbyor ba)* in defense of what was later taken by Tibetan authors to be the philosophical view *(lta ba)* of the Madhyamaka.

In the present paper, I intend to take a close look at several of those passages from the PPMV that seemed most relevant to Tibetan doxographers in general, and to Tsong kha pa in particular, and to reexamine, from a critical, historical point of view, Candrakīrti's own words. In the end, I shall claim that a close reading of the original Sanskrit of his work, understood in its proper historical context (that is, in terms of what came before, and not after it was composed), strongly suggests that Candrakīrti would have had very specific and trenchant objections to his being referred to as a "Prāsaṅgika-Mādhyamika."

We will probably never know who coined the enormously influential terms *Rang rgyud pa* (*Svātantrika) and *Thal 'gyur ba* (*Prāsaṅgika). They do not figure among the vocabulary used during the early dissemination of Buddhism in Tibet, but it seems likely that it was the translator Pa tshab nyi ma grags (1055–1145?) who began to use them in conjunction with his study of Candrakīrti.[8] An earlier concern with "pragmatic" versus logical argumentation was preserved in these new terms, which apparently were then applied to the same two groups of Indian authors.[9] The shift in terminology was no doubt seen as a refinement based on further study of Candrakīrti.[10] There is certainly no question about the fact that it was due to the force of Candrakīrti's writing that Tibetan scholars felt compelled to revise the old classifications. Moreover, although to a certain extent scholarly opinion varied on the meaning and implications of Candrakīrti's work, the Tibetans were virtually unanimous in judging his texts to be the pinnacle of Madhyamaka thought. Where Candrakīrti was perceived to disagree with another commentator—either explicitly or implicitly—his word was invariably taken as the final authority. This was especially significant in the context of his criticism of Bhāvaviveka, for it was there, in the first chapter of the PPMV, that he drove home the central features of his interpretation of Nāgārjuna that figured so prominently in later Tibetan doxographical literature. The distinction between Bhāvaviveka and Candrakīrti—that is, the twofold division of Indian Madhyamaka into *Rang rgyud pa* and *Thal 'gyur ba*—became, in a very real sense, the linchpin around which the Tibetan doxographical tradition revolved.

In this literature, schools and subschools are defined on the basis of the tenets they hold. According to a prominent eighteenth-century dGe lugs pa doxographic manual, these tenets are to be regarded as "established conclusions" that one "will not pass beyond."[11] The minimum requirement for membership in a school or subschool is that an author must actively promote his own views, both defending those views against the views of his opponents and seeking to establish them on their own merits. The most obvious significance of the names *Rang rgyud pa* and *Thal 'gyur ba*—and the one most relevant to the present discussion—has to do specifically with the method by which a Mādhyamika philosopher accomplishes this purpose. In its most fundamental (etymological) sense, the difference between the two schools is said to rest on their distinctive rhetorical styles, and on the philosophical implications of this rhetoric. Bhāvaviveka insists on the necessity for a formal autonomous argument through which the Mādhyamika's tenet or thesis is established as an independently valid conclusion. Bhāvaviveka further insists that the argument through which the Mādhyamika's thesis is established must be explicitly stated to his opponent. Candrakīrti, on the other hand, rejects Bhāvaviveka's use of inferential reasoning. For the most part he favors a type of reductio ad absurdum where one's thesis is not developed through the use of independently valid arguments, but rather by using the opponent's own words against him. When the untenable consequences *(prasaṅga)* in his assertions are drawn out, the opponent is left "logically speechless," and for Candrakīrti—within the doxographic context—this very inability to respond is taken as sufficient evidence that the Mādhyamika's thesis has been established.

In turning toward an historically grounded understanding of Candrakīrti, and away from the scholastic view of Indian Buddhism presented by Tibetan doxographers, the first thing we want to notice is that, strictly speaking, *grub mtha'* texts contain no account of "early Indian Madhyamaka." Louis Dumont has defined history as "un ensemble de changements significatifs, un developpement,"[12] but here we find authors whose work defines a span of half a millennium or more of spirited philosophical activity placed side by side under the same rubric, as if nothing of real significance had occurred during the intervening years.[13] What is important about these authors, from the Tibetan perspective, is that they can be interpreted as saying essentially ("in essence") the same thing. And although Candrakīrti is fiercely critical of Bhāvaviveka, even this potentially fractious difference is resolved by assigning both of them to the same overarching school. Tibetan doxographers (like their Indian predecessors) were interested in what Mimaki calls "a synthetic understanding" of doctrinal positions,[14] and what we find in their scholastic manuals is the description of two subschools, each defined first of all by the assertion of its own tenets and second by its acceptance of a common nucleus of tenets that characterizes the all-encompassing school. The pieces (schools, subschools, and tenets) all fit neatly together in a single, seamless picture called "Madhyamaka"—an aerial photograph taken from the high Himalayas, untouched by the disruptive influence of time.[15]

We have seen that a tenet *(siddhānta, grub mtha')* is literally an "established conclusion," a hypothesis marking some point "that one will not pass beyond." Tenets are not fluid lines of thought that change and develop, nor are they merely a style of conversation, like Socratic dialogue. They are, in effect, timeless atomic units of meaning ("resolved, established, fixed"), and the schools that take shape around them stand outside of history in a timeless realm created by the doxographers' imagination and presented as explanation or exegesis. In *grub mtha'* taxonomic schemes these schools and their tenets are set into a hierarchy that presumes "a certain uniformity to the [Indian] textual tradition,"[16] itself reflecting the uniformity of truth and reality in which the exegetical project as a whole is anchored. Clearly this does not mean that Tibetans always agreed among themselves on how best to analyze and interpret Indian texts, only that the presuppositions embodied in their method of analysis (what Gadamer calls "the interest bound together with knowledge")[17] preclude recognition of any authentic change over time, and so of anything that could meaningfully be referred to as an early period in the development of Indian commentaries. By "early period" I mean a period of time defined by historically unique ideas or methods, a period significantly distinct—that is, cut off or hidden—from subsequent exegesis. From the perspective of Tibetan *grub mtha'* the Indian tradition may incorporate any number of competing interpretations, each one more or less distant from "the correct view of emptiness;"[18] what it may not contain is an early period separated from later exegesis by an unbridgeable intellectual or methodological rupture in which something significant was left behind, lost, or forgotten.

In direct contrast to the concerns of orthodox scholasticism, critical historiography is founded on the presupposition that history is irredeemably shaped by inconsistency, imperfection, change, and loss. Historians strive to uncover and display the very deeds and events that are most problematic for the writing of orthodox exegets. In discussing how traditional scholars dealt with inconsistencies in the Gospels, Elaine Pagels comments, "Jewish teachers in antiquity, like many Christians after them, turned to theological ingenuity rather than historical or literary analysis to account for contradictions in the texts."[19] Johannes Bronkhorst cites this comment and adds, "This directs our attention to an important feature of religious traditions: they may preserve inconsistencies, but are at the same time likely to explain them away."[20] For Darwin "the primary proofs of evolution are the oddities and imperfections that must record pathways of historical descent,"[21] and this is precisely the sort of thing Lambert Schmithausen has in mind when he insists that for the historian "instances of incoherence must be taken seriously and explained."[22] Inconsistency and imperfection are marks of the individual acting in history, and for the historian of ideas the primary act is the act of writing. Schmithausen acknowledges this in his own methodological manifesto: "I presuppose that the texts I make use of are to be taken seriously, in the sense that one has to accept that they mean what they say, and that what they mean is reasonable within its own terms."[23]

In working to develop a critical intellectual history of early Indian Mahāyāna, then, the focus of our attention must shift from "tenets" and "schools"—the fundamental categories of Tibetan scholastic doxography—to individual authors and their own original words. To accomplish such a shift in attention is unquestionably much more difficult than it may seem at first glance, for the stability and eloquence of the later tradition's view of itself is mesmerizing. And yet, the world revealed through the lens of critical historiography is far removed from the "carefully contrived ideal paradigm"[24] presented by orthodox Tibetan scholars. No doubt something is sacrificed in turning away from this timeless image, but the effort to recognize and map isolated periods in the development of Indian Buddhist thought can only proceed through "the very complex task of textual analysis."[25]

Given Nāgārjuna's severely skeptical attitude toward anything that might have been taken as a metaphysical ground for the Buddhist doctrine of his time, it seems reasonable to assume that his writing would not have found an immediate and secure place in any orthodox tradition. Furthermore, although the scriptures on which his ideas were based had probably attained quasi-canonical status by the first or second century C.E., it is likely that they would not have been accepted as the authentic Word of the Buddha by the community at large. In fact many of the most important Prajñāpāramitā texts were being actively composed during this period. It was a time of immense turmoil and change within the Indian Buddhist world. Discussion of the bodhisattva, the supremacy of the Buddha and his supranormal perception, the welfare of all beings, and of course, the "perfection of wisdom" had set in motion a groundswell of new ideas that was sweeping away the ancient and hard-won sense of a uniform Buddhist tradition fostered in the canon. All the evidence currently available suggests that the Buddhist intelligentsia were divided among themselves not simply on minor points of interpretation, but on fundamental issues of religious practice and philosophical orientation. Several centuries were required before the revolutionary changes underway would be assimilated, categorized, and comfortably assigned their respective niches in an all-embracing Mahāyāna orthodoxy.

It is historically significant that we find no reference to a philosophy called "Madhyamaka" either in the writings of Nāgārjuna or in those of his immediate disciple, Āryadeva.[26] But there is more, for if we take them at their word (take what they say "seriously," as Schmithausen has it), then there is every indication that these authors were philosophically and religiously indisposed to the promulgation of any "established conclusion beyond which one will not pass"—not to mention the founding of an orthodox school of systematic, speculative thought built around the defense of such tenets. In his *Yuktiṣaṣṭikā,* Nāgārjuna wrote,

> It is strange indeed that exponents of universal impermanence, those who follow the Buddha's path, should so desperately cling to things by quarreling.
>
> When, on close inspection, neither "this" nor "that" can be found, what wise man will argue for the truth of either?[27]

These are not the words of a system builder, piling up tenets like bricks. Nor are these:

> Convinced that impermanent things are like the moon's reflection in water, neither true nor false, one is not carried away by philosophical views.[28]

Almost fifteen centuries later the Tibetan doxographer dKon mchog 'jigs med dbang po will tell us that the "insider" (i.e., the orthodox Buddhist) is distinguished from other philosophers or religious practitioners not because he sees clearly the pointlessness of all such disputation, but precisely because he espouses a particular set of tenets.[29] And yet, for Nāgārjuna himself,

> Great men have no position and therefore no quarrel; for those who have no position, where is the opposing position?

> In taking any stand whatsoever one is seized by the writhing snakes of emotional attachment. They alone are free, whose mind has no place to stand.[30]

And finally, a well-known verse from the *Vigrahavyāvartanī* (VV):

> If I had any thesis *(pratijñā, dam bca')*, then I would have some fault. Because I have no thesis I am entirely faultless.[31]

The list could be extended indefinitely by culling passages from Nāgārjuna's other compositions, but the verses cited above are sufficient insofar as they contain instances of three key terms that express, very explicitly, what is to be shunned by the wise man. The last verse is particularly relevant, and deserves close attention. The Tibetan word for "thesis" *(dam bca')* is a noun corresponding to the past passive participle *dam bcas pa* (literally, "bound" or "fixed," from the root *'cha' ba*). *Dam bcas pa* is used as an adjective in a key passage from the *Grub pa'i mtha'i rnam par bzhag pa rin po che'i phreng ba,* where a tenet is defined as a "fixed meaning" *(dam bcas pa'i don).* In that text the Buddhist is described as a proponent of specific tenets, that is (to be etymologically precise), the Buddhist is said to hold and defend "a meaning derived from scripture and reason that has been resolved, established, and fixed in the manner of a thesis." But to go about one's philosophical business in this way is exactly the "fault" that Nāgārjuna strives to avoid—or so it would seem on the basis of his own words.

The three centuries following Nāgārjuna saw the production of a number of commentaries on his major treatise, the *Mūlamadhyamakakārikā* (MMK). Unfortunately many of these are presently unavailable. Accounts of the content of these lost treatises, combined with the study of other texts that have survived, paint a heterogeneous picture in which no consensus was reached on the interpretation of his thought. As Ruegg explains, "The existence of such commentaries by leading authorities of the Vijñānavāda clearly indicates that Nāgārjuna's work was not considered to be the exclusive property of the Mādhyamikas in the narrow sense of a particular school, and that it was regarded as fundamental by Mahāyānist thinkers of more than one tendency."[32] In fact, once we free ourselves from the uncritical habit of reading Indian sources through scholastic categories provided by later doxographers it becomes immediately evident that there were no Mahāyāna schools during this early period, only "Mahāyān-ist thinkers" who represented various "tendencies." From roughly the second through the fifth centuries there was obviously a tremendous interest in Nāgārjuna's work, but it is equally obvious that his ideas had not yet been clearly distinguished from those of Asaṅga and Sthiramati,[33] much less codified into an individual school with its own uniquely authoritative tenets. At this stage in the intellectual history of Indian Buddhism Nāgārjuna had not yet been conscripted to serve the interests of any particular philosophical thesis or view. A good deal of historical and philological research remains to be done before the significance of this observation will take hold.

In tracing the historical origins of the idea of a "school of Madhyamaka," one particular author commands our immediate attention: while framing his own critical reading of Buddhapālita's *Mūlamadhyamakavṛtti,* Bhāvaviveka simultaneously developed a comprehensive interpretation of Nāgārjuna's thought that marked a profound and irreversible exegetical turn, for from that time on the MMK was safely incorporated into the mainstream Indian Buddhist tradition, where it could only be understood as the presentation of a fixed thesis or system of tenets, that is, the authoritative view of an orthodox philosophical school.

So far as we know at present Bhāvaviveka is responsible for first appropriating the word *madhyamaka* as the name of a philosophical system or school that advocated specific tenets. Shotaru Iida suggests that the Madhyamaka did not become a "full-fledged school of thought" until Bhāvaviveka wrote his *Madhyamakahṛdayakārikā* (MHK) in which he formulated his "basic position" and defended it against other Buddhist and non-Buddhist schools.[34] However, if we accept the definition of a school provided in Tibetan doxographies, then it would not be going too far to say that Bhāvaviveka invented both the name and the school in a single stroke, for he not only lifted the term *madhyamaka* from the title of Nāgārjuna's primary work, but he seems also to have been the first of Nāgārjuna's commentators explicitly to associate this term with the formulation of a specific philosophical thesis *(pratijñā/dam bca')* or position *(pakṣa/phyogs).*[35] This required the working out of a complicated system of formal inferential reasoning that had not played a part in Nāgārjuna's own treatises, where, as we have seen, the assertion of any thesis, position, or view was self-consciously eschewed. In accomplishing this task there is no doubt that Bhāvaviveka sought to align his interpretation of Nāgārjuna ideologically and methodologically with his own elder contemporary, the logician and epistemologist Dignāga (ca. 480–540). Dignāga represented a powerful current of thought that was ascendant among Indian intellectuals during the first centuries of the common era. He had already abbreviated the five-stage inference of the *Nyāyasūtra* as part of an overall effort to incorporate the use of autonomous reasoning into Buddhism, and Bhāvaviveka simply adopted this logical form to his own ends.[36]

Bhāvaviveka's relationship with the Tibetan definition of a school as a collection of "tenets" is not merely formal or coincidental, however. He is the acknowledged progenitor of the entire genre of doxographical literature in India and Tibet, although in this project as well he was following the lead provided by Dignāga's *Pramāṇasamuccaya.*[37] Both authors were almost certainly influenced by Bhartṛhari, whose *Vākyapadīya* is clearly a *saṃgraha,* or collection of views or philosophies (*darśanas*).[38] Having forged the conceptual tools necessary to shape the intellectual tendencies of Mahāyānist thinkers into "tenets," in his extensive scholastic treatises Bhāvaviveka then set about organizing these tenets into schools and placing the schools themselves into an overarching taxonomic scheme that incorporated the ancient Buddhist principle of hierarchical truth values embedded in one all-encompassing Truth.[39] He needed to find a thesis and a position in Nāgārjuna's work because these are the terms in which a tenet is defined; without a thesis there would be no tenet, and without any tenet there would be no school of Madhyamaka and therefore no place for Nāgārjuna in the Buddhist tradition. Given the intellectual context in which he was writing, he was very likely also inspired by Bhartṛhari in his appropriation of the word *darśana* as the generic term for a "way of seeing" and so, by extension, a particular fixed philosophical system or school.[40] In all of this Bhāvaviveka was evidently laboring on behalf of conservative elements in the community to organize, harmonize, synthesize, and domesticate the welter of ideas that were circulating freely about in the Buddhist world of his day. His success in this respect was astounding, but it was achieved at a cost, and so far as we know only one individual seems to have had any idea just how steep the price may have been.[41]

Candrakīrti lived almost a century after Bhāvaviveka, but the intervening years were decisive. By the first half of the seventh century Nāgārjuna's potentially dangerous proclamations had been almost completely domesticated by Buddhist exegetes and any real threat to orthodoxy was largely a thing of the past. Despite severe criticisms of his predecessor's "addiction to logic" *(prīyānumānatā)*[42] Candrakīrti's ideas nevertheless took shape in an intellectual environment structured around an uncritical acceptance of the ahistorical, scholastic view of tradition presented in Bhāvaviveka's writing. He took for granted Bhāvaviveka's use of the word *madhyamaka,* which he further associated with a particular philosophical system or school called *śūnyatādarśana* or *madhyamakadarśana.*[43]

Nāgārjuna had referred in his writing to *sūnyavāda,*[44] but never to *śūnyadarśana.* The words *vāda* and *darśana* seem to have been used interchangeably by Bhāvaviveka,[45] but there are sound historical arguments against Ruegg's recommendation that they be treated as synonyms for the purpose of interpreting Nāgārjuna's own writing. First of all, according to Halbfass *darśana* is not a part of the vocabulary of ancient Indian sūtras and their commentaries, including those of Nāgārjuna.[46] Bhartṛhari himself did not use the word in any strict doxographic sense; rather, "his work shows us this doxographic usage *in statu nascendi* and in preliminary stages of development."[47] *Vāda* (from the root *vad,* to speak) means simply "speech," "discourse," or "discussion," and in the centuries preceding Bhartṛhari the term had "obviously no specific reference to the method or subject-matter of philosophy."[48] There is every indication that for Nāgārjuna a *śūnyatāvādin* was merely "a person who talks about emptiness." Whether he intended the word to be understood in any more technically binding sense is especially doubtful given his persistent warnings about identifying oneself with any particular philosophical stance. The word *darśana* would have been especially suspect to him in this respect because of its close etymological association with another Sanskrit word, *dṛṣṭi.*[49]

In the excerpts from Nāgārjuna's writing cited above, the wise man, convinced that things are impermanent and so neither true nor false, "is not carried away by a *dṛṣṭi.*" Even more than the other two terms with which it is aligned, *dṛṣṭi* functions throughout the corpus of Nāgārjuna's work as the paradigmatic emblem of what is to be avoided.[50] Moreover, all of his Indian commentators down through the centuries were careful to follow the Master's lead in this respect. Candrakīrti himself was adamant about the dangers of holding any *dṛṣṭi,* but this did not stop him from using the word *madhyamaka* as the formal name of a *darśana.*[51] In his time it had become commonplace to speak in terms of philosophical schools or systems (*darśanas*), and it was equally commonplace to understand Nāgārjuna's thought as defining one such system—albeit the "highest"—among others. All of this was Candrakīrti's unacknowledged inheritance from Bhartṛhari, Dignāga, and Bhāvaviveka; but it came with invisible strings attached, for every diatribe he penned against their addiction to logic and their reification of Nāgārjuna's thought was vitiated by metaphysical presuppositions about truth and reality epitomized in his own use of the word *darśana.* Candrakīrti sits uncomfortably on the cusp between two worlds: behind him lie some five centuries of enormous creativity, the intellectual fruits of a loosely structured community of strikingly original "Mahāyānist thinkers"; ahead of him the orthodox tradition stretches away into a future when Tibetan scholars translating his own writing would not consistently distinguish between the two words *dṛṣṭi* and *darśana.*[52] For the modern historian of ideas his work is a bridge thrown up between these two worlds and, not surprisingly, a minefield of irony and contradiction.

According to Candrakīrti, Nāgārjuna's analysis *(vicāra)* is not conducted "out of fondness for debate"[53]—that is, out of any desire to assert and defend one's own thesis against that of an opponent. Rather it is intended solely as a means to liberation from the compulsion to grasp at one view while pushing away another:

> Attachment to one's own philosophical view and aversion to the view of another is itself evidence of reified thinking. When one sets aside attachment and aversion and analyzes [all views], he will quickly find liberation.[54]

In Candrakīrti's writing the Middle Path emerges as an attitude of nonclinging based on the understanding that there is nothing (no form of ontological reality or epistemological truth) that should be held onto and defended, either conventionally speaking or in any deeper (ultimate) sense. "Truth" and "reality" are seen as equally indeterminate at both levels, and the search for any kind of absolute certainty *(niścaya)*[55]—logical or otherwise—is soteriologically misguided, as it only perpetuates the root problems of attachment and aversion. This is evident in the following passage from the PPMV, part of an imaginary conversation with a Buddhist philosopher who, given the context, is almost certainly intended to represent the position of Bhāvaviveka. Candrakīrti speaks first:

> If we allowed for any real certainty *(niścaya)* whatsoever then either it would have to arise from some valid means of knowledge or else it would not. But we do not allow for any certainty. How is that? There could be certainty if there were some possibility of uncertainty as its opposite. When we do not allow for any real uncertainty, however, then, in the absence of its opposite, how could there be certainty? [Discussion of certainty] without reference to its partner would be like [arguing whether] a donkey's horn is long or short. Moreover, when we do not allow for any certainty then why would we imagine some valid means of knowledge? What would it serve to establish? How many such valid means of knowledge would there

be? What would be their characteristics, their objects? Would they arise out of themselves, out of another, or from both? Or perhaps from no cause at all? None of this is of the slightest concern to us.

[Bhāvaviveka] If you allow for no certainty whatsoever, then why does your statement about things not arising from self, etc., appear to be certain?

[Candrakīrti] This statement is certain for worldly people who interpret it in terms of arguments familiar to them. It is not certain for those with deep insight (*ārya*s).

[Bhāvaviveka] Do those with deep insight really have no conclusive argument (*upapatti:* proof, demonstrated conclusion)?

[Candrakīrti] Who can say whether they do or they don't? For those with deep insight the truth of the highest meaning is a state of silence. This being so, how is there any possibility of discursive thinking out of which we might find either a conclusive argument or no real argument at all?[56]

According to Candrakīrti, it is absolutely essential that this compulsive desire, or need, for certainty—and its contrary, the fear of uncertainty—be seen for what they are, insurmountable obstacles to any real appreciation of Nāgārjuna's philosophy, for they only serve to reinforce the tendency to crave and cling:

In asserting a conclusion one expresses the desire to establish in others the same certainty *(niścaya)* that he himself possesses. [To fulfill this desire] one must convince someone else through that very argument by which his own conclusion was reached. The operating principle is, in this sort of activity, that in order to assert any conclusion one must compel the other person to accept the argument accepted by oneself. This is not so [for a Mādhyamika]. When he addresses someone else there is no possibility of resorting to any reason or example [of his own], so the inference by which his conclusion is reached necessarily corresponds to a thesis [held only by his opponent]. He therefore [provisionally] accepts a position that is unproven and is to that extent in contradiction even with himself

> *(svātmānam evāyaṃ kevalaṃ visaṃvādayan);* under the circumstances he is surely incapable of establishing any certainty in someone else. Is there, however, any clearer problem than the incapacity to prove the conclusion asserted on one's own behalf? What purpose is served by producing a counter inference [of our own]?[57]

Not only would a counter inference serve no purpose, it would expose the Mādhyamika to the very difficulties he seeks to uncover in his analysis of other people's views, positions, or theses:

> Others may be confounded by the unfavorable consequences [of their own arguments], but not us. We have no thesis of our own, and so it is impossible for us to fall into contradiction with any tenet (*siddhānta:* "established conclusion").[58]

Any thesis can be shown to rest on irresolvable internal contradictions, and when that thesis underlies a tenet that itself forms the cornerstone of one's philosophical system, then those internal contradictions fatally compromise the integrity of the project as a whole. Therefore, the Mādhyamika confines himself to a critique that depends on no thesis or tenet that might itself be subject to further critique. But if this is true, then it is essential to note that the words of a "Mādhyamika" must themselves lack the defining characteristic of any philosophical school or system of thought *(darśana),* an "unfavorable consequence" that lands Candrakīrti—and the entire doxographical tradition that endorses his writing as the most authoritative expression of Madhyamaka thought—in just the sort of predicament he was determined to avoid in the first place by not holding a thesis.

Either Nāgārjuna founded a school, or he did not. Candrakīrti clearly wants it both ways: he wants the Madhyamaka to be a school without tenets. Of course—as Bhāvaviveka well knew—this is impossible, and so we find Candrakīrti periodically attempting to slip a tenet in through the back door by treating Nāgārjuna's lack of thesis as if it were a formula or an abstract philosophical principle instead of an entirely pragmatic, ad hoc procedure. As if, to put it another way, Nāgārjuna's writing was rooted in the methodical application of fixed rules or the conviction that one is in the presence of "established conclusions," rather than in a particularly acute sensibility for the nuances of human emotion and thought—a difference that is analogous in significant respects to the difference between a logical proof and a poem, painting, or literary work.[59]

And yet in fairness to Candrakīrti one must acknowledge that the tension is unavoidable. We can feel it throughout the MMK. There can be no question that Nāgārjuna saw himself as carrying on the work of the Buddha, and to this extent he was confronted with a similar problem—both Nāgārjuna and Candrakīrti belonged to a tradition that could perpetuate itself only through a strategy that simultaneously undermined its own claim to convey some form of absolute (logical or otherwise ahistorical) truth. Nāgārjuna, however, was in one important sense a revolutionary. He embraced this disturbing irony and placed it at the center of his work, and in doing so he self-consciously placed himself at the beginning of tradition—or completely outside of it—for in a very real sense he was not "explaining" or "interpreting" the Buddha's words, but rather, doing with language what the Buddha had done. Unlike Candrakīrti his Buddhism is not self-consciously framed as exegesis or commentary. Certainly both of them are walking a rhetorical tightrope, weaving and bobbing high above the audience of readers on a precarious string of words. The difference is that for Nāgārjuna the whole project has the appearance of a virtuoso at work. He seems to delight in the danger, never committing himself to any particular conceptual formulation, always regaining his balance at the last moment with an unanticipated turn of phrase. As Robinson puts it in commenting on the MMK: "Its elements are few and its operations are simple, though performed at lightening speed and with great dexterity."[60] In contrast, reading Candrakīrti one cannot avoid the impression that he is secretly afraid of falling. One senses in his work the apprentice's characteristic lack of confidence. What is a source of inspiration and delight in Nāgārjuna continually threatens to become, for Candrakīrti, a matter of teeth-clenching principle, as if he were constantly fighting the urge to crouch down and grab the rope. In his writing the ironic tension is occasionally a palpable distraction. At times we can not help feeling that, despite the exaggerated tone of polemical confidence, behind it all Candrakīrti is haunted by the fear that far below there really is a cold, hard ground—the thesis, tenet, or "view," something to be proved, something that must be there, just out of sight, along with its ontological referent, the reality expressed by the word.

Nevertheless, some of Candrakīrti's most provocative writing is directed at his preeminent foil, Bhāvaviveka, and where the critique rages most fiercely he forgets his fear of heights and almost dances on the wire. Bhāvaviveka's assertion of nonerroneous conventional statements *(avitathālokavyāvahāra)* is for Candrakīrti a paradigmatic example of clinging, as is his belief in a kind of "real conventional experience" *(tathyasaṃvṛti)* containing both truth *(satya)* and valid knowledge *(pramāṇa)*.[61] Any such belief implies the possibility of making conclusive statements expressing a true thesis about a real object, but Candrakīrti repeatedly stresses that this is not the business of the Mādhyamika. His statements have as their only function the annulment of someone else's thesis *(parapratijñāniṣedhaphalatvā)*.[62] They have no independent ontological or epistemological force; such language is of exclusively practical value and is to be understood entirely on the basis of its success in undermining someone else's claim to knowledge and certainty. Like the teaching of the buddhas, the Mādhyamika's statements are motivated by compassion *(anugraha)*[63] and not by a desire to prevail or "get it right"—to out-logicize the logicians. Their purpose is merely to serve as an aid to liberation by destablilizing the linguistic/conceptual grounds of attachment and aversion. This purpose is the sole and final aim of a very strict soteriological pragmatism that is radically incommensurable with Bhāvaviveka's logical method. To appreciate just how distrustful Candrakīrti was of this method we need to look closely—and with a fresh, historically attuned eye—at the language he uses in chapter 1 of the PPMV, where his remarks are directed explicitly at Bhāvaviveka's use of autonomous reason intended to establish an inferential thesis. Here we find him at his best, entirely caught up in the activity of a pure critique. He has no fear of falling, no time to worry about principles, tenets, or ground:

> If someone else will not relent even though confronted with an admitted self-contradiction, then he is shameless and is not about to relent when presented with new reasons and examples. We should not bother engaging in discussion with a person like this, who is incapable of thinking clearly. It follows that the Ācārya [Bhāvaviveka] merely displays his own addiction to inferential reason by introducing it where it has no place. It is inappropriate for a Mādhyamika to use independently established inferences because it is impossible [for him] to accept either a position of his own or one of another.[64]

Candrakīrti then quotes a verse from Āryadeva's *Catuḥśataka* (CŚ) regarding the difficulty of refuting someone who holds no position, followed by two stanzas from Nāgārjuna's VV. The passage closes with a rhetorical question:

> When a Mādhyamika does not set forth any independently established inference, why then does [Bhāvaviveka] bring to bear an independent thesis against the Sāṃkhya?[65]

For a definitive answer to his own question we need only look a few pages ahead.

In the relevant passage Bhāvaviveka has just suggested that it is the duty of commentators to present cogent and binding logical arguments in support of Nāgārjuna's writing. Candrakīrti denies this uncategorically. After first pointing out that Nāgārjuna himself did not do so in his own autocommentary on the VV, he goes on to say,

> Even though a Logician may take the side of the Madhyamaka school out of a desire to parade the extent of his own dialectical skill, it is evident that the presentation of autonomous reasoning becomes, for him, an enormous reservoir where faults pile up one after another.[66]

Here we have it: as far as Candrakīrti is concerned, Bhāvaviveka is not a Mādhyamika at all, he is merely a Logician *(tārkika)* taking the side of the Madhyamaka school *(aṅgīkṛtamadhyamakadarśana)* out of a desire to show off his mastery of the canons of logic *(tarkaśāstrātikauśalamātram āviścikīrṣayā)*. Like Dignāga, who was the reference point for virtually every important methodological choice he made, Bhāvaviveka is, in Candrakīrti's eyes, nothing but a Logician. And, like all Logicians, he is primarily motivated not by compassion *(anugraha)* but rather by a profound desire, or need, for philosophical certainty.

If we can educate ourselves to read Candrakīrti's words as they must have appeared in their own historical context, and not through the lens of subsequent ahistorical doxographic exegesis, then the text of the PPMV is unambiguous on this point. Candrakīrti does not recognize, either implicitly or explicitly, two subschools of Madhyamaka:

> Whoever speaks in terms of independently valid logical arguments (inferences) reaps some fault. We do not rely on them, because the only fruit of our arguments is the annulment of someone else's thesis.[67]

Let us presuppose for the moment, along with Schmithausen (whom I cited earlier), "that the texts [we] make use of are to be taken seriously, in the sense that one has to accept that they mean what they say, and that what they mean is reasonable within its own terms."[68] At least two conclusions are apparently inescapable:

First, the labels *Thal 'gyur ba* and *Rang rgyud pa*—commonly translated into Sanskrit by contemporary Western scholars as Prāsaṅgika and Svātantrika—must be judged not only anachronistic but philosophically problematic as applied to a period in the intellectual history of Indian Buddhism when, so far as we know, not one of Nāgārjuna's commentators was prepared to acknowledge, even provisionally, the existence of two distinct and viable interpretations of the MMK. From approximately the second up through the seventh century as preserved in extant sources, there is not the slightest suggestion that any of Nāgārjuna's commentators would have been sympathetic to the idea that there were any "subschools" of Madhyamaka. And in particular, from Candrakīrti's point of view, to say that there are two kinds of Madhyamaka is like saying that there are two kinds of baseball: one in which the ball is struck with a bat, and another where the players kick it around the field. This is not a trivial point. Which brings us to the second conclusion:

If as rigorously critical historians we are interested in understanding Candrakīrti through the medium of his own words in the context of his own time and place, and not in terms of a conceptual grid fastened upon him by later generations of Tibetan doxographers, then I believe we must begin by seeing and accepting the fact that he excluded uncategorically Bhāvaviveka from membership in this school. In Candrakīrti's eyes Bhāvaviveka does not represent some kind of viable (albeit inferior) alternative reading of Nāgārjuna. In Candrakīrti's eyes Bhāvaviveka is a Tārkika, not a Mādhyamika, and if his use of independently valid logical arguments in the *Tarkajvālā* and other treatises were to be accepted as authoritative—even in some qualified sense—it would amount to a fatal subversion of Nāgārjuna's entire project. In other words, according to Candrakīrti it's not that Bhāvaviveka doesn't get it right, or even that he doesn't quite get it right. He simply does not get it.

For my part, I am persuaded that Candrakīrti's uncompromising refusal to allow the MMK to be reduced to a series of doctrines, tenets, or logical formulas is an attempt to read Nāgārjuna as "soteriologically pragmatic," in the spirit of the *Kalama Sutta* and the *Majjhima Nikāya*.[69] In any case, his rejection of Bhāvaviveka's logical reading was clearly sabotaged largely by his own uncritical acceptance of a powerful new doxographic vocabulary that effectively transformed Nāgārjuna's writing into a "philosophical system" or "school" *(darśana)*. Where there is a system or school there must be tenets, and where there are tenets there is most definitely something to prove. This same vocabuarly—as appropriated and elaborated upon by the Tibetans—would eventually be turned to a particularly curious purpose when it was used to extol Candrakīrti as the preeminent interpreter of Nāgārjuna's work. And so—in what amounts to a deeply ironic twist of fate—Candrakīrti was posthumously awarded highest honors from an orthodox scholarly tradition that could sustain its authority only by refusing to take seriously what he had himself insisted upon: Nāgārjuna is not in the business of providing rational arguments designed to substantiate, prove, establish, or make certain anything.

It seems to me that, in the present context, the most serious problem with the doxographic project in general is that it is predicated on the assumption that Buddhist philosophy must, by definition, be concerned with the preservation and explication of tenets *(siddhānta, grub mtha')*. The terms Prāsaṅgika and Svātantrika cannot do otherwise than embody this premise, and despite (or better: because of) the fact that they further imply that there is more than one kind of Madhyamaka, the force of Candrakīrti's central point continues to be either diminished or altogether lost.

Notes

1 Notable exceptions are certain rNying ma pa and Bon po schemes; see Mimaki (1982): 8.

2 Ibid.: 38.

3 Ruegg (1981): viii. See also his remarks in Ruegg (1980): 279.

4 Mimaki (1982): 3.

5 Ibid.: 53. Tibetan doxographers derived the new terminology through a process of extrapolation from Indian sources that were considered to provide the philosophical justification for its use.

6 It is the opinion of the present author that the expression "Indo-Tibetan Buddhism," which has achieved common currency among contemporary Buddhologists, derives its authority largely on the basis of a tacit assumption that Tibetan scholars stand in some sort of historically privileged position vis-á-vis the Indian sources. If this were not the case, then one wonders, for example, why the corollary "Indo-Chinese Buddhism" has no place in academic discourse, despite the fact that the Chinese Buddhist tradition is in every respect based on the translation and interpretation of Indian literature. Fortunately all

of this is beginning to be subjected to critical reflection. In addition to the present volume, cf., for example, the introduction to Dreyfus (1997); Tillemans (1990): 14ff.; Tillemans (1995): 641–642; and my own earlier discussion in Huntington (1995b): 693–696. The following comments of José Cabezón are relevant: "It is interesting that disciplines that pride themselves on critical distance from their object of study often implicitly incorporate many of its assumptions and presuppositions without being aware of the fact that this is the case. Buddhist Studies is no exception here, uncritically recapitulating in its scholarly literature many traditional Buddhist presuppositions." Cabezón (1995): 261. In the accompanying note Cabezón specifically mentions "the adoption of the fourfold siddhānta schema as an explanatory mechanism." He also provides a number of useful references on the subject.

7 Tsong kha pa makes this explicit in his *lHag mthong chen mo,* where he discusses the development of Madhyamaka in India and Tibet. Cf. Tsong kha pa, *rJe tsong kha pa'i gsung dbu ma'i lta ba'i skor,* vol. 1 (Sarnath ed.): 17.

8 Mimaki (1982): 44–45. Mimaki also holds out the unlikely possibility that Tsong kha pa was responsible for inventing these terms. Ibid.: 38–39.

9 See the charts in ibid.: 27–29 for distribution of these two groups.

10 This is the explanation given by Tsong kha pa. He refers in particular to certain passages in PPMV. Cf. Lopez (1987): 57.

11 The expressions shown here are lifted from the translation of dKon mchog 'jigs med dbang po's *Grub pa'i mtha'i rnam par bzhag pa rin po che'i phreng ba* in Hopkins and Sopa (1976): 53–54. The full passage reads as follows: "The etymology for 'tenet' *(grub mtha', siddhānta)* is: a tenet is a meaning which was made firm, decided upon, or established in reliance on scripture and/or reasoning and which will not be forsaken for something else.... 'Established conclusion' *(grub mtha')* signifies one's own established assertion which is thoroughly borne out by scripture and reasoning. Because one will not pass beyond this assertion, it is a conclusion." Cf. dKon mchog 'jigs med dbang po, *Grub pa'i mtha'i rnam par bzhag pa rin po che'i phreng ba* (n.d.): 4: *grub pa'i mtha ste / rigs pa'i lung gis rab tu bstan par rang gi 'dod pa grub pa ni / de las phar yang 'gro ba med pas na mtha'o / zhes gsungs pa ltar lung rigs gang rung la brten nas thag bcad cing grub pa 'am dam bcas pa'i don de nyid rang gi blo ngor tshul de las gzhan du 'dod pa med pas na / grub pa'i mtha' zhes brjod pa'i phyir //.*

12 Dumont (1964): 32.

13 Cf. Qvarnström (1988): 13: "...the doxographical genre neglects historical developments and presents a fixed system..."

14 Mimaki (1982): 38.

15 In her presentation of Tsong kha pa's distinction between "Mādhyamikas of the model texts" *(gzung phyi mo'i dbu ma pa)* and "Partisan Mādhyamikas" *(phyogs 'dzin pa'i dbu ma pa),* Elizabeth Napper speaks of "the chronology of the commentators who commented on Nāgārjuna's thought." Napper (1989): 164 and 268ff. However, what this distinction refers to is not historical change, but rather the classical Indian rubrics of "root text" (*mūlagrantha,* in this case the

original compositions of Nāgārjuna and Āryadeva), and a whole variety of exegetical literature *(vṛtti, bhāṣya, chāya)* that is necessarily parasitic (here, the commentaries of Buddhapālita, Bhāvaviveka, Candrakīrti, etc.).

16 Cabezón (1990): 15.

17 Gadamer (1976): 92: "One of the fundamental structures of all speaking is that we are guided by preconceptions and anticipations in our talking in such a way that these continually remain hidden and that it takes a disruption in oneself of the intended meaning of what one is saying to become conscious of the prejudices as such...the basic prejudices are not easily dislodged and protect themselves by claiming self-evident certainty for themselves, or even by posing as supposed freedom from all prejudice...the interest that is bound together with knowledge is overlooked." The most fundamental "interest" of the doxographical project—what amounts, in that literature, to a "self-evident certainty"—is a view of the Indian Buddhist tradition in which nothing essential is ever changed, much less lost.

18 Hopkins (1983): 321.

19 Pagels (1988): xxii.

20 Bronkhorst (1993): 64.

21 Ibid.: 63, referring to the writing of Stephen Gould, whom he goes on to cite: "'This principle of imperfection is a general argument for history, not a tool of evolutionary biologists alone. All historical scientists use it...'"

22 Schmithausen (1981): 200.

23 Ibid.

24 The phrase here is borrowed from Schopen (1991): 5.

25 Hayes (1986): 167. The full context of his remarks is worth citing at length: "Despite the efforts of later Indian and Tibetan academics to classify Buddhist doctrines into a highly artificial schema of four schools—two Hīnayāna and two Mahāyāna—with well-defined dogmatic boundaries, Indian philosophical schools were constantly evolving. Particularly in the highly creative period to which Vasubandhu, Diṇnāga and Dharmakīrti belonged, it can practically be said that each of the men whose works survive down to the present day was a school unto himself.... To settle a problem of how to interpret a specific passage or how to construe a particular technical term, we must set stereotypes aside altogether and engage in the very complex task of textual analysis." Elsewhere he continues (ibid.: 172): "If the book [under review] succeeds in anything it is to show, albeit inadvertently, the bankruptcy of treating the philosophers under discussion as spokesmen of doctrinaire schools rather than treating the schools as heuristic categories into which individuals, who differ considerably from one another, can provisionally be placed for pedagogical purposes."

26 Murti (1960): 87, and Iida (1980): 30.

27 *Yuktiṣaṣṭikā: / sangs rgyas lam la brten nas ni // kun la mi rtag smra ba rnams // rtsod pas dgnos rnams mchog gzung bas // gnas pa gang yin de rmad do /* (41) */ 'di 'am de 'o zhes gang du // rnam par dpyad nas mi dmigs na // rtsod pas 'di 'am de bden zhes // mkhas pa su zhig smra bar 'gyur /* (42). Lindtner (1987 repr.): 112.

28 *Yuktiṣaṣṭikā: / gang dag brten nas dngos po rnams // chu yi zla ba lta bur ni // yang dag ma yin log min par // 'dod pa de dag bltas mi 'phrog /* (45). Ibid.: 114.

29 dKon mchog 'jigs med dbang po, *Grub pa'i mtha'i rnam pa bzhag pa rin po che'i phreng ba* (n.d.), 4–5: *grub pa'i mtha' zhes brjod pa'i phyir / de la dbye na gnyis / phyi rol pa dang / nang ba'o /.*

30 *Yuktiṣaṣṭikā: che ba'i bdag nyid can de dag // rnams la phyogs med rtsod pa med // gang rnams la ni phyogs med pa // de la gzhan phyogs ga la yod /* (50) */ gang yang rung ba'i gnas rnyed nas // nyon mongs sbrul gdug g.yo can gyis // zin par gyur te gang gi sems // gnas med de dag zin mi 'gyur /* (51). Lindtner (1987 repr.): 114–116.

31 VV: *yadi kā cana pratijñā syān me tata eṣa me bhaved doṣaḥ / nāsti ca mama pratijñā tasmān naivāsti me doṣaḥ //.* Ibid.: 80.

32 Ruegg (1981): 49.

33 Ibid.

34 Iida (1980): 32.

35 See, e.g., PrP 1.1, p. 11, quoted by Candrakīrti in PPMV 1.1 (Vaidya ed.) 25ff; re: position, see: TJ 3.26, f. 64b. Cf. Ruegg (1981): 65, on both terms. He may have been following an earlier commentator, Devaśarman (ibid.: 62), but we will probably never know for sure.

36 Cf. Qvarnström (1988): 3, and Lindtner (1987 repr.): 78, n. 24. Bhāvaviveka's TJ and *Madhyamakaratnapradīpa* contain frequent references to Dignāga's PS. See TJ 8.68 for an instance of Bhāvaviveka's own distinctive threefold argument: thesis *(pratijṇā):* there is fire on the mountain; cause *(hetu):* because of smoke; example *(dṛṣṭānta):* as in a kitchen. See Ruegg (1981): 36–37, n. 93, and 64–66 for further details.

37 Qvarnström (1988): 6 and (1989): 99–100.

38 Cf. Kelly (1992): 172–173. Dignāga actually quotes at least two verses from the *Vākyapadīya* in chapter 5 of his PS, as well as *Vākyapadīya* 3.53–85 in his *Traikālyaparīkṣā.* On this last reference (for which I am indebted to Sara McClintock) see Frauwallner (1959): 145ff, and Biardeau (1964): 256. Also cf. Lindtner (1993): 200 and 205: "I have no doubt that future research will show that Dignāga and Dharmakīrti are heavily indebted to Bhartṛhari for much of their technical terminology."

39 Cf. the distinction between *nītārtha* and *neyārtha,* found in the Pāli suttas and throughout the Mahāyāna corpus.

40 Halbfass (1988): 268.

41 Lopez (1987): 57–58, where he is discussing the *Legs bshad snying po:* "Tsong-kha-pa writes...that although Bhāvaviveka found many faults with Buddhapālita's commentary to Nāgārjuna's *Treatise on the Middle Way,* he did not disagree with him on the selflessness of persons and phenomena. Bhāvaviveka's commentator, Avalokitavrata, also finds no disagreement between Buddhapālita and Bhāvaviveka concerning the conventional and ultimate nature of phenomena.... Tsong-kha-pa goes on to note that none of the great Svātantrikas—Jñānagarbha, Śāntarakṣita, Kamalaśīla—found any difference between the selflessness of their own system and that of the system of Buddhapālita and

Candrakīrti. Candrakīrti did not assert that there was any difference between himself and Buddhapālita concerning the ultimate and conventional. However he, and he alone among the great Mādhyamikas, distinguishes the system that he shares with Buddhapālita from that of the other Mādhyamikas.... Candrakīrti thus contends that his understanding of the doctrine of emptiness is unique and is not shared by others...."

42 PPMV (Vaidya ed.) 5,23.

43 Ibid.: 150,10 and 217,27; also Ruegg (1981): 1, n. 3; 2, n. 6.

44 VV 69, *Vaidalyaprakaraṣa* 1. See Lindtner (1987 repr.).

45 Qvarnström (1988): 7.

46 Halbfass (1988): 265.

47 Ibid.: 268.

48 Ibid.

49 *Dṛṣṭi* is an abstract noun made by the addition of a suffix (one of a class of *kṛt pratyayas)* directly to the verbal root *dṛś,* whereas *darśana* is a present active participle made from the same root by a different process. In this sense, *dṛṣṭi* may be understood as a particular "view," whereas *darśana* is "a way of seeing."

50 Cf. Halbfass (1988): 272: "*Dṛṣṭi,* 'speculation,' 'theorizing,' 'conceptualization,' implies soteriological negligence and irresponsibility, and in general a waste of time. Beyond that, it also stands for the representational, reifying and possessive positing of objects and the relations between objects, the projection and reflection of that primeval 'thirst' which attaches us to the world of passion and pain, the formation of a network of ideas in which the owner himself, the thinking and theorizing subject, gets caught."

51 Ruegg (1981): 2, n. 6.

52 See Yamaguchi (1974): part 1, 96; part 2, 110.

53 MAv 6.118: *bstan bcos las dpyad rtsod la chags pa'i phyir/ ma mdzad....* La Vallée Poussin (1907–1912): 231; trans. in Huntington (1989): 171.

54 MAv 6.119: */ rang gi lta la chags dang de bzhin du // gzhan gyi lta la 'khrug gang rtog pa nyid // de'i phyir 'dod chags khong khro rnam bsal te // rnam dpyod* (LVP has *dbyod*) *pa na myur du grol bar 'gyur/.* La Vallée Poussin (1907–1912): 232; trans. in Huntington (1989): 171.

55 This important word, used repeatedly in the first chapter of the PPMV, carries the following connotations: ascertainment, fixed opinion, conviction, resolution, resolve. Cf. Monier-Williams Sanskrit-English Dictionary, 561.

56 PPMV (Vaidya ed.) 19,16–29: *yadi kaścin niścayo nāmāsmakaṃ syāt, sa pramāṇajo vā syād apramāṇajo vā / na tv asti / kiṃ kāraṇam ? ihāniścayasaṃbhave sati syāt tatpratipakṣas tadapekṣo niścayaḥ / yadā tv aniścaya eva tāvad asmākaṃ nāsti, tadā kutas tadviruddhāviruddho niścayaḥ syāt saṃbandhyantaranirapekṣatvāt, kharaviṣāṇasya hrasvadīrghatāvat / yadā caivaṃ niścayasyābhāvaḥ, tadā kasya prasiddhyarthaṃ pramāṇāni parikalpayiṣyāmaḥ ? kuto vaiṣāṃ saṃkhyā lakṣaṇaṃ viṣayo vā bhaviṣyati—svataḥ parata ubhayato 'hetuto vā samutpattir iti sarvam etan na vaktavyam asmābhiḥ // yady evaṃ niścayo nāsti sarvataḥ, kathaṃ punar idaṃ niścitarūpaṃ vākyam upalabhyate bhavatām—na svato nāpi parato na*

dvābhyāṃ nāpy ahetuto bhāvā bhavantīti ? ucyate / niścitam idaṃ vākyaṃ lokasya svaprasiddhayaivopapattyā, nāryāṇām / kiṃ khalu āryāṇām upapattir nāsti ? kenaitad uktam asti vā nāsti veti / paramārtho hy āryāṇāṃ tūṣṇīṃbhāvaḥ / tataḥ kutas tatra prapañcasaṃbhavo yadupapattir anupapattir vā syāt ?

57 Ibid. 6,17–22: *yasmād yo hi yam arthaṃ pratijānīte, tena svaniścayavadanyeṣāṃ niścayotpādanecchayā yayā upapattyā asāv artho 'dhigataḥ saivopapattiḥ parasmai upadeṣṭavyā / tasmād eṣa tāvan nyāyaḥ—yat pareṇaiva svābhyupagatapratijñātārthasādhanam upādeyam / na cāyaṃ (cānena ?) paraṃ prati / hetudṛṣṭāntāsaṃbhavāt pratijñānusāratayaiva kevalaṃ svapratijñātārthasādhanam upādatta iti nirupapattikapakṣābhyupagamāt svātmānam evāyaṃ kevalaṃ visaṃvādayan na śaknoti pareṣāṃ niścayam ādhātum iti / idam evāsya spaṣṭataraṃ dūṣaṇaṃ yaduta svapratijñātārthasādhanāsāmarthyam iti kim atrānumānabādhodbhāvanayā prayojanam ?*

58 Ibid. 7,24–25: *prasaṅgaviparītena cārthena parasyaiva saṃbandho nāsmākam / svapratijñāyā abhāvāt / tataś ca siddhāntavirodhāsaṃbhavaḥ /.*

59 Cf. Sells (1994): 216 *et passim* on the distinction between kataphatic and apophatic writing, and Huntington (1995a) on both Sells and the application of literary critical (anti-) theory to the interpretation of Nāgārjuna. More recently, Jeff Humphries, a professor of Comparative Literature at Louisiana State University, has published a book titled *Reading Emptiness,* which he describes, in part, as follows (1999: 31–32): "It was conceived in answer to a graduate student's question. All of her teachers, she said, read works of literature in quite different ways, according to different theories or methods, including the antitheory theory, according to which all theories are bad; most of these theories led to contradictory, even mutually exclusive results when applied to the same text. One professor gleefully embraced every theory, applying each, willy-nilly, to the poor poem until his students reeled in dizzy confusion. Where then, she asked, was the truth of the literary text? Must not only one of these readings really be the best one? How to tell which? And what about the text itself? How can it have any value unless there is only one correct reading of it?... Buddhist thought may even provide Western literary theory with what the graduate student...found missing from her education: insight into the nature of literary truth." In this context he explains that "Buddhist thought has not often been considered by students and scholars of literature, partly because of the pervasive idea that textuality implies a kind of mediation inimical to the 'direct experience' that Buddhist practice seeks to achieve, and also because of the traditional disciplinary boundaries, according to which Buddhism is the exclusive province of a small community of specialists in religious studies." Ibid.: 31. The book explores, from the perspective of a literary critic whose earlier publications are on Villon, Proust, Stendahl, Poe, and Flannery O'Connor, many issues directly relevant to the present paper.

60 Robinson (1972): 326.

61 Cf. TJ 3.12, f. 60a. Cited in Ruegg (1981): 75, n. 244.

62 PPMV (Vaidya ed.) 11,7.

63 Ibid. 11,22.

64 Ibid. 5,21–24: *atha svābhyupagamavirodhacodanyayāpi paro na nivartate, tadā nirlajjatayā hetudṛṣṭāntābhyām api naiva nivarteta / na conmattakena sahāsmākaṃ vivāda iti / tasmāt sarvathā priyānumānatām evātmanaḥ ācāryaḥ prakaṭayati asthāne 'py anumānaṃ praveśayan / na ca mādhyamikasya sataḥ svatantram anumānaṃ kartum yuktaṃ pakṣāntarābhyupagamābhāvāt //.*

65 Ibid. 6,7–8: *yadā caivaṃ svatantrānumānabhidhāyitvaṃ mādhyamikasya tadā kutaḥ...svatantrā pratijñā yasyāṃ sāṃkhyāḥ pratyavasthāpyante /.* Notice that Candrakīrti has here treated the words *anumāna* and *pratijñā* as synonyms.

66 Ibid. 8,13–14: *ātmanas tarkaśāstrātikauśalamātram āviścikīrṣayā aṅgīkṛta-madhyamakadarśanasyāpi yat svatantraprayogavākyābhidhānaṃ tad atitarām anekadoṣasamudāyāspadam asya tārkikasyopalakṣyate /.*

67 Ibid. 11,6–7: *svatantram anumānaṃ bruvatām ayaṃ doṣo jāyate / na vayaṃ svatantram anumānaṃ prayuñjmahe parapratijñāniṣedhaphalatvād asmad anumānānām /.*

68 Schmithausen (1981): 200.

69 There is abundant evidence to suggest that among the earliest followers of the Buddha were those who more or less side-stepped any theoretical problems by interpreting his teaching in entirely practical terms: truth is whatever "works" (whatever is conducive to liberation), and what works for one person may very well not work for another. This is, for instance, the position of the *Kalama Sutta,* where we are told to "reject any doctrine when you yourself realize that its acceptance leads to misfortune and suffering...." (*Aṅguttara Nikāya,* II.191). It follows that truth is not necessarily one or many in any significant sense. A radical version of this position might dispense altogether with the notion of truth, looking upon any sustained concern with the issue as symptomatic of an unhealthy attachment to what is, in the final analysis, nothing but a theoretical abstraction that will inevitably distract one from the real problem of liberation. According to the *Majjhima Nikāya* (I.431) certain questions were not answered by the Buddha because "they were not practical, not related to what is fundamental to the spiritual life, not conducive to *nibbidāya,* dispassion, cessation, peace, higher knowledge, awakening or *nirvāṇa.*"

This approach is also suggested by two well-known parables found in the same text. In the first a man is counseled by the Buddha that some types of questions are not conducive to living the spiritual life; to insist on pursuing such purely theoretical questions is pointless and, indeed, altogether misguided—as if, being wounded by an arrow, one were to insist on knowing "how and by whom the shaft was made, what was the material, who shot it and so forth before having the point removed." (Ibid., I.429.) The second is the famous parable of the raft: "I preach a doctrine *(dhamma)* comparable to a raft, useful for crossing over but not to be clung to.... Those who understand [my] doctrine to be like a raft should discard it as well, to say nothing of what is not [my] doctrine *(adhamma)*...." (Ibid., I.134.) From this perspective all doctrinal formulations are of exclusively pragmatic value. Any actual statement of doctrine is always potentially dispensable and, indeed (as is the case with Candrakīrti), both the desire for or the belief in the absolute truth or certainty of such statements is ultimately viewed as an obstacle to liberation.

3. Metaphysics for Mādhyamikas

TOM J.F. TILLEMANS

In general, if one held that particulars *(rang mtshan, svalakṣaṇa)* were ultimately established, one would be a realist *(dngos smra ba)*. Those who hold that [particulars] are not ultimately established, but *are* established in transactional usage *(tha snyad du grub pa)*, are Svātantrika-Mādhyamikas, while the position of the two [Prāsaṅgika] masters [viz., Buddhapālita and Candrakīrti] is that [particulars] are not established even in transactional usage.[1]—Tsong kha pa

Let us say that metaphysics in the pejorative sense is a confused conception of what legitimates our practices; confused because metaphysics in this sense is a series of pictures of the world as containing various independent demands for our practices, when the only real legitimation of those practices consists in showing their worthiness to survive on the testing ground of everyday life.[2]—M. Johnston

Is there a difference such as that suggested above by Tsong kha pa, or indeed any important difference at all, between the Svātantrika and the Prāsaṅgika branches of the "Middle Way" school of Buddhism? I don't think we need to be terribly worried by the fact that "Svātantrika" and "Prāsaṅgika" are most likely invented terms, modern Sanskrit translations of the terms *Rang rgyud pa* and *Thal 'gyur ba* that were found exclusively (or, at least, almost exclusively) in indigenous Tibetan scholastic writings and not in Indian works.[3] Indeed, inventing un-Indian terms for Mādhyamika schools would be intelligent and creative if the schools they described were worth differentiating. Still there is no obviousness to the proposition that the differences between Svātantrika and Prāsaṅgika *are* worth elaborating upon or that they are of any major philosophical interest.

Tsong kha pa certainly made much of the distinction, arguing that the main point was that the Svātantrika had a different account of what there is on the level of customary truth *(saṃvṛtisatya),* or transactional usage *(vyavahāra),* from that of the Prāsaṅgika.[4] In fifteenth-century Tibet certain philosophers skeptical of Tsong kha pa's positions, such as Go rams pa bsod nams seng ge (1429–1489), had granted that Svātantrika and Prāsaṅgika used different logical techniques to prove voidness *(śūnyatā)* and ultimate truth—the former generally opting for positive proofs, the so-called "autonomous logical reasons " *(svatantrahetu),* to prove such theses and the latter using reductio ad absurdum, i.e., *prasaṅga*—but had maintained that there was no difference between them when it came to their ways of proving customary truths, and (what is especially important) that there was no difference at all in their ontologies, be it on the level of customary or ultimate truth.[5] The supposed difference between the two schools was therefore taken to be relatively minor, a question of tactics of proof rather than any divergence over what there is. And although I don't know of any contemporary writers on Buddhist studies who would want to defend Go rams pa's Mādhyamika philosophy *in toto,* there is nowadays often skepticism about attempts to impute different ontologies to the Mādhyamika schools.

Above all, a target of skepticism is Tsong kha pa's oft-repeated doctrine that Svātantrikas accept that in customary truth, or (equivalently) in transactional usage, things are established by their intrinsic natures *(tha snyad du rang bzhin gyis grub pa),* or by their own particular characters *(tha snyad du rang gi mtshan nyid kyis grub pa);* these principles clearly make use of, and interpret, key Indian terms, namely, *svabhāva* and *svalakṣaṇa,* that figure in numerous other contexts, mostly negative, in Mādhyamika argumentation. Equally suspect for many is a third principle that Tsong kha pa attributes to the Svātantrika, namely, that, in transactional usage, things are established "from their own side" *(tha snyad du rang ngos nas grub pa).* Although *rang ngos nas grub pa* almost certainly does not translate any Sanskrit original term, its basic sense is relatively clear. It is often glossed by the term *rang gi sdod lugs kyi ngos nas grub pa,* "things established from the perspective of the way they themselves are," and seems to signify what one often expresses by the richly charged English term "objective fact," viz., something that is as it is, independently of, or unaffected by, what we believe, feel, think, and say about it.[6] For Tsong kha pa and the dGe lugs pa scholastic, these three principles are mutually implicative and hence equivalent, with Svātantrikas accepting all three as characterizing how things exist on the level of customary (but not ultimate) truth. Prāsaṅgikas, on the other hand, supposedly accept none of them, not even on the level of the customary and transactional.

Now, typically when philosophers speak seriously of "intrinsic natures/properties," "things in themselves," "particulars," "objectivity," they are convinced they are providing an ontology, viz., a description of the most general and fundamental features of the universe that must exist to somehow legitimate, or ground, our ordinary ways of talking and acting, and even our scientific methods. It is very difficult to imagine that a Svātantrika-Mādhyamika's philosophical project would be radically otherwise, if indeed notions like "establishment by intrinsic natures," etc., were to have a predominant place in his system (as Tsong kha pa maintains they do). Certainly, when Tsong kha pa depicts Svātantrikas as holding that worldly things (but not sheer falsities) are correctly "findable" *(rnyed rgyu yod pa)* by the world in the bases upon which these things are conceived *(brtags gzhi),* he is attributing to these Mādhyamikas an ontological account of why and how certain customary truths can be true. The question, then, is whether Svātantrikas and Prāsaṅgikas *are* genuinely different in what, if anything, they take to be general features of all being that ground our ordinary practices, i.e., their metaphysics.

While it would be nice to be able to offer neutral, incontrovertible, literal, Indian textual evidence that speaks for itself, perhaps even clearly using the terms *tha snyad du rang bzhin gyis grub pa / *vyavahāratas svabhāvena siddha,* etc., and thus roundly refuting an adherent of a Go rams pa–style skeptical position, I am very doubtful that any such definitive textual passage is to be found. The best Indian quotation cited by Tibetans is a very problematic passage from Bhāvaviveka (6th c. C.E.) discussed by Tsong kha pa in his *Drang nges legs bshad snying po:* Tsong kha pa then informs us candidly that this passage was about the clearest evidence *he* could find in support of his position that Svātantrikas accepted intrinsic natures on the level of customary truth.[7] At any rate, it seems that the passage wasn't probative at all for Tibetans like Go rams pa, and indeed it is probably hard to imagine it speaking for itself to anyone other than already convinced adherents of the dGe lugs pa position. Tsong kha pa gives virtually no other *arguments* worthy of the name to prove that the Indian authors themselves had the positions on customary truth that he attributes to them, although he does consecrate an enormous amount of energy to elaborating what these positions are and what consequences they entail. This is in a way very typical Tsong kha pa: as is the case for his doctrine of "recognizing the object to be refuted" *(dgag bya ngos 'dzin),* he seems to have elaborated many of his most fertile and sweeping philosophical ideas and interpretive schemes on the basis of the slimmest, and sometimes even misconstrued, Indian textual evidence.[8] *Our problem, then, is to see if we can arrive at some of the broad outlines of Tsong kha pa's position on the Indian authors, but on our own, relying on sympathetic, and above all systemically sound, readings of the Indian texts.*

It may sound a bit cavalier to many schooled in philology to even bother with a position unbacked by a modicum of *hard textual evidence* in the Indian works, but I don't think that paucity of such evidence generally matters all that much when we are evaluating very wide-ranging choices of interpretations.[9] At any rate, let me state my own methods at the outset and ignore the vexing question of what is sober and what isn't. The central distinctions between Svātantrika and Prāsaṅgika philosophers will be made by using *systemic* arguments turning on their allegiance to, or independence from, the school of Buddhist logic and its major metaphysico-epistemological preoccupations. In the case of the two eighth-century Indian Svātantrikas whom I will be primarily investigating, i.e., Kamalaśīla and Śāntarakṣita, they had a massive and clear debt to the logicians, Dignāga and Dharmakīrti, and were avowed adherents of the Buddhist logic school. Indeed their Svātantrika philosophy is largely an attempt to resituate the metaphysics, epistemology, and logic of Dharmakīrti by placing them, intact, on the level of customary truth, while the Nāgārjunian dialectic, voidness, and Mādhyamika standpoint are applied to the ultimate status of things. The Prāsaṅgika, Candrakīrti, by contrast, had no such debt at all to the logicians and hence could embrace an entirely different philosophical project. In short, I think that we can find good reasons to say that the labels "Svātantrika" and "Prāsaṅgika" capture significant differences in systems of thought. These differences between Indian Mādhyamika schools will be seen as much more than a choice of logical techniques and will concern major questions of metaphysics, notably the acceptance of particulars *(rang mtshan, svalakṣaṇa)* that is intimately tied in with a foundationalist philosophy of perception.

A final disclaimer. In what follows, I'll speak of "Svātantrika" and "Prāsaṅgika" without presupposing a ready answer as to precisely which individual historical thinkers were members of which school. Given the systemic approach I adopt, however, I think it will turn out to be reasonable to place at least certain so-called Sautrāntika-Svātantrikas, like Bhāvaviveka and his commentator, Avalokitavrata, in the same school as

Kamalaśīla and Śāntarakṣita, even though the former accept external objects on the level of customary truth and the latter reject them. On the other hand, I haven't any idea as to why one really should end up grouping Buddhapālita and Śāntideva along with Candrakīrti in a common Indian Prāsaṅgika school; "Indian Prāsaṅgika" in what follows, will therefore only mean Candrakīrti and perhaps his commentator, Jayānanda.[10]

Foundationalism, the Given, and Particulars

A number of years ago, in the third chapter of my *Materials for the Study of Āryadeva, Dharmapāla and Candrakīrti* (= *Materials),* I tried to present a collection of philosophical points of difference between the Svātantrika and Prāsaṅgika systems of thought, focusing on their respective acceptance and rejection of a "given," i.e., "the sort of entity naturally suited to be *immediately present to consciousness.*"[11] Of course one can complain that the notion of a given is not itself without some controversy and is not agreed upon by all. It would, however, be quite bizarre to take that fact as a reason for dismissal, unless one went to the coherent but extreme position of shunning all use of contemporary analytic philosophy's key ideas whatsoever. In any case, problems of the given and those of empiricism in general are some of the dominant and most creatively developed themes in Anglo-American philosophy, so that in spite of there being different philosophical stances on what is entailed, there certainly is much more than a vague idea as to what the issue is. As Wilfrid Sellars explained it in his "Empiricism and the Philosophy of Mind," the article that remains the starting point for discussions of this notion,

> One of the forms taken by the Myth of the Given is the idea that there is, indeed *must be,* a structure of particular matter of fact such that (a) each fact can not only be noninferentially known to be the case, but presupposes no other knowledge either of particular matter of fact, or general truths; and (b) such that the noninferential knowledge of facts belonging to this structure constitutes the ultimate court of appeals for all factual claims—particular and general—about the world.[12]

The given is thus often viewed as the necessary ontological correlate to foundationalism. It is seen as the metaphysics integral to the epistemological view that there are self-authenticating, or intrinsically credible, cognitions—perceptions—which constitute the final court of appeal upon which inferential understanding depends for its justification and without which there would be an infinite regress, one understanding supporting another without end. The given is what these foundational perceptions grasp and know; it is the *purely particular,* known without prior reliance on concepts or any general truths.

I won't repeat here all the complex discussion in *Materials* where I applied these notions to the Svātantrika-Prāsaṅgika question, although I would stand by its main points. Nor will I restate the various textual passages that I had cited in *Materials* in support of my argument. Suffice it to reiterate here that in all the logicians' and the Svātantrikas' systems, particulars *(svalakṣaṇa),* be they accepted as external or as only mental, are the sort of thing *naturally suited to be present to noninferential awareness,* and hence can be considered as a type of given—this is what is involved in Buddhists saying that particulars are *the* exclusive objects of perception. As is well known, logicians took these particulars to be external objects *(bāhyārtha)* when they adhered to the Sautrāntika's stance, as did so-called Sautrāntika-Svātantrikas, like Bhāvaviveka. The logician's final position, however, was that of a Yogācāra idealist for whom there were only mental entities—particulars were appearances, or images *(ākāra)* to perceptual consciousness, and were genuinely real. Not surprisingly, in the Yogācāra-Svātantrika system of Śāntarakṣita and Kamalaśīla, appearances *(snang ba, pratibhāsa)* to perception *(pratyakṣa)* end up being the customary-truth counterparts to the particulars of the Buddhist logician's Yogācāra ontology.[13] Again, they can be said to be naturally suited to be present to only noninferential awareness, i.e., perception, and are thus the main candidates for a given. *The only significant point of difference between the Yogācāra-logician and Yogācāra-Svātantrika on the question of particulars and perceptions of them seems to be that the particulars are fully real for the former and are relegated to the level of merely customary existent entities for the latter.*

Noteworthy too is the fact that for the logicians, and especially for Śāntarakṣita and Kamalaśīla in *Tattvasaṃgraha(pañjikā)* 25 (TSP 25), the *Svataḥprāmāṇyaparīkṣā,* there is a clear recognition that perception serves a foundational role for thought, that at least some perception must be intrinsically credible (i.e., must be *svataḥ prāmāṇya*), and that without foundations there would be an infinite regress *(anavasthā).*[14] And, in what seems to embody another aspect of foundationalism, we find the frequent argument in Śāntarakṣita's *Madhyamakālaṃkāravṛtti* (MAV) that appearances, or "appearing objects" *(snang ba'i don),* are necessary conditions for inferential thought in that they provide the actual subject *(dharmin)* without which there can be no debate; they are known by perception, and indeed must be so known by all concerned if subsequent inferential reasoning is to be justified as pertaining to things in the world, rather than to just our imagined "superimpositions" *(samāropa).*[15] As Kamalaśīla makes plain by citing key verses from Dignāga and Dharmakīrti in his discussion of the problem of "unestablished loci" *(āśrayāsiddha),* these appearances are the Mādhyamika version of the *svadharmin* ("[proponent's] own subject"), which Dharmakīrti discusses at length in *Pramāṇavārttika* (PV) 4.136–148—they are, for a logician and Svātantrika alike, what must be perceptually known and accepted by both parties as a *vastu* ("entity") for subsequent inferential thought to be about anything at all.[16]

This much will have to suffice to set up the contrasts we seek and enables us to turn to the other side of the ledger. What is important to note is that for the Prāsaṅgika, Candrakīrti, there is a deliberate rejection, in his *Prasannapadā* 1 (PPMV 1), *Madhyamakāvatārabhāṣya* 6 (MAvBh 6) and *Catuḥśatakaṭīkā* 13 (CŚ 13), of the very notion of particulars, of the logician-inspired account of the perception which has access to them,[17] and of the necessity that there be commonly known perceptible appearances for inference to function.[18] *None of those above-mentioned important Svātantrika themes are accepted by Candrakīrti. Indeed, it is around the rejection of those themes that he constructs much of his distinctive philosophy.*

Finally, it's probably fair to say that in its most general formulation the problem of there being or not being foundations for knowledge can be seen (as, for example, in John McDowell's *Mind and World*) as essentially turning on the acceptance or rejection of a dichotomy between conceptual schemes and the perceptual data upon which they are based. If conceptual thought is not to "spin freely"[19] and is to give us reliable information about the world, it must meet some resistance in perceptual experience, a given, be it external particulars, sense impressions, or what have you, to which it has privileged and purely receptive access.

This is also, I think, one of the most promising ways to look at the Svātantrika-Prāsaṅgika distinction, and was—in essence if perhaps not sufficiently in words—one of the main themes that I was trying to develop in chapter 3 in *Materials.* An acceptance of a type of dichotomy between conceptual schemes and experiential intake is extremely important for the Buddhist logicians and their Svātantrika descendants. As is well-known, logicians make a radical dichotomy between perception and conceptual thought;

indeed thinkers like Dharmottara explicitly formulate this dichotomy in terms of arbitrariness and nonarbitrariness, recognizing that conceptual thought is "not fixed" *(aniyata)* and is free to think what it will, while perception is fixed *(niyata)* and is not free in the way that thought is.[20] And it is corresponding rigidly to that distinction between unfree, receptive, perception and free, inventive, thought that they make a distinction between the particulars *(svalakṣaṇa)* that are the objects, and causes of, perception, and universals *(sāmānyalakṣaṇa)*, which are the invention of conceptualization. Significantly, the Svātantrikas accept, and integrate into their system, the logician's definition of perception—viz., "what is free of conceptualization and nonerroneous" *(kalpanāpoḍham abhrāntam)*. It is clear that they too subscribe to the dichotomy and its implicit ontology. On the Prāsaṅgika side, Candrakīrti's outright rejection of the logician's definition of perception, his possible acceptance of the view that certain perceptions like *mānasapratyakṣa* ("perception by the mental faculty [alone]") are even conceptual,[21] and his insistence that perception itself is also fundamentally mistaken about its objects and largely invents their mode of being all suggest strongly that he is deliberately blurring the dichotomy between conceptual schemes and the perceptual given that is so important to his Svātantrika counterparts. When the distinction between conceptual thought and perception is deliberately fudged, that between the inventions of thought and the objects of perception is too—not surprisingly, Candrakīrti ends up having no use at all for foundationalist holdovers like appearances-cum-particulars.

Possible Objections

There is, however, a clear risk in my approach. To put the matter succinctly: *if* it is meaningful to say that particulars are a kind of perceptual given for the logicians, it should also be meaningful to say that they are for Svātantrikas like Śāntarakṣita and Kamalaśīla. And if that's so, then we might make a case, along the lines of *Materials,* that the respective acceptance or rejection of particulars and foundational perceptions is one of the major differences between Svātantrika and Prāsaṅgika philosophy. On the other hand, if the idea of a perceptual given is inapplicable to the major logicians inspiring Śāntarakṣita and Kamalaśīla, the rest of our approach comes adrift. So, before we can see the Svātantrika-Prāsaṅgika distinction as turning on foundationalism and the given, we need to reexamine a number of arguments, actual and possible, as to why these notions supposedly are *inapplicable* or don't show much of significance in the matter at hand.

A look at Georges Dreyfus' objections

In 1996 Georges Dreyfus published an article, "Can the Fool Lead the Blind? Perception and the Given in Dharmakīrti's Thought," in which he argued, inter alia, that logicians, like Dharmakīrti, do *not* subscribe to a given and are thus not actually real empiricists, in spite of the prima facie attractiveness of attributing to them these views. Dreyfus consecrates a good deal of energy to showing that Buddhist logicians accept that memory and other conceptual processes are necessary for perception to yield knowledge, and that, for the logicians, memory and such processes are not fully reliable. From this necessary dependence upon unreliable factors, he then seems to conclude that the perception is not a fully certain knowledge, which is what it would have to be if it were to be knowledge of a given.

Now, part of Dreyfus' argument turns on the idea that any foundational knowledge of a given would have to be something indubitably certain—I don't think that this is so, but I'll wait until the next section to take up that argument. There is, however, another recurrent theme, which we see in the following representative quotes:

> Perception in isolation cannot provide useful knowledge unless it is supplemented by perceptual judgments, which are nothing but memories induced by previous experience.
>
> ...[P]erception is limited to a bare sensing which does not directly produce any useable information.
>
> Perception is unable in and of itself to bring about ordinary knowledge, which cannot be reduced to experience, contrary to what empiricists argue. To produce knowledge, perception requires the cooperation of perceptual judgments, which are memories.[22]

The essential point here would seem to be that depicting Dharmakīrti (or Svātantrikas) as subscribing to a given or "myth of the given," makes no sense because, for them, mere perception of such a given would not itself be, or directly bring about, *ordinary and useful* knowledge, or (what is the same thing according to the Buddhist) knowledge in the strong sense of the term implied in the notion of *avisaṃvādi jñānam* ("reliable/non-belying cognition").[23] As for "ordinary knowledge" not being *reducible* to experience, I'm not sure that I get what this means for Dreyfus—it is somewhat of a new formulation figuring at the end of the article. But judging from Dreyfus' own elaboration, it seems to come down to the oft-stated theme that perception alone is insufficient: other conceptual thought processes are psychologically needed to arrive at propositional knowledge upon which we can profitably act. Put in this way, I think that it must immediately strike us as very doubtful that intelligent foundationalists and subscribers to the myth *must,* or even do, ever advocate that perception *alone* directly brings about our *ordinary, useful knowledge* of things. What they are advocating, at least on Sellars' characterization, is that there is a type of non-inferential knowledge of sense contents, call it "being conscious/aware of sense contents," that presupposes no concepts, memory, learning, and so forth. However, getting to "ordinary knowledge," which is a knowledge that such and such is thus and so, does involve conceptual processes. Compare Sellars' formulation in his "Empiricism and the Philosophy of Mind":

> They [i.e., sense-data philosophers] have taken givenness to be a fact which presupposes no learning, no forming of associations, no setting up of stimulus-response connections. In short, they have tended to equate *sensing sense contents* with *being conscious,* as a person who has been hit on the head is *not* conscious, whereas a newborn babe, alive and kicking, *is* conscious. They would admit, of course, that the ability to know that a *person,* namely oneself, is *now,* at a certain time, feeling a pain, *is* acquired and does presuppose a (complicated) process of concept formation. But, they would insist, to suppose that the simple ability to *feel a pain* or *see a color;* in short, to sense sense contents, is *acquired* and involves a process of concept formation, would be very odd indeed.[24]

Whether we think that this is a good way or an impossible way to do epistemology is another matter. It is probably true, as Robert Brandom puts it in his "Study Guide" to Sellars (1997), that the myth of the given turns on a blurring of the distinction between sentience and sapience, i.e., between having some sensory input (as does presumably every animal who is awake) and having experiential knowledge.[25] The fact is, however, that people of an empiricist bent have consecrated considerable energy and ingenuity to doing epistemology in this way and have thought that perceptual awareness is not just one of the many animal functions necessary for cognition to occur, but is itself a type of cognition of a certain kind of thing. I think that Dharmakīrti is one of these empiricists, and I think that Śāntarakṣita and Kamalaśīla are too.[26]

Certainly, a Buddhist logician recognizes that *ordinary knowledge* is not a matter of *pure perception of particulars alone,* and this recognition does, as Dreyfus points out, lead him into an exegetical tangle about how to preserve the idea of perception being *avisaṃvādi jñānam* and hence genuinely useful knowledge. Leaving aside this strong sense of knowing, however, it is clear from the texts that Dharmakīrti and his school do recognize that perception *apprehends* or *grasps* (cf. the Sanskrit verbal root *grah*) information in a way in which a thoroughly noncognitive, insentient process (like, e.g., digestion) would not; equally there's little doubt that the Buddhist logician recognizes that particulars *appearing* to perception is itself also very much a *cognitive* event, although not itself full-fledged knowledge qua *avisaṃvādi jñānam.* In that sense, Dharmakīrti does accord, like the sense-data theorist, a *type of epistemic status* to this basic consciousness of data which everyone who is "alive and kicking" has. Like Sellars' empiricist, the Buddhist logician accepts that "sensing is a *cognitive* or *epistemic* fact."[27]

In this vein a minor detail concerning the philosophical allegory alluded to in the title of Dreyfus' article actually takes on a certain importance. The allegory that Sa skya Paṇḍita uses to characterize nonconceptual perception is that it is like a fool, one who sees but is unable to verbalize and intelligently describe; conceptualization, on the other hand, is like a blind speaker, in that it is articulate but lacking in itself even the most rudimentary experiential cognition. The point is that perception for the Buddhist *is* cognitive, but rudimentary. Contrast this image with the Kantian maxim that anti-foundationalists so frequently cite: *intuitions without concepts are blind.*[28] The Buddhist logician is saying pretty much the opposite: it is concepts that are blind, while sense intuition does see, albeit unintelligently. It is worth our while to stress that the major anti-given, anti-foundationalist strategies in contemporary American philosophy are precisely *not* what the Buddhist logician is advocating.

Historically speaking, what seems to have happened is that Dharmakīrti inherited and clearly accepted the two-*pramāṇa* ("means of valid cognition") system of his predecessors with its radical separations between perception and conceptualization, and between perceived particulars and invented universals. His school then had to address itself, *within that same context,* to bridging the gap between the Buddhist version of perception and genuine propositional knowledge. Dharmakīrti's own solution consisted largely in introducing the idea of a perceptual judgment *caused* by the initial nonpropositional perception—without such judgments no one could arrive at ordinary knowledge like "This is such and such a type of thing," knowledge upon which we can act in practical life. These "perceptual judgments following upon perception," i.e., the *pratyakṣapṛṣṭhalabdhaniścaya,* would themselves be conceptual thoughts, but their nonarbitrariness would be guaranteed by their causal connection with perception. Other people, East and West, inclined to foundationalism, would have other solutions. (For example, Sellars discusses the essential empiricist position that if sense contents are sensed at all, they are "sensed as being of a certain character, and...the fact that it is of this character [must] be noninferentially known."[29]) Arguably, Śāntarakṣita, in the *Tattvasaṃgraha* (TS) and *Madhyamakālaṃkāra* (MA), is also addressing the problem of how perception can be knowledge in introducing the idea of a perception of X also being itself nonconceptually aware that it is seeing X; this "reflexive awareness" *(svasaṃvedana)* is said to be the necessary condition for any event or thing to be cognitive, rather than simply insentient.[30] At any rate, whatever be the version of how perception can be cognitive and result in ordinary knowledge, the fact that these tentative solutions are being proposed at all to this conundrum suggests strongly that we should look upon Dharmakīrti, and the Svātantrikas too, as attempting to solve the fundamental questions which so many empiricists who accepted the given, nonpropositional knowledge, knowledge by acquaintance, foundationalism, etc., would have to struggle with. The Buddhist is, in his own way, going down what will become a well-travelled road trodden by empiricists. It's probably not surprising that he ran into serious difficulties needing quite complicated remedies. But that he had what are for us now rather daunting difficulties is not an argument to show that he came to abandon the project of a foundationalist empiricism or, what is even weirder, that he never had it in the first place.[31]

A second possible objection: perception of a given would have to be completely indubitable and unassailable, but perception is not unassailable for a Svātantrika.

It could also be argued that while Svātantrikas do accept *kalpanāpoḍham abhrāntam* ("what is free of conceptualization and is nonerroneous") as the definition of perception *(pratyakṣa),* neither they nor their logician forefathers hold that perception is definitively immune to any and all criticism.

In that sense, perception would not yield access to a given, if what we meant by "given" was the content of such an *indubitable and incorrigible* awareness. A number of major modern philosophers, especially the logical positivists, have indeed wanted to link the quest for the given with the quest for utter incorrigibility. In *Materials,* when I on occasion spoke of the given as "unassailable," I could well have been taken as uncomfortably close to this position. It is what one finds in, for example, H. H. Price's *Perception,* C.I. Lewis' *Mind and the World,* and in Bertrand Russell's idea of knowledge by acquaintance with sense-data, as developed in his *Problems of Philosophy.* In any case, it has been quite frequent that empiricists take the perception of the given as the *indubitable* foundation, the resting place where doubts about truth would finally and completely come to an end, because (so the argument goes) although one can doubt whether something is composed of such and such material, is long or is red, one cannot doubt at all that it at least *looks* red to us. We cannot possibly be wrong about our own sense-contents stripped down to raw feels, or at least so say several empiricists who have adopted an epistemology where there must be something utterly certain if there is to be anything else which is even probable.

True, the Svātantrikas (and the logicians for that matter) do adopt a type of sliding-scale of analysis (to use Sara McClintock's phrase), so that what is accepted on a lower perspective is not so on a higher—we have a significantly different system and a different ontology each time we move the scale up a notch. And this sliding-scale approach in Buddhist logic and in Svātantrika philosophy would indeed make talk of foundations impossible if they had to be for once and for all incorrigible and utterly unassailable by *any* reasoning used. But, in fact, it is hard to see why such utter incorrigibility *must* be essential to talk about foundations. I think that Michael Williams has it right in saying,

> Epistemologically basic beliefs provide ultimate terminating points for chains of justification, but this seems at most to imply that these beliefs must be such that one can be *justified* in holding them without being able to supply independent justification. Nothing has been said to incline us to the view that such beliefs enjoy absolute safety. They may be prima-facie justified, but defeasible.[32]

All that the Buddhist or other foundationalists actually need in their epistemology are foundational understandings which are prima facie, or intrinsically, credible and which stop the regress of justifications—these understandings may still be somehow defeasible by higher-level critique like what we find in idealism or in the Mādhyamika.

It might be replied, however, that all this is to misunderstand the nature of Kamalaśīla's approach: he could be prepared to argue from several different standpoints on varying occasions only if he was himself committed to none. Advancing different versions of the foundational understandings and the given would thus come at the price of not being ontologically committed to any (or perhaps indeed to any customary thing at all)—in short, the Svātantrika would have to be seen as using talk of appearances in a purely tactical way. I don't think this follows and I would generally resist this, and many other, attempts to explain seeming anomalies in Buddhist texts by appealing to an all-pervasive pragmatism.[33] Agreed, Kamalaśīla's approach often seems to turn largely on matters of pedagogical convenience and intelligibility, and it generally is simpler and more intuitive to talk initially to people about external particulars, rather than adopting straight off an idealist, not to mention Mādhyamika, perspective. (I think one may see a somewhat similar thing when an analytic philosopher who is attracted to nominalism as the final word on how mathematics is to be done still goes on talking on several occasions about abstract entities like sets, as a pedagogically simpler *façon de parler.*[34]) However, it does not follow from *this* that Kamalaśīla had no position himself which he would take as the *right* account of the ordinary world, or that he refused to commit himself on how ordinary things correctly existed. He recognized that they had a way of being which made some beliefs about them right and others wrong; indeed, he, like other Svātantrikas (and in contrast to Candrakīrti), maintained that customary truths *could* be correct *(tathyā)* or incorrect *(mithyā),* and that it was only a "means of valid cognition" *(pramāṇa)* understanding things as they were which decided the question. Whatever the tactical reason for Kamalaśīla's varied approaches, he thus had a metaphysics grounding true and false versions of the ordinary world, and this metaphysics consisted principally in the idealism, the view of radical impermanence, and the *svalakṣaṇa* ontology that he inherited from the logicians. This is clear in the passage from the *Sarvadharmaniḥsvabhāvasiddhi* that we will translate below.

There is, undeniably, a certain slipperiness in the Yogācāra-Svātantrikas' all-inclusive, ecumenical approach, according to which there is, at some time or another, a lower or higher place for virtually every Buddhist school of thought. However, if we do feel a bit lost in pinning down the Svātantrikas' own views as to what is foundational, there is the consolation that the general problem of understanding Buddhist hierarchical systems is nothing new.

Arguably we are confronted by the same types of difficulties in understanding Dharmakīrti's switch from Sautrāntika to Yogācāra,[35] and perhaps also in understanding what so many Mahāyāna Buddhist philosophers are actually advocating when they seem to accept some things from one point of view, i.e., customary truth, and not another, i.e., ultimate truth. As far as I can see, a Svātantrika like Kamalaśīla just wants to conserve a place for an *exceptional* number of competing accounts of the customary, including even idealism, whereas many other Mahāyānists would not be quite *that* inclusive. Of course I can't easily *resolve* the complex problems that a Buddhist has in proceeding in such a way, but equally I don't think I need to do so in order to show that some Buddhists accepted foundational perceptions and their content and yet also held a hierarchical approach as to what these foundations were taken to be by different philosophers of different levels of sophistication. The fact remains that many Mahāyānists thought that *they* could manage with sliding-scale approaches and yet still have positions of their own.

Realism and Its Holdovers

So much for one angle on the Svātantrika-Prāsaṅgika question, i.e., the metaphysics of particulars and the given that is implicit in the Svātantrikas' foundationalist philosophy of perception. I would now think that there may well be another approach to distinguish the logician-inspired program of the Svātantrika from that of the Prāsaṅgika, one which would account reasonably well for the dGe lugs pa idea that Svātantrikas held that, in customary truth or transactional usage, things had certain properties "intrinsically" *(rang bzhin gyis)* and "from their own side" *(rang ngos nas),* or objectively. Broadly speaking, this is the question of affinities with realism. Putting the two approaches together we get the following picture: that being a Svātantrika, as opposed to a Prāsaṅgika, means sharing the foundationalism of the logicians as well as endorsing certain holdovers of their, and the other lower Buddhist school's, realism.

One of the most extraordinary ideas in Tsong kha pa and the dGe lugs pa tradition is that Svātantrika philosophers not only accept that customary things are established intrinsically, from their own side, etc., but in so doing end up in a very subtle way being *like* realists, i.e., "advocates of real entities" *(dngos smra ba),* and hence essentially in the same camp as all lower Buddhist schools and perhaps even non-Buddhists. Of course, Tsong kha pa is not saying that Svātantrikas *are* themselves *dngos smra ba.* Nonetheless, the *rapprochement* is very clear. In texts like *Drang nges legs bshad snying po,* we find passages like:

> Our position is that one will inevitably have to use autonomous [arguments] *(rang rgyud)* if one accepts that things are established by their intrinsic natures as explained in the *Saṃdhinirmocanasūtra,* just as do our realist coreligionists and [Svātantrikas] such as Bhāvaviveka and others.[36]

Indeed, as we see in the quote from Tsong kha pa with which we began this article, the realist *(dngos smra ba)* and Svātantrika supposedly do not differ so much in their ontology, i.e., *what* they accept as existing, but instead on the level of truth to which this ontology is assigned—the former accepts *svalakṣaṇa, svabhāva,* etc., as ultimate, while the latter accepts them as customary. And in key contexts concerning the Svātantrika-Prāsaṅgika debates, the Svātantrika *are* regularly grouped together with the lower Buddhist schools under the designation *rang rgyud pa man chad* ("[thinkers] from Svātantrika on down"), these all being contrasted with the Prāsaṅgika. Odd as it may seem to us, Tsong kha pa and his followers, in effect, divided all Buddhist philosophy into two significant camps: realists and Svātantrikas on the one hand and Prāsaṅgikas on the other. It's worth examining what is behind this. Here is Tsong kha pa's own succinct formulation in his *dBu ma dgongs pa rab gsal:*

> Thus although there is no way things are *(sdod lugs)* that is not brought about in virtue of things appearing to the mind, in this [Svātantrika] tradition it is not contradictory that the way things are which is so brought about is something existent, not just simply a linguistic designation *(ming du btags pa tsam min pa).* And therefore, in one's understanding, there should be a major difference between what the two Mādhyamika traditions are refuting.[37]

The basic ideas in this and other related passages can be unpacked as follows:

1. Both Mādhyamika schools recognize that customary things are mind-dependent, or "brought about by the mind" *(blo'i dbang gis bzhag pa),* in that such things do not exist independently of a cognizing mind.

2. Svātantrikas hold that although customary existent things are not really independent of the cognizing mind, they are nonetheless more than just mere ways of speaking and thinking; true talk and thought is about *something existent in itself that is more than a purely linguistic fiction.* The customary entity is thus established intrinsically, from its own side *(rang ngos nas)* or from the point of view of how the things themselves are *(rang gi sdod lugs kyi ngos nas).*

3. Prāsaṅgikas do not even accept this limited ontology in 2, and hence have nothing whatsoever to do with things being established from their own side and other such equivalent notions.

4. Where the affinities with realism *(dngos po smra ba)* come in is the acceptance of things being more than linguistic fictions, i.e., that they exist in themselves, or from their own side.

A number of difficult questions immediately arise: Does this give a plausible account of what we find in Indian texts? *If* Tsong kha pa is fairly characterizing the Indian authors, does the Svātantrika-Prāsaṅgika difference actually have anything to do with what *we* would term "realism"?

Let me take the second question first and begin with a disclaimer: probably no fully satisfactory answer to this question about the applicability of the label "realism" can be provided. Anglo-American philosophy after Michael Dummett has seen several very sophisticated philosophical versions of realism being debated, so that it is something of a live issue as to which one best captures our ordinary and intuitive notions and deserves to be called "realism." Nonetheless, if we provisionally adopt John Haldane's and Crispin Wright's "fair characterization of an intuitive realism,"[38] the fundamental core of realism is a fusion of two ideas, deference to the independent and objective facts that make true beliefs true and the self-assurance that we can know these facts. The deference typically consists in an acceptance of an external world existing independently of us, of our concepts, attitudes, descriptions, and beliefs; the self-assurance is the confidence that at least in some favorable circumstances we can come to know this independent world of facts as it is.

Now, straight off, what should be clear is that no Mādhyamika, be he Svātantrika or Prāsaṅgika, will countenance there being a genuinely real external world completely independent of mind—in that sense, both schools clearly are *not* realist, when the term is used in the full sense following

Haldane's and Wright's criteria. We can also understand how contemporary writers, like Mark Siderits, would see the Mādhyamikas as all being *anti-realists* in their denial of a mind-independent reality to which beliefs, when true, must correspond.[39] Even the Tibetan dGe lugs pa scholastic, as we saw, would never countenance calling Mādhyamikas "realists" *(dngos smra ba).* Is it not then just simply incomprehensible to look for a Svātantrika-Prāsaṅgika difference in terms of what we have been terming "affinities with realism," and don't we find our way back to Go rams pa's skepticism about the supposed metaphysical angles to this difference?

I think it's worth persevering through our initial sense of anomaly. There is a subtle sense, at least on Tsong kha pa's interpretation, in which the Svātantrika accepts a *mind-created* appearance to perception as being also quite independent of how we conceptualize it or describe it, and about which we can come to be right or wrong in a way that isn't just a matter of what we believe, think, feel, or say. There is, thus, in a limited way, deference to something like objective facts in the Svātantrika position. And there is also the self-assurance that we can, with a means of valid cognition *(pramāṇa),* get those facts right. The Prāsaṅgika, by contrast, in rejecting that there are any such facts existing independently of what we think or say to be the case does not endorse even this limited deference of his Svātantrika coreligionist.

I don't know if the Svātantrika position is seriously defensible, nor, fortunately, is it my responsibility to take on that task. But perhaps it is of use here to imagine an approximate parallel in another context that would seem to illustrate the essentials of their view. Since Locke, people have argued about whether secondary qualities, like color and taste, are mind-invented. Now, someone might say that they are indeed invented, but are still to be distinguished from purely language-created fictions (such as the characters in novels) in that the twin ideas of deference and self-assurance do apply. This type of "deference-theorist" might argue, for example, that when a wine taster says that such and such a *grand cru* has a lingering taste of berries, is full-bodied or sharp in its attack, he could be shown to be wrong even though he might sincerely believe what he says he tastes: the right answer about tastes would be right because of properties that those tastes have independently of what the taster might think or say. (The same theorist would presumably argue that it is not for nothing that wine tasters have to gain their knowledge through a long acquaintance with wine and that the art of wine tasting isn't just a matter of "talking the talk.") I personally don't know of anyone writing about secondary qualities who does hold this position, but perhaps it is a plausible middle way between complete mind-independence and pure invention—I would have to leave the matter to those better versed in the literature on this subject. In any case, the "deference-theorist's" adversary might reply that whatever the explanation we might give for a taster's being right or wrong, there is no fact to the matter or entity to which we defer or to which we have access, other than the deep-seated ideas and linguistic practices that we and our peers have about secondary qualities.

Let us now go back to first hard question, the applicability of Tsong kha pa's account to Indian texts. Consider the following very typical passage from the *Sarvadharmaniḥsvabhāvasiddhi* of the Svātantrika Kamalaśīla.

> One should analyze the production of entities with logic *(rigs pa, yukti)* and scripture *(lung, āgama)*. Suppose it were thought, "Why should we analyze it, when [a fact such as] the production of sprouts and the like being conditioned by seeds and so forth is just simply admitted *(grags pa)* by everyone from cowherds on up? The intelligent should not analyze in order to ascertain the natures of entities, because [if they did] it would follow that there would be no end [to such analysis] and that they would not [actually] be intelligent." This is not right, for they would not ascertain [things] through means of valid cognition *(tshad ma, pramāṇa)*, and moreover it is possible that what is [generally] admitted is wrong. Otherwise [if analysis using means of valid cognition were unnecessary], no one who applied himself to what he had himself admitted would ever end up being unreliable about anything at all. To take some examples: it is [generally] admitted that perishing is something that has a cause [although this is actually wrong],[40] and though people [generally] admit that matter and the like are external objects, this can be invalidated by a means of valid cognition if it is subjected to analysis. In the same way here too [with regard to the production of entities], what people admit could also turn out to be deceptive, and hence one really should analyze it. As for scripture without any logic, it would be of no attraction to the intelligent. It is scripture grounded by logic that cannot lead astray, and so first of all we should analyze [things] logically.[41]

The passage turns on a version of the ideas of deference and self-assurance that we have taken to be central to realism: establishing or proving some proposition depends upon the facts and upon a means of valid cognition *(pramāṇa)*, i.e., a way of knowing the facts, and not upon our simply accepting the proposition or generally thinking it is so. Knowledge is of things which can be, and often are, quite other than what we might think or say they are, as Kamalaśīla attempts to show by citing a number of cases on which the ordinary man believes one thing, but actually has customary truth quite wrong. Kamalaśīla is in effect endorsing the logician's emphasis on *pramāṇas* as being grounded in reality and being able to serve as a nonarbitrary corrective to beliefs, even though for him as a Mādhyamika this "reality" is not ultimate, and is itself defeasible by Mādhyamika-style dialectic.

It's far from sure that the adversary spoken about by Kamalaśīla was the historical Candrakīrti. Fortunately, however, nothing much in our argument depends vitally on us making such a definite identification. For our purposes what counts is that the passage does represent an adversary holding a type of Prāsaṅgika-like position, even if Kamalaśīla is somewhat unsympathetic in his depictions. The adversary's emphasis on no analysis of convention and on what is simply admitted *(grags pa)* seems in keeping with Candrakīrti's position, in *Madhyamakāvatāra* (MAv) 6.32–33 and 35, on production and causality being simply the unanalyzed and ordinarily admitted phenomenon of one thing leading to another, stripped of theoretical additions like cause and effect being identical or different—in this discussion Candrakīrti's stance is in stark contrast to the Svātantrika.

More generally, Candrakīrti seems to lack the deference to grounding facts of his Svātantrika adversary. As we saw earlier, Kamalaśīla and other Svātantrikas have no qualms about characterizing propositions as correct *(tathya)* or incorrect *(mithyā) tout court,* i.e., without taking into account people's particular views. On the other hand, in the MAv 6.24–25, we see that Candrakīrti takes pains to reject this: there are no customary truths which are, or could be, right or wrong objectively in this way, i.e., for a universal, ideal audience of the rational; they are so only "relative to the world" *('jig rten la ltos pa)* and in dependence upon the world's beliefs.[42] In fact, it is a controversial point if, and to what degree, Candrakīrti relies on *pramāṇas* at all, with some commentators, like the Kashmirian, Jayānanda, and certain Tibetans, often depicted as attributing to Candrakīrti fundamentally a no-*pramāṇa* stance.[43] At any rate, the *pramāṇas* that we could attribute to Candakīrti are not ones in the spirit of the Svātantrikas and logicians, i.e., they would not be *underpinned* by facts that are so irrespective of what people might believe and say.

How much then does the dGe lugs pa account of the Svātantrika's affinities with realism and Prāsaṅgika's resolute rejection of such affinities accord with the Indian texts? It probably has to be said that Tsong kha pa's own position on *prasaṅga*-method, *pramāṇas, paraprasiddhahetu* ("reasons accepted by [only] the adversary") and the Prāsaṅgika's no-thesis stance is a very complex one bearing a problematic relationship with elements of Candrakīrti's own texts, notably with the first chapter of the PPMV. I have dealt with some of these considerations in an earlier article, "Tsong kha pa *et al.* on the Candrakīrti-Bhāvaviveka Debate."[44] It does seem that there is an overly baroque transformation of Prāsaṅgika thought largely due to the extreme reluctance on Tsong kha pa's part to take some of Candrakīrti's claims at their radical face value, and especially due to his own attempt to harmonize Prāsaṅgika philosophy with that of the logicians. In particular, in making Prāsaṅgikas adopt a *logician*'s positions on things being established by *pramāṇas,* Tsong kha pa introduces into Candrakīrti's philosophy a kind of lingering deference to objective facts which I think a simpler and more literal reading of Candrakīrti just does not bear out. *It is ironic that Tsong kha pa, who more than anyone brought out differences between Svātantrika and Prāsaṅgika, read Candrakīrti as being de facto an adherent of Buddhist logic.* That said, the introduction into the Svātantrika-Prāsaṅgika debate of notions of customary establishment due to intrinsic natures or characters, or from [the object's] own side and from the perspective of the way things themselves are, may well be considered a superb insight: it gives us the tools to make sense of several passages in both Svātantrika and Prāsaṅgika texts as turning on holdover issues of realism and objectivity that arise even within the Mādhyamika philosophy of a mind-dependent world.

I see two ways to take Candrakīrti's philosophy. First of all, the Svātantrika might be depicted as claiming that judgments about customary truth should be like what the first Kantian *Critique* had termed *convictions (Überzeugung),* valid for all rational beings in an (idealized) universal audience because not dependent on subjectively held ideas and attitudes. The corresponding depiction of the Prāsaṅgika would be to say that he recognizes only *persuasions (Überredung)* that work for particular groups of people in particular contexts, but not for all objectively in an idealized audience. This advocacy of persuasions to the exclusion of convictions could then be taken pejoratively, in keeping with the Kantian spirit, as resulting in a kind of skepticism, i.e., a view that understandings are always nothing but "a mere semblance" *(ein blosser Schein),* with only "private validity" *(Privatgültigkeit),* never justified by the objective facts and metaphysical underpinnings they would need in order to be serious and genuine.[45] And indeed there have been such skepticism-oriented readings of Candrakīrti, from Edward Conze to B.K. Matilal.[46] A second, more sympathetic picture, however, would be to say that Candrakīrti accepts that the world has its own agreed-upon standards of true and false, real and unreal, and that these common criteria do lead to shared understandings, and perhaps even new and more sophisticated knowledge.[47] Still this consensus or shared "persuasions" about customary truth would not be underpinned by objective facts, appearances-cum-particulars, or any other such metaphysical constructs. Not only would it be impossible to ground our ordinary beliefs, practices, and language games in such a fashion, but the ordinary man's approach to causality, the external world, perception, etc., would provide all the justificatory criteria we would ever need: all the rest would be superfluities thought up by those who, as the *Catuḥśatakaṭīkā* puts it, are "intoxicated" *(smyos par gyur ba)* by such things and are "completely unversed in the mundane."[48] If that's right, Candrakīrti could well be a genuinely extraordinary figure in Indian philosophy: a type of quietist, or perhaps minimalist, whose philosophy promotes only *le libre retour à l'empirique sublimé,* and recognizes neither possibility nor need for metaphysics at all.[49]

Notes

1 *rTsa ba shes rab kyi dka' gnas chen po brgyad,* (Sarnath ed.) 6; (Collected Works) 572: *spyir rang mtshan don dam du grub par 'dod na / dngos smra bar 'gyur la / don dam du ma grub kyang tha snyad du grub par 'dod pa dbu ma rang rgyud pa dang / tha snyad du'ang ma grub pa slob dpon gnyis kyi bzhes pa'o //.*

2 Johnston (1993): 85. Cf. the characterization of a "metaphysical picture" in Johnston (1997): 175: "a concrete instance of the idea of an independent demand in the things themselves."

3 See Ruegg (1981): 58, and the introduction to Mimaki (1982).

4 I have followed Mark Siderits in adopting the term "customary" for *saṃvṛti,* instead of "conventional." "Customary" can perhaps better emphasize that *saṃvṛti* is what is usual, habitual, surface-level. In any case, whatever be the translation, it is important that *saṃvṛtisatya* is not misunderstood as being just a purely conventional and arbitrary agreement in the way in which the moon's being called "that which has a rabbit" *(śaśin)* is just a *purely conventional* agreement. What is true for the world, be it the impermanence of phenomena or the

law of cause and effect, is so not just because of simple conventional agreements on arbitrary words—whether we are Svātantrika or Prāsaṅgika, *saṃvṛtisatya* is deeper than that. On Dignāga's and Dharmakīrti's accounts of the moon-*śaśin* type of convention and of "common recognitions" *(prasiddhi)* of language use, see Tillemans (2000): 153 et seq. As for the term, *vyavahāra* / *tha snyad* (which is used interchangeably in Madhyamaka philosophy with *saṃvṛtisatya),* I have opted for Ruegg's translation, "transactional usage." See, e.g., Ruegg (1981): 16.

5 Go rams pa, in his *lTa ba'i shan 'byed,* adopts the perspective that there is no difference between Svātantrika and Prāsaṅgika on matters of customary truth and that Prāsaṅgikas do even accept the use of "autonomous reasons" *(svatantrahetu)* in debates about customary truth. See *lTa ba'i shan 'byed* (Tokyo ed.) f. 34a4–5: *tha snyad kyi rnam bzhag la / thal rang gi khyad par 'byed pa ni min te / tha snyad kyi rnam bzhag la rang rgyud kyi gtan tshigs thal 'gyur ba rnams kyis kyang khas len pa'i phyir /* "Concerning the presentation of transactional usage, there is no difference to be made between Prāsaṅgika and Svātantrika. This is because Prāsaṅgikas too accept autonomous reasons *(rang rgyud kyi gtan tshigs, svatantrahetu)* [as being proper] for the presentation of transactional usage." When arguing with a realist *(dngos smra ba)* about voidness and ultimate truth, however, the Prāsaṅgika maintains (contrary to the Svātantrika) that no commonly agreed upon terms can be found, and hence that an autonomous reason cannot be used. Note too that in Go rams pa's *lTa ba'i ngan sel* (his critique of Tsong kha pa's *rTsa shes dka' gnas chen po brgyad*), we find a clear rejection of Tsong kha pa's key position that the issue between Svātantrikas and Prāsaṅgikas turns on the former accepting particulars *(rang mtshan, svalakṣaṇa)* on the level of customary truth. See ff. 41a4–41b2 of the *lTa ba'i ngan sel: mkhas rlom dag rang rgyud pas rang gi mtshan nyid kyis grub pa'i chos bsgrub dgos pas rang rgyud kyi gtan tshigs khas len la thal 'gyur bas de bsgrub mi dgos pas rang rgyud kyi gtan tshigs khas mi len pa yin no zhes smra ba ni phyogs gar yod tsam yang ma mthong ba ste / rang rgyud pas mtha' bzhi'i skye ba bkag pa'i dam bca' bsgrub pa'i skabs su rang gi mtshan nyid kyis grub pa'i chos sgrub par thal ba'i phyir ro //* "Those who have the conceit that they are learned say that the Svātantrikas accepted autonomous reasons because they needed to prove dharmas established by their particular characters *(rang gi mtshan nyid, svalakṣaṇa),* but that Prāsaṅgikas did not need to prove such things and hence did not accept autonomous reasons. One cannot see that there is any point whatsoever [in this position], for [if true] it would absurdly follow that when the Svātantrikas proved the thesis consisting in the negation of the four points *(mtha' bzhi, catuṣkoṭi)* of production, they would then be proving dharmas which were established by their particular characters *(svalakṣaṇa).*"

6 My use of "objective" here corresponds to what Searle calls the "epistemic" sense of "objective"; see Searle (1995): 8–9.

7 This long passage has been translated by M. David Eckel in his article in the present volume. See p. 179–182 in the present volume.

8 Williams (1995) brings this out nicely in analyzing Tsong kha pa's use of Śāntideva's *Bodhicaryāvatāra* 9.140 as an Indian textual source for the doctrine of recognizing the object to be refuted.

9 To take a Western parallel, to stake everything on there being or not being *that* kind of evidence would be to ensure a rather flat, unsympathetic perspective on a philosopher, much as if one dismissed a contemporary philosopher's penetrating analysis of Kant or Plato because the formulation of the explanation was not to be found clearly present in the original German or Greek.

10 Some methodological remarks and anticipated objections: In order to avoid accusations of question-begging, it's no doubt better to stay within the Indian context at the key stages of the argument and avoid taking indigenous Tibetan sources as unproblematically authoritative on the interpretation of Indian texts. In short, the Tibetan scholastic literature can provide hypotheses, and even extremely valuable inspiration, but not proof. Second, as it is certainly not clear that there are *unified* Svātantrika and Prāsaṅgika schools having precisely the members that the Tibetan *grub mtha'* texts say they have, it seems prudent to concentrate first of all on specific writers and their works, resisting the temptation to zig-zag unselfconsciously between the several philosophers that Tibetan authors traditionally consider to be Svātantrika or Prāsaṅgika. For the present purposes these two varieties of question-begging can be avoided by focusing on major Indian figures—Śāntarakṣita and Kamalaśīla on the Svātantrika side and Candrakīrti on the Prāsaṅgika—sketching out certain general features of what I'll call their "Svātantrika/Prāsaṅgika philosophy" based on their texts. It will have to remain an open question for now as to how many of those features also apply to the numerous other thinkers grouped under the rubrics in question. That said, given more space I would argue that the sometimes maligned Tibetan classifications could well be justifiable in their grouping of Bhāvaviveka and Avalokitavrata under the Svātantrika label. These latter thinkers seem to have the same logician's ontology (minus idealism) and foundationalism as their Yogācāra-Mādhyamika counterparts. Furthermore, Bhāvaviveka has an *apoha* theory in MHK 5.60–68 which looks like a direct precursor of Dharmakīrti's position in PV 1.64 and other verses.

11 The definition is that of Rorty (1979; 1980 repr.): 104. For my earlier presentation of the Svātantrika-Prāsaṅgika question as well as various textual passages supporting the argument, see Tillemans (1990): 37–53.

12 See Sellars (1997): 68–69. Different variants on this characterization figure throughout "Empiricism and the Philosophy of Mind." Cf. also R. Brandom's characterization in the "Study Guide," ibid.: 122.

13 Cf. for example the discussion of "appearances" in Kamalaśīla's *Sarvadharmaniḥsvabhāvasiddhi,* P 313a8–313b3: *gal te dngos po thams cad rang bzhin med pa nyid yin na / 'o na ni de'i tshe de dag yul dang dus la sogs pa nges par sngon po dang / phya le ba la sogs pa'i ngo bor snang ba ji ltar mi 'gal zhe na ma yin te / 'khrul ba'i rnam par shes pa la snang ba'i gzugs bzhin du brdzun pa yang snang ba'i phyir ro // ji ltar 'khrul ba'i rnam par shes pa la snang ba'i rnam pa rnams don dam*

par rang bzhin med pa yin yang yul dang dus la sogs pa nges par snang ba ltar gzhan dag kyang de dang 'dra bas mi 'gal ba nyid do // "[Objection:] But if all entities *(dngos po)* were without intrinsic natures *(rang bzhin),* then why isn't it contradictory that they appear *(snang ba)* as having intrinsic natures *(ngo bo)* such as being blue, flat, etc., i.e., as restricted to [specific] places, times, and so forth? [Reply:] No, it isn't [contradictory], because they do appear even though they are deceptive, just like the forms that appear to erroneous consciousnesses. Just as images *(rnam pa, ākāra)* appearing to erroneous consciousnesses are actually without any intrinsic natures, but nonetheless appear as though restricted to [specific] places, times and so forth [i.e., appear as particulars], so too the other things [i.e., customary truths] are similar to these [images appearing to erroneous consciousnesses] and thus there is no contradiction [in entities being without intrinsic natures and yet appearing as though restricted to specific places and times]."

We see the allusion to particulars in Kamalaśīla's use of the phrase "restricted to [specific] places, times, and so forth" *(yul dang dus la sogs pa nges pa, deśakālādiniyata),* a formula which is also found in several places in his other Mādhyamika works, such as the *Madhyamakāloka.* This formula to characterize particulars is especially important in Dharmakīrti's descriptions of particulars *(svalakṣaṇa)* in works such as the PV and *Hetubindu* (HB). In the HB, for example, Dharmakīrti describes particulars as "things restricted to [specific] places, times, [one] intrinsic nature, and [one] state" *(deśakālasvabhāvāvasthāniyata),* but this more elaborate description is routinely also compacted to formulations like *niyatadeśakāla(tva),* as we see in the PVSV to PV 1.35. See HB 26*.12–13 (ed. Steinkellner), trans. in Steinkellner (1967): vol. 2, p. 67; PVSV *ad* k. 35 (ed. Gnoli): 23, trans. Mookerjee and Nagasaki (1964): 85–86. See also the explanations in Dreyfus (1997): 70–71. Matthew Kapstein informs me that the formula also figures regularly in other Yogācāra-Vijñaptimātratā literature.

14 Following the account in TS 25.2956 et seq., a cognition of, say, fire, is justified and confirmed by another cognition which directly perceives the ability of this firelike thing to actually burn and have the practical efficacy *(arthakriyā)* expected of fire; the regress is avoided because this perception, at least in people thoroughly used to how fire functions, will supposedly immediately recognize itself as being a genuine cognition of such efficacy due to the cognition's own reflexive awareness *(svasaṃvedana, ātmasaṃvedana)* by which it perceives itself. In short, a perception of the object's efficacy needs no other confirming cognition and serves to anchor validity once and for all—it is thus the final arbiter and dispeller of doubt. Cf. TS 2965–2967: *tasmād arthakriyābhāsaṃ jñānaṃ yāvan na jāyate / tāvad ādye apramāśaṅkā jāyate bhrāntihetutaḥ // anantaraṃ phalādṛṣṭiḥ sādṛśyasyopalambhanam / mater apaṭutetyādi bhrāntikāraṇam atra ca // kāryāvabhāsivijñāne jāte tv etan na vidyate / sākṣād vastunibaddhāyāḥ kriyāyāḥ prativedanāt //* "Therefore, so long as there is not yet a cognition to which the practical efficacy [of the object] appears, there will remain the doubt that the initial [cognition] was not valid, for there could be causes for error. Now, in the

case of this [initial cognition] there could be causes for error, such as, among others, the fact that no effect might be seen right afterwards, that we might perceive [the cognition] to be similar [to wrong cognitions], or that the mind is dull. However, when there is a cognition to which the effect [of the object] appears, then there will be no such [cause for error], for there is a direct experience of the action which is necessarily connected with the real entity [itself]."

15 Śāntarakṣita argues that if there were not at least a datum of appearance which, qua appearance, would be cognized by "scholars, women, and children," then "the locus [i.e., the subject] of the reason would be unestablished." Kamalaśīla, commenting on this problem of the locus being unestablished, states that "although one refutes superimpositions of a real intrinsic nature, one does not refute the intrinsic nature of the subject." The passage might in itself seem to lend some support for Tsong kha pa's idea that the Svātantrika rejects real or ultimate intrinsic natures but accepts customary ones, but this would be going far on relatively slim textual evidence. What does emerge from the passage and the subsequent argumentation, however, is that the subject is a perceptual appearance which everyone has in common and that this customary subject can be accepted as established, even though the Mādhyamika would deny that it has any ultimate intrinsic nature. This customary subject is not, however, to be taken in the way that philosophers, like Vaiśeṣikas or others, might *think* it is, for such conceptions are just pure creations of thought only in keeping with theories. See MA and MAV, P 73b5–74a6; D 75a1–7: *gzhung gis bskyed pa'i bye brag gi*[a] *// chos can spangs nas mkhas pa dang // bud med byis pa'i bar dag la // grags par gyur pa'i dngos rnams la // bsgrub dang sgrub pa'i dngos po 'di // ma lus yang dag 'jug par 'gyur // de lta min na gzhi ma grub // la sogs lan ni ji skad gdab // bdag ni snang ba'i ngang can gyi*[b] */ / dngos po dgag par mi byed de // de lta bas na sgrub pa dang // bsgrub bya gzhag pa 'khrugs pa med // rjes su dpag pa dang rjes su dpag par bya ba'i tha snyad thams cad ni phan tshun mi mthun pas grub pa'i mthas*[c] *bskyed pa chos can tha dad pa*[d] *yongs su btang ste / mkhas pa dang bud med dang byis pa'i bar gyi mig dang rna ba la sogs pa'i shes pa la snang ba'i ngang can gyi phyogs sgra la sogs pa'i chos can la brten nas 'jug go // de lta ma yin na du ba dang / yod pa la sogs pa'i me dang mi rtag pa nyid la sogs pa bsgrub par 'dod pa thams cad kyi gtan tshigs kyi gzhi 'grub par mi 'gyur te / bsgrub*[e] *pa'i chos can yan lag can dang / nam mkha'i yon tan la sogs pa'i ngo bo rnams ma grub pa'i phyir ro // . . . kho bo yang mig la sogs pa'i shes pa la snang ba'i ngang can gyi dngos po ni mi sel mod*[f] *kyi / shes rab dang ye shes kyis dpyad na chu shing gi sdong po bzhin du snying po bag tsam yang mi snang bas don dam par mi 'dod do // de lta bas na snang ba'i don ma bkag pa nyid kyis mngon par zhen pa med pa'i bsgrub pa*[g] *dang / sgrub pa'i tha snyad 'jug pas chos thams cad rang bzhin med par smra ba la gnod pa ci yang med do //* ([a]D. *gis*—[b]P. *gyis*—[c]P. *mi mthun pa'i mthas*—[d]P. *pa'i*—[e]D. *sgrub pa'i*—[f]P. omits *mod*—[g]P. *sgrub pa)* "[MA] Setting aside subjects *(dharmin)* to which treatises give rise, [logical] entities consisting of means of proof *(sādhana)* and what is to be proved *(sādhya)* will all function correctly on the basis of the entities recognized by [everyone] from scholars to women and

children. Otherwise, there would be criticisms like that the locus *(āśraya)* [of the reason] would be unestablished. I do not refute entities as they appear, and thus there is nothing that perturbs the establishment of means of proof *(sādhana)* [i.e., logical reasons and examples] and what is to be proved *(sādhya)*. [MAV:] We should set aside the different subjects *(dharmin)* brought into being by philosophical theories *(siddhānta)* as their usages about what infers and is inferred are in mutual conflict. [Instead] we apply ourselves in dependence upon a subject, like places, sounds and so forth, as they appear to visual and auditory consciousnesses of [everyone from] scholars to women and children. Otherwise loci of the logical reasons for all who wish to prove things like smoke and existent fire or impermanence will be unestablished *(asiddha)*, for the intrinsic natures of subjects to be proven like [Nyāya-Vaiśeṣika notions such as] wholes *(avayavin)* or qualities of space *(ākāśaguṇa)*, are not established.... But while we do not eliminate the entity as it appears to the visual consciousness and other [direct perceptions], if we analyze [it] with insight and wisdom, then like [illusions] such as plantains *(kadalī)*, not the slightest essence will appear, and thus we do not accept them ultimately. Thus, by not negating the appearing object, we apply ourselves on the basis of usages of *sādhana* and *sādhya* which are not invented conceptually *(mngon par zhen pa med pa)*, and thus there is no invalidation whatsoever when we assert that all things are without intrinsic nature."

16 See *Madhyamakāloka* (MĀ), P 188b–189a, where Kamalaśīla cites Dignāga's definition of a thesis (PS 3.2), as well as PV 3.136–137 and 141–143. On these verses from Dignāga and Dharmakīrti and the problem of *āśrayāsiddha,* see Tillemans (2000): 194–210.

17 See, e.g., CŚ 13, translated in Tillemans (1990): 176–179. On the rejection of *svalakṣaṇa,* see, e.g., MAvBh *ad* MAv 6.36: *de'i phyir rang gi mtshan nyid kyi skye ba ni bden pa gnyis su char du yang yod pa ma yin no* / "Hence, from the point of view of either of the two truths, there is no production of particulars."

18 The latter theme becomes known in Tibetan accounts as the question of *chos can mthun snang ba* ("concordantly appearing subjects"); see Tillemans and Tomabechi (1995), n. 25, and the references therein. The relevant passage in Candrakīrti is PPMV (La Vallée Poussin ed.) 28–30; see Tillemans (1990), n. 107.

19 The formulation is that of McDowell (1998), where the whole issue is linked up with Kant's characterization of conceptual thought, or the understanding, as being "spontaneous," to be contrasted with the imposition of data upon the receptive sensory intuition.

20 See Dharmottara's *Nyāyabinduṭīkā ad Nyāyabindu* 1.5 (ed. D. Malvania): 49.1–50.1: *aniyatapratibhāsatvaṃ ca pratibhāsaniyamahetor abhāvāt / grāhyo hy artho vijñānaṃ janayan niyatapratibhāsaṃ kuryāt / yathā rūpaṃ cakṣurvijñānaṃ janayan niyatapratibhāsaṃ janayati / vikalpavijñānaṃ tv arthān notpadyate / tataḥ pratibhāsaniyamahetor abhāvād aniyatapratibhāsam / kutaḥ punar etad vikalpo arthān notpadyata iti / arthasannidhinirapekṣatvāt* / "The fact that the [conceptual] image is not fixed is due to there being no cause for fixing the

image. Indeed, if the apprehended [i.e., perceived] object [i.e., the particular] gave rise to the consciousness, then it would produce a fixed image, just as visible form *(rūpa),* when it gives rise to the visual consciousness, gives rise to a fixed image. Conceptual thought, however, does not arise from the object [i.e., the particular] and thus, because there is no cause for fixing the image, the image is unfixed. [Objection:] But how do we know this, i.e., that conceptual thought does not arise from the object. [Reply:] It is because there is no dependence upon the object being nearby [for conceptual thought to arise]." The discussion turns on the Dharmakīrtian idea of conceptual thought and language having unrestricted *yogyatā,* or "fitness"—in short, we can think about and linguistically designate what we will as we will. See Tillemans (2000): 219–228.

21 See Tillemans (1990), n. 428.

22 Dreyfus (1996): 211, 213, 224.

23 Dharmakīrti's PV 2.1 notoriously defines a "means of valid cognition" *(pramāṇa)* as "reliable/non-belying cognition" *(avisaṃvādi jñānam),* and then explains this latter notion (i.e., *avisaṃvādana*) as consisting in there being "confirmation of practical efficacy" *(arthakriyāsthiti).* Dreyfus (1996): 213, in explaining this passage, rightly makes the connection between *avisaṃvādi jñānam* and the "practical ability to lead us towards successful practical actions." See also Tillemans (1999): 6–7 and 19, n. 6, on *arthakriyāsthiti.*

24 Sellars (1997): 20.

25 See Brandom (1997): 121–122: "In its most familiar form, the Myth of the Given blurs the distinction between sentience and sapience. This is the distinction between being aware in the sense of being merely *awake* (which we share with nondiscursive animals—those that do not grasp concepts), on the one hand, and on the other hand, being aware in a sense that involves *knowledge* either by *being* a kind of knowledge, or as potentially serving to *justify* judgements that so qualify. The 'idea that a sensation of a red triangle is the very paradigm of empirical knowledge' is a paradigm of the sort of conflation in question. The Myth of the Given is the idea that there can be a kind of *awareness* that has two properties. First, it is or entails having a certain sort of *knowledge*—perhaps not of other things, but at least that one is in that state, or a state of that kind—knowledge that the one whose state it is possesses simply in virtue of being in that state. Second, it entails that the capacity to have that sort of awareness, to be in that sort of state, does not presuppose the acquisition of any *concepts*—that one can be aware in that sense independently of and antecedently to grasping or mastering the use of any concepts (paradigmatically through language learning)."

26 The idea of "reflexive awareness" *(svasaṃvedana),* so crucial in Dharmakīrti, Śāntarakṣita, and Kamalaśīla (and so utterly rejected in Candrakīrti), does in effect embody the two properties of the awareness that Brandom speaks about (see n. 25 above). When one has a perception of red, the very same cognition is also nonconceptually, nonlinguistically, aware *that* one is perceiving red, or in other words, *that* one is in that type of a state. This "reflexive awareness"

inherent to perception is, if we wish to be exact in our description of Dharmakīrti's empiricism, the two-propertied awareness that drives the myth of the given. See also n. 30 below.

27 Sellars (1997): 17. The italics are those of Sellars.

28 See Richard Rorty's introduction to Sellars (1997): 3.

29 Sellars (1997): 17.

30 Cf. Paul W. Williams (1998): 6: "If it is seeing blue but it is not conscious of seeing blue then, it is argued [by Śāntarakṣita] there is no real seeing blue at all." See p. 6, n. 8, and pp. 19–23, 31–32.

31 It looks to me that Dreyfus is using this backhanded type of argument where the fact that Dharmakīrti ran into serious problems with his own foundationalist empiricist principles somehow counts against him having them at all. Cf. Dreyfus (1996): 214: "This conclusion [viz., that perception depends on conceptualization to be knowledge] is not, however, acceptable to Dharmakīrti, for it completely undermines the foundational role of perception in his system. It furthermore threatens to make his account circular, for the epistemological support of conceptuality [for Dharmakīrti] was supposed to lie in perception, the unproblematic foundation of knowledge. This foundation, however, can never be secured since the epistemological validity of perception seems to rely on the collaboration of concepts."

32 M. Williams (1999): 62. See also the section on "foundationalism without infallibility" in Dancy (1989): 62–65, which goes in the same direction. Interestingly enough, Sellars' discussion does not seem to turn on the given and foundations being absolutely indubitable, nor does that of McDowell. Cf. the remark on Sellars' "Empiricism and the Philosophy of Mind" in Putnam (1994): 115: "[A]n examination of that essay shows that questions of *certainty* [Putnam's italics] play almost no role in Sellars' discussion."

33 For some discussion on Dharmakīrti's pragmatism, see Tillemans: (1999): 6–12.

34 Not just philosophers of mathematics, but a well-known nominalist writer on aesthetics does this sort of thing. See Nelson Goodman (1968): xiii: "Frequently some result of my own earlier philosophical work has been brought to bear here, but I have tried not to regrind old axes. For instance, if some of the following pages violate the principles of nominalism, that is only because it seems unnecessary for me to show, for present purposes, how a nominalistic version may be formulated."

35 On the complex hierarchy of positions and the "ascending scale of analysis" in Dharmakīrti, see Dunne (1999): sec. 3.1, and Dreyfus (1997): 83–105.

36 *Drang nges legs bshad snying po* (Sarnath ed.) 184: *rang gi lugs ni dgongs 'grel las gsungs pa ltar rang gi mtshan nyid kyis grub pa 'dod na ni nges par rang rgyud bya dgos te / rang sde dngos por smra ba rnams dang legs ldan la sogs pa bzhin no /.*

37 *dBu ma dgongs pa rab gsal* (Sarnath ed.) 136: *de ltar na blo la snang ba'i dbang gis bzhag pa min pa'i sdod lugs med kyang / de'i dbang gis bzhag pa'i sdod lugs ming du btags pa tsam min pa cig yod pa lugs 'di la mi 'gal bas / dbu ma pa gnyis kyi dgag bya la blo'i ngor mi 'dra ba chen po 'ong ngo //.*

38 See pp. 3–5 in the introduction to J. Haldane and C. Wright (1993).

39 See Siderits (1989): 236–238 and Siderits (1988).

40 In the background of the argument is the Buddhist logicians' position that moment by moment perishing is an inherent feature of things and is not caused by external factors.

41 P 312a8–312b6: *rigs pa dang lung dag gis dngos po rnams kyi skye ba dpyad par bya'o // gal te 'di snyam du myu gu la sogs pa'i skye ba sa bon la sogs pa'i rkyen can gnag rdzi yan chad la grags pa kho na yin na de la dpyad par bya ci dgos / dngos po'i bdag nyid gtan la phab pa la ni rtog pa dang ldan pa rnams dpyad par rung ba ma zin te / thug pa med par thal bar 'gyur ba'i phyir dang / rtog pa dang mi ldan pa nyid du thal bar 'gyur ba'i phyir ro snyam du sems na / de ni rigs pa ma yin te / tshad mas gtan la ma phab pa'i phyir dang / grags pa yang log par srid pa'i phyir ro // de lta ma yin na rang la grags pa'i ngor byas te 'jug pa rnams su yang gang la yang bslu bar mi 'gyur ro // de la dper na 'jig pa yang rgyu dang ldan pa nyid du grags la / gzugs la sogs pa yang phyi rol gyi don nyid du grags zin kyang / dpyad pa byas na tshad mas gnod pa srid pa de bzhin du 'di la yang grags pa brdzun pa'i ngo bo yang srid pas dpyad par bya bar rung ba nyid do // de la lung rigs pa dang bral ba ni rtog pa dang ldan pa rnams rangs par mi 'gyur la / rigs pas brtan por byas pa'i lung yang don gzhan du drang bar mi nus pas de'i phyir re zhig rigs pas dpyad par bya'o //.*

42 See Tillemans (1990): 46 and 50.

43 See Yoshimizu (1993a): 208–211. In *Drang nges legs bshad snying po* (Sarnath ed.) 183, Tsong kha pa describes what seems to be Jayānanda's position: *yang kha cig tshad mas grub pa'i don thams cad du med pas pha rol pos khas blangs pa'am blangs pa'i mthar thug pa la brten pa'i thal 'gyur gyis log rtog 'gog la / bden pa rnam par bcad tsam gyi bden med bsgrub rgyu med pa rang rgyud kyi rtags dang dam bca' med pa'i don du 'dod do /* "Also, some people maintain that the [Prāsaṅgika's] point of there not being autonomous logical reasons or theses is that since there is nothing anywhere that is established by a *pramāṇa,* [the Prāsaṅgika] refutes wrong views by means of absurd consequences *(prasaṅga)* that rely on what the adversary believes or upon what ends up ensuing from his beliefs, and [in this way] [things] being true is just simply negated, but not being true does not have to be proved."

44 Tillemans (1992).

45 See *Critique of Pure Reason,* trans. by P. Guyer and A. W. Wood (1997): 685: "If it is valid for everyone merely as long as he has reason, then its ground is objectively sufficient, and in that case taking something to be true is called *conviction.* If it has its ground only in the particular constitution of the subject, then it is called *persuasion.* Persuasion is a mere semblance, since the ground of the judgment, which lies solely in the subject, is held to be objective. Hence such a judgment also has only private validity, and this taking something to be true cannot be communicated. Truth, however, rests upon agreement with the object, with regard to which, consequently, the judgments of every understanding must agree."

46 Cf., e.g., Conze (1959): 124–125: "The Madhyamika school flourished in India for well over 800 years. About 450 A.D. it split into two sub-divisions: one side, the *Prasangikas,* interpreted Nagarjuna's doctrine as a universal scepticism, and claimed that their argumentations had the exclusive purpose of refuting the opinions of others; the other side, the Svatantrikas, maintained that argument could also establish some positive truths."

47 Mark Siderits sees in Candrakīrti a "no-theory" stance where what counts is simply what we now say—the result is that Candrakīrti supposedly rejects "the possibility that our linguistic practices might allow of alteration and improvement. Once again, customary practices are thought of as brutely given and to be taken at face value." (Siderits [1989]: 243). This certainly is one way in which Candrakīrti might be read, especially if we weight heavily some passages concerning the rejection of "production from other." The fact remains, however, that Candrakīrti, in commenting upon Āryadeva's CŚ, does recognize that the way the world takes certain important aspects of customary truth is inconsistent with other features and principles they would accept. Thus, for example, the world thinks the body is clean, but this belief is shown to be inconsistent in that the world also recognizes that most, or all, of the individual parts, taken separately, are repulsive and dirty. A more interesting way to take the "no-theory" stance is "no theory accepting metaphysical entities." This leaves open the possibility that the world could apply its procedures to discover new things and reform inconsistencies.

48 See Tillemans (1990): vol. 1, pp. 53, 177.

49 Quietism is a term for Wittgenstein's lucid avoidance of substantive philosophy, as in *Philosophical Investigations,* 133: "The real discovery is the one that makes me capable of stopping doing philosophy when I want to." See McDowell (1998): 175–178. I am using "minimalism" here in the sense of Mark Johnston (1997): 149–150: "the view that metaphysical pictures of the justificatory undergirdings of our practices do not represent the real conditions of justification of those practices." I owe the impetus to seeing Candrakīrti as a minimalist to the philosopher, Roy W. Perrett, who developed such an interpretation in a lecture at the 12th conference of the International Association of Buddhist Studies, in Lausanne, August 1999. The characterization of the Mādhyamika's philosophical project as *le libre retour à l'empirique sublimé* is that of Paul Demiéville in his preface to J. May (1959).

4. The Role of the "Given" in the Classification of Śāntarakṣita and Kamalaśīla as Svātantrika-Mādhyamikas

SARA L. MCCLINTOCK[1]

The opinion which is fated to be ultimately agreed upon by all who investigate, is what we mean by the truth, and the object represented in this opinion is the real. That is the way I would explain reality.[2]—C. S. Peirce

THERE IS PERHAPS a certain irony in choosing to discuss the Tibetan classifications of Śāntarakṣita and Kamalaśīla in terms of the contemporary philosophical idea of the given. After all, a possible criticism of the Tibetan doxographers is that the categories they use to describe the various types of Indian Buddhism are anachronisms not indigenous to the Indian texts. And, indeed, it is our very purpose in this volume to investigate the question of whether two of the most famed Tibetan classifications of Indian Madhyamaka—those of the Svātantrika and the Prāsaṅgika—are at all useful or valid in the evaluation of Indian Madhyamaka sources.[3] So to introduce yet another foreign term, the still greater anachronism that is the "given," might seem antithetical to our project of trying to disentangle the already complicated web of Tibetan interpretations in order to see whether and how such interpretations relate to the Indian traditions they purport to explain. Throwing the given into the mix only increases the obstacles faced, especially when we consider the enormous lack of agreement concerning the concept in contemporary philosophy.

Yet, ironically again, it may be precisely the given's controversial nature that allows it to be useful in analyzing philosophical arguments spanning India and Tibet, two distinct historical-cultural contexts. Why? Because in recognizing that there is hardly any agreement on what the given *is*, we also come to see that there is significantly greater agreement concerning what the given is supposed to *do.* Concerning what the given *is,* Wilfrid Sellars, a seminal critic of the idea, says that all of the following have at times been held to be the given: "sense contents, material objects, universals, propositions, real connections, first principles, even givenness itself."[4] When it is possible for such diverse entities to be construed as the given, then what makes one or another of these things the given must be some further property (or properties) that these things may be argued to have such that each of these things may serve as the given on one or another epistemology. In other words, the properties requisite to the given on this reading turn out to have something to do with its *function.*

We get a sense of Sellars' idea about the function of the given from his statement that "the point of the epistemological category of the given is, presumably, to explicate the idea that empirical knowledge rests on a 'foundation' of noninferential knowledge of matter of fact."[5] In other words, an entity plays the role of the given as long as that entity is understood to meet two conditions: a) that it provide a foundation for empirical knowledge and b) that it do so noninferentially. This twofold function is what is key for the given, while the details of what counts as the given, along with what counts as "providing a foundation for empirical knowledge noninferentially," may be left purposely unspecified. Whatever fulfills the function of the given *is* the given, and any philosophical system asserting some entity or experience that fulfills this function is a system that asserts the given. Although it is possible to construe things differently, in this paper I will adopt the above two criteria as providing the basic parameters for what counts as the given.

Seeing the given in this light, it is reasonable to consider its role even in the works of philosophers who antedate its explicit formulation by many centuries. Furthermore, it seems beneficial to do so, especially in the context of investigating the Svātantrika-Prāsaṅgika distinction, where one can quite easily and fruitfully construe some Tibetan understandings of the difference between the two "schools" as hinging upon the acceptance or rejection of what we can fairly describe as a variety of the given in the aforementioned sense. Discussing the Svātantrika-Prāsaṅgika distinction in these terms helps us to deepen our appreciation of some of the philosophical issues involved, and it provides a convenient term ("the given") with which to analyze those issues. As long as we refrain from prematurely ascribing any particular variety of the given to the authors we are studying, and commence instead by seeking to discover for ourselves what (if anything) functions as the given in their works, then the idea of the given can become a handy tool of inquiry, rather than a superfluous or even detrimental anachronism.[6]

In this paper, I use the idea of the given as a means to evaluate a claim, found in various dGe lugs pa sources, that Svātantrika-Mādhyamikas uphold a subtle ontological commitment on the conventional level which tarnishes their status as Mādhyamikas. According to this claim, Svātantrika-Mādhyamikas commit the error of allowing natures *(svabhāva, rang bzhin)* to stand conventionally. Because they negate natures on the ultimate level, Svātantrikas may still be considered Mādhyamikas; their erroneous postulation of conventional natures, however, must be recognized as a flaw in their Madhyamaka system.[7] In this paper, I attempt to evaluate this normative dGe lugs pa claim in relation to Śāntarakṣita and Kamalaśīla, two eighth-century Indian Mādhyamikas with strong ties to the Buddhist epistemological *(pramāṇavāda)* tradition, by means of an analysis of the role of the given in their thought. But before we turn to this specific program, we should pause to make some brief comments on the role of the given in the Buddhist epistemological tradition more generally.

The Given and the Buddhist Epistemological Tradition

Whether the Buddhist epistemological tradition should be seen as embracing a variety of the given is a contentious issue.[8] At first glance, Dharmakīrti's theory of perception certainly *seems* to resemble empiricist projects that explicitly advocate the given, where the given corresponds to the first item in Sellars' list: sense contents.[9] While those who accept sense contents as the given differ in numerous details, they do generally agree that there is something, often called a sense-datum, that is immediately (i.e., noninferentially) and nonconceptually presented, or *given,* to perceptual or sense consciousness. In the words of H. H. Price, one of the foremost sense-data theorists, consciousness of the sense-data that are given "is not reached by inference, nor by any other intellectual process (such as abstraction or intuitive induction), nor by any passage from sign to significate."[10] Whether and to what degree sense-data correspond to external objects, and in what manner they may be considered reliable, depend on a theorist's other epistemological and ontological presuppositions. But in one way or another, those who accept sense-data as the given also accept that it is our *immediate knowledge* of these data that provides the foundation for the remainder of empirical knowledge.

In a classical sense-data theory, such as that of C. I. Lewis, there are thus two elements in the knowing process: the immediate apprehension of that which is given to consciousness and the subsequent interpretation of that apprehension.[11] Of these, only the second element is propositional and can be true or false; the apprehension of the given, in contrast, is irrefragable and inherently certain, although not in a propositional sense.[12] Lewis maintains that without such a twofold structure of knowledge—without there being something that is simply *given* to experience—no beliefs could ever be justified.[13] This formulation in Lewis' thought exemplifies the frequent connection between the given and foundational theories of justification, where some beliefs are independently and intrinsically justified, while other beliefs derive their justification either entirely or in part in dependence upon those more basic beliefs.[14] When the given is understood as part of a foundationalist theory of justification, as it almost invariably is, the given provides the warrant for the basic beliefs that themselves ground further empirical knowledge. The given is thus that which prevents an infinite regress in the process of the justification of true beliefs.

The problem with this scenario for those like Sellars who reject the given is that as soon as we try to express what we know when we apprehend the given, we have no choice but to invoke propositional judgments (e.g., "I see a round red lump over there"), and these judgments are far from being nonconceptual or immediate.[15] In short, for some critics of the given, "[w]hatever validates or invalidates our judgments must be capable of standing in logical relations to them, and nothing lacking propositional content can enter into such relations."[16] At best, then, the given could be a theoretical entity postulated to *explain* empirical knowledge; but in that case, not being directly known but only theoretically postulated, its qualities as immediate and irrefragable are called strongly into question, as is its ability to provide a foundation for all further knowledge. It is this dilemma, in part, that prompts Sellars to conclude that the immediate and nonpropositional knowledge associated with theories of the given is no more than a seductive myth.[17]

Now, an initial reading of the Buddhist *pramāṇavāda* tradition indicates that the contents of perceptual awareness might very well qualify as a variety of the given. For one thing, Dharmakīrti and his followers, including Śāntarakṣita and Kamalaśīla, hold that perception *(pratyakṣa)* is a kind of nonerroneous *(abhrānta)* and nonconceptual *(nirvikalpa)* awareness *(jñāna)*, which, with the help of other factors, can and does lead to correct propositional judgments *(niścaya)*.[18] As a mental state, perception is also decidedly noninferential, thus aligning perceptual apprehension with that aspect of the given. Although it is true that Dharmakīrti maintains inference *(anumāna)* to be as reliable as perception in terms of its status as a means of trustworthy awareness *(pramāṇa),* inference *is* dependent upon perception to function.[19] The prioritization of perceptual awareness in the pursuit of knowledge in this way resembles the prioritization of the given by sense-data theorists, and seems to echo their foundationalist tendencies. Further, for the majority of the Buddhist *pramāṇavāda* philosophers, it is possible to conceive of the immediate object of perception as a sense-datum or "image in awareness" *(ākāra).*[20] In Dharmakīrti's system, which relies on a causal theory of perception, the sense-datum is the effect of a particular *(svalakṣaṇa),* whose very causal efficacy *(arthakriyā)* ensures that it is real. Perception thus has an aura of infallibility, which brings to mind some empiricists' claims that apprehension of the given is irrefragable or immune to doubt.

Other aspects of the Buddhist *pramāṇavāda* tradition's theory of perception, however, speak against interpreting that tradition as embracing the given. We have just seen how a number of modern critics assert that when we say that we *know* the given, we have already entered into the world of propositional knowledge that throws into doubt the very notion of the given. In the Buddhist epistemological tradition, we find (in seeming concert with many foundationalist theories of justification) that perception can be a warrant for propositional knowledge. Although perception itself is nonconceptual, it still serves as the primary, though not exclusive, cause for the conceptual judgments that arise from it. At the same time, perception *qua* means of trustworthy awareness, or *pramāṇa,* is said to occur *only when a corresponding correct judgment arises directly or indirectly as its result.* Now, only those perceptual judgments will arise for which the conditions exist in the mindstream wherein the perceptual awareness occurs. In this sense, we only see (or know) what we are already conditioned to see (or know). Thus, even though Buddhist epistemologists understand perception as nonerroneous, nonconceptual awareness—as a kind of direct and full-blown encounter with the real—there are good grounds for caution in referring to the contents of perception as the given, since perceptual awareness alone seems unable to ground or justify basic beliefs.[21]

Indeed, most of the problems that arise when one construes the image in perceptual awareness as the given in the Buddhist epistemological tradition are problems connected with that tradition's theory of justification, meaning their theory of how one attains certainty regarding propositional judgments.[22] These problems, while fascinating, are beyond the scope of this investigation. Although it is clear that a thorough-going examination of the given in the Buddhist *pramāṇavāda* tradition has to consider how propositional knowledge arises from nonconceptual awareness, our present inquiry is not primarily oriented toward such epistemological puzzles, but concerns rather a dispute over ontological commitments in the Madhyamaka context. Of prime import in this investigation is not the given as a means for the justification of true beliefs, but rather another quality associated with the given: its seemingly invariable connection to the *real*. Thus, when I speak of the image in perceptual awareness as the given, I intend to highlight the image's role in providing evidence for some degree of unassailable reality. That is, because the image in perceptual awareness arises through a causal process, the image can thereby be understood as *restricted* by its cause, in that it does not arise willy-nilly but rather only in the presence of its cause; it is this restriction that enables perception to function as an ultimate, and noninferential, check for knowledge, since the presence of the image depends on the presence of its cause. With this much accepted, the point of contention then centers upon the ontological commitments that such a model implies. Of course, ontological commitments may impact epistemological theory, and we shall find ourselves returning to the theme of foundations at the end of this essay. Yet our main concern shall be to answer the following normative question: does postulating the given on the model of the Buddhist epistemologists necessarily imply an ontological commitment on the part of a Mādhyamika that, from a Madhyamaka perspective, should be deemed in Tsong kha pa's terms "unsuitable"?

The dGe lugs pa Claim: Objection to the Given

In turning now to the dGe lugs pa claim that the system of the Svātantrika-Mādhyamikas is subtly flawed, I should begin by clarifying that the presentation in this paper of what I am calling "the dGe lugs pa claim" does not aspire to reflect the views of *all* the Tibetan and Mongolian thinkers who have worked under the aegis of the dGe lugs pa institutional banner. Secondary literature on Madhyamaka in Tibet has too often assumed an unwarranted univocality in the dGe lugs pa tradition, and I am anxious not to contribute to this infelicitous trend.[23] I emphasize, therefore, that my depiction of the dGe lugs pa claim in this section does not reflect an exhaustive study of the full range of sources on this topic. It is instead a distillation of my readings in selected indigenous Tibetan sources, which I note where appropriate, and the available secondary literature. My focus is on the views of mKhas grub dge legs dpal bzang, with reference as well to his teacher, Tsong kha pa blo bzang grags pa, and to the later doxographer, lCang skya rol pa'i rdo rje.[24]

My primary goal in this portrayal of the dGe lugs pa claim is to show that the claim itself can be understood as an objection to what amounts to the idea of the given in the form of sense contents. For the dGe lugs pa scholars under consideration, acceptance of the given is extremely problematic, although not for the same reasons as it is for contemporary philosophers like Sellars. That is, while Sellars and company reject the given on epistemological grounds, the dGe lugs pa objection is rooted in ontological concerns. In short, for these Buddhists, the notion that there is something—anything—that is immediately and nonerroneously given to consciousness implies the existence of something unassailably real; yet these thinkers also maintain that acceptance of an unassailably real entity is antithetical to the highest expression of Buddhist thought, Madhyamaka.[25] Thus, anyone who accepts what could be described as the given cannot be a Mādhyamika, or at least cannot be a Mādhyamika in the truest and best sense of the term, but must instead be some type of "realist" *(dngos por smra ba),* i.e., a philosopher who accepts unassailable reality in any form, whether objective or subjective.[26] The apparent acceptance of a version of the given in perceptual consciousness by such thinkers as Bhāvaviveka, Jñānagarbha, Śāntarakṣita, and Kamalaśīla thus relegates them, in the eyes of these dGe lugs pa critics, to dubious sorts of Mādhyamikas.

At this point, we should nuance our presentation of the dGe lugs pa claim in one crucial regard; once we have done so, it will be easier to understand how Tsong kha pa and his followers can continue to admit Bhāvaviveka and the other Svātantrikas into the Madhyamaka fold. The crucial point here revolves around the distinction of the two truths, for Tsong kha pa and others charge Svātantrikas with acceptance of the given not on the ultimate level, but only conventionally. The key ontological difference between Svātantrikas and Prāsaṅgikas on this view, then, is entirely a matter of how they understand conventional reality, and especially how they understand the nature of that which appears to conventional perceptual awareness. Tsong kha pa maintains that the Svātantrikas go wrong as Mādhyamikas when they allow the given to play a role in conventional awareness and in the conventional ascertainment of right and wrong. Prāsaṅgikas like Candrakīrti, in contrast, get it right when they insist that even the conventional is devoid of the given, that perceptual awareness (at least in the case of unenlightened beings) is not free from the imputations of beginningless ignorance, and that any attempt to ground conventional judgments in the given is futile and misguided. In other words, as the best kind of Mādhyamikas recognize, entities do not appear to the mind of an ordinary being "just as they are."[27] Rather, such appearances are already shaped by the primordial erroneous presuppositions (i.e., the ignorance) of that being's mind, and as such, they are unsuited to ground empirical or any other sort of knowledge.[28]

Another helpful approach to understanding the dGe lugs pa claim is through an examination of the so-called "object of refutation" *(dgag bya)*. The object of refutation is that which a Mādhyamika must refute or negate in order to successfully complete the process of rejecting the unassailably real. Tsong kha pa and many of his followers typically discuss the object of refutation in terms of six nearly equivalent expressions: they say that the object of refutation is that which is "truly established" *(bden par grub pa)*, "ultimately established" *(don dam par grub pa)*, "really established" *(yang dag par grub pa)*, "established from its own side" *(rang ngos nas grub pa)*, "established by its own character" *(rang gis mtshan nyid kyis grub pa)*, and "established by its own nature" *(rang bzhin gyis grub pa)*.[29] As Helmut Tauscher points out, these six ways of speaking about the object of refutation fall neatly into two groups of three. The first group, starting with "truly established," is concerned with the ontological status of entities; the second group, starting with "established from its own side," has to do with the status of entities as they are subjectively cognized.[30] Many dGe lugs pas, including Tsong kha pa, understand the two groups of expressions to represent a "gross" *(rags pa)* and a "subtle" *(phra mo)* object of refutation, respectively.[31] Significantly, Svātantrikas are said to commit the error of allowing the *subtle* object of refutation to stand on the conventional level. That is, conventionally they make the mistake of accepting that perceptual objects possess real natures *(svabhāva)* which have a mode of existence *(sdod lugs)* independent of the mind's constructive and interpretive functions. Once again, the Svātantrikas' downfall as Mādhyamikas hinges on their acceptance of a form of the given.

Evidence for the dGe lugs pa Claim: mKhas grub's View

What evidence do the dGe lugs pa authors under consideration adduce in support of their claim that Svātantrikas accept real natures conventionally? Simply put, they hold the clincher to be that Svātantrikas, unlike Prāsaṅgikas, employ a form of argument known as an independent, or autonomous, inference *(rang rgyud kyi rjes su dpag pa, svatantrānumāna)*. An autonomous inference for these dGe lugs pa authors is one in which the elements of the inference, including the subject *(chos can, dharmin)*, the evidence *(gtags, hetu)*, and the examples *(dpe, dṛṣṭānta)*, are all "established as appearing similarly" *(mthun snang du grub pa)* for both the proponent and the opponent in the debate.[32] According to this claim, autonomous inferences are unsuitable for a Mādhyamika when arguing against a realist opponent, since using them would require that the Mādhyamika assent to the realist's understanding of the manner in which the subject and so on are established to appear. For most non-Mādhyamika Indian philosophers, entities like subjects, evidence, and examples are held to be established by virtue of their natures *(bhāva, svabhāva)*, which are, in some sense of the term, unassailably real; but for Mādhyamikas, there are no such unassailably real natures that can serve to establish these subjects and so on. A Mādhyamika and a realist therefore can *never* agree on the question of how subjects and so on are established to appear. For this reason, these dGe lugs pa authors argue that a good Mādhyamika will use only 1) reductio-style reasonings *(thal 'gyur, prasaṅga)* or 2) inferences based on reasons that are acknowledged by the opponent alone *(gzhan grags kyi rjes su dpag pa, *paraprasiddhānumāna)*. We shall refer to this second form of reasoning as "opponent-acknowledged inference."

Starting with Bhāvaviveka, however, Svātantrikas notoriously *do* (or at least *seem* to) employ autonomous inferences; accordingly, they must also accept that there is something that is unassailably real, at least conventionally, even if they refuse to admit doing so.[33] On this reading, that which the Svātantrikas accept to be unassailably real conventionally is a particular *(rang mtshan, svalakṣaṇa)*, awareness of which is immediately and non-erroneously given to consciousness in the act of perception *(mngon sum, pratyakṣa)*. All of this adds up to a less-than-perfect Madhyamaka position on the dGe lugs pa view. In the *sTong thun chen mo*, mKhas grub clarifies the line of reasoning that links autonomous reasoning with acceptance of a real particular and the given (without, of course, using the contemporary terminology of the given). In the pages that follow, I will quote from this text at length, considering a key passage that intends to illustrate the fundamental differences between Prāsaṅgikas and Svātantrikas by focusing on autonomous reasoning. For simplicity, I leave untranslated the technical term *tshad ma* (Sanskrit: *pramāṇa*), which has the general signification of a "(means of) valid cognition."[34] The passage in question commences as follows:

> Regarding the presentation of autonomous propositions and evidence, it is not sufficient that the subject of inquiry *(shes 'dod chos can),* which is the locus wherein some particular property *(chos)* is posited, simply be established by a *tshad ma* for the proponent as well as for the opponent. Rather, it is definitely necessary that [that subject of enquiry] be established as appearing similarly in the philosophical systems *(lugs)* of both the proponent and the opponent. And it is necessary that the three characteristics of the evidence that confirms the proposition be established by a *tshad ma* such that they also are established as appearing similarly in the systems of both the proponent and the opponent. Furthermore, for the subject to be established as appearing similarly in the systems of both the disputants, it is necessary that the method for establishing the subject through a *tshad ma* [also] be established to appear similarly in the systems of both disputants. [35]

Here we see mKhas grub laying down the basic conditions that must be in place to correctly employ an autonomous inference on his view. The most notable feature of these conditions is the requirement that the subject, evidence, and examples all be "established as appearing similarly" *(mthun snang du grub pa)* for both parties in the debate. This stipulation recalls the general principle of Indian Buddhist debate logic that the three characteristics of the evidence *(trirūpahetu)*[36] in an inference-for-others *(parārthānumāna)* must be acknowledged by both parties to the debate.[37] But on mKhas grub's reading there is also the *added* requirement that the subject and other elements in the inference must be "established as appearing similarly."[38] What is noteworthy is the insistence that even the *means* (i.e., the *tshad ma*) by which the elements of the inference come to be established for the parties in the debate must be established as appearing similarly. In other words, for mKhas grub it is central to the definition of an autonomous inference that the two parties *understand exactly the same thing in exactly the same way* when they assert that the subject and the evidence and so on are established by a *tshad ma.*

Immediately following this presentation of autonomous inference, mKhas grub unambiguously asserts a key point about realists, namely that for realists, perception, which is an immediate and nonerroneous means of valid cognition, or *tshad ma,* necessarily has real particulars as its object. He says:

> In the philosophical system of the realists *(dngos smra ba),* perceptible *(mngon gyur pa)* subjects, such as form, are necessarily established through the *tshad ma* perception; and it is held that the *tshad ma* perception necessarily is a *tshad ma* that directly reliably knows its own reliably-known object *(rang gi gzhal bya),* a particular *(rang mtshan).*[39]

Remember that "realists" here refers to those who accept any kind of unassailably real entity. For mKhas grub, it is obvious that such persons also accept that there is a trustworthy means (a *tshad ma*) of knowing that real entity, and they accept that that trustworthy means is perception. That which perception knows is a particular (this could be an entity external to the mind or it could be a sense-datum, depending on the type of realist); the particular itself is unassailably real.

Apart from the references to realists and *tshad ma,* the above statement by mKhas grub could very nearly represent a contemporary depiction of the given—especially a depiction in which sense perception is held nonerroneously and immediately to know real particulars like sense-data. In this empiricist-style description, it is our immediate, infallible, nonconceptual, perceptual knowledge ("acquaintance" in Russell's terms) that is held to be the basis of the remainder of empirical knowledge.[40] Strikingly, mKhas grub's passage continues in a vein that reflects this same idea, asserting that for realists, even inferential knowledge is ultimately grounded in perception:

> When one apprehends something remote *(lkog gyur),* such as the ocular faculty,[41] as the subject [of the inference], the *tshad ma* that directly knows that subject is an inference; nevertheless, [that knowledge] must indirectly come down to *(thug)* a perception. Regardless of whether or not one applies the term 'particular' to the object for which that inference is a *tshad ma,* all realists are the same in asserting that that reliably known object is established in its objective mode of being *(yul gyi sdod lugs)* which is not posited just nominally. Therefore, in a realist system, it is asserted that a *tshad ma* that reliably knows a subject [of an inference] is necessarily a *tshad ma* for a subject that is established by its own character *(rang gi mtshan nyid kyis grub pa).* And in the system of a realist, it is accepted that a *tshad ma* is necessarily a nonerroneous awareness with regard to the reliably known object for which it is a *tshad ma.* Therefore, they accept that when the subject of the evidence is

established by a *tshad ma,* that subject is necessarily an object which has been found by a *tshad ma* that is nonerroneous with regard to its own object.[42]

Here mKhas grub introduces the all-important qualification "being established by its own character" *(rang gi mtshan nyid kyis grub pa),* which, as we have seen, is one of the properties that an entity must have if it is to be unassailably real. This amounts as well to an entity being established in its own "mode of being" *(sdod lugs),* which means that the entity exists in some fashion that is more than just nominal. When entities are established in this way, as mKhas grub maintains that they are for realists, perception may then be deemed nonerroneous, since the real and fixed nature of entities will reliably govern which images will arise in awareness as the results of those entities. The combination of a causal model of perception with the notion that entities are established to have an independent mode of being thus leads to a position in which the objects of sense perception are *given* to consciousness in the form of sense contents.

Argument and Debate in the Absence of the Given: mKhas grub's View

For a true Mādhyamika, however, *nothing is or ever can be given to consciousness.*[43] This is because there is no unassailably real mode of being that can permit the qualification "being established by its own character" to apply to an entity. For mKhas grub, an important consequence of this fact is that an entity that is established by its own character can *never* be known by any kind of trustworthy awareness or valid cognition *(tshad ma)* simply because *such an entity does not exist.* The nonexistence of the given therefore has profound implications for the manner in which a Mādhyamika can debate against a realist. mKhas grub explains:

Thus, because in the system of the Prāsaṅgikas it is not possible that even conventionally [something can be] established by its own character, there cannot be even a conventional *tshad ma* that reliably knows an object that is established by its own character. Therefore, it is not possible that a method for establishing a subject by a *tshad ma* be established to appear similarly either [just] for the realists or for both systems. This is why [Prāsaṅgikas] induce a definitive awareness which realizes the lack of any unassailable reality *(bden med)* in the mind streams of opponents by means only of

> opponent-acknowledged inferences and reductio-style arguments [but not through autonomous inferences].[44]

The lack of a *tshad ma* that knows an entity that is established by its own character prevents the Mādhyamika from accepting a subject that is established to appear similarly for both parties in the debate. Although the subject may be established conventionally by a *tshad ma* for the Mādhyamika, it is not established in a manner *at all* similar to the manner in which it is established for the realist opponent.[45] Accordingly, then, autonomous inferences cannot be used by a Mādhyamika in a debate with a realist.

On Tsong kha pa and mKhas grub's views, the forms of argument left to the Mādhyamika who wishes to convince a realist opponent that entities lack any unassailable reality or nature are opponent-acknowledged inferences and reductio-style demonstrations. Of these two forms of argument, the reductio-style (Sanskrit: *prāsaṅgika*) demonstration begins not with something commonly established for both parties but rather with something established for the opponent alone.[46] Then, relying on the connections among entities acknowledged by the opponent, the proponent draws out or deduces a consequence undesired for the opponent.[47] This type of argument seems well suited to Madhyamaka thought, and Nāgārjuna is of course famous for his use of *prasaṅgas*.[48] But in Tsong kha pa's and mKhas grub's view, the best kind of Mādhyamika is not restricted to *prasaṅgas*, for even a Prāsaṅgika can legitimately use an opponent-acknowledged inference, a type of reasoning that resembles autonomous inference, except that the three characteristics of the evidence are presented in accordance with the opponent's view alone. In this Tibetan exegesis, which Tom Tillemans judges "very credible,"[49] Candrakīrti, as a representative of the Prāsaṅgikas, can still legitimately use the inferential apparatus of the Indian epistemological traditions, as long as he removes the stipulation that the evidence, examples, and so on be acknowledged as established by both parties in the debate.

mKhas grub next goes on to summarize the dGe lugs pa claim concerning the Svātantrika appeal to the given, condensing the salient points of the arguments examined thus far:

> If we express this briefly and in a manner that is easy to understand [sic!], it is as follows: the meaning of autonomous evidence *(rang rgyud kyi rtags)* is that one presents a logical reason which proves the property to be proved *(bsgrub bya'i chos)* which the proponent wishes to [cause the opponent to] infer. [One presents this reason]

in relation to a subject which is established as appearing similarly in the systems of both the proponent and the opponent, [that subject] being an object that is found by a *tshad ma* that is nonerroneous with regard to its object, which [itself] is established by its own character. As for an opponent-acknowledged inference, [it occurs when], although the method for establishing the subject by a *tshad ma* is not established to appear similarly for both the proponent and the opponent, that subject is established in general *(spyir)* by a *tshad ma* in the system of the proponent and by a *tshad ma* in the system of the opponent; [under these circumstances, an opponent-acknowledged inference occurs when] a logical reason is presented in accordance with *('khris nas)* the subject, the presence of the evidence in the subject *(phyogs chos),* and so on that are accepted as established by a *tshad ma* in the system of the opponent.[50]

This passage states the most significant *formal* aspects of the dGe lugs pa claim. That is, while opponent-acknowledged inference may resemble autonomous inference in its external structure, its distinguishing characteristic is that it dispenses with what Tillemans has called the "*metalogical* requirement" that the subject and the triply characterized evidence be acknowledged by both parties in the debate (i.e., that they be *ubhayaprasiddha*).[51] But the dGe lugs pa claim goes beyond that, for as Tillemans elsewhere remarks, on Tsong kha pa and mKhas grub's views, opponent-acknowledged evidence "is *not* explained in the usual Candrakīrtian way as one where the terms are *only* acknowledged by the opponent—the Buddhist himself can accept the terms—but rather where the terms are grasped in different manners due to differing positions on whether or not *pramāṇa*s are mistaken with regard to *svalakṣaṇa.*"[52] In other words, opponent-acknowledged inference differs crucially from autonomous inference in that, unlike the latter, it does not require that the subject, evidence, and so on be established *in the same manner* for both parties to the debate. This mechanism allows a Mādhyamika proponent to advance autonomous-*style* inferences against a realist opponent while avoiding the problem that occurs when advancing a truly autonomous inference, whereby the Mādhyamika proponent would be *forced* into accepting the given—and the unassailable reality that the given entails.

Śāntarakṣita, Kamalaśīla, and the Given

We turn now to our central question: does the dGe lugs pa claim concerning the Svātantrika acceptance of the given and the corresponding taint of realism apply in the case of Śāntarakṣita and Kamalaśīla? To address this question, we must break it into several subsidiary inquiries. In the first place, we need to determine more clearly whether and how it is correct to speak of Śāntarakṣita and Kamalaśīla as accepting some form of the given. I shall argue in what follows that it *is* correct to see them as accepting a given on the definition adopted in this paper, insofar as they, like Dharmakīrti, understand perception to provide a noninferential foundation for (or check on) empirical knowledge. Next, we must see whether mKhas grub's characterization of autonomous inference corresponds to autonomous inference as it is conceived by Śāntarakṣita and Kamalaśīla. I argue that it *does not,* as the Indian authors differ from mKhas grub in their understanding of what it means for the subject of a debate to appear similarly. Finally, we shall consider whether Śāntarakṣita and Kamalaśīla's acceptance of the given—and the use to which they put it—implies an ontological commitment antithetical to the Madhyamaka perspective. This is the crux of the matter and by far the most difficult problem to resolve. My argument is that Śāntarakṣita and Kamalaśīla probably should *not* be seen as upholding a subtle ontological commitment on the conventional level, since they reject the given at the highest levels of conventional philosophical analysis. The idea of distinct levels of analysis is key here, so we begin with some observations concerning this philosophical method.

The Sliding Scale of Analysis

The method of the sliding scale of analysis is vital to Śāntarakṣita and Kamalaśīla's philosophical program. This tool, similar to that of other (especially Buddhist) Indian epistemologists, permits these authors to move among apparently contradictory ontological and epistemological schemes, even within the purview of a single philosophical treatise. Dreyfus has described this method in the case of Dharmakīrti as a "strategy of ascending scales of analysis,"[53] saying that insufficient attention to this strategy has often resulted in an oversimplification of Dharmakīrti's thought on the part of both modern and traditional interpreters.[54] The same can be said for Śāntarakṣita and Kamalaśīla. The texts that form the focus of this investigation—Śāntarakṣita's *Madhyamakālaṃkāra* (MA), *Madhyamakālaṃkāravṛtti* (MAV), and *Tattvasaṃgraha* (TS) and Kamalaśīla's commentaries on these works, the *Madhyamakālaṃkārapañjikā* (MAP) and *Tattvasaṃgrahapañjikā* (TSP)—all exhibit the method of sliding scale of analysis.[55] In these works, we can discern three distinct levels of philosophical analysis, each with ostensibly conflicting ontologies and epistemologies. How can we account for this? Kajiyama, I think, was right when he assessed the significance of the method to be "that lower doctrines were not simply rejected, but admitted as steps leading to understanding of the highest one."[56] Each level of analysis is both a refinement and a corrective of the preceding level, which is itself judged accurate only to a certain degree.

Let us describe the method and then move on to see how it affects our understanding. First, there are certain fundamental theorems or principles that pertain throughout all the levels of analysis.[57] Among the most important of these is a theorem concerning the necessary conditions of a real thing *(vastu):* a real thing must be capable of causal functioning (i.e., it must be both an effect and a cause).[58] A corollary is that being capable of causal functioning entails being capable of producing an image in perceptual awareness. From these premises, it is accepted that whatever is real can be perceived, since whatever is real can cause an image of itself to arise in awareness.[59] At the first level of analysis, the Sautrāntika level, the principles of the causal efficacy of the real and the causal theory of perception contribute to an acceptance of the given that is in many ways quite similar to that of the classical sense-data theories as sketched above.[60] Likewise, the theory of justification developed on this level of analysis shares a foundationalist flavor with empiricist theories accepting the given, since immediate and nonerroneous awareness *(jñāna)* of a real particular *(svalakṣaṇa)* provides the ultimate check on what does and does not count as valid empirical knowledge. On this level of analysis, which is used extensively in the TS and the TSP, as well as in the opening section of the MA and its commentaries, the given can be fairly said to possess an invariable connection to the real.[61]

The second level of analysis is that of the Yogācāra or Vijñānavāda, a nondualist perspective that rejects objects of knowledge external to the mind. The given, which is the core of the Sautrāntika epistemology, here undergoes a degree of deterioration in terms of the strength of its connection to the real. That is, on the first level of analysis, the given provided a foundation for empirical knowledge because it gave immediate knowledge of real, causally functioning external particulars. Now, however, the authors apply new lines of analysis to show that the Sautrāntika model of perception is irredeemably flawed, since one can demonstrate conclusively that objects of knowledge external to the mind are not possible. The arguments are complex, and proceed along two main lines, which I will attempt to sketch briefly.

The first line of argument seeks to demonstrate the impossibility of external objects of knowledge. It starts with the theorem that a real entity must be singular,[62] and then asks whether the external particular that is supposedly known in perception (via the given) may be singular. Now the given often occurs as an appearance of gross and extended entities, but the singularity of such entities is logically ruled out, as they obviously have parts (as is understood from the fact that it is possible for such an entity to be partially hidden).[63] Only infinitesimal, partless particles *(paramāṇu),* it seems, have a chance at being the real entities known in perception. If these are really partless, however, they can never aggregate, as aggregation requires that the aggregating entities have parts, even if those are understood just as front and back, top and bottom, and so forth.[64] The images of gross entities that appear in perceptual awarenesses thus cannot be accounted for by the aggregation of partless particles. This leads to the conclusion that an external cause for the image in awareness cannot exist.[65]

The second line of reasoning seeks to establish the nonduality of awareness, through an analysis of whether it is possible for that which is known in perception to be different in nature from the awareness in which it appears.[66] After a great variety of twists and turns, this investigation concludes that what is known in perception cannot be radically different (i.e., external and material) from the awareness that knows it, in essence because there could be no point of contact between the two.[67] What is known in awareness can be only awareness itself, which is always singular and nondual, despite its appearance in terms of a subjective aspect *(grāhakākāra)* and an objective aspect *(grāhyākāra).* It is the latter element, the objective aspect of awareness, that is the given at this level of analysis. The given still possesses an invariable connection to the real—now understood to be nothing other than mind—but this connection is less direct. The dualist Sautrāntika system is thus shown to be *less rational* than the nondualist Yogācāra system that denies objects external to the mind, even though the Sautrāntika system is still "workable" when one sets aside considerations of the reality of external objects.[68] Other elements of the earlier system, notably the basic contours of the theories of inference and justification, and a variety of basic theorems, carry over to this level of analysis more or less unchanged.[69]

The third, and final, level of analysis is that of the Madhyamaka. Here,

Śāntarakṣita and Kamalaśīla analyze the given even more vigorously than before and from a different angle. Their aim this time is to show that neither objects *nor* the mind is actually real. Although, once again, the arguments are too complex to present fully, the basic strategy involves an investigation into two distinct strands of the Yogācāra tradition, one in which the images in awareness are real *(satyākāravāda)* and one in which the images in awareness are unreal *(alīkākāravāda)*.[70] Relying again on the idea that the real is necessarily singular, Śāntarakṣita and Kamalaśīla conclude that neither Yogācāra position withstands analysis, and they arrive at a position in which *neither* the image in awareness, *nor* the mind that knows the image, can be upheld as real.[71] The conclusion is that, on the Madhyamaka level of analysis, there is nothing that is unassailably real.[72] There is no knower, nothing known, and therefore *a fortiori* also nothing that is given. If there remain any images in awareness, these have now utterly lost their invariable connection with the real.

The gusto with which Śāntarakṣita and Kamalaśīla reject unassailable reality at this level of analysis is so intense that even their critics are constrained to admit their status as Mādhyamikas. It remains to be seen, uhowever, whether their philosophical method of adopting provisional allegiances to a variety of "givens" on the sliding scale of analysis is incompatible with their Madhyamaka view, and therefore also inappropriate to them as Mādhyamikas. One way to get at this question is through an analysis of the ways in which perception is, and is not, nonerroneous.

Nonerroneous Perception on the Sliding Scale of Analysis

Recall that perception *(pratyakṣa, mngon gyur)* is the trustworthy awareness *(pramāṇa, tshad ma)* which, on the lower levels of analysis, is held to immediately apprehend the given in such as way as to provide a check on what counts as valid knowledge conventionally. It is characterized as nonerroneous *(abhrānta)* and nonconceptual *(nirvikalpa)* awareness *(jñāna)* of the given, its perceptual object, the image in awareness *(ākāra)*. Here, we are concerned mostly with the "nonerroneous" component of this characterization, since it is this aspect of perception that implies that the given has an invariable connection to the real. For the dGe lugs pa authors we have considered, it is clear that Svātantrikas accept that which they *should* reject—namely, conventionally unassailably real entities that are in some fashion given to perceptual awareness—for the simple reason that they accept that there is something known nonerroneously in perception. And, although they concede that Svātantrikas do not explicitly admit their acceptance of the conventionally unassailably real, these dGe lugs pa critics nonetheless do assert that Svātantrikas can be shown to accept it de facto on the basis of their commitment to nonerroneous perception.[73]

But do Śāntarakṣita and Kamalaśīla understand perception to be nonerroneous in the manner claimed by these dGe lugs pa authors on any or all of the levels of analysis? We can start by agreeing, as shown above, that these Indian authors accept the given on each of the first two levels of analysis, where, in both cases, the given may be described as an immediately apprehended, causally produced image in awareness. On the Sautrāntika level, the given is produced by a real, external particular; on this view, the images in awareness have "similarity" *(sārūpya)* with the external particulars that are their causes, which similarity accounts for the nonerroneous nature of perception. When similarity is absent (as, for example, when the sense faculties are injured), the image in awareness is no longer trustworthy in regard to external entities; the image therefore no longer counts as the given in relation to the appearing objects, just as the awareness itself does not count as perception. On the Yogācāra level of analysis, the cause of the given is no longer external to the mind, but is postulated to be caused by the ripening of internal imprints *(vāsanā)* existing beginninglessly in the mind due to a beginningless series of previous experiences.[74] As before, the given is immediately and nonconceptually known in perception. But now the "similarity" of the image to its cause is diminished, and perception *is* now recognized as mistaken *(bhrānta)* with respect to at least one aspect of the given: its dualistic appearance as external, material, extended in space, and so on.[75] Śāntarakṣita and Kamalaśīla seem unbothered by this diminished similarity, probably because they are content now to rely on a different understanding of what it means to be nonerroneous, where the emphasis is on the perceptual image being correspondent *(saṃvāda)* or trustworthy *(avisaṃvāda)* at the same time as being nonconceptual.[76] The given still possesses a connection to the real, but it is no longer nonerroneous in such a thorough-going fashion.

For an image to be correspondent or trustworthy in this context means that the appearance accords sufficiently well with other images in one's awareness that one can confidently rely upon it to achieve one's goals.[77] Although the images in perceptual awareness no longer possess *sārūpya* with their causes, they *are* still causally produced, and as such they are still formed and restricted by their causes.[78] Even though an image of a patch of blue does not arise from a group of causally functioning external blue particulars, it does arise from a causally functioning internal particular, namely an imprint for the arisal of an image of a patch of blue. The arisal of images in perception is thus not an arbitrary affair (and to that degree it is *real*); rather, it is rooted in karmic imprints and ignorance.[79] This regularity of the causal process of perception is at least in part what accounts for mKhas grub's assertion that the blue appearing in awareness is, for the Yogācāra system, "established by its own characteristic," even though it does not exist in the manner in which it appears.[80]

When we move to the Madhyamaka level of analysis, things get considerably more complex. The problem at this level of analysis, as we have said, is that there is nothing left of the model of perception that has operated up to this point, since both objects of knowledge and the mind have been shown through analysis to be unreal. However, this much analysis alone does not get rid of appearances or images in awareness, i.e., that which up to now has served as the given. In his *Tattvāloka,* a Madhyamaka text, Kamalaśīla remarks:

> Perception is not at all established to have a truly real object, since the form and so on that are seen are false, like [that which is seen by] one who has an eye disease.[81]

Perception no longer is nonerroneous or even trustworthy in any manner. Yet sense contents still appear. What does this mean? Madhyamaka, after all, is the highest level of analysis, which purports to tell us about the way things really are, characteristics that imply that Madhyamaka is ultimate. At the same time, Madhyamaka remains a human construct, a linguistic endeavor, a transaction aimed at communication—in short, Madhyamaka as a philosophical system remains conventional. One may arrive at the Madhyamaka level of analysis through reasoning, but without cultivation of one's understanding through meditation one will still lack *nonconceptual* realization, one will remain in the realm of the conventional, and one will not have eliminated the ignorance that causes images to appear. One will know (analytically) that whatever appears as "given" is in fact erroneous, and one will realize (conceptually) that there is, and can be, *no* given, but one will not be free of appearances, because one will still be influenced by primordial ignorance.

Appearances thus have different values on the different levels of analysis. On the Sautrāntika level, appearances testify to real, external particulars. On the Yogācāra level, they testify to the reality of the mind. On the Madhyamaka level, they testify to nothing other than the continued presence of ignorance in the mind. Appearances serve as the given on the first two levels of analysis, but they do not on the third, where there is no given. Appearances, for Mādhyamikas, are *mere appearances.* They are like dreams in which certain things appear to be true. So how can they play a role in logic and debate? To address this question, let us turn now to the consideration of the role of appearances and the given in that *bête noire* of the Prāsaṅgikas, autonomous inference.

Autonomous Inference on the Sliding Scale of Analysis

We have seen that for mKhas grub and other dGe lugs pas, a Mādhyamika who uses autonomous inferences in a debate with a realist is understood to tacitly accept some form of realism, if only conventionally, since autonomous inferences can occur only when the elements of the inference are established in the same manner for both parties to the debate. This means that in a debate with a realist, one can use an autonomous inference only if one accepts that the subject, evidence, and so on exist in the same manner that the realist understands them to be established. My contention is that Śāntarakṣita and Kamalaśīla have a different understanding of autonomous inference, one that dispenses with the metalogical requirement that all elements in the inference be established as appearing similarly *(mthun snang du grub pa)* as mKhas grub understands this requirement. While it is true that they accept that the elements of the debate must be established similarly for both parties, there is no evidence that they hold that the elements must be established *in precisely the same fashion,* as mKhas grub requires.[82]

A fairly simple argument for this assertion could be made by pointing to the many arguments in the TS and the TSP that rely upon proof statements in the form of autonomous inferences offered on the Sautrāntika level of analysis. Granted, such arguments are clearly thought to operate on a model in which the given plays an important role, since, due to its invariable connection to the real, it provides a check on what can and cannot be asserted in the argument. But at the same time these arguments always proceed, sometimes explicitly, by *ignoring* or *suppressing* certain tenets that the authors elsewhere uphold as "true" on the Yogācāra level of analysis. The result is that such arguments end up relying on subjects, reasons, and examples that the authors actually accept only provisionally, even though the inferences themselves have the usual formal properties of an autonomous inference.[83] In such cases, the reasoning in question begins to look less like the autonomous inference criticized by mKhas grub, and more like the opponent-acknowledged inference *(gzhan grags kyi rjes dpag pa)* he judges more suitable for Mādhyamikas.

An example is an argument, directed at Uddyotakara among others, against the notion that a gross object *(sthūla)* is known in perception. Here, the opponent maintains that if gross objects did not exist, there could be no perception of trees and so on, since the infinitesimal particles that make up these entities are not themselves perceptible.[84] Śāntarakṣita responds that in fact the particles *are* perceptible, but only when they act together in such a way as to mutually support one another in becoming perceptible (that is, when they come together so as to produce an image in awareness).[85] He emphasizes that one determines only those aspects of the partless particle for which the causes for determination exist;[86] and Kamalaśīla notes that one does not have a determination of all aspects of those particulars, because one is not trained to see those aspects, or because one's mind is not sufficiently sharp, and so on.[87] Yet setting all such detail aside, it is clear that this is an argument by which Śāntarakṣita and Kamalaśīla hope to establish that what is known in perception is partless, momentary, external particulars, and that there can be therefore no such thing as a gross object.

But we know that on the Yogācāra level of analysis Śāntarakṣita and Kamalaśīla *reject* such external particulars! Should this fact not invalidate their autonomous inferences in such arguments? To address such qualms, Kamalaśīla quite explicitly tells us that the argument concerning perception was made only having provisionally accepted *(abhyupagamya)* the existence of external objects, even though from the Vijñānavāda perspective such objects are not established. He then goes even further, saying that the blue and so on seen in perception have the nature of appearances that are just *erroneous awarenesses,* since they are devoid of having either a singular or a plural nature.[88] Thus, we have a very clear example of Śāntarakṣita and Kamalaśīla using what looks to be an autonomous inference (i.e., "Those infinitesimal particles which arise as mutually supportive are not beyond the senses, because they are the objects of the senses"), but where they do not accept the subject (infinitesimal particles), the quality to be proved (that they are perceptible), or the reason (because they are the objects of the sense faculties) *even conventionally* at another, higher level of analysis.

Autonomous Inference and the Commonly Appearing Subject

What, then, is to prevent us from concluding that *all* apparently autonomous inferences advanced by these thinkers are in fact understood as provisional when regarded from the higher Madhyamaka level of analysis? Why cannot *all* their inferences actually be opponent-acknowledged, autonomous in name alone? Well, for one thing, there is Śāntarakṣita's famous statement, "I do not refute the entity which appears,"[89] which he makes to rebuff the charge, leveled against the Madhyamaka, of the technical fault in debate logic of "subject failure" or the "unestablished basis" *(āśrayāsiddha)*.[90] Kamalaśīla's commentary on Śāntarakṣita's statement reinforces the impression of a philosophical system in which the given (here, the "entity which appears") is established by means of its own character conventionally:

> Someone may think: The fault of [the reason having] an unestablished basis (i.e., *āśrayāsiddha*) does not pertain to that reason which is applied in relation to a subject *(chos can = dharmin)* that appears in order to refute a superimposed aspect [of that subject]. But you refute the subject that is appearing! Therefore, why would the fault of *āśrayāsiddha* and so forth not pertain to you? To this [objection, Śāntarakṣita replies]: "I do not [refute the entity that appears]" and so on. We have established the refutation of the superimposition of an ultimate nature on this appearing subject, but we do not refute the nature *(rang gi ngo bo = svarūpa, svabhāva)* of the subject; therefore, it is the same [as the first scenario suggested by the opponent].[91]

Tillemans has pointed to the final sentence of this passage as being "one of the strongest quotations one can find for arguing that Indian Svātantrikas—and not just Tibetans—accepted that objects had to conventionally have properties by their own-nature for logic to function."[92] I agree that this passage confirms Śāntarakṣita and Kamalaśīla's commitment to natures on the conventional level (but this is no "news flash," since they often use the idea of *svabhāva* in inferential reasoning), but I am less sure that this acceptance indicates an *ontological* commitment, as mKhas grub insists, so long as the natures are accepted only provisionally.

That is, mKhas grub's argument depends, in part, on the idea that the subject in an autonomous inference must be established as appearing commonly for both parties in the debate. And here, as in the commentaries, we find Śāntarakṣita and Kamalaśīla insisting that their Madhyamaka arguments are not open to the charge of subject failure precisely because the subjects of the arguments appear in the awarenesses of both parties to the debate. But there is an important distinction between the two formulations of what it means to appear commonly, for mKhas grub rje specifically requires that the subject be established as appearing commonly according to the *philosophical systems (lugs)* of both the proponent and the opponent,[93] while Śāntarakṣita emphasizes that inferences should be formulated "having *precluded* the various subjects that are produced through mutually incompatible philosophical systems."[94] The idea is that the subject of an inference should not be derived from the application of philosophical theories, but should rather be such things as appear to and are "acknowledged by scholars and woman on down to children."[95] Entities that have been qualified in ways that arise through philosophical theorizing—and this would, on reflection, include any form of the given—are purposefully and emphatically excluded from being the subject of a debate.

This move on the part of Śāntarakṣita and Kamalaśīla is reminiscent of Bhāvaviveka's appeal in the *Prajñāpradīpa* (PrP) to a "general" *(sāmānya)* subject, such as sound, which is devoid of philosophical qualifications, such as "being a quality of space" *(ākāśaguṇa)* and so on.[96] This was a position for which Bhāvaviveka argued in an attempt to find a subject for the debate upon which he, as a Mādhyamika, could agree with a realist like a Sāṃkhya. Candrakīrti was critical of the idea, as he thought it left Bhāvaviveka with an impossible subject that was neither conventional nor ultimate. It is not clear whether Candrakīrti's critique would apply to Śāntarakṣita. In any case, whether he knew of Candrakīrti's critique or not, Śāntarakṣita is evidently aware that his position might be considered damaging to his Madhyamaka perspective.[97] Śāntarakṣita therefore defends his approach by reference to what he calls the application of "non-imaginatively determined conventions":

> Therefore, due to not refuting the appearing entity, because one applies non-imaginatively determined *(mngon par zhen pa med pa)* conventions of the property to be proved *(sādhyadharma)* and the evidence *(sādhana),* there is absolutely no harm to the philosophical position that all *dharmas* are without a nature.[98]

Kamalaśīla clarifies that applying "non-imaginatively determined conventions" means constructing an inference "without relying on a subject and so forth from the perspective of one's own philosophical system."[99] One interesting way to read this statement is to consider that the implication is that while one may not construct an inference from the perspective of one's own philosophical system, one *may* do so from the perspective of *another's* philosophical system. On this reading, Śāntarakṣita and Kamalaśīla appear to come rather close to mKhas grub's idea that opponent-acknowledged inferences alone are appropriate for Mādhyamikas.

For Candrakīrti, there can be no given because all ordinary awareness is mistaken, since its object is unreal. Thus, there can be no autonomous inference. Śāntarakṣita and Kamalaśīla likewise believe that all ordinary awareness is mistaken, but they still accept autonomous inference (on the basis of appearances) because they recognize that, even as Mādhyamikas, they are still ensconced in conventional reality. That is, even the Madhyamaka analysis of the ultimate nature of things is *still just conventional.* Even Mādhyamikas experience dualistic images, and thus Mādhyamikas, too, can find conventional agreement concerning appearances with others whose minds are afflicted by a similar form of ignorance. The common appearances that they use as the subjects of the debate are understood, even *known,* not to be unfailing indicators of reality. But they are still the locus of conventional consensus, and for that reason they are also the natural starting point for investigation and debate. One starts, of necessity, with what appears, and one proceeds to scrutinize those appearances to see if they contain or imply any unassailable reality. Through this method, one arrives at a series of increasingly accurate appraisals of what appears, ending up eventually at a Madhyamaka perspective, since no appearance can withstand thorough-going analysis and scrutiny. Having made the important ascertainment that appearances contain no reality, the philosopher can still go on to discuss and debate appearances, in the same way in which non-philosophers quite easily agree concerning all kinds of aspects *their* appearances. Indeed, when seeking to convince an opponent of the lack of unassailable reality in all things, one is constrained to start with appearances, and to begin the reasoning process from there.

Obviously, this begs many questions. For one thing, how do two persons come to agree upon a subject for debate? A truly satisfactory answer to this question would require an extensive excursion into Śāntarakṣita and Kamalaśīla's theory of reference (via their theory of exclusion, or *apoha*). Time and space do not permit such a digression, but we can get an idea of how such agreement might come about from the evocative final verses of the *Śabdārthaparīkṣā* of the TS. In that chapter, Śāntarakṣita attempts to establish that even though words may elicit the arisal of images in awareness, they do not (and cannot) refer to real external particulars. But, an objector asks, what then is it about the image in each person's awareness that is the same, such that they can mutually communicate (as we observe them to)? The answer is that it is only the mistaken, imaginative determination *(adhyavasāya)* of these images as referring to the same unreal, external objects that the two parties have in common.[100] Śāntarakṣita illustrates his point with an example: he says that two ordinary people can communicate effectively in the same way that a person who sees two moons due to an eye disease can obtain agreement from another person afflicted with a similar disease to the statement that there are two moons.[101] Although this argument occurs in the context of an investigation of verbal reference and conceptual determinations, it is instructive that Śāntarakṣita describes what is the same about images in awareness by means of the metaphor of nonconceptual perceptual error. This indicates that Śāntarakṣita and Kamalaśīla understand agreement concerning the subject of a debate to come about through a shared participation in some form of error.

The key point is that even Mādhyamikas experience dualistic appearances, for intellectual discernment of the lack of unassailable reality is not by itself a sufficient antidote to the primordial ignorance that is the dominant cause of such appearances.[102] Only an advanced practioner, a buddha or a high-level bodhisattva, has the kind of purified vision in which appearances are not brought about by error, if they even have appearances at all. Thus, even when his realist opponents have a different *intellectual* understanding of the elements involved in an inference—including, most significantly, the manner in which these elements are established to appear—a Mādhyamika can still, due to a primordial ignorance shared with others, find some common ground from which to begin the dialectical process of demonstrating that unassailably real natures do not exist. In many cases, when dealing with unschooled or dense opponents, one may be required to "descend" to a lower level of analysis and assume some grosser form of unassailable reality—such as external particulars or mental imprints—in order to convince the opponent of some basic truth, such as the momentariness of all things. Yet as a Mādhyamika, one will always be keenly aware that *no* autonomous inference *at any level* is ever anything more than provisional. The important thing is not what appears to one; the important thing is that one applies analysis to that appearance. Through the application of analysis, one provides one's opponent and oneself with the opportunity and the means to throw off the shackles of all types of realism and to begin in earnest the path of meditation on the naturelessness *(niḥsvabhāvatā)* of all things.

Conclusions

I set out in this paper to evaluate a normative claim, advanced by some dGe lugs pa authors, which holds that the philosophical methods of the so-called Svātantrika-Mādhyamikas are incompatible with the Madhyamaka rejection of unassailable reality. The specific charge is that by allowing appeal to the given to play a role in philosophical investigation, Svātantrikas (unwittingly) accede to an ontological commitment on the conventional level that is inappropriate for them as Mādhyamikas. My aim has been to evaluate this claim in relation to Śāntarakṣita and Kamalaśīla by means of an examination of the given in their philosophy, especially in terms of the role it plays in autonomous inference, a tool of reasoning that, for the dGe lugs pa thinkers in question, the best kind of Mādhyamikas necessarily reject. Having discovered some significant ways in which the given embraced by Śāntarakṣita and Kamalaśīla differs from the given that is rejected by mKhas grub and others, the question now becomes how to evaluate the situation.

In the first place, it seems clear that the acceptance of a variety of givens on the sliding scale of analysis does function to curtail what one may justifiably say about conventional reality in any particular context or conversation. That is, there is no doubt that there are definite checks on what one may say about the conventional for these thinkers, and some of those checks are provided by the direct and immediate apprehension of appearances, which may act as a form of the given. In such cases, the given may be appealed to as evidence in a debate, which can act in various ways (e.g., directly or through contradiction) to establish or refute some thesis. Or, the given may serve as the subject of a debate, in the absence of which no debate or even conversation can even occur. Without some form of the given, Śāntarakṣita and Kamalaśīla's philosophical program would fall apart, for there would be nothing to talk about, not to mention no means to justify what one said. All this lends support to an interpretation of these authors as making some kind of implicit, albeit provisional, commitment on the conventional level. But is this really an ontological commitment, as the dGe lugs pa authors claim? It seems more like an epistemological or perhaps even a rhetorical commitment, which would lead the authors to an ontological commitment only if they accepted that perception is nonerroneous on all levels of analysis (which they seem *not* to do).

Furthermore, the way the authors use the given suggests that they are not really interested in providing a *foundation* for empirical knowledge, but rather that they care more about ascertaining the nature of reality through reason. For them, the given is less a foundation for knowledge than a testing ground for reason, an experience one investigates to discover ultimate or metaphysical realities, the most important of these being, of course, the utter absence of all forms of unassailable reality, conventionally and ultimately. While it is true that the given provides a check on what one can assert conventionally, by itself this does not render it an infallible indicator of any particular unassailable reality. As a matter of fact, conventional reality, *and therefore also the given,* is *not* infallible or unassailable, a finding that can itself be demonstrated through analysis. But for this demonstration to occur, one must begin with the conventional and then apply analysis to it. Once this has been done, one can then use the conventional as a field for dialectical reasoning, offering inferences that start out from whatever can be agreed upon to appear to oneself and others in order to help others arrive at the Madhyamaka perspective.

This seems a far cry from a philosophical system designed to provide a foundation for empirical knowledge. Still, Śāntarakṣita and Kamalaśīla do seem interested both in attaining knowledge and in justifying knowledge once it is found. The knowledge sought, however, is not empirical, but metaphysical, and its cornerstone is not the given, but is *reason* and the human ability to analyze reality.[103] For while the given does not remain the same on all the levels of the sliding scale of analysis—and, at the highest level, it even disappears—the formal elements of reasoning do. Even the definition of perception does not really change. What changes from level to level is the status of appearances. On the lower levels of analysis, appearances are straight-forwardly the given. At the highest level of analysis, they are mere appearances. At that point, while there is no given, there may still be nonerroneous perception. In that case, nonerroneous perception is not what appears to ordinary persons, but is only the difficult-to-fathom perception that directly and nonconceptually knows the absence of unassailable reality of all things, an object of knowledge so extraordinary, so abstract, and so removed from the conventional that it could *never* play the role of the given, whose function is to ground basic empirical beliefs.

Our evaluation of the dGe lugs pa claim depends entirely on what we think Śāntarakṣita and Kamalaśīla understand the given *to do.* Does it give access to unassailable reality, or not? This is clearly not an easy question to answer. But we do well, I think, to recognize that the mere appeal to sense contents and to perception as part of a theory of justification does not, in itself, require that these Mādhyamikas accept a conventional form of the unassailably real. In an interesting passage at the outset of his famous essay, "Empiricism and the Philosophy of Mind," Sellars observes that the argument against givenness does not involve a repudiation of the difference between inference and observation:

> I presume that no philosopher who has attacked the philosophical idea of givenness or, to use the Hegelian term, immediacy, has intended to deny that there is a difference between *inferring* that something is the case and, for example, *seeing* it to be the case. If the term "given" referred merely to what is observed as being observed, or, perhaps, to a proper subset of the things we are said to determine by observation, the existence of "data" would be as noncontroversial as the existence of philosophical perplexities. But, of course, this just isn't so. The phrase "the given" as a piece of professional—epistemological—shoptalk carries a substantial theoretical commitment, and one can deny that there are "data" or that anything is, in this sense, "given" without flying in the face of reason.[104]

Sellars' criticism of the given is not that of mKhas grub, and his concerns are decidedly not ontological but epistemological. His point here, however, can still be applied analogically to our present discussion. That is, to the degree that objects of perception (i.e., appearances) carry with them a substantial theoretical (i.e., ontological) commitment, they are problematic, while to the degree that the do not, they must remain noncontroversial. One way to think about Śāntarakṣita and Kamalaśīla's use of the given (if it can still be called that) is to see that it is not a conclusion or even a premise of reasoning, but only a necessary propaedeutic, which does not require any particular ontological commitment, and which, by virtue of the conventional reliability of the causal process, stands always and only as a *provisional* check on one's findings in the search for truth and one's attempt to convince others of that truth once it is found.

Notes

1 My thanks go to Helmut Krasser, Georges Dreyfus, John Dunne, Tom Tillemans, and Leonard van der Kuijp for their careful reading and insightful criticisms of two previous versions of this paper.

2 Buchler (1940; 1955 repr.): 38.

3 Throughout this paper I use the names Svātantrika and Prāsaṅgika to represent the Tibetan terms *Rang rgyud pa* and *Thal 'gyur ba.* I realize that in choosing to employ Sanskrit translations for what are most likely indigenous Tibetan terms, I risk giving the impression of a tacit recognition of their historical and philosophical legitimacy before the investigation into them has even begun. My choice to employ the Sanskrit translations, however, rests primarily on the fact that their use has become standard in the scholarly literature on the topic. Further, I believe that these Sanskrit terms represent the terms that Tibetans would most likely use to describe their classifications of Indian Madhyamaka if they were speaking to traditional Indian scholars. As such, these terms can be seen as mere translations, which one employs for convenience, in a manner similar to the way in which one might represent the Sanskrit term *saugata* by the English word "Buddhist." The use of the Sanskrit terms alone thus does not automatically compel one to accept their validity as names of real schools or movements in India, or even their validity as pointing to real philosophical differences. The crucial point is the care with which the terms are used, not the language in which they are expressed.

4 Sellars (1956; 1997 repr.): 14.

5 Sellars (1956; 1997 repr.): 15.

6 A secondary benefit of utilizing the given in these investigations is to allow the ancient Buddhist texts to speak more meaningfully to modern readers. It is not only that the use of the given as a tool of analysis highlights structural similarities in the epistemological enterprises of philosophers from diverse places and times; it is also that the category of the given may provide a kind of bridge that allows communication between two seemingly utterly distinct worlds: that of contemporary thought and that of ancient Buddhist philosophy. Tillemans (1997: 13) has convincingly argued for the necessity of this kind of careful introduction of contemporary language in the interpretation of ancient texts: "La méthode philologique, conçue à la manière étroite des *Geisteswissenschaften* du XIXe siècle, est donc souvent critiquée, à juste titre, parce qu'elle ne répond pas d'une façon adéquate à notre besoin de savoir ce que veut dire le texte. Il est inévitable, dans cette quête de sens, que nous interprétions les textes dans des termes et schémas qui sont d'une importance fondamentale dans la pensée actuelle. Autrement dit, nous ferons des interprétations que nous soutiendrons comme correctes, parce que rigoureusement justifiées par l'évidence textuelle, tout en admettant que les termes seraient parfaitement inconnus aux auteurs historiques eux-mêmes." Cf. also the remarks of Matilal (1971: 11): "Philological

research is of course essential. However, for philosophical studies, it should be treated not as an end but as a means to an end."

7 Tsong kha pa compares Svātantrikas to wayward monks, who, despite transgressing certain rules of the monastic order, are nonetheless still accepted—though perhaps grudgingly—as members of the monastic community. See *Drang nges legs bshad snying po* (Drepung Loseling ed.) 187: *mkhas pa de dag kyang chos bden par yod pa'i grub mtha' rigs pa'i sgo du mas 'gog cing bden med du legs par zhal gyis bzhes pas dbu ma pa ni yin no / dbu ma pa yin na rang rgyud bya mi rigs par gsungs pa dang mi 'gal te / bcas ldan gyi dge slong gis bcas pa dang 'gal bar mi rigs kyang de dang 'gal ba tsam gyis dge slong min mi dgos pa bzhin no //.*

8 Dreyfus (1996) and Tillemans (1990) are the only works to date of which I am aware that make a significant start at this interpretive project. The two works are quite different, however. Dreyfus argues that Dharmakīrti "does not subscribe to what Wilfrid Sellars calls the Myth of the Given" (210). His reasoning takes into account the role of memory (in the form of previous perceptual judgments) in the production of empirical knowledge. As Dreyfus explains (224), "Perception is unable in and of itself to bring about ordinary knowledge, which cannot be reduced to experience, contrary to what empiricists argue." Tillemans' contribution takes a different tack. He presents a picture in which Dharmakīrti, as a representative of the epistemological school of Indian Buddhism, accepts that the images *(ākāra)* in perceptual awareness are nonconceptually and nonerroneously given to awareness. Tillemans contrasts this approach with that of Candrakīrti, whom he says is nearly alone among Indian Buddhists in "arguing for the position that there is no perceptual given at all." (1990): 67–68. In this paper, my interest in ontological commitments prompts me to follow Tillemans' lead, although I find many things with which to agree in Dreyfus' assessment that perceptual awareness is not the given for Dharmakīrti. See also the contribution by Tillemans in the present volume.

9 Despite what Sellars has said about the wide variety of entities that can be considered the given, it is the first item on his list, sense contents, that so many twentieth-century philosophers (especially pre-Sellars) have explicitly construed as the given. It is also this form of the given upon which Sellars chooses to focus his critique, although he does so having insisted that his argument against sense-datum theories is only "a first step in a general critique of the entire framework of givenness" (1956; 1997 repr.): 14.

10 Price (1932; 1950 ed.): 3.

11 See, e.g., Lewis (1929; 1956 ed.): 38: "There are in our cognitive experience, two elements, the immediate data such as those of the sense, which are presented or given to the mind, and a form, construction, or interpretation, which represents the activity of thought."

12 Lewis (ibid.: 52) speaks of the twofold knowing process in relation to the given element in the perception of a pen: "My designation of this thing as 'pen' reflects my purpose to write; as 'cylinder' my desire to explain a problem in

geometry or mechanics; as 'a poor buy' my resolution to be more careful hereafter in my expenditures. These divergent purposes are anticipatory of certain different future contingencies which are expected to accrue, in each case, partly as a result of my own action. The distinction between this element of interpretation and the given is emphasized by the fact that the latter is what remains unaltered, no matter what our interests, no matter how we think or conceive. I can apprehend this thing as pen or rubber or cylinder, but I cannot, by taking thought, discover it as paper or soft or cubical." See Haack (1993: 34–51) for an interpretation of Lewis as undermining his own theory of sense-data as utterly certain through his own appeal to memory and other factors in the arisal of judgments. See also Lewis (1929; 1956 edition: 50): "In whatever terms I describe this item of my experience, I shall not convey it *merely* as given, but shall supplement this by a meaning which has to do with relations, and particularly with relations to other experiences which I regard as possible but which are not just now actual.... The infant may see it as much as I do, but still it will mean to him none of these things I have described it as being...."

13 See, e.g., Lewis (1929; 1956 ed.: 38–39): "If there be no datum given to the mind, then knowledge must be contentless and arbitrary; there would be nothing which it must be true to. And if there be no interpretation or construction which the mind itself imposes, then thought is rendered superfluous, the possibility of error becomes inexplicable, and the distinction of true and false is in danger of becoming meaningless."

14 See Haack (1993: 14–17) for a definition of foundationalism along these lines, as well as a helpful delineation of a range of foundationalist positions, including what she describes as weaker and stronger versions.

15 See, for instance, Williams (1999: 31), a student of Sellars, who describes the dilemma as follows: "that in so far as the content of immediate experience can be expressed, the sort of awareness we have in our apprehension of the given is just another type of perceptual judgment and hence no longer contact with anything which is *merely given.* But if the content of immediate experience turns out to be ineffable or nonpropositional, then the appeal to the given loses any appearance of fulfilling an explanatory role in the theory of knowledge: specifically, it cannot explicate the idea that knowledge rests on a perceptual foundation."

16 Williams (1999): 194. See also Sellars' well-known remark (1956; 1997 repr.: 76): "The essential point is that in characterizing an episode or a state as that of *knowing,* we are not giving an empirical description of that episode or state; we are placing it in the logical space of reasons, of justifying and being able to justify what one says."

17 I should note that Sellars' arguments involve many more steps than I am able to represent here.

18 Dharmakīrti's classic definition of perception occurs at NB 1.4: *tatra pratyakṣaṃ kalpanāpoḍham abhrāntam /.* For Dignāga's position, see Hattori (1968). For a study and partial translation of Śāntarakṣita and Kamalaśīla's chapter on

perception in the TS and TSP, see Funayama (1992). For a helpful exegesis of some aspects of the role of *niścaya* in perception in Dharmakīrti's thought, see Dunne (1999: ch. 5).

19 Although he rejects the characterization of Dharmakīrti as empiricist, Dreyfus (1996: 210) remarks that "Dharmakīrti holds that the only other form of knowledge, inference, is valid only due to its reliance on perception."

20 Throughout this paper, I shall use the translation "image in awareness" or simply "image" to represent the Sanskrit technical term *ākāra* (Tibetan: *rnam pa*). This translation is not without problems, and other possibilities (such as "form," or even "content") present themselves. The problem with how to translate *ākāra* may reflect an ambiguity concerning the term in the tradition itself. On the one hand, an *ākāra* sometimes seems to refer simply to the image or experience that arises upon the contact of a sense organ with a real particular. On the other hand, an *ākāra* can sometimes take on a more limited meaning, in which it signifies only that *aspect* of a perception for which a subsequent correct propositional determination *(niścaya)* arises. If the *ākāra* is *only* the aspect of the perception that one comes to "know" (in a propositional sense), then its status as the given may be questioned. If, however, the *ākāra* is (at least in some contexts) simply that nonconceptually apprehended image in awareness (as it seems to be represented in various contexts), then referring to the *ākāra* as the given is less problematic.

21 This characterization of the Buddhist theory of perceptual judgments reflects the thinking of Śāntarakṣita and Kamalaśīla as found in the *Tattvasaṃgraha* (TS) and *Tattvasaṃgrahapañjikā* (TSP). In those works, the authors argue that only that aspect of the perceived object for which there arises a corresponding judgment *(niścaya)* or ascertainment *(parāmarśa)* counts as the means of trustworthy awareness "perception" *(pratyakṣa)*. See, e.g., TSP *ad* TS 1972ff *(bahirarthaparīkṣā)*, where Kamalaśīla defends Śāntarakṣita's proof (TS 1966–1968) that external atoms cannot be the objects of perception: *pratyakṣam aviśeṣeṇotpannam api sad yatraivāṃśe yathā parigṛhītākāraparāmarśaṃ janayati sa eva pratyakṣaṃ iṣyate vyavahārayogyatayā yatra tu na janayati tad gṛhītam apy agṛhītaprakhyam* / "That is to say, when unqualified perception arises, it is asserted according to appropriate convention as 'perception' only in relation to that component for which it produces a concordant determination of the 'apprehended' image; but in relation to that [component for which] it does not produce [that kind of determination], then even though [all aspects of the object of perception] are 'apprehended,' they are spoken of as 'unapprehended.'"

Likewise, the idea that conceptual ascertainment does not necessarily arise in the wake of perceptual awareness is stated, among other places, at TSP *ad* TS 458 *(sthirabhāvaparīkṣā)*. In this case, the context is a discussion of the impossibility of a permanent entity. The Buddhist critique (TS 457) holds that the present state of existence of a permanent entity must be either the same as or different from its previous state of existence. If it is different, then the entity's permanence has been disproved. If it is the same, then why is it not apprehended at the time when the previous state of existence is apprehended? In response to this critique, the interlocutor tries to appeal to the Buddhists' own position by suggesting that the previous existence *is* apprehended but is simply *said* not to be apprehended. Kamalaśīla rejects this, noting it is not that some aspects of the real thing (e.g., momentariness) are not apprehended in any given instance of perceptual awareness, but rather only that some aspects are not conceptually ascertained: *syād etat / yathā kṣaṇikatvaṃ śabdāder avyatiriktam api sat tadgrahaṇe saty apy agṛhītam ucyate / tadvad idam api bhaviṣyatīti / tad ayuktam / na hi śabde dharmiṇi gṛhīte 'pi tadavyatireki kṣaṇikatvam agṛhītam iti vyavasthāpyate / kiṃ tu gṛhītam api tanniścayotpattikāraṇābhāvād aniścitam ity abhidhīyate / na hy anubhavamātrād eva niścayo bhavati / asyārthitvābhyāsasādguṇyādisāpekṣatvāt* / "Someone might think the following: Even though momentariness is not different from sound, it is said to be unapprehended, even when there is the apprehension of that [sound]. Likewise, such should be so in this case as well. This is not correct. For we do not postulate that even when the subject *(dharmin)* sound is apprehended, momentariness, which is not different from it, is not apprehended. What then? We say that even though it *is* apprehended, it is not ascertained due to the nonexistence of the causes that would give rise to an ascertainment of it. For it is not the case that just through mere experience *(anubhava)* there is ascertainment, since that [ascertainment] depends upon such things as interest *(arthitva),* habituation *(abhyāsa),* good qualities *(sādgūṇya)* and so on."

22 The theory of *pramāṇa* is closer to a theory of justification than a theory of truth. This is because true statements are not *pramāṇa*s, but can themselves be verified through *pramāṇa*s.

23 Hopkins (1999) is one recent, and welcome, departure from this trend.

24 A number of the most important sources by these authors on the question of the Svātantrika-Prāsaṅgika distinction have been translated into English. I would like especially to acknowledge four translators whose efforts have greatly aided my understanding of these texts: Jeffrey Hopkins, Robert A. F. Thurman, Donald S. Lopez, Jr., and José I. Cabezón. I would also like to thank Geshe Lhundrub Sopa of Madison, Wisconsin, for his oral commentary on Tsong kha pa's *Drang nges legs bshad snying po* in July and August 2000.

25 The phrase "unassailably real" is not a translation of a Sanskrit or Tibetan technical term but is my attempt to capture the meaning behind a range of expressions, including, for example, the Tibetan phrase *bden par grub pa,* or "truly established." That the rejection of *bden par grub pa* is seen as a cornerstone of the Madhyamaka is evident in a passage by lCang skya that defines a Mādhyamika (*Grub mtha' thub bstan lhun po'i mdzes rgyan,* Lhasa ed.: 209): *chos thams cad la don dam par grub pa'i yod mtha' dang / tha snyad du yang med pa'i chad mtha' legs par 'gog cing bden med du grub par zhal kyis bzhes pa'i rang sde ni dbu ma pa'o //* "A Mādhyamika is one of our own [i.e., a Buddhist] who, refuting well both the extreme of existence, which is that all *dharma*s are ultimately established, and the extreme of nihilism, which is that even conventionally [all

dharmas] do not exist, accepts that the lack of true existence *(bden med)* is established *(grub)*." My phrase "unassailably real" is also intended to reflect the idea that a "truly established" entity should be "able to withstand rational analysis which analyzes reality" *(de kho na nyid dpyod pa'i rigs pas dpyad bzod pa)*. Cf., e.g., mKhas grub, *sTong thun chen mo:* 145.

26 In the *sTong thun chen mo,* mKhas grub refers repeatedly to "realists" *(dngos por smra ba),* and even "Buddhist realists" *(rang sde dngos por smra ba),* whom he contrasts with Prāsaṅgika-Mādhyamikas *(dbu ma thal 'gyur ba)*. See, e.g., *sTong thun chen mo:* 91, where realists are characterized as holding that "if things are not established inherently, then they will necessarily not be established at all" *(dngos po rang bzhin gyis ma grub na gtan nas ma grub dgos pas...)*.

27 That one can have knowledge of things *just as they are* is one of the key areas of dispute between those who accept and those who reject the given. For Bertrand Russell's commitment to this notion, see below, n. 40.

28 Tsong kha pa clarifies that ordinary perception, while it may *seem* to be free from error, is in fact not so. See, e.g., *dGongs pa rab gsal* (Sarnath ed.) 101b3f: *da lta gzugs sgra sogs lnga rang gi mtshan nyid kyis grub par dbang shes la snang ba ni / ma rig pas bslad pa yin pas shes pa de dang / gzugs brnyan dang brag cha sogs snang ba'i dbang shes rnams la / phra rags tsam ma gtogs pa snang yul la 'khrul ma 'khrul la khyad par med cing.* Cited in Tauscher (1995): 142, n. 299. Cf. also mKhas grub, *sTong thun chen mo:* 121: *mig shes chos can / khyod gzugs kyi rang bzhin la mi bslu ba'i shes pa yin par thal / de la tshad ma yin pa'i phyir / rtags khas blangs / khyab pa yang khas blangs te / tshad ma'i mtshan nyid du mi bslu ba smos pa'i phyir ro // 'dod na mig shes chos can / khyod gzugs kyi rang bzhin la bslu bar thal / khyod la gzugs rang gi mtshan nyid kyis grub par snang ba gang zhig / rang gi mtshan nyid kyis grub pas stong ba de gzugs kyi rang bzhin yin pa'i phyir / zhes bya ba yin no //.* Trans. in Cabezón (1992): 119.

29 mKhas grub adds two more into the mix: "established autonomously" *(rang dbang du grub pa)* and "established substantially" *(rdzas su grub pa)*. See *sTong thun chen mo:* 177.

30 Tauscher (1995): 125. It is not clear to me whether all six phrases possess corresponding Sanskrit equivalents or not. Tillemans (1982: 111) maintains that at least some of them "are very probably Tibetan inventions."

31 Tauscher (1995): 132.

32 For in-depth treatments of Tsong kha pa's interpretations of autonomous inferences, see Hopkins (1989) and Yotsuya (1999). See also the contribution by Yoshimizu in the present volume.

33 Tsong kha pa, mKhas grub, and lCang skya are all aware that their analysis of the Svātantrika position would not be accepted by the philosophers in question. What they urge, however, is that the acceptance of an unassailably real nature conventionally is an unavoidable consequence of the Svātantrika's use of autonomous inference.

34 The term *tshad ma* is a translation of the Sanskrit term *pramāṇa,* which derives from the verbal root *pramā,* meaning in this context "to ascertain" or "to know

indubitably." In its broadest sense, a *pramāṇa* is the instrument or means by which one may be justified in regarding a particular instance of awareness as an instance of indubitable knowing. Unlike non-Buddhist Indian theorists, Buddhist epistemologists hold that the *pramāṇa* that serves to justify a cognitive episode as an instance of indubitable knowing does not differ from the episode itself. This distinction has led some modern authors to translate the term *pramāṇa* differently in different contexts; see, e.g., Dreyfus (1997: 528, n. 23): "I translate *pramāṇa* as 'means of valid cognition' when used in the Nyāya sense of the word and as 'valid cognition' when understood according to Buddhist ideas." While such a procedure is not without reason, it does tend to gloss over fact that the term *pramāṇa* is used and understood *across* sectarian lines, suggesting that at least some aspect of this term is shared by Buddhist and non-Buddhist authors alike. In addition, it may also be useful to point out that although for the Buddhists a *pramāṇa* is not different from the cognitive episode that it certifies, it nonetheless does not thereby give up its character of serving as the *means* of arriving at that certification. Thus, even though the means and the end are not distinct, there may still be Buddhist contexts where it is appropriate to speak of *pramāṇa* as a means, since a cognitive episode is certified as an instance of indubitable knowledge *by virtue of the fact* that it is a *pramāṇa*.

35 See, e.g., *sTong thun chen mo:* 317: *gzhi gang gi steng du khyad par kyi chos gang dam 'cha' ba'i gzhir gyur pa shes 'dod chos can de nyid snga rgol gyi tshad mas kyang grub phyi rgol gyi tshad mas kyang grub pa tsam gyis mi chog gi / snga rgol phyi rgol gnyi ga'i lugs la mthun snang du grub pa zhig nges par dgos shing dam bca' de nyid sgrub pa'i rtags kyi tshul gsum yang snga rgol phyi rgol gnyi ga'i lugs la mthun snang du grub pa'i sgo nas tshad mas grub pa dgos so // de yang rgol ba gnyi ga'i lugs la chos can mthun snang du 'grub pa la chos can tshad mas grub tshul rgol ba gnyi ga'i lugs la mthun snang du grub pa dgos shing / ....*

36 The three characteristics of the evidence are three relations involving the evidence that must be verified in order for an inference to successfully function. The form of an inference is as follows: A certain subject is qualified by a certain predicate because that subject possesses a certain property (i.e., the evidence). The three necessary relations are 1) that the evidence be a property of the subject *(pakṣadharmatā, phyogs chos);* 2) that the predicate exist wherever the evidence exists *(anvayavyāpti, rjes khyab);* and 3) that the evidence not exist wherever the predicate does not exist *(vyatirekavyāpti, ldog khyab).* Probative or valid evidence in an inference must be reliably shown to be qualified, or characterized by, these three relations.

37 See PV 4.1–12 (translated and commented upon in Tillemans [2000: 9–24]), where Dharmakīrti gives his interpretation of the term *svadṛṣṭa* in Dignāga's definition (in PS 3.1) of an inference-for-others *(parārthānumāna).* In PV 4.1, Dharmakīrti states that Dignāga introduces the term *svadṛṣṭa* in order to eliminate the mistaken view (attributed to some Sāṃkhyas) that an inference-for-others can proceed when the evidence in the inference is recognized *only* by the

opponent and not by the proponent. The following *kārikās* elaborate on this principle, and also contain an interesting discussion on the distinct logical structures of an inference-for-others and a *prasaṅga* or reductio-style argument.

38 This seems likely to be an innovation developed in Tibet. See Tillemans (1989a): sec. f.

39 *sTong thun chen mo:* 317: ...*dngos smra ba'i lugs la gzugs la sogs pa chos can mngon gyur pa rnams mngon sum tshad mas 'grub dgos la / mngon sum tshad ma yin na rang gi gzhal bya rang mtshan dngos su 'jal ba'i tshad ma yin pa'i khyab par 'dod cing /*

40 Russell (1912; 1997 repr.: 48) states that "All of knowledge, both knowledge of things and knowledge of truths, rests upon acquaintance as its foundation." To better understand what Russell means by acquaintance, consider the following (ibid.: 46): "We shall say that we have *acquaintance* with anything of which we are directly aware, without the intermediary of any process of inference or any knowledge of truths. Thus in the presence of my table I am acquainted with the sense-data that make up the appearance of my table—its colour, shape, hardness, smoothness, etc.; all these are things of which I am immediately conscious when I am seeing and touching my table. The particular shade of colour that I am seeing may have many things said about it—I may say that it is brown, that it is rather dark, and so on. But such statements, though they make me know truths *about* the colour, do not make me know the colour itself any better than I did before: so far as concerns knowledge of the colour itself, as opposed to knowledge of truths about it, I know the colour perfectly and completely when I see it, and no further knowledge of it itself is even theoretically possible. Thus the sense-data which make up the appearance of my table are things with which I have acquaintance, things immediately known to me just as they are."

41 The term "remote" indicates an entity that can be known only inferentially. The term is part of a well-known trio of epistemological concepts that taken together encompass all possible objects of knowledge: the epistemically perceptible *(pratyakṣa, mngon sum),* the epistemically remote *(parokṣa, lkog gyur),* and the epistemically radically inaccessible *(atyantaparokṣa, shin tu lkog gyur).* The ocular faculty (and the other sense organs) are generally considered by Buddhists to be knowable through inference, and not directly through perception.

42 *sTong thun chen mo:* 317–318: *mig la sogs pa lkog gyur chos can du bzung pa'i tshe na yang / chos can de nyid dngos su 'jal ba'i tshad ma rjes dpag yin kyang brgyud nas mngon sum la thug dgos shing / rjes dpag de nyid gang la tshad mar song ba'i gzhal bya la rang mtshan gyi tha snyad 'dogs sam mi 'dogs gang yin yang sla'i / zhal bya de ming tsam gyis bzhag pa ma yin pa'i yul gyi sdod lugs su grub par 'dod pa la dngos smra ba thams cad khyad par med pas / dngos smra ba'i lugs la chos can 'jal ba'i tshad ma yin na rang gi mtshan nyid kyis grub pa'i chos can la tshad mar song bas khyab par 'dod pa yin zhing / dngos smra ba rnams kyi lugs la tshad ma yin na rang gang la tshad mar song ba'i gzhal bya de la ma 'khrul pa'i shes pa yin*

pas khyab pa'i phyir rtags kyi chos can de tshad mas grub na chos can de nyid rang gi gzhal bya la ma 'khrul pa'i tshad ma'i rnyed don yin pa'i khyab par 'dod pa yin no //

43 We have already noted (see n. 8 above) that Tillemans argues that Candrakīrti does not accept any form of the given. Although Tsong kha pa does not use the contemporary language, he concurs that Candrakīrti does not accept that awareness of sense-data or any other image in awareness can be nonerroneous. See the quotation from the *dGongs pa rab gsal* above, n. 28.

44 *sTong thun chen mo:* 318: *des na thal 'gyur ba'i lugs la rang gi mtshad nyid kyis grub pa tha snyad du yang mi srid pa'i phyir rang gi mtshan nyid kyis grub pa'i gzhal bya 'jal ba'i tshad ma tha snyad du yang med pas dngos smra ba dang dnyi ga'i lugs la chos can tshad mas grub tshul mthun snang du grub pa mi srid pa'i phyir gzhan la grags kyi rjes dpag dang thal 'gyur tsam gyi sgo nas pha rol po'i rgyud la bden med rtogs pa'i nges shes skyed par byed pa yin no //.*

45 mKhas grub emphasizes that the fundamental difference between a Prāsaṅgika and a realist of any kind (including the realism-tainted Svātantrikas) is that the former does not accept that a *tshad ma* is nonerroneous in regard to its object being established by its own characteristic. Although subjects can be validly "found" by conventional trustworthy awarenesses *(tha snyad pa'i tshad ma)*, they are not found in a manner at all similar to the way that they are established or found by realists. This means that a subject that is established as appearing similarly is not possible for a Prāsaṅgika. See, e.g., *sTong thun chen mo:* 329–330: *de yang dbu ma rang rgyud pa dag gzugs sogs tha snyad du yang bden par ma grub par 'dod cing / tshur mthong gi mig gi rnam par shes pa la sogs pa rnams gzugs sogs kyi rang gi mtshan nyid la ma 'khrul ba'i tshad mar 'dod kyang / gzugs sogs tha snyad du bden par ma grub na tha snyad du rang gi mtshan nyid kyis kyang ma grub dgos shing / de ltar na rang gi mtshan nyid kyis grub par snang ba'i mig shes sogs 'khrul par khas len dgos pas / gzugs sogs rnams 'khrul pa'i tshad mas rnyed don du 'dod dgos la / de ltar na dngos smra ba'i lugs la ni gzugs sogs rnams rang gi mtshan nyid kyis grub pa'i gzhal bya la ma 'khrul pa'i tshad mas rnyed don yin pas khyab pa'i phyir chos can mthun snang du grub pa mi 'thad pas / rang rgyud kyi rtags 'god par mi rigs so zhes rigs pas phul nas / chos thams cad bden med du khas len pa dang rang rgyud khas len pa la 'gal ba ston pa yin la / dbu ma pa yin na rang rgyud khas len par mi rigs pa'i rgyu mtshan kyang 'di nyid yin no //.* Trans. in Cabezón (1992): 282.

46 It is interesting that for Kamalaśīla in the TSP, a consequentialist *(prāsaṅgika)* proof *(sādhana)* is not *only* refutational in function. At TSP *ad* TS 3308, Kamalaśīla states that the proof of the Buddha's knowledge of all things whatsoever is *prāsaṅgika,* and he contrasts this with the primary *(mukhya)* proof of the Buddha's knowledge of the means to attain liberation and heaven.

47 See PV4.12bcd for Dharmakīrti's explanation of the mechanics of a *prasaṅga: parakalpitaiḥ prasaṅgo dvayasambandhād ekābhāve 'nyahānaye //.* Trans. in Tillemans (2000: 21): "An [absurd] consequence is [drawn] by means of the other's conceptual constructs *(parakalpitaiḥ);* as the [consequence's] two terms

are necessarily connected, it serves to negate the second term in the absence of the first." Manorathanandin (PVV 417) illustrates this definition with an example: *parakalpitaiḥ sādhanaiḥ prasaṅgaḥ kriyate yathā sāmānyasya paropagatānekavṛttitvād anekatvam āpādyate na tv ayam pāramārthiko hetus trairūpyābhāvāt /*. Trans. in Tillemans (2000: 22): "A consequence is drawn by means of *sādhanas* which are the other's conceptual constructs, as in the following case: 'It follows that a universal *(sāmānya)* is many [different things] *(anekatva)*, because, as the other accepts, it is present in a multitude *(anekavṛtti)* [of particulars]'. This, however, is not really a [valid] reason, because it lacks the triple characterization *(trairūpya)*."

48 See, e.g., Ruegg (1981): 36–42.

49 Tillemans (1992): 317.

50 *sTong thun chen mo:* 317–318: *des na mdor bsdus te go bde bar brjod na / rang gi mtshan nyid kyis grub pa'i gzhal bya la ma 'khrul pa'i tshad mas rnyed don yin par snga rgol phyi rgol ngyi ga'i lugs la mthun snang du grub pa'i chos can gyi steng du / snga rgol gang la dpag 'dod zhugs pa'i bsgrub bya'i chos sgrub byed kyi gtan tshigs su bkod pa / zhes pa rang rgyud kyi rtags kyi don yin la / chos can de nyid tshad mas 'grub tshul snga rgol phyi rgol gnyi ga'i mthun snang du grub pa med kyang spyir chos can de nyid snga rgol gyi lugs la'ang tshad mas grub phyi rgol gyi lugs la'ang tshad mas grub cing chos can dang phyogs chos sogs phyi rgol {gyi?} lugs la tshad mas grub pa'i khas blangs la 'khris nas bkod pa'i gtan tshigs ni gzhan la grags kyi rjes dpag ces bya'o //.*

51 Tillemans (1992): 317.

52 Tillemans (1989a): 1.

53 Dreyfus (1997): 49, 86, *et passim*. Although I agree with Dreyfus' characterization of the scale of analysis as "ascending," in that each level of analysis supersedes the previous level in terms of its accuracy, I think it is important to emphasize that a person with a higher level of understanding can (and indeed *should*) "descend" to a lower level of analysis for the purposes of debate. That is why I prefer the image of a "sliding" scale of analysis to that of an "ascending" scale. On Dharmakīrti's shifting philosophical method, see also Dunne (1999): ch. 3.

54 Dreyfus (1997): 83.

55 A premise of my ongoing work on these texts is that they ought to be studied in conjunction, an approach that unfortunately has been rarely taken in modern scholarship. Although it is true that the two sets of texts are probably aimed at different audiences—with the MA, MAV, and MAP speaking primarily to Buddhists and the TS and TSP to both Buddhists and non-Buddhists—it is also evident that the Madhyamaka works take for granted the study and understanding of the longer and more epistemologically oriented treatises. Likewise, even though the TS and TSP stop at the Yogācāra level of analysis, they contain a sufficient number of comments concerning the superiority of the Madhyamaka level of analysis to serve as a good indication that the authors of the TS and TSP hoped that their readers would "graduate" to the Madhyamaka

perspective. See, e.g., TSP *ad* TS 1916–17, where Kamalaśīla glosses Śāntarakṣita's reference to "some wise persons" *(sudhiyaḥ kecid)* as Mādhyamika Mahāyānists *(sudhiyo mahāyānikāḥ / kecid iti mādhyamikāḥ)*. See the discussion in McClintock (2002): 68–76.

56 Kajiyama (1978): 117. Kajiyama's assessment of the sliding scale of analysis as having a practical (and thus pedagogical purpose) is similar to the idea behind the study of Tibetan *grub mtha'* literature as described by Hopkins (1996): 171: "Systems of tenets, therefore, are primarily studied not to refute other systems but to develop an internal force that can counteract one's own *innate* adherence to misapprehensions....the stated aim of studying different schools of philosophy is to gain insight into the fact that many of the perspectives basic to ordinary life are devoid of a valid foundation. This leads the adepts to then replace these with well-founded perspectives."

57 In this simplified presentation of the sliding scale of analysis, I cannot go into all of the a priori principles and general theorems that inform the earliest levels of philosophical analysis. They include such notions as the law of contradiction, the law of the excluded middle, and also some important ideas about identity and difference.

58 This principle finds clear expression in NB 1.15. *arthakriyāsāmarthyalakṣaṇatvād vastunaḥ /* which is probably the source for the quotation in MAV *ad* MA 8: *don byed nus pa la dngos po'i mtshan nyid /*. The principle that causal functioning is the defining feature of real things is also succinctly stated in a negative form in TSP *ad* TS 385: *yat sarvasāmarthyaśūnyaṃ tad avastu yathā vandhyāputraḥ /*.

59 It is less clear whether an entity *must* be perceived to be real for these thinkers. There are indications for both a positive and a negative response to this query, and more work needs to be done to arrive at a satisfactory answer. For an interesting preliminary analysis in relation to Dharmakīrti, see Dunne (1999): ch. 3, especially the section entitled "The Perceptible as Ultimately Real."

60 Kamalaśīla refers to this level of analysis as Bahirārthavāda and Sautrāntika at various places throughout the TSP. For another perspective on the similarity of the Sautrāntika level of analysis with sense-data theories, see Matilal (1986): 248–250.

61 mKhas grub cites the pervasive use of *pramāṇavāda* style reasoning in the works of these authors as evidence that Śāntarakṣita and Kamalaśīla endorse the idea of real things being established in terms of their own characteristics. See *sTong thun chen mo:* 148: *der ma zad zhi 'tsho yab sras kyis tshad ma sde bdun gyi rang lugs kyi rigs pa phal che ba dbu sems gnyis kyi thun mong ba yin par tshad chen dang dbu ma snang ba las bshad pas kyang dngos po rang gi mtshan nyid kyis grub pa bzhed par nges so //*. "In addition, Śāntarakṣita and his son [i.e., Kamalaśīla] have explained in the *Great Pramāṇa* [i.e., the TS] and the *Madhyamakāloka* that most of the reasoning of the system of the seven logical treatises [of Dharmakīrti] is common to both Madhyamaka and Yogācāra. Therefore, it is definite that they also accept that real things *(dngos po)* are established by their own characteristics."

62 More precisely, the theorem states that a real entity must be either singular or plural; however, since plurality is thought to rest upon the existence of real singular entities, the actual demonstration revolves around an investigation of the possibility of singularity.

63 See TS 1972–1978 and TSP *ad cit.* See also MA 10.

64 See TS 1989–1991 and TSP *ad cit.* Cf. MA 11–13. For a study of these arguments as initially developed by Vasubandhu, see Kapstein (1988).

65 See TS 1992–1996 and TSP *ad cit.* Cf. MA 14.

66 Śāntarakṣita and Kamalaśīla follow Dignāga and Dharmakīrti in rejecting even on the Sautrāntika level of analysis that the object known in perception is separate from the awareness itself. The best known argument for this rejection is the so-called *sahopalambhaniyama*-inference. Using this reasoning, one argues that the object of awareness and the awareness itself cannot be different, because they are always necessarily apprehended together *(sahopalambhaniyamāt).* The reasoning itself does not refute real external particulars, which can still be inferred (on the Sautrāntika level of analysis) as having a kind of causally efficacious existence; nonetheless, the argument is an important step in the eventual refutation of external objects. See TS 2029–2030 and TSP *ad cit.* for Śāntarakṣita and Kamalaśīla's treatment. See also Iwata (1991) for a detailed study of this reasoning in the larger Buddhist *pramāṇavāda* tradition.

67 See MA 18 = TS 2001: *tad asya bodharūpatvād yuktaṃ tāvat svavedanam / parasya tv artharūpasya tena saṃvedanaṃ katham.* In the MAP (Ichigō, 75) Kamalaśīla clarifies that the purpose of this verse is to show that external objects of knowledge are illogical: *phyi rol rig pa'i bya ba mi rung bar bstan pa'i phyir.* See also TS 1358–1360 (the final three verses of the *Pratyakṣalakṣaṇaparīkṣā*) and TSP *ad cit.*

68 For a statement that it is *more* rational to accept a mentalist *(vijñaptimātra)* perspective than a materialist one, see TS 1887 and TSP *ad cit.*

69 There is a necessary shift in the understanding of perception, however. We treat this in the section entitled "Nonerroneous Perception on the Sliding Scale of Analysis" below.

70 Some later commentators, such as Bodhibhadra, refer to these two strands of the Yogācāra as *sākāravāda* and *nirākāravāda,* respectively. This terminology is confusing because it is also widely used to classify Indian philosophical thought more generally into positions that do and do not accept that ordinary awareness is endowed with an image. The point in the Yogācāra context is not whether awareness is endowed with an image, but whether the image that appears in the awareness of ordinary beings is *real.* If it is judged to be unreal *(alīka),* then images will not occur in the awareness of awakened beings; if, however, images are real *(satya),* then there will be nothing to prevent them from arising in the awareness of buddhas and so on. Since Śāntarakṣita and Kamalaśīla reject both of these analyses of images and awareness, it may not be appropriate to see them (as some, including some Tibetans, have done) as following *either* form of the Yogācāra, even conventionally. For more on *sākāra-*

/*satyākāravāda* and *nirākara-/alīkākāravāda* see Kajiyama (1965: *passim*), (1966: 154–58), and (1978: 125–29); Mimaki (1976); Moriyama (1984); and Tillemans (1990: 41–42; 51, n. 113). For some reflections on how the classification plays out in Tibet, see Dreyfus (1997: 433–38).

71 For a useful overview of the arguments leading to these conclusions as they are presented by Śāntarakṣita, Kamalaśīla, and Haribhadra, see Moriyama (1984): part I.

72 Śāntarakṣita's classic statement of the lack of unassailable reality of all things is found in the opening verse of his MA (Sanskrit preserved in *Bodhicaryāvatāra*; see Ichigo ed., 22): *niḥsvabhāvā amī bhāvās tattvataḥ svaparoditaḥ / ekāneka-svabhāvena viyogāt pratibimbavat //* "These entities that are postulated by ourselves and others are ultimately without any nature, because they have neither a single nor a multiple nature, like a reflection."

73 mKhas grub repeatedly acknowledges that the critique of Svātantrikas as tainted by realism on the conventional level is a critique that must be forced upon them, not something they will admit to willingly. See especially *sTong thun chen mo:* 180–185.

74 See, e.g., TS 1889: *abahistattvarūpāṇi vāsanāparipākataḥ / vijñāne pratibhāsante svapnādāv iva nānyataḥ //* "Forms that lack any true externality appear in awareness through the ripening of imprints, just as in a dream, and not otherwise."

75 See, e.g., TSP *ad* TS 2041–2043 for a statement that awareness of what seems to be an entity external to the mind is erroneous awareness: *kevalam avidyā-vaśād aviṣayam evābhūtākāropadarśakaṃ jñānaṃ bhrāntaṃ jāyate /* "[In the case of the apparent awareness of an external entity] it is just that through ignorance an erroneous awareness that has no object at all *(eva)* arises presenting an unreal *(abhūta)* image."

76 See TSP *ad* TS 1311: *abhrāntamatrāvisaṃvāditvena draṣṭavyam na tu yathāvasthitālambanākāratayā / anyathā hi yogācāramatenālambanāsiddher ubhayanayasamāśrayeṇeṣṭasya pratyakṣalakṣaṇasyāvyāpitā syāt / avisaṃvāditvaṃ cābhimatārthakriyāsamarthārthaprāpaṇaśaktikatvam....* "Here [the word] 'non-erroneous' *(abhrānta)* should be understood in the sense of 'trustworthy' *(avisaṃvāda)* and so on. It should not be [understood] in terms of the notion that images [in perception] have an objective basis *(ālambana)* that is established in the way [that the images appear]. [This must be the case] because otherwise, since on the Yogācāra view the objective basis *(ālambana)* is not established, the definition of perception—which is asserted as the basis of both systems [i.e., Sautrāntika and Yogācāra]—would not apply *(avyāpin)* [to both systems]. Being trustworthy means having the capacity to cause one to obtain an *artha* which is capable of the desired causal functioning *(arthakriyā)*." This final statement clearly harkens back to PV 2.1bff.: *arthakriyāsthitiḥ / avisaṃ-vādanam....* "Trustworthiness is the cognition *(sthitiḥ)* of [the desired] causal functioning." On the interpretation of this statement and on the role of *arthakriyā* in Dharmakīrti's PV and PVSV, see Dunne (1999): ch. 5.

77 In this sense, perception here draws closer to inference *(anumāna)* in terms of

its trustworthiness *(prāmāṇya)*. See Tillemans (1999): 8–11 for a discussion of *bhrānta* and *abhrānta* in terms of isomorphism, congruence, and correlation.

78 See TSP *ad* TS 1978 (674,24–675,14–17): *athābhimatārthakriyāvabhāsi jñānam evārthakriyāsaṃvādaḥ / tadāyam anyathāpi bāhyārthālambanam antareṇāpi sambhāvyata iti tathā hetor anaikāntikataiva / katham anyathāpi sambhāvyate / ity āha sāmarthyaniyamād dhetor iti / hetoḥ samanantarapratyayasya sāmarthyabhedaniyamāt / kaścid eva hi samanantarapratyayaḥ kiñcid vijñānaṃ janayituṃ samartho na sarvaḥ sarvam / yathā bhavatā bāhyo 'rtha iti tata eva niyamaḥ siddhaḥ //*. Cf. also TSP *ad* TS 1627–1628.

79 We have already noted that for Śāntarakṣita and Kamalaśīla images in awareness arise on the Yogācāra level of analysis through the ripening of imprints. We learn at TSP *ad* TS 151 that when it comes to conceptual *(savikalpika)* awarenesses, the image in awareness arises through ignorance, which is defined in that context as an "imprint for an incorrect imaginative determination" *(vitathābhiniveśavāsanā)*. In MA 44 and the commentaries on it, Śāntarakṣita and Kamalaśīla expand on this approach, implying that on the Yogācāra level of analysis even the nonconceptual images in perceptual awareness arise through a similar kind of error. MA 44: *ci ste thog ma med rgyud kyi / bag chags smin pas sprul pa yi / rnam pa dag ni snang ba yang / nor bas sgyu ma'i rang bzhin 'dra //:* "Well, [on the Yogācāra view] although there is the appearance of images which are manifested through the ripening of imprints [existing] beginninglessly in the mental stream, because [they arise] through a mistake, their nature is similar to an illusion." Kamalaśīla explains the nature of the mistake in MAP *ad cit.: dmigs pa bden par 'dod pa'i shes pa la snang ba'i rnam pa 'di dag kyang thog ma med pa'i srid par 'byung ba can dngos po la mngon par zhen pa'i bag chags yongs su smin pa'i mthus snang ngo //*. "But although these images appear to an awareness that is asserted to have a real object, they appear by the force of the ripening of the imprints for the imaginative determination *(abhiniveśa)* of real entities which arise in beginningless *saṃsāra*." See also *Abhisamayālaṃkāra* 626, 13–14 (Wogihara).

80 In discussing the Yogācāra (or *sems tsam pa*) understanding, mKhas grub says: *sngon po sngon po'i tha snyad kyi gzhir rang gi mtshan nyid kyis ma grub kyang sngon po sngon por rang gi mtshan nyid kyis grub pa ltar / dbang shes la sngon po sngon po'i tha snyad 'jug pa'i gzhi'i snang tshul ltar rang gi mtshan nyid kyis ma grub kyang sngon po sngon por snang ba'i snang tshul ltar rang gi mtshan nyid kyis grub la / snang tshul de ltar 'dzin pa'i rtog pas zhen pa ltar yang rang gi mtshan nyid kyis grub pa'o //*. Trans. in Cabezón (1992): 61. The idea that the object of perception should exist in the manner in which it appears has an obvious "svātantric" air about it. Nonetheless, it is interesting that although Candrakīrti criticizes this standard model of perception in the CŚ, he does accept the principle that whatever exists in a manner *different* from how it appears is deceptive. Tillemans (1990: 47) demonstrates that Candrakīrti uses this principle "to show that any perception by an ordinary being is erroneous, because something will appear as real or as having a *svabhāva,* whereas it is in fact void."

Tillemans also argues (1990: 43) that in rejecting the nonerroneous status of perception (i.e., in rejecting the given) Candrakīrti distinguishes himself from Svātantrikas, who are characterized by some Tibetans as "holding that things are illusions, but that even *qua* illusions they do have an 'objective mode of being' *(don gyi sdod lugs)*." This analysis seems close to that of mKhas grub.

81 *Tattvāloka,* D 258b3ff: *rab rib can bzhin gzugs la sogs / brdzun pa rnams ni mthong ba'i phyir / yang dag pa yi dngos po'i don / mngon sum 'ga' yang grub pa med //.* Cf. MĀ D 168bff.: *gang yang mngon sum gyi yul ni dngos po yin pa'i phyir ro zhes smras pa gang yin pa de yang ma grub pa yin te / 'di ltar tshu rol mthong ba rnams kyi mngon sum gang yin pa de ni rab rib can gyi mngon sum bzhin du gzugs la sogs pa brdzun pa'i yul can yin pa nyid kyis dngos po'i ngo bo nyid yang dag pa pa'i yul can nyid du rigs pa ma yin no //.* "And the statement that 'because it is an object of perception it is a real thing' also is not established, since whatever is perceived by ordinary persons has a false object, i.e., form and so on, in the manner of the perception of a person with an eye disease. Therefore, it is not correct that [perception] has an object which is an authentic *(yang dag pa pa ≈ bhāvika)* real nature of a real thing."

82 See TS 304 and TSP *ad cit.* for affirmation of the authors' acceptance of the requirement that the reason in an autonomous inference must be established for both parties to the debate (i.e., the requirement of *ubhayaprasiddha*). Here, Kamalaśīla argues that the evidence "being produced" offered by a Sāṃkhya opponent in a failed autonomous inference is not successful because it is not established for the Buddhist, who has a different understanding of production than does the Sāṃkhya (i.e., the Buddhist does not accept that production entails the production of an already existent entity). While it is true that the reason is here judged inadmissible because it is understood differently by the two parties, Kamalaśīla gives no indication that the two parties necessarily ascertain or establish the reason through the exact same process in order for the reason to be valid (so that, for instance, the two parties would necessarily have to agree about such issues as the nature and reality of objects of perception).

83 Śāntarakṣita and Kamalaśīla argue this way quite consciously, often expressly qualifying what seem to be autonomous inferences as presented only by means of a provisional acceptance *(abhyupagamaṇa)* of some element of the inference; I have noted at least twenty overt instances of this technique in the TSP.

84 TS 561a–c: *sthūlārthāsambhave tu syān naiva vṛkṣādidarśanam / atīndriyatayāṇūnāṃ /* "But if there were no gross object, a tree and so on would not be seen, because infinitesimal particles are beyond the senses." Kamalaśīla indicates that the opponents here include Uddyotakara and Bhāvivikta.

85 TS 583: *anyonyābhisarāś caivaṃ ye jātāḥ paramāṇavaḥ / naivātīndriyatā teṣāṃ akṣāṇāṃ gocaratvataḥ //* "Those infinitesimal particles which arise as mutually supportive are not beyond the senses, because they are the objects *(gocara)* of the senses." Kamalaśīla explains: *asiddham aṇūnāṃ atīndriyatvaṃ viśiṣṭāvasthāprāptānām indriyagrāhyatvāt /* "It is not established that infinitesimal particles are beyond the senses, because [those particles] that have attained a particular

state are apprehended by the senses." For an analysis of this idea in Dharmakīrti, see Dunne (1999): ch. 3.

86 TS 586–587: *sarveṣām eva vastūnāṃ sarvavyāvṛttirūpaṇām / dṛṣṭāv api tathaiveti na sarvākāraniścayaḥ // akalpanākṣagamye 'pi nirāśe 'rthasvalakṣaṇe / yadbhedavyavsāye 'sti kāraṇaṃ sa parīyate //* "All real things whatsoever have a nature *(rūpa)* of exclusion from all [other real things]. Even when seen, the determination 'it is thus' does not occur for all aspects. Even though the particular thing which is understood by nonconceptual perception is partless, only that for which the cause for its determination exists is [so] apprehended *(parīyate).*"

87 The explanations, found in TS 586–587 and TSP *ad cit.*, are closely modeled on Dharmakīrti's PVSV *ad* PV 1.58. This is just one of many instances in the TS and TSP where the PVSV appears to be a fundamental source. Cf. PVSV *ad* PV 1.58: *kiṃ punaḥ kāraṇaṃ sarvato bhinne vasturūpe 'nubhavotpattāv api tathaiva na smārto niścayo bhavati / sahakārivaikalyāt / tataś ca / pratyakṣeṇa gṛhīte 'pi viśeṣe 'ṃśavivarjite / yadviśeṣāvasāye 'sti pratyayaḥ sa pratīyate // yady apy aṃśarahitaḥ sarvato bhinnasvabhāvo bhāvo 'nubhūtas tathāpi na sarvabhedeṣu tāvatā niścayo bhavati / kāraṇāntarāpekṣatvāt / anubhavo hi yathāvikalpābhyāsaṃ niścayapratyayān janayati / yathā rūpadarśanāviśeṣe 'pi kuṇapakāminībhakṣyavikalpāḥ / tatra buddhipāṭavaṃ tadvāsanābhyāsaḥ prakaraṇam ity ādayo 'nubhavād bhedaniścayotpattisahakāriṇaḥ / teṣām eva ca pratyāsattitāratamyādibhedāt paurvāparyam / yathā janakatvādhyāpakatvāviśeṣe 'pi pitaram āyāntaṃ dṛṣṭvā pitā me āgacchati nopādhyāya iti /.* Dunne (1999: ch. 4) translates as follows: "'But why is it that, even though one has had a [perceptual] experience of the nature of a real thing *(vasturūpe)* that is distinct from all other [things], one does not have a mnemonic determination of it as such?' Because the supporting conditions are lacking. And therefore, even though one has apprehended through perception a distinct [entity] *(viśeṣa)* that is [ultimately] devoid of parts, one cognizes that distinctive aspect *(viśeṣa)* for the determinative cognition of which there is the supporting condition. [PV 1.58] Although one has experienced an entity that has no parts and whose nature-*svabhāva* is distinct from all other things, one does not thereby determine all [its] distinctive qualities *(bheda)* because [such a cognition] depends on other causes. That is, [perceptual] experience produces determinate cognitions *(niścayapratyaya)* in accord with [one's mental] conditioning [for favoring the formulation of certain] concepts. For example, even though there is no difference in that [they are all] seeing matter, [when an ascetic sees the body of a dead woman], he conceives it to be a corpse; [a lustful man] conceives it to be a woman; and [a hungry dog] conceives it to be food. In such cases, the acuity of the intellect, the conceptual imprints to which one is accustomed, the context, and other such factors are the supporting conditions that [account for] the arisal of different determinations from a [single] perceptual experience. And because of their [varying degrees of] association *(pratyāsatti)* and priority *(tāratamya),* [some determinations] occur before others. For example, even though there is no difference between the fact that the person one is seeing is one's parent and the fact that

he is one's teacher, upon seeing one's father coming, one thinks, 'my father is coming'; one does not think, 'my teacher is coming.'"

88 TSP *ad* TS 586–587: *etac ca sarvaṃ parmāṇūnāṃ siddhiṃ bāhyasya cārthasya prayakṣatvasiddhim abhyupagamyoktam / yasya tu vijñānavādino na bāhyo 'rtho nīlādirūpatayā pratyakṣasiddhaḥ / svapnādau vināpi bāhyam arthaṃ tathāvidha-nīlādipratibhāsopalambhena saṃśayāt / tasya ca nīlādirūpasyaikānekasvabhāva-śūnyatvena bhrāntijñānapratibhāsātmakatvāt / nāpi parmāṇavaḥ siddhāḥ teṣāṃ paurvāparyāvasthāyitayā digbhāgabhedinām ekatvāsiddheḥ / taṃ prati kathaṃ nīlādirūpatayā paramāṇūnāṃ pratyakṣatvaṃ paurvāparyasya vānupalakṣaṇam bhrāntinimittenārthāntarasamāropād iti śakyaṃ vaktum //.*

89 MA 78ab: *bdag ni snang ba'i ngang can gyi / dngos po dgag par mi byed de /.*

90 "Subject failure" is Tillemans' gloss on the logical fallacy of the "unestablished basis" *(āśrayāsiddha)* in the Buddhist *pramāṇavāda* tradition. An example of subject failure occurs when one tries to assess the proposition "The present king of France is bald." In Tillemans' words (1998: 111), this proposition "is either false or neither true nor false, depending upon one's philosophical analysis, *because* there is no such king to whom we can ascribe baldness." Subject failure is a downfall in most forms of Indian debate; understandably, anti-realist Mādhyamikas are particularly open to the charge. For a brief overview of *āśrayāsiddha,* in post-Dharmakīrtian Buddhist thought in India, see Funayama (1991). For aspects of the development of Kamalaśīla's position, see Tillemans and Lopez (1998): 117, n. 8.

91 MAP *ad* MA 76–77 (Ichigō ed.: 255): *di snyam du gang zhig chos can snang ba la brten nas sgro btags pa'i rnam pa dgag pa'i phyir sgrub pa sbyor bar byed pa de la ni gzhi ma grub pa la sogs pa nyes pa'i glags mi thod na / khyod ni chos can snang ba 'gog par byed de / de lta na khyod la ci'i phyir gzhi ma grub pa la sogs pa'i glags mi thod snyams pa la / bdag ni zhes bya ba la sogs pa smos te / chos can snang ba 'di la yang rang bzhin yang dag par sgro btags pa dgag pa sgrub par byed kyi / chos can gyi rang gi ngo bo 'gog par ni ma yin pas mtshungs so //.* Cf. also MAV *ad* MA 67–68: *byis pa'i gnas skabs nas bzung ste / thams cad mkhyen pa'i ye shes kyi bar du myong ba gang ma brtags gcig pu na yid du 'ong ba'i rang bzhin la ni kho bos bkag pa med de /…//.*

92 Tillemans (1982): 122, n. 18.

93 See above, p. 134ff.

94 MAV *ad* MA 76–68 (Ichigō ed.: 256): *phan tshun mi mthun pa'i grub pa'i mthas bskyed pa chos can tha dad pa yongs su btang ste /….* Śāntarakṣita makes the same point in the TS, where he states that the subject of a debate should be "that commonly acknowledged and unanalyzed *artha* that appears in the awareness even of fishermen." See TS 2736–2738: *dharmibhedavikalpena yāśrayāsiddhir ucyate / sānumālakṣaṇājñānād dharmitvaṃ bhāsino yataḥ // avicāraprasiddho 'rtho yo 'yaṃ jñane 'vabhāsate / śanakāder api proktā tāvanmātrasya dharmitā // tatraiva hi vivādo 'yaṃ sampravṛttaḥ pravādinām / icchāracitabhede tu na vivādo 'sti kasyacit //.*

95 MA 76: *gzhung gis bskyed pa'i bye brag gi / chos can spangs nas mkhas pa dang / bud med byis pa'i bar dag la / grags par gyur pa'i dngos rnams la //.*

96 See Yotsuya (1999): 93, n. 72.

97 Candrakīrti's presentation and refutation of Bhāvaviveka's idea of the general subject occurs in PPMV (La Vallée Poussin ed.): 28–30. See Yotsuya (1999): 92–104. See also Tillemans (1990): 47, n. 107. mKhas grub cites and explains this passage in *sTong thun chen mo:* 325–329.

98 MAV *ad* MA 76–78 (Ichigō ed.: 256): *de lta bas na snang ba'i don ma bkag pa nyid kyis mngon par zhen pa med pa'i bsgrub pa dang / sgrub pa'i tha snyad 'jug pas chos thams cad rang bzhin med par smra ba la gnod pa ci yang med do //.*

99 MAP *ad* MA 76–78 (Ichigō ed.: 257): *rang gi grub pa'i mtha'i sgo nas chos can la sogs pa la brten pa med pa /.*

100 TS 1209: *svasya svasyāvabhāsasya vedane 'pi sa varttate / bāhyārthādhyavasāye yad dvayor 'pi samo yataḥ //.*

101 TS 1210: *timiropahatākṣo hi yathā prāha śaśidvayam / svasamāya tathā sarvā śābdī vyavahṛtir matā //.*

102 See TSP *ad* TS 3338 (Shastri ed.: 1060): *yat punar utkam anumānabalāvadhāritanairātmyānām api samutpadyante rāgādaya iti / tad ayuktam / yasmād bhāvanāmayaṃ sphuṭapratibhāsatayā nirātmakavastusākṣātkārijñānam avikalpakaṃ pramāṇaprasiddhārthaviṣayatayā cābhrāntaṃ tan nairātmyadarśanam ātmadarśanasyātyantonmūlanena pratipakṣo varṇito na śrutacintāmayam //* "But the following might be urged: even for those [persons] for whom selflessness has been ascertained by the strength of inference, [negative mental states such as] passion and so on arise. [Answer:] This is not right. For that vision of selflessness which is produced through meditation *(bhāvanāmaya),* which, because it appears clearly, is a nonconceptual awareness that directly apprehends the real thing, 'selflessness' *(nirātmaka),* and which, because its object has been established by a trustworthy means of awareness, is nonerroneous *(abhrānta)* is described as the antidote due to completely uprooting the vision of the self. [The vision of selflessness] which is produced through study and contemplation is not [the antidote]."

103 This may be in keeping with Jñānagarbha's position. See Eckel (1986).

104 Sellars (1956; 1997 repr.): 13.

5. The Satisfaction of No Analysis: On Tsong kha pa's Approach to Svātantrika-Madhyamaka

MALCOLM DAVID ECKEL

As every beginning student of Buddhism knows, Buddhists love to make lists. If you open a book on Buddhist teaching, you do not turn many pages before you learn that the Buddha taught four noble truths. If you turn a few more pages, you learn that the second truth is explained by a twelvefold chain of causes and the fourth by an eightfold path. This is not a tradition for the numerically challenged, nor is it a tradition for those who dislike complex systems of classification. I doubt that I will reveal a professional secret if I say that the proliferation of intellectual distinctions can be one of the least appealing aspects of Buddhist thought. There are times when the subtlety of distinctions within distinctions, like Winston Churchill's riddle wrapped in a mystery inside an enigma, is more likely to produce confusion than clarity. As often as not, readers are left to wonder why such small issues seemed to warrant so much attention. For those who find the profusion of categories perplexing, let it simply be said that perplexity is precious. If the classifications were obvious and the categories clear, there would be nothing to learn. It is only the unexpected concepts and puzzling details that force readers to confront the remoteness of the text and start the painstaking process of understanding.

For many students of Indian philosophy, this process begins, either directly or indirectly, with one of the classic Indian philosophical compendia.[1] These compendia have a venerable history, going back at least to the sixth century. They also have the advantage of organizing the major schools, concepts, and disputes in a distinctively Indian way. At first they look stable and formulaic, but behind these seemingly static systems lies a world where philosophers once negotiated the thrust and counterthrust of philosophical debate. To outsiders, the moves may now seem predictable and tightly circumscribed, like the moves of an ancient chess game. But someone who is sensitive to the nuances of the game can see strokes of genius and acts of imagination in the sacrifice of a bishop or the advance of a pawn. The only way to see an act of imagination in a complex and sophisticated game is to know the background of the game and read each play against the tradition that produced it—to know which moves are possible, which moves are expected, and which moves turn the game in unexpected directions.

If this is true of Indian philosophy in general, it is even more true of the categories used to classify individual traditions, like the Madhyamaka, or "Middle Way," school in India and Tibet. The Madhyamaka tradition was already five or six hundred years old in the eighth century, when Kamalaśīla won the debate at bSam yas and established the influence of Madhyamaka thought in the monastic culture of central Tibet. With many vicissitudes and a few key exceptions, the Madhyamaka tradition has dominated formal philosophical discourse in Tibet for more than a millennium, so much so that the moves on the Madhyamaka chessboard seem thoroughly mapped and predictable. The predictability, however, is an illusion. There is still as much room for surprise on the chessboard of Madhyamaka as there is on the chessboard that has bishops and rooks, as long as someone knows the subtleties of the game. This was even more true in the formative years of Tibetan philosophy, when Tibetan scholars we just beginning to explore the sources of the Indian Madhyamaka and map the possibilities of the game. To understand how someone can operate creatively within the established categories of Tibetan Madhyamaka, there is no better strategy than to look back at the early period in the Tibetan tradition and see how its earliest practitioners used their sources, classified their options, defined the key disputes, and laid out the rules of the game.

This paper will focus on one particularly influential text in the history of Tibetan philosophy and will attempt to answer a simple question: How did the author use his Indian sources to classify and map the intellectual options in the Madhyamaka tradition? The text is the *Drang dang nges pa'i don rnam par phye ba'i bstan bcos legs bshad snying po* (lit., *The Essence of Eloquence: A Treatise on the Differentiation of Interpretable and Definitive Meanings;* also known simply as the *Legs bshad snying po*),[2] written by Tsong kha pa (1357–1419) in 1407–1408 in his hermitage above Se ra Monastery, north of Lhasa.[3] Tsong kha pa's importance as the founder and intellectual inspiration for the dGe lugs pa monastic tradition is well known. The importance of *The Essence of Eloquence* also is well known. It was not Tsong kha pa's longest Madhyamaka work, and it was not even his last, but its conciseness and the force of its arguments have made it, in Jeffrey Hopkins's words, "*the* central source of philosophical fascination for a long tradition of Ge-luk-ba scholarship."[4]

The purpose of this essay is not simply to contribute to the understanding of Tsong kha pa's text, as influential as the text and its author may be, but to identify some of the ways Tsong kha pa took creative liberties with his sources, saw possibilities in their words that may previously have been overlooked, and shaped the possibilities of Tibetan debate just as a chess master crafts new variations on established patterns of play. This is an essay, in other words, about the creative appropriation of tradition. I also should add that this is intended, in a literal sense, to be an *essay.* Without knowing much more about the centuries of Madhyamaka interpretation that intervened between the time of Bhāvaviveka (6th c.) and Tsong kha pa (14th c.), it is difficult to speak with any confidence about Tsong kha pa's originality. How much of Tsong kha pa's apparent innovation should be attributed to his teacher Red mda' ba gzhon nu blo gros (1349–1412), for example, rather than to his own critical imagination is impossible to know without a thorough study of Red mda' ba and his sources. This essay is intended to be a "tentative effort in learning or practice" in the sense suggested by *Rollin's Ancient History* (1827): "These were considered only as essays preparatory to the great design."[5] But it also is meant to be a "specimen, sample, or example" of the work that still remains to be done on the language and texture of Tibetan appropriations of the Indian philosophical tradition.

Tsong kha pa's Account of Svātantrika-Madhyamaka

It is commonly assumed among scholars of Buddhism that there are two kinds of Madhyamaka, called Svātantrika and Prāsaṅgika. It also is assumed that the distinction between them involves a disagreement about logical procedure: Svātantrikas are said to hold what Edward Conze once called the "well-nigh incredible thesis" that Mādhyamikas should maintain valid, independent *(svatantra)* inferences,[6] while Prāsaṅgikas focus their logical labors on showing that opponents' assertions lead to untenable conclusions *(prasaṅga).*[7] Tsong kha pa respected this logical distinction, but for him the key difference between the Svātantrikas and the Prāsaṅgikas did not lie in the form of their arguments but in their approach to the elusive and problematic category of conventional truth. According to Tsong kha pa, all Mādhyamikas agreed that nothing could be established ultimately, or from the point of view of ultimate truth *(don dam par, paramārthataḥ),* but Mādhyamikas did not agree about what it meant to say that things are "established" or "accepted" *(grub pa, siddha)* or "presupposed" *(khas len pa, abhyupagata)* in a conventional sense.[8]

To someone who is not familiar with the internal problematic of the Madhyamaka tradition, this issue might seem to be nothing more than a small, intramural dispute between philosophers who otherwise are indistinguishable on important matters of belief and practice. But it was natural for Tsong kha pa to take the issue seriously. The issue had to do, first of all, with the understanding of a crucial verse in Nāgārjuna's *Mūlamadhyamakakārikās* (MMK, lit., *Root Verses on the Middle Way*), the founding text of the Madhyamaka school. In Nāgārjuna's account of the relationship between conventional and ultimate truth, he said, "It is impossible to teach the ultimate without being based on the conventional, and without understanding the ultimate, it is impossible to attain *nirvāṇa.*"[9] To understand ultimate truth was the goal of Madhyamaka thought, and teaching about the ultimate required a careful appropriation of conventional truth. But the problem of conventional truth had to do with more than teaching. It also touched on a series of basic Buddhist concerns about the world of practice, action, and everyday life: How can a person be serious about the conventional issues of life and still cultivate the awareness that the ordinary concepts of things have no more ultimate significance than a dream? What kinds of questions can be asked about conventional things? How closely can someone analyze them? At what point does a person simply have to be satisfied with the appearance of things and ask no more confusing questions about what they really are?

As its long title indicates *(The Essence of Eloquence: A Treatise on the Differentiation of Interpretable and Definitive Meanings),* Tsong kha pa's text begins with a question about scriptural interpretation: Which sūtras should be considered definitive and which ones need further interpretation? Tsong kha pa identifies two possible Mahāyāna strategies to answer this question. The first, in the *Saṃdhinirmocana (Untying the Knot* or *Revealing the Hidden Intention) Sūtra,* leads Tsong kha pa to an analysis of the Yogācāra doctrine of "three natures" *(trisvabhāva).* The second, in the *Akṣayamatinirdeśa (The Teaching of Akṣayamati) Sūtra,* leads him to his analysis of the Madhyamaka doctrine of "two truths" *(satyadvaya).* Each section of the text begins as a discussion of scripture and then gives way to a discussion of reality itself.

Within the Madhyamaka section there are, of course, two parts: the first discusses Svātantrika, and the second, Prāsaṅgika. We would expect the concept of conventional truth to figure prominently at the beginning of both these parts, and that is precisely what happens. Tsong kha pa starts his discussion of Svātantrika with an argument by Bhāvaviveka[10] (generally regarded as the "founder" of the Svātantrika tradition) against the Yogācāra approach to "imagined nature" *(parikalpitasvabhāva),* the first of the three natures. Tsong kha pa then returns to the concept at the beginning of his section on the Prāsaṅgikas. In that section the purpose is not to show the difference between Yogācāra and Madhyamaka but to draw a clear line between the work of Candrakīrti (the most influential Prāsaṅgika theorist) and his Svātantrika predecessors. In both cases, the concept of conventional reality serves as the key criterion of distinction.

Tsong kha pa's argument leads us back to an Indian passage that is buried, like a forgotten footnote, at the end of the twenty-fifth chapter of Bhāvaviveka's *Prajñāpradīpa* (PrP, lit., *Lamp of Wisdom*), his commentary on Nāgārjuna's MMK.[11] The twenty-fifth chapter has to do with *nirvāṇa.* The last verse of this chapter says, "The cessation of all grasping *(sarvopalambhopaśama)* is the auspicious *(śiva)* cessation of discursive ideas *(prapañcopaśama);* the Buddha taught no Dharma anywhere to anyone."[12] As often happens in Madhyamaka sources, the issue of teaching coincides again with the issue of reality, in this case the reality of *nirvāṇa* itself. In his commentary, Bhāvaviveka introduces this verse with the argument of an objector: "*Nirvāṇa* must ultimately exist, because the Buddha taught the Dharma so that [*nirvāṇa*] could be attained."[13] For Bhāvaviveka, the problem with this objection lies in the claim that the Buddha taught the Dharma. If this statement is intended to be conventional, it cannot be used establish the *ultimate* existence of *nirvāṇa.* If it is intended to be ultimate, it is false, as the verse itself indicates: from the ultimate point of view, the Buddha did not teach the Dharma to anyone. Bhāvaviveka quotes the verse, uses it as the occasion for some intriguing comments about the Buddha's silence,[14] then introduces another objection about the nature of reality. This objection comes from a Yogācāra opponent: "If it is true that 'the cessation of all grasping is the auspicious cessation of discursive ideas,' then it is impossible to repudiate *(apavāda)* dependent *(paratantra)* [nature], which is the means by which this [cessation] is attained."[15] This objection then elicits Bhāvaviveka's full analysis of the Yogācāra doctrine of three natures.

Bhāvaviveka's analysis of the three natures has its share of obscurities, but the underlying point is quite simple. Bhāvaviveka focuses on Yogācāra views about the *reality* of the three natures. According to the Yogācāra objector, imagined nature *(parikalpitasvabhāva)* does not exist (or is not real), while dependent nature *(paratantrasvabhāva)* and absolute nature *(parinispanna-svabhāva)* do exist (or are real). Bhāvaviveka criticizes these two claims by analyzing them from the point of view of the Madhyamaka doctrine of two truths. If the Yogācāra objector says that imagined nature does not exist, is this negation meant to be ultimate or conventional? If it is meant to be ultimate, the Yogācāra position is no different from the Madhyamaka. If it is conventional, it involves, in Bhāvaviveka's words, a "repudiation" or "unjustified denial" *(apavāda)* of real things: it denies things that are conventionally real.

What kind of thing does Bhāvaviveka have in mind when he says, against the Yogācāra, that imagined nature must be conventionally real? What does he think are "imagined" things? He suggests an answer to this question by the way he handles the time-honored Indian maxim of the snake and the rope. When someone walks down a road on a dark night, sees a coiled rope and mistakes it for a snake, the imagined "snake" does not exist in that place on the road where there is a coiled rope. But, Bhāvaviveka insists, this does not mean that snakes are completely nonexistent. There may be snakes elsewhere, on other dark roads, and it is a useful conventional skill to distinguish imagined snakes from real snakes before they sink their conventional teeth into your conventional foot and bring your conventional life to a conventional end. Bhāvaviveka puts the point like this: "To say that no snake exists even conventionally *(vyavahāreṇa)* is contradicted *(viruddha)* by common sense (or by a point that is generally accepted, *prasiddha*)."[16] This conventional point is matched by a corresponding point about the Yogācāra definitions of dependent and absolute nature. If the Yogācāra claim about the existence of dependent and absolute nature is intended to be conventional, there is no problem. Bhāvaviveka agrees that they exist conventionally. But if the claim is intended to be ultimate, it involves a "superimposition" *(samāropa)* or unwarranted reification, and it is subject to all the customary Madhyamaka arguments against the ultimate reality of anything, including the ultimate itself.

Tsong kha pa takes the raw material of this argument and extracts a formula that has had far-reaching implications for Tibetan understanding of the Madhyamaka tradition. According to Tsong kha pa, when Bhāvaviveka says that the Yogācāra denial of imagined nature contradicts something that is generally accepted" *(prasiddha),* Bhāvaviveka indicates that for him conventional snakes are "generally accepted." Bhāvaviveka makes the same point in his analysis of the standard syllogism, where he says simply that conventional entities, like coiled snakes, are "accepted" or "established" *(siddha)* conventionally. Tsong kha pa puts the word "established" *(siddha)* together with the Yogācāra claim that imagined nature is "empty of identity" *(lakṣaṇaniḥsvabhāva)* and, with a few associative leaps, says that, for Bhāvaviveka, things are *established with their own identity (rang gi mtshan nyid kyis grub pa, *svalakṣaṇasiddha) conventionally.* This formula becomes the key to Tsong kha pa's distinction between Svātantrika- and Prāsaṅgika-Madhyamaka.

To see how Tsong kha pa arrives at this crucial point, it is helpful to look at the full text of his argument:[17]

> When Bhāvaviveka explains Nāgārjuna's intention, how does he explain the two kinds of ultimate no-self? This becomes clear when one understands how he specifies the three identities *(mtshan nyid, lakṣaṇa).* In the *Prajñāpradīpa* he says:
>
> > In this case, if you say that imagined nature *(kun brtags pa'i ngo bo nyid, parikalpitasvabhāva),* which consists of mental or verbal speech about "material form," does not exist, this is a repudiation *(skur pa 'debs pa, apavāda)* of a real entity *(dngos po, vastu),* because it is a repudiation of mental or verbal speech.
>
> If the imagined [nature] that is mentioned in the [Yogācāra] claim that imagined nature has no identity *(mtshan nyid ngo bo nyid med do, lakṣaṇaniḥsvabhāva)* consists of the thought or act of speech that attributes natures *(ngo bo, svabhāva)* and particular characters *(khyad pa, viśeṣa)* [to things], then both [the thought and the act of speech] are included in the aggregates *(phung po, skandha).* [Bhāvaviveka] says that it is a repudiation [of real things] for there to be no identity *(mtshan nyid ngo bo nyid, lakṣaṇasvabhāva)* in dependent *(gzhan dbang, paratantra)* [nature]. Therefore, he must think that dependent [nature] has identity.
>
> In the *Saṃdhinirmocana [Sūtra]* it says that if something is not established *(grub pa, siddha)* with its own identity *(rang gi mtshan nyid, svalakṣaṇa),* then it is empty of identity *(mtshan nyid ngo bo*

nyid med pa, lakṣaṇaniḥsvabhāva). Since these [Svātantrikas?] also determine the meaning of this sūtra, it is clear that they think that dependent [nature] has a nature that is established with its own identity.

In the *Prajñāpradīpa,* [Bhāvaviveka] takes as his [opponent's] preliminary position *(phyogs snga, pūrvapakṣa)* the claim that imagined [nature] has no identity because it is not included in the five [categories] that consist of names *(ming, nāma),* distinguishing marks *(rgyu mtshan, nimitta),* concepts *(rnam par rtog pa, vikalpa),* correct knowledge *(yang dag pa'i ye shes, samyagjñāna),* and thusness *(de bzhin nyid, tathatā).* In the *Saṃgraha* it says that [imagined nature] is not included in these five categories. In that [text] names are said to exclude [imagined nature], and distinguishing marks are said to be the basis of designation for imagined nature (i.e., the reality to which it refers). If imagined [nature] is not a real entity *(dngos po, vastu)* it cannot be one of the first four categories *(chos, dharma),* and if it is conceptually constructed, it cannot be thusness. In the *Madhyāntavibhāga* it says that names are imagined, but Sthiramati explains that this refers to the objects referred to by words, not to the words themselves. In that [text] it says that distinguishing marks are dependent [nature], but it intends [to refer only to] the distinguishing marks of conditioned states *('du byed),* since the *Saṃgraha* says that these [distinguishing marks] can also be unconditioned.

Svabhāva (own nature), *prakṛti* (original nature), *svalakṣaṇa* (own identity) and so forth are often mentioned in Prāsaṅgika treatises in relation to conventional existence, and there are many [references to conventional reality being] *svabhāvāsiddha* (not established with their own nature), *svabhāvānutpanna* (not arising with their own nature), *vastvasiddha* (not established as a real thing), and so forth, in the treatises of this Master [Bhāvaviveka], so it seems difficult to distinguish between the two. But this explanation of the presence or absence of identity in the teachings of the *Saṃdhinirmocana* is the clearest source for the [claim that] this Master thinks that things are established with their own identity conventionally.

Therefore he thinks that [it is possible to] understand the definition of the two forms of no-self completely without understanding that persons and phenomena are empty *(niḥsvabhāva)* in such a way that they are not established with any identity of their own. There will be a later explanation of the negandum *(dgag bya, pratiṣedhya)* that he attributes to both kinds of no-self when he uses a kind of negation that does not apply merely to something that is established with its own identity. In the *Prajñāpradīpa* it says,

> If [the opponent] says that the objects imagined by these two [mental or verbal speech] do not exist at all, like the snake [imagined] in place of a rope, [our response is that] these imagined [objects] do not not exist. When the mind is confused by similarity, the object that it imagines may not exist right there [in the place where it seems to appear], but this does not mean that it does not exist when there is a coiled snake conventionally.

This shows that the example is flawed when [an opponent] claims that imagined [nature] is not an act of designation but is the object that is imagined when an ordinary person applies words or concepts, like the snake that is imagined in place of a rope.

This means that, when someone thinks a rope is a snake, it is not reasonable to use this nonexistent, imagined object as an example for the nonexistence (*mtshan nyid ngo bo med pa, lakṣaṇasvabhāvābhāva,* literally, nonexistence with identity) of the object that is imagined as having a nature *(ngo bo, svabhāva)* or particular character *(khyad par, viśeṣa)* when someone designates material form, and so forth, as being "this" or "that." This is because the [Mādhyamika] opponent can respond to this by saying that the object *(yul, viṣaya)* that is grasped when someone thinks that material form is material form exists conventionally, even though the object that is grasped when someone thinks that material form is feeling does not exist, just as the object that is grasped when someone thinks that a snake is a snake exists conventionally, even though the object that is grasped when someone thinks that a rope is a snake does not exist.

Here existence and nonexistence mean existence and nonexistence with identity *(mtshan nyid ngo bo, lakṣaṇasvabhāva),* so he is saying that the object that is imagined as having a nature or particular character does not have nonexistent identity conventionally.

If he is saying that it contradicts common sense *(grags pas gnod*

> *pa, prasiddhaviruddha)* conventionally for there to be no snake where there is a coiled snake, then he must be saying [that it also contradicts common sense] for no object to be grasped when someone thinks that a coiled snake is a snake conventionally.
>
> He does say, however, that someone who denies that there ultimately is any real entity agrees with the Madhyamaka. In other words, the Madhyamaka approach is to say that, when someone thinks that the coiled snake is a snake, the object that is grasped does not have real identity ultimately. So he says in the *Prajñāpradīpa* that anyone who intends to claim that anything whose nature or particular character is imagined has no identity should accept the reasoning of the Madhyamaka.[18]

Why does Tsong kha pa make so much of an argument that seems to appear as an afterthought in Bhāvaviveka's text? One reason has to do with Tsong kha pa's historical situation. Like other Tibetan philosophers in the thirteenth and fourteenth centuries, a century or two after Muslim incursions led to the destruction of the great Indian monasteries, Tsong kha pa faced the diversity of the Indian Mahāyāna without any definitive Indian guide. The scriptures and their commentaries took widely different approaches to fundamental questions, and Tsong kha pa needed a model that could set the Indian traditions in order and distinguish which was correct. He found this model in the Indian philosophical compendium—the *siddhānta* or "doctrine" text—with individual chapters on different philosophical traditions and a critical procedure to distinguish right from wrong. When he looked to India for an example of this kind of text, Bhāvaviveka loomed particularly large. The earliest known model for a *siddhānta* text in the Buddhist tradition (perhaps in all of Indian philosophy) was Bhāvaviveka's *Madhyamakahṛdayakārikā*s (MHK, lit., *Verses on the Heart of the Middle Way*) with their commentary, the *Tarkajvālā* (TJ, lit., *Flame of Reason*).[19] When Tsong kha pa turned to Bhāvaviveka to distinguish Madhyamaka from Yogācāra, he was turning to one of the key figures in the history of Indian philosophical classification, not only for the Mahāyāna but for all the major Indian traditions, including the Hīnayāna (which he called the tradition of the "Disciples" or *śrāvaka*s) and Brahmanical traditions such as the Sāṃkhya, Mīmāṃsā, and Vedānta.

Although it was natural for Tsong kha pa to use Bhāvaviveka to help him distinguish the Madhyamaka from the Yogācāra, it is less clear why he chose to focus on the account of the Yogācāra in the twenthy-fifth chapter of the PrP. He could just as well have used the longer and more detailed account of the Yogācāra in the fifth chapter of the MHK and TJ.[20] One reason for his choice might be the relationship between the PrP and the sources of the Madhyamaka tradition itself. The twenty-fifth chapter of the PrP was not an independent text but a commentary on the verses of Nāgārjuna. Perhaps he thought that the best way to drive a wedge between the Madhyamaka and Yogācāra interpretations of scripture was with a Madhyamaka attack on Yogācāra interpretations of Nāgārjuna. In any case, the seemingly marginal position of Bhāvaviveka's comments about the Yogācāra in the PrP should not obscure their importance. Together with the fifth chapter of the MHK, they set the stage for all later interpretation of the relationship between these two Mahāyāna traditions.

Tsong kha pa's use of Bhāvaviveka to refute the Yogācāra has a double function in his own text. It sets the Madhyamaka apart from the Yogācāra position discussed earlier in the text, but it also looks forward to the discussion that lies ahead. In the passage just quoted, Tsong kha pa says that Prāsaṅgikas and Svātantrikas at first seem hard to distinguish: they use words like "own nature" *(svabhāva),* "original nature" *(prakṛti),* and "own identity" *(svalakṣaṇa)* in similar ways. But he goes on to say that Bhāvaviveka's explanation "of the presence or absence of identity in the teachings of the *Saṃdhinirmocana* is the clearest source for the [claim that] this Master thinks that things are established with their own identity conventionally." The net effect of these words is to say that Bhāvaviveka's attack on the Yogācāra is going to give Tsong kha pa the tool he needs to split the Svātantrika from the Prāsaṅgika. Much depends on this distinction, not just for Tsong kha pa's understanding of Madhyamaka, but for our own understanding of Tsong kha pa. To understand Tsong kha pa's critical procedure and to see how he shapes the concept of Madhyamaka, we have to look at the way he uses his sources. We have to ask, in other words, whether Tsong kha pa gives an accurate reading of Bhāvaviveka's approach to conventional reality.

Bhāvaviveka on Conventional Reality: The Indian Evidence

Tsong kha pa argues that Bhāvaviveka thinks things like coiled snakes are *established with their own identity (rang gi mtshan nyid kyis grub pa, *svalakṣaṇasiddha) conventionally.* When we look back at Bhāvaviveka's own work with this formula in mind, the first thing we notice is that Bhāvaviveka himself does not use these words in this way. Tsong kha pa does not cite any passages where Bhāvaviveka actually uses this formula to characterize his own position. He has had to piece the formula together by implication from Bhāvaviveka's criticism of the Yogācāra. Tsong kha pa indicates as much in his comments about the interpretation of the *Saṃdhinirmocana Sūtra:*

> In the *Saṃdhinirmocana [Sūtra]* it says that if something is not established *(grub pa, siddha)* with its own identity *(rang gi mtshan nyid, svalakṣaṇa),* then it is empty of identity *(mtshan nyid ngo bo nyid med pa, lakṣaṇaniḥsvabhāva).* Since these [Svātantrikas?] also determine the meaning of this sūtra, it is clear that they think that dependent [nature] has a nature that is established with its own identity.

Tsong kha pa refers to the interpreters of the *Saṃdhinirmocana* in the plural, without identifying Bhāvaviveka directly or quoting from one of his works. One reason for the plural might be that the singular alone does not work. Bhāvaviveka himself does not mention the *Saṃdhinirmocana* in his own account of the Yogācāra and does not draw the conclusion from it that Tsong kha pa alleges.

Reading Tsong kha pa's passage from the point of view of the Indian sources, you could argue that Tsong kha pa forces Bhāvaviveka to say something that would have seemed unnecessary to him and might even have made him uncomfortable. In effect, Tsong kha pa says that, when Bhāvaviveka rejects the Yogācāra view about the nonexistence of imagined nature, he has to commit himself to *the Yogācāra view* of its existence. That is, he has to commit himself to the position that imagined nature exists, conventionally, in precisely the same way dependent nature does, with its own identity *(svalakṣaṇa).* But it is a cardinal principle in Bhāvaviveka's work to insist that, when he denies his opponents' assertions, he does not have to commit himself to its opposite.[21] He is prepared to accept that coiled snakes that are not falsely superimposed on coiled ropes have *some* conventional reality, but his method does not require him to accept the Yogācāra definition of that reality. Nor does he seem eager to accept this aspect of the Yogācāra as a stepping-stone to something else. In the fifth chapter of the MHK, he compares the Yogācāra approach to the doctrine of mind-only *(citta-mātra)* to people who cover themselves with mud before they take a bath.[22] If they really want to be clean, he says, it is better for them to stay out of the mud in the first place. Looking at Bhāvaviveka in his own right, without the lens of Tsong kha pa's interpretation, we have to ask how plausible it is that this thinker, who was so committed to removing misconceptions about "own-nature" *(svabhāva),* would bathe in the mud of "own-identity" *(svalakṣaṇa)* before washing it away.

Once this is said, however, it also is important to acknowledge that Bhāvaviveka shows a remarkable willingness to specify precisely what he thinks is conventionally real. Sometimes he does this in a way that is almost guileless; sometimes he does it with such subtlety that one suspects he is making a wry Madhyamaka joke. An example of the former appears from time to time in his commentary on Nāgārjuna's MMK. As is well known, Bhāvaviveka thinks that Mādhyamikas are obligated to construct independent *(svatantra)* syllogisms. Among the rules for a valid syllogism is the requirement that the basis or locus *(āśraya)* of the properties in the syllogism be accepted *(siddha)* by both parties. This means that, when one person is trying to convince another that there is fire on a mountain, both of them have to agree that there is a mountain. Here the mountain is the basis *(āśraya)* of the syllogism and fire-possession is the inferred property *(sādhyadharma).* Bhāvaviveka argues that there are no mountains ultimately, so the mountain that functions as the basis of the syllogism has to be accepted *(siddha)* conventionally if it is to be accepted at all.

This is fine for mountains, perhaps, but what about more problematic categories like the self *(ātman)*? Is there any accepted basis *(siddhāśraya)* for Nāgārjuna's assertion at the beginning of the eighteenth chapter of the MMK, "If [the self] were different from the aggregates, it would not have the characteristics of the aggregates"?[23] In keeping with his commitment to independent syllogisms, Bhāvaviveka transforms this line into the following assertion: "Ultimately a self that is different from the aggregates does not exist."[24] Bhāvaviveka acknowledges that this new assertion presents an obvious problem: "Some think that because the Mādhyamikas do not accept the self as a real category, it is wrong for us to apply attributes *(viśeṣaṇa)* to it, just as [it is wrong] to describe the son of a barren woman as black or white."[25] He responds by specifying what he means by "self" conventionally: "We use the word 'self' because of the process of rebirth. The term *(prajñapti)* 'self' is used to refer to consciousness *(vijñāna),* so we speak of consciousness as being the self. The Lord himself spoke this way when he said: 'A disciplined mind is happy, and with a disciplined mind one attains happiness.' In another sūtra [he said]: 'The self is the self's protector; what other protector can there be? With self well-disciplined, a wise man attains *nirvāṇa.*' Therefore, since we accept the self conventionally in a general sense, there is no fault in our rejecting attributes that we do not accept."[26] He qualifies his position by saying that he only accepts consciousness as a self "in a general sense" *(sāmānyena),* but he is not reluctant to say that the word "self" refers to something from a conventional point of view.[27]

The question of reference comes up again in a more subtle and complex way in Bhāvaviveka's response to Dignāga's theory of *apoha* ("exclusion") in the fifth chapter of the MHK. For Bhāvaviveka the Yogācāra includes not just the works of Asaṅga and Vasubandhu but the system of Buddhist logic formulated by Dignāga in the *Pramāṇasamuccaya* (PS, lit., *Compendium of the Means of Valid Knowledge*). A significant feature of this system is Dignāga's theory of language. According to Dignāga, words acquire their meaning not by referring directly to an object but by their "exclusion of the other" *(anyāpoha,* or, simply, *apoha).* A common example of Dignāga's position is the word "cow." Dignāga argues that the word cannot refer directly to a cow, since all reality is momentary; it can only exclude things that are not cows. The meaning of the word consists simply of this exclusion. There is no need to go into the details of Bhāvaviveka's response to this position. It is sufficient simply to note that he attacks Dignāga's concept of "exclusion" by constructing a familiar Madhyamaka dilemma: if there is no real cow, the act of exclusion cannot be a property of a cow, and if the act of exclusion belongs to something other than a cow, it cannot function as a way of referring to a cow.[28]

The most surprising aspect of Bhāvaviveka's argument against *apoha* is not that he finds it objectionable but that he uses it as an occasion to outline his own position about the conventional relationship between words and objects. What does he think words refer to? He says that they name an "emptiness of that which is dissimilar" *(vijātīyena śūnyatvam).*[29] This specific type of emptiness functions as a universal *(sāmānya)* in two ways: by distinguishing a particular thing from other things that reside in different continua *(vijātīya)* and by creating a perception of similarity in anything that resides in the same continuum *(tulyajātīya).* The key to this concept lies in the relationship between a particular instance of emptiness and the object in which it resides. Strictly speaking, an emptiness *(śūnyatvam)* is nothing more than an absence *(abhāva),* like the absence of a pot on a table. What we call the absence of a pot is nothing more than the surface of the table, minus the pot. The same is true of the emptiness that Bhāvaviveka takes to be the meaning of words: the emptiness of that which is dissimilar, in the end, is equivalent (conventionally) to the thing itself. Bhāvaviveka puts it this way: "'Cowness' is not different from the dewlap, and so forth [that are the specific features of a cow]. And what is this? It is not different from the thing itself *(bhāvasvabhāva).*"[30]

John Dunne and Tom Tillemans have pointed out that Bhāvaviveka's analysis of Dignāga is very similar to Dharmakīrti's and may mark an important stage in the evolution of the *apoha* theory from Dignāga to Dharmakīrti.[31] Dharmakīrti argues that words do not refer to a mere exclusion (as Dignāga says) but to a particular that possesses a universal.[32] What intrigues me most about Bhāvaviveka's argument is not its historical significance, as important as that is, but rather the insight it gives us to Bhāvaviveka's philosophical imagination. There is a strong sense of symmetry that connects this form of emptiness (the emptiness of that which is dissimilar) with the emptiness that characterizes ultimate reality. What is ultimate reality for Bhāvaviveka? Emptiness of self or, to use the more precise formula, emptiness of intrinsic nature *(svabhāvaśūnyatvam).* What conventional reality do words refer to? Emptiness of other, or to be precise, emptiness of whatever is dissimilar *(vijātīyena śūnyatvam).* In both cases, the nature of the thing is equivalent to an emptiness. I take this to mean that even when Bhāvaviveka is specifying the conventional meaning of a term, he does it in a way that mirrors its emptiness. One form of emptiness recalls the other and reminds the reader that both belong to a system of two truths.

When Bhāvaviveka approaches conventional reality with this degree of complexity, it is difficult to give a simple evaluation of Tsong kha pa's reading of his position. It is important to recognize, first of all, that Tsong kha pa has forced Bhāvaviveka in a direction that is foreign to his own way of thinking. Bhāvaviveka does not refer to conventional reality as "established with its own identity," and there are good reasons to think that he would have resisted this approach. On the other hand, there is no question that Bhāvaviveka thinks it useful and even logically necessary to specify the reference of conventional terms. You can argue that Tsong kha pa distorts Bhāvaviveka's position for his own intellectual purposes, but you can argue just as plausibly that Tsong kha pa draws implications from Bhāvaviveka's work that would have eluded even Bhāvaviveka, but were present implicitly in his work. Either way, whether Tsong kha pa's argument is read as a distortion of the Indian sources or as a careful elaboration of their implications, it is clear that Tsong kha pa's text is more than a slavish reproduction of the Indian tradition. It is a strong act of philosophical interpretation, and it is an interpretation that prepares him for an equally strong reading of Bhāvaviveka's opponents and successors.

Tsong kha pa on the Distinction between Svātantrika- and Prāsaṅgika-Madhyamaka

When Tsong kha pa finishes his analysis of the Svātantrika, the next step is to distinguish Bhāvaviveka's method from the Prāsaṅgika method of Candrakīrti. To do this, he looks more deeply at the implications of the formula he extracted from Bhāvaviveka's work. "What does it mean," he asks, "to grasp something as established with its own identity *(rang gi mtshan nyid kyis grub pa, svalakṣaṇasiddha)*?" The answer is important enough, once again, to quote in its entirety:

> First of all, there are philosophers whose method is to search *(btsal)* for the meaning *(don)* of the conventional term *(tha snyad btags pa)* "person" in the conventional sentence, "A certain person performs a certain action and experiences a certain result," and ask whether this person is the same as the aggregates or different from them. When they find *(rnyed)* that one position or the other is possible, they have a place to put *('jog sa)* the [word] "person," and they can refer to it as the accumulator of karma, and so forth. If they do not find [any such possibility], they cannot posit [such a person], and they are not content *(tshim pa)* with the mere conventional term *(tha snyad btags pa tsam)* "person." When they have analyzed *(dpyod pa)* or searched for a referent *(btags pa'i btags gzhi)* for this conventional term and then posit [its existence], they are positing a person that is established with its own identity *(rang gi mtshan nyid kyis grub pa)*. All Buddhists from the Vaibhāṣikas to the Svātantrikas hold this position.[33]

A close look at the terminology of this passage shows how persuasive Tsong kha pa can be when he plays with the formulas of Buddhist philosophical rhetoric. He starts with a sequence of ordinary actions drawn from ordinary life. Think of a cook in a kitchen who picks up a spoon or a student in a library who picks up a book. Where should the spoon be stored? Where should the book be shelved? To answer these questions, you have to "search" *(btsal)* for the right "place" *(sa)*. When you "find" *(rnyed)* it, you can "put" *('jog)* the spoon or the book away. Tsong kha pa's words suggest that the language of Madhyamaka starts right here, in ordinary life, and then the process of reflection forces readers to ask serious questions about what these seemingly transparent actions and words actually mean.

The first hint of a movement toward analytical discourse in this passage (apart from the word "person," which already situates the passage in the midst of Buddhist discourse about the self), is the word *'jog*. In ordinary language it means to "put, place, settle, assign,"[34] but an informed reader of this text would hear it as an echo of the technical expression *rnam par 'jog pa*, the Tibetan equivalent of the Sanskrit *vyavasthāpana*, which means to "establish, determine, or define." Robert A. F. Thurman translates the word as "posit," and he is certainly right that it acquires this technical force as the paragraph develops. The slide toward analytical discourse is reinforced by the rest of the paragraph. "Searching" *(btsal)* is equated with "analyzing" *(dpyod)*, and "putting" or "positing" *('jog)* is equated with establishing something as having its own identity.[35]

Carried along by Tsong kha pa's subtle slide from ordinary experience to the technical language of philosophy is a group of wayward Buddhists who make the mistake of not being "content" *(tshim)* with "mere" *(tsam)* words. The sly echo in the phrase *tsam gyis mi tshim* seems to function as a way of leading the reader into another area of technical discourse from eighth-century Indian Madhyamaka. Indian sources after the time of Dharmakīrti commonly define relative or conventional truth with a three-part formula: relative truth "satisfies without analysis" *(avicāramanohara)*, "arises dependently" *(pratītyasamutpanna)*, and is "capable of effective action" *(arthakriyāsamartha)*.[36] To a reader who is familiar with the literature of this period, Tsong kha pa's simple words carry enormous weight. He is saying that Svātantrika-Mādhyamikas are not *satisfied* to accept conventional truth *without analysis* but insist on analyzing conventional things until they can find something that is *established with its own identity*. By insisting on this kind of analysis, they are contradicting one of the most basic and widely-acknowledged features of conventional truth.

What does Tsong kha pa mean by suggesting that someone should be *satisfied with no analysis*? Does he mean that we should close up shop, call off the rest of the day's work, and take a long walk in the woods? Or are there questions we can ask about the words we use or the things we do that stop short of this prohibition against analysis? Tsong kha pa responds to this question by carrying out a close reading of a key passage in the first chapter of Candrakīrti's *Prasannapadā* (PPMV).[37] The argument is precipitated by an opponent who wants to say that "hardness" is the "intrinsic identity" *(svalakṣaṇa)* of earth, even though there ultimately is no difference between the intrinsic identity called "hardness" and earth itself. The opponent gives two examples, "the body of a pestle" and "the head of Rāhu," and argues that these two expressions play a legitimate role in conventional usage, even though a pestle is nothing but a body, and Rāhu, the demon who swallows the moon when there is an eclipse, is nothing but a head. Candrakīrti argues that the words "body of a pestle" and "head of Rāhu" can be used to answer legitimate questions in ordinary usage *(laukikavyavahāra)*. If someone mentions the word "body" or "head," he says, it is perfectly understandable for someone else to ask, "Whose body?" or "Whose head?" These questions can express legitimate curiosity. But there is no reason for anyone to be curious about hardness and earth: everyone knows that earth is hard.[38]

Well, then, isn't this also true about Rāhu and the pestle? When we look closely, don't we "find" *(upalambha)* that Rāhu is identical to his head and the pestle to its body? For Candrakīrti, this attempt to *find* something is the crux of the problem.[39] He says: "In ordinary usage *(laukike vyavahāre)* one does not engage in this kind of analysis *(itthaṃvicāra)*, and ordinary things exist without analysis."[40] In other words, we can ask lots of interesting questions about conventional reality and learn a great deal from the answers, but we cannot find exactly what words refer to without straying into the domain of ultimate truth, where ultimately there is nothing to find.

The Satisfaction of No Analysis

This concept of analysis lets Tsong kha pa draw a sharp distinction between the Svātantrikas and the Prāsaṅgikas: one group *analyzes* things conventionally and the other does not. The distinction conveys a satisfying sense of clarity, but it poses a problem. If we look closely at Tsong kha pa's Indian sources, we find that the distinction is not as sharp as it appears in Tsong kha pa's text. By the eighth century, the concept of no analysis seems to have become a standard feature of Madhyamaka, regardless of a thinker's traditional affiliation. Jñānagarbha, an eighth-century Mādhyamika who is considered part of the Svātantrika lineage, says that relative truth exists "as it is seen" or "as it is presented to cognition" *(yathādarśana)*, and he insists that it cannot be analyzed.[41] His teacher, Śrīgupta, defines conventional things by saying, "They satisfy only when they are not analyzed, from such things other things seem to arise, and such things produce specific effective action."[42] Śāntarakṣita uses the same formula in the *Madhyamakālaṃkāra* (MA, lit., *Ornament of the Middle Way*): "Whatever satisfies only when it is not analyzed, has the property of arising and ceasing, and is capable of effective action is considered relative."[43] The same formula appears in sources that would normally be ascribed to the Prāsaṅgika branch of the school, such as Atiśa's *Satyadvayāvatāra* (lit., *Introduction to the Two Truths*): "A phenomenon *(dharma)* which arises and is destroyed, which only satisfies when it is not analyzed *(avicāraramaṇīya),* and is capable of efficiency *(arthakriyāsāmarthyavat)*—is maintained to be the genuine relative truth."[44] By the time of Tsong kha pa the concept of no analysis gave very little critical leverage to distinguish between Svātantrika and Prāsaṅgika views of conventional truth.

Fortunately Tsong kha pa notices this problem and has a ready response: he focuses on the words of Jñānagarbha's definition of conventional reality as "as it is seen" or "as it is perceived" *(yathādarśana),* and says that Svātantrikas attribute conventional existence to things only when they are "seen" in reliable sense perception. Tsong kha pa argues that Jñānagarbha's "seeing" constitutes the Svātantrikas' "searching for and finding" the conventional identity of things. Prāsaṅgikas, in contrast, treat things as conventionally real through the mere application of conventional terms, without attempting to find the reference of their terms.[45]

By focusing on the phrase *yathādarśana,* Tsong kha pa does indeed identify a crucial aspect of Jñānagarbha's epistemology. Jñānagarbha divides the two truths between the two most important means of valid cognition, perception *(pratyakṣa)* and inference *(anumāna),* just as Dignāga and Dharmakīrti did, but he turns them upside down. Dignāga and Dharmakīrti say that perception gives access to ultimate truth, while inference gives access only to conventional truth.[46] Jñānagarbha says that conventional truth is a product of perception *(pratyakṣa)* and ultimate truth a product of rational investigation *(nyāya).*[47] On the face of it, this seems to be a very odd use of the distinction between inference and perception. Inference, after all, uses words, and it is virtually an axiom in Buddhist philosophy that words obscure and falsify their objects. (Bhāvaviveka indicates as much in his own analysis of the meaning of words.) But Jñānagarbha is saying simply that perception itself, with its presumption of real objects, can only be viewed as a conventional activity. And the way to cut through the illusion of perception is not to use some other form of perception, but to analyze the nature of things in the style of Nāgārjuna and his great commentators. Eventually this process of rational analysis, which Jñānagarbha's commentator calls the "expressible ultimate" *(paryāyaparamārtha),* leads to the cessation of all concepts, a cessation that can only be represented (if it can be represented at all) by silence.[48] Jñānagarbha's commentator refers to the final cessation of concepts as the "inexpressible ultimate" *(aparyāyaparamārtha).* Jñānagarbha illustrates this cessation with the well-known story of Vimalakīrti's silence.[49] When Jñānagarbha refers to conventional truth as *yathādarśana,* he is not using words casually or loosely. The term expresses the actual structure of his epistemology and his understanding of the two truths.

By isolating this feature of Jñānagarbha's thought, Tsong kha pa seems to have settled the matter for good, if it were not for one further complication. Candrakīrti goes on from the passage about the head of Rāhu, in a section that Tsong kha pa did not discuss, and presents his own positive understanding of the means of cognition *(pramāṇa).* We would expect nothing less from a philosopher whose world was so decisively shaped by both Buddhist and Hindu logicians. Candrakīrti concludes with the following comments:

> These [four means of cognition] are established *(sidhyanti)* in such a way that they depend on one another. When there are means of cognition, there are objects of cognition, and when there are objects of cognition, there are means of cognition. The means and the objects of cognition are not established *(siddhi)* as having any intrinsic nature *(svabhāva).* So let ordinary usage *(laukikam)* be just as it is seen *(yathādṛṣṭam),* and enough with this *prasaṅga*! We will now explain the subject at hand, establishing *(sthitvā)* the Dharma teaching of the Lord Buddhas on ordinary vision *(laukike darśane).*[50]

These are the words Candrakīrti chose to state his final position about the means of cognition, and they are virtually the same words Jñānagarbha uses to express his view of conventional truth: the *pramāṇa*s are a form of ordinary usage, just "as it is seen" *(yathādṛṣṭam).*[51]

Conclusion

What can we conclude from this excursion through Tsong kha pa's sources? It seems that the topic of no-analysis, as satisfying as it may be, did not mark as sharp a distinction between Svātantrika and Prāsaṅgika in India as it later did in Tibet. This is not surprising when there apparently was so little formal awareness of a distinction between the different traditions or schools of Madhyamaka in India. Disagreements there certainly were, but the lines were fluid, and crucial terminology seems to have belonged to a common body of exploration rather than to isolated, competing factions in a larger school. The decisive distinction between Svātantrika and Prāsaṅgika clearly owes as much to Tibetan analysis of the Indian tradition as it does to the Indian tradition itself.

It is not necessary to be content, however, with a merely negative conclusion about Tsong kha pa's relationship to his sources. Indian texts give us a measure of the analytical transformation Tibetans had to bring to bear on their interpretation of the Indian Madhyamaka. Tsong kha pa's reading of the concept of "no-analysis" was not transmitted from India ready-made. He or his predecessors had to work with the concept, the way a sculptor works with a newly quarried stone, before they could use it to build their system of classification. The real question posed by these sources is whether Tsong kha pa's intellectual labors, or the labors of others who preceded him, exposed a form that already lurked inside the stone or whether he formed a figure in his own imagination and used his chisel to impose it on the raw surface of his materials.

A strictly literal reading of the Indian sources favors the second option. Bhāvaviveka did not actually say that conventional reality is "established with its own identity," and the Svātantrikas are not the only ones who say that conventional reality exists "as it is seen." To use these as the key criteria for distinguishing Svātantrika from Prāsaṅgika requires some heavy blows from the chisel, to say nothing of the omission of contrary evidence from the work of Candrakīrti himself. This literal reading of the evidence suggests that Tsong kha pa imposed an order on the tradition that is absent in the tradition itself. Reading the evidence this way certainly has its advantages. It preserves the integrity of the Indian sources, it recognizes the fluidity and indeterminacy of the process of interpretation, and it makes room for Tsong kha pa to shape the sources in his own distinctive way. But does it do justice, in the end, either to the Indian sources or to Tsong kha pa's own understanding of the tradition?

To answer this question it would be better to think of Tsong kha pa not as a sculptor but as a judge.[52] When supreme court justices deliver a novel reading of the Constitution, there are always critics who suggest that the decision is no more than the arbitrary creation of a group of justices, influenced perhaps by the demands of a particular segment of American society. The suspicion, of course, has its validity. *Brown vs. The Board of Education,* the famous decision that overthrew the practice of racial segregation, required a significant shift in political ethos and depended on changes in American society that put old assumptions about inequality in doubt. But the decision would not have been possible, in an epistemological and judicial sense, if it did not elaborate a legal principle embodied in the "equal protection" clause of the Constitution. No matter how deeply buried the principle may have been, in the text of the Constitution or in constitutional litigation, the principle had a certain logic and led eventually to a certain outcome.

The same can be said of Tsong kha pa's reading of the texts that now are recognized as belonging to the Svātantrika and Prāsaṅgika branches of the Madhyamaka tradition. His reading of the distinction was influenced, no doubt, by intellectual or social factors quite remote from the Indian tradition. But the important question—the question that lets Buddhist philosophy be philosophy in the same way that Constitutional law is law rather than an arbitrary exercise of the will—is whether there is something in the *ideas* of Bhāvaviveka, Candrakīrti, Jñānagarbha, and other Mādhyamikas of the sixth through ninth centuries in India that requires certain kinds of intellectual distinctions, even when the authors fail to be consistent about the distinctions themselves.

We have already seen that Bhāvaviveka shows a distinctive willingness to specify the reference of words conventionally. He is not clumsy about it, and he may even do it with a sense of irony, but he does accept the challenge of identifying "in general" *(sāmānyena)* the objects that lie behind his words. It is not unreasonable for someone to focus on this aspect of Bhāvaviveka's thought and elaborate it into a principle of classification. The same can be said about Jñānagarbha's use of the term *yathādarśana* ("as it is seen"). Candrakīrti may use the same (or a similar) term at a crucial point in his own argument, but the term does not have the same integral function in his epistemology. Jñānagarbha's use of the word "vision" *(darśana)* in his definition of conventional truth helps map the relationship between the two truths and the two essential means of cognition. For Candrakīrti the word appears at the end of his argument as little more than an afterthought. There is nothing in the earlier stages of his work to suggest that it has any importance. If the word were omitted from Jñānagarbha's text, the whole argument would crumble. If it were omitted from Candrakīrti's, it would hardly be missed. It is not necessary to take Tsong kha pa's argument as a distortion of the Indian sources. We also can read it as a plausible and careful study of their implications. But no matter how we read the argument, it is still an interpretation. Tsong kha pa does not reproduce the Indian sources verbatim; he works with them to serve the needs of his own system of classification.

I said earlier that this investigation of Tsong kha pa's text has implications not just for the study of Tibetan philosophy but for the study of the Buddhist tradition as a whole. One implication, of course, has to do with the question of cross-cultural transmission. Tsong kha pa gives a limited but significant example of a process that goes on whenever the Buddhist tradition enters a new culture. The sources have to be culled, interpreted, and put in order for them to be useful in a new context. But the implication that seems most intriguing has to do less with the form of the transmission than with its substance. The study of Buddhist epistemology has become so specialized in recent years that it has begun to seem like a sleepy backwater, only marginally related to the mainstream of Buddhist studies. The same might be said about the study of Tsong kha pa and his sources. In my opinion, nothing could be farther from the truth. It takes only a moment of reflection to realize that Tsong kha pa's search for a clear understanding of conventional truth has to do with one of the fundamental concerns of Buddhist life.

In thought and in practice, the Buddhist tradition involves an exploration of negation. The reasons for this are buried in the tradition's Indian origins and in the idea that freedom from *saṃsāra* comes from cutting the cognitive ties—the troublesome tendencies toward reification—that bind a person in the cycle of death and rebirth. But complete negation, like complete skepticism, is a contradiction in terms. It has to have its limits. So the same question appears in one form of the Buddhist tradition after another: What is left over when the negation is done, and what language or verbal strategy is appropriate to express it?

One delightfully subtle strategy lurks in these pages of Tsong kha pa's text. He begins one of his most important statements about the Svātantrikas with words drawn from ordinary life: he says that Svātantrikas and other misguided Buddhists are "not content *(tshim pa)* with the mere conventional expression *(tha snyad btags pa tsam)* 'person.'" Later he says that the dispute between Svātantrikas and Prāsaṅgikas can be distilled into a dispute about what is excluded by the word "mere" *(tsam, mātra)*. In this setting, the word "mere" *(mātra)* carries formidable intellectual force, but it speaks so quietly that is easily overlooked.[53] The word "mere" is the perfect philosophical diminuendo. It is like a withdrawal into the quiet routine of everyday life when heavy philosophical labors are done. The Dalai Lama used it at Harvard when, after a long and mind-numbing lecture on the intricacies of the no-self doctrine, he referred to himself *bdag tsam,* the "mere self." It also echoes through the literature of Zen in ways that others, no doubt, can trace as well as I. The word "mere" is a place where philosophy comes back down to earth and situates itself in ordinary life, satisfied with the cessation of its questions. This process of cessation is what Tsong kha pa tried to pin down in the pages of his text. The effort now seems arcane, accessible to only the most intense philological labors, but the effort is not far from the heart in many traditions of Buddhist practice.

Notes

1 Perhaps the best known of the traditional compendia is Sāyaṇa Mādhava's *Sarvadarśanasaṃgraha.* Examples of the genre in English include Chatterjee and Datta (1968) and Hiriyanna (1932).

2 References to and quotations from the *Legs bshad snying po* are taken from the Ngag dbang dge legs Delhi ed. The full text has been translated in Thurman (1984). For an analysis of comparable issues in Tsong kha pa's *Lam rim chen mo,* see Ruegg (1991). See also the commentary on mKhas grub rje's *sTong mthun skal bzang mig 'byed* in Ruegg (1983).

3 On the composition of the text and its relationship to Tsong kha pa's other Madhyamaka works, see Hopkins (1999): 6–25.

4 Hopkins (1999): 15.

5 This definition (with its illustrative quotation) and the one that follows are taken from the *Oxford English Dictionary* (1971), s.v. "essay."

6 Conze (1967).

7 David Seyfort Ruegg has pointed out that the names Svātantrika and Prāsaṅgika are, to a large degree, a Tibetan creation. They represent Sanskritized versions of the Tibetan terms *Rang rgyud pa* and *Thal 'gyur ba* and were not used to name distinct branches of the Madhyamaka school in the Sanskrit sources that are now available. See Ruegg (1981): 58. Ruegg has since pointed out that Jayānanda, the commentator on Candrakīrti's MAv, seems to use the word Svātantrika to refer to the position Candrakīrti opposes in the PPMV, his commentary on the MMK of Nāgārjuna. Jayānanda refers to Candrakīrti's own position simply as the Madhyamaka.

8 Some of the logical aspects of this question are explored in Tillemans (1992) and Tillemans and Lopez (1998).

9 MMK (de Jong ed.) 24.10: *vyavahāram anāśritya paramārtho na deśyate / paramārtham anāgamya nirvāṇaṃ nādhigamyate //.*

10 There has been a great deal of discussion about the proper form of this important philosopher's name. "Bhāvaviveka" has come down to us from La Vallée Poussin's edition of Candrakīrti's PPMV. There also is good evidence, however, for the forms Bhavya and Bhāviveka. A useful summary of the complex and contradictory evidence for the name of Bhāvaviveka or Bhavya can be found in

Lindtner (1995): 37–65. Recent manuscript discoveries suggest that the proper form of the name is almost certainly Bhāviveka. See Yonezawa (2001a): 26. Here I will use the form Bhāvaviveka simply because it is the most widely recognizable, if not necessarily the most correct.

11 The full text of chapter 25 of Bhāvaviveka's commentary on the MMK has been translated in Eckel (1980). The appendix on the Yogācāra appeared in Eckel (1985).

12 MMK 25.24: *sarvopalambhopaśamaḥ prapañcopaśamaḥ śivaḥ / na kva cit kasya cit kaścid dharmo buddhena deśitaḥ //.*

13 PrP D 239a7–239b1: *gzhan dag gis smras pa / don dam par mya ngan las 'das pa ni yod pa kho na yin te / de thob par bya ba'i phyir bcom ldan 'das kyis / bsam pa dang / mos pa dang / dus dang / yul la ltos pas chos bstan pa'i phyir ro //.*

14 For commentary on the significance of Bhāvaviveka's views about the Buddha's silence, see Eckel (1992): ch. 3.

15 PrP app. (Lindtner ed. 1995): 79: *rnal 'byor spyod pa pa dag gis smras pa / dmigs pa thams cad nyid zhi zhing / spros pa nyer zhi zhi ba ste / sangs rgyas kyis ni gang du yang / su la'ang chos 'ga' ma bstan to // zhes bya ba ni bden na de rtogs par bya ba'i thabs gzhan gyi dbang la skur pa 'debs pa de ni mi rung ste //.* A widely quoted Yogācāra source for this argument is found in a verse from the *Mahāyānābhidharma Sūtra:* "There is a primordial element *(dhātu)* that is the basis *(samāśraya)* of all phenomena *(dharma);* because this [element] exists, all states [of rebirth] exist, as well as the attainment of *nirvāṇa.*" This verse is quoted by, among others, Bhāvaviveka and Sthiramati. See Eckel (1985): 55.

16 PrP app. (Lindtner ed., 1995): 80–81: *sbrul med do zhe na ni grags pa'i gnod par 'gyur ro //.* See Eckel (1985): 50.

17 There is no agreed set of equivalents for many of the technical terms which appear in this passage, so I will follow customary usage and give the key terms in parentheses. This is a translation from Tibetan, not from Sanskrit, so the terms appear first in Tibetan and then, where necessary or appropriate, in the nearest Sanskrit equivalent.

18 *Legs bshad snying po* (Delhi ed.) ff. 577–580: *legs ldan 'byed kyis 'phags pa'i dgongs pa bkral ba la don dam pa bdag med gnyis ji ltar bshad pa ni slob dpon 'dis mtshan nyid gsum gtan la phab tshul shes na gsal te / de yang shes rab sgron ma las // de la 'dir gal te gzugs zhes bya bar yid la brjod pa dang tshig tu brjod pa'i kun brtags pa'i ngo bo nyid gang yin pa de med do zhe na ni / dngos po la skur pa 'debs [578] pa yin te yid la brjod pa dang tshig tu brjod pa la skur pa 'debs pa'i phyir ro // zhes kun brtags la mtshan nyid ngo bo nyid med do zhes smra ba'i kun brtags de ngo bo dang khyad par du 'dogs pa'i rtog pa dang ming la byed na de gnyis phung por gtogs pas gzhan dbang la mtshan nyid ngo bo med pa'i skur 'debs su bshad pas gzhan dbang la mtshan nyid ngo bo nyid yod par bzhed do // de yang dgongs 'grel las rang gi mtshan nyid kyis ma grub pas mtshan nyid ngo bo nyid med par bshad cing 'di dag kyang mdo de'i don gtan la 'bebs pa yin pas gzhan dbang la rang gi mtshan nyid kyis grub pa'i ngo bo yod par bzhed par gsal lo // shes rab sgron ma las kun brtags ming dang rgyu mtshan dang rnam par rtog pa dang yang dag pa'i ye*

shes dang de bzhin nyid lnga po gang gi yang khongs su mi gtogs pas mtshan nyid ngo bo nyid med pa'o zhes phyogs snga blangs pa ni / bsdu ba las / de lnga'i khongs su mi gtogs par bshad pa yin la / der ming ldan min du bshad la rgyu mtshan kun brtags kyi gdags gzhir bshad cing kun brtags dngos por med pas chos bzhi ma yin la / rtog pas btags pa tsam du zad pas de bzhin nyid kyang ma yin no // dbus mtha las / ming kun brtags su bshad pa ni ming gis btags pa'i don yin gyi ming gi ngo bo min par blo brtan gyis bshad do // der rgyu mtshan gzhan dbang du bshad pa yang 'du byed kyi rgyu mtshan la dgongs te de la 'dus ma byed kyang bsdu ba las bshad pas so // des na chos lngar mi gtogs pa'i rgyu mtshan gyis mtshan nyid ngo bo nyid med pa yin kyang der mi gtogs pa mtshan nyid ngo bo nyid med pa'i don min no // tha snyad du yod pa la yang de'i ngo bo nyid dang rang bzhin dang de'i rang gis mtshan nyid sogs su thal 'gyur ba'i gzhung nas bshad pa yang mang la rang gi ngo bo nyid kyis ma grub pa dang ngo bo nyid kyis ma skyes pa dang rdzas su ma grub pa la sogs pa slob dpon 'di yi gzhung na'ang mang bas dbye dka' bar snang na'ang dgongs 'grel las gsungs pa'i mtshan nyid ngo bo nyid yod med kyi don bshad pa 'di nyid slob dpon 'dis dngos po la rang gi mtshan nyid kyis grub pa tha snyad du bzhed pa'i khungs gsal shos yin no // de'i phyir gang zag dang chos la rang gi mtshan nyid kyis grub pa'i rang bzhin med par ma rtogs kyang bdag med gnyis mtshan nyid tshang bar rtogs par bzhed la / rang gi mtshan nyid kyis grub pa tsam min pa'i ji 'dra zhig bkag pas bdag med gnyis su 'jog pa'i dgag bya ni 'chad par 'gyur ro // yang shes rab sgron ma las / ci ste gang yang rung bas de gnyis kyis don kun brtags pa de med de dper na thag pa la sbrul gyi blo bzhin no zhe na ni / kun brtags pa med pa ma yin te / de la rnam pa 'dra bas blo gros 'khrul pas kun brtags pa'i don med kyang tha snyad du sbrul 'khyil pa la de med pa ma yin pa'i phyir ro // zhes kun brtags de 'dogs byed min gyi byis pa gang yang rung bas ming dang rtog pas btags pa'i btags don yin la de la mtshan nyid ngo bo nyid med de thag pa la sbrul du btags pa bzhin zhes zer na dper mi 'thad pa'i skyon ston no // de'i don ni gzugs la sogs pa la 'di dang 'di'o zhes ngo bo dang [580] khyad par du btags pa'i don de mtshan nyid ngo bo nyid med pa'i dper thag pa la sbrul lo snyam du btags pa'i btags don med pa 'jog pa mi rigs te / de la pha rol pos thag pa la sbrul lo snyam du bzung ba de'i don med kyang sbrul 'khyil ba la sbrul lo snyam du bzung ba'i don tha snyad du yod pa bzhin du gzugs la tshor ba'i snyam du bzung ba'i yul med kyang gzugs la gzugs so snyam du bzung ba'i yul tha snyad du yod do zhes smra bar nus pa'i phyir ro // 'dir yod med ni mtshan nyid ngo bo nyid yod med yin pas gzugs sogs la ngo bo dang khyad par du btags pa'i yul tha snyad du mtshan nyid ngo bo nyid med pa min zhes pa'o // ci ste tha snyad du sbrul 'khyil ba la sbrul med na ni grags pas gnod par gsungs te tha snyad du sbrul 'khyil ba la 'di sbrul lo snyam du bzung ba'i yul de med na zhes pa'o // don dam par dngos po sel na dbu ma pa'i rjes su smra ba yin te zhes gsungs te / sbrul 'khyil ba la sbrul lo snyam du bzung ba'i yul de don dam par mtshan nyid ngo bo nyid med par smra na dbu ma pa'i lugs su 'gyur zhes pa'o // des na ngo bo dang khyad par du kun brtags pa'i kun brtags mtshan nyid ngo bo nyid med par ston 'dod pas ni dbu ma'i rigs pa 'dod par bya'o zhes shes rab sgron ma las gsungs te //.

19 On the origins of philosophical compendia in the Indian tradition, see Folkert (1993): parts 2 and 3.

20 The Sanskrit text of the verse portion of this chapter has been edited by Lindtner (1995). The Tibetan translation of the TJ commentary is found in D, vol. *Dza,* ff. 40b–329b. For a translation of this chapter, with commentary, see Hoornaert (1999, 2000, 2001a, 2001b).

21 Bhāvaviveka distinguishes between *prasajyapratiṣedha* (verbally-bound negation) and *paryudāsapratiṣedha* (nominally-bound negation). The first form of negation (for example: "Brahmins should not drink liquor") does not commit a person to the assertion of the opposite. The second form of negation (for example: "He is a non-brahmin") does require such a commitment. Bhāvaviveka insists that his negations function in the first way, not the second. The *locus classicus* for Bhāvaviveka's distinction between *prasajyapratiṣedha* and *paryudāsapratiṣedha* is his commentary on the word "not" *(na)* in MHK 3.26. The verse reads: *tatra (bhūtasvabhāvaṃ) [hi] norvyādi paramārthataḥ / kṛtakatvād yathā jñānaṃ hetumattvādito 'pi vā //.* See Heitmann (1998): 29. "Here earth and so forth do *not* ultimately have the nature of gross elements, because they are produced or because they have causes, and so forth, like knowledge." To explain the meaning of the word "not," he says (D 59b3–6): *'dir min zhes bya ba'i dgag pa 'di ni med par dgag pa'i don du gzung gi ma yin par dgag pa'i don du ni mi gzung ngo // med par dgag pa dang ma yin par dgag pa zhes bya ba de gnyis kyi bye brag ji lta bu zhe na / ma yin par dgag pa ni dngos po'i ngo bo nyid dgag pas de dang 'dra ba de las gzhan pa'i dngos po'i ngo bo nyid sgrub par byed pa ste / dper na 'di bram ze ma yin no zhes dgag pas bram ze de 'dra ba de las gzhan pa bram ze ma yin pa dka' thub dang thos pa la sogs pas dman pa'i dmangs rigs yin par bsgrubs pa lta bu'o // med par dgag pa ni dngos po'i ngo bo nyid tsam zhig 'gog par zad kyi de dang 'dra ba de ma yin pa gzhan gyi dngos po sgrub par mi byed pa ste / dper na bram zes chang btung bar mi bya'o zhes bya ba de tsam zhig 'gog par zad kyi de las gzhan pa'i btung ba btung ngo // zhe'am mi btung ngo zhes mi brjod pa lta bu'o //* "Here the word 'not' should be taken as a verbally-bound negation *(prasajyapratiṣedha).* It should not be taken as a nominally-bound negation *(paryudāsapratiṣedha).* What is the difference between these two kinds of negation? A nominally-bound negation negates one thing in order to affirm something else that is similar to it. For example, the negation 'He is a non-brahmin' affirms something else that is similar to a brahmin, such as a non-brahmanical ascetic or a *śūdra* who is deficient in learning. A verbally-bound negation just negates something; it does not affirm anything else that is similar to it. For example, the negation 'Brahmins should not drink liquor' functions just as a negation; it does not tell whether [brahmins] should drink anything else." This passage appears in Iida (1980): 84. Further discussion of the distinction between these two kinds of negation can be found in Matilal (1971): 162–165, and in Kajiyama (1966): 38–39. See also Eckel (1987): 126.

22 Bhāvaviveka uses the "maxim of washing away mud" *(paṅkaprakṣālaṇanyāya)* in MHK 5.54 and the accompanying commentary.

23 MMK 18.1cd: *skandhebhyo 'nyo yadi bhaved bhaved askandhalakṣaṇaḥ //.*

24 D 179b6: *'dir rjes su dpag pa ni don dam par bdag gzugs la sogs pa'i phung po las gzhan pa med de /.*

25 D 180b2–3: *ci ste yang la la 'di snyam du dbu ma pas bdag tshig gi don nyid du khas ma blangs pa'i phyir de'i khyad par bstan pa mi rigs te / dper na mo gsham gyi bu'i sngo bsangs dang / dkar sham nyid la sogs pa bzhin no snyam du sems na /*. A full translation of this chapter of Bhāvaviveka's commentary can be found in Eckel (1980): 192–264.

26 D 180b3–5: *yang 'byung ba'i srid pa len pa'i phyir bdag ces bya te / rnam par shes pa'i yul la bdag tu tha snyad gdags pa'i phyir rnam par shes pa la bdag tu brjod de / de ltar yang bcom ldan 'das kyis / sems dul ba ni dge ba ste // dul ba'i sems kyis bde ba thob // ces gsungs nas mdo sde gzhan las / bdag gi mgon ni bdag nyid yin // gzhan ni mgon du su zhig 'gyur // mkhas pa bdag ni legs dul bas // mtho ris dag kyang 'thob par 'gyur // zhes gsungs pas / de'i phyir tha snyad du bdag spyir khas blangs pas khyad par ma grags pa sel ba'i phyir skyon med do //.*

27 The exact force of the word *spyir / sāmānyena* is not clear. The most obvious way to take it is as a reference to the self as a "universal" *(sāmānya)* rather than as a "particular" or as an "intrinsic identity" *(svalakṣaṇa)*. If so, it gives another reason to be suspicious of Tsong kha pa's claim that Bhāvaviveka accepted the existence of things "with intrinsic identity" *(svalakṣaṇena)* conventionally. On Bhāvaviveka's view of universals, see the next paragraph.

28 The argument appears in MHK 5.66–68 and in the accompanying commentary.

29 See MHK 5.62–65 and commentary.

30 TJ *ad* MHK 5.63: *ba lang nyid ces bya ba de lkog shal la sogs pa dag las gzhan pa ni ma yin te / 'o na ji lta bu zhe na / dngos po'i rang gi ngo bo nyid las tha mi dad pa yin no /.*

31 Private communication in response to earlier drafts of this essay.

32 See PV 1 *(svārthānumānapariccheda)*, vv. 64ff.

33 *Legs bshad snying po* (Delhi ed.) f. 609: *'di la thog mar grub mtha' smra ba'i lugs brjod par bya ste / gang zag 'dis las 'di byas so // 'bras bu 'di myong ngo zhes pa'i tha snyad btags pa la rang gi phung po 'di nyid gang zag yin nam 'on te de dag las don gzhan zhes gang zag gi tha snyad btags pa de'i don btsal te / don gcig pa'i don tha dad la sogs pa'i phyogs gang rung zhig rnyed nas gang zag de 'jog sa byung na las gsog pa po la sogs par 'jog nus la / ma rnyed na 'jog mi nus pas gang zag gi tha snyad btags pa tsam gyis mi tshim par de'i tha snyad gang la btags pa'i btags gzhi de ji ltar yin dpyad cing btsal nas 'jog na gang zag rang gi mtshan nyid kyis grub par 'jog pa yin te / rang sde bye brag tu smra ba nas dbu ma rang rgyud pa'i bar thams cad kyis de bzhin du 'dod do //.*

34 Das (1902).

35 Note also that the word *sa* ("place") prepares the way for the word *gzhi* (Skt. *āśraya*), "basis" or "locus," and *rnyed pa* anticipates the important term *dmigs pa (upalambha* or *upalabdhi)*, "grasp" or "apprehend."

36 References to this formula in Madhyamaka literature can be found in Eckel (1987): 137–138. The dating of this formula is complicated by its appearance in the *Madhyamakaratnapradīpa*. If this text is attributed to the Bhāvaviveka who wrote the PrP and lived in the sixth century, the formula must have been available in the sixth century. For an argument to this effect, see Lindtner (1980):

27–37. It seems more plausible to leave Dharmakīrti's date in the seventh century and assign the *Madhyamakratnapradīpa* to a second Bhavya in the eighth century or beyond. See Ruegg (1981): 66. The idea that reality can "satisfy only when it is not analyzed" *(avicāritaramaṇīya)* plays a significant role in Jayarāśi's *Tattvopaplavasiṃha (The Lion that Annihilates [All] Principles)*, a Carvāka work from the late eighth century. See Franco (1994). In a review of Franco, de Jong (1989) notes other examples of the concept in Madhyamaka literature from the eighth century and beyond. The relationship between the Madhyamaka and the larger tradition of Indian skepticism is a topic that needs further exploration. Franco concludes his remarks about this relationship by saying, "it is certainly remarkable that Jayarāśi criticizes all schools of thought except one, the Madhyamaka" (xiii).

37 La Vallée Poussin ed., 67–68.

38 Assuming, of course, that "everyone" is knowledgeable about the Indian theory of the gross elements.

39 Unfortunately, this is not the place to discourse at length on the importance of *anupalambha* or *anupalabdhi* ("no grasping," "no apprehension," or simply "no finding") in Mahāyāna literature. Compare, for example, *Madhyānta-vibhāga* 1.6 ("Based on apprehension, there arises no apprehension") or *Mahāyānasūtrālaṃkāra* 9.78 ("Nonexistence is the supreme existence, and complete no-apprehension is considered the supreme apprehension"). One can gauge the importance of *anupalambha* for the Madhyamaka tradition in a passage like MHK 4.23–24, where Bhāvaviveka argues that the practice of *anupalambha* is the distinguishing feature of the Mahāyāna.

40 PPMV (La Vallée Poussin ed.) 67.7–8: *laukike vyavahāra itthaṃvicārāpravṛtter avicārataś ca laukikapadārthānāṃ astitvāt /.*

41 *Jñānagarbha's Commentary*, v. 21. The Tibetan translation of *yathādarsana (ji ltar snang ba)* emphasizes the aspect of "appearance." The Sanskrit comes closer, as Jñānagarbha evidently intended, to the active language of "seeing" as an example of *pratyakṣapramāṇa*. For this reference and those that follow, see Eckel (1987): 89 and 137–138.

42 D, vol. *ha*, 41b1: *ma brtags gcig pu nyams dga' ste // de 'dra las 'byung de bzhin no // dngos po de dag de lta bu'i // don bya de dang de byed do //.*

43 MA 64: *ma brtags gcig pu nyams dga' zhing / skye dang 'jigs pa'i chos can pa / don byed pa dag nus rnams kyi / rang bzhin kun rdzob pa yin rtogs //.*

44 Trans. from Lindtner (1981).

45 *Legs bshad snying po* (Delhi ed.) f. 615: *dbu ma rang rgyud pa rnams ni tha snyad 'dogs pa'i blo'i dbang gis gzugs 'tshor la sogs pa 'jog mi nus la gnod pa med pa'i dbang po'i shes pa la sogs pa la snang ba'i dbang gis tha snyad du yod pa 'jog nus par 'dod pas blo'i dbang gis bzhag ma bzhag gi blo la yang khyad par che'o /* "According to the Svātantrikas, it is not possible to posit the existence of the aggregates on the basis of a cognition that applies conventional terms, but it is possible to posit conventional existence on the basis of vision *(snang ba)* in reliable sense cognition. There is, therefore, a big difference between the

cognitions *(blo)* that posit or do not posit [existence] on the basis of cognition." Tsong kha pa's *snang ba'i dbang gis* normally would correspond to the Sanskrit **ābhāsavaśena* rather than *darśanavaśena,* but the phrase is based on a formula from Jñānagarbha, where *ji ltar snang ba* is used by the Tibetan translator to represent the Sanskrit *yathādarśana.* See Eckel (1987): 110.

46 See Hattori (1968): 24. Cf. Dharmakīrti, PV 3 *(pratyakṣaparicchedа),* v. 3.

47 Jñānagarbha makes this point in vv. 3 and 4 of his *Satyadvayavibhaṅga* (SDV, lit., *Distinction Between the Two Truths*). SDV 3cd: *ji ltar snang ba 'di kho na / kun rdzob....* "Only what is consistent with the way things are seen *(yathādarśana)* is relative *(saṃvṛti).*" SDV 4abc: *slu ba med pas rigs pa ni / don dam yin te kun rdzob min / de ltar mi slu min phyir te /* "Since it cannot be contradicted *(avisaṃvāda),* reason *(nyāya)* is ultimate *(paramārtha)* and not relative *(saṃvṛti).*" For further discussion of this distinction, see Eckel (1987).

48 The distinction between the two kinds of ultimate is discussed in Eckel (1987): 112–113. The *locus classicus* for this distinction is the third chapter of Bhāvaviveka's TJ (D 60b4–5): *don dam pa ni rnam pa gnyis te / de la gcig ni mngon par 'du byed pa med par 'jug pa 'jig rten las 'das pa zag pa med pa spros pa med pa'o / gnyis pa ni mngon par 'du byed pa dang bcas par 'jug pa bsod nams dang ye shes kyi tshogs kyi rjes su mthun pa dag pa 'jig rten pa'i ye shes zhes bya ba spros pa dang bcas pa ste /* "There are two kinds of ultimate: The first is effortless, transcendent *(lokottara),* free from impurity, and free from discursive ideas *(niṣprapañca).* The second is accessible to effort, consistent with the prerequisites of merit and knowledge, pure, and accessible to discursive ideas *(saprapañca);* it can be referred to as worldly knowledge *(laukikajñāna).*"

49 See *The Teaching of Vimalakīrti (Vimalakīrtinirdeśasūtra).*

50 PPMV (La Vallée Poussin ed.) 75: *tāni ca parasparāpekṣayā sidhyanti / satsu pramāṇeṣu prameyārthāḥ / satsu prameyeṣv artheṣu pramāṇāni / no tu khalu svābhāvikī pramāṇaprameyayoḥ siddhir iti tasmāl laukikam evāstu yathādṛṣṭam ity alaṃ prasaṅgena / prastutam eva vyākhyāsyāmaḥ / laukika eva darśane sthitvā buddhānāṃ bhagavatāṃ dharmadeśanā //*. The textual status of the last clause in the La Vallée Poussin edition, from *laukika eva* to *dharmadeśanā,* is questionable. It does not appear in the sDe dge and Peking editions of the Tibetan translation, and Anne MacDonald has noted (in a private communication) that, while the clause is attested in other Nepali manuscripts, it is included with other material that suggests a scribal insertion. Cf. D, vol. *'a,* 25b5–6: *de'i phyir* [P add *de ltar*] *tshad ma bzhi las 'jig rten gyi* [*gyis* P] *don rtogs par *rnam par** [P om.] *'jog pa yin no // de dag kyang phan tshun ltos* [*bltos* P] *pas 'grub par 'gyur te / tshad ma dag yod na gzhal bya'i don dag tu 'gyur la / gzhal bya'i don dag yod na tshad ma dag tu 'gyur gyi / tshad ma dang gzhal bya gnyis ngo bo nyid kyis grub pa ni yod pa ma yin no // de'i phyir mthong ba ji lta ba bzhin du 'jig rten pa nyid yin la rag ste / spros pas chog go // dkyus ma nyid bshad par bya'o //*.

51 Georges Dreyfus has asked whether the word *yathādṛṣṭam* means the same thing to Candrakīrti that *yathādarśanam* means to Jñānagarbha. In SDV 3–4, Jñānagarbha distinguishes relative truth, which was based on vision *(darśana),*

from ultimate truth, which is based on reason *(nyāya)*. In other words, he thinks that relative truth is a matter of perception *(pratyakṣa)*, while ultimate truth is a matter of inference *(anumāna)*. So the question about the meaning of "vision" distills into a question about the meaning of perception. Evidently Candrakīrti differs from Dharmakīrti by accepting the possibility that perception can be conceptual and also mistaken (as in the perception of a double moon). Jñānagarbha apparently does not adopt Dharmakīrti's view that perception is unmistaken *(abhrānta)*. (His views on this point have to be inferred from the commentary on v. 8.) On the possibility of conceptual perception, Jñānagarbha seems to have agreed with Candrakīrti against Dharmakīrti, when he says that "there are two kinds of vision, conceptual and nonconceptual" (commentary on verse 3: *mthong ba ni rnam pa gnyis te rnam par rtog pa dang bcas pa dang / rnam par rtog pa med pa'o*). These two points are not definitive, but they suggest greater kinship between Jñānagarbha and Candrakīrti than is generally recognized. For further discussion of Candrakīrti's view of perception, see Siderits (1980–81).

52 Paul J. Griffiths has explored the implications of this analogy in Griffiths (1994): ch. 1.

53 Paul Williams has pointed out that this word has attracted significant commentary in Tibetan literature (1980).

Part 2: Examining the Distinction in the Tibetan Tradition

6. Phya pa chos kyi seng ge as a Svātantrika

HELMUT TAUSCHER[1]

THE DIVISION of the Madhyamaka school of philosophy into Prāsaṅgika and Svātantrika was "invented" in Tibet during the time of the "later propagation of the doctrine" *(phyi dar),* probably by Pa tshab nyi ma grags (b. 1055) or by those in the circles around him.[2] This distinction became very popular both within the Tibetan tradition and also later among Western scholars, and a tendency developed to treat this distinction as if it had existed and served as the basis for "subschools" of the Madhyamaka, or at least distinct exegetical traditions already in India. The question of whether and to what extent such an assumption is justified shall not be touched upon in this paper which aims rather at a preliminary investigation of Phya pa chos kyi seng ge's Madhyamaka position, based on his *dBu ma shar gsum gyi stong thun,* or *Shar gsum stong thun* for short. As Phya pa is regarded not only as one of the leading scholars from the early period of the "later propagation" but also as a close adherent of the Svātantrika tradition, his position could be expected to be illuminating for the development of the Prāsaṅgika-Svātantrika distinction. However, Phya pa's *Shar gsum stong thun* does not deal with this distinction directly, but only with the validity of the use of *prasaṅga* and *svatantra* reasoning in Madhyamaka. Therefore, this paper has to be restricted primarily to the question of how, to what extent, and according to which criteria Phya pa is to be classified as a Svātantrika.

Phya pa chos kyi seng ge (1109–1169) is reported to have "written many refutations of the works of the Ācārya Candrakīrti,"[3] but no treatise that by its title could be recognized as being polemical in nature is mentioned among his works in the *Blue Annals* or in A khu rinpoche's *Tho yig,*[4] or, to the best of my knowledge, in any other source. Provided that the statements by 'Gos lotsāva and Shākya mchog ldan do not merely reflect a later Tibetan classification of Phya pa chos kyi seng ge as a strict Svātantrika, it has, therefore, to be assumed that these "many refutations" are to be found within his commentaries on such Madhyamaka treatises as the *Bodhicaryāvatāra, Satyadvayavibhaṅga* (SDV), *Madhyamakāloka* (MĀ), *Madhyamakālaṃkāra* (MA), and *Uttaratantra,* or within his "long" and "short summary of Madhyamaka" *(dBu ma bsdus pa che chung).*

Of all his works, however, only one is presently known to be extant, namely the above-mentioned and newly discovered *dBu ma shar gsum gyi stong thun* or *dBu ma de kho na nyid kyi snying po,* which can hypothetically be identified with the "long summary of Madhyamaka" mentioned by 'Gos lotsāva and A khu rinpoche.[5] It shows Phya pa chos kyi seng ge as a follower of the Madhyamaka tradition represented by the "three Svātantrika-Madhyamaka (teachers) from the East" *(dbu ma rang rgyud pa shar gsum),*[6] Jñānagarbha, Śāntarakṣita, and Kamalaśīla, who strongly emphasized the method of *svatantra* according to Dignāga and Dharmakīrti within Madhyamaka argumentation.

The *Shar gsum stong thun* consists of three main sections: "Ascertainment of the objects of cognition" *(shes bya nges bar bya ba),* "Mahāyāna practice," and "The stage of the Buddha" *(buddhabhūmi).* The first of these, which covers some 85 percent of the entire text, is a discussion of the two realities *(bden pa gnyis).* It contains two main subdivisions: "Distinction *(dbye ba)* of the two realities" and "Definition/characteristics *(mtshan nyid)* of the two realities." The greatest part of this latter section is dedicated to the "Negation of true[ly established] entities" *(yang dag pa'i dngos po dgag pa)* (sec. 125.1 of the topical outline presented at the end of this article), consisting of a "Refutation of the object of negation being negated by *prasaṅga*" *(dgag bya thal 'gyur gyis 'gog pa sun dbyung ba)* (125.11) and a presentation of "How an [independant] syllogism negates discursive development" *(rjes dpag gis spros pa 'gog pa'i tshul)* (125.12). The first of these subsections comprises as main topics an "Exposition of the opponent's [i.e., the Prāsaṅgikas'] system" *(gzhan kyi lugs dgod pa)* (125.111); a discussion as to why "It is not correct not to accept the use of *svatantra*" *(rang rgyud kyi sbyor ba khas mi len pa mi 'thad pa)* (125.112.1); a discussion as to why "A *prasaṅga* is unable to negate a realistic position" *(thal 'gyur gyis dngos por smra ba 'gog mi nus pa)* (125.112.2); and a short presentation of Phya pa's own system *(rang gi lugs rnam par gzhag pa)* (125.113). The second subsection (125.12) presents mainly a detailed discussion of the independent syllogism suited to proving the all-pervading emptiness, structured according to its individual parts: *dharmin, sādhya, hetu, pakṣadharmatā,* and *vyāpti.*[7]

General Remarks on the Subdivisions of the Madhyamaka School from the Eleventh through the Thirteenth Centuries in Tibet

In doxographic works of the early period of the "later propagation" the Prāsaṅgika-Svātantrika distinction plays only a comparatively modest role.[8] The following is a brief overview.

The rNying ma pa scholar Rong zom chos kyi bzang po (11th c.) does not know these categories at all; presumably he composed his texts before Pa tshab or his followers established the Prāsaṅgika-Svātantrika distinction. Rong zom distinguishes merely between Yogācāra-Madhyamaka *(rnal 'byor spyod pa'i dbu ma)* and Sautrāntika-Madhyamaka *(mdo sde [spyod pa'i] dbu ma)*[9] and between sGyu ma lta bur 'dod pa (dbu ma), which maintains the ultimate essence of phenomena to be real in the way of an illusion, and Rab tu mi gnas par 'dod pa (dbu ma), which holds the view that phenomena are verbally designated, but do not exist in the way they are designated.[10]

The Sa skya pa master Grags pa rgyal mtshan (1147–1216) likewise does not utilize this division when discussing the Madhyamaka school in his *rGyud kyi mngon par rtogs pa rin po che'i ljon shing (= Rin che ljon shing).* Yet Go rams pa bsod nams seng ge (1429–1489) does so when he refers to and quotes Grags pa rgyal mtshan within the discussion of the system of the "former [scholars]" *(snga rabs pa)* in his *rGyal ba thams cad kyi thugs kyi dgongs pa zab mo dbu ma'i de kho na nyid spyi'i ngag gis ston pa nges don rab gsal (= Nges don rab gsal).* Here, without mentioning Prāsaṅgika, he identifies with Svātantrika two of Grags pa rgyal mtshan's five subdivisions regarding the interpretation of conventional reality *(saṃvṛtisatya),* viz., Sautrāntika-Madhyamaka and Yogācāra-Madhyamaka. Go rams pa also introduces the division between Prāsaṅgika and Svātantrika with regard to the ultimate reality *(paramārthasatya),* stating, however, only that there is no difference in their ways of understanding it.[11]

Discussing the system of the two realities in a tantric context, however, Grags pa rgyal mtshan does distinguish Prāsaṅgika and Svātantrika. In the section on the respective sorts of cognition, i.e., conventional *(saṃvṛti)* and absolute *(paramārtha),* he initially mentions four methods of ascribing them to different kinds of persons: the methods of the *śrāvaka*s, the Yogācārins, "[those who hold] cessation *(vicceda)* not to be definitely fixed" *(rgyun chad rab tu mi gnas pa),* and "[those who hold] the unity [of ?] not to be definitely fixed" *(zung 'jug rab tu mi gnas pa).*[12] In the actual discussion, however, the last two methods are called "Prāsaṅgika" and "Svātantrika" respectively; they are distinguished according to their not accepting or accepting the division into "conceptual" or "corresponding" *(paryāya, rnam grangs [pa] / mthun pa)* and "nonconceptual" or "actual/real" *(aparyāya, rnam grangs ma yin pa / dngos) paramārtha.*[13] Grags pa rgyal mtshan also introduces the concept of a "corresponding *saṃvṛti*" *(rnam grangs kyi kun rdzob)* for the pure worldly gnosis of the Buddha, a notion unknown to me from Indian sources.

According to Grags pa rgyal mtshan, the Prāsaṅgika classifies the various sorts of cognitions in the following way. The cognition of ordinary beings, which is to be defined as defiled ignorance, is only *saṃvṛti.* In the case of the three kinds of *ārya*s, i.e., śrāvaka-arhats, pratyekabuddhas, and bodhisattvas below the seventh stage, "gnosis in (contemplative) concentration" *(samāhitajñāna),* which is nonconceptual cognition of the absolute reality *(paramārthasatya)* without any mental activity, is *paramārtha;* "succeedingly gained gnosis" *(pṛṣṭhalabdhajñāna),* which is gained immediately after the *samāhitajñāna* upon leaving contemplative concentration, has *saṃvṛtisatya* as its object, without, however, the notion of "existing in an absolute sense"; it is classified as *saṃvṛti.* The buddhas' gnosis is exclusively *paramārtha,* as they permanently remain in contemplative concentration. This, Grags pa rgyal mtshan argues, is incorrect, because it contradicts the commonly accepted fact that the buddhas stay in "nonabiding *nirvāṇa*" *(apratiṣṭhitanirvāṇa),* which means that they are equally established in *saṃsāra* and *nirvāṇa* and have access to *saṃvṛti* and *paramārtha* alike.

On Grags pa rgyal mtshan's analysis, the Svātantrika agrees with the above system regarding the gnosis of the three kinds of *ārya*s. The cognition of ordinary beings, however, although *saṃvṛti* in general, is regarded as "corresponding *paramārtha*" when the true nature of phenomena, their nonorigination, is concerned. The buddhas' nonconceptual gnosis, being *paramārtha* in general, is similarly considered "corresponding *saṃvṛti*" when it is pure worldly gnosis. Thus the presuppositions are fulfilled, viz., that the buddhas stay in *apratiṣṭhitanirvāṇa,* and their gnosis, without showing any change, is *paramārtha;* that they permanently remain in concentration; and that even "corresponding *paramārtha*" really is *paramārtha.*[14]

Grags pa rgyal mtshan's nephew, Sa skya paṇḍita kun dga' rgyal mtshan (1182–1251), or Sa paṇ, in his *Thub pa'i dgongs pa rab tu gsal ba (= Thub dgongs rab gsal)* takes up the concept of a "corresponding *saṃvṛti*" and mentions the fourfold division of reality into "corresponding" and "actual" *saṃvṛti* and *paramārtha* as a distinctive feature of the Svātantrika.[15]

In his *gZhung lugs legs par bshad pa,* Sa paṇ divides Madhyamaka with regard to the interpretation of *paramārtha* into sGyu ma lta bu and Rab tu mi gnas pa, and divides the latter into Svātantrika and Prāsaṅgika exclusively on grounds of the methodological difference of accepting or not accepting the triple characterization *(trairūpya)* of a valid reason for proving the ultimate, without, however, specifying different sorts of *rab tu mi gnas pa.*[16]

An unidentified early Tibetan master *(kha cig)* who held that the Prāsaṅgikas should be counted among the "Mādhyamikas of fundamental texts" *(gzhung phyi mo [pa]'i dbu ma pa),*[17] as they have no affirmation *(khas len)* at all, is mentioned by Go rams pa.[18]

These few examples cannot, of course, provide a comprehensive survey. Nevertheless, to some extent the outlines presented by Grags pa rgyal mtshan and Sa skya paṇḍita can be assumed to be representative for the time. The rather limited relevance of the categories "Prāsaṅgika" and "Svātantrika" for establishing subdivisions of the Madhyamaka school in these early texts does not, of course, mean that no discussion related to this topic existed at that time. In the way it is presented in Phya pa's *Shar gsum stong thun,* the discussion focuses mainly on the question of whether or not a thesis or proposition *(pratijñā, dam bca')*/affirmation *(abhyupagama, khas len)*/philosophical position *(pakṣa, phyogs)* is maintained, and related problems. This point, however, is not particularly stressed in *grub mtha'* texts; it is reflected only in Sa paṇ's *gZhung lugs legs par bshad pa* and in the position of the early Tibetan master mentioned by Go rams pa. On the other hand, the question of whether the division into "conceptual" or "corresponding" and "nonconceptual" or "actual/real" *paramārtha* is accepted does not appear at all in Phya pa's discussion.

Strictly speaking, this discussion is not about the distinction of subschools, but rather about the question of whether a thesis of one's own can legitimately be maintained within Madhyamaka philosophy. This question, however, is inseparably connected with the issue of the use of reductio ad absurdum *(prasaṅga)* or of independent syllogism *(svatantra)* for proving ultimate reality. For this reason and on account of the way Phya pa deals with this topic (see p. 220 ff. below), I shall tentatively and for the sake of convenience refer to the distinction that centers on the question of whether an own thesis is denied or maintained as the "old Prāsaṅgika-Svātantrika distinction" in analogy to Tani's "old Prāsaṅgika,"[19] and in contrast to a "new," i.e., dGe lugs pa distinction, which will be discussed below. This does not imply that the distinction as such was commonly accepted at any time; already Sa skya paṇḍita in his *mKhas pa rnams 'jug pa'i sgo* argues against the denial of a philosophical tenet *(grub mtha')* as being characteristic of the Madhyamaka position.[20]

Phya pa chos kyi seng ge on the Use of Prasaṅga *and (Implied)* Svatantra

Pa tshab nyi ma grags is not only the probable "inventor" of the Prāsaṅgika-Svātantrika distinction; the propagation of Candrakīrti's works in Tibet is to a great extent due to his activities as a translator and teacher.[21] Phya pa chos kyi seng ge, being fifty-four years junior to him and having "written many refutations of the works of the Ācārya Candrakīrti," must have been familiar with the works and activities of Pa tshab,[22] and it can be assumed that he also knew about the distinction of Prāsaṅgika and Svātantrika. However, neither of these terms occur in the *Shar gsum stong thun*, although Phya pa spends much effort on the discussion of the use and validity of *prasaṅga* and *svatantra* for negating an absolutely real entity and for proving ultimate reality. In other contexts his arguments are very "*prasaṅga*-like," hypothetically accepting the opponent's position and showing its absurd consequences, which cannot be accepted by the opponent himself,[23] but in the context of absolute reality he accepts only *svatantra* reasoning as a valid method.

Phya pa, whose impact on the development of the Tibetan *pramāṇa* tradition has been studied and valued elsewhere,[24] is related by Shākya mchog ldan to have classified the *prasaṅgas* into eighteen types, five of which do not imply a *svatantra* as a contraposition, three of which imply a *svatantra* of "own type" *(rang rigs),* and ten of which imply a *svatantra* of "heterogeneous type" *(gzhan rigs).*[25] This classification was taken over by Sa skya paṇḍita in a slightly extended form, which was then handed down by Shākya mchog ldan and Go rams pa.[26] The "implied independent syllogism" *(rang rgyud 'phangs pa)* is the same as the "reversed reductio ad absurdum" *(prasaṅgaviparyaya)* of the Indian *pramāṇa* tradition. The *prasaṅga* hypothetically uses the opponent's proposition as a logical reason, in order to show an unavoidable consequence that is acceptable for neither the opponent nor the proponent. The *prasaṅgaviparyaya,* on the other hand, uses the negation of this unacceptable consequence as a logical reason that negates the logical reason of the *prasaṅga* and, thereby, the opponent's proposition;[27] in this case the logical reason, i.e., the negation of the unacceptable consequence, is accepted by both parties. Thus the syllogism is considered to be "independent" *(svatantra)* by Phya pa and the "old" tradition; in the dGe lugs pa tradition this is not necessarily the case (see p. 229, n. 76).

Here, in the *Shar gsum stong thun* we meet with some of these types of "implying *prasaṅgas*" and "implied *svatantras*" in Phya pa's own writing, which not only sheds light on Phya pa's general position regarding the use of *svatantra* and *prasaṅga,* but also helps in evaluating his contribution to the development of the classification of *prasaṅgas*.[28]

Establishing the Relation Between the Two Realities

In discussing the relation between the two levels of reality, Phya pa refutes the position that emptiness and the conventional are non-identical in nature *(stong pa nyid dang kun rdzob ngo bo gcig ma yin pa)* in the traditional and well-known way through argumentation *(rigs pa)* and authoritative scripture *(lung)*.[29] The second of these one would expect to consist mainly of quotations from *Saṃdhinirmocanasūtra* (SNS) 3.3–5, but surprisingly, this section does not contain a single quotation. Instead, Phya pa merely refers to the four unacceptable consequences *(prasaṅga)* of this position that are pointed out in the sūtra, and then formulates a *prasaṅga* together with its "implied *svatantra*" or *prasaṅgaviparyaya,* in each case. Only this method, Phya pa argues, is able to refute the opponent's position. The "consequences" discussed in the *Shar gsum stong thun* are not to be found in SNS in the form presented by Phya pa. They are merely loose renderings of the sūtra's message. Similarly, the respective arguments are not taken from the sūtra; apparently they are Phya pa's own.

1) The consequence that understanding suchness (tathatā) would not negate discursive development (prapañca) of appearing phenomena:

If one explicitly affirms that emptiness is not the same in nature as appearing phenomena, one implicitly affirms that someone who understands emptiness does not thereby understand the nature of appearing phenomena, and

> consequently he does not eliminate the imputation *(samāropa)* of an [ultimately] real nature on appearing phenomena, as he does not understand their nature, just as comprehending sound as impermanent does not remove doubt with regard to ether being permanent.

> This [*prasaṅga*] being accepted, with *(na)* the implied *svatantra* with the logical reason of essential property *(rang bzhin gyi rtags kyi rang rgyud 'phangs pa),* "He understands their substance [by understanding emptiness], because he removes imputation [of an ultimately real nature] on appearing phenomena through [its] removal by the experience establishing imputation [of an ultimately real nature] as being removed," it is implicitly established that the object of valid cognition, i.e., emptiness, too, and appearing phenomena are identical in substance.[30]

2) The consequence that emptiness would not be suited to being the true property:

> The statement, "Emptiness would not be the true property *(chos nyid)* of appearing phenomena, as it does not consist in the nature of appearing phenomena, just as permanence is not the true property of something impermanent," is a *prasaṅga* [with the logical reason] of nonperception of the pervading property *(khyab byed mi dmigs pa'i thal ba).*
>
> Its implication *('phangs pa),* "[Imputation of an ultimately real nature] is removed by establishing [emptiness] as [their] true property through inference; therefore, as it is the true property, [emptiness] is the nature of appearing phenomena," [operates with] a conventionally proving logical reason of essential property *(tha snyad sgrub pa'i rang bzhin gyi rtags).*[31]

In both these first two cases, the *prasaṅgas* correspond to the fourth of Sa paṇ's "*prasaṅgas* implying a heterogeneous *svatantra*" (no. 13 in Go rams pa's account), namely, the *prasaṅga* [with the logical reason] of nonperception of the pervading property *(khyab byed ma dmigs pa'i thal 'gyur)* implying a *svatantra* with the logical reason of essential property *(rang bzhin gyi gtan tshigs).*

The addition of "conventionally proving" to "logical reason of essential property" in one case does not denote a distinction, but rather a general description that applies to the logical reason or the *svatantra* in all cases in this context, regardless of whether it is explicitly mentioned or not.[32]

3) The consequence that for appearing phenomena the mere negation of a real thing would not be suited to being the intrinsic nature (svabhāva):

> In case of [the opponent] affirming suchness to be pervaded by being different from the conditioned *(saṃskāra),* the statement, "This mere negation of person *(pudgala)* and entity *(dharma)* for the conditioned would not be suchness, because [suchness] is not different from the conditioned," is a *prasaṅga* with the logical reason ascertained by valid cognition, refuting an affirmed pervasion.[33]

This appears to be the only case where no implied *svatantra* is given, and the *prasaṅga* as such is called "refuting" and "with the logical reason ascertained by valid cognition." Hypothetically this could mean that it was classified as a valid non-implying *prasaṅga* with the logical reason of perception of the pervading property *(*khyab byed dmigs pa'i thal 'gyur mi 'phen pa).* However, no such category seems to be known, and it is not evident why this particular *prasaṅga* should be "non-implying."

My translation of the *prasaṅga*'s specification is doubtful, and it has to be suspected that the text of the manuscript is not only incomplete[34] but also corrupt in this place. Apparently the passage containing the formulation of the respective implied *svatantra* is missing from the manuscript, and what appears as the specification of the *prasaṅga* should actually refer to the implied *svatantra.* Under this assumption the *prasaṅga* could be classified as corresponding to the second of Sa paṇ's "*prasaṅga*s implying an heterogeneous *svatantra*" (no. 14 according to Go rams pa's account; see n. 26), namely, the *prasaṅga* with the logical reason of perception of the essential property *(rang bzhin dmigs pa),* implying a *svatantra* with the logical reason of nonperception of the pervading property *(khyab byed ma dmigs pa).* Here it could be in the form of "The mere negation of person and entity for the conditioned is suchness, because suchness is not pervaded by being different from the conditioned; therefore the conditioned and suchness are non-different in nature," or something similar. The same classification of the *prasaṅga* can be made in the following case.

4) The consequence that the gnosis of the Buddha would be defiled and pure at the same time:

If it is affirmed that the conditioned and emptiness are totally different, it is also to be affirmed that the omniscient one perceives them totally differently. Thus, taking the conditioned as an object, the Buddha's gnosis would be defiled, because it has as its object a "real thing," which is different from emptiness; and perceiving emptiness, which is different from the conditioned, his gnosis would at the same time be pure; thus defilement and purification would occur simultaneously in one mental continuum, because it embraces a "real thing" as well as perceives emptiness.

This [*prasaṅga*] being accepted, with *(na)* the implied *svatantra* of nonperception of the pervading property *(khyab byed mi dmigs pa),* "There is not simultaneous defilement and purification for the Buddha, because this is invalidated by authoritative scripture; therefore the conditioned and emptiness are not seen separately," it is explicitly established that the Buddha does not see [them] differently; in this case it is implicitly established that the objects, too, do not exist differently.[35]

SNS 3.3–5 does not argue merely against the two realities being different. It in fact argues against the position that "the characteristic of the conditioned and the characteristic of the ultimate are non-different or different" *('du byed kyi mtshan nyid dang / don dam pa'i mtshan nyid tha dad pa ma yin pa'am / tha dad pa zhes zer ba).* This leaves room for various interpretations like the "difference of negated identity" *(gcig pa bkag pa'i tha dad)* between the two realities, which means that they are "undeterminable as being the same or different" *(de nyid dang gzhan du brjod du med pa),* or the two realities being "identical or different in no way whatsoever" *(gcig tha dad gang yang ma yin pa).* Phya pa takes the sūtra as refuting that they are non-different with regard to the characteristic distinction *(ldog pa, vyāvṛtti)*[36] and different in nature; he determines the two realities as "identical in nature and different with regard to the characteristic distinction" *(ngo bo gcig la ldog pa tha dad pa).*

In his chapter "Avoiding the unacceptable consequences taught in authoritative scripture for the (own system)" *(de [= rang gi lugs] la lung nas gsungs pa'i thal ba spang ba)*[37] Phya pa argues that the consequences from the sūtra cannot apply to "identical in nature," but rather they must be formulated against the concept "identical with regard to the characteristic distinction." Here he proceeds in the same manner as above: for each of the "consequences" he formulates a *prasaṅga* loosely connected with the statements of the sūtra and adds an implied *svatantra.*[38]

1) In this case the statement, "It follows that emptiness would be suited to being cognized by direct perception of ordinary beings, because it is non-different from appearing phenomena with

regard to the characteristic distinction," is a *prasaṅga* with the logical reason of the essential property *(rang bzhin kyi rtags);* [the statement] "[Emptiness] is not non-different from appearing phenomena with regard to the characteristic distinction, because it is not suited to being cognized by direct perception [of ordinary beings]," is a conventionally proving [*svatantra* with the logical reason] of nonperception of the pervading property *(khyab byed mi dmigs pa).*[39]

2) The statement, "Emptiness would be a support *(ālambana)* for the obstructions *(āvaraṇa),* because it is non-different from appearing phenomena with regard to the characteristic distinction," is a *prasaṅga* [with the logical reason] of the essential property *(rang bzhin);* and the statement, "[Emptiness] is not non-different from appearing phenomena with regard to the characteristic distinction, because it is not a support for the obstructions," is an implied *svatantra* [with the logical reason] of nonperception of the pervading property *(khyab byed mi dmigs pa).*[40]

Just as above, the *prasaṅgas* in these two cases are of the type appearing as the second "*prasaṅga* implying an heterogeneous *svatantra*" in Sa paṇ's list as related by Shākya mchog ldan.

3) The statement, "It follows that also physical *(rūpin)* and nonphysical phenomena would be without divisions, because they are non-different from emptiness with regard to the characteristic distinction," is a *prasaṅga* [with the logical reason] of the perception of pervasion through the contradictory *('gal bas khyab pa dmigs pa);* and the statement, "[Physical and nonphysical phenomena] are not non-different from emptiness with regard to the characteristic distinction, because they have divisions," is a *svatantra* [with the logical reason] of perception of a contradictory pervading property *(khyab byed 'gal ba dmigs pa).*[41]

4) [The formulation of] the consequence that it would not be necessary to seek emptiness in a way other than through seeing and hearing, viz., through contemplative endeavor, because it is non-different from appearing phenomena with regard to the characteristic distinction, is a *prasaṅga* [with the logical reason] of the

> perception of pervasion through the contradictory *('gal bas khyab pa dmigs pa);* and the statement, "[Emptiness] is not non-different from appearing phenomena with regard to the characteristic distinction, because it is necessary to seek it through an endeavor which is not [seeing and hearing]," too, is a *svatantra* [with the logical reason] of perception of a contradictory pervading property *(khyab byed 'gal ba dmigs pa).*
>
> Thus, there is the opportunity to imply four conventionally proving *(tha snyad sgrub) svatantras* [in this case].[42]

The type of *prasaṅga* used in these latter two instances appears—in a form that could be considered an alternative formulation of the one given here—only in Go rams pa's exposition (*gzhan rigs 'phen pa,* no. 12) of Sa paṇ's classification: a *prasaṅga* [with the logical reason] of the perception of a contradictory pervaded property *('gal ba'i khyab bya dmigs pa'i thal 'gyur).* Shākya mchog ldan mentions three types of related *prasaṅgas*: the *prasaṅgas* [with the logical reason] of the perception of the pervaded property being in contradiction to the intrinsic nature, the cause, and the effect, respectively *(rang bzhin, rgyu* and *'bras bu dang 'gal ba'i khyab bya dmigs pa'i thal 'gyur),* which imply a *svatantra* [with the logical reason] of the perception of the intrinsic nature, the effect, and the cause being in contradiction to the pervading property *(khyab byed dang 'gal ba'i rang bzhin dmigs pa, 'bras bu dmigs pa* and *rgyu dmigs pa'i rang rgyud)* respectively (nos. 5, 9, 10). The first two are also contained as separate types in Go rams pa's list (nos. 3 and 6), but not the third one, *'bras bu dang 'gal ba'i khyab bya dmigs pa'i thal 'gyur,* implying a *khyab byed dang 'gal ba'i rgyu dmigs pa'i rang rgyud.*[43]

Negating Absolutely Real Entities

The greater part of *Shar gsum stong thun* is dedicated to the "Negation of true[ly established] entities" *(yang dag pa'i dngos po dgag pa),*[44] and this chapter, as a whole, deals with the question of whether this negation can be achieved by the use of *prasaṅga* or of *svatantra.* Phya pa's position can be summed up in a simple statement: It is exclusively by using a *svatantra* that one is able to negate truly established, absolutely real entities; a *prasaṅga* is either inefficient or, in fact, a *svatantra.*[45]

Denying its efficiency,[46] Phya pa argues in a first subchapter that "(a *prasaṅga*) is totally unable to negate the object of negation" *([thal 'gyur gyis] dgag bya gtan dgag mi nus pa).*[47] Provided that the contradiction shown in the valid *(rnal ma) prasaṅga,* "From eternal existence it follows that origination is meaningless" *(ye nas yod pas skye ba don myed du thal zhes pa... thal ba rnal ma)* is based not only on mere conventional affirmation, but upon the very nature of the objects of cognition, it can be utilized to negate two different concepts.

1) When initial origination *(da gdod skye ba)* is negated on grounds of eternal existence being the very nature of the objects of cognition, "the actual formulation [of the consequence] itself is a *svatantra* argumentation" *(dngos su brjod pa nyid rang rgyud kyi rtags su 'gyur).*[48] Eternal existence established as the very nature of the objects of cognition is the property of the subject *(pakṣadharma)* which is pervaded by being contradictory to initial origination, and being empty with regard to initial origination is the property to be proved *(sādhyadharma).*

2) When eternal existence is negated on grounds of initial origination being the very nature of the objects of cognition, however, Phya pa states that "the implication through the *prasaṅga* is a *svatantra* argumentation" *(thal bas 'phangs pa rang rgyud gyi rtags su 'gyur ro).*[49] In any other case the *prasaṅga* is meaningless and inefficient.

These two examples being formally identical, it is not evident why the *prasaṅga* should *be* a *svatantra* in one case and *imply* one in the other. It could be assumed that *'phangs pa* / *'phen pa* is understood to be added even if it is not mentioned, but then, what is the purpose of the emphasis "the formulation *itself*" (*brjod pa* nyid)?

The second subchapter is introduced by the title "A *prasaṅga* does not negate all discursive development *(prapañca)*" *(thal 'gyur gyis spros pa mtha' dag mi khegs pa).*[50] In listing the titles of the subchapters at the beginning of the chapter, however, Phya pa gives a slightly expanded form, adding, "Even if [it were hypothetically accepted that] it is able [to negate the object of negation]" *([dgag bya dgag] nus kyang).* Of course, this could also mean "although a *prasaṅga* is able to negate [some aspects of the object of negation], it does not negate *all* discursive development," but then again, what would be the purpose of stressing in the title of the first subchapter that it is "*totally (gtan [nas])* unable"? No obvious solutions to either of these quandaries present themselves.

In this second subchapter, Phya pa argues that in the case of negating origination according to its four alternatives, viz., from itself, from another, and so on, by way of a *prasaṅga,* it is doubtful whether these four kinds of origination are ascertained as being impossible or possible. In the second case, i.e., when origination is being ascertained as possible, discursive development is not negated at all, and in the first case, i.e., when origination is being ascertained as impossible, the pervasion of all discursive development by the four kinds of origination is either ascertained or not ascertained.

> In the first case, the ascertainment of the nonexistence of the pervaded through ascertaining that the pervading property does not exist is a *svatantra* argumentation; in the second case, any discursive development not pervaded by the four alternatives is not negated.
>
> Or, the pervading property of discursive development is negated or not negated by the *prasaṅga.* In the first case the pervading property is not perceived (i.e., the *prasaṅga* which should, according to the above mentioned classification, be of the type "perception of the essential property" [*rang bzhin dmigs pa*], implies a *svatantra* of nonperception of the pervading property [*khyab byed ma dmigs pa*]*)*; in the second case the doubt regarding the possibility of discursive development is not abolished.[51]

Although in this chapter, too, Phya pa operates with the implied *svatantra* or *prasaṅgaviparyaya,* he mentions the possibility of such an implication only once, and that in such a way that it is weakened by the preceding statement. The reason might be that here, discussing the means of negating absolutely real entities, he wants to make perfectly sure that an argumentation with *prasaṅgaviparyaya* is taken as *svatantra* reasoning, in order to support his theory that absolutely real entities can be negated only by a *svatantra.*

Phya pa chos kyi seng ge on the Prāsaṅgika-Svātantrika Distinction

As stated above, Phya pa does not use the terms Prāsaṅgika and Svātantrika in his text. Nevertheless, the description and refutation of the system of the opponent, "the teacher Candrakīrti, etc.,"[52] evokes the impression that he does not merely argue for or against the use of *svatantra* or *prasaṅga,* but thinks of actual subdivisions or at least clearly distinct exegetical traditions of the Madhyamaka school that could be designated by these terms.

In this context Phya pa deals with three arguments brought forward by the opponent against the use of *svatantra* in proving ultimate reality. They are along the lines of the four positions refuted by Tsong kha pa in the *Lam rim chen mo* in the course of discussing whether the object of negation by reasoning *(rigs pa'i dgag bya)* should be negated by *prasaṅga* or *svatantra*. Unlike Tsong kha pa and the dGe lugs pas, Phya pa takes these arguments as actually representing Candrakīrti's position. Thus, for Phya pa they are distinctive features of the opponent's system, which could very well be called "Prāsaṅgika."

1) The subject (dharmin) is not accepted by both parties:
As false appearing phenomena are not established for a realist, and truly real appearing phenomena are not established for a Mādhyamika, the main argument of the opponent runs, it is inappropriate to use a *svatantra* when refuting a realist position. However, the opponent adds one argument that seems to point towards ontological and epistemological implications in the use of *svatantra:*

> Even if one admits the substratum to appear, the [property] to be proved [according to] one's wish *(zhe 'dod)* is not to be proved; therefore a logical reason proving it and a *svatantra* showing the logical reason are not correct, because a Mādhyamika affirms it in no way whatsoever, as it represents an extreme, no matter which of [the alternatives] "existent," "nonexistent," "both" and "neither" has been affirmed.[53]

The ontological aspect of this argument is not explicitly taken account of in Phya pa's refutation. Instead, in rather general terms he maintains that the same argument could be held against the use of *prasaṅga* as well:

> As an illusory person *(pudgala)* is not established for a realist, and a person fit to withstand analytical investigation is not established for a Mādhyamika, there is no common agreement *(mthun snang)* regarding the person to be refuted; therefore it is not correct to apply a *prasaṅga* to it.[54]

The whole discussion evokes the impression of referring to the actual person of the disputant rather than to the concept of *pudgala*, and this impression is confirmed by Shākya mchog ldan, who paraphrases and criticizes the entire chapter "Refutation of the opponent's system" (*de* [= *gzhan gyi lugs*] *sun dbyung ba;* sec. 125.112) in his *Lung rigs rgya mtsho.* Shākya mchog ldan also establishes a clear connection with the ontological significance of the argument; this, however, might be due to dGe lugs pa influence. (The "refutation" here represents Phya pa's position.)

> To the refutation, "Then, as the disputant applying a *prasaṅga* to anything, too, does not exist, a *prasaṅga* is not correct either," others reply that then the disputant was affirmed to exist. To this it is replied: [Neither is correct] because in this context [these] very severe wrong concepts are abandoned by [determining] the disputant about to refute anything [as taken to] exist for *(ngor)* erroneous *saṃvṛti,* even though he does not exist according to the Mādhyamika's own system, and determining the argument *(rigs pa)* refuting it, too, as taken to exist for erroneous *saṃvṛti,* even though it does not exist according to the Mādhyamika's own system....
>
> In short: In an absolute sense both the negation of what is to be negated and the proof of what is to be proved are, indeed, not affirmed. [However] Candra[kīrti] maintains that at the time of a Mādhyamika's mental and verbal activity *(shes brjod kyi tha snyad 'dogs pa)* no proof of what is to be proved is affirmed, but a mere verbal expression negating what is to be negated is made.[55]

As for the epistemological aspect of the opponent's initial argument, Phya pa deals with it in basically the same way as above: it could be held against the use of a *prasaṅga* with the same justification as against the use of a *svatantra:*

> As the appearance of the person [maintained] by the realist, too, is the object of worldly cognition, but the Mādhyamika, who affirms this in no way whatsoever, does not see a person, the application of a *prasaṅga* formulation to it is not correct. If a *prasaṅga* is applied, even though the person is not seen by oneself, an [independent] syllogism *(rtags)* [too, can] be applied, even though the substratum does not appear to oneself.[56]

2) The Madhyamaka does not accept a thesis (pratijñā) of its own:

On the basis of *Vigrahavyāvartanī* (VV) 29 and *Catuḥśataka* (CŚ) 16.25, which say that the Madhyamaka does not propose a thesis of its own and consequently is irrefutable, the opponent argues that both a logical reason proving a thesis and a *svatantra* argumentation showing the logical reason are not correct, and therefore discursive development *(prapañca)* is not to be abolished by a *svatantra.*[57] Phya pa replies with three arguments:

[A] *Negation of wrong concepts [by prasaṅga] is not correct (log rtogs 'gog mi 'thad pa):*

Objection: As there is nothing to be proved for a Mādhyamika, it is not correct to apply an [independent] syllogism.

[Answer:] As for the opponent there is no wrong concept which does not agree with the very nature of the objects of cognition, it is not correct to formulate a *prasaṅga* negating it.

Objection: The assumption of an absolutely real thing is a wrong concept which does not agree with the very nature of the objects of cognition.

[Answer:] Well, affirming being empty with regard to an absolutely real thing as the very nature of the objects of cognition violates [the principle of] the lack of a thesis.[58]

[B] *Rejection of both direct contraries is not correct (dngos 'gal gnyi ga 'dor ba mi 'thad pa):*

If in an absolute sense one does not accept both a thing and being empty with regard to it, how do [you] negate the acceptance of both?

Objection: The proof itself of the one is the rejection of the other; therefore it is contradictory to affirm both.

[Answer:] The negation itself of the one is the proof of the other; therefore it is contradictory not to affirm both.

Objection: This is not established.

[Answer:] [Your] above [statement] is not established either.[59]

This second discussion could be taken as evidence for Phya pa accepting appearing phenomena as conventionally established in themselves, provided Shākya mchog ldan's addition[60] is justified and the initial question actually contains Phya pa's own position. This, however, does not seem to be the case. The last part of the dialogue quoted rather indicates that Phya pa confronts his opponent, the "Prāsaṅgika," with a—hypothetical or actual—position of a realist and, by hypothetically advocating this position, shows that the Prāsaṅgika's approach is insufficient to negate the realist. A tendency towards this kind of procedure can occasionally be observed in other contexts as well.[61]

Similarly, his third argument would clearly indicate Phya pa's ontological position and, in addition, establish him as a proponent of an own thesis in Madhyamaka and as being under the very strong influence of Yogācāra philosophy, yet only if one takes the introductory question to reflect Phya pa's opinion.[62]

[C] *Mere cognition which is [not ?]*[63] *fit to withstand analytical investigation cannot be negated (dpyad [mi ?] bzod pa'i shes pa tsam dgag mi nus pa):*

How do the proponents *(smra ba dag)* of the lack of a thesis negate the opinion *(smra ba)* that only the absolute existence of clear mind established by experience exists as the only thesis?

Objection: [We negate it by] conducting the analysis, "is it one or many, originated or not originated, permanent or impermanent?"

[Answer:] Also the conducting [of this analysis] itself has to be analyzed, "is it a real thing or empty with regard to it?"

Objection: We affirm neither.

[Answer:] We, too, do not affirm any special quality whatsoever for the absolute[ly existing] clear [mind].

Objection: With an existing being *(ngo bo)* it is not correct not to affirm any special quality whatsoever.

[Answer:] With two direct contraries it is not correct to reject both.

> Objection: As being direct contraries, too, [they] are established [only] for the world, whereas for us [they] are not established.
>
> [Answer:] [Concepts like] not exceeding being permanent and impermanent, or not exceeding being one and many, etc., too, are established [only] for the world, whereas for us [they] are not established.
>
> Objection: One cannot reject the pervaded and the pervading ascertained by non-invalidated experience.
>
> [Answer:] One can also not reject direct contraries established by non-invalidated experience.[64]

In general, on account of these passages it seems to be impossible to determine whether and in which respect Phya pa agrees with the message of VV 29 and CŚ 16.25, or whether and to what extent he maintains an own thesis for the Madhyamaka. Here, the only thing obvious is that he does not accept the lack of such a thesis as an argument against the use of *svatantra.* However, he seems to tend towards taking *śūnyatāvāda* as a "thesis."

The third of the opponent's arguments points again to an ontological-epistemological aspect implied in the use of *svatantra.*

3) *Logical reason (liṅga), the [fact that the logical reason is a] property of the subject (pakṣadharma[tā]) and pervasion (vyāpti) are not ascertained by valid cognition (pramāṇa):*

This passage offers Phya pa's definition of valid cognition *(pramāṇa).* The opponent maintains that the message of MAv 6.30, which states that a worldly cognition cannot be valid cognition, results in "the consequence that whatever is valid cognition is a cognition which sees [ultimate] reality" *(tshad ma yin na bden pa mthong ba'i blor thal lo).*[65]

On this basis the argument runs:

> Objection: Perception *(pratyakṣa)* and inference *(anumāna)* themselves are worldly cognition but not valid cognition, therefore it is not correct that they ascertain [the fact that] the logical reason is a property of the subject and pervasion [of the logical reason by the property to be proven].

> [Answer:] The statement, "Origination follows to be meaningless, because the result is existent in the cause," [brought forward] against the proponent [of the theory] that the result is existent in the cause, too, is not a valid *prasaṅga,* therefore it is not correct to negate a wrong concept of others with it.
>
> Objection: This *[prasaṅga]* has the ability to prove the proposition [to be] unacceptable [for the opponent], because of the general characteristics of a *prasaṅga* as such, [namely] the logical reason and pervasion being established for the opponent; therefore it is not established not to be a valid *prasaṅga.*
>
> [Answer:] Perception and inference, too, have the general characteristics of valid cognition as such, [namely] contradiction with the [wrong] conceptual imputation on a subject previously not comprehended *(rtogs pa)* by a cognition that is nonerroneous with regard to [that] subject; therefore it is not correct that they are not valid cognition.[66]

Against the "Prāsaṅgika's" definition of valid cognition Phya pa objects:

> In the case of a valid *prasaṅga,* too, an affirmed logical reason and pervasion are ascertained and [the logical reason] removed *(bsal bar 'gyur)* from the proposition by valid cognition.
>
> Objection: This is without pervasion, because also a *prasaṅga* is possible where [the logical reason and] pervasion are affirmed and [the logical reason] removed from the proposition by its own words.[67]
>
> [Answer:] [Your above-stated] consequence that [whatever is valid cognition] is a cognition which sees [ultimate] reality, is without pervasion as well, because it is not contradictory that even a perception and an inference investigating *('jal ba)* a conventional [reality] *(saṃvṛti[satya])* and an inference investigating ultimate reality *(paramārthasatya),* which [all] do not *see* [ultimate] reality, have [the characteristics of valid cognition].[68]

Apart from this controversy on the definition of valid cognition, the discussion runs very much along the by now well-known lines, i.e., the arguments brought forward against the use of *svatantra* apply rather to the *prasaṅga.*

> Objection: Logical reason and pervasion are seen by worldly cognition but are not established for *(bas)* a Mādhyamika, who does not affirm anything whatsoever, therefore the Mādhyamika does not apply an [independent] syllogism *(rtags).*
>
> [Answer:] Logical reason and pervasion, though being affirmed [hypothetically by the Mādhyamika], are seen by the world but are not seen by the Mādhyamika, therefore it is not correct that the Mādhyamika should apply a *prasaṅga.*
>
> Objection: Even worldly cognition examining conventionally belongs to the very tradition *(rgyud)* of Madhyamaka, which in an absolute sense does not affirm anything whatsoever; therefore, [hypothetically?] affirming the logical reason and pervasion, [worldly cognition examining conventionally] is established exactly for that person who advocates Madhyamaka.
>
> [Answer:] For this very reason the [fact that the logical reason is a] property of the subject and pervasion, too, are established exactly for that person who advocates Madhyamaka.[69]

The Prāsaṅgika-Svātantrika Distinction According to dGe lugs pa Interpretation

In dGe lugs pa *grub mtha'* literature, the Prāsaṅgika-Svātantrika distinction is the common and main division of Madhyamaka. No other Tibetan teacher or tradition has put as much emphasis on and analytical effort into this topic or offered such detailed argumentations as Tsong kha pa and other proponents of the dGe lugs pa school. The basic distinctive feature is, of course, the same as in the older texts; the designations for the main divisions of Madhyamaka are derived from their methods of proving reality through reasoning, either by means of *prasaṅga* or of *svatantra,* respectively. Thus, lCang skya rol pa'i rdo rje (1717–1786) defines a Svātantrika as

> a Mādhyamika who affirms the triple characterization of a logical reason for proving nonreality as established in itself *(rang ngos nas grub pa),*

and a Prāsaṅgika as

> a Mādhyamika who, without affirming independent syllogism, asserts that an inferential consciousness comprehending nonreality is generated merely through what is approved by others.[70]

The present paper is not the place to discuss Tsong kha pa's and the dGe lugs pas' arguments against the use of *svatantra* reasoning in detail.[71] Within their tradition this topic is considered to be one of the crucial and most difficult points in Madhyamaka exegesis, and as such it is included in the *dBu ma'i rtsa ba'i dka' gnas chen po brgyad kyi brjed byang* of rGyal tshab dar ma rin chen. Here, this text can serve as a summary.

Regarding the subdivision of Madhyamaka rGyal tshab uses the terms Svātantrika and Prāsaṅgika, but alternatively he introduces the expressions "those who make ultimate reality *(de kho na nyid)* comprehended by means of affirming an independent *(rang rgyud, svatantra)* logical reason *(rtags)*" and "those who generate the comprehension of ultimate reality without affirming this [independent logical reason] by means of a logical reason acknowledged by others *(gzhan grags, paraprasiddha).*"[72] He defines these two types of logical reason in the following way:

> A [logical reason] that is, without depending on what is affirmed by others, autonomously supplied with the triple characterization *(trairūpya)* established by a valid cognition *(pramāṇa)* which is non-erroneous with regard to the object of [its special] mode of apprehension is [called] "independent," and
>
> a [logical reason] that is, on the contrary, supplied with the triple characterization ascertained by a valid cognition in dependence on what is affirmed by others is called "a logical reason *(gtan tshigs)* acknowledged by others."[73]

The crucial point is that—as indicated in rGyal tshab's definition quoted above—the valid cognition establishing the triple characterization is either accepted by oneself or solely by the opponent, but not the triple characterization ascertained by valid cognition as such. rGyal tshab continues:

> Some hold that it is Prāsaṅgika [method] to negate wrong concepts of others through the triple characterization [of a valid logical reason] affirmed by others, or through what merely amounts to [such] an affirmation *(khas blangs pa'i mthar thug pa tsam)*,[74] and Svātantrika [method] to do so through the triple characterization ascertained by valid cognition; ...it has been exhaustively explained in detail elsewhere that this is not correct.[75]

This means that according to dGe lugs pa interpretation the "reversed reductio ad absurdum" *(prasaṅgaviparyaya)* is not to be considered a *svatantra,* as it is done by Phya pa and the "old" tradition, but is in fact part of the *prasaṅga* reasoning.[76] Tsong kha pa, who is to be considered as strict a Prāsaṅgika as Phya pa is said to be a Svātantrika, states in the *rTsa she ṭik chen,*

> In the case of implying *prasaṅga*s such as: "If a sprout is affirmed to have an intrinsic nature established in itself, it will not arise in dependence upon the seed, because it exists by its own nature," there are very many [instances] of proving a thesis *(dam bca')* which is the reverse of the logical reason in the *prasaṅga,* having used the reverse of the [proved] property in the *prasaṅga* as the logical reason [in a *prasaṅgaviparyaya* like]: "Because it arises in dependence, the sprout does not have an intrinsic nature established in itself."
>
> In this case, further, a pure negative determination *(vyavaccheda)* of the existence [of something] in itself proposed by the opponent is being made, but no other property is proved; in this respect all [these instances] are alike.[77]

In the view of the dGe lugs pas, the difference between Prāsaṅgika and Svātantrika is not restricted to their methodological approaches; different identifications of the "object of negation" *(dgag bya)* are implied.[78] This technical term refers in a general way to that which is opposed to reality and its realization; its identification provides the criteria for distinguishing "existent" from "nonexistent," and thus constitutes a basis for ontology.

In his *Lam rim chen mo* Tsong kha pa states:

> The learned ones from the time of the later propagation of the doctrine in the Land of Snow applied the two designations "Prāsaṅgika" *(thal 'gyur ba)* and "Svātantrika" *(rang rgyud pa)* to Mādhyamikas. As this is in accordance with the *Prasannapadā* it is not to be considered their invention. Thereby the distinction of whether or not they conventionally accept external objects [established through their own characteristic][79] is ascertained, and when they are named according to [their respective] manners of generating the theory of ascertaining the ultimate *(paramārtha)*, i.e., emptiness *(śūnyatā)*, in a mental continuum *(saṃtāna)*, too, the distinction of Prāsaṅgika and Svātantrika is ascertained.[80]

The characteristic feature of the Svātantrikas' acceptance of an independent syllogism, Tsong kha pa argues, is their acceptance of an "own characteristic" *(svalakṣaṇa)* that is conventionally established in itself *(tha snyad du rang gi ngo bos grub pa'i rang mtshan);* this coincides with the Svātantrikas' specific interpretation of the object of negation *(dgag bya)*.[81]

According to dGe lugs pa exegesis, this object of negation is generally specified by six concepts.[82] Although they are more or less synonyms, they form two groups. The first one, "established as real" *(bden par grub pa, satyasiddha),* "established in an absolute sense" *(don dam par grub pa, paramārthasiddha),* and "truly established" *(yang dag par grub pa, samyaksiddha),* relates to an ontologically absolute status of appearing phenomena, implying independence from causes and conditions; the second, "established in itself" (lit., "through its own nature") *(rang gi ngo bos* or *rang ngos nas grub pa, svarūpasiddha / svabhāvasiddha),* "established through its own characteristic" *(rang gi mtshan nyid kyis grub pa, svalakṣaṇasiddha),* and "established through its intrinsic nature" *(rang bzhin gyis grub pa, svabhāvasiddha),* refers to objects in relation to their cognizing subjects. "Own nature" and "own intrinsic nature" denote the very own status and mode of existence of the objects, being independent from others, namely from conventional cognitions.[83]

The Prāsaṅgikas take both of these groups as equally being attributes of the object of negation, while the Svātantrikas accept only the first one, *bden par grub pa,* etc. This means that the latter assume appearing phenomena as established in themselves, through their own-being and through their own characteristic. This, however, implies existence in an absolute sense, even if it is accepted only conventionally.

In addition, the Svātantrikas accept nondefective sense consciousness conventionally as nonerroneous with regard to the appearing object *(snang yul)*. This, too, is shown by the fact that they accept things to be established in themselves, because they appear that way.[84] Only the objects have to be distinguished as being correct or false, according to whether or not they have causal efficiency corresponding to their appearance. In that way they constitute, according to the SDV, correct *(samyak)* and false *(mithyā)* *saṃvṛti*.[85]

The Prāsaṅgikas, on the other hand, do not accept this distinction with regard to the object aspect of *saṃvṛti*, and they consider every sense cognition of someone not enlightened to be erroneous, because they perceive their objects as established through their own characteristic, regardless of whether they perceive objects that are "correct" or "false" from a worldly point of view. There exists only the difference between subtle and gross error with regard to the appearing object.[86]

However, no Indian master classified as Svātantrika explicitly advocates the conventional existence of anything "in itself," "through its own characteristic," or "through its own-being," and Indian Mādhyamikas do not seem to have been aware of any exegetical differences in this respect.[87] The only exception might be Candrakīrti, but his description of his own system as unique even among Mādhyamikas[88] might not point to the Prāsaṅgika-Svātantrika distinction as clearly as Tsong kha pa seems to interpret it. As an introduction to a quotation from the relevant passage he states that Candrakīrti explains his own way of positing the ultimate *(paramārtha)* and the conventional *(saṃvṛti/sāṃvṛta)* as being in agreement with Buddhapālita, who explains the intentions of Nāgārjuna correctly, and diverging from that of other Mādhyamikas;[89] Buddhapālita is not even mentioned by Candrakīrti in this context. That means that the dGe lugs pa interpretation of the Svātantrikas' position is the result of Tsong kha pa's interpretive efforts and skills and his awareness of possible implications of their methodological approach.[90]

Of course, Tsong kha pa's views are not unanimously accepted by all Tibetan scholars. Go rams pa, for example, opposes them strictly. The main difference between the two systems of Madhyamaka, he argues, lies exclusively in the method of proving the ultimate in argumentation,[91] and

> for the statement of those who pretend to be scholars: "Svātantrikas affirm independent syllogism, because [according to their system] they have to prove phenomena established through their own

characteristic, while Prāsaṅgikas do not affirm independent syllogism, because they do not have to prove this" no basis is to be found anywhere, as this would mean that Svātantrikas prove phenomena established through their own characteristic when they prove the thesis of negated origination according to the four alternatives.[92]

To What Extent and According to Which Criteria Is Phya pa to Be Classified as a Svātantrika?

Methodology

On the basis of the method applied for proving the ultimate, Phya pa chos kyi seng ge is certainly a strict Svātantrika, but only if one distinguishes between the use of reductio ad absurdum and independent syllogism according to the "old" interpretation, taking an argumentation with a *prasaṅgaviparyaya* as *svatantra* reasoning. If, however, one considers the dGe lugs pas' specifications of *svatantra* reasoning, this question is not to be answered so clearly; the mere fact that Phya pa insists on the use of "implying *prasaṅgas*"/"implied *svatantras*" would not be sufficient to label him a Svātantrika.

Similarly, if my assumption regarding the original form of the corrupt text of *Shar gsum stong thun* 6,15–17 is correct and the specification "with the logical reason ascertained by valid cognition" should not, as it appears to do, refer to the *prasaṅga* but to an implied *svatantra* (p. 215 above; nn. 33 and 34), this would merely show that Phya pa holds the opinion rejected by rGyal tshab, namely that the logical reason of a *svatantra* is ascertained by valid cognition, and that of a *prasaṅga* by what is acknowledged by others (n. 75). This, in turn, could be taken as evidence for Phya pa affirming "the triple characterization of a logical reason for proving non-reality as *established in itself*" (n. 70), or using "a logical reason that is, without depending on what is affirmed by others, *autonomously* supplied with the triple characterization established by a valid cognition that is nonerroneous with regard to the object of [its special] mode of apprehension" (n. 73).

In these Svātantrika definitions by lCang skya and rGyal tshab, however, the emphasis lies on "established *in itself*" and "autonomously." The question is: Do these specifications really apply to Phya pa's interpretation of *svatantra*? We will have to return to this problem below.

The "Old" Prāsaṅgika-Svātantrika Distinction

The topics that form the core of this "old" distinction are closely and inseparably connected with the question of the methodology applied; in the *Shar gsum stong thun* they are discussed in the context of defending the use of *svatantra* for proving the ultimate (see p. 220ff.).

If one takes, as Phya pa obviously does, the positions he argues against as doctrines of the "Prāsaṅgika," i.e., of the "Ācārya Candrakīrti, etc.," Phya pa has certainly to be considered a Svātantrika. However, from a dGe lugs pa perspective the whole matter looks different.

Basically, these topics correspond to the four *pūrvapakṣas* in Tsong kha pa's *Lam rim chen mo* within the lengthy discussion of "Negating the (object of negation by reasoning) by *prasaṅga* or *svatantra*" *(de [= rigs pa'i dgag bya] 'gog pa te thal rang gang gis byed pa['i tshul])*,[93] ascribed to Jayānanda, "a (?) *lotsāva*, pupil of this scholar" *(paṇ ḍi ta de'i slob ma lo tstsha ba dag)*—identified, among others, as Khu lotsāva,[94]—"present-day (scholars) who consider themselves Prāsaṅgika-Mādhyamikas" *(da lta dbu ma thal 'gyur bar 'dod pa dag)*, and "Mādhyamikas of early times, Tibetan scholars following the Ācārya Candrakīrti" *(sngon gyi dbu ma pa slob dpon zla ba'i rjes su 'brang pa'i bod kyi mkhas pa)*.

Tsong kha pa and his successors strictly object to the positions that a thesis is unacceptable for the Madhyamaka, that the Madhyamaka does not have its own system, and that nothing is established by valid cognition, etc. This has all been dealt with elsewhere,[95] and it shall not be a topic of this paper. Here it may suffice to note that for the dGe lugs pa tradition this position is not a distinctive feature of the Prāsaṅgika, but a misconception of it, or rather of Madhyamaka in general. 'Jam dbyangs bzhad pa, for example, explicitly states that proponents of this theory are not to be considered Mādhyamikas, even if they consider themselves to be so.[96]

Since from a dGe lugs pa perspective these arguments do not represent Prāsaṅgika doctrine, the mere fact of refuting them would not testify to Phya pa being a Svātantrika, in the same way his methodological approach *alone* would not.

Ontology and Epistemology

In order to classify Phya pa as a Svātantrika according to the dGe lugs pa distinction, it would be necessary that he, as mentioned above, advocate "the triple characterization of a logical reason for proving non-reality *established in itself*" (see n. 70) and that he thereby accept "an own characteristic *(svalakṣaṇa),* which is conventionally established in itself" (n. 81). That means the main emphasis has to be laid on the ontological and epistemological implications of the Prāsaṅgika-Svātantrika distinction maintained by the dGe lugs pas.

As no Svātantrika would explicitly claim a *svalakṣaṇa* conventionally established in itself, and thus it is not to be expected that this question is directly dealt with in a text like the *Shar gsum stong thun,* it might be difficult to determine Phya pa's respective position with certainty on the basis of such a summarizing text with its concise way of presenting arguments, unless one be equipped with the analytical skill of Tsong kha pa. In any case, further and more intensive analysis of this text than has been possible up to now will be necessary. At the present stage it must suffice to point out some possible points of departure, as has already been done above (p. 220ff.).

These instances, however, seem not to provide any clear evidence for classifying Phya pa a Svātantrika according to the criteria of the dGe lugs pa distinction. In the two cases that indicate the acceptance of anything as conventionally established in itself it is at least doubtful whether the acceptance of both a thing and its emptiness (see [B], p. 223 above) and of the absolute existence of clear mind (see [C], p. 224 above) actually represent Phya pa's own position.

With regard to the ontological-epistemological status of the logical reason, the specification "with the logical reason ascertained by valid cognition" referring to an implied *svatantra* in contrast to an implying *prasaṅga* (p. 215; n. 33 and 34) could be, as stated above, interpreted as implying the notion of "the triple characterization of a logical reason *established in itself.*" However, the concluding part of the discussion of whether the logical reason *(liṅga),* the fact that the logical reason is a property of the subject *(pakṣadharmatā),* and pervasion *(vyāpti)* are ascertained by valid cognition in the *Shar gsum stong thun* suggests that Phya pa advocates an ontological status of the individual parts of a syllogism that resembles dGe lugs pa interpretation, i.e., as *not* established in themselves or through their intrinsic nature. Even worldly cognition examining conventionally, Phya pa argues, is accepted by the Madhyamaka, which in an absolute sense does not affirm anything whatsoever; therefore, also *pakṣadharmatā* and *vyāpti* are established for a Mādhyamika (p. 227; n. 69). However, this argument is in contradiction to the claim expressed by dGe 'dun grub pa, viz., that "the logical reason and [its] pervasion [by the property to be proven] are established for the cognition, and not the [fact that the logical reason is a] property of the subject and pervasion [of the logical reason by the property to be proven]" (n. 67).

In addition, the "Prāsaṅgika's" definition of valid cognition *(pramāṇa)* presented in this passage, viz., "a cognition that sees [ultimate] reality" *(bden pa mthong ba'i blo)* (n. 65) would be unacceptable from a dGe lugs pa point of view. His "general characteristics of a *prasaṅga* as such," namely "the logical reason and pervasion being established for the opponent" reveal the same wrong understanding referred to by rGyal tshab in his *dBu rtsa dka' gnas* (n. 75). Phya pa's definition of valid cognition as "contradiction with the [wrong] conceptual imputation on a subject previously not comprehended *(rtogs pa)* by a cognition that is nonerroneous with regard to [that] subject" (p. 226; n. 66), on the other hand, corresponds to dGe lugs pa views, however with the exception of interpreting *pramāṇa* as a "new" cognition.[97]

With regard to the ontological position in general, striking similiarities on important basic topics are to be perceived between Phya pa and Tsong kha pa. As they are relevant for the topic of the present paper only indirectly, they shall only be mentioned here and have to be dealt with in detail separately. The following topics are concerned in particular:

The basis of distinction (dbye gzhi) of the two realities: Phya pa defines it as "the mere basis of definition pointed out as an object of cognition" *(shes byar mtshon pa'i mtshan gzhi tsam),* Tsong kha pa as "the mere object of cognition" *(shes bya tsam).*[98]

The difference between the two realities: Phya pa lays great emphasis on determining the two realities as "identical in nature and different with regard to the characteristic distinction" *(ngo bo gcig la ldog pa tha dad pa).*[99] Equally, in Tsong kha pa's Madhyamaka exegesis the same determination is of utmost importance, as it provides a basis for his interpretation of "neither existent nor nonexistent" as meaning "neither existent in an absolute sense nor nonexistent conventionally," which is understood as referring to both realities and thus represents the essence of his ontology.[100] Apparently this position was unique for the time of Phya pa as well as of Tsong kha pa.

Identification of the object of negation: For Tsong kha pa's understanding of conventional existence *(tha snyad du yod pa),* which relates to both realities, it is crucial that only absolute existence *(don dam par yod pa)* is to be negated, but not conventional reality *(saṃvṛtisatya)* in the sense of conventionally real things or existence as such *(yod pa tsam),* for this would imply either substantialism or nihilism. The same is stressed also by Phya pa.[101]

The knowability of ultimate reality (paramārthasatya): Both masters argue for *paramārthasatya* as an object of cognition *(shes bya).*[102]

Other Criteria

Early Sa skya pa masters mention accepting or not accepting the division into "conceptual" *(paryāya)* and "nonconceptual" *(aparyāya) paramārtha* and *saṃvṛti* as criteria to distinguish Svātantrika and Prāsaṅgika (nn. 14 and 15). In a dGe lugs pa distinction this feature is irrelevant; although the concept of dividing *paramārtha* in this way was developed within texts attributed to the Svātantrika-Madhyamaka, Tsong kha pa, too, accepts it with regard to *paramārtha,* without, however, fully incorporating it into his Prāsaṅgika system. He also establishes a clear connection between these two kinds of *paramārtha* and excluding negation *(paryudāsa[pratiṣedha], ma yin dgag)* and pure negation *(prasajyapratiṣedha, med dgag)*[103] respectively. Both of them are "real" *paramārtha,* endowed with dualistic appearance in the one case, and without it in the other.[104] In general, however, i.e., without applying this distinction, *paramārtha(satya)* has to be classified as pure negation.

In *Shar gsum stong thun* Phya pa does not make this distinction with regard to either of the two realities. He does hold, however, that only the pure negation is ultimate reality *(paramārthasatya, don dam bden pa),* as it is the only thing that is real as an object of a valid cognition investigating the ultimate *(mthar thug 'jal ba'i gzhal byar bden pa),* which is his definition of *paramārthasatya.*[105]

One single argument within his refutation of the opinion that *paramārthasatya* is not an object of cognition might point to the concept underlying this division of *paramārthasatya,* but it is not approved of by Phya pa.

> Objection: [The fact that something which is not real in an investigation of the ultimate *(mthar thug dpyad na)* is *saṃvṛtisatya*] is ascertained through simultaneously determining the usual designation *(spyod pa'i brda)* [of *saṃvṛtisatya*] by accepting that something [which is not real in an investigation of the ultimate] is pervaded by [being] *saṃvṛtisatya.*
>
> [Answer:] [In the case of] "fit to withstand analytical investigation" being pervaded by *paramārthasatya,* too, it is like that. If one holds

> it to be *saṃvṛti,* because emptiness is a substance not fit to withstand analytical investigation, the appearing phenomenon would be *paramārthasatya,* because it was a substance fit to withstand analytical investigation.[106]

A dGe lugs pa would mention the division of *saṃvṛti(satya)* into a correct *(samyak)* and a false *(mithyā)* one as being typical of the Svātantrika system. The acceptance of correct *saṃvṛti(satya)* depends on the assumption that worldly cognition is correct cognition and on accepting an own characteristic *(svalakṣaṇa)* established in itself, and is thus representative of the respective ontological-epistemological position.

Phya pa chos kyi seng ge clearly accepts this division as such, without, however, putting much emphasis on it. He merely gives his definitions, without any discussion.

> An erroneous apprehended object *(gzung yul)* [being] an object of [a cognition] not investigating the ultimate is false *saṃvṛti;* what is not an erroneous apprehended object [being] an object of [a cognition] not investigating the ultimate is correct *saṃvṛti.*[107]

For Phya pa himself this is not a point of controversy with "the Ācārya Candrakīrti, etc."; for their system he postulates the same division, quoting—again without any discussion—MAv 6.25, 6.26, and 6.28.[108]

The only discussion in this context is on refuting a wrong interpretation of correct *saṃvṛti* based on Jñānagarbha's SDV 8.[109] At the present stage I am unable to identify the proponent of this interpretation, but it certainly has nothing to do with a possible distinction of Prāsaṅgika and Svātantrika.

Concluding Summary

In regard to the Prāsaṅgika-Svātantrika distinction of the Madhyamaka school of philosophy one has to distinguish two methods. Although both methods exhibit the use of *prasaṅga* or *svatantra* reasoning as the basic distinctive feature, they are essentially different. The "old" method centers on the question of whether an own thesis *(pratijñā)* is denied or maintained, and it takes any proof by means of the triply characterized *(trairūpya)* logical reason established by valid cognition to be *svatantra* reasoning. The second method, i.e., the "dGe lugs pa distinction," on the other hand, concentrates on the question of whether an own character *(svalakṣana)* established in itself is denied or accepted—with all its ontological and epistemological implications—and it takes only a reasoning where the triple characterization of the logical reason is established by valid cognition autonomously, without depending on what is acknowledged by others to be *svatantra.*

Phya pa chos kyi seng ge appears to be somewhere in between these. On the one hand he is—regardless of the fact that he does not use the terms Prāsaṅgika and Svātantrika at all—clearly indebted to the "old" distinction, and according to it he is a Svātantrika. On the other hand his views show a number of correspondences in particular with the ontological and epistemological position of Tsong kha pa, and at the present stage I cannot see any convincing reason to classify him as a Svātantrika according to the "dGe lugs pa distinction," unless his disagreement with dGe 'dun grub pa regarding the question of whether the fact that the logical reason is a property of the subject and pervasion of the logical reason by the property to be proven should be established for a Madhyāmika or the logical reason and its pervasion by the property to be proven should be established, turns out to be of major importance in this respect. It could be that Phya pa simply was not yet in the position to declare—as Tsong kha pa did—the current interpretations of his time as misconceptions with regard to the Prāsaṅgika.

However, it has to be stressed again that this paper represents a preliminary study of Phya pa's work; further and more detailed and intensive studies, including the works of his immediate students, might change the present impression and reveal a different picture.

Abbreviated Topical Outline (sa bcad) *of the* dBu ma shar gsum gyi stong thun

The chapter titles given here are not in all cases strict translations of the Tibetan; in particular in chapters that are not relevant for the present paper, the titles given merely indicate the content of the respective chapter. Nevertheless, additions to the Tibetan wording are indicated by square brackets; alternative formulations to be found within the text are given in round brackets. Figures within parentheses denote the number of subdivisions in the respective chapter. For the topical outline (in Tibetan) in full detail see *Shar gsum stong thun* (pp. xxv–xxxiii).

1 (2)	Ascertainment of the objects of cognition	1,12–125,22
11 (4)	Distinction of the two realities	1,15–15,16
111	Basis of the distinction	1,17–2,2
112 (6)	Meaning of the distinction	2,3–13,16
112.1	Negation of a difference in nature of the two realities	2,7–14
112.2 (2)	Negation of the "difference of negated identity"	2,15–9,17
112.21 (3)	Negation of a difference between emptiness and the conventional	2,18–7,14
112.211	Through argumentation	2,20–5,14
112.212 (4)	Through authoritative scripture	5,15–7,8
112.213	Authoritative scripture proving the two realities to be one [in nature]	7,9–14
112.22 (3)	Negation of [the assumption] that emptiness being of the same nature as the conventional is not *paramārthasatya*	7,15–9,17
112.3	Negation of an identity with regard to the characteristic distinction	9,18–10,5
112.4	Presentation of the own system	10,6–12

112.5	Avoiding the [unacceptable] consequences taught in authoritative scripture for the own system	10,13–12,20
112.6	Avoiding the mistake that from the two realities being of identical nature it would follow that absolute[ly real] entities are established	13,1–16
113	Ascertainment of the number of the two realities	13,17–14,15
114	Meaning of the names of the two realities	14,16–15,16
12 (5)	Definitions of the two realities	15,17–125,22
121 (2)	Individual definitions of the two realities	15,21–24,3
121.1 (3)	The own system	16,1–18,3
121.2 (2)	Negation of the opponent's system	18,4–24,3
121.21 (2)	Negation of a differently assumed definition of *paramārthasatya*	18,7–22,17
121.22	Negation of a differently assumed definition of correct *saṃvṛtisatya*	22,18–24,3
122 (2)	Basis of the definition	24,4–35,7
123 (7)	Avoiding polemics regarding the basis of the definition	35,8–57,17
124	Valid cognition ascertaining the basis of the definition	57,18–58,2
125 (2)	Valid cognition ascertaining the definition being contained therein (Ascertainment of the basis of definition of *paramārthasatya* in the form of an excluding negation, to be empty with regard to being established by logical analysis)	58,3–125,22
125.1 (2)	Negation of true[ly established] entities	58,5–124,9

125.11 (4)	Refutation of the object of negation being negated by *prasaṅga*	58,7–77,20
125.111 (4)	Exposition of the opponent's system	58,9–64,15
125.111.1	Distinction of erroneous and nonerroneous cognition by the Ācārya Candrakīrti, etc.	58,12–59,10
125.111.2 (3)	Twofold distinction of reality according to that	59,11–61,3
125.111.3	Refutation of discursive development being negated by *svatantra*	61,4–62,14
125.111.4	Negation of discursive development by *prasaṅga*	63,1–64,15
125.112 (3)	Refutation of the opponent's system	65,1-76,5
125.112.1 (3)	It is not correct not to accept the use of *svatantra*	65,4–69,20
125.112.11	The lack of a commonly accepted subject is not fit as its reason	65,7–66,6
125.112.12 (3)	The lack of an own thesis in Madhyamaka is not fit as its reason	66,7–67,17
125.112.121	Negation of wrong concepts [by *prasaṅga*] is not correct	66,10–14
125.112.122	Rejection of both direct contraries is not correct	66,15–67,3
125.112.123	Mere cognition that is [not ?] fit to withstand analytical investigation cannot be negated	67,4–17
125.112.13	The lack of the logical reason, the [fact that it is a] property of the subject, and pervasion being ascertained by valid cognition is not fit as its reason	68,1–69,20
125.112.2 (3)	A *prasaṅga* is unable to negate a realistic position	70,1–72,15

2 (2)	Means of persevering Mahāyāna practice	126,1–138,18
21 (3)	Means based on *saṃvṛtisatya*	126,9–135,7
211	Taking refuge in the [three] jewels	126,11–128,2
212	Production of the mind of enlightenment	128,3–22
213 (3)	Completing the perfections	129,1–135,7
22 (3)	Insight based on *paramārthasatya*	135,8–138,18
221 (3)	Insight through hearing	135,11–138,4
222	Insight through thinking	138,5–10
223	Insight through contemplation	138,11–18
3 (4)	The stage of the omniscient Buddha	139,1–145,18
31	*dharmakāya* and *rūpakāya*	139,4–142,16
32	Definition of the three *kāya*s	143,1–19
33	Ascertaining the number of the three *kāya*s	144,1–13
34	Differences among the three *kāya*s	144,13–145,18

Notes

1 I wish to thank my colleagues Helmut Krasser and Ernst Steinkellner for their critical remarks and suggestions, and Anne MacDonald for correcting my English.

2 See Tauscher (1995): n. 4.

3 Roerich (1949): 334. See also Shākya mchog ldan's comments in his *dBu ma'i byung tshul*, 234,6: ...*zla ba'i bstan bcos kyi tshig don gnyis ka la dgag pa'i rnam grangs shin tu mang po yod pa'i bstan bcas mdzad* /

4 See Roerich (1949): 334, and Chandra (1963): 637–830, nos. 11076, 11317–11321, 11473, 11803–11806, 11910.

5 A manuscript (hereafter, MS) of this text was discovered by Leonard van der Kuijp, who left a photocopy of it with me in 1995. My edition was published in 1999 in Vienna; references to the work in this article are to this edition (or, occasionally, to the MS).

6 See Tauscher (1999): nn. 2 and 3.

7 For an overall structure of the text see the abbreviated topical outline *(sa bcad)* at the end of the body of this paper.

8 For a more comprehensive survey of various *grub mtha'* texts, see Mimaki (1982): 27ff.

9 *Grub mtha' brjed byang:* 341,3 and 343,4; *lTa ba'i brjed byang:* 208,6 and 209,4.

10 *lTa ba'i brjed byang,* 230,4–231,4: *dbu ma'i lta ba mdor bsdu na / ma ya ste sgyu ma lta bur 'dod pa dang / a bra ti sti te rab tu mi gnas par 'dod pa'o // de la sgyu ma lta bu ni... bsdus na dngos po rnams kyi chos nyid ni / ngo bo nyid sgyu ma lta bu'i chos nyid ni bden no zhes 'dod do // rab tu mi gnas pa ni chos thams cad la ming dang brda dang tha snyad kyi mtshan nyid sna tshogs sa brtan cing / rnam par bzhag kyang ji lta bu'i mtshan nyid du'ang gnas pa mi 'grub ste / ... rab tu shin tu mi gnas pa zhes bya'o //*

In his *Tattvaratnāvalī* (1,17–17) Advayavajra gives the terms *māyopamādvayavādin (sgyu ma lta bur gnyis su med par smra ba)* and *sarvadharmāpratiṣṭhānavādin (chos thams cad rab tu mi gnas par smra ba),* according to Mimaki (1982): 33, n. 66. This method of dividing Madhyamaka would require a closer investigation than is possible and necessary within this article: Rong zom and Advayavajra seem to connect *sgyu ma lta bu* to *paramārtha,* and *rab tu mi gnas pa* to *saṃvṛti.* Contrary to this usage, Grags ba rgyal mtshan seems to apply *rab tu mi gnas pa* to *paramārtha* (see n. 12), while *sgyu ma lta bu* is said about *saṃvṛti* (*Rin che ljon shing,* 49a6: *kun rdzob sgyu ma lta bur bstan pa ni / ...*). Sa skya paṇḍita uses both categories in the context of *paramārtha* (see n. 16).

11 See *Rin che ljon shing,* 30a1ff.; *Nges don rab gsal,* 26a6f. and 28a2–4. Cf. Mimaki (1982): 31f.

12 The exact meaning of these two terms is not clear to me. They might refer to *paramārtha* taken as pure negation *(prasajyapratiṣedha, med dgag)* or excluding negation *(paryudāsa [pratiṣedha], ma yin dgag),* if one understands "cessation" as *nirvāṇa* = *paramārtha* as such, i.e., actual *paramārtha* = pure negation, and "union" as the combination of an appearing thing and its emptiness = conceptual *paramārtha* = excluding negation. In this case, however, the term "union" *(zung 'jug, yuganaddha)* for the combination of an appearing thing and its emptiness would seem problematic or at least unusual. All this, however, is mere speculation, and since this question is beyond the scope of the present paper, it will not be investigated further.

13 Cf. *Nges don rab gsal,* 23b6f. For these two kinds of *paramārtha* see Tauscher (1988), and (1995): 291–326.

14 *Rin che ljon shing,* 42b1–43a4: *blo gnyis po de gang zag gang gi rgyud la ldan zhe na / 'di la bzhi / nyan thos kyi 'dod tshul dang / rnal 'byor spyod pa'i 'dod tshul dang / rgyun chad rab tu mi gnas pa'i 'dod tshul dang / zung 'jug rab tu mi gnas pa'i 'dod tshul lo // dang po ni de la nyan thos sde pa dag... // yang rnal 'byor spyod pa dag... // dbu ma thal 'gyur ba dag ni so so skye bo'i blo thams cad ni kun rdzob 'ba' zhig yin la / 'phags pa gsum gyi mnyam gzhag ni don dam pa yin / rjes spyod kun rdzob kyi blo yin no // sangs rgyas ni dus rtag tu mnyam par gzhag pa yin pas don dam pa 'ba' zhig go zhes ser ro // de'ang yang dag pa ma yin te / sangs rgyas*

rnams ni mi gnas pa'i mya ngan las 'das pa la bzhugs pa ma yin par thal bar 'gyur ba'i skyon yod do // ... // yang dbu ma rang rgyud pa dag so so'i skye bo'i dus nas chos can shes pa'i blo thams cad kun rdzob kyi blo yin la / chos nyid shes pa de'ang kun rdzob yin mod kyang rigs pas skye med du shes pa de chos nyid / skye med du shes pa'i sangs rgyas kyi thugs dang cha 'dra bas mthun pa'i don dam zhes bya'o // 'phags pa gsum gyi shes pa ni mnyam gzhag don dam yin la / rjes spyod kun rdzob yin no // sangs rgyas kyi thugs rnam par mi rtog pa ni don dam pa yin la / dag pa 'jig rten pa'i ye shes ni ye shes la dmigs nas rnam grangs kyi kun rdzob yin no // des na mi gnas pa'i mya ngan las 'das pa'ang yin la / ye shes res 'jog tu mi btab pas don dam ste / rtag tu mnyam par gzhag pa'ang yin te / 'di la'ang mthun pa'i don dam pa de la don dam pa nyid du gol bar mi bya'o //

15 *Thub dngos rab gsal,* 62a4–6: *dbu ma rang rgyud pa dag bden pa gnyis la rnam grangs pa dang rnam grangs ma yin pa gnyis gnyis bzhi yod pa las so so'i skye bo'i blo ma dpyad pa'i ngor snang ba rnam grangs ma yin pa'i kun rdzob / dpyad pa'i ngor bden pa rnam grangs pa'i don dam pa / 'phags pa gsum gyi rnam par mi rtog pa'i ye shes rnam grangs ma yin pa'i don dam pa / dag pa 'jig rten pa'i ye shes rnam grangs kyi kun rdzob ces bya ba gsungs pa ni...*; cf. Tauscher (1995): n. 496 (without reference to *Rin che ljon shing*).

16 *gZhung lugs legs bshad,* 146b6, 147a2–4: *don dam gyi sgo nas dbu ma sgyu ma lta bu dang rab tu mi gnas pa gnyis yin / ... / dbu ma rab tu mi gnas pa'i lugs kyis rang la longs spyod dam sgrib bya gang yang med la / gzhan gyi khas len 'gegs pa la gnyis te / tshul gsum tshad mas grub pa las byung ba'i spros pa gcod byed kyi rigs pa la brten nas gzhan gyi khas len 'gegs pa ni rang rgyud yin la / tshul gsum tshad mas grub par khas mi len zhing khas blangs su bkod nas gzhan gyi log rtog 'gegs pa ni thal 'gyur ba yin no //*

17 This term is traditionally applied to Nāgārjuna and Āryadeva. Cf. Tauscher (1995): 4f., n. 5. Their VV 29 and CŚ 16.25 represent the basis for the position that a Mādhyamika does not maintain any thesis of his own. See p. 222ff. above.

18 See *Nges don rab gsal,* 24a6: *kha cig thal 'gyur ba ni khas len thams cad dang bral bas de'i phyir gzhung phyi mo pa'i dbu ma pa'o zhes zer ro //*

19 See Tani (1992): 289ff.

20 See Jackson (1987): vol. 1, 269,20–270,22 (text); vol. 2, 340f. (trans.). Cf. Ruegg (1983): 231.

21 Cf. Roerich (1949): 341ff. The canon contains Pa tshab's translations of the following works of Candrakīrti: *Prasannapadā* (D 3860), *Madhyamakāvatāra* (D 3861), *Madhyamakāvatārabhāṣya* (D 3862) and *Catuḥśatakaṭīkā* (D 3865). In the Peking edition he is named as the revisor of the last, not as its co-translator (P 5266), and Roerich (1949): 342 lists *Yuktiṣaṣṭikāvṛtti* (D 3864) instead of *Catuḥśatakāṭīkā* among the texts translated by Pa tshab.

22 There occurs, however, a little problem of textual history in this respect. Most of Phya pa's quotations from the MAv in the *Shar gsum stong thun* exhibit considerable deviation from Pa tshab's translation as contained in the canon (D 3861 and 3862, P 5262 and 5263), and they do not agree with the older translation of Nag tsho tshul khrims rgyal ba (P 5261) either.

23 See, e.g., *Shar gsum stong thun,* 20,4ff., negating the position that ultimate reality is not an object of cognition.

24 See Jackson (1987): 105–107, 129–131, 168–173, 181–183; Kellner (1997): 501f.; Onoda (1986) and (1992); Tillemans (1989b): 265f.; and van der Kuijp (1978), and (1983): 59–96.

25 See Onoda (1986): 80.

26 See Onoda (1986): 81f. and (1992): 85f.

27 For *prasaṅga* and *prasaṅgaviparyaya* in general see, e.g., Iwata (1993) and Kajiyama (1966): 114ff.

28 Observations in this respect will only be mentioned but not investigated and discussed in detail in this paper.

29 *Shar gsum stong thun,* 2,20–7,8; sec. 112.211 and 112.212 of the topical outline.

30 Ibid.: 6,4–8: *...des snang ba la bden pa'i dngos po'i sgro 'dogs mi gcod par thal te snang ba'i bdag nyid mi 'jal ba'i phyir / sgra mi rtag par rtogs pa[s] nam mkha' rtag par dogs pa mi sel ba bzhin no // de 'dod na sgro 'dogs sel bar grub pa'i myong bas bsal bas snang ba la sgro 'dogs sel bas de'i rdzas 'jal lo zhes pa'i rang bzhin gyi rtags kyi rang rgyud 'phangs pa na gzhal bya stong pa nyid kyang snang ba dang rdzas gcig par shugs la grub pa yin no //*

31 Ibid.: 6,10–13*: stong pa nyid snang ba'i ngo bor mi gnas pas snang ba'i chos nyid ma yin par 'gyur te rtag pa mi rtag pa'i chos nyid ma yin pa bzhin no zhes bya ba ni khyab byed mi dmigs pa'i thal ba yin la / de la rjes dpag gis chos nyid du grub pas bsal bas chos nyid yin pas snang ba'i ngo bo yin no zhes 'phangs pa ni tha snyad sgrub pa'i rang bzhin gyi rtags so //*

32 Cf. below (n. 42); for the term as such, cf. *tha snyad sgrub kyi rtags yang dag,* Onoda (1992): 170 and 78.

33 *Shar gsum stong thun,* 6,15–17: *de bzhin nyid la 'du byed las gzhan yin pas [khyab pa] khas len na 'du byed la gang zag dang chos khegs pa tsam de de bzhin nyid ma yin par 'gyur te 'du byed las gzhan ma yin pa'i phyir zhes [bya] ba [ni] khyab pa khas blangs pa rtags tshad mas nges pa'i sun 'byin pa'i thal ba'o /[/]*

34 Usually the manuscript of *Shar gsum stong thun* has a double *shad* at the end of each section, but not so in this case. The second *shad* is missing together with the *"bzhi ba ni"* introducing the following paragraph. Obviously, a passage of uncertain length is missing in addition, which could not be taken into account in the edition.

35 *Shar gsum stong thun,* 7,3–8: *...kun nas nyon mongs pa dang rnam byang rgyud cig la dus cig du ldan par 'gyur te / bden pa'i dngos por yang zhen la stong pa nyid kyang mthong ba'i phyir ro // de 'dod na lung gis gnod pas sangs rgyas la kun nas nyon mongs dang rnam byang dus cig tu myed pas 'du byed dang stong pa nyid so sor gzigs pa myed ces pa'i khyab byed mi dmigs pa'i rang rgyud 'phangs pa na sangs rgyas kyis tha dad du ma gzigs par dngos su grub pa na yul yang tha dad du mi gnas par shugs la grub pa yin no //*

36 This term refers to the "exclusion of others" *(anyāpoha, gzhan sel;* cf. *Grub bzhi rnam bshad,* 104,3: *de gnyis ngo bo gcig pa gang zhig / ldog pa'am gzhan sel bltos nas tha dad yin pa'i phyir)* and thus to qualities or properties something does not

have. Nevertheless, in the given context I prefer the more positive expression "characteristic distinction" to commonly used renderings like "exclusion," "reverse," and so on.

37 *Shar gsum stong thun,* 10,13–12,20; sec. 112.5.

38 This passage has previously been overlooked and is not taken into account in Tauscher (1999).

39 *Shar gsum stong thun,* 12,3–5: *'di ltar stong pa nyid 'di so so'i skye bo'i mngon sum gyis gzhal du rung bar thal te snang ba dang ldog pa tha mi dad pa'i phyir zhes pa rang bzhin gyi rtags kyi thal ba yin la / mngon sum gyi gzhal rung ma yin pas snang ba dang ldog pa tha mi dad ma yin zhes pa tha snyad sgrub pa'i khyab byed mi dmigs pa'o //*

40 Ibid.: 12,6–8: *yang stong pa nyid snang ba dang ldog pa tha mi dad pas sgrib pa'i dmigs par 'gyur zhes pa{'i}*[a] [*rang bzhin gyi*] *thal ba* [*yin*] *dang* [/] *sgrib pa'i dmigs pa ma yin pas snang ba dang ldog pa tha mi dad ma yin zhes pa{'i rang bzhin gyi thal bas}*[a] *khyab byed mi dmigs pa'i rang rgyud 'phen pa'o //*

[a]To be deleted. – The text is apparently corrupt here; upright square brackets contain emendations that do not appear in the edition.

41 Ibid.: 12,9–11: *yang gzugs can dang gzugs can ma yin pa la sogs pa'ang stong pa nyid dang ldog pa tha mi dad pas rnam dbye myed par thal lo zhes pa 'gal bas khyab pa dmigs pa'i thal ba yin la / rnam dbye yod pas stong pa nyid dang ldog pa tha mi dad ma yin zhes pa khyab byed 'gal ba dmigs pa'i rang rgyud do //*

42 Ibid.: 12,12–15: *yang stong pa nyid snang ba dang ldog pa tha mi dad pas mthong ba dang thos pa las gzhan du sgom pa'i 'bad pas btsal mi dgos par thal ba ni 'gal bas khyab pa dmigs pa'i thal 'gyur yin la [de min] pa'i 'bad pas btsal dgos pas snang ba dang ldog pa tha mi dad ma yin zhes pa'ang khyab byed 'gal ba dmigs pa'i rang rgyud yin te / tha snyad sgrub pa'i rang rgyud bzhi 'phen pa'i go skabs ni yod do //*

43 On merely formal grounds this could mean that the unspecified *'gal bas khyab pa dmigs pa'i rang rgyud* of Go rams pa's list (and also *Shar gsum gyi stong thun*?) corresponds to Shākya mchog ldan's *'bras bu dang 'gal ba'i khyab bya dmigs pa'i thal 'gyur.* The logical reason in the example given above, "because it is non-different from appearing phenomena with regard to the characteristic distinction," however, does not justify this classification. If it is to be specified at all, it rather seems to represent a *rang bzhin dang 'gal ba'i khyab bya dmigs pa'i thal 'gyur,* implying a *khyab byed dang 'gal ba'i rang bzhin dmigs pa'i rang rgyud.*

The terms *rang bzhin* and *rgyu dang 'gal ba'i khyab bya dmigs pa'i thal 'gyur* are indicated by Onoda (see n. 26 above) as belonging "most likely" to "Phya pa's eighteen *thal 'gyur*" but *'bras bu dang 'gal ba'i khyab bya dmigs pa'i thal 'gyur* is not. From the above it is, however, rather to be suspected that Phya pa himself has not introduced this specification of different types of *'gal ba'i khyab bya dmigs pa'i thal 'gyur* at all, or only at a later stage of his life. Unfortunately nothing is known about the relative chronology of his works. For different types of *'gal dmigs* reasons in Phya pa's system, see Kellner (1997): 501f.

44 *Shar gsum stong thun,* 58,5–124,9; sec. 125.1.

45 This theory is in contradiction to the position of Kamalaśīla, as presented by

Tsong kha pa in his *dBu ma rgyan gyi zin bris,* namely that it is not sufficient to negate such entities by just *prasaṅgas (thal 'gyur tsam)* and that both methods should by applied. See Tillemans (1984b): 384 and 367. See also the following note. In this context it might be interesting to notice that Phya pa, who is hardly ever mentioned by name in dGe lugs pa literature, is related in Tsong kha pa's *dBu ma rgyan gyi zin bris* to hold a *svatantra* as inappropriate for refuting nonexistent subjects imputed by non-Buddhists (see Tillemans [1984b]: 365 and 383). I am unable to offer any explanation for this rather strange statement by Tsong kha pa.

46 *Shar gsum stong thun,* 70,1–72,15; sec. 125.112.2: "A *prasaṅga* is unable to negate a realistic position" *(thal 'gyur gyis dngos por smra ba 'gog pa mi nus pa/... 'gog mi 'thad pa).* Shākya mchog ldan quotes this title as "A *prasaṅga* alone..." *(thal 'gyur rkyang pas...)* (*Lung rigs rgya mtsho,* 14.519,7). In this form it would correspond to Kamalaśīla's position mentioned in the previous note, but Phya pa's arguments do not seem to support this amendment. Cf. also Tauscher (1999): 392.

47 *Shar gsum stong thun,* 70,4–72,3; sec. 125.112.21. This section was dealt with in Tauscher (1999), which primarily presented a very preliminary introduction to this newly discovered text. Some points have had to be reconsidered.

48 Ibid.: 70,19f.

49 Ibid.: 71,2f.

50 Ibid.: 72,4–11; sec. 125.112.22.

51 Ibid.: 72,8–11: *dang po ltar na khyab byed mi dmogs par nges pas khyab bya myed par nges pa rang rgyud kyi rtags su 'gyur la / gnyis pa ltar na bzhi pos ma khyab pa'i spros pa ma khegs par 'gyur ro // gzhan yang spros pa'i khyab byed thal bas khegs sam ma khegs / dang po ltar na khyab byed mi dmigs par 'gyur la / gnyis pa ltar na spros pa srid pa'i dogs pa mi chod par 'gyur ro //*

52 Ibid.: 58,9–64,15; sec. 125.111 and 65,1–76,5; sec. 125.112.

53 Ibid.: 61,15–17: *gzhi snang du chog kyang bsgrub bya rang gi zhe 'dod bsgrub du myed pas de sgrub pa'i rtags dang rtags ston pa'i rang rgyud kyi ngag mi 'thad de / yod pa dang myed pa dang gnyi ga dang gnyi ga ma yin pa gang khas blangs kyang mtha' yin pas dbu ma pa ci'ang khas mi len pa'i phyir ro //*

54 Ibid.: 65,9–11: *sgyu ma lta bu'i gang zag dngos por smra ba la ma grub la / dpyad bzod pa'i gang zag dbu ma pa la ma grub pas sun dbyung ba'i gang zag la mthun snang myed pas de la thal ba 'god pa mi 'thad do //*

55 *Lung rigs rgya mtsho,* 14.524,4–525,1: ***...de'i tshe gang la thal ba 'god pa'i rgol ba yang yod pa ma yin pas thal 'gyur yang mi 'thad do*** *zhes sun 'byin la gzhan dag gis lan 'debs pa ni / de'i tshe rgol ba yod par khas len pa yin la / 'dir lan ni / skabs der gang sun dbyung bar bya ba'i rgol ba dbu ma pa rang gi lugs la yod pa ma yin yang / kun rdzob 'khrul ngor yod pa yin la / de sun 'byin par byed pa'i rigs pa yang / dbu ma pa rang gi lugs la yod pa ma yin yang / kun rdzob 'khrul ba'i ngor yod par 'dzin du bcug pas log par rtog pa shin tu che ba dag bzlog pa'i phyir ro // ... // mdor na don dam par ni dgag bya 'gog pa dang / bsgrub bya sgrub pa gnyis ka khas mi len mod / dbu ma pa'i shes brjod kyi tha snyad 'dogs pa'i tshe*

bsgrub bya sgrub pa khas mi len gyi dgag bya 'gog pa'i tha snyad tsam zhig ni byed par zla bas bzhed pa yin te /

56 *Shar gsum stong thun,* 66,2–4: *dngos por smra ba'i gang zag snang pa nyid 'jig kyang rten pa'i blo'i yul yin gyi ci'ang khas mi len pa'i dbu ma pas gang zag mthong pa myed pas de la thal ba'i ngag 'god pa mi 'thad do* // *rang gis gang zag ma mthong yang thal ba 'god na rang la gzhi mi snang yang rtags 'god do* //

57 Ibid.: 62,8–14.

58 Ibid.: 66,10–14: *dbu ma pa la bsgrub du myed pas rtags 'god pa mi rigs so zhe na* / *pha rol po la shes bya'i gshis dang mi mthun pa'i log rtogs myed pas de 'gog pa'i thal ba brjod pa mi rigs so* // *don dam pa'i*[a] *dngos por 'dod pa shes bya'i gshis dang mi mthun pa'i log rtogs yin no zhe na* / *'o na don dam pa'i dngos pos stong ba shes bya'i gshis su khas blangs pa dam bca' myed pa nyams so* //
[a] *pa'i* : *po'i* (MS)

59 Ibid.: 66,15–19: *don dam par dngos po dang des stong ba gnyi ga mi 'dod na* / *gnyi ga 'dod pa ji ltar dgag* / *gcig bsgrubs pa nyid gzhan dor ba yin pas gnyi ga khas len pa 'gal lo zhe na* / *gcig bkag pa nyid gcig shos bsgrubs pa yin pas gnyi ga khas mi len pa 'gal lo* // *de nyid ma grub zhe na* / *snga ma'ang ma grub po* //

60 Shākya mchog ldan seems to take "the acceptance of both" as Phya pa's own position; see *Lung rigs rgya mtsho,* 14.519,2: *...kho bos gnyis ka yod par smras na ji ltar dgag* /

61 See, e.g., *Shar gsum stong thun,* 4,3ff.

62 Shākya mchog ldan's paraphrase of *Shar gsum stong thun* (see n. 64) does not offer any hint in this respect; his refutation of it has not yet been analyzed sufficiently.

63 According to Shākya mchog ldan; see *Lung rigs rgya mtsho,* 14.519,2: *dpyad mi bzod pa'i shes pa tsam dgag mi nus pa.*

64 *Shar gsum stong thun,* 67,4–17: *dam bca' myed par smra ba dag dam bca' gcig du myong bas grub pa'i blo gsal ba don dam du yod pa kho na yod par smra ba ji ltar dgag* / *gal te blo de gcig pa 'am du ma 'am skyes sam ma skyes sam rtag gam mi rtag ces brtag pa byed* [*pas dgag go zhe*] *na* / *byed nyid la'ang bden pa'i dngos po yin nam des stong ba yin zhes brtag pa bya'o* // *bdag cag la khas len gang yang myed do zhe na* / *bdag cag kyang gsal ba don dam pa la*[a] *khyad par gang yang khas len pa myed do* // *ngo bo yod la khyad par gang yang khas mi len pa mi 'thad do zhe na* / *dngos 'gal gnyis la gnyi ga 'dor ba mi 'thad do* // *dngos 'gal nyid du'ang 'jig rten pa la grub pa yin gyi bdag cag la grub pa myed do zhe na* / *ngo bo yod pa la rtag pa dang mi rtag pa las mi 'da' ba 'am cig dang du ma las mi 'da' ba la sogs pa'ang 'jig rten pa la*[b] *grub pa yin gyi bdag cag la grub pa myed do* // *gnod myed kyi myong bas khyab bya khyab byed du nges pa dor mi nus so zhe na* / *gnod myed kyi myong bas dngos 'gal du grub pa'ang dor bar mi nus so* //
[a] *don dam pa la* : *don dam las* (MS); cf. 67, n. 59.
[b] *la* : *las* (MS); see 67, n. 60.

Cf. *Lung rigs rgya mtsho,* 14.519,4–6: *myong ba gsal rig gi ngo bo yod pa kho na yod par smras na cis 'gog* / *'o na gcig dang du ma gang du yod ce na* / *'o na khyed rang ltar na* / *de nyid bden par grub ma grub gang yin* / *kho bo cag la khas len gang yang med do ce na* / *nged la yang khyad gzhi de la khyad chos gang yang med do* //

khyad gzhi khas blangs nas khyad chos khas mi len pa 'gal lo zhe na / 'o na bden grub bkag nas bden stong khas mi len pa yang 'gal lo //

65 *Shar gsum stong thun,* 69,3.

66 Ibid.: 68,14–20: *mngon sum dang rjes dpag nyid 'jig rten pa'i blo yin gyi tshad ma ma yin pas rtags kyi phyogs chos dang khyab pa nges byed du mi 'thad do zhe na / rgyu la 'bras bu yod par smra ba la rgyu la 'bras bu yod pa'i phyir skye ba don myed par thal zhes pa'ang thal 'gyur rnal ma ma yin pas des gzhan gyi log rtogs 'gog par mi 'thad do // de la thal 'gyur tsam gyi spyi'i mtshan nyid rtags dang khyab pa pha rol la grub pas dam bca' mi 'dod pa*[a] *sgrub nus pa yod pas de thal ba rnal ma ma yin par ma grub po zhe na / mngon sum dang rjes dpag la'ang tshad ma tsam gyi spyi'i mtshan nyid don la mi 'khrul ba'i blos sngar ma rtogs pa'i don la sgro 'dogs dang 'gal ba yod pas tshad ma ma yin par mi 'thad do //* [a]*mi 'dod par* would be preferable.

Cf. Phya pa's definition of valid cognition as related by Go rams pa: "(1) A valid means of cognition entails a *de novo* cognition of its own object of purposeful action which has not been previously cognised; and (2) While [a valid means of cognition] entails a nondelusive mode of apprehension *('dzin-stags)* and the capacity to eliminate conceptual accretions *(sgro-'dogs, samāropa),* then,..."; trans. by van der Kuijp (1983): 78.

67 Cf. dGe 'dun grub pa, *Rigs pa'i rgyan,* 134b2–4: "The characteristics of a *prasaṅga* are: logical reason and pervasion established for the cognition of the opponent, and a formulation which shows the logical reason falling into a removal *(bsal ba 'bab pa)*[a] from the proposition. Further, the *prasaṅga* is not suitable when there is no removal [of the logical reason] from the proposition, and the [fact that the logical reason is a] property of the subject is not established when [this removal] is there; therefore it is said: 'Logical reason and [its] pervasion [by the property to be proven] are established for the cognition,' and it is not said: 'The [fact that the logical reason is a] property of the subject and pervasion [of the logical reason by the property to be proven] are established for the cognition.'" *(thal 'gyur gyi mtshan nyid / rtags dang khyab pa pha rol po'i blo ngor grub cing / dam bca' la bsal ba 'bab pa'i rtags ston pa'i ngag / de yang dam bca' la bsal ba med na thal 'gyur du mi rung la / yod na phyogs chos mi 'grub pas / phyogs chos dang khyab pa blo ngor grub pa zhes ma smos par rtags dang khyab pa blo ngor grub pa zhes smos pa yin no //)*

[a]The translation of this term is tentative. According to the explanation of *Tshig mdzod chen mo (bsal ba 'bab pa / dam bca' la gnod pa ste khas len mi nus pa /),* it is a technical term denoting a fault of the proposition.

68 *Shar gsum stong thun,* 69,4–9: *thal 'gyur rnal ma yin na'ang rtags khas blangs pa dang khyab pa tshad mas nges pa dang dam bca' la bsal bar 'gyur ro // de khyab pa myed de khyab pa khas blangs pa dang dam bca' la rang gi tshig gis bsal pa'i thal 'gyur yang srid pa'i phyir ro zhe na / bden pa mthong pa'i blor thal ba'ang khyab pa myed de / kun rdzob 'jal ba'i mngon sum dang rjes dpag dang don dam pa'i bden pa 'jal ba'i rjes dpag bden pa ma mthong ba la'ang yod pa mi 'gal ba'i phyir ro //*

69 Ibid.: 69,15–20: *rtags dang khyab pa 'jig rten pa'i blos mthong pa yin gyi ci'ang khas mi len pa'i dbu ma bas grub pa myed pas dbu ma bas rtags bkod pa myed do zhe*

na / rtags dang khyab pa khas len par yang 'jig rten pas mthong gi dbu ma bas mthong ba myed pas dbu ma bas thal ba 'god bar mi rigs so // tha snyad 'jal ba'i 'jig rten pa'i blo'ang don dam par ci yang khas mi len pa'i dbu ma nyid kyi rgyud du gtogs pas rtags dang khyab khas len par dbu mar smra ba'i gang zag nyid la grub[a] *pa yin no zhe na / de nyid kyis na phyogs kyi chos dang khyab pa'ang dbu mar smra ba'i gang zag nyid la grub pa yin no //* [a]*grub : sgrub* (MS); see 69, n. 64.

70 *mDzes rgyan* (Sarnath ed.) 326,8f.: *...bden med sgrub pa'i rtags kyi tshul gsum rang ngos nas grub par khas len pa'i dbu ma pa de dbu ma rang rgyud pa'i mtshan nyid du bya'o //* Cf. Lopez (1987): 295. Ibid. 408,14–16: *...rang rgyud khas mi len par gzhan grags tsam gyis bden med rtogs pa'i rjes dpag bskyed par 'dod pa'i dbu ma pa de thal 'gyur ba'i mtshan nyid ces byas ....* Cf. Hopkins (1987): 362.

71 For a recent study of this topic, see Yotsuya (1999).

72 *dBu rtsa dka' gnas,* 323,6–324,1: *yang na rang rgyud kyi rtags khas len pa'i sgo nas de kho na nyid rtogs par mdzad pa dang / de khas ma blangs par gzhan grags kyi rtags kyi sgo nas de kho na nyid kyi rtogs pa skyed pa'i dbu ma pa gnyis su 'bye'o //*

73 Ibid.: 324,1f.: *...gzhan gyi khas blangs la ma ltos par rang dbang du 'dzin stangs kyi don la mi 'khrul ba'i tshad mas bzhag pa'i tshul gsum dang ldan pa la rang rgyud dang / de lta min par gzhan gyis khas blangs la ltos nas tshad mas nges pa'i tshul gsum dang ldan pa la gzhan grags kyi gtan tshigs zhes pa'o //*

74 The rendering of this term follows David Seyfort Ruegg's translation of *dBu rtsa dka' gnas,* being prepared for publication in Vienna.

75 *dBu rtsa dka' gnas,* 324,2f.: *kha cig / tshul gsum gzhan gyis khas blangs pa'am / khas blangs pa'i mthar thug pa tsam gyis gzhan gyi log rtog 'gog pa thal 'gyur ba dang / tshul gsum tshad mas nges pa'i sgo nas byed pa rang rgyud pa zhes 'dod pa dang / ...ni mi 'thad pa rgyas par gzhan du gsungs zin pas...*

76 For Tsong kha pa on *prasaṅgaviparīta* and *prasaṅgaviparyaya,* see Ruegg (1991): 292ff.; for *prasaṅga* and inference according to dGe lugs pa interpretation in general, see Yoshimizu (1996): 172ff.; for the "old" and "new" interpretation of *prasaṅga* and *svatantra,* see Tani (1992): 289ff.

77 *rTsa she ṭik chen,* 175a6–8: *myu gu la rang gi ngo bos grub pa'i rang bzhin yod pa khas len pa na sa bon la brten nas 'byung bar mi 'gyur te / rang gi ngo bos yod pa'i phyir zhes pa'i thal ba 'phen pa lta bu la ni brten nas 'byung ba'i phyir myu gu la rang gi ngo bos grub pa'i rang bzhin med do zhes thal chos bzlog rtags*[a] *su byas nas thal rtags bzlog pa'i*[b] *dam bca' sgrub pa shin du mang ngo*[c] *// de la yang gzhan gyis dam bcas pa'i rang gi ngo bas yod pa rnam par bcad pa tsam zhig byed kyi chos gzhan mi sgrub pa ni thams cad la 'dra'o //*

[a]*rtags : brtags.*

[b]*pa'i : pa di.*

[c]*mang ngo* (T, Zh, Sarnath [1975]): *med do.*

Cf. Ruegg (1991): 294; Yotsuya (1999): 39f.

78 For a detailed discussion of the different interpretation of the object of negation by the Prāsaṅgika and Svātantrika, see Tauscher (1995): 122–152.

79 According to Tsong kha pa's Prāsaṅgika-Madhyamaka exegesis, the mere conventional existence *(tha snyad du yod pa)* of external objects is not to be denied;

the crucial point, however, is to distinguish this existence from an existence established by its own characteristic *(rang gi mtshan nyid kyis grub pa, svalakṣaṇasiddha),* which is not to be accepted even conventionally. Cf. Tauscher (1995): 56ff., 122ff.

80 *Lam rim chen mo* (Peking ed.) vol. *kha,* 6b6f. (cf. *Lam rim chung ba:* 279a8f.): *gangs ri'i khrod kyi phyi dar gyi mkhas pa rnams dbu ma pa la thal 'gyur ba dang rang rgyud pa gnyis kyi tha snyad byed pa ni tshig gsal dang mthun pas rang bzod mi bsam mo // des na tha snyad du phyi rol 'dod mi 'dod gnyis su nges la don dam pa stong pa nyid nges pa'i lta ba rgyud la bskyed tshul gyi sgo nas ming 'dogs na'ang / thal rang gnyis su nges pa yin no //*

81 See *Lam rim chen mo* (Peking ed.) vol *kha* 76a8f.: *rang rgyud kyi rtags rang gi lugs la zhal gyis bzhes pa'i rgyu mtshan yang tha snyad du rang gi ngo bos grub pa'i rang mtshan yod pa 'di yin pas rang rgyud kyi rtags rang lugs la 'jog mi 'jog ni dgag bya shin tu phra pa 'di la thug pa yin no //* Cf. *Legs bshad snying po* (Loseling ed.) 173,13–15: *rang gi lugs ni dgongs 'grel las gsungs pa ltar rang gi mtshan nyid kyis grub pa 'dod na ni nges par rang rgyud bya dgos te / rang sde dngos por smra ba rnams legs ldan la sogs pa bzhin no //*

82 *sTong thun chen mo,* 177,3, and *Blo gsal sgron me,* 201,4f. give a list of ten terms, while the *dBu ming rnam grangs,* 425,4–426,2 gives a list of eighteen terms to specify the object of negation. Cf. Tauscher (1995): n. 263.

83 See *Lam rim chen mo* (Peking ed.) vol. *kha,* 53a3f.: *de la gzhan la rag ma las pa zhes pa ni / rgyu rkyen la rag ma las ma yin gyi yul can tha snyad ba'i shes pa la gzhan zhes bya ste de'i dbang gis bzhag pa min pas gzhan la rag ma las pa'o // des na rang dbang ba zhes bya ste yul de dag gi rang rang gi gnas lugs sam sdod lugs thun mong min ba'i ngo bo'o // de nyid la rang gi ngo bo dang rang gi rang bzhin zhes bya'o //*

84 Cf. lCang skya rol pa'i rdo rje, *mDzes rgyan* (Sarnath ed.) 325,20–326,4: *de yang rang rgyud pa'i lugs la dbang shes gnod med rnams tha snyad du snang yul la ma 'khrul pa yin la / de ltar ma 'khrul pa'i rgyu mtshan yang gnod med kyi shes pa rnams la gzugs sogs rang gi ngo bos grub par snang zhing gzugs sogs kyang rang gi ngo bos grub par zhal gyis bzhed pa nyid la thug go //*

85 Cf. *Lam rim chung ba,* 303a7ff.: *dbu ma rang rgyud pa dag shes pa rang gi mtshan nyid kyis grub par snang ba'i snang ba ltar du yod par nges pas / yul can la yang dag log pa gnyis mi 'byed par / yul du snang ba la ji ltar snang ba ltar gyi rang gi mtshan nyid kyis yod med 'byed pa rnams ni / bden gnyis las / snang du 'dra yang don byed dag // nus pa'i phyir dang mi nus phyir // yang dag yang dag ma yin pa'i // kun rdzob kyi ni dbye ba byas //* [SDV 12] *zhes gzungs pa ltar bzhed do //*

86 Cf. *dGongs pa rab gsal* (Peking ed.) 101b3f.: *da lta gzugs sgra sogs lnga rang gi mtshan nyid kyis grub par dbang shes la snang ba ni / ma rig pas bslad pa yin pas shes pa de dang / gzugs brnyan dang brag cha sogs snang ba'i dbang shes rnams la / phra rags tsam ma gtogs pa snang yul la 'khrul la khyad par med cing / …*

87 Cf. Hopkins (1989): 12: "More, bluntly, one might say that the evidence for a difference in the view of emptiness between Chandrakīrti and Bhāvaviveka is so thin that even great Indian scholars did not notice it."

88 MAvBh, 406,9ff. For a translation of the passage quoted by Tsong kha pa see Thurman (1984): 288, and Hopkins (1989): 13.

89 *Legs bshad snying po* (Loseling ed.) 132,13–16, *zla ba grags pas ni / sangs rgyas bskyangs kyis 'phags pa'i dgongs pa ji lta ba bzhin du bkral bas de dang rang gi don dam pa dang kun rdzob pa'i 'jog tshul khyad par med par bzhed la / rang gi lugs ni dbu ma pa gzhan gyis bkral ba dang thun mong ma yin par bshad de /*

90 For a detailed discussion of this topic see Hopkins (1989); cf. Tauscher (1995): 40ff.

91 See *lTa ba ngan sel,* 40a4: *des na 'di gnyis kyi khyad par gyi gtso bo ni don dam sgrub byed kyi rigs pa bkod tshul gyi sgo nas 'jog ste /*

92 *lTa ba ngan sel,* 41a3–5: *mkhas rlom dag rang rgyud pas rang gi mtshan nyid kyis grub pa'i chos bsgrub dgos pas rang rgyud kyi gtan tshigs khas len la thal 'gyur bas de bsgrub mi dgos pas rang rgyud kyi gtan tshigs khas mi len pa yin no zhes smra ba ni phyogs gar yod tsam yang ma mthong ba ste / rang rgyud pas mtha' bzhi'i skye ba bkag pa'i dam bca' bsgrub pa'i skabs su rang gi mtshan nyid kyis grub pa'i chos sgrub par thal ba'i phyir ro //*. For the opinion criticized here cf. *Legs bshad snying po* (Loseling ed.) 173,13–15 (see n. 81 above). See also the references in Yoshimizu (1996): 175, n. 345.

93 *Lam rim chen mo* (Peking ed.), vol. *kha,* 59a2–84a5, translated in Wayman (1978): 283–336; the *pūrvapakṣa*s are stated at vol. *kha,* 59a8–62a7 and refuted at *kha,* 62a7–70b7 (Wayman [1978]: 284–309).

94 See Ruegg (1983): 228.

95 E.g., Ruegg (1983) and Yoshimizu (1993a); see also Yoshimizu (1996): 102, n. 28; Tauscher (1995): 154f.

96 *Grub mtha' chen mo,* 18,3f. and 647,4; see Tauscher (1995): 154, n. 321.

97 See Yoshimizu (1996): 100.

98 See *Shar gsum stong thun,* 1,17–2,2; sec. 111, for Tsong kha pa's position in Tauscher (1995): 181–187; cf. also Tauscher (1990): n. 17.

99 *Shar gsum stong thun:* 2,3–13,16; sec. 112 (cf. p. 216ff. above).

100 Cf. Tauscher (1995): 56–72, 187–194. Phya pa's way of treating this topic seems to have influenced scholars of later times, in particular Tsong kha pa and the dGe lugs pas. In his *Lam rim chung ba* Tsong kha pa states that "many of the former [Tibetan scholars] propound the two realities to be of the difference of negated identity, while some/someone accept(s) the two to be identical in nature and different with regard to the characteristic distinction" (300b1–3: *'di la snga rabs pa mang po...bden gnyis ni gcig pa bkag pa'i tha dad du smra la / kha cig ni de gnyis ngo bo gcig la ldog pa tha dad du 'dod do //*). In 'Jam dbyangs bzhad pa's *dBu 'jug mtha' dpyod* (522,6): those propagating the difference of negated identity are identified, in an inserted gloss, as "rNgog lotsāva and his pupils(s), etc." *(rNgog yab sras sogs).* The *"sras"* might refer here to Khyung rin chen grags (cf. Tauscher [1995]: n. 352), the "grand-teacher" of Phya pa chos kyi seng ge. Those/the one accepting the two realities to be identical in nature and different with regard to the characteristic distinction I have never seen identified in later literature, but it is possible that Phya pa is meant.

Phya pa's structuring the arguments against the positions of the two realities being different in nature and identical with regard to the characteristic distinction according to SNS III,3–5 is not to be found in Tsong kha pa's works, but is found almost identically in later dGe lugs pa writing (see, e.g., *Grub mtha' legs bshad* by Ngag dbang dpal ldan [b. 1779]: 99,1–102,5).

Drawing upon the same passages from SNS, which seem to have served as the *locus classicus* for this discussion ever since Phya pa, other authors propound the two realities to be "identical or different in no way whatsoever" (see *dBu 'jug mtha' dpyod,* 523,3: *...gzhan dag na re / bden gnyis ngo bo gcig dang tha dad gang yang ma yin par thal / de re re la skyon bzhi bzhi yod pa'i phyir / dgongs 'grel las /* ...). On the same basis Rong ston shes bya kun rig (1367–1449) maintains "identity or difference in no way whatsoever," with the implication of the "difference of negated identity" *(gcig pa bkag pa'i tha dad)* on a conventional level (see *Rigs lam kun gsal,* 10b1ff.; cf. Tauscher [1995]: 191, n. 395). This position is already held by Sa paṇ, *Thub dgongs rab gsal,* 63a4–6. Dol po pa shes rab rgyal mtshan (1292–1361) postulates the "difference of negated identity" in general without distinguishing a conventional and an ultimate level (see *bKa' bsdu gtan tshig,* k. 12–14b [366,6–367,2] and *bDen gsal nyi ma,* 12a1–13a2).

101 See *Shar gsum stong thun,* 82,16–20. However, the *mChan bzhi* of Ba so chos kyi rgyal mtshan *et al.* (283,5) identifies Phya pa *(Bya ba)* together with rNgog lotsāva *(Lo chen)* as the "some former scholars" *(sngon gyi mkhas pa 'ga' re)* mentioned in *Lam rim chen mo,* (Peking ed.) vol. *kha* 25a7f., who propound a too broad identification of the object of negation and thus hold *saṃvṛtisatya* to be nonexistent; cf. Tauscher (1995): 165.

102 *Shar gsum stong thun,* 18,7–22,17; sec. 121.21, for Tsong kha pa's position Tauscher (1995): 326–341.

103 In Tauscher (1995), I have chosen the translations "ausgrenzende Negation," based on the "literal" meaning of the term *paryudāsa* and its usage in Indian traditions like the Mīmāṃsā, and "reine Negation" *(prasajyapratiṣedha)* instead of the more common renderings "presuppositional, implicative, relative" and "non-presuppositional, non-implicative, absolute negation" for merely practical reasons. Here, I maintain these translations for contextual reasons as well as for the sake of convenience; the renderings "inclusive negation" for *paryudāsa* and "exclusive negation" for *prasajyapratiṣedha* would, in fact, match Phya pa's interpretation better. These specifications would, however, no longer refer to "a property other than the negated one" but to the probative aspect of the negation.

In the *Shar gsum stong thun* (85,14–87,12) he strongly objects against interpreting these negations as implying and not implying a property other than the negated one: in the case of *prasajyapratiṣedha* this would mean a too broad definition, and the definition of *paryudāsa* would be impossible (86,18f.: *...myed dgag gi mtshan nyid ha cang khyab pa dang ma yin dgag gi mtshan nyid mi srid pa kho na yin no*). Phya pa defines *paryudāsa* as something that is only proof (cf. 85,20: *...sgrub pa thams cad ma yin dgag yin pa'i phyir*) or a combination of negation and proof, and *prasajyapratiṣedha* as something that is exclusively negation (87,9–12: *sgrub pa 'ba' zhig pa dang dgag sgrub tshogs pa ma yin dgag* *yin la dgag pa 'ba' zhig pa myed dgag yin pas myed dgag gi mtshan nyid ni ldog pa de kha yar nges pa na dgag pa 'ba' zhig par blos zhen par bya ba yin la / ma yin dgag gi mtshan nyid ni ldog pa de kha yar nges pa na sgrub pa'i cha ma dor bar zhen par bya ba yin no*).

Apparently this interpretation is indebted to Bhāvaviveka, who takes negation to be the main aspect of *prasajyapratiṣedha* and proof the main aspect of *paryudāsa* (see PrP 48b6f.: *bdag las ma yin zhes bya ba'i dgag pa 'di ni med par dgag pa'i don du lta bar bya ste / dgag pa gtso che ba'i phyir... // ma yin par dgag pa yongs su bzung na ni de sgrub pa gtso che ba'i phyir...*; cf. Tauscher [1995]: 296, n. 593). Whether this interpretation of negation is of relevance for the Prāsaṅgika-Svātantrika distinction will have to be subject to separate studies.

104 See Tauscher (1995): 305–323.

105 See *Shar gsum stong thun*, 16,20: *don dam bden pa'i mtshan nyid ni mthar thug 'jal ba'i tshad ma'i yul du bden pa ste /* 17,19f.: *...myed dgag kho na mthar thug 'jal ba'i gzhal byar bden pa'i mtshan nyid dang ldan par 'dod pas....* For the translation of *gzhal bya* with "object of a valid cognition" see 124,11f., where *gzhal bya* is opposed to *tshad ma* in the same way as *shes bya* to *shes pa* and *brjod bya* to *rjod byed.*

106 Ibid.: 22,12–15: *de la kun rdzob kyi bden pas khyab pa 'dod pas spyod pa'i brda lan cig zhugs pas nges so ce na / dpyod bzod la don dam pa'i bden pas khyab pa'ang de dang 'dra'o // stong nyid dpyad mi bzod pa'i rdzas yin pas kun rdzob par smra na snang ba dpyad bzod pa'i rdzas yin pas don dam gyi bden par 'gyur ro //*

107 Ibid.: 18,1–3: *thar thug mi 'jal ba'i yul 'khrul pa'i gzung yul ni log pa'i kun rdzob yin la / mthar thug mi 'jal ba'i yul 'khrul pa'i gzung yul ma yin pa ni yang dag pa'i kun rdzob po //*

108 Ibid.: 60,1–13; sec. 125.111.22.

109 Ibid.: 22,18–24,3; sec. 121.22.

7. Tsong kha pa's Reevaluation of Candrakīrti's Criticism of Autonomous Inference

CHIZUKO YOSHIMIZU[1]

Introduction

CANDRAKĪRTI's (7th c.) criticism of autonomous inference *(svatantrānumāna)* in his *Prasannapadā* (PPMV) and the development of that criticism by Tibetan Madhyamaka interpreters have both strongly attracted modern scholars in the last two decades, not only because of their historical significance but also because of the complexity of the arguments themselves.[2] This criticism is also closely related to (1) the later Tibetan classification of the Madhyamaka tradition into *Rang rgyud pa* (*Svātantrika)[3] and *Thal 'gyur ba* (*Prāsaṅgika) as well as to (2) the question of whether the Mādhyamika should prove his own propositional thesis *(pratijñā, dam bca')* or philosophical position *(pakṣa, phyogs)* by formulating an inferential statement, for both issues originated in the controversy between Bhāviveka[4] (5th c.) and Candrakīrti. In this paper, I will discuss the problem of how Tsong kha pa (1357–1419), a great Tibetan Madhyamaka master, interpreted Candrakīrti's criticism of autonomous inference with reference to these two issues. In light of the different historical circumstances in which he worked and his own Madhyamaka interpretation, Candrakīrti's discussion receives a new value and meaning in the works of Tsong kha pa. I intend to reveal Tsong kha pa's systematic shifting of the values of autonomous inference, as well as his interpretation of Candrakīrti's arguments against it.

As for the division between the two Madhyamaka systems, (1) although the division seems to have been already acknowledged in Tibet at the time of Tsong kha pa,[5] he introduced a new criterion for distinguishing the theoretical and methodological difference between the Svātantrika and the Prāsaṅgika systems in accordance with their interpretations of the three kinds of nonsubstantiality *(triniḥsvabhāvatā)* taught in the *Saṃdhinirmocana-*

sūtra (SNS).[6] Specifically, for Tsong kha pa, the Svātantrika conventionally accepts that which is established as a real self-characteristic *(rang gi mtshan nyid kyis grub pa),*[7] while the Prāsaṅgika accepts this kind of real self-characteristic neither ultimately nor conventionally. From this standpoint, Tsong kha pa then reinterprets Candrakīrti's criticism of autonomous inference, as Matsumoto and Yotsuya have clarified through their detailed investigations of his commentaries on the first chapter of the PPMV (especially on PPMV 29,7–30,14) as preserved in the *Lam rim chen mo* and the *Legs bshad snying po.*[8] Both scholars point out that by connecting autonomous inference with conventionally established self-nature or self-characteristic, Tsong kha pa demonstrates the difference between the ontological positions of the Prāsaṅgika and the Svātantrika as well as the former's superiority over the latter.[9] For according to Tsong kha pa's own Madhyamaka interpretation, Bhāviveka's employment and Candrakīrti's rejection of autonomous inference are grounded in their respective ontologies. In this way, Tsong kha pa reinterprets *svatantrānumāna* as an inferential proof that presupposes the acceptance of what is established as a real self-characteristic *(rang gi mtshan nyid kyis grub pa)* either ultimately or conventionally, and Bhāviveka is reinterpreted as a Svātantrika-Mādhyamika who makes use of an autonomous inference on the ground of his acceptance of this kind of proof.[10]

Under this specification, however, Candrakīrti's arguments against Bhāviveka's use of autonomous inference might be thought to lose their point. That is, Candrakīrti argues that Bhāviveka—or whoever claims to be a Mādhyamika—is in no position to prove his theory of the nonsubstantiality or nonorigination of things, since, for him, things never exist in ultimate reality. Hence, according to Candrakīrti, Bhāviveka's autonomous inference is fallacious, since the subject of his inference is not ultimately existent nor is it established for Bhāviveka himself. Yet, for Tsong kha pa, Bhāviveka's use of autonomous inference is legitimate and theoretically well-grounded on the Svātantrika ontological system, in which things are conventionally accepted as real self-characteristic. Insofar as Tsong kha pa maintains this position, it follows that the ultimate nonexistence of things should not and does not prevent Bhāviveka from stating an autonomous inference. In fact, Tsong kha pa seems to find Bhāviveka's fault in his ontological *assumptions* rather than in his use of autonomous inference per se.[11]

This theoretical inconsistency between Candrakīrti and Tsong kha pa has puzzled scholars. One can understand, on the one hand, that Tsong kha pa reinterprets Candrakīrti's arguments and applies them to the direct criticism of Bhāviveka's acceptance of self-characteristic; but on the other hand, one might doubt whether Tsong kha pa's interpretation is appropriate, as Tsong kha pa constructs his criticism on the ground of his own definition of the Svātantrika ontology. For it is not Candrakīrti but Tsong kha pa who constricts the definition of the Svātantrika-Mādhyamika as conventionally accepting a real self-characteristic. Tsong kha pa faults Bhāviveka for this Svātantrika position, but it is Tsong kha pa himself who defines it and ascribes it to him.[12]

Those who investigate Tsong kha pa's interpretation of Candrakīrti's criticism of autonomous inference cannot help facing this problem. One possible solution, which I would like to propose here, is that Tsong kha pa composed his commentary with a totally different intention from that of Candrakīrti. That is, Tsong kha pa never thought of criticizing Bhāviveka's use of autonomous inference, since he understood that it was reasonable for this Svātantrika master to propound an autonomous inference. Instead, what he really intended was to make clear why Candrakīrti or the Prāsaṅgika does *not* propound an autonomous inference. For this purpose, he reinterprets Candrakīrti's arguments against autonomous inference and applies them to explain the reason for the Prāsaṅgika's rejection thereof.

This hypothesis is bolstered by the fact that in the *Lam rim chen mo* Tsong kha pa presents his commentary on PPMV 1 together with a thorough refutation of the incorrect or false interpretations of the Madhyamaka logical method:[13] The first half of the large section entitled "Ascertainment of the meaning of *prasaṅga* and autonomous inference" *(thal rang gi don ngos bzung ba)*[14] is devoted to this refutation under the title "Refutation of others' positions" *(gzhan lugs dgag pa)*[15] and the latter half under the title "Establishment of our own position" *(rang lugs bzhag pa)*.[16] In other words, this section as a whole can be said to deal with the aforementioned question (2), i.e., whether a Mādhyamika should use inferential statements to establish his position. One reads therein of Tsong kha pa's determined opposition to the notion that the Prāsaṅgika should on no account formulate a probative reasoning to prove his own thesis or philosophical position.[17]

This also links up with Tsong kha pa's own way of classifying the Madhyamaka systems (i.e., question 1): By eliminating the simple drawing of a distinction between the two Madhyamakas on the basis of whether one proves his own doctrinal position or solely refutes that of his opponent, Tsong kha pa demonstrates that the Prāsaṅgika *may* employ an inferential proof to make his substantialist opponent understand the Madhyamaka doctrine of the nonorigination or nonsubstantiality of things.

Furthermore, supposing that *svatantrānumāna* be an inference that presupposes the acceptance of real self-characteristic as Tsong kha pa maintains, a sound probative reasoning *not* based on such a substantial thought is assured a place for the Prāsaṅgika, too. As many scholars have extensively discussed, Tsong kha pa in this way freely admits, in addition to *prasaṅga* reasoning, an inferential proof as well as two kinds of valid means of cognition *(tshad ma, pramāṇa)* in his own Prāsaṅgika system.[18] In other words, Tsong kha pa holds that Candrakīrti never intended to declare his opposition to *all* kinds of probative inference, but rather only to the *svatantrānumāna,* which requires or implies a real self-characteristic.

From this perspective, Tsong kha pa explicitly disproves the negative interpretations of the Prāsaṅgika position with regard to inferential reasoning before entering into Candrakīrti's discussion of autonomous inference. What is important here is that those negative views are asserted on the authority of Candrakīrti, especially of his criticism of autonomous inference in PPMV 1. That is to say, those who held the position that Candrakīrti does not allow the (Prāsaṅgika-)Mādhyamika to propound a thesis of his own are supposed to have maintained that it is *for this reason* that Candrakīrti rejects the use of autonomous inference. Tsong kha pa, however, disagrees with this assessment. Hence it is indispensable for Tsong kha pa to show the *correct* or *real* reason for Candrakīrti's rejection by *correctly* reinterpreting his own words in the PPMV.[19]

The following is my attempt to identify some substantial modifications that Tsong kha pa makes to Candrakīrti's original discussion, and clarify that all of them properly serve his purpose to explain why the Prāsaṅgika does not admit an autonomous inference.

1. The shift of focus: Who should not propound an autonomous inference, Bhāviveka or a Prāsaṅgika-Mādhyamika?

In his PPMV, Candrakīrti introduces the following autonomous probative statement *(svatantraprayogavākya),* which is originally set forth by Bhāviveka to defeat the Sāṃkhya theory of origination from self:

> [A] Ultimately *(paramārthataḥ),* the inner sense-fields have not originated from themselves, because [they] are [already] existing, like mental factors.[20]

According to Candrakīrti, this reasoning incurs faults in both the proposition *(pakṣadoṣa)* and the logical reason *(hetudoṣa),* since the subject *(dharmin),* viz., inner sense-fields, is not established for Bhāviveka himself due to his Madhyamaka position of not accepting its ultimate existence.[21] Responding to a possible objection from Bhāviveka that the subject and the probandum of his statement are of an unspecified, general character *(sāmānya),* which is free of the qualifications as "ultimate existent" or "conventional existent," and are therefore established in common for himself and his substantialist opponent,[22] Candrakīrti appeals to the same faults again a few pages later in PPMV 1.[23] To sum up, according to Candrakīrti, Bhāviveka—or whoever claims to be a Mādhyamika—should not propound this kind of autonomous probative reasoning to demonstrate to a substantialist opponent his own theory of nonorigination or nonsubstantiality, for it is impossible for him either to set forth a subject of an unspecified general character or to share a subject with his opponent. This suggests that in setting forth an autonomous probative statement Bhāviveka cannot avoid violating the logical rule of common establishment *(ubhayasiddhatva),* which he himself accepts as necessary.[24]

In contrast to Candrakīrti, Tsong kha pa, in his introductory remarks[25] to the same passage,[26] indicates his own understanding of Bhāviveka *not only* as the proponent of the inferential proof of nonorigination, but also as the opponent who is destined to be refuted by the Prāsaṅgika-Mādhyamika:

> [B] Here [in PPMV 29,7–30,11 Candrakīrti] shows how the subject *(chos can, dharmin)* [of Bhāviveka's autonomous inference] that obtains as commonly appearing *(mthun snang du grub pa)* [for both the Mādhyamika and] his opponent cannot be established. This "opponent" refers in the present context of the PPMV to the [Sāṃkhya] opponent, whose assertion of origination from self is to be refuted, but also, in general *(spyir),* to both the substantialist, who asserts that entities *(dngos po rnams)* ultimately *(don dam par)* have [real] self-nature *(rang bzhin),* and the Svātantrika, who asserts that they have the self-nature which is conventionally *(tha snyad du)* established as their own [real] characteristic *(rang gi mtshan nyid kyis grub pa'i rang bzhin).*[27]

The expression "in general," in my reading, connotes "in the general context of PPMV 1," but not "in the general case apart from the PPMV." That is, by saying "in general," Tsong kha pa presumably suggests that the interpretation of Bhāviveka as the opponent is more generally applicable to the whole discussion in PPMV 1 and better represents Candrakīrti's intention than the interpretation of Bhāviveka as the proponent. Actually, in both the *Lam rim chen mo* and *Legs bshad snying po,* when elucidating Candrakīrti's words, Tsong kha pa assigns the role of the opponent to Bhāviveka, as Matsumoto and Yotsuya have successively revealed.[28] In other words, in Tsong kha pa's commentaries, it is the Prāsaṅgika who plays the role of the proponent of an inferential statement instead of the Svātantrika Bhāviveka, who is regarded, even if being a Mādhyamika, as one of "those who assert that the self-nature exists" *(rang bzhin yod par smra ba).*[29] This is no doubt the most substantial modification that Tsong kha pa makes to the discussion of the PPMV. What underlies this shift of roles is, in my opinion, his strong intention to clarify the reason for the Prāsaṅgika's rejection of autonomous inference, since the shifting of roles necessarily results in rearranging the focus of the entire discussion from an explanation of why Bhāviveka—or whoever claims to be a Mādhyamika—should not propound an autonomous inference to an explanation of why the Prāsaṅgika does not do it.

Yet there remains a controversial problem. Whereas Matsumoto seems to understand Tsong kha pa's entire discussion to proceed within such a modified framework, Yotsuya explicitly argues that Tsong kha pa still partly retains Candrakīrti's original framework by assigning Bhāviveka the role of the proponent, especially in his commentaries on the passages in question.[30] Candrakīrti begins this section with the following refutation:

> [C] This is not so [i.e., the subject or the property-possessor *(dharmin)* of an unqualified general character *(sāmānya)* is not established for Bhāviveka himself]. Because precisely when *(yadaiva...tadaiva)* the negation of origination is intended as the probandum [or the property to be proven] *(sādhyadharma)* in the [inference] here in question, this [master, viz., Bhāviveka] himself has acknowledged that its locus *(ādhāra),* viz., the subject [or the property-possessor], which obtains its own existence solely by a mistaken [cognition] *(viparyāsa),* is destroyed, for mistaken [cognition] and unmistaken [cognition] are distinct [from each other].[31]

In this passage, Candrakīrti denies the possibility of Bhāviveka's putting forward the subject of an unqualified general character by indicating the self-contradiction this would entail; for the subject, which is established by a mistaken cognition on the Madhyamaka view, must be qualified as conventional. The rule of common establishment is, for Candrakīrti, thus concerned with the qualification of the ontological status of the subject as either ultimate or conventional, where the ultimate existent is the object of unmistaken cognition and the conventional existent is that of mistaken cognition.[32]

Let us reconsider Tsong kha pa's commentary on this passage in the *Lam rim chen mo,* which seems to have convinced Yotsuya that Tsong kha pa adopts Candrakīrti's original framework (i.e., where Bhāviveka is understood as the proponent) here.[33] It should be noted that Tsong kha pa employs the reading *de'i tshe de kho nar (*tadā tattvataḥ)* instead of *de'i tshe kho nar (tadaiva)* in accordance with one Tibetan version corresponding to the current sDe dge edition.[34]

> [D] Bhāviveka himself has acknowledged that the locus of the property to be proven, viz., [the property-possessor or] the subject such as eyes or visible matter, is in reality *(de kho nar)* destroyed, that is to say, not established. What sort of thing is the subject? It is that which obtains its own existence *(bdag gi dngos po)* solely through a mistaken [cognition] contaminated by ignorance. In other words, it is the object established solely by such a conventional knowledge *(tha snyad pa'i shes pa)* as eye-cognition. The way in which [Bhāviveka] has acknowledged [the nonestablishment of the property-possessor or the subject] is as follows: In the case *(de'i tshe)* in which the negation of origination in ultimate reality *(don dam par)* is dependent, as the property to be proven, upon those [property-possessors such as eyes and visible matter], it would be contradictory that the [property to be proven] is dependent upon [them], insofar as they were established in reality *(de kho nar).* [Question:] Granting that [Bhāviveka] thus acknowledges, what would then follow from that? [Answer:] Those [things] such as visible matter, which are neither established in reality *(de kho nar)* nor real objects *(de kho na nyid kyi don),* are inappropriate as objects to be obtained by a nonerroneous cognition *(ma 'khrul pa'i shes pa),* so that they are [the objects] to be obtained by a conventional cognition *(tha snyad pa'i shes pa),* that is the cognition *(yul can)* apprehending false [objects]. Hence, these [conventional cognitions] as well are erroneous [cognitions] contaminated by ignorance. Accordingly, the object which is obtained by a nonerroneous cognition cannot appear to an erroneous cognition, and the object which appears to

> an erroneous cognition is not [the object which is] obtained by a nonerroneous cognition, for the two [kinds of cognitions], i.e., mistaken, erroneous cognition and unmistaken, nonerroneous cognition, are distinct [from each other] in their way of operating in relation to objects through excluding from [one's] own object [the other's] own object.[35]

At first sight, Tsong kha pa's argument does not seem to differ from that of Candrakīrti and well concurs with his own tenet, too, that the Svātantrika does not accept on the ultimate level what is established as a real self-characteristic, which is to be cognized by an unmistaken cognition or nonerroneous valid cognition for such a characteristic. It is true that the subject is not ultimately established for Bhāviveka in contrast to his substantialist opponent. To this extent, Yotsuya's interpretation that Tsong kha pa criticizes Bhāviveka's use of autonomous inference, supposing Bhāviveka himself to be a proponent, on the ground of the ultimate nonestablishment of the subject for him seems to be plausible,[36] but there remains a problem. If Yotsuya was right, it would follow that Tsong kha pa here contradicted his own fundamental view that the Svātantrika adopts an autonomous inference on the ground of his acceptance of the conventional establishment of real self-characteristic. In other words, Tsong kha pa would have stated in the *Lam rim chen mo* the two inconsistent ideas that Bhāviveka *cannot* formulate an autonomous inference because the subject is *not* ultimately established for him, and that Bhāviveka *can* do it because the subject *is* conventionally established for him. Yotsuya's interpretation incurs this contradictory consequence.

A crucial point which nevertheless motivated Yotsuya's interpretation is that this ultimate nonestablishment of the subject results in Bhāviveka's violation of the rule of common establishment, since, for his substantialist opponent, the subject is ultimately established. Yet I suppose that Tsong kha pa makes it possible for Bhāviveka to state an autonomous inference without violating this rule by making another important modification to Candrakīrti's thought, i.e., the modification of the rule of common establishment itself. That is, in the *Lam rim chen mo,* Tsong kha pa ascribes "common establishment" *(ubhayasiddhatva)* or "establishment in common appearance" *(mthun snang du grub pa)* to the similarity of the valid means of cognition *(tshad ma, pramāṇa),* which establishes the constituent elements of an inference:

> [E] The [subject's] "being established as commonly appearing" *(mthun snang du grub pa)* also means that it is established for the proponent, too, by a valid means of cognition of the same kind as the valid means of cognition by which it is established for the opponent.[37]

A valid means of cognition to which the subject appears is a nonconceptual direct perception *(mngon sum, pratyakṣa)*. If the subject, such as eyes or visible matter, appears similarly to the direct perceptions of both proponent and opponent, the condition for the common establishment is fulfilled. Then, the valid means of direct perceptions, too, are established as commonly appearing for them. And what appears in the direct perception of the substantialists and the Svātantrika is, according to Tsong kha pa, nothing other than that which is established as a real self-characteristic *(rang gi mtshan nyid kyis grub pa)*.[38]

Consequently, there are two kinds of direct perception: For those who accept the existence of real self-characteristic as it appears, it is nonerroneous *(ma 'khrul ba, abhrānta)*, whereas for those who do not accept such a real self-characteristic, it is erroneous *('khrul ba, bhrānta)*. In other words, their respective ontological positions determine the nonerroneous or erroneous character of direct perception. The similarity of this character of direct perception then becomes the criterion for the subject's common establishment in Tsong kha pa's system, which he applies as well to Candrakīrti's arguments in his commentary [D] by identifying "unmistaken" and "mistaken" with "erroneous" and "nonerroneous." He has already given a previous indication of this interpretive move in his introductory remarks:

> [F] As regards the manner in which the sense-field of visible matter, which is posited as the subject [of Bhāviveka's inferential statement] is established, it must be established by a valid means of direct perception *(mngon sum tshad ma)*, viz., the eye-cognition that apprehends it. Furthermore, this [eye-cognition] must be nonerroneous, since, if it is not established as nonerroneous *(ma 'khrul ba)* for them *(de dag)* [i.e., substantialists and the Svātantrika],[39] it is inappropriate as direct perception for establishing an object *(don)*. [The idea that] the nonconceptual *(rtog med)* [cognition] is established as nonerroneous necessarily presupposes in their system that [a thing] appears [as] being established as a [real] self-characteristic *(rang gi mtshan nyid kyis grub pa)* [and as being] the basis *(sa)* with

regard to which [the nonconceptual cognition] has come to be nonerroneous, and that [this thing] exists as it appears. If that is the case, a valid means of cognition *(tshad ma)* of the same kind as that which establishes the subject for the opponent *(phyi rgol)* is inappropriate for the proponent [i.e., the Prāsaṅgika], since [in his system] there exists no valid means of cognition which establishes the [subject that is established as a real self-characteristic] because there exists no [self-]nature which is established as a [real] self-characteristic even on the conventional level *(tha snyad du'ang)* in any thing whatsoever *(chos gang la'ang)*. With this intention, this master [i.e., Candrakīrti] refuses autonomous inference [in contrast to Bhāviveka, who puts forward the subject of an {unspecified} general character, taking it as necessary that the subject of an inferential statement is established as commonly appearing *(mthun snang du grub pa)* for both Mādhyamika and his substantialist opponent[40]].[41]

It is instructive to compare this with Candrakīrti's system, in which:

1) The chief criterion for the subject's common establishment is the ontological question of whether the subject is ultimately existent or existent only conventionally.

2) The object of an unmistaken cognition is an ultimate existent and that of a mistaken cognition is a conventional existent.

In contrast, Tsong kha pa offers different interpretations:

1') The chief criterion for the subject's common establishment is the ontological question of whether the subject is existent *as it appears to cognition,* i.e., as being established as a real self-characteristic, or not.

2') The object of a nonerroneous valid means of cognition is what is established as a real self-characteristic (either ultimately or conventionally) and that of an erroneous cognition is what is not established as a real self-characteristic.

Accordingly, for Tsong kha pa, the nonestablishment of the subject on the ultimate level does not cause any violation to the rule of common establishment for Bhāviveka, who accepts the real self-characteristic on the conventional level, because he shares the same appearance of the subject with his substantialist opponent. In this manner, Tsong kha pa has substituted his own criterion for common establishment based on the appearance of real self-characteristic for the criterion of Candrakīrti, which is based on the distinction between ultimate and conventional existents.

Thus considered, in his aforecited commentary [D] on PPMV 29,7–30,2 [C], Tsong kha pa, on the one hand, allows that Bhāviveka has acknowledged that the object of a mistaken cognition is not ultimately existent; but, on the other hand, Tsong kha pa understands this as solely implying that the object of an erroneous cognition is unreal in the sense of not being established as a real self-characteristic, having identified "unmistaken" with "nonerroneous" and "mistaken" with "erroneous." This identification means that Tsong kha pa substitutes the criterion for common establishment 1' for 1 and the ontological qualification of the object of the two kinds of cognition 2' for 2. In short, for Tsong kha pa, Bhāviveka's position just serves to illustrate the plain idea that the object of an erroneous cognition is unreal. Tsong kha pa possibly intends to say: "Because even the Svātantrika master Bhāviveka acknowledges that an erroneous cognition does not establish a real existent, it is completely reasonable that the proponent Prāsaṅgika, for whom all conventional cognitions are erroneous with regard to a real self-characteristic, cannot share the subject with his substantialist opponents including the Svātantrika, for whom conventional cognitions are valid for and nonerroneous with regard to a real self-characteristic. Therefore, the Prāsaṅgika never propounds an autonomous inference."

In this way, it is safe to interpret Tsong kha pa's commentary [D] on the PPMV passage [C], if obviously deviating from Candrakīrti's intention, within the modified framework, in which the Prāsaṅgika plays the role of the proponent of an inferential statement, in conformity with his own system exposed in the introductory remarks [B] and [F]. Tsong kha pa is consistent in thinking that the Svātantrika *can* properly formulate an autonomous inference, unless he abandons his ontological position of accepting real self-characteristic on the conventional level. The ultimate nonestablishment of the subject, according to Tsong kha pa, never prevents Bhāviveka from propounding an autonomous inference to his substantialist opponent.

Moreover, this interpretation is well-supported by his commentary on the same passage in the *Legs bshad snying po,* where he reads *de'i tshe kho nar (tadaiva)* correctly and presents the following explanation:

> [G] In answer to the [objection from Bhāviveka, Candrakīrti] refutes [the subject of an unspecified general character] by having shown the reasoning *(rigs pa)* as follows: Bhāviveka himself has acknowledged that the self-nature *(rang gi ngo bo)* of [the property-possessor or] the subject, such as eyes, is not obtained by a mere mistaken [cognition] *(phyin ci log tsam)* [but obtained by an unmistaken cognition].[42] And the unmistaken and the mistaken are distinct [from each other], in other words, directly contradictory *(dngos 'gal).* The meaning of these [arguments] is as follows: It is inappropriate to posit mere eyes, etc., *(mig sogs tsam),* which are free of the qualification as to the two kinds of reality *(bden gnyis),* as the subject for proving the nonorigination of eyes, etc., from themselves. Namely, the valid means of cognition *(tshad ma)* which cognizes this [property-possessor or] subject is a nonerroneous cognition with regard to the self-nature *(rang bzhin)* of eyes, etc., and unmistaken cognition [consists in] the mode *(gnas skabs)* of being nonerroneous with regard to the self-nature, since, [insofar as] the object *(yul)* that is obtained by this [unmistaken cognition] is concerned, there exists no mistaken object of the cognition *(shes bya phyin ci log),* which is a false appearance [in the sense that the object] appears, in spite of its being nonexistent as a [real] self-characteristic, as such.[43]

This passage strongly suggests that there can be a common establishment of the subject for both Bhāviveka and his substantialist opponent,[44] and again "unmistaken" and "mistaken" are identified with "nonerroneous" and "erroneous," although it is indisputable that Tsong kha pa misreads the original text by connecting *pracyutiḥ (nyams par 'gyur ba)* with *āsādita-(rnyed pa),* as Tillemans has analyzed.[45] Yet I tentatively suppose that Tsong kha pa has made this bold change rather intentionally, after having found out the correct Tibetan translation of *tadaiva,* viz., without *de kho nar,* which must have been favorable for him to express his thought, for he thereby did not need to consider the case of the ultimate level. In other words, if it is not concerned with ultimate reality, the text can properly be reinterpreted to allow Bhāviveka's acceptance of the subject's being established by an unmistaken cognition. This is, in my opinion, the same idea as Tsong kha pa has tried to convey in a tricky way in his *Lam rim chen mo.*[46]

To conclude, in both the *Lam rim chen mo* and *Legs bshad snying po,*

Tsong kha pa shifts the focus of Candrakīrti's criticism of autonomous inference from a critique centering on Bhāviveka's fault in employing autonomous probative statements to a more general critique of autonomous inference from the Prāsaṅgika ontological viewpoint, aiming at clarifying the reason why the Prāsaṅgika rejects the use of autonomous inference. He achieves this shift through modifying not only the framework of the discussion (i.e., by making Bhāviveka the opponent rather than the proponent),[47] but also by modifying the meaning of the rule of common establishment.

2. *The focus: Why does the (Prāsaṅgika-)Mādhyamika not propound an autonomous inference?*

The question of what sort of reasoning "autonomous inference" refers to in the earlier Indian Madhyamaka tradition has been clarified to a large extent by modern scholars through the analysis of Bhāviveka's and Candrakīrti's usage of the terms *svatantra (rang dbang, rang rgyud)* and *svatantrānumāna (rang rgyud kyi rjes dpag)*.[48] It is most likely that Candrakīrti adopted them from Bhāviveka. In the PPMV, although Candrakīrti gives no clear definition of these terms, the following two ideas may be specified:

1) Autonomous inference is an inferential proof *(sādhana)* based on one's own doctrinal position *(pakṣa)* or thesis *(pratijñā)*. It is opposed to a reasoning solely to negate another's thesis *(parapratijñāniṣedha);*

2) Or, it is an inferential proof based on what is established for oneself, i.e., based on the property-possessor *(dharmin)* and its properties *(dharma)* that are established for the proponent himself *(svaprasiddha)* independently from others. It contrasts with a reasoning based on those that are established solely for others *(paraprasiddha).*

Accordingly, on the question here under investigation, i.e., why the (Prāsaṅgika-)Mādhyamika does not propound an autonomous inference, one can formulate Candrakīrti's possible answers as follows:

1') because he has no doctrinal position or thesis of his own, nor any valid means of cognition to prove it;[49]

2') or because there is nothing to be established for himself by valid means of cognition.[50]

CŚ 16.25 and VV 29 and 30, which Candrakīrti cites as authoritative scriptural evidence for his positions,[51] also support the views 1' and 2'. It can be said that both views presuppose the Madhyamaka's fundamental ontology of the nonestablishment of any existents in ultimate reality. In other words, Candrakīrti's main point is that since whatever is cognized by a mistaken cognition is unreal and there is no valid means of cognition for real existents, neither the property-possessor nor the property in Bhāviveka's inferential statement is established as ultimately real for himself.

In the later development of Madhyamaka tradition, these basic ideas of Candrakīrti came to require more precise interpretation, especially in connection with the theoretical distinction between the Prāsaṅgika and the Svātantrika. 1' mainly developed into the negative Prāsaṅgika interpretations, to which I have adverted in the introduction of this paper, whereas 2' occasioned further logico-epistemological investigations. In this regard, it is interesting to note that Phya pa chos kyi seng ge (1109–1169) enumerates and counters the following three "Prāsaṅgika" arguments against autonomous inference: There is (1) neither a common appearance of a subject *(chos can mthun snang med pa)* for the Prāsaṅgika and his substantialist opponent; (2) nor a propositional thesis *(dam bca', pratijñā);* (3) nor a logical reason *(rtags, liṅga)* the [three characteristics *(tshul gsum, trirūpa)*] of which, viz., its being a property of the subject of thesis *(phyogs chos, pakṣadharmatā)* and having [two kinds of] pervasion *(khyab pa, vyāpti),* are ascertained by a valid means of cognition.[52] Jayānanda as well is reported to have considered autonomous inference to be based on a logical reason with the three characteristics that are established by a valid means of cognition for the proponent himself, and *prasaṅga* reasoning to be based on those which are acknowledged solely by others.[53] Moreover, the character of valid means of cognition has come to be explained on the ground of the ontological status of its object. Some scholar, for instance, is said to have insisted that the Prāsaṅgika may conventionally propound a probative statement *(bsgrub pa'i ngag),* having denied both valid means of direct perception and inference that functions by virtue of a real entity *(dngos po stobs zhugs, *vastubalapravṛtta).*[54] dBus pa blo gsal byang chub ye shes (14th c.) also ascribes the essential difference between the Prāsaṅgika and the Svātantrika to their acceptance and rejection of both the logical reason *(rtags, liṅga)* and the valid means of cognition that function by virtue of a real entity.[55]

From these observations with regard to its historical background, one can gain greater clarity concerning *svatantrānumāna* in Tsong kha pa's Madhyamaka system. For him, autonomous inference is an inferential proof based on the constituents that are established as a real self-characteristic by a valid means of cognition for the proponent himself. Accordingly, the Prāsaṅgika does not employ it on the ground of his rejection of such a self-characteristic. This is no doubt a modification of the basic ideas 2 and 2'. In other words, Tsong kha pa has revised them with ontological and epistemological clarification. What is important here is, again, that through these modifications, he can successfully eliminate views 1 and 1', which were in his day widely accepted as authoritative Prāsaṅgika tenets in Tibet. Thus considered, it is surely safe to say that Tsong kha pa's theory of the two Madhyamaka logical positions owes much to the preceding historical developments,[56] although at first glance it seems very original and peculiar to him.

Let us now return to Tsong kha pa's commentary on the PPMV and analyze the structure of his theory more accurately. In the *Lam rim chen mo* he explains it several times:

> [H] Therefore, in their system [of the Svātantrika], the unsullied *(gnod med)* sensory cognitions *(dbang shes)* to which the self-nature that is established as a [real] self-nature *(rang gi ngo bos grub pa'i rang bzhin)* appears are also conventionally nonerroneous with regard to the appearing object *(snang yul)*. Moreover, the conventional cognitions that apprehend such a self-nature as existent in a sprout, etc., are nonerroneous with regard to the conceptual objects *(zhen yul)*. If it were not the case and they considered these [cognitions] to be erroneous, how can there be a valid means of cognition *(tshad ma)* which is established as commonly appearing *(mthun snang du grub pa)* in both systems of substantialists and [the Svātantrika]?[57]

> [I] If you accept [to use] an autonomous inference, you must prove a probandum *(bsgrub bya)*, after having accepted the valid means of cognition for real self-characteristic *(rang mtshan)* as commonly appearing *(mthun snang du)* for both proponent and opponent, by means of [a logical reason] the three characteristics *(tshul gsum)* [of which] are established in common for both [of them] by this [sort of a valid means of cognition]. If that is the case, it follows that [the constituents of an inferential statement] such as subject *(chos*

> *can)* are not established [for the Prāsaṅgika as commonly appearing for himself and his substantialist opponent] since [he does] not have such a valid means of cognition [for a real self-characteristic].[58]

The points of these statements correspond well to those of the aforecited introductory remarks [F]. That is to say, Tsong kha pa's theory that the Svātantrika states an autonomous inference based on his ontological position of the conventional existence of real self-characteristic can be analyzed as follows:

a) The Svātantrika conventionally accepts a real self-characteristic;

b) Therefore, he accepts a nonerroneous valid means of cognition for real self-characteristic;

c) Therefore, he shares with his substantialist opponent not only a common appearance of valid means of cognition but also that of the subject, logical reason, and example of his inferential statement;

d) Therefore, he can properly make use of an autonomous inference.

Although the stress seems to be placed on the epistemological explanation of how an autonomous inference is applied, it is clear that the ontological status of the object plays a decisive role in determining the character of the cognition as well as the entire process. In his *Legs bshad snying po,* Tsong kha pa simplifies all these points by saying,

> [J] [According to] our system, if one accepts what is established as a [real] self-characteristic *(rang gi mtshan nyid kyis grub pa)* as stated in the *Saṃdhinirmocanasūtra,* one must necessarily formulate an autonomous [inference] *(rang rgyud),* as the Buddhist substantialists and [the Svātantrikas] such as Bhāviveka do.[59]

> [K] Autonomous [inference] *(rang rgyud)* refers to an inference which one performs to understand a probandum *(bsgrub bya),* after having ascertained the way in which the two property-possessors *(chos can gnyis)*[60] as well as the three characteristics of logical reason are established, [i.e., the way of their being established] independ-

> ently *(rang dbang du)* by the mode of existence of the object *(don gyi sdod lugs nas)* through a valid means of cognition *(tshad ma)* without depending on *(ma 'khris par)* what is accepted by the opponent.[61]

Although there is no mention of the rule of common establishment in this definition, it should hold among substantialists and the Svātantrika, for whom the subject, etc., are established in the same way, i.e., by the mode of existence of entity or in the form of real self-characteristic.[62]

To sum up, we can reconstruct Tsong kha pa's reasons for explaining the Prāsaṅgika's rejection of autonomous inference:

a') The Prāsaṅgika accepts no real self-characteristic even conventionally.

b') Therefore, he accepts no nonerroneous valid means of cognition for a real self-characteristic;

c') Therefore, he shares with his substantialist opponent neither a common appearance of a valid means of cognition, nor that of the subject, logical reason, and example of his inferential statement;

d') Therefore, he does not propound an autonomous inference.

It is for these reasons, in Tsong kha pa's view, that Candrakīrti refuted Bhāviveka's argument for autonomous inference, but by no means for the reason that he has no thesis of his own. This is what Tsong kha pa aims to establish by reinterpreting Candrakīrti's criticism of autonomous inference through the introduction of two substantial modifications, i.e., the shift of focus by changing the roles of proponent and opponent, and the redefinition of the meaning of the rule of common establishment as well as of autonomous inference. Thus reevaluating Candrakīrti's discussion, Tsong kha pa has clarified the difference between the logical methods of the two Madhyamaka schools on the basis of their respective ontologies, whereby he has not only defined his own position as to questions 1 and 2 presented at the beginning of this paper, but also demonstrated a *correct* interpretation of the most authoritative text for Prāsaṅgikas, viz., the PPMV. In this way, all the problematics were closely connected with each other and have effected a great systematic change of Madhyamaka interpretation.

I will conclude this paper by summarizing Tsong kha pa's main points in his reinterpretation or reevaluation of Candrakīrti's criticism of autonomous inference:

1. Autonomous inference is an inferential proof the constituents of which are established as real self-characteristic either ultimately or conventionally by valid means of cognition for the proponent himself.

2. Common establishment means that the constituents such as subject of an autonomous inference are commonly established as a real self-characteristic by a valid means of cognition for both proponent and opponent.

3. Bhāviveka, as a Svātantrika master, can properly propound an autonomous inference to his substantialist opponent because he conventionally accepts that which is established as a real self-characteristic, and therefore fulfills the condition for the common establishment.

4. In the PPMV, Candrakīrti criticizes Bhāviveka not only as the proponent of an inferential statement, but also as one of the substantialist opponents to be refuted by the Prāsaṅgika.

5. Candrakīrti criticizes autonomous inference because he accepts neither ultimately nor conventionally that which is established as a real self-characteristic, but not because he thinks that the Mādhyamika has no thesis of his own.

Appendix: Some Remarks on the Phrase rang gi mtshan nyid kyis grub pa

The main controversial points in the interpretation of this phrase are what *rang gi mtshan nyid* refers to, and what the instrumental *kyis* signifies. Although it is clear that *rang gi mtshan nyid kyis grub pa* connotes an establishment in reality or a real existent, there are two different usages, which may inform us concerning what is modified by this phrase: (1) there is a use wherein characteristic or nature X of thing Y is *rang gi mtshan nyid kyis grub pa;* (2) there is a use wherein thing Y is *rang gi mtshan nyid kyis grub pa.* I have considered the usage 1 to be based on the expression *rang gi mtshan nyid kyis rnam par gnas pa['i mtshan nyid],* or "characteristic that exists as a self-characteristic," in opposition to that of *ming dang brdas rnam par gzhag pa'i mtshan nyid,* "characteristic postulated by means of names and conventions," both of which are found in the SNS. In the expression *rang gi mtshan nyid kyis grub pa'i rang mtshan,* which appears often in Tsong kha pa's works with slight modifications (see the list in Yoshimizu [1993b]: 121–125), *rang gi mtshan nyid kyis grub pa* defines the ontological status of the second *rang mtshan,* and *kyis* qualifies the mode of its establishment, for the second *rang mtshan* alone does not necessarily refer to a real existent. According to the Yogācāra system, even *svalakṣaṇa* or *svabhāva* in the sense of "essential characteristic" *(svabhāvalakṣaṇa)* could be unreal and conceptually constructed *(parikalpita)* in the same way as other attributive characteristics *(viśeṣalakṣaṇa)* such as arising and cessation. Hence *rang gi mtshan nyid kyis grub pa'i rang mtshan* is to be interpreted to mean that an essential characteristic of a thing, e.g., the characteristic "being pot" of a pot, is established *as* that thing's real characteristic or in the form of real self-characteristic. In case 2, on the other hand, it seems more appropriate to think that *rang gi mtshan nyid* refers to an intrinsic and essential characteristic of thing Y, and that *kyis* denotes the ground of its establishment. If one says that thing Y, e.g., a pot, is *rang gi mtshan nyid kyis grub pa,* it means that a pot is established *by* its own characteristic, i.e., *by* its intrinsic nature, or by its nature, in short. Popular translations such as "by self-characteristic," "by way of its own character," "by virtue of self-character," and the like, which are almost synonyms of "by itself," "by nature," "unaided," "independently," or "intrinsically,"can be understood in this sense and may also connote something real, since whatever is established intrinsically, not depending on others, is considered to be real in the Madhyamaka system. In Tibetan, the phrase may also be a synonym of *rang ngos nas grub pa* ("being established from its own side"), as Tauscher (1995: 124, n. 262) has indicated. This second usage is, however, assumed to have developed from the first one, for it is probably an abridged and simplified expression of the idea, "Thing Y has characteristic X that is established as its real characteristic" (cf. Yoshimizu [1993b]: *loc. cit*). Although it is possible to accept the most simple rendering such as "being established by itself" for both cases 1 and 2, my principle in the present paper has been to adopt, insofar as tenable, the closest translation to its presumable original meaning, as I have done in my previous papers (cf. Yoshimizu [1993b]: 93). For *rang gi mtshan nyid,* I employ more literal renderings, such as "its real characteristic" or "real self-characteristic." In this regard, it is not acceptable as Fukuda (2000) claims, neither clarifying the meaning of the word *rang gi mtshan nyid,* nor investigating Tsong kha pa's understanding of its Yogācāra usage, that the instrumental *kyis* denotes a ground or reason. For the Yogācāra usage of the word *lakṣaṇa,* see Schmithausen (2000).

Notes

1 My thanks are due to Profs. Leonard van der Kuijp, Georges Dreyfus, and Sara McClintock for their valuable suggestions regarding both content and English expressions. The responsibility for any errors, of course, remains mine.

2 Ejima (1980): 178–200; Ruegg (1983), (1986), (1991), (2000); Matsumoto (1986), (1997); Cabezón (1988); Hopkins (1989); Tillemans (1989a), (1992); Yotsuya (1992), (1999); Tanji (1992): 235–301; and Chu (1997) should all be referred to with regard to this subject, among which the present paper is indebted in particular to Matsumoto (1986) and Yotsuya (1999). For other relevant studies, see *Selected Secondary Literature Cited* in Yotsuya (1999: 175–187). According to Yonezawa (1999), the part of PPMV 1 here under discussion is treated in the **Lakṣaṇaṭīkā,* an anonymous commentary on the PPMV, the palm-leaf manuscript of which has been published and studied by Yonezawa (1999), (2001a) and (2001b). As for the Sanskrit text of PPMV 1, some important emendations have been made by MacDonald (2000), based mainly on an invaluable palm-leaf manuscript from Nepal.

3 Besides Jayānanda's (11th c.) use of the term *rang rgyud pa* in his MAvṬ (D 281a6, 281b6 [*dbu ma rang rgyud pa*], 282a2 [*rang rgyud pa*], 282b3 [*rang rgyud du smra ba*]), Yonezawa (1999: 1022; 2001a: 26) has reported that the **Lakṣaṇaṭīkā* gives Bhāviveka the appellation *svatantrasādhanavādin.* This text is supposed to have been composed earlier than the last quarter of the eleventh

century, for, according to Yonezawa (2001a: 6ff. and 26), its palm-leaf manuscript was presumably copied during the last decade of the eleventh century and the first quarter of the twelfth century under the supervision of Abhayākaragupta, who was active at Vikramaśīla at that time.

4 The name of this master is transmitted threefold: Bhāviveka, Bhāvaviveka, or Bhavya. In the present paper, I shall provisionally adopt Bhāviveka in accordance with Ejima's proposal (1990, cf. Yoshimizu 1994: 295, n.2) and its appearance in the **Lakṣaṇaṭīkā.*

5 In the earlier Tibetan tradition, the division into Svātantrika and Prāsaṅgika was just one of various distinctions of Madhyamaka doctrines. Cf., e.g., Mimaki (1982): 27–54, and Ruegg (2000): 23 *infra.* Pa tshab nyi ma grags (1055?-?), a great translator of Candrakīrti's works, is said to have employed the appellations *rang rgyud phyogs* and *thal 'gyur gyi phyogs.* See Matsumoto (1981): 207, n. 1, and Mimaki (1982): 45, n. 110.

6 Cf. Yoshimizu (1992a), (1993b), (1993c) and (1994).

7 For some more remarks on the phrase *rang gi mtshan nyid kyis grub pa,* which I have extensively discussed in Yoshimizu (1992a), (1993b), (1993c) and (1994), see the Appendix at the end of the body of this paper (275–276).

8 See Matsumoto (1986) and Yotsuya (1999).

9 Matsumoto (1986): 492, and Yotsuya (1999): 111.

10 Cf., e.g., *Lam rim chen mo* (Delhi ed.) 425a5ff. (P 76a7): *slob dpon legs ldan 'byed la sogs pa / chos rnams la rang gi ngo bos grub pa'i rang gi mtshan nyid tha snyad du bzhed pa'i dbu ma pa rnams / rang rgyud kyi rtags rang gi lugs la zhal gyis bzhes pa'i rgyu mtshan yang tha snyad du rang gi ngo bos grub pa'i rang mtshan yod pa 'di yin pas rang rgyud kyi rtags rang lugs la 'jog mi 'jog ni dgag bya shin tu phra ba 'di la thug pa yin no //* "Since the reason why the Mādhyamikas such as the master Bhāviveka, who conventionally accept that things have the self-characteristic which is established as their own [real] nature, accept an autonomous reasoning in their own system is also found in the [point that] the self-characteristic which is established as a [real] self-nature conventionally exists. [The question as to why the Svātantrika] sets forth an autonomous reasoning and why [the Prāsaṅgika] does not in their respective system leads to this extremely subtle [issue of] what is to be negated." Cf. also Chu (1997): 162 *infra.*

11 The discussion in *Lam rim chen mo* (Delhi ed.) 423a1ff. (P 74a8ff.) reflects this idea of Tsong kha pa (cf. Matsumoto [1986]: 491; Yotsuya [1999]: 140): *gal te tha snyad du yang rang gi ngo bos grub pa'i rang bzhin med pa'i phyogs la de ltar yin mod kyang / kho bo cag ni tha snyad du de ltar mi 'dod pas rang rgyud kyi chos can la sogs pa yod pa'i phyir phyogs skyon med yod do snyam na // tha snyad du de 'dra ba'i rang bzhin yod pa mi 'thad pa ni sngar yang bshad cing da dung yang 'chad pas lan de ni rigs pa ma yin no //* "[The Svātantrika] may conceive: That may well be the case [i.e., that it is impossible to state a faultless proposition based on an autonomous inference] in [your Prāsaṅgika] system, according to which there is no self-nature which is established as a [real] self-nature even conventionally. Yet [for us] there exists the subject, etc., of an autonomous

[inference], since we conventionally do not assert as such [i.e., we conventionally accept the self-nature]. Hence there is a faultless proposition [for us]. [Tsong kha pa says:] I have explained before that [even] conventionally it is incorrect that the self-nature as such exists, and I will now explain [that] again. Therefore, [your] reply is not reasonable." Matsumoto (1986: 492) has already indicated that this is a criticism of the Svātantrika *system* rather than of autonomous inference per se.

12 Matsumoto (1986: 492) has noted that Tsong kha pa's criticism of autonomous inference would finally result in a simple clarification that the Prāsaṅgika never states an autonomous inference, but not that the Svātantrika should not propound it. In this regard, he has expressed his doubts that Tsong kha pa's criticism of autonomous inference could bring about a mere demonstration of the difference between the Prāsaṅgika and Svātantrika ontology.

13 For the four kinds of false interpretation refuted in the *Lam rim chen mo* (Delhi ed.), see, e.g., Tillemans (1982): 120 n. 11; Ruegg (1983): 228f., (2000): 156–168, 189–193; and Yoshimizu (1993a): 209 *infra*.

14 *Lam rim chen mo* (Delhi ed.) 404a6–433b6.

15 Ibid. (Delhi ed.) 404b4–419a1.

16 Ibid. (Delhi ed.) 419a1–433b6.

17 The most negative view of the Prāsaṅgika position is represented by the third of four false interpretations, namely, that the Prāsaṅgika has, even conventionally, neither a thesis of his own nor a valid means of cognition *(tshad ma, pramāṇa)*. The second false interpretation ascribed to Khu lo tsā ba mdo sde 'bar (11th c.), which holds that the Prāsaṅgika should not propound any thesis when investigating ultimate reality, also receives Tsong kha pa's intense critique (*Lam rim chen mo* [Delhi ed.] 409a1–410a2). Cf. Ruegg (1983): 228f., (2000): 161, and Yoshimizu (1993a): 210f. Despite the fact that both interpretations have been criticized by many other earlier and later Tibetan masters including Go rams pa bsod nams seng ge (1429–1489), as I have indicated in Yoshimizu (1993a), Matsumoto (1997) has repeated his identification of the third interpretation with the "theory of freedom from extremes as the middle view" *(mtha' bral la dbu ma smra ba)* propounded by Sa skya pa scholars including Go rams pa.

18 For the details of his argument, see, e.g., Ruegg (1983), (1986), (1991), (2000): sec. 3; and Tillemans (1992).

19 Those who hold the third false interpretation, for instance, maintain that, according to Candrakīrti's view, whoever has his own thesis to be proven is to be regarded as a Svātantrika. In the following statement, Tsong kha pa clearly indicates his intention to remove this misunderstanding by showing a *correct* interpretation of PPMV 1: (*Lam rim chen mo* [Delhi ed.] 413b2f. [P66b3f.]): *'on kyang rang bzhin med pa'i dam bca' yod na* rang rgyud par 'gyur ro zhes pa'i dogs pa skye ba ni shin tu bden pa zhig ste / 'di ni ches shin tu phra ba'i dka' gnas su snang ba'i phyir ro // de'i lan ni rang lugs 'jog pa'i skabs su 'chad par 'gyur ro //* [*P: *yod na dang*] "Nonetheless, it is very natural that you wonder whether one

should be a Svātantrika if he has the thesis of nonsubstantiality [as his own], for this seems to be an extremely subtle difficult point. I will give an answer to this [question later] in the section where [I will] present our own position." "The section where [I will] establish our own position" refers to nothing other than the section where he presents his commentary on the PPMV. Tillemans (1992: 324) has also justly remarked that the strict criticism of negative Madhyamaka position inevitably turns on the interpretation of the text such as PPMV 1.

20 PPMV (La Vallée Poussin ed.) 25,9–26,2: *na paramārthata ādhyātmikāny āyatanāni svata utpannāni, vidyamānatvāt, caitanyavad iti.* (= PrP, D 49a2f.)

21 See PPMV (La Vallée Poussin ed.) 27,7ff.: *api ca yadi saṃvṛtiyotpattipratiṣedhanirācikīrṣuṇā viśeṣaṇam etad upādīyate, tadā svato *'siddhādhāraḥ pakṣadoṣa āśrayāsiddho vā* hetudoṣaḥ syāt / paramārthataḥ svataś cakṣurādyāyatanānām anabhyupagamāt.* (*...* emended according to Tanji [1988]: 153, n. 220 and Yotsuya [1999]: 89: *asiddhādhāre pakṣadoṣa āśrayāsiddhau vā*) "Moreover, if this qualification ['ultimately' in Bhāviveka's inferential statement] is applied because [Bhāviveka] wants to exclude [the possibility] that origination is negated [even] conventionally, there would then occur for [Bhāviveka] himself the fault in the proposition that its locus is not established, or the fault in the logical reason that it is not established in its substratum, for the inner sense-fields such as eyes are not ultimately accepted by [Bhāviveka] himself." Ibid.: 28,1ff.: *ucyamāne 'pi parair dravyasatām* eva cakṣurādīnām abhyupagamāt prajñaptisatām anabhyupagamāt parato 'siddhādhāraḥ pakṣadoṣaḥ syād iti na yuktam etat /* (*emended according to de Jong [1978]: 31; Tanji [1988]: 153, n. 225; and Yotsuya [1999]: 91: *vastusatām*) "Even supposing that it were stated [that 'ultimately there is no origination of conventional eyes, etc.,' there would [still] be the fault in the proposition that its locus is not established, from the standpoint of the opponent, since the [substantialist] opponents admit eyes, etc., to be existent exclusively as substance, but do not admit [their] being existent [merely] as designation. Thus, this [statement] is incorrect."

22 See PPMV (La Vallée Poussin ed.) 28,4–29,7 (cf. Yotsuya [1999]: 92–96): *atha syāt / yathānityaḥ śabda iti dharmadharmisāmānyam eva gṛhyate na viśeṣaḥ...evam ihāpi dharmimātram utsṛṣṭaviśeṣaṇaṃ grahīṣyata iti cet /* "[Bhāviveka] may assert: [When stating] that sound is impermanent, only a general [nature] of the subject and the probandum is apprehended [by the Buddhist proponent and the Vaiśeṣika opponent], not the particular [nature such as being ultimate or conventional].... In the same manner, in the present [inferential statement] too, a mere subject, which is free of any qualification, is to be apprehended." Bhāviveka indeed makes a similar assertion in PrP, D 180b5 (cf. Kajiyama [1967]: 297; Ejima [1980]: 189): *de'i phyir tha snyad du bdag spyir khas blangs pa'i khyad par ma grags pa sel ba'i phyir skyon med do //* "Therefore, because with regard to the self in general, which is conventionally accepted, we deny its unacknowledged qualification, there is no fault [in our inferential statement]."

23 PPMV (La Vallée Poussin ed.) 29,7–30,16. Trans. and commented in Tillemans (1989a): 5f., (1992): 316, n. 5; Tanji (1988): 23ff.; and Yotsuya (1999): 99–105.

24 This logical rule is mentioned by Dignāga in his PS 2.11 and its *Vṛtti* (Kitagawa [1973]: 481) and is cited in Prajñākaragupta's *Pramāṇavārttikabhāṣya* 647,9: *dvayoḥ siddhena dharmeṇa vyavahārād viparyaye / dvayor ekasya cāsiddhau dharmyasiddhau ca neṣyate //* as well as in the *Nyāyamukha* (Katsura [1977]: 124). For further references, see Ruegg (1991): 286, n. 20, and (2000): 245, n. 20. Bhāviveka himself states in PrP, D 182b2f. (Kajiyama [1967]: 302, and Ejima [1980]: 190): *gzhan gyi phyogs 'ba' zhig la grags pa'i phyogs kyi chos kyis ni bsgrub par bya ba'i don bsgrub mi nus par nges par gzung ste / gang yang rung ba la ma grub pa'i phyir gzhan gyi phyogs la ma grub pa bzhin pas....* "The subject of the proposition that is acknowledged solely in the system of the opponent is ascertained to be unable to prove the object to be proven. Because it is not established in one case [i.e., in the system of the proponent] like that which is not established in the system of the opponent. Therefore..." As for the Tibetan development *mthun snang du grub pa,* see, e.g., Tillemans (1982): 121, n. 18, (1989a); Hopkins (1989); and Ruegg (1991). Matsumoto (1986: 479) has drawn attention to Jñānagarbha's SDV 18 as the notion's possible Indian source (SDV D 2b2f., Eckel [1987]: 173: *rgol ba gnyi ga'i shes pa la // ji tsam snang ba'i cha yod pa // de tsam de la brten nas ni // chos can chos la sogs par rtog //*). Tillemans (1982: 121, n. 18) has also adduced the expression *mthun par...snang ba* from its *Vṛtti* (SDVV D 5b4, Eckel [1987]: 160).

25 *Lam rim chen mo* (Delhi ed.) 420b4–421b1.

26 PPMV (La Vallée Poussin ed.) 29,7–30,11.

27 *Lam rim chen mo* (Delhi ed.) 420b5–421a1 (P 72b2ff., cf. Yotsuya [1999]: 122f.): *'dir phyir rgol gang dang mthun snang du grub pa'i chos can mi 'grub pa'i mi 'grub lugs ston pa'i phyir rgol de ni tshig gsal las gsungs pa'i skabs 'dir ni bdag skye 'gog pa'i phyi rgol yin mod kyang spyir ni dngos po rnams la don dam par rang bzhin yod par 'dod pa'i dngos por smra ba dang tha snyad du de dag la rang gi mtshan nyid kyis grub pa'i rang bzhin yod par 'dod pa'i rang rgyud pa gnyis ka yin no //*

28 See Matsumoto (1986) and Yotsuya (1999).

29 See *Lam rim chen mo* (Delhi ed.) 421a2 (P 72b5): *rang bzhin yod par smra ba zhes pa ni dngos por smra ba dang rang rgyud pa gnyis ka la go bar bya'o //*

30 See Matsumoto (1986): 492. For the details of Yotsuya's interpretation, see the table in Yotsuya (1999): 166–170.

31 PPMV (La Vallée Poussin ed.) 29,7–30,3 (cf. Tillemans [1989a]: 5; Chu [1997]: 161; and Yotsuya [1999]: 99): *na caitad evam / yasmād yadaivotpādapratiṣedho 'tra sādhyadharmo 'bhipretaḥ / tadaiva dharmiṇas tadādhārasya viparyāsamātrāsāditātmabhāvasya pracyutiḥ svayam evānena aṅgīkṛtā / bhinnau hi viparyāsāviparyāsau //.*

32 This idea of ultimate and conventional reality is formulated in MAv 6.23 (cited by Prajñākaramati in the *Bodhicaryāvatārapañjikā* 174,27): *samyagmṛṣādarśanalabdhabhāvaṃ rūpadvayaṃ bibhrati sarvabhāvāḥ / samyagdṛśāṃ yo viṣayaḥ sa tattvaḥ mṛṣādṛśāṃ saṃvṛtisatyam uktam //* "All things bear a twofold nature,

which is obtained through right and wrong sight. The object of those who see in a right way [i.e., saints] is said to be [ultimate] reality, and that of those who see wrongly [i.e., ordinary people] is conventional reality." For this distinction between the two kinds of reality, too, Tsong kha pa has proposed a different interpretation, according to which ultimate reality is cognized not only by saints but also by ordinary people through a right analytical reasoning *(rigs shes)* and conventional reality is cognized by saints, too, through a conventional valid means of cognition *(tha snyad pa'i tshad ma)*. This valid means of cognition, which is finally regarded as erroneous with regard to the self-characteristic, corresponds to "mistaken cognition" here in question. Cf. *dGongs pa rab gsal* (Peking ed.) 108a3–5, 108b 2ff., cited in Yoshimizu (1990): 112, 114; and Tauscher (1995): 199f.

33 Matsumoto (1986), on the other hand, does not mention Tsong kha pa's commentaries in either the *Lam rim chen mo* or *Legs bshad snying po* (viz., the passages [D] and [G]) on the passage [C] of the PPMV.

34 As for this reading, cf. Hopkins (1989): 19–24; Tillemans (1989a): 7f.; and Yotsuya (1999): 128ff., n. 43.

35 *Lam rim chen mo* (Delhi ed.) 421b1–6 (P 73a3–73b1; cf. Hopkins [1989]: 19f.; Tillemans [1989a]: 6; Chu [1997]: 168ff.; and Yotsuya [1999]: 128–131): ... ***bsgrub bya'i chos kyi rten chos can*** *mig gam gzugs la sogs pa ni de kho nar* ***nyams par gyur pa*** *ste ma grub par legs ldan 'byed* ***'dis rang nyid kyis khas blangs pa*** *yin no // chos can ji 'dra ba snyam na ma rig pas bslad pa'i* ***phyin ci log tsam gyis bdag gi dngos po rnyed pa*** *ste / mig gi shes pa la sogs pa'i tha snyad pa'i shes pa tsam gyis grub pa'i don no // khas blangs lugs ni don dam par* ***skye ba bkag pa*** *de chos can de dag la* ***bsgrub bya'i chos su*** *brten pa* ***de'i tshe*** *ste / de'i phyir te / de* ***kho nar*** *grub na de brten pa 'gal ba'i phyir ro // 'o na de ltar khas len mod des cir 'gyur snyam na / de kho nar ma grub cing de kho na nyid kyi don yang ma yin pa'i gzugs la sogs pa de dag ni ma 'khrul ba'i shes pas rnyed pa'i don du mi rung bas yul can brdzun pa 'dzin pa'i tha snyad pa'i shes pas rnyed pa yin pas de dag kyang ma rig pas bslad pa'i 'khrul ba yin no // des na ma 'khrul bas rnyed pa'i don 'khrul shes la mi snang la / 'khrul shes la snang ba'i don ma 'khrul ba'i shes pas rnyed pa ma yin te* ***phyin ci log*** *'khrul shes* ***dang phyin ci ma log pa*** *ma 'khrul ba'i shes pa gnyis rang rang gi yul phan tshun spangs* pa'i sgo nas yul la 'jug pa'i* ***tha dad pa yin*** *pa'i phyir ro //* (*P: *spyangs*)

36 See Yotsuya (1999): 128.

37 *Lam rim chen mo* (Delhi ed.) 420a4f. (P 71b7f.): *mthun snang du grub pa'i don yang phyir rgol la tshad ma ji 'dra ba zhig gis grub pa'i tshad ma de 'dra ba zhig gis snga rgol* la'ang grub pa'o //* (*P: *sngar rgol*) For Tsong kha pa, the common establishment of the subject further indicates the common establishment of the valid means of cognition. In fact, he often uses the expressions *mthun snang du grub pa'i mngon sum* or *tshad ma mthun snang du grub pa*. Cf. ibid. 422b5f. (P 74a6f.): *rang gi ngo bos grub pa'i rang bzhin med par smra ba dang dngos por smra ba gnyis la gzugs kyi skye mched chos can du bzhag pa'i tshe ma 'khrul ba'i mngon sum mthun snang du ma grub pas gnyis ka'i lugs la mthun snang du grub pa'i chos

can sgrub byed kyi tshad ma med pas...; 426a3f.(P 77a2f.): *de dag dang rang gi ngo bos grub pa'i rang bzhin med par smra ba'i dbu ma pa'i lugs gnyis la mthun snang du grub pa'i mngon sum ma 'khrul ba med pa yin no //*; 429a2f. (P 79b3f.): *rang rgyud khas len na rang mtshan la tshad mar gyur pa'i tshad ma rgol gnyis ka'i mthun snang du khas blangs nas;* and 430b1f. (P 80b7f.): *des na kho'i lugs dang rang gi lugs gnyis la rang gi ngo bos grub pa'i gzhal bya 'jal ba'i tshad ma mthun snang du grub pa khas blangs ma byung bas* (cited in Matsumoto [1986]: 488).

38 Cf., e.g., *Lam rim chen mo* (Delhi ed.) 422a2f. (P73b3f., cf. Yotsuya [1999]: 133): *rtog med kyi shes pas bzung ba ni* snang ba tsam la bya dgos pas rang gi mtshan nyid du gzugs sogs snang ba'o //* (*P: *na*) "Since [the object to be] apprehended by a nonconceptual [direct] cognition must be an appearing [object] alone, visible matter, etc., appear [to the cognitions of the sense-fields] as a self-characteristic." It is assumed that Tsong kha pa has adopted this idea basically from the Pramāṇa school, but negated the real existence of self-characteristic, following Candrakīrti (cf. Yoshimizu [1992a], [1993b], [1993c], and [1994], especially [1992a]: 651, nn. 59 and 62). In *Lam rim chen mo* (Delhi ed.) 420b4, he formulates the same proposition as [A], substituting the subject "eyes" by "visible matter" and the example "mental factors" by "pot" *(gzugs kyi skye mched ni bdag las skye ba med de yod pa'i phyir mdun na gsal ba'i bum pa bzhin no).* Tsong kha pa often exemplifies the subject "sense-field" by "visible matter" besides "eyes," presumably because "visible matter" fits better for the explanation of common appearance in a perception than "eyes." This is in fact one of Tsong kha pa's tricks, as Matsumoto (1986: 484) has noted. However, this modification does not always take place. Cf. *Lam rim chen mo* (Delhi ed.) 419b6f. (P 71b4): *...dbu ma pas mig la sogs pa nang gi skye mched dam gzugs la sogs pa phyi'i skye mched rnams bdag las skye ba med par ...*; 421b1 (P 73a3): *chos can mig gam gzugs la sogs pa....*

39 Cf. *Lam rim chen mo* (Delhi ed.) 421a2 cited above in n. 29, where they are designated *rang bzhin yod par smra ba.*

40 Cf. Ibid. 420a3f. (P 71b6f.): *...mig dang gzugs tsam zhig chos can du 'jog ste dbu ma pa dang dngos por smra ba gnyis kyis bdag las skye ba yod med la sogs pa'i khyad par gyi chos dpyod pa'i gzhi yin pas gnyis ka'i mthun snang du grub dgos pa'i phyir ro snyam du bsam pa'o //*

41 Ibid. 421a2–5 (P 72b5–73a1; cf. Chu [1997]: 164f., and Yotsuya [1999]: 124f.): *gzugs kyi skye mched chos can du bzhag pa de 'grub lugs ni de 'dzin pa'i mig gi shes pa'i mngon sum tshad mas 'grub dgos la / de yang ma 'khrul bar de dag gis ma grub na don bsgrub pa'i mngon sum du mi rung bas ma 'khrul ba dgos so // rtog med ma 'khrul bar 'grub pa ni de dag gi lugs la gang la ma 'khrul bar song sa de'i rang gi mtshan nyid kyis grub pa de snang zhing snang ba ltar yod pa la nges par bltos so* // de ltar na phyi rgol** la tshad ma ji 'dra ba zhig gis chos can grub pa'i tshad ma de ni snga rgol la mi rung ste chos gang la'ang rang gi mtshan nyid kyis grub pa'i ngo bo tha snyad du'ang med pas de sgrub byed kyi tshad ma med pa'i phyir ro snyam du slob dpon 'dis dgongs nas rang rgyud 'gog pa yin no //* (*P: *bltas so;* **P: *phyir rgol*)

42 Yotsuya's rendering (1999: 156) of this phrase *(phyin ci log tsam gyis rnyed pa min par)* by "not found only by mistaken [cognition], [but also by unmistaken cognition]" is doubtful, since it would not be acceptable for Bhāviveka that some subject is established by a mistaken cognition and another subject by an unmistaken cognition, or that one subject is established by both kinds of cognition. Cf. Hopkins' translation (1989a: 21) "not found by mere erroneous [consciousness]" and Tillemans' "not found by a simple erroneous [cognition]" (1989a: 7). As for this passage, cf. also *Legs bshad snying po* (Delhi ed.) 92b1f. (P 165a6f.) and Ruegg (2000): 279f.

43 *Legs bshad snying po* (Delhi ed.) 90a6–90b3 (P163b2–5, cf. Hopkins [1989]: 21f.; Tillemans [1989a]: 7; and Yotsuya [1999]: 156f.): *de'i lan du mig sogs kyi chos can gyi rang gi ngo bo de phyin ci log tsam gyis rnyed pa min par legs ldan rang nyid kyis khas blangs la / phyin ci log ma log tha dad pa ste dngos 'gal yin pa la sogs pa'i rigs pa bstan nas bkag go // de dag gi don mig sogs bdag las mi skye bar sgrub pa'i chos can du bden gnyis kyi khyad par dor ba'i mig sogs tsam gzhag tu mi rung ste / chos can de 'jal ba'i tshad ma ni mig sogs kyi rang bzhin la ma 'khrul ba'i shes pa yin la shes pa phyin ci ma log pa rang bzhin la ma 'khrul ba'i gnas skabs te / des rnyed pa'i yul na shes bya phyin ci log rang mtshan gyis med bzhin du der snang ba'i rdzun snang med pa'i phyir ro //.*

44 Hopkins (1989: 23) and Yotsuya (1999: 129, n. 43), who have fully investigated these different readings in the *Lam rim chen mo* and the *Legs bshad snying po,* nevertheless take Bhāviveka as the proponent to be criticized.

45 See Tillemans (1989a): 8.

46 Refer to his own statement in *Legs bshad snying po* (Delhi ed.) 92b3f. (P165b1f.): *rten chos can de kho nar grub pa nyams par khas blangs pa'i steng nas kyang gzhan du bshad pa dang bshad tshul 'di gnyis mi mthun kyang rang rgyud 'gog pa'i grub mtha' mi mthun pa min no //* "I have exposed [the same passage of the PPMV] elsewhere [viz., in the *Lam rim chen mo*] from the viewpoint that [Bhāviveka] has acknowledged that the locus, [viz.,] the subject, which is established in reality [i.e., ultimately], is destroyed. Although the two ways of exposition [of the *Lam rim chen mo* and the *Legs bshad snying po*] are not identical, the theory to refute the autonomous [inference] is not inconsistent." This may sound like an excuse, but I do not think that his basic position differs in the two works. In this regard, one should say that Yotsuya's interpretation (1999: 147, 157) of this passage [G], that Tsong kha pa faults Bhāviveka for his use of autonomous inference from the viewpoint of the Prāsaṅgika, is not persuasive either.

47 Besides the discussions in the *Lam rim chen mo* and the *Legs bshad snying po* on PPMV (La Vallée Poussin ed.) 29,7–30,8 here under reconsideration, Yotsuya (1999: 140 and 162f.) has characterized Tsong kha pa's commentary in *Lam rim chen mo* (Delhi ed.) 423a1f. and *Legs bshad snying po* (Delhi ed.) 93a1–4 as proceeding within the original framework in which the Svātantrika plays the role of proponent. As seen above (n. 11), *Lam rim chen mo* 423a1f. indeed deals with the case that the Svātantrika propounds an autonomous inference, but Tsong kha pa's remark seems to suggest solely the Prāsaṅgika's rejection thereof on the

ground of his nonacceptance of the conventionally real self-nature. Hence, it is more reasonable to understand *Lam rim chen mo* 423a1f. as well to deal with the question of whether the Prāsaṅgika propounds an autonomous inference or not. *Legs bshad snying po* (Delhi ed.) 93a1–4 (P165b5f.) is also apparently concerned with the Prāsaṅgika position, the key sentence of which runs as follows (cf. Yotsuya [1999]: 161): *'di la legs ldan la sogs pa rang rgyud pa rnams kyis...don dam par dang bden par yod med kyis khyad par du ma byas pa'i spyi chos can du gzung rgyu yod ces sgrub mi nus te / rang gi ngo bo yod na bden par yod pa'i don yin pa'i phyir ro //* "The Svātantrikas such as Bhāviveka cannot prove, [opposing] to this [Prāsaṅgika position], that there is a reason for adopting as a subject [something of] a general [character], which is unspecified either as being ultimate and real existent or non-existent, since, [for the Prāsaṅgika], if [something] exists [by] its own nature, it is an object that exists in reality." In my reading, this sentence neither implies that the Svātantrika cannot share a common subject with substantialists, nor that he cannot propound an autonomous inference, because, for Tsong kha pa, the criterion for common establishment (i.e., common appearance) is not whether the subject ultimately exists or not. Furthermore, it is the Prāsaṅgika, not the Svātantrika, who represents the position that whatever is existent by its own nature *(rang gi ngo bo[s] yod pa)* is identical with a real existent *(bden par yod pa)*, as Yotsuya himself has noted (1999: 110, n. 1). Presumably Tsong kha pa is arguing here: "The Svātantrika cannot prove to the Prāsaṅgika that there is a possibility even for the Prāsaṅgika to share a common subject with his substantialist opponent, since the Prāsaṅgika considers that which is existent by its own nature to be identical with the ultimate existent in contrast to the Svātantrika, who takes them to be different." In other words, Tsong kha pa carefully leaves room for the Svātantrika to adopt a subject which appears in common with his substantialist opponent, while refuting this possibility for the Prāsaṅgika.

48 See the studies cited above in n. 2, especially Yotsuya (1999): 47–72 (ch. 3: The meaning of the term *svatantra* [*rang (gi) rgyud* or *rang dbang*]).

49 Cf. PPMV (La Vallée Poussin ed.) 16,2 (as for the Sanskrit text, cf. Matsumoto [1997]: 374 and 399, n. 78, and Yotsuya [1999]: 55): *na ca mādhyamikasya svataḥ svatantram anumānaṃ kartuṃ yuktaṃ pakṣāntarābhyupagamābhāvāt /* "And it is illogical for the Mādhyamika to state an autonomous inference by himself, since he does not accept any other position [to be proven]"; and PPMV (La Vallée Poussin ed.) 23,3: *nāsmākaṃ svapratijñāyā abhāvāt /* "There is no thesis of our own." For the meaning of *pakṣāntara,* which is usually understood to refer to a position other than the origination from self, Tsong kha pa gives the unique explanation that it refers to "that which is established as a [real] self-characteristic" *(Lam rim chen mo* [Delhi ed.] 428b5: *rang gi mtshan nyid kyis grub pa'i don).* Cf. also *Lam rim chen mo* (Delhi ed.) 415a6, and Matsumoto (1997): 363f. Matsumoto (1997: 374, 378, 382 *infra*) has proposed to interpret the word *svatantram* in PPMV (La Vallée Poussin ed.) 16,2 adverbially as meaning "independently" or "by itself," and *svatas* and *svatantram* as synonyms that

denote "based on one's own thought *(mata)* or thesis *(pratijñā)*" or "established for oneself" *(svataḥ-siddha)* in accordance with Bhāviveka's usage thereof. His conclusion that Candrakīrti accepts no assertion for the Mādhyamika may correctly describe Candrakīrti's thought in its single aspect, but this thought itself is definitely asserted by Candrakīrti. In other words, no one could have doubts that Candrakīrti has expressed in his works many thoughts and assertions of his own as to various issues of Madhyamaka philosophy (cf. also Ruegg [2000]: 129–132). As Matsumoto (1997: 373) himself has admitted, Candrakīrti actually uses the terms *pratijñā* and *pakṣa* in different senses in the PPMV (cf. also Ruegg [1983]). Accordingly, I should like to confine myself in the present paper to setting forth these ideas of Candrakīrti, viz., 1, 2, 1', and 2', as working hypotheses. It is also not acceptable that Matsumoto has identified Candrakīrti's position of denying any assertion with the "theory of freedom from extremes as the middle view" *(mtha' bral la dbu ma smra ba)* (cf. n. 17 above).

50 Cf. PPMV (La Vallée Poussin ed.) 18,1f.: *kuto 'smākaṃ vidyamānatvād iti hetur* / "How can the logical reason 'because [the sense-fields] are [already] existent' arise for us?"; and PPMV (La Vallée Poussin ed.) 18,5–9 (cf. Tanji [1988]: 14; Yotsuya [1999]: 64f.; and MacDonald [2000]: 172f.): *athāpi syāt / mādhyamikānāṃ pakṣahetudṛṣṭāntānām asiddheḥ svatantrānumānābhidhāyitvāt...* "[Bhāviveka] may assert: [It may be accepted that] the Mādhyamikas do not propound an autonomous inference, since [for them] neither a proposition, nor a logical reason, nor an example is established"; and PPMV (La Vallée Poussin ed.) 34,13 (cf. Tanji [1988]: 29): *asti sā ca svaprasiddhenaiva hetunā, na paraprasiddhena...* "Yet the [refutation of an inference] occurs solely with regard to the logical reason which is established for oneself, not [the logical reason which] is established for others."

51 VV 29,30 (cited in PPMV [La Vallée Poussin ed.] 16,7–10 and 30,7f.): *yadi kā cana pratijñā syān me tata eṣa* me bhaved doṣaḥ / nāsti ca mama pratijñā tasmān naivāsti me doṣaḥ // yadi kiṃ cid upalabheyaṃ pravartayeyaṃ nivartayeyaṃ vā / pratyakṣādibhir arthais tadabhāvān me 'nupālaṃbhaḥ //* (*emended according to VV, Tanji [1988]: 132, n. 134) "If there were any thesis for me, it follows that there would be this fault for me. Yet there is no thesis for me. Hence there is no fault for me. If I did cognize something by [a valid means of cognition] such as direct perception, I would make an affirmation or negation. For me, however, there is no such [a cognition]. Therefore I cannot be censured." CŚ 16.25 (cited in PPMV [La Vallée Poussin ed.] 16,4f.): *sad asat sadasac ceti yasya pakṣo na vidyate / upālaṃbhaś cireṇāpi tasya vaktuṃ na śakyate //* "It is forever impossible to censure the [person] who has no proposition of [positing something as] being existent, nonexistent, or both existent and nonexistent." Tsong kha pa repeatedly explains in his *Lam rim chen mo* (e.g., Delhi ed., 413b3–416a2) that neither these verses, VV 30 in particular, nor Candrakīrti's negative statements about thesis and valid means of cognition support view 1', for they solely negate their establishment as a real self-characteristic.

52 *Shar gsum stong thun* 65, 4ff.: *dang po (=rang rgyud kyi sbyor ba khas mi len pa*

mi 'thad pa) la gsum ste / chos can la mthun snang myed pa rgyu mtshan du mi rung pa dang / dam bca' myed pa rgyu mtshan du mi rung pa dang / rtags phyogs chos dang khyab pa tshad mas nges pa myed pa rgyu mtshan du mi rung ba'o // Cf. also Phya pa's discussion in ibid.: 65–69.

53 According to *Lam rim chen mo* (Delhi ed.) 405b6f. (P 60a8f.): *'dis ni tshul gsum tshad mas grub pa'i rtags kyis byed na rang rgyud dang tshul gsum khas blangs kyi mthar thug pa tsam gyis byed na thal 'gyur du 'dod par snang ngo //* See also MAvṬ D 120a5: *'dir thal 'gyur gyi mtshan nyid ni gzhan gyis khas blangs pa'i sgo nas gzhan la mi 'dod pa ston pa gang yin pa ste /*; D 120b3: *gzhan yang rang rgyud kyi gtan tshigs kyi phyogs la gal te gtan tshigs dang / bsgrub par bya ba dag la tshad mas khyab pa grub na de'i tshe rang rgyud sgrub byed du 'gyur pa yin la /* This position of Jayānanda is criticized by Tsong kha pa as the first of the four false interpretations of the Madhyamaka logical method in the *Lam rim chen mo*. Cf. nn. 17 and 19 above; Ruegg (1983): 228, (2000): 156ff.; and Yoshimizu (1993a): 210 *infra*.

54 According to *Lam rim chen mo* (Delhi ed.) 407b6–b3 (P 62a4ff.): *sngon gyi dbu ma slob dpon zla ba'i rjes su 'brang ba'i bod kyi mkhas pa kha cig ni… / rigs pas rnam par dpyad pa'i rang gi mtshan nyid kyis gzhal bya dang tshad ma'i rnam gzhag khas len pa'i dngos po stobs zhugs kyi tshad ma mngon rjes gnyis ka bkag nas tha snyad du ma dpyad pa'i 'jig rten grags pa'i tshad ma dang gzhal bya khas blangs nas dbu ma pa rang gis phyir rgol la bsgrub pa'i ngag bkod pa'i sgo nas gtan tshigs yang dag gis bden par med pa'i don sgrub par byed do //* This is the fourth false interpretation to be attributed to rMa bya byang chub brtson 'grus (?-1185). Cf. Ruegg (1983): 229, (2000): 163–168; Williams (1985): 208; and Yoshimizu (1993a): 210ff. For the Tibetan interpretation of the cognition termed *dngos po stobs zhugs kyi tshad ma* or *rjes dpag*, see, e.g., Yoshimizu (1996): 170.

55 *Blo gsal grub mtha'* 178, 15–18 *ad* 12.11: *de la 'di gnyis kyi khyad par dngos ni chos thams cad rang gi ngo bos stong par smra ba gang zhig rang rgyud la grub pa'i dngos po stobs zhugs kyi rtags dang tshad ma khas len pa dang mi len pa nyid du gnas pa'i phyir gtan tshigs kyi dbye bar bzhed do //*. Translated in Mimaki (1982): 179.

56 For the early Tibetan Madhyamaka interpretations of the logical method, cf. Ruegg (2000): 156–193.

57 *Lam rim chen mo* (Delhi ed.) 425b1f. (P 76b1ff.): *des na khong rnam pa'i lugs la rang gi ngo bos grub pa'i rang bzhin snang ba'i dbang shes gnod med rnams kyang tha snyad du snang yul la ma 'khrul la / de lta bu'i rang bzhin myu gu sogs la yod par 'dzin pa'i rtog pa'ang zhen yul la ma 'khrul ba yin te / de lta ma yin par de dag 'khrul bar bzhed na dngos por smra ba rnams dang gnyis ka'i lugs la mthun snang du grub pa'i tshad ma gang yod //*.

58 Ibid. 429a2f. (P 79b3ff.): *rang rgyud khas len na rang mtshan la tshad mar gyur pa'i tshad ma rgol ba gnyis ka'i mthun snang du khas blangs nas des grub pa'i tshul gsum gnyis ka la grub pas bsgrub bya bsgrub dgos la / de ltar na tshad ma de med pas chos can la sogs pa rnams ma grub par 'gyur ro //*.

59 *Legs bshad snying po* (Delhi ed.) 86b6f. (P 160b3f., cf. Yotsuya [1999]: 70): *rang gi lugs ni dgongs 'grel las gsungs pa ltar rang gi mtshan nyid kyis grub pa 'dod na*

ni nges par rang rgyud bya dgos te / rang sde dngos por smra ba rnams dang legs ldan la sogs pa bzhin no //.

60 This presumably refers to the two property-possessors set forth as a subject and an example, e.g., inner sense-fields and mental factors, in Bhāviveka's inference, as Katano and Khangkar (1998: 169) have suggested, whereas Yotsuya (1999: 70) has inferred that they are *chos can* and *chos*. According to the parallel passage from mKhas grub dge legs dpal bzang po's *Tong thun chen mo* 165b6f. cited in Matsumoto (1986: 502f.), the ascertainment of *chos can, rtags, dpe,* and *tshul gsum* comes into question.

61 *Legs bshad snying po* (Delhi ed.) 94a2f. (P 166b3f., cf. Yotsuya [1999]: 71): *phyi rgol gyi khas blangs la ma 'khris par tshad mas don gyi sdod lugs nas rang dbang du chos can gnyis dang rtags kyi tshul rnams grub tshul nges par byas nas bsgrub bya rtogs pa'i rjes dpag skyed pa zhig rang rgyud kyi don yin no //*

62 The fact is that Tsong kha pa does not speak of the rule of common establishment or common appearance in the relevant discussion in his *Legs bshad snying po.* Yet this rule thus properly finds its place in the formulation of an autonomous inference. In this sense, it can be said that this rule is one of the conditions of autonomous inference, but also a natural consequence of the ontological agreement between the proponent and the opponent. Hence I dissent from Matsumoto's assumption (1986: 500–504) that Tsong kha pa has abandoned the rule of common appearance *(mthun snang)* in his *Legs bshad snying po,* whereas in the *Lam rim chen mo* it has functioned as a principle or a *Merkmal* of autonomous inference. According to Matsumoto, Tsong kha pa employs, instead, the concept "the way of being established by the mode of existence of the object by a valid means of cognition" *(tshad mas don gyi sdod lugs nas grub tshul)* in the *Legs bshad snying po,* as seen in [K]. Statement [K] is, however, an accurate definition of autonomous inference, and a similar definition appears in the *Lam rim chen mo* as well. See, e.g., *Lam rim chen mo* (Delhi ed.) 433b5 (P 83b7): *de ltar na sngar bshad pa lta bu'i tshad mas rgol ba gnyis ka la grub pa'i rtags kyis bsgrub bya bsgrub pa la rang rgyud rtags dang....* "In this manner, [the inferential proof] which proves the probandum by a logical reason that is established for both parties through such a kind of valid means of cognition as explained above [i.e., through a valid means of cognition for real self-characteristic] is [defined as] autonomous inference and..." Removing the phrase *rgol ba gnyis ka la,* this is not essentially different from the definition given in [K]. The rule of common appearance is not adduced in the *Legs bshad snying po* presumably because it necessarily holds between the Svātantrika and substantialists. Therefore, as to the question of whether Prāsaṅgikas can state an autonomous inference with regard to conventional occurrences, one can answer that they are in a position to state an inference, but it never becomes *autonomous* inference. In the same manner, Tsong kha pa's comment in the *Lam rim chen mo,* "For the time being, I will leave aside the investigation of whether the autonomous inference is needed or not among Prāsaṅgika-Mādhyamikas on the occasion of formulating an inference to make each other understand something to the

extent of [conventional reality]" *(Lam rim chen mo* [Delhi ed.] 421b6f. [P 73a2]: *dbu ma thal 'gyur ba nang phan tshun du ji snyad pa'i don 'ga' zhig rtogs pa'i rjes dpag bskyed pa'i yan lag tu rang rgyud dgos mi dgos kyi dpyad pa ni re zhig bzhag go)* is not to be interpreted to imply the possibility of their employing an autonomous inference, even if they have a common appearance of their subject, etc. For, that which commonly appears to the Prāsaṅgikas cannot be a real self-characteristic. How can they then employ an autonomous inference?

8. Two Views on the Svātantrika-Prāsaṅgika Distinction in Fourteenth-Century Tibet

JOSÉ IGNACIO CABEZÓN

Introduction

THE PROLIFERATION of doctrinal interpretations, their coalescence into schools, and their doxographical classification by exegetes who sought to bring order to the messiness of doctrinal diversity is of course a phenomenon well known to the history of religion. For the traditional scholar, such doxographical classifications serve as an important organizing principle of knowledge—as a method of identifying different currents of interpretation within the tradition, and of ordering them, sometimes hierarchically, and sometimes not. When approached critically, such doxographical schemes can be as useful to the contemporary scholar as they are to the traditional scholar. However, our concern with history and our awareness of the political implications of religious ideologies force contemporary scholarship to face certain issues and questions that, if not unknown, were certainly less emphasized in the traditions that we study. Among these are the following:

1. To what extent are doxographical categories reflective of actual historical trends, and to what extent do they represent imaginative reconstructions of history? For example, central to the doxographical process is the ascription of a fixed "school"-identity to a group of individuals and their texts. To what extent do such individuals and/or texts recognize themselves as belonging to such a school? To what extent does such a move represent a reading into history of an order that is otherwise absent there?

2. Of course, that a certain group of historical figures and their body of texts do not identify *themselves* as belonging to a certain school

or movement does not imply that they cannot or should not be so considered by later scholars. On the one hand, such a grouping, even if it never explicitly identifies itself as a distinct school, may have enough internal coherence to be convincingly treated as a distinct intellectual movement. On the other, even when the homogeneity falters and a group of texts seems to resist being classified as belonging to a single school, there may be other reasons (e.g., pedagogical ones) for being grouped together. The point is that every classification—so long it is not utterly spurious—has its merits. It illuminates certain things, but at the same time, it misses or hides certain things. Here, it seems to me, it is the responsibility of the scholar to tread a critical middle path, being aware of the limits of classificatory schemes while at the same time checking the impulse to dismiss them. On the one hand, part of the task of the contemporary scholar is to explore the fissures of a doxographical category in an attempt to find *where* the homogeneity falters, and to read within those fissures or cracks the heterogeneity that the category occludes. But even imperfect categories have their uses, and so, on the other hand, it is part of the scholar's task to elucidate the (e.g., social) uses of such schemes, even when (perhaps especially when) they are questionable.

3. The previous two points have assumed that there is unanimity concerning doxographical classification, but that is of course far from being so. Different later schools will disagree, sometimes vehemently, over the way of divvying up the doctrinal pie. And even when certain categories (e.g., Svātantrika-Prāsaṅgika) come to be generally agreed upon as at least nominally valid distinctions, in many cases this surface agreement gives way to a heated polemic concerning (a) who gets included in which category, (b) the definitions and limits of the categories, and (c) how strong the distinction really is. The point here is twofold. First, attention must be paid to the *divergence* of doxographical schemes; and second, exploring this divergence of opinion can be extremely illuminating, not only in regard to the figures and texts being classified, but also in regard to those who are doing the classifying as well.

4. Given the importance of doxography to sectarian identity, it is important to investigate the role that doxographical distinctions play in the rise and development of religious institutions as social and political entities. Here, too, it seems to me, there is a middle way to be tread, for while granting that there are socio-political motivations and implications to religious ideologies (e.g., to doxography), and while acknowledging the validity and usefulness of such forms of analysis, *pace* Nietzsche and Foucault, the history of thought cannot be reduced to the history of power. Put another way, there is more at stake than politics in doxographical disputes.

5. Finally, any scholarship on this topic that is at all self-aware, at one point or another, will be forced to confront the issue of *its own,* even if secular, "doxographical" presuppositions. By this I mean not only our tendency to reduplicate traditional doxographical distinctions un-self-critically in our own scholarship, but, more important, our own penchant to classify the world in distinct ways. What categories and organizational presuppositions form the basis for our own ordering of the material that we study (e.g., in a historical analysis that seeks to construct a continuous and unbroken genealogy of influences, or even in the very distinction "traditional" versus "contemporary")? How are these schemes and categories constructed and differentiated? How does one come to be privileged over another?

To sum up, doxographical distinctions can be as useful to contemporary scholars as they are to traditional ones, although often in different ways. For the former, questions of history, social and institutional practices, and politics will take the inquiry in directions that are often different from those of the latter. Even then, however, vigilance as regards reductionism serves as a kind of corrective to the tendency to be dismissive of traditional doxography, as does the realization that *we too* operate with implicit doxographical-like presuppositions of our own.

Now the Madhyamaka (itself a doxographical category) has been the object of considerable doxographical subschematization, both in India and especially in Tibet. David Seyfort Ruegg has discussed how the Madhyamaka, in its "middle period" in India, was variously understood to be either undifferentiated, or else differentiated principally in terms of historical figures, e.g., the followers of Bhāvaviveka versus those of Śāntarakṣita.[1] By the eleventh century there seem to arise more thematic divisions like the one between the *māyopamādvayavādin* and the *sarvadharmāpratiṣṭhānavādin.*[2] Although it is true that the Svātantrika-Prāsaṅgika distinction seems to be virtually unknown to the Indian Madhyamaka tradition (a search of the ACIP database's dBu ma section of the bsTan 'gyur would seem to confirm this),[3] it is worth mentioning that Jayānanda's (fl. latter half of the 11th. c.)[4] *Madhyamakāvatāraṭīkā* (MAvṬ) does use the word Svātantrika twice in contexts where it clearly refers to advocates of a position that he sees Candrakīrti as opposing.[5] Nonetheless, it is interesting, and significant, that he calls *his own* position simply "the Madhyamaka" *(dbu ma),* without specifying it as Prāsaṅgika.[6]

In Tibet, as both Ruegg and Mimaki have shown,[7] the early (eighth- to ninth-century) distinction between Yogācāra- and Sautrāntika-Mādhyamikas eventually gives way to a plethora of different classificatory schemes, including, during the period of the later spread of the doctrine *(phyi dar),* the Svātantrika-Prāsaṅgika distinction. Mimaki has investigated Tibetan classificatory schemes of Indian Madhyamaka from the early period through the eighteenth century.[8] What has not been so fully explored is the Tibetan tendency to coin their own, often catchy, names for their particular school's version of the "view" *(lta ba).* That this was already a well-established pattern by the fifteenth century is witnessed by listings of those various nomenclatures in texts by Rong ston pa shes bya kun rig (1367–1449),[9] and mKhas grub dge legs dpal bzang (1385–1438),[10] who tend to portray the Tibetan penchant for dividing "the view" in this way as a kind of faddishness. Whether the Madhyamaka as a field of knowledge is (at least in Tibet) unique in regard to its susceptibility to this kind of partition, and if so, why, is an interesting issue, but one that I am content to leave here as an open question.

The main subject of this essay, however, is not *the plethora* of divisions and subdivisions of Tibetan Madhyamaka, but one in particular: the Svātantrika-Prāsaṅgika distinction. Our discussion below will focus on the debates between Sa skya pas and dGe lugs pas in the fourteenth and fifteenth centuries concerning the Svātantrika-Prāsaṅgika distinction, but before proceeding to that it is perhaps worth briefly mentioning something of how the distinction was understood in earlier times. The classical Indian locus for the distinction is, of course, the discussions between Buddhapālita, Bhāvaviveka, and Candrakīrti, in their respective commentaries on the *Mūlamadhyamakakārikā* (MMK), over the type of reasoning Mādhyamikas can and should use to bring their opponents to an understanding of emptiness.[11] Buddhapālita uses chiefly *prasaṅga*-type arguments aimed at demonstrating the absurdity in his opponents' positions. Bhāvaviveka criticizes Buddhapālita, claiming that *prasaṅgas* are insufficient, and argues for using independent *(svatantra)* syllogisms. Candrakīrti not only defends Buddhapālita's use of *prasaṅgas*, but also criticizes Bhāvaviveka's notion of *svatantra* syllogisms as incompatible with the Mādhyamika view as a whole. In India, as mentioned above, this disagreement over Madhyamaka method does not seem to have given rise to a full-blown doxographical distinction between Svātantrikas and Prāsaṅgikas. In Tibet, on the other hand, the disagreement between Bhāvaviveka and Candrakīrti on this issue was seen by some as representing a radical split in the Madhyamaka. The divergence of views between Bhāvaviveka and Candrakīrti on this issue became the basis upon which to elaborate yet other differences between these two, and other later, Indian figures, which in turn would eventually lead to the construction of the Svātantrika and Prāsaṅgika as distinct schools.

The investigation of the Svātantrika-Prāsaṅgika distinction in Tibet can take different (though related) routes. One such form of analysis is *descriptive/historical*. It seeks to elucidate how Tibetans went about distinguishing the Indian Madhyamaka sources into these two subschools. Under this rubric one might explore when the Svātantrika-Prāsaṅgika distinction first appears in Tibet, what the relationship of this particular scheme is to other schemes for partitioning the Madhyamaka, and how these two subschools were variously identified, distinguished, and subschematized at different points in time.[12] Once this terrain has been mapped, however, there still remains the *textual* question of whether (and if so which) of the Tibetan doxographical schemes best accords with the actual Indian textual evidence, and this constitutes a form of analysis different from, though dependent upon, the analysis of the descriptive/historical sort. When *this* has been accomplished, however, there still remains the *normative* issue of the *philosophical* validity of the various claims being made. How sound are the arguments being made for the superiority of the Svātantrika over the Prāsaṅgika, or vice versa? Which of these two schools, in their various interpretations, seems to present us with a more plausible picture of, e.g., the workings of reason? Finally, there is a mode of analysis that is concerned not with charting the various doxographical permutations, nor with assessing the extent to which they correspond to the Indian sources, nor with their philosophical plausibility, but rather with the *socio-political motivations and implications* of doxography as an ideology. What role does the philosophical valorization or devalorization of the Svātantrika and Prāsaṅgika as interpretations of the Madhyamaka serve in the construction of Tibetan sectarian identity? To what extent is a strong Svātantrika-Prāsaṅgika distinction important to the construction of a particular Tibetan school's identity? How and why do some Tibetan scholars align themselves with one of the two schools over the other? How and why do other scholars de-emphasize the Svātantrika-Prāsaṅgika distinction as essential to the construction of their own school's sense of identity? Clearly, all of these forms of analysis are related, and yet I believe that it is heuristically useful at the outset to separate them, even if they remain only implicit in what is to follow.

The Svātantrika-Prāsaṅgika Distinction in Tibet Prior to Rong ston pa and Tsong kha pa

In Tibet the tendency to separate out the tradition of Candrakīrti (to whom the names of Buddhapālita and Śāntideva are often conjoined) from that of other Indian Mādhyamika exegetes—from Bhāvaviveka, and from the "three teachers from the East" (dBu ma shar gsum), that is Jñānagarbha, Śāntarakṣita, and Kamalaśīla—probably began in earnest with the translations of Candrakīrti's main Madhyamaka works in the late eleventh century. Aside from Jayānanda, mentioned above, especially important in this regard are the figures of rNgog blo ldan shes rab (1059–1109), who is usually identified as the first major Tibetan proponent of the Svātantrika teachings, and Pa tshab nyi ma grags (b. 1055), who is considered the main proponent of Candrakīrti's Prāsaṅgika.[13] Until the Madhyamaka works of these two important figures become available, however, we cannot be sure of *how* or of *the extent to which* they *understood themselves* as upholding two distinct Madhyamaka traditions.

Several Madhyamaka writings of figures in rNgog's lineage are just recently available. Gro lung pa blo gros 'byung gnas (late 11th to early 12th c.), one of rNgog's chief disciples, has an extensive section on Madhyamaka in his *bsTan rim chen mo,* but, perhaps because it is not a work dedicated exclusively to the Madhyamaka, Gro lung pa does not take up the Svātantrika-Prāsaṅgika question in any significant way there.[14] Now Gro lung pa's student, Phya pa chos kyi seng ge (1109–1169), whose *dBu ma shar gsum gyi stong thun* has recently been found by Leonard van der Kuijp, and edited by Helmut Tauscher, clearly favors the later Indian "Svātantrika" tradition, whether or not he calls himself a "Svātantrika." More than that, however,

Phya pa's work is an elaborate attack on Candrakīrti, especially as regards the latter's views concerning the validity of *prasaṅga,* and the lack of validity of *svatantra,* reasoning. Finally, Phya pa is criticized for his attack on Candrakīrti by his student rMa bya pa byang chub brtson 'grus (= brTson 'grus seng ge = rTsod pa'i seng ge), who the *Blue Annals*[15] informs us switched at one point from Phya pa's Madhyamaka tradition to the tradition of Pa tshab and Jayānanda. rMa bya pa's commentary to the MMK, the *dBu ma rtsa ba shes rab kyi 'grel pa 'thad pa'i rgyan,* clearly rejects the position of "those Mādhyamikas who advocate *svatantras*" *(rang rgyud du smra ba'i dbu ma pa).*[16]

To summarize, the Tibetan Madhyamaka literature of the eleventh to twelfth centuries evinces the beginnings of the Svātantrika-Prāsaṅgika distinction as a proto-doxographical category. Even if the distinction is not seen as important by all writers, and even if the terms "Svātantrika" and "Prāsaṅgika" have yet to emerge as the basis for Tibetan sectarian affilitation, at the very least there was one important, even if solitary, figure, Phya pa, who upheld the use of *svatantras*, and a host of others, from Jayānanda to rMa bya pa, who rejected them.

How the Svātantrika-Prāsaṅgika distinction was utilized in the doxographical schematization of the Madhyamaka in the late twelfth through the thirteenth centuries is a complex matter.[17] Suffice it to say that the distinction was utilized by many doxographers, although at times only implicitly.[18]

Of course, our knowledge of the history of the Svātantrika-Prāsaṅgika distinction in the eleventh through the thirteenth centuries is incomplete not only because we lack many of the important Madhyamaka texts of this period, but because many of the texts available to us have yet to be fully explored. Hence, simply knowing that a particular figure utilized the distinction tells us nothing about the doctrinal content of the distinction (i.e., on what basis the distinction was made), nor does it tell us anything about what preference, if any, that figure had for one of these schools over the other.

Whatever the situation may have been in earlier centuries, it would seem that in the period and schools that most interest us here, the Sa skya and dGe lugs traditions of the fourteenth to fifteenth centuries, the Svātantrika-Prāsaṅgika distinction was well established as a major—and for the dGe lugs pas, at least, *the only valid*—doxographical subschematization of the Madhyamaka. The fact that important figures of this period, specifically Red mda' ba gzhon nu blo gros[19] (1349–1412) and Tsong kha pa blo bzang grags pa (1357–1419), viewed Candrakīrti's Prāsaṅgika as *the only* valid interpretation of the Madhyamaka, and as the true purport of the Buddha's teachings *(gsung rab kyi dgongs pa)*—a position that may well go as far back as Jayānanda and Pa tshab—leads to a hard Svātantrika-Prāsaṅgika distinction. Perhaps less well known is the countermovement among some Sa skya pas to suggest a softer distinction between Svātantrikas and Prāsaṅgikas, one that does not imply such a radical split in the Madhyamaka, and that does not require a choice between Candrakīrti and the rest of the Indian Madhyamaka tradition. This latter perspective was represented by such figures as Rong ston shes bya kun rig (1367–1449) and Go rams pa bsod nams seng ge (1429–1489). In the remainder of this paper I intend to examine the evolution of this debate principally in the thought of two figures: Tsong kha pa and Rong ston pa.

Tsong kha pa on the Svātantrika-Prāsaṅgika Distinction

That Tsong kha pa dedicates so much energy to elaborating the Svātantrika-Prāsaṅgika distinction is due in large part to the fact that he wishes to affiliate himself with the Prāsaṅgika position. But this is not the only reason. By focusing attention on this particular distinction he is of course suggesting that it is the *Indian* debates on the correct interpretation of the Madhyamaka that are worth pursuing. Implicitly, he is claiming that the various other distinctions elaborated by Tibetans are unhelpful to the understanding of the Madhyamaka view. This, of course, is consistent with Tsong kha pa's general position that it is the Indian textual tradition that should serve as the source of all doctrine.

More than that, however, Tsong kha pa wants to make sure that the Svātantrika position is rejected for the right reasons. In particular, he wants to make sure that in the rejection of *svatantras*, syllogistic reasoning (not just *prasaṅgas*) and valid cognitions *(tshad ma)* are preserved. In Candrakīrti's defense of Buddhapālita, the former not only defends the latter's use of *prasaṅgas*, he also criticizes Bhāvaviveka's use of *svatantras*. The question for later interpreters becomes what *svatantras* are, and why for Mādhyamikas *svatantra* forms of reasoning are disallowed. Many Tibetan scholars before Tsong kha pa claimed that *svatantras* are rejected because Mādhyamikas, having no positions of their own, use only *prasaṅga* forms of reasoning, that is, forms of reasoning that, "based on what their opponents accept, evoke a consequence that is unacceptable to their opponents."[20] According to this interpretation, to offer a *svatantra* syllogism to prove emptiness, as Bhāvaviveka urges, would require Mādhyamikas to accept certain theses of their own, that is, to accept theses independently *(svatantra)* of what the opponent accepts. It would mean that Mādhyamikas would have to accept the opposite of the position they are rejecting, thereby vitiating the character of emptiness as an absolute negation *(med dgag tsam)*. Moreover, it would require that Mādhyamikas accept that the different constituents of the syllogism (the subject and so forth), and the trimodal criteria (*tshul gsum* = the pervasion and so forth) that make syllogisms valid, are established by valid cognitions *(tshad ma)*.[21] Now accepting such theses, it is claimed, violates the Madhyamaka dictum against having any position of one's own, but more specifically, it violates the Madhyamaka tenet that things are simply to be accepted as they are by the world, without epistemological grounding. Since positing *svatantra*s, so it is claimed, requires not only the acceptance of theses, but also, additionally, their epistemological grounding in valid cognition, they are to be rejected by Mādhyamikas. This, or a version of it, would seem to be the position of Jayānanda,[22] and possibly that of Red mda' ba.[23]

Now Tsong kha pa finds this interpretation of *svatantra*s, and these reasons for their rejection, *un*acceptable because he believes that syllogistic forms of reasoning—with all of its formal constituents, including the trimodal criteria *(tshul gsum)* and their establishment by valid cognitions—are appropriate *even in the context of an ultimate analysis*. If this is the case, then *svatantra*s must be something more than mere syllogistic reasoning, and so Tsong kha pa embarks on a project of trying to show that *svatantra*s are syllogisms that contain within them the assumption of independent existence.[24] This, in fact, will be Tsong kha pa's strategy for distinguishing Svātantrikas from Prāsaṅgikas generally: to show that, whether or not Svātantrikas explicitly accept "existence by virtue of own characteristic" *(rang gi mtshan nyid kyis grub pa)* at the conventional level, many of their other tenets—their use of the qualifier "conventionally" in their repudiation of inherent existence, their distinction between true and false conventionalities *(yang log kun rdzob)*,[25] their positing of a form of personal identity that is not the "mere I," and so forth—are indicative of a kind of crypto-realism that makes them inferior to the Prāsaṅgikas. In this way, what began in India as a debate about the forms of reasoning that Mādhyamikas can and should use becomes for Tsong kha pa the locus for constructing a much more elaborate partition of the Mādhyamikas that goes far beyond the issue of the logical strategies Mādhyamikas should use, extending to all facets of the Madhyamaka as a philosophical system.

Tsong kha pa and his teacher Red mda' ba have quite different theories of the Madhyamaka, but however they may differ, both are what we might call "hard doxographers." By this I mean not only that they organize Buddhist doctrine into a hierarchically arranged and fixed number of schools of tenets *(siddhānta, grub mtha')*,[26] but also that they see what distinguishes one school from another as real, substantive, and irreconcilable differences. In Red mda' ba's words, "the texts of the four schools of tenets are mutually contradictory...and only the Madhyamaka path of the freedom from extremes *(mtha' bral dbu ma'i lam)* is the true purport of all of the Tathāgata's teachings.... All of the special beliefs (held by the various philosophers of the different schools) from the Vijñānavādins on down are not established even as conventional truths.... The system of the Ārya Nāgārjuna is the only correct interpretation of the Tathāgata's word."[27] Both Red mda' ba and Tsong kha pa agree that Candrakīrti's Prāsaṅgika is the only unequivocally correct interpretation of Nāgārjuna, making the Prāsaṅgika school, and this school alone, the Buddha's true intention.

In contrast to this hard doxographical approach there was in Tibet a softer one, an approach that saw the distinctions between the different schools of tenets as less radical—as more a matter of emphasis than as something based on rigid metaphysical distinctions. This soft doxographical approach tended more toward holism. It stressed the continuities between one school—and both within and across schools, between one figure—and the next. Where differences did exist, they were often seen as trivial, or even when not trivial, at least as having little if any impact on the different schools' ability to accomplish what was most important, the understanding of reality and the acquisition of liberative knowledge. Those Tibetans in the soft doxographical tradition included Rong ston pa, his student Go rams pa, and perhaps others,[28] and to this tradition we now turn.

Rong ston pa on the Svātantrika-Prāsaṅgika Distinction[29]

In a previous article on Rong ston pa,[30] I discussed his view on the Svātantrika-Prāsaṅgika distinction as a subtheme of his position on the Madhyamaka doctrine of thesislessness *(dam bca' med pa)*. To summarize that discussion, it is Rong ston pa's position that there is no substantial difference between Svātantrikas and Prāsaṅgikas either as regards the subtlety of the object they refute *(dgag bya)*,[31] or as regards their belief concerning the nature of logical reasoning as it applies to conventional reality.[32] In particular, Rong ston pa believes that to claim that the Svātantrikas accept, and that Prāsaṅgikas reject, *svatantra* forms of syllogistic reasoning *in general* is incorrect, since both Svātantrikas and Prāsaṅgikas accept *svatantras* in the analysis of the conventional world. "The Prāsaṅgikas' claim that *svatantra* theses are invalid [is a claim] they make with regard to *ultimate* forms of analysis. With regard to the establishment of the *conventional*, [even the Prāsaṅgikas believe that] there are *svatantra* theses and reasons."[33]

Rong ston pa acknowledges that there is a more than superficial difference between Svātantrikas and Prāsaṅgikas as regards the necessity, and even the appropriateness, of using syllogistic reasoning in an ultimate analysis, that is, in an analysis of reality that culminates in an understanding of emptiness.

> What is the difference between the Prāsaṅgikas and the Svātantrikas? When they engage the realists in examining the nature [of reality, Prāsaṅgikas] do not accept *svatantra* reasons; instead, they eliminate the misconceptions of others by means of *prasaṅgas*. [The Svātantrikas, on the other hand,] believe that even if it is permissible to first posit a reason by means of a *prasaṅga*, later it must be sustained by means of a *svatantra*.[34]

The fact that Prāsaṅgikas reject *svatantras*, however, does not imply that they reject syllogistic reasoning even in regard to the ultimate, or that they use exclusively *prasaṅga* forms of reasoning that only point out the absurdity in the opponent's position. Prāsaṅgikas, for example, use "inference based on what is established for others" *(gzhan la grags pa'i rjes dpag)*,[35] which, Rong ston pa implies, is the Prāsaṅgika analogue of the *svatantra*. Rong ston pa explains:

> What is the difference between "inference based on what is established for others" and *svatantra* inference? In a syllogism that establishes a *svatantra* thesis, the trimodal criteria are ascertained. [In an inference] based on what is established for others, for the sake of eliminating the misconceptions of the opponent, one states as the reason what the others accept, without establishing any thesis independently *(rang dbang du)*.[36]

Svātantrikas believe that an understanding of emptiness requires the use of *svatantras*, that is, formal syllogistic reasoning that satisfies the trimodal criteria.[37] For Rong ston pa, what makes someone a Svātantrika is the insistence that emptiness can be understood "only by relying upon a reason that has its trimodal criteria *(tshul gsum)* established by means of a valid cognition, so that there is [for Svātantrikas] no question of the need for a *svatantra* reason."[38] Prāsaṅgikas, on the other hand, believe that "when one analyzes the ultimate there is nothing *to* be established by means of a *svatantra* reason, [a reason] that takes as its object the quality accepted by [Mādhyamikas themselves] *(rang gis mngon par 'dod pa'i chos),* and that is sought to be inferred in regard to a subject *(chos can)* that is established by the valid cognitions of both parties [the Mādhyamikas and their opponents]."[39] In short, for Prāsaṅgikas, there *is* no trimodal criteria that *can be* established by both Mādhyamikas and their opponents, making the Svātantrika insistence on such a formal reason inappropriate. That in the context of analyzing reality there is, for example, no subject *(chos can)* established for both parties is, according to Rong ston pa, a direct corollary of the fact that "for the Mādhyamika at that time there is not even the appearance of a subject."[40] According to Rong ston pa, if a subject were to be established for the Mādhyamika in the context of an ultimate analysis, then that subject would have to withstand reasoned analysis *(rigs pas brtag bzod),* thereby vitiating its lack of true existence. So why do Prāsaṅgikas repudiate *svatantras*? It is because "in the context of analyzing reality, the basis upon which the analysis is conducted is not established for the Mādhyamika, so that with respect to such a [basis] there is no belief in a quality to be proven *(sgrub chos)* as the opposite of the quality to be repudiated *(dgag chos)*."[41]

But this does not mean, as stated previously, that Prāsaṅgikas do not use syllogistic reasoning. Consider the following exchange with an opponent:

> [Rong ston pa's own position:] That which is to be proven *(sādhya, sgrub bya)* is [the fact that] the conventional is like an illusion, and ultimately, the freedom from proliferations, and so forth; what proves this *(sādhana, sgrub byed)* is scripture and reasoning, as explained in the texts. [Opponent:] But aren't *svatantra* reasons rejected? How then can you accept such things as "that which is to be proven" and "that which proves"? [Rong ston pa:] Even though *svatantra* reasons are rejected, we do not repudiate "that which is to be proven" and "that which proves" as mere labels *(btags pa tsam)*.... Therefore, a reason *(gtan tshig),* which is like the moon in water, [causes] an opponent *(phyir rgol),* who is like a magical illusion, to understand that which to be proven *(sgrub bya),* which is like a dream.[42]

As long as the conventional, illusory-like quality of syllogistic reasoning is upheld, such reasoning is not problematic, even, it would seem, in regard to emptiness. This illusory-like quality of logic is maintained, says Rong ston pa, by the Mādhyamikas' commitment to restricting themselves to the beliefs of the opponent and of the world. It is transgressed when there is an insistence that the various parts of the syllogism must be established by *pramāṇas*.[43] It is not, therefore, the syllogistic structure of reasoning that is problematic for the Prāsaṅgika, but rather the additional claim made by the Svātantrikas that the components of, and relations within, the syllogism—the subject, thesis, reason, pervasion etc.—must be ascertained *by means of valid cognition*. This is what makes a syllogism a *svatantra*. Prāsaṅgikas repudiate such epistemologically grounded syllogisms because they believe that in the context of an ultimate analysis such grounding contradicts the Mādhyamika claim that nothing can withstand reasoned analysis.

For Rong ston pa, then, Svātantrikas and Prāsaṅgikas differ from each other only with respect to the epistemological requirements necessary to make syllogisms that prove emptiness valid. But though Svātantrikas may require formal syllogisms with specific properties (in particular, the valid ascertainment of the trimodal criteria), this does not, according to Rong ston pa, and contra Tsong kha pa, commit them to accepting any form of independent existence, subtle or otherwise. Disagreement between Svātantrikas and Prāsaṅgikas regarding the details of the reasoning used to prove emptiness, therefore, does not for Rong ston pa put the Svātantrikas at a disadvantage as regards their understanding of emptiness. "Concerning their beliefs about the ultimate, the Mādhyamikas of the Noble Land [of India] are for the most part in agreement in regard to how they identify [emptiness]; they do not differ, in so far as all of them accept the freedom from proliferations."[44]

Go rams pa's Position in the lTa ba'i shan 'byed

Go rams pa bsod nams seng ge (1429–1489), a student of Rong ston pa, generally follows his teacher on the major points concerning the Svātantrika-Prāsaṅgika distinction. In the present context his work is of interest because it fills in some of the gaps in Rong ston pa's position. That, like Rong ston pa, he is a soft doxographer, can be seen by examining the *lTa ba'i shan 'byed,* one of his most important and popular works. The *lTa ba'i shan 'byed* is a polemical text whose goal it is to argue for the superiority of his interpretation of the Madhyamaka—which Go rams pa, following Red mda' ba, Rong ston pa, and other earlier Sa skya pa figures, calls the "Freedom from Proliferations" *(spros bral)* theory of the Madhyamaka—vis-à-vis two rival interpretations prevalent in his day, that of the founder of the Jo nang pa tradition, Dol po pa shes rab rgyal mtshan[45] (1292–1361), and that of Tsong kha pa (see above). The Madhyamaka theories of these latter two figures were known, respectively, as the "Emptiness of What Is Other" *(gzhan stong)* and, as we have seen, the "Prāsaṅgika" *(thal 'gyur pa)*.

In good Madhyamaka fashion, Go rams pa's strategy in the *lTa ba'i shan 'byed* is to argue for his version of the Madhyamaka by situating it as the middle way between what he considers to be Dol po pa's eternalism and Tsong kha pa's nihilism. The nature of the Svātantrika-Prāsaṅgika distinction forms an essential part of this argument, albeit more in regard to Tsong kha pa than in regard to Dol po pa.

Dol po pa, we now know,[46] repudiated the Svātantrika-Prāsaṅgika division of the Madhyamaka as a valid doxographical distinction. He sees such a distinction as an aberration that arises in later historical periods, one that is flawed because it goes counter to the earlier textual tradition. However, Dol po pa's repudiation of the distinction is based more on metaphysical than exegetical grounds. He sees the distinction as somehow introducing or tainting the purity of the absolute—as contradicting the unitary and unequivocally ultimate nature of the absolute by "mixing it with...composite factors." Dol po pa is willing to grant that the absolute (and therefore the Madhyamaka) can be called by different names, but he insists that these various names are mere designations of something that is in reality singular in meaning and in "taste." For Dol po pa, then, any substantive Svātantrika-Prāsaṅgika distinction is invalid not so much because it contradicts the textual evidence as because it threatens the univocal oneness of the ultimate truth.

Tsong kha pa, on the other hand, argues, as we have seen, for a strong Svātantrika-Prāsaṅgika distinction, and opts, of course, for his interpretation of Candrakīrti's Prāsaṅgika as the highest Madhyamaka view *(lta ba mthar thug pa)*. Tsong kha pa elaborates the Svātantrika-Prāsaṅgika distinction in a number of different contexts throughout his works. Ontologically, he sees Svātantrikas like Bhāvaviveka as underestimating the extent of what is to be refuted in the Madhyamaka critique, thereby clinging to a subtle form of reification that he calls "existence by virtue of own characteristic" *(rang gi mtshan nyid kyis grub pa)*. In the words of Tsong kha pa's student, mKhas grub rje, "In comparison to what it is that the Prāsaṅgikas consider the object to be refuted, what the Svātantrikas here posit is much more crude *(shin tu rag pa)*."[47] Thus, Tsong kha pa argues for a strong distinction between these two subschools of the Madhyamaka, and opts for the Prāsaṅgika over the Svātantrika interpretation as *the* correct one.

Now Go rams pa's view concerning the Svātantrika-Prāsaṅgika distinction is a kind of intermediary position between Dol po pa's and Tsong kha pa's. Contra Dol po pa, he is willing to grant the validity of the distinction generally, but contra Tsong kha pa, he does not believe that the distinction is a very strong one. In his words, "there is no difference between the two, that is, between Prāsaṅgikas and Svātantrikas, in regard to the way they accept the ultimate." Specifically, Go rams pa rejects the position put forward by the dGe lugs pas that the Svātantrikas' acceptance of *svatantras* commits them to accepting a subtle form of inherent existence (existence by virtue of own-characteristic), and that this condemns them to a kind of crypto-realism.[48] Like Rong ston, Go rams pa believes that in the analysis of the conventional world both Prāsaṅgikas and Svātantrikas rely on, and accept, *svatantras*. In that sense, there is, he believes, no wholesale repudiation of *svatantras* even on the part of Prāsaṅgikas.[49] *Svatantras* are problematic for Prāsaṅgikas only in the context of an analysis of reality. This, he states, "is what distinguishes Prāsaṅgikas and Svātantrikas, namely, that *in the context of analyzing reality,* [the latter] does, and [the former] does not accept *svatantras*."[50] Go rams pa defines a *svatantra* (autonomous) thesis as "that which is proven by a reason that is established by means of a valid cognition in such a way that the proponent has a desire to infer the specific property based upon a subject that is established in common for both parties."[51] This he contrasts with two forms of reasoning used by Prāsaṅgikas: (1) "inference based on what is acceptable to the other" *(gzhan la grags kyi rjes dpag),* which "refers to [forms of reasoning] in which the two—subject and predicate—as well as the reason and pervasion are all accepted only by the opponent [of the syllogism] and not by the proponent,"[52] and (2) *prasaṅga* (reductio) forms of reasoning,[53] in which the proponent is likewise not interested in establishing any independent thesis based upon a commonly held subject, but instead is concerned only with pointing out the absurdity and contradictions in the position that is held by his or her opponent. For Go rams pa, except for these forms of argumentation, which are idiosyncratic to the Prāsaṅgikas, all syllogistic reasoning is essentially svatantric in character, and is acceptable even to Prāsaṅgikas, except of course in the analysis of emptiness.

Why do Prāsaṅgikas reject autonomous syllogisms—*svatantras*—in the context of an analysis of reality, that is, in an analysis that culminates in the understanding of emptiness? Go rams pa answers this question much in the same way as his teacher Rong ston pa, invoking the fact that Prāsaṅgikas maintain that the various parts of the syllogism do not appear to Madhyamakas and their opponents in the same way (indeed, to Madhyamakas in certain specific contexts *not at all*).[54] Hence, the fact that Prāsaṅgikas believe that in the analysis of reality the subject of the syllogism does not even appear *(snang tsam nyid kyang ma grub pa)* is what leads them to reject *svatantras*, since it is precisely the appearance of the subject to both parties in common *(chos can mthun snang)*[55] that is the defining characteristic of an autonomous syllogism.[56]

Even though Go rams pa takes Rong ston pa's side on most issues, there is at least one point on which he disagrees with his master, and he makes no attempt to hide this. This particular exchange between Go rams pa and his teacher is interesting, on the one hand, because it demonstrates the critical spirit that pervades the Tibetan philosophical tradition. Although rare for a student to admit that his position actually contradicts that of his master, it is not unheard of, as this passage clearly shows us. On the other hand, the exchange is interesting because it reveals another reason why some Madhyamaka exegetes rejected *svatantras*. Here is the passage from Go rams pa's *lTa ba'i shan 'byed:*

> In this regard [Rong ston] Shes bya kun rig has said:
>
>> If one is a Madhyamaka, it is incorrect to utilize autonomous syllogisms that prove the arising [of one thing] from another in the wake of the [Prāsaṅgika's reductio] refutation of [the fact that things] arise from themselves. This is because [Madhyamakas] do not believe in the arising [of one thing] from another, which is the opposite of the position that they arise from themselves.
>
> Despite his having said this, I think that it is incorrect, since this is the section of the dispute concerning whether or not there exist autonomous [syllogisms] that prove the nonexistence of [the fact that] things arise *from themselves.*[57]

Rong ston pa appears to be arguing that Madhyamakas should not use autonomous syllogisms since it commits them to accepting the opposite of the positions they repudiate. In this case, to rely on an autonomous syllogism after the first extreme position (the arising of things from themselves, *bdag skye)* has already been refuted using reductio arguments (which is what Bhāvaviveka demands of Buddhapālita) would force the Madhyamaka to accept the position that things arise from other things *(gzhan skye),* which of course is the second extreme, and equally unacceptable to the Madhyamaka. Go rams pa, however, rejects this as a reason for abandoning the use of autonomous syllogisms, maintaining that it is possible to reject *svatantras* simply on the basis of epistemo-logical arguments that make reference only to the terms operative in the repudiation of the extreme of self-arising. The use of *svatantras*, he implies, could not commit those who use them to accepting the opposite of what they reject, in this case, "the arising of one thing from another," since this would create a substantive divide between Prāsaṅgikas and Svātantrikas, and vitiate against the soft doxographical distinction that he is attempting to preserve. All of this goes to show that the position of the soft doxographer is a precarious one. On the one hand, they must account for the differences between the philosophical views found in the Indian texts themselves, but they must do so in a restrained fashion, that is, in a way that does not provide fodder for the creation of hierarchies.

Go rams pa, it seems to me, sees the problem with the Svātantrika position to lie in its insistence on the universal applicability of logic, that is, in its refusal to notice that there are contexts in which formal syllogistic reasoning is (a) unnecessary, and (b) actually inappropriate. Syllogistic reasoning is sometimes unnecessary because other forms of reasoning (i.e., reductio arguments, "inference based on what is acceptable to the other party") can also bring about knowledge. In the context of arguments leading to the knowledge of reality, however, *svatantra*—that is syllogistic—forms of reasoning, or we might say formal logic, are actually inappropriate, because on this occasion the context prohibits that the criteria operative in such reasoning (the common acceptance of the syllogisms' various parts and relationships) simply cannot be met. However, contra Tsong kha pa, neither Go rams pa nor, for the most part, Rong ston pa see *svatantras* as instrinsically flawed. If Svātantrikas like Bhāvaviveka are critiqued by Candrakīrti, it is, they claim, because Bhāvaviveka is a logical universalist, which is to say that he believes that logic is everywhere equally applicable, and independent/autonomous *(svatantra)* of context—that is, independent of who is arguing with whom, or what they are arguing about. By contrast, Prāsaṅgikas are contextualists, not only because they discern when and *when not* to rely on formal syllogistic reasoning, but also because, more generally, they understand the provisional character of logic, aware of the fact that it is to be used fluidly, as a flexible means rather than as an end that governs philosophical discourse under all circumstances. There are, then, for Prāsaṅgikas no fixed means of leading their opponents to an understanding of reality, no set formulas. Since reality is beyond linguistically describable positions arrived at by fixed logical means, no form of language (including the language of logic) is privileged. Notice, however, that this characterization of the Svātantrika-Prāsaṅgika distinction emphasizes their methodological differences, and that it specifically refuses to draw any metaphysical implications from these differences.[58] All of this, of course, is to say that Go rams pa, like Rong ston pa, is a soft doxographer.

Conclusion

It is of course difficult to know what precisely motivated hard and soft doxographers to take the positions that they did. That Tibetan scholars argued for or against a sharp distinction between Prāsaṅgikas and Svātantrikas out of deep intellectual convictions can hardly be denied, but were there other—social and political—motives behind such positions? Ascertaining motivation is always a difficult thing to do. To quote Jayānanda in a different context, "because of our prolonged grasping at mistaken causal patterns, we are trapped in error even about what we ourselves know…[how much more so] about the particularities of another's mind."[59] But whether or not it is possible to speak of *motivations* for specific doxographical moves, it is clear that the hard and soft positions on the Svātantrika-Prāsaṅgika distinction had clear socio-political *implications*. Counterfactually, had Tsong kha pa not convincingly argued for a substantive distinction between Prāsaṅgikas and Svātantrikas, it of course would have been impossible for him to have convincingly argued for the superiority of the former over the latter, or for his particular interpretation of the former. And if *that* had not taken place, one wonders, given the importance of establishing a unique Madhyamaka view to the construction of sectarian identity, whether the then nascent dGe lugs pa school would have fared as well as it did. That there is a relationship between the elaboration of a particular school's unique and credible interpretation of the Madhyamaka and its rise to prominence is something that did not go unnoticed by Tibetans themselves. Tāranātha (1575–1635), for example, complains in his *History of the Kālacakra* about "many who were obsessed with the provisional meaning *(neyārtha, drang don)* and were concerned with having the highest view, and gaining reputation, power, and large entourages."[60]

Similarly, one cannot help but see in the soft doxographical position of Rong ston pa and Go rams pa not only a disagreement with Tsong kha pa over how substantial the Svātantrika-Prāsaṅgika distinction really is, but, given Tsong kha pa's position, a challenge to the very foundations of his interpretation of the Madhyamaka, and therefore to the viability of the dGe lugs pa tradition as a whole. For if Rong and Go were right—if the Svātantrika-Prāsaṅgika distinction was less sharp, and the Madhyamaka as a whole more unified, than Tsong kha envisioned—then Tsong kha pa was founding his entire Madhyamaka theory on shaky, and perhaps nonexistent, ground. Rong and Go's views on the Svātantrika-Prāsaṅgika distinction therefore had potentially devastating consequences for the dGe lugs pas, which is undoubtedly why they drew the attention of later dGe lugs pa polemicists like Se ra rje btsun chos kyi rgyal mtshan (1469–1546).[61]

Of course, it is one thing to say that the debate over this particular doxographical distinction had potential social and political consequences for the parties involved, and quite another to claim that the debate can be reduced to socio-political factors. The very passion, commitment to detail, and tremendous integrity of the debate itself would seem to suggest that it was carried out not so much for political motives as for one that, in our postmodern age, is becoming increasingly difficult for us to recognize: the search for what is true.

Notes

1 See Ruegg (1981): 58.

2 An almost identical distinction is known in Tibet at about the same time: e.g., to Rong zom chos kyi bzang po (11th c.), who accepts it, and to rNgog blo ldan shes rab (1059–1109), who, according to Tsong kha pa and mKhas grub rje, rejects it; see Ruegg (1981): 59n, and Cabezón (1992): 89, 439, n. 270. The Tibetan version of this distinction is as follows: *sGyu ma lta bu* ("Illusory-like"; or *sGyu ma rigs grub,* "Those Who Use Illusory-like Reasoning") and *Rab tu mi gnas pa* ("Non-abiding"). Sa skya Paṇḍita (1182–1251) accepts this as a division of the ultimate *(don dam),* and places Svātantrikas and Prāsaṅgikas under the category of the *Rab tu mi gnas pa'i dbu ma pa,* although Ba' ra ba (1310–1391) considers the *dBu ma sgyu ma lta bu* and *Rab tu mi gnas pa* to be identical to the Svātantrikas and Prāsaṅgikas, respectively; see Mimaki (1982): 32–34, esp. n. 67.

3 Given that there are errors in this textual database, any broad conclusions like the present one must of course be taken as provisional.

4 See Ruegg (1981): 113–114 for more on this important figure, and concerning the text.

5 See Jayānanda, MAvṬ (ACIP ed.) 281a: *de la kha cig ces bya ba ni dbu ma rang rgyud pa'o /* and 282a: *yang rang rgyud pa la skyon gzhan bstan par bya ba'i phyir/ gzhan yang zhes bya ba la sogs pa gsungs te, 'dis zhes bya ba ni rang rgyud pas so /.*

6 This is not to say that Jayānanda does not prefer—as does Buddhapālita, whom he defends—the use of *prasaṅgas*. In the same text, ibid. 120a, he defines a *prasaṅga* as "that which, using what others accept, demonstrates for those others something that they do not [otherwise] believe," and then (120b) states: "It is correct to refute the other side by means of what they accept. Otherwise, if, as is the case with the partisans of *svatantra* syllogisms, the pervasion in regard to the predicate and reason is established by means of a valid cognition *(tshad ma),* then it becomes a *svatantra* proof.... Therefore, please understand that the pervasion is established simply by means of what the world accepts, and not by valid cognitions; and so how is it incorrect for *prasaṅga* syllogisms to refute the other side?" Moreover, it is "because Mādhyamikas do not use *svatantra* inferences that they do not have *svatantra* theses [of the sort that claim] 'neither outer nor inner phenomena arise from themselves'" (121b). These passages tell us several things about the position of Jayānanda: (1) what he finds problematic is not the formal structures of syllogistic reasoning, like the existence of a pervasion, but the fact that those structures are claimed by some (i.e., by Svātantrikas) to be established by valid cognitions; (2) he takes quite literally the claim that Mādhyamikas have no independent theses of their own, even as regards something as trivial as the fact that things do not arise from themselves, and this he sees as a corollary of the fact that they repudiate independent forms of syllogistic reasoning; so 3) the fact that Mādhyamikas have no theses of their own is, in the end, due to the fact that they use, e.g., *prasaṅgas*, that is, a) forms of reasoning that do not require them to posit any epistemic (i.e., *pramāṇic*) foundation over and above those established by worldly conventions, and b) forms of reasoning that "result only in the refutation of the other's thesis, carrying with it no consequences related to that which is the opposite of the absurdity *(thal bar 'gyur ba las bzlog pa'i don)*" (f. 123a). On a passage from Pa tshab (b. 1055), who collaborated with Jayānanda on various translation projects, a passage that seems to uphold views similar to those of Jayānanda, see Cabezón (1997): 101–102.

7 See Ruegg (1981): 59, and Mimaki (1982).

8 Mimaki (1982).

9 See Rong ston, *Nges don rnam nges,* 105.

10 *sTong thun chen mo,* 112–114, and Cabezón (1992): 112–114.

11 See Lopez (1987); Tillemans (1992); and Cabezón (1994): ch. 7.

12 These are the types of questions dealt with, for example, in Mimaki's ([1982]: 27–54) valuable study of the way in which, principally in Tibet, various, mostly

siddhānta, texts subdivided the Madhyamaka, not only into Svātantrika and Prāsaṅgika, but in other ways as well.

13 On rNgog, see Roerich (1976): 328–341, and on Pa tshab, Roerich (1976): 341–344. Although we do not have any of the works of Pa tshab available to us, we do know that he was aware of, and utilized, the Svātantrika-Prāsaṅgika distinction in his writings, and that he distinguished the two schools on the basis of whether or not they accept "valid cognitions [whose efficacy derives from] the force [of their relation] to real things" *(dngos po stobs zhugs kyi tshad ma):* Svātantrikas accepting such valid cognitions, and Prāsaṅgikas rejecting them. See Mimaki (1982): 45, n. 110.

14 Gro lung pa does mention (*bsTan rim chen mo*-2: 390a) the position of certain "previous scholars" *(sngon gyi slob dpon)* who advocate the sole use of *prasaṅgas* and repudiate *svatantras*, but his own views in this regard remain unclear to me. Over and above the texts of Nāgārjuna and Āryadeva, the Madhyamaka texts that he mentions, like the MHK and the PrP, both texts of Bhāvaviveka, would seem to put him squarely into the Svātantrika camp. However, Gro lung pa also mentions Buddhapālita in his introduction to the Madhyamaka section. What is most significant, perhaps, is the fact that nowhere in the *bsTan rim chen mo* does Gro lung pa mention Candrakīrti. Be that as it may, Gro lung pa never uses terms like "Svātantrika" and "Prāsaṅgika" in the *bsTan rim chen mo* to refer to his own or others' views.

15 See Roerich (1976): 343.

16 See especially *dBu ma rtsa ba shes rab kyi 'grel pa 'thad pa'i rgyan,* 41–45.

17 See Mimaki (1982): 31–35.

18 For example, Bu ston (1290–1364) uses the term Prāsaṅgika but not Svātantrika, although the two other subdivisions that he places in apposition to Prāsaṅgika (Sautrāntika- and Yogācāra-Madhyamaka), and the figures that he lists in those latter two subdivisions, correspond perfectly to what other, both contemporary and later, scholars consider Svātantrikas. Likewise, Bo dong (1376–1451) does not seem to explicitly use either Svātantrika or Prāsaṅgika, but once again, his two main subdivisions of the Madhyamaka ("Those who use logic" and "Those who use worldly conventions"), in terms of the historical personages he lists in each category, correspond to what others would call Svātantrikas and Prāsaṅgikas. See Mimaki (1982): 33–35. Although it is possible to "read" the Svātantrika-Prāsaṅgika distinction into schemes of these sorts, and although other Tibetans will themselves do so, the fact that some authors refuse to explicitly use terms like "Svātantrika" cannot simply be dismissed as unimportant, since it is sometimes indicative of quite important doctrinal positions.

19 Hence, Red mda' ba states (*De kho na nyid gsal sgron* 28) that Candrakīrti, "having seen that *the correct interpretation* of the Ārya [Nāgārjuna] is found in the system of Buddhapālita...undertook a defense of Buddhapālita's text." Red mda' ba states that he will not treat the issue of the difference between Svātantrikas and Prāsaṅgikas in any detailed way in that text because (ibid.: 28) "I have written about it elsewhere." It is difficult to know precisely, therefore,

how Red mda' ba elaborated this distinction, although we have clues from other portions of the *De kho na nyid gsal sgron* (104–105). That Red mda' ba takes a position that is more akin to that of the earlier tradition of Jayānanda and rMa bya pa, and different from that taken by Tsong kha pa and Rong ston pa is discussed in Cabezón (1997): 100. That Tsong kha pa was Red mda' ba's student, and that they both advocated Candrakīrti's Prāsaṅgika as the highest Madhyamaka view, should therefore not be taken as implying that the two represented identical interpretations of Candrakīrti.

20 This is Jayānanda's definition of a *prasaṅga* (MAvṬ [ACIP ed.] 120a): *dir thal 'gyur gyi mtshan nyid ni gzhan gyis khas bslang pa'i sgo nas gzhan la mi 'dod pa ston pa gang yin pa ste /.* See n. 6 above.

21 On the Prāsaṅgika doctrine of valid cognitions, see Yoshimizu (1996).

22 See MAvṬ (ACIP ed.) 120a-123a.

23 See *De kho na nyid gsal sgron,* 104–105, 184–190. A similar position is cited as belonging to an unidentified opponent *(kha cig)* by rMa bya pa, and rejected (*dBu ma rtsa ba shes rab kyi 'grel pa 'thad pa'i rgyan,* 41–42). rMa bya pa characterizes the Svātantrika position as "claiming that [the two truths] are ascertained by a valid cognition that is [derived from] the force of [their relation] to real things *(dngos po stobs zhugs)* as understood by both parties, that is, by a valid cognition that is nonerroneous in regard to the way it apprehends [things] *('dzin stangs mi 'khrul pa).*" (Ibid.: 41). rMa bya pa believes that even if Mādhyamikas have no theses or valid cognitions that prove them "in the context of reasoning that analyzes and examines the ultimate," (although later he seems to equivocate on this point, see ibid.: 43) that they do have theses, and accept valid cognitions, in regard to the conventional world. For example, Madhyamakas accept the four classical Madhyamaka forms of valid cognitions (direct perception, inference, scripture, and analogy) "as understood by their opponents or by the world, although even conventionally they find unacceptable valid cognitions that are [derived from] the power of [their relationship] to real objects." (Ibid.: 42). So for rMa bya pa, Mādhyamikas do use inferences in regard to which the trimodal criteria are established, but "not in an independent *(rang rgyud du)* fashion, that is, in such a way that one posits one's own position *(rang phyogs)* qua probandum as true, that is, as [proven], by a reason that is established for both [parties] by virtue of being [derived from] the power [of their relationship] to real things.... Even though conventionally Mādhyamikas do offer both positive and negative [arguments] about what, in the context of their own minds *(rang gi blo ngor),* they have unilaterally ascertained *(mtha' gcig du nges pa),* these [arguments] are established only by the valid cognitions accepted by the opponent. They do not, even conventionally, unilaterally ascertain anything established by [valid cognitions] that [derive from] the force of [their relationship] to real objects, nor do they offer arguments for a position opposite [to that of the opponent]. That is how they avoid both *svatantra*s and "positive probative" *prasaṅga*s *(sgrub byed 'phen pa'i thal 'gyur).*" (Ibid.: 43–44). See also Yoshimizu (1996): 16–18, and esp. n. 70.

24 See Newland (1992): 90–91. Hence, the later dGe lugs pa doxographer, dKon mchog 'jigs med dbang po (1728–1791) will state: "Why are they called 'Svātantrikas'? Because they refute real things by relying upon a correct reason in regard to which the trimodal criteria are established *from their own side (rang ngos nas)*"; Mimaki (1977): 97, my translation and emphasis. For the dGe lugs pas, then, a *svatantra* is more than simply a valid syllogism; it is a syllogism that carries assumptions about the reality of its own formal structures.

25 See *sTong thun chen mo:* 443–449, and Cabezón (1992): 366–370. See also Yoshimizu (1992b).

26 These are of course the classical four schools: Vaibhāṣika, Sautrāntika, Yogācāra/Cittamātra, and Madhyamaka; see Mimaki (1977), (1982), and Sopa and Hopkins (1982).

27 *De kho na nyid gsal sgron,* 30–34.

28 See Cabezón (1997): 102, n. 22, where I mention Mi bskyod rdo rje. Se ra rje bstun pa (1469–1546) criticizes Shākya mchog ldan for holding similar soft-doxographical views; see the former's *lTa ba nga (sic) ngan pa'i mun sel,* 309ff.

29 This discussion of Rong ston pa's position is based on his two major Madhyamaka works available to me, his commentary on Nāgārjuna's MMK, the *dBu ma rtsa ba'i rnam bshad zab mo'i de kho na nyid snang ba* (or *De kho na nyid snang ba*), and his commentary on Candrakīrti's MAv, the *dBu ma la 'jug pa'i rnam bshad nges don rnam nges* (or *Nges don rnam nges*). For other of Rong ston pa's Madhyamaka works that may perhaps be extant, see Jackson (1988): xiv–xv, xviii–xix.

30 Cabezón (1997).

31 Consider the following exchange between a dGe lugs pa–like opponent and Rong ston pa in *De kho na nyid snang ba,* 25–26. "[Opponent:] Even though it is true that they [Svātantrikas] do not *explicitly (dngos su)* advocate inherent existence *(rang bzhin yod pa),* according to the Prāsaṅgikas, they become advocates of inherent existence [because of the other tenets they accept]. [Reply:] Well then, how would you answer the charge that according to the Svātantrikas, the Prāsaṅgikas are advocates of the fact that phenomena exist inherently? [Opponent:] That is not the case, since the Prāsaṅgikas reject the fact that even conventionally phenomena exist inherently. [Reply:] But even the Svātantrikas reject [this], so how can you distinguish between them [in this way]?" And in response to the dGe lugs pa charge that the Svātantrikas, by affixing the qualifier "ultimately" to their refutation of arising, implicitly accept that conventionally there is inherent arising, Rong ston pa states (ibid.: 27) that, despite differences in wording, there is no difference between what Bhāvaviveka and Candrakīrti are repudiating in their refutation of arising *(skye 'gag):* "They are making the same point, since there is no difference between [Bhāvaviveka's claim that] there is no arising ultimately *(don dam par skye ba med pa)* and [Buddhapālita's claim that] there is no arising when analyzed by reasoning *(rigs pas dpyad na skye ba med pa).*"

32 As he states in *De kho na nyid snang ba,* 34, "In positing conventional phenom-

ena, (even for the Prāsaṅgikas) there are *svatantra* theses and reasons. This is because there is [for them such a thing] as establishing, by means of valid cognition, the trimodal criteria in regard to the proof *(sgrub byed)* of an object they themselves seek to have inferred with respect to a subject that is established for both parties by means of valid cognition." This makes it clear that for Rong ston pa, a *svatantra* is no more and no less than a simple syllogism where the terms are established for both parties. Where using such a form of inferential reasoning becomes inappropriate is in the context not of the conventional world, where, by definition, agreement presumably exists about the terms, but in the context of proving emptiness, where such agreement does not exist between Mādhyamikas and their opponents. The reason why Prāsaṅgikas reject *svatantras*, then, has to do with the use of syllogistic reasoning in the context of proving emptiness, and not with anything intrinsic to syllogistic reasoning itself.

33 Ibid.: 31.

34 *Nges don rnam nges,* 74.

35 For examples of this form of reasoning, see ibid.: 77–78.

36 Ibid.: 83–84.

37 For Tsong kha pa, *svatantras* are more than mere syllogisms, since they conceal within them certain implicit ontological assumptions concerning the objects being manipulated in the syllogism. Hence, those who use *svatantras*, even if unaware of this, are crypto-realists in so far as they hold the different parts of the syllogism and their relationships to exist independently. However, this is not so for Rong ston pa, for whom a *svatantra* is simply a trimodal syllogism with no hidden realist assumptions, crypto- or otherwise.

38 *De kho na nyid snang ba,* 31– 32; *tshul gsum tshad mas grub pa'i rtags la rten dgos pa'i phyir / rang rgyud kyi rtags gdon mi za bar bya dgos so /.*

39 Ibid.: 32; *don dam la dpyod pa de'i tshe / rgol ba gnyis ka'i tshad mas grub pa'i chos can la rang gis mngon par 'dod pa'i chos dpag 'dod kyi yul du gzung nas rang rgyud kyi rtags kyis sgrub par byar med de /.*

40 Ibid.: 32; *de'i tshe dbu ma pa'i ngor chos can snang ba tsam yang med pa'i phyir/.* This position is critiqued in dGe lugs pa sources, but Go rams pa defends it in *lTa ba'i shan 'byed* (Varanasi ed.) 113–114.

41 *Nges don rnam nges,* 83.

42 Ibid.: 74–75. For a similar claim concerning the labeled nature of the *sādhya,* see Gro lung pa's (c. 1100) *bsTan rim chen mo*-2, f. 392a. There are in fact several points of similarity between the Madhyamaka works of Rong ston pa and the *bsTan rim chen mo* of Gro lung pa, including a commitment to the inexpressibility *(brjod du med pa)* of the ultimate. There are, however, some radical differences. Gro lung pa is a staunch supporter of the view that the ultimate is an absolute negation *(med dgag),* whereas Rong ston pa views the absolute/affirming negation *(med dgag/ma yin dgag)* debate as an argument between "those who are attached only to positions qua names" *(ming gi phyogs re tsam la mngon par zhen par zad do),* which is to say that the debate is for him nothing but a semantic squabble; see *Nges don rnam nges,* 106. In addition, Gro

lung pa (*bsTan rim chen mo*-2, f. 352B) maintains that "it is not the case that the subject, etc., do not appear to the valid cognition that refutes real things because [that valid cognition] does not comprise a refutation of the basis [i.e., the subject] as something that is nonexistent." This too puts him at odds with Rong ston pa, who believes that for Mādhyamikas, the subject of the syllogism that proves emptiness cannot appear.

43 That it is really the insistence on, or repudiation of, the epistemic grounding of syllogisms in valid cognition that is at issue as regards the difference between Svātantrikas and Prāsaṅgikas is a view that Rong ston pa shares with Jayānanda; see MAvṬ-1 (ACIP ed.) 120a-120b. The former may well have relied on the latter in his composition of *Nges don rnam nges.*

44 *Nges don rnam nges,* 105.

45 See Ruegg (1963), Broido (1989), Kapstein (1992), and Stearns (1999) for more on this important figure and his views.

46 See Stearns (1999): 146–149.

47 *sTong thun chen mo,* 140; Cabezón (1992): 141.

48 *lTa ba'i shan 'byed* (Varanasi ed.) 114: *des na rang rgyud pas mtha' bzhi'i skye ba dgag pa'i skabs su / rang rgyud khas blangs pa yin pas / de'i tshe rang gi mtshan nyid kyis grub pa'i chos bsgrub pa la rang rgyud dgos pa yin ces pa ni log rtogs zhugs pa'i gzhi tsam yang mi 'dug /.*

49 Ibid. 109: *tha snyad kyi rnam bzhag la / thal rang gi khyad par 'byed pa ni min te / tha snyad kyi rnam bzhag la rang rgyud kyi gtan tshigs thal 'gyur ba rnams kyis kyang khas len pa'i phyir /.*

50 Ibid. 111: *des na thal rang gi khyad par ni gnas lugs la dpyod pa'i skabs su rang rgyud khas len dang mi len pa la 'jog pa ni gnad kyi don yin te /.*

51 Ibid. 107–108: *chos can rgol ba gnyis kyi mthun snang du grub pa'i steng du / snga rgol gyis khyad par gyi chos la dpag 'dod zhugs nas / tshad mas grub pa'i gtan tsigs kyis bsgrub pa bya ba ni rang rgyud kyi dam bca' /.*

52 Ibid. 100: *chos can gnyis dang / gtan tshigs dang khyab pa thams cad phyir rgol go nas khas bslangs pa yin gyi / snga rgol gyis khas bslangs med pa /.*

53 See ibid. 107–109.

54 Go rams pa, ibid. 101, citing a passage from Tsong kha pa's *Legs bshad snying po,* then goes on to claim that Tsong kha pa's position is contrary to the Prāsaṅgika view, and in fact coincides with the Svātantrika position, in so far as Tsong kha pa maintains that valid reasons, etc., even in the context of proving emptiness, must be held not only by the opponent, but by the Madhyamaka proponent as well. Whether or not Go rams pa is here misinterpreting Tsong kha pa, however, remains to be seen, for even if Tsong kha pa's interpretation of the *chos can mthun snang/ma snang* doctrine is different from Go rams pa's, the former nonetheless *does* have a method of making sense of this.

55 See, e.g., *lTa ba'i shan 'byed* (Varanasi ed.) 108.

56 The question of course then becomes whether in Rong and Go's view Svātantrikas, by virtue of not only accepting but indeed insisting upon the use of *svatantras* in the analysis of reality, commit themselves to the existence of the

various parts of the syllogism within the reasoning consciousness that analyzes reality. If so, this would seem to imply that the various parts of the syllogism, together with their relations (the trimodal criteria) should be real, since that is, according to Rong and Go, the implication of existing within the cognitive purview *(rig ngor)* of a form of analysis that is searching for reality. To claim, however, that Svātantrikas believe the parts and relations of such syllogisms to be real would seem to be tantamount to the dGe lugs claim that Svātantrikas *are crypto-realists.* So Rong and Go seem to be caught on the horns of a dilemma: either admit that there is a real difference between Prāsaṅgikas and Svātantrikas, or else come up with another way of distinguishing between them. Go rams pa is aware of this problem, as witnessed by this passage in *lTa ba'i shan 'byed* (Varanasi ed.) 112: *gnas lugs la dpyod pa'i skabs su rang rgyud pas rang rgyud kyi gtan tshigs khas len ces pa'i don yang / myu gu bdag las skye ba med par bsgrub pa'i rang rgyud kyi gtan tshig khas len ces pa'i don yin gyi / rang rgyud kyi gtan tshigs rang ldog nas gnas lugs dpyod pa'i rig ngor grub pa'i don la 'khrul par mi bya'o /* "What does it mean [to say that] in the context of analyzing reality Svātantrikas believe in autonomous syllogisms? It means that they believe in an autonomous syllogism that proves that sprouts do not arise from themselves. But do not get confused, it does *not* mean that [they believe that] autonomous syllogisms generally exist within the cognitive purview [of a consciousness] that analyzes reality." By this, it would appear, Go rams pa seems to be addressing the issue just raised: namely, whether his way of distinguishing between Prāsaṅgikas and Svātantrikas commits him to accepting that Svātantrikas believe that syllogisms exist in reality. He attempts to argue his way out this by making a distinction *(zhib cha):* Svātantrikas believe that autonomous syllogisms must be used in this particular case (that is, in the portion of the analysis of reality that seeks to prove that things do not arise from themselves), and not in general (that is, not in the analysis of reality in general, which presumably consists of the repudiation of the four extremes taken as a whole).

57 *lTa ba'i shan 'byed* (Varanasi ed.) 98: *'di la shes bya kun rig gi zhal snga nas / dbu ma pa yin na / bdag skye bkag nas gzhan skye sgrub pa'i rang rgyud kyi gtan tshigs bya mi rigs te/ bdag skye las phyogs gzhan gzhan skye khas bslangs pa med pa'i phyir / ces bsungs kyang/ 'dir bdag skye med par sgrub pa'i rang rgyud yod med rtsod pa'i skabs yin pas mi 'thad par sems so /.*

58 This, of course, is in stark contrast to the view of Tsong kha pa that we have already discussed, but it is also in stark contrast to the views of, e.g., sTag tshang lo tsa ba (b. 1405), who is a quite different breed of doxographer. Like Go rams pa and Rong ston pa, sTag tshang believes that *svatantras* are nothing more than ordinary syllogistic reasoning. Unlike the former, however, this leads him to throw out syllogistic reasoning altogether, and, indeed, to throw out the notion of valid cognition *(tshad ma),* upon which syllogistic reasoning is founded; see Cabezón (1992): 391–392 for a brief listing of some of sTag tshang's positions. For sTag tshang, then, being a Madhyamaka is incompatible with upholding any epistemo-logical system. So we have here, then, three

incommensurable views concerning *svatantras* and their acceptability (or lack thereof): (1) *svatantras* are just ordinary syllogistic arguments, and therefore generally acceptable (Rong ston pa and Go rams pa); (2) *svatantras* are just ordinary syllogistic arguments, and therefore unacceptable (sTag tshang); and (3) *svatantras* are not ordinary syllogistic arguments—while the latter are acceptable, the former are not (Tsong kha pa).

59 MAvṬ (ACIP ed.) 120b.

60 This is a paraphrase of Tāranātha's position in Stearns (1999: 60), who then goes on to identify the object of Tāranātha's displeasure as the dGe lugs pas. Tāranātha's text is unavailable to me.

61 See *lTa ba nga (sic) ngan pa'i mun sel.*

9. Would the True Prāsaṅgika Please Stand? The Case and View of 'Ju Mi pham

GEORGES B. J. DREYFUS

THE ARTICLES in this volume attest to the complex issues involved in the Svātantrika-Prāsaṅgika distinction in a variety historical contexts. In concluding this collection, it may be helpful to examine a more recent Tibetan view on this topic, that of the rNying ma scholar 'Ju Mi pham rgya mtsho (1846–1912), known also simply as Mi pham. The discussion of a recent perspective is appropriate at the end of this volume, since it can help provide a synopsis of the involved nature of the Svātantrika-Prāsaṅgika distinction, underlying the fact that while the distinction may not be entirely groundless, it is far from self-evident.

Mi pham offers a nuanced treatment of the Svātantrika-Prāsaṅgika distinction. In this article, I start by describing the Tibetan scholarly context in which Mi pham operates, a context dominated by Tsong kha pa's views and the criticisms that were raised against them. Although Mi pham is in many ways sympathetic to these criticisms, he is also influenced by the eclectic or ecumenical *(ris med)* movement in which his work takes place and hence he cannot simply be classified as a critic of Tsong kha pa. I describe Mi pham's complex relation to this context and examine his own approach to Madhyamaka, focusing on his interest in the school of Madhyamaka thought often described as Yogācāra-Svātantrika-Madhyamaka, a school which emphasizes the affinities between Madhyamaka and Yogācāra approaches. Finally, I examine Mi pham's understanding of the Svātantrika-Prāsaṅgika distinction itself and contrast it with other perspectives. I conclude with a few remarks on the involved nature of the Svātantrika-Prāsaṅgika distinction and some of the problems it raises.

The Tibetan Scholarly Context

The scholarly context out of which Mi pham's ideas concerning the Svātantrika-Prāsaṅgika distinction arise is dominated by the opposition between Tsong kha pa's views and those of his critics. This opposition is a result of the influence of Tsong kha pa's interpretations of Madhyamaka and the strength of the reactions these interpretations provoked. This is not to say that Tsong kha pa created the Svātantrika-Prāsaṅgika distinction. The distinction was already well known before him, though its exact importance and status at that time is hard to estimate, since relatively little is known about pre–Tsong kha pa Tibetan Madhyamaka.[1] The Svātantrika-Prāsaṅgika distinction and the superiority of the latter seem to have been first asserted by the translator Pa tshab nyi ma grags (1055–1145?) and to have been widely adopted by later authors. Klong chen rab 'byams pa (1308–1363), for instance, stressed the importance of the Prāsaṅgika view in the practice of the Great Perfection (*rdzogs chen,* lit., Great Completion), a topic to which we will return. Thus, by Tsong kha pa's time, the preeminence of the Prāsaṅgika view was already firmly inscribed in the rhetorical field of the Tibetan tradition. Tsong kha pa in turn greatly contributed to the domination of the Prāsaṅgika view, which he considered to entail a different understanding of emptiness due to which it was far superior to the Svātantrika. For Tsong kha pa, a correct understanding of the distinction between the two views is basic to a sound interpretation of Madhyamaka. It is the sign that one has properly understood the profundity of the Madhyamaka view. This is not the place to discuss Tsong kha pa's understanding of this topic.[2] Nevertheless, two key points must be kept in mind if one wants to evaluate Mi pham's perspective.

First, for Tsong kha pa, there is a substantive difference in the view of the ultimate between the two subschools. This difference is reflected in the difference in their respective understandings of the object that is to be negated *(dgag bya)* during the process of ascertaining emptiness. For Tsong kha pa, the Svātantrika view still holds to a certain idea of objectivity and is thus unable to eliminate fully the object of negation as understood by the Prāsaṅgika.[3] In particular, the Svātantrika holds that phenomena exist objectively (*rang gi mtshan nyid kyis grub pa,* lit., are established by their own characteristics) on the conventional level and that this objective existence should not be negated; otherwise, if one *were* to negate this conventional objective existence, the Svātantrika argues, the conventional validity of phenomena would be jeopardized. By contrast, on Tsong kha pa's interpretation, the Prāsaṅgika view *does* negate this objective existence while nevertheless still preserving the conventional validity of phenomena. Thus, according to Tsong kha pa, the Svātantrika negation is partial and coarse: it leaves out the more subtle object of negation, objective existence, which only the Prāsaṅgika approach is able to negate. The startling but irresistible conclusion is that the Prāsaṅgika is the only fully correct Madhyamaka view. The Svātantrika view of emptiness is partial and thus not sufficient by itself to lead even to liberation.

Second, and probably even more significant for the understanding of the Indian sources, there are other related important philosophical differences between the Prāsaṅgika and the other schools, differences captured by what Tsong kha pa describes as the "eight difficult points" *(dka' gnas brgyad)* of the Prāsaṅgika philosophy, explained briefly below. Together these eight points set apart Candrakīrti's view from other Madhyamaka interpretations, particularly those of Bhāvaviveka and his followers, and authorize the description of Candrakīrti's view as that of a separate school, the Prāsaṅgika.

Tsong kha pa's dominant place in the intellectual history of post-fifteenth century Tibet and his aggressive promotion of Prāsaṅgika as the supreme Madhyamaka view were key elements in reinforcing the preeminence of Prāsaṅgika in Tibetan Buddhism. His promotion of Prāsaṅgika greatly contributed to the configuration of the rhetorical field in which the supremacy of the Prāsaṅgika became firmly inscribed. Henceforth, instead of being just Candrakīrti's interpretation of Nāgārjuna, the Prāsaṅgika came increasingly to be seen as the pinnacle of Buddhist philosophy, the only fully accurate view in the nontantric aspects of the tradition. Any other view, even if it is Madhyamaka, came to be seen as necessarily inferior.

At the same time, the reception of Tsong kha pa's interpretation of Madhyamaka was far from unanimous. Some well-established scholars such as rGyal tshab dar ma rin chen (1364–1432) and mKhas grub dge legs dpal bzang po (1385–1438) were attracted by the intellectual power and brilliance of his explanations. Not all scholars, however, were equally taken by his interpretations, and gradually opposition started to be expressed, particularly among the Sa skya tradition, the school to which Tsong kha pa and his early disciples belonged. Some of the first scholars to voice their opposition were Rong ston shākya rgyal mtshan (1367–1449) and the translator sTag tshang (1405–?), both of whom assailed Tsong kha pa's interpretations as being innovations without sufficient grounding in the tradition. Their critiques were taken over and amplified by later philosophers such as

Go rams pa bsod nams seng ge (1429–1489), gSer mdog paṇ chen shākya mchog ldan (1428–1509), and the Eighth Kar ma pa Mi bskyod rdo rje (1504–1557). Together, these figures provided a powerful and well-articulated critique of Tsong kha pa's interpretations around which his opponents rallied. This is not to say that these thinkers were united on every issue but that they formulated a series of clear and similar positions that stood in sharp contrast with Tsong kha pa's views. In this way, the field of Tibetan Madhyamaka became polarized between Tsong kha pa's followers, the school that came to be known as the dGe lugs, and their opponents.

This polarization, which reflected the political situation of the country, has tended to play an important role in the later developments of Tibetan schools.[4] This is not to say, however, that all scholars have automatically aligned their views with those of the one of the two camps. Throughout the history of the tradition there have been independent thinkers such as Nga ri paṇ chen padma dbang rgyal (1487–1542), the Fifth Dalai Lama (1617–1682), gTer bdag gling pa (1646–1714), and others who blurred the lines between traditions. This antisectarian stance became particularly significant during the nineteenth century in eastern Tibet, when an eclectic or nonsectarian *(ris med)* movement developed around the charismatic personalities of 'Jam mgon kong sprul (1813–1899), 'Jam dbyangs mkhyen brtse'i dbang po (1820–1892), and Dza dpal sprul (1808–1887). Disgusted by the rivalries that had previously torn apart religious traditions and their political allies, these teachers promoted an inclusive approach in which all traditions were accorded some validity.

This ecumenical movement had a strong influence on the non–dGe lugs schools. It led to the revival of the scholarly traditions of these schools and to the development of new institutions of higher learning, the commentarial schools *(bshad grwa)*. It is in this context that Mi pham's thought must be understood. The nonsectarian movement has been in many ways a means for non–dGe lugs pa schools to counter the dGe lugs pa hegemony. As such, the movement has been at times critical of dGe lugs pa ideas and practices. This critical stance is taken, however, less as expressing a deep sense of opposition than as allowing the formulation of a distinct non–dGe lugs viewpoint that can compete with the dominant dGe lugs tradition.

Mi pham is an important participant in this nonsectarian movement, and his views are typical of it. He is at times critical of Tsong kha pa and in many ways he shares the view of the thinkers I describe as "Tsong kha pa's critics." But he is also careful not to oppose entirely Tsong kha pa, who is venerated by so many in Tibet. Mi pham is keen to show that he is able incorporate some of Tsong kha pa's ideas in a broad-minded synthesis that can include the views of important Tibetan philosophers. In this eclectic synthesis, Tsong kha pa's views are reconciled with the ideas of other Tibetan scholars, including some of the proponents of extrinsic emptiness *(gzhan stong)* despite the fact that these views are usually thought to be radically at odds.

Nevertheless, despite this openness, Mi pham is in limited agreement with Tsong kha pa, and on many key issues he sides with the latter's critics. In fact, his views often appear to be based on the positions of Go rams pa, one of Tsong kha pa's most virulent critics.[5] Accordingly, Mi pham rejects the two key aspects of Tsong kha pa's critique of Svātantrika mentioned above: the assertion of a difference in the view of emptiness between Svātantrika and Prāsaṅgika, and the eight difficult points that single out the Prāsaṅgika view. Let me first explain Mi pham's position with regard to these two key points before going on to explore the particularities of Mi pham's own view.

The Rejection of Tsong kha pa's Object of Negation

The first and most important issue on which Tsong kha pa's critics agree is the rejection of his assertion that there is a substantive difference between the Svātantrika and the Prāsaṅgika understanding of emptiness. The critics argue that in as much as the Svātantrika-Prāsaṅgika distinction is laid out in Indian texts, it is not couched in terms of a difference in the view of emptiness. Candrakīrti, for instance, does not accuse his opponent Bhāvaviveka of having a different view of emptiness or of not understanding emptiness but, rather, of not understanding the methods appropriate to its realization. Moreover, these critics argue, it is highly counterintuitive to imagine that such venerable figures as Bhāvaviveka and Śāntarakṣita, who have been counted in India and in Tibet among the great masters of the Madhyamaka tradition, had an inferior understanding of emptiness to that of Candrakīrti, who stood almost alone as a Prāsaṅgika. Is it feasible to posit that there is a correct view of emptiness, that of the Prāsaṅgika, that had not been comprehended by almost the totality of the important Indian Madhyamaka thinkers?

This rejection of Tsong kha pa's first key point, i.e., the assertion of a substantive difference in the view of the ultimate, is shared by all of the major critics of Tsong kha pa, though it is expressed with varying degrees of vigor. Some of these critics are emphatic and even strident in their rejection of this point. Mi bskyod rdo rje, perhaps the most vocal, says,

> Here in Tibet, however, prattlers led astray by errors pertaining to faulty direct perception and inference talk, with regard even to Mādhyamikas such as Bhāvaviveka and Candrakīrti, about a higher and lower theory *(lta ba)* and comprehension *(rtogs pa)* and also about a right and wrong philosophical doctrine *(grub mtha'= siddhānta)*. But if this were correct, those described as inferior would in fact not be Mādhyamikas at all; for so long as the meaning of Madhyamaka remains unrealized in such a way, there would be nothing but the mere names "Madhyamaka" and "Mādhyamika," as is the case with [the names] *Alīkākāra-Madhyamaka* and *Alīkākāra-Mādhyamika.*[6]

For Mi bskyod rdo rje, the idea that there is a difference in the view between Svātantrika and Prāsaṅgika is simply preposterous, for that would imply that the inferior view, the Svātantrika, would not really be Madhyamaka.

Mi pham is more moderate in his tone, but he agrees in substance with this view. He states that there is no difference in the richness *(skyed pa)* of the views of these two philosophies. Both views come to the same point, emptiness, which is understood as the freedom from any assertion *(khas len thams cad dang bral ba)* and the freedom from any elaboration pertaining to the four extremes (*mtha' bzhi spros bral,* more on this shortly).[7] If one of the two views were different, it would have to eliminate a supplementary elaboration *(spros pa, prapañca)* that is not included in the four extremes, and as Mi pham puts it politely but firmly, "this is hard to imagine."[8] Thus, for Mi pham, it makes no sense to posit any substantive difference between the two views, for both constitute the complete elimination of any possible elaboration. What more could emptiness mean?

This first difference between Tsong kha pa and his critics is probably the most significant in terms of the objectives of these authors, who aim at providing proper guidance for the realization of emptiness but disagree on how to do so. For Tsong kha pa, emptiness is a negation *(dgag pa, pratiṣedha)* and must be understood in terms of the negation of a putative object of negation *(dgag bya)*. Tsong kha pa describes such a putative object within the Prāsaṅgika context as inherent existence *(rang bzhin gyis grub pa)*, existence from the side of the object *(rang ngos nas grub pa)*, or objective existence *(rang gi mtshan nyid kyis grub pa)*. The understanding of emptiness presupposes the identification of such an object whose nonexistence is then demonstrated by the various Madhyamaka reasonings. This, for Tsong kha pa, is how to realize emptiness.

For Mi pham and Tsong kha pa's critics, this approach to emptiness is questionable. For them, emptiness is not, at least in its ultimate expression, a negation. If emptiness were a negation, it would consist of the rejection of a proposition and hence would be conceptual. How could a conceptual fabrication stand as the ultimate nature of things? Moreover, a negation exists only in opposition to an affirmation. Hence, if emptiness were a negation, it would have to exist on the same level as other conventional phenomena and would be just another elaboration, a phenomenon captured by dichotomies such as "is" and "is not." Finally, the idea of identifying a special object of negation does not make much sense, for what is this object? Is it the first extreme *(mtha', koṭi)* mentioned in Madhyamaka reasonings, the positive extreme, usually spelled out as *existence (yod pa, bhāva)*? If this were the case, the understanding of emptiness that would result from its negation would be partial, leaving out the negation of the other extremes, particularly of the second, the negative extreme, usually spelled out as nonexistence *(med pa, abhāva)*. If the object of negation were not the first extreme (existence), what would it be?

For these thinkers, emptiness is not the negation of a putative object of negation, for emptiness is beyond any description and hence transcends both affirmation and negation. This is not to deny, however, the special role of negation in the process of understanding emptiness. To understand emptiness one must negate all the extremes.[9] First, one must refute existence, the positive extreme variously described as inherent existence *(rang bzhin gyis grub pa)*, true existence *(bden par grub ba)*, or more simply, existence *(yod pa)* or production *(skye ba)*, etc. Such a refutation, however, is not emptiness in its ultimate expression but only a proximate ultimate *(mthun pa'i don dam)* or a figurative ultimate *(rnam grang pa'i don dam)*. This figurative ultimate is important, for its realization can lead to the insight into the actual ultimate. Hence, it is often presented as emptiness in Madhyamaka texts. But such descriptions cannot be taken literally, for they are still prisoners of the essentialist temptation to pin down reality through a determinate description. To conceive of ultimate truth as being merely the fact that phenomena do not exist intrinsically is to assume a negative essence and to remain a captive of binary oppositions. In order to understand reality to its fullest extent, we need to go beyond this negative description and negate the second, or negative, extreme as well. For it is only when one leaves behind *all* the extremes that one can be said to understand emptiness in its ultimate expression.

In this perspective, which sees emptiness in terms of freedom from any elaboration and stresses the ineffability of ultimate truth, Tsong kha pa's idea of emptiness as the negation of a putative object of negation is problematic. It seems to be only a partial understanding of emptiness. And if the idea of emptiness as the negation of an object of negation is rejected, Tsong kha pa's first key point that there is a difference in the object of negation between Svātantrika and Prāsaṅgika falls by the wayside. Once one understands emptiness as the transcendence of all four extremes, it makes no sense to argue that there is a substantive difference between Svātantrika and Prāsaṅgika on the basis of a difference in their conceptions of the object of negation. Either the Svātantrika rejects the four extremes and offers a true Madhyamaka insight, or it does not and is unfit to be counted as Madhyamaka.

The Rejection of Tsong kha pa's Eight Difficult Points

The second point of opposition between Tsong kha pa and his critics concerns the former's assertion that there are other related important philosophical differences between Svātantrika and Prāsaṅgika. Tsong kha pa summarizes these differences under the heading of "the eight difficult points" *(dka' gnas brgyad)* that characterize the Prāsaṅgika philosophy and separate it from its rivals. These eight points are: the refutation even on the conventional level of (1) a store-consciousness *(ālayavijñāna, kun gzhi rnam shes)* distinct from the six consciousnesses and (2) self-cognition *(rang rig, svasaṃvitti)*; (3) the rejection of autonomous probative arguments[10] *(rang rgyud kyi sbyor ba, svatantraprayoga)* to generate the view of emptiness; (4) the assertion of the existence of external objects on the same level as cognition; (5) the assertion that the disciples *(śrāvaka)* and the self-realizers *(pratyekabuddha)* comprehend the selflessness of phenomena; (6) the assertion that the grasping to the self of phenomena is a negative emotion *(nyon mongs, kleśa)*; (7) the assertion that disintegration *(zhig pa)* is an impermanent thing; and (8) the consequent uncommon presentation of the three times.[11] For Tsong kha pa, these are the significant philosophical differences that establish the Prāsaṅgika as a separate school.[12]

Not surprisingly, Tsong kha pa's critics reject his claim that there are significant doctrinal differences between the two subschools and downplay the Svātantrika-Prāsaṅgika distinction, arguing that Tsong kha pa has exaggerated its importance. For these thinkers, the Svātantrika-Prāsaṅgika distinction does not involve significant philosophical issues but mostly concerns conflicting interpretations of some passages in Nāgārjuna as well as different approaches to the understanding of emptiness. In particular, these critics are keen to reject Tsong kha pa's eight difficult points and have devoted large sections in their Madhyamaka works to this refutation. Shākya mchog ldan, for instance, argues that there is nothing significant about these eight points. Whether or not Candrakīrti rejected the existence of a self-cognition and a store-consciousness on the conventional level (like Go rams pa, Mi pham, and most non–dGe lugs thinkers, Shākya mchog ldan believes that he did not) is meaningless as far as the understanding of emptiness is concerned. Thus, to call these uncommon characteristics of the Prāsaṅgika is sheer exaggeration *(lhur blang ba).*[13]

Not all of Tsong kha pa's critics are so extreme in denying any philosophical significance to the differences between Svātantrika and Prāsaṅgika. Go rams pa, for instance, recognizes some differences between these two subschools, but he carefully downplays the importance of these differences and presents them as relatively minor. He provides his own list of sixteen differences between these two approaches, a list that aims to replace Tsong kha pa's eight. Go rams pa takes special care not to concede any validity to Tsong kha pa's eight difficult points. He argues against some of them at great length in several of his works, particularly against the first three and most important of Tsong kha pa's eight points.[14] This is obviously not the place to discuss in detail these points, which would require significant analysis. A brief discussion of a few of these points may be in order, however, since they are central to the Svātantrika-Prāsaṅgika distinction and throw some light on Indian sources.

The most directly relevant to a discussion of the Svātantrika-Prāsaṅgika distinction is the third point concerning Candrakīrti's well-known rejection of Bhāvaviveka's use of autonomous arguments in establishing emptiness. Historically, this is the starting point of the differences that came to be described by later Tibetan scholars as the Svātantrika-Prāsaṅgika distinction. Bhāvaviveka criticized Buddhapālita's previous commentary on Nāgārjuna's *Prajñāmūla* or *Mūlamadhyamakakārikā* (MMK) for failing to formulate the autonomous formal arguments encapsulating Nāgārjuna's arguments. Candrakīrti replied that Bhāvaviveka was at fault, not Buddhapālita. It is improper, argued Candrakīrti, for Mādhyamikas to use autonomous arguments when arguing about the ultimate with non-Mādhyamikas.[15]

Most Tibetan scholars consider the issue of autonomous argument as central to the Svātantrika-Prāsaṅgika distinction. For Tsong kha pa the crucial and difficult point is the meaning of *autonomous.* Tsong kha pa points to Bhāvaviveka's statement that *autonomous* means *independent,* and deduces from this that what Bhāvaviveka means is *objectively established (rang gi mtshan nyid kyis grub pa).*[16] For Tsong kha pa, an argument is autonomous if, and only if, it takes as the referents of its terms objectively established phenomena. Thus, the use of such an argument has ontological implications, for since the Svātantrika view accepts arguments that rest on the existence of objectively established phenomena, it must accept the existence of these phenomena conventionally. By contrast, the Prāsaṅgika view rejects autonomous arguments because it denies the existence of objectively established phenomena. Hence, Tsong kha pa concludes that the implications of the acceptance or refusal of autonomous arguments go well beyond the methodology necessary to approach emptiness and has ontological implications. Whereas the Svātantrika view accepts that phenomena exist objectively, the Prāsaṅgika view denies this and takes this objective existence as the object to be negated in the process of ascertaining emptiness.[17]

Tsong kha pa's critics reject this interpretation of the argument between Bhāvaviveka and Candrakīrti. They contend that autonomous and objective are not the same and that the dispute is not about Madhyamaka ontology, but just about the kind of arguments that Mādhyamikas can use when arguing about the ultimate. For them, an argument is autonomous if its terms are established as appearing similarly *(mthun snang du grub pa)* to both parties involved in the debate. Such an argument works independently of the particular perceptions of the parties and hence is called *autonomous.* By contrast, a statement of consequence *(prasaṅga, thal 'gyur)* or an other-intended argument *(*paraprasiddhaprayoga, gzhan grags kyi sbyor ba)* is different in that it deals with the opponent on his own terms and thus does not presuppose any commonality between the two parties.

According to this interpretation, what separates Svātantrika and Prāsaṅgika is just the question of whether autonomous arguments are allowable in the search for the ultimate. The Svātantrika contends that they are and that they should be used, whereas the Prāsaṅgika denies this, arguing that there cannot be any commonality between Mādhyamikas and their adversaries when debating the nature of the ultimate. For a Prāsaṅgika, there is no subject or example on which both parties can agree in a debate concerning the ultimate. The Mādhyamika sees any conventional phenomenon as unreal whereas his adversary sees it as real. There is no subject established as appearing similarly *(mthun snang du grub pa)* to both parties.

Hence, any autonomous argument provided in the context of the ultimate fails to be valid since its subject is not established for at least one of the two parties. Autonomous arguments have no place in this context. They can be used, however, in conventional investigations, and their use does not by itself have any ontological implication.[18] Hence, the Svātantrika-Prāsaṅgika distinction is not ontological but purely pragmatic, and hence much less dramatic than Tsong kha pa would have it.

Before leaving this question, which is addressed by several authors in this volume, let us notice that contrary to other authors such as Go rams pa and Shākya mchog ldan, who expend great efforts refuting Tsong kha pa on this point and offering their own views, Mi pham is not very explicit on this question. In accordance with his antisectarian stance, Mi pham is not prone to criticize Tsong kha pa and adopts a broad-minded standpoint. He also seems to think that the meaning and implications of autonomous arguments are secondary issues in the dispute between Svātantrika and Prāsaṅgika, the main issue being how to approach emptiness.[19]

Another issue is, for Mi pham, more important than that of autonomous arguments, namely, Candrakīrti's alleged rejection of self-cognition *(sva-saṃvitti, rang rig).* For Tsong kha pa, this is a philosophically significant point for at least two reasons. First, it plays an important role in establishing the nature of the ultimate. Self-cognition, the nonthematic awareness that we have of our own mental states, is the cornerstone of the Cittamātra *(sems tsam)* or Mind-Only system and supports that school's thesis that cognition is real whereas external objects are not. Hence, the refutation of the existence of self-cognition is a decisive step in the refutation of the Mind-Only system and the establishment of a strong difference between this school and Madhyamaka. Second, self-cognition is an important and problematic philosophical topic on its own right, concerning the nature of reflexivity. We all seem to feel that we know what we experience or think without having to reflect on this. The doctrine of self-cognition seeks to account for this feeling of immediacy that we have with respect to our own mental states by positing a nonobjectifying awareness of our mental states. For Tsong kha pa, the postulation of such an awareness is problematic, for it seems to imply the kind of self-presence of the mind to itself that would entail an essentialism incompatible with the radical Madhyamaka insight. It is this radical antifoundationalism that Tsong kha pa reads in Candrakīrti's refutation of self-cognition.

Tsong kha pa's critics are united in rejecting this point, arguing that Tsong kha pa has read too much into Candrakīrti's apparent denial of self-cognition. Its refutation, like that of the store-consciousness, must be understood from an ultimate standpoint, for both phenomena exist conventionally. Mi pham shares this view. Although he is more ecumenical and less vocal on other issues, he is particularly vigorous on the issue of self-cognition, to which he has devoted numerous pages in his Madhyamaka works. This is not the place for a detailed examination of this topic, which deserves and has received extensive analysis.[20] Nevertheless, a few points need to be made to highlight Mi pham's view on this topic, which is itself symptomatic of his approach in attempting to bridge the gap between Madhyamaka and Yogācāra.

Mi pham's Madhyamaka Approach

The relation between Madhyamaka and Yogācāra has been one of the most contentious and important issues in the Tibetan philosophical tradition for several centuries. This issue concerns not just the relation between these two philosophical traditions, or schools of tenets, but also the body of scriptures that each Tibetan school considers as foundational. Should one rely on the second turning of the wheel, and the Prajñāpāramitā literature, or should one rely on the third turning of the wheel, such as some of the *Tathāgatagarbha* sūtras and the Yogācāra literature?[21] This question was raised by Dol po pa shes rab rgyal mtshan (1292–1361), who argued that the true view, the so-called "Great Madhyamaka," is to be found in the third turning of the wheel. Tsong kha pa responded vigorously by stressing the primacy of the second turning of the wheel and emphasizing the distance and incompatibility between Madhyamaka and Yogācāra. For him, one of the most important Madhyamaka ideas is that of the conventional validity of the external world, which he holds to be a central theme of Candrakīrti's works, particularly of his *Madhyamakāvatāra* (MAv).[22]

It is in the context of this debate that Mi pham steps in to offer his view, which reflects his attempt to formulate a rNying ma perspective that concurs with the scholarly standards instituted by Tsong kha pa and his critics. In accord with his nonsectarian orientation, Mi pham also attempts to find a middle ground between Tsong kha pa and his critics, though here again he mostly tilts toward the latter group. Hence, in contrast to Tsong kha pa, Mi pham minimizes the distance between Madhyamaka and Yogācāra, and offers a Madhyamaka view in which the centrality of the mind and the fact that the external world exists as its mere display are stressed. In that, he is quite close to the Mind-Only tradition, as he recognizes in his commentary on Śāntarakṣita's *Madhyamakālaṃkara* (MA), the *dBu ma rgyan gyi 'grel ba.*[23] He does make, however, an important distinction between Madhyamaka and Mind-Only as he understands it, namely that, while emphasizing the centrality of the mind, as a Mādhyamika Mi pham also seeks to ward off its reification.

We may wonder about the reasons behind Mi pham's orientation. Why is he interested in a view in which Madhyamaka and Yogācāra are in close proximity rather than in opposition? I believe that the answer is to be found in Mi pham's commitment to the rNying ma tradition of the Great Perfection and his wish to expound a Madhyamaka view well suited to this tradition. In the Great Perfection, the ultimate is not just the emptiness described by the Madhyamaka treatises but also the clear and knowing quality of the mind. A typical expression of this view is found in the threefold description of the ground *(gzhi)* found in the texts of the Great Perfection. There, ground or reality in its most basic aspect is depicted as having a nature *(ngo bo)* that is pristine *(ka dag),* an inherent quality that is spontaneous *(lhun grub),* and an activity (*thugs rje,* lit., a compassion) that is uninterrupted *(dgag med).*[24] Particularly relevant here are the first two characteristics. The first, that of the ultimate's pristine nature, refers to the empty quality of the ground, which is variously glossed as *reality (chos nyid, dharmatā), the ultimate (don dam),* and so on. Proponents of the Great Perfection, especially Klong chen pa, explain this empty quality in accordance with the Madhyamaka view. The second quality refers to the clarity of awareness, which is described as *self-arisen wisdom (rang byung ye shes), self-cognition (rang rig), clear light ('od gsal),* and so on. Together these two qualities provide a view of the ultimate as being not just empty but also luminous, that is, as having the nature of pristine awareness.

This twofold description of reality is by no means unique to the rNying ma Great Perfection. It is found in other non–dGe lugs Buddhist traditions in Tibet such as the bKa' brgyud Mahāmudrā or the view of inseparability of *saṃsāra* and *nirvāṇa* of the Sa skya Lam 'bras tradition.[25] Such a view, which is more specifically connected to the esoteric aspect of those traditions, is extensively described in the Indian and Tibetan tantric literature. It is also present in certain texts of the exoteric tradition, particularly those associated with the third turning of the wheel that propound a view of reality in which some interpretation of the doctrine of emptiness is combined with the idea that the mind is luminous. In the Great Perfection, particularly as it has been interpreted by Klong chen pa, this empty aspect is identified as the emptiness taught in the Madhyamaka texts and is combined with the understanding of the luminosity of the mind.

Although the Great Perfection view is not the explicit topic of Mi pham's Madhyamaka works, it is present in the background, as is revealed in another of Mi pham's texts, the *Nges shes sgron me*. There the connection with the Great Perfection is made explicit, as we shall later see. But even in the Madhyamaka texts where the connection remains only implicit, Mi pham propounds a Madhyamaka interpretation that prepares the way to the Great Perfection. As mentioned above, the view of the Great Perfection presents a twofold view of the ultimate as both empty and luminous, a view that differs from the view set forth by Nāgārjuna in his five or six Madhyamaka texts. Among the Indian Madhyamaka interpretations, the closest to the Great Perfection view seems to be Śāntarakṣita's view, which came to be described by Tibetan doxographers as Yogācāra-Svātantrika-Madhyamaka. This view emphasizes the centrality of the mind, presenting phenomena as its display, but only on the conventional level. The mind itself is presented as empty, thereby avoiding its reification. In this way, reality is described by focusing on the mind and its emptiness. Such a description is well suited as a propaedeutic for the Great Perfection view of reality as both empty and luminous.

Mi pham cannot, however, completely adopt this Yogācāra-Svātantrika-Madhyamaka view, for at least two reasons. The first pertains to the general configuration of the rhetorical field of the post–Tsong kha pa Tibetan tradition in which such a view, being a subclassification of the Svātantrika, is seen as inferior. To adopt openly this view would be tantamount to an admission of the inferiority of one's standpoint. This was particularly true during Mi pham's time, when the dGe lugs hegemony was overwhelming. dGe lugs pa centers of higher learning set the scholarly standards, and dGe lugs pa texts, particularly those of Tsong kha pa, largely determine the contours of acceptable philosophical language. In such a context, holding a Svātantrika view, which is almost universally considered as inferior, would have been highly problematic, something as odd as a physicist holding onto the supremacy of Newtonian physics in this century.

The second reason pertains to the configuration of the rNying ma tradition as it came to be understood during the nonsectarian movement when, under the influence of 'Jigs med gling pa (1730–1798) and his followers, the role of Klong chen pa came to be seen as preponderant. Mi pham shares this perspective and takes Klong chen pa as providing authoritative guidance in the field of Madhyamaka philosophy, which is to be established in accordance with his interpretations. This is also the case for the Svātantrika-Prāsaṅgika distinction, which Klong chen pa addresses in his works.[26] There Klong chen pa expresses a clear preference for the Prāsaṅgika, which he presents as providing the most radical approach for understanding the ultimate. In particular, the Prāsaṅgika emphasis on reality as being utterly beyond any determination, its rejection of philosophical categories, and its denial of any objectively established phenomena are seen as useful in the context of the Great Perfection where there is a danger of reifying the mind. To ward off this danger, Klong chen pa emphasizes the empty side and chooses what he sees as the more radical Prāsaṅgika interpretation.[27]

Let us notice that this preference is far from obvious. One of the other great rNying ma thinkers, Rong zom paṇḍita (11th–12th c.), had expressed a different orientation. Although he did not make the distinction between Svātantrika and Prāsaṅgika, Rong zom had a clear preference for Śāntarakṣita's view, which he described as Yogācāra-Madhyamaka and contrasted favorably with Bhāvaviveka's Sautrāntika-Madhyamaka.[28] Thus, for Rong zom, it is the view that came to be classified later as Yogācāra-Svātantrika-Madhyamaka that is to be preferred in the context of the Great Perfection. This contrasts with Klong chen pa's preference for the Prāsaṅgika and his refusal to embrace Śāntarakṣita's Madhyamaka.[29]

The preference for Candrakīrti's Prāsaṅgika became important in the later rNying ma tradition. Rather than being just a personal choice made by Klong chen pa under the influence of his Sa skya pa background, it came to be seen as expressing the central standpoint of the tradition. This choice was all the more convenient in that it was congruent with the dominant dGe lugs pa view, which strongly emphasized the Prāsaṅgika primacy. Hence, as a follower of Klong chen pa living in a period of dGe lugs pa political and intellectual hegemony, Mi pham came to be quite naturally committed to the Prāsaṅgika interpretation. And yet he is also sympathetic to the Yogācāra-Madhyamaka view. How can he reconcile these two approaches?

To begin, Mi pham minimizes the differences between Śāntarakṣita and Candrakīrti, arguing that the latter's view is quite close to and compatible with the former's. Mi pham also argues for the importance of Śāntarakṣita's view by laying out five special features of his MA. Among those five contributions, the first three are particularly relevant. First is the adoption on the conventional level of Dharmakīrti's distinction between specifically characterized phenomena *(svalakṣaṇa, rang mtshan)* and generally characterized phenomena *(sāmānyalakṣaṇa, spyi mtshan)*.[30] Second is the assertion that self-cognition and store-consciousness exist on the conventional level. Third is the assertion that phenomena exist as the manifestation of the mind *(sems kyi rnam 'phrul)* on the conventional level. These three features all point in the same direction: specifically, they emphasize the role of the mind in Madhyamaka philosophy, and the compatibility between Madhyamaka and Yogācāra. Let me discuss these three features before moving on to a consideration of Mi pham's view of the Svātantrika-Prāsaṅgika distinction.

The first feature of Śāntarakṣita's MA, as delineated by Mi pham, establishes a general framework, borrowed from Dharmakīrti, to comprehend conventional phenomena in a way that favors a match between Madhyamaka and Yogācāra. This is done by first introducing the idea that certain phenomena, in this case conceptual fictions, exist only as mere appearances of the mind. The third feature of Śāntarakṣita's text highlighted by Mi pham then extends this mind-made status to *all* phenomena, which are then also described as manifestations of the mind. Mi pham recommends such a view on the conventional level, for it provides a sound comprehension of cyclic existence and liberation. He says,

> From the point of view of the ultimate nature that is free from all objects, signs, and elaborations, [statements such as] "the appearance is [just] mind" are not borne out, [for] such [nature] is the ultimate that is beyond designation. But if as long as one remains an ordinary person one [must] settle for a [system of] convention, then there is nothing superior to the designation of conventional appearances [as being merely mind]. [This is so] because the existence of the external world is refuted by reasonings and Mind-Only is established by reasonings. Moreover, when one investigates the phenomena posited by mere conceptuality, [one realizes that] they are not established in any way. And yet there is this irrefutable appearance which is incontrovertibly experienced from one's point of view and is thus established by the sheer power of facts as the appearance of the mind or the own-appearance.[31]

For Mi pham, phenomena are to be viewed as mere appearances of the mind. This is quite similar to the way they are described in the Mind-Only literature, the main difference being that for him they exist as such only on the conventional level. This is similar, though not identical, to the Great Perfection where phenomena are viewed as the displays of pristine awareness *(rig pa'i rtsal)*. There phenomena are presented not just as the manifestation of ordinary conventional mental states, but as relating to the pristine awareness that is the ultimate nature of these states.

The second feature of Śāntarakṣita's text highlighted by Mi pham, the existence of self-cognition, strengthens this framework by establishing the centrality of mind as the experiencer of objects that exist as its mere display. Here again, there seems to be an implicit connection with the Great Perfection. *Self-cognition* is an important term in this tradition, where it is used as an epithet for the ground. Such a self-cognition, which is also identified with pristine wisdom *(ye shes, jñāna),* is not identical to the self-cognition posited by Dharmakīrti and Śāntarakṣita as a way to explain mind's reflexivity. Nevertheless, there seems to be a connection. On the most obvious level, the notion of self-cognition strengthens the Yogācāra-Madhyamaka framework that Mi pham sees as favorable ground for the ideas of the Great Perfection. It also introduces the kind of experience of the mind that is central to the practice of the Great Perfection, as when Mi pham speaks of "this irrefutable appearance which is incontrovertibly experienced from one's point of view and is thus established by the sheer power of facts as the appearance of the mind or the own-appearance."[32] Moreover, the epistemological notion of self-cognition seems to prepare the way for the Great Perfection idea that the ground is self-aware and suggests a relation between ordinary reflexivity and transcendent gnosis.[33] Finally, the assertion of the existence of self-cognition is a way to minimize the differences between Śāntarakṣita's and Candrakīrti's views and argue for their compatibility. For if Candrakīrti's rejection of self-cognition, a notion that plays a central role for Mi pham, were to affect the conventional level, the dGe lugs pa case that the Prāsaṅgika is a separate school would receive some confirmation. By denying this, Mi pham builds a case for a more modest distinction between Svātantrika and Prāsaṅgika.

These three features represent some of the contributions made by Śāntarakṣita and his tradition as understood by Mi pham. They are important for Mi pham's interpretation of Madhyamaka, which presents a view rooted in the great Indian commentaries *(śāstra)* held in high regard in the Tibetan tradition but also well suited to the Great Perfection view. This approach is quite different from that of Tsong kha pa, who emphasizes the texts associated with the second turning of the wheel and is quite happy to limit his Madhyamaka interpretation to Nāgārjuna's and Candrakīrti's views as he understands them. Mi pham's view is more oriented toward the texts and ideas of the third turning of the wheel. In doxographical terms, this means an interest in the Yogācāra-Svātantrika tradition, though he is, or claims to be, a Prāsaṅgika. But is he? And what does it mean to be a Prāsaṅgika for Mi pham?

Mi pham on the Svātantrika-Prāsaṅgika Distinction

To answer this question we need to examine the fourth uncommon feature of Śāntarakṣita's text highlighted by Mi pham, the distinction between the figurative ultimate and the actual ultimate *(rnam grangs ma yin pa'i don dam).*[34] The figurative ultimate is usually explained as being emptiness as understood by conceptual thought. It differs from the actual ultimate, which is the object of direct perception. Mi pham explains it in this way:

> Accordingly, the figurative ultimate is one of the two polar opposites in the combined pair of conventional production and ultimate nonproduction. It is first the object of the language and thought contained in studying and thinking. [Such an ultimate] is figurative because it is the pole contrasted with conventional existence and is [thus] to be counted as belonging to the ultimate. Moreover, it is the element that is to be enumerated in opposition to conventional [truth] when one enumerates the two truths. It is ultimate because it is merely a door that is proximate to the final ultimate or because if one meditates on it one will be able to destroy the grasping to things which is fed by the power of the imprints left by timeless habituation. One should realize that from the perspective [of the figurative ultimate] there are theses such as "there is no production" and that such an investigation merely produces the certainty found in the [conceptual] practice of post-meditative state *(rjes thob).* From the point of view of the actual ultimate nature, *nonproduction,* which is opposed to production, is merely the conceptual reflection of the thought that eliminates the other [i.e., the opposite]. Therefore, [only] the extremely pure meaning of the primordial wisdom of the noble ones which has overcome all the objects of thought and language and is beyond all extremes such as production or nonproduction is the matchless nonfigurative ultimate. From its point of view, there is no thesis whatsoever. Because it is close to this [actual ultimate] and in accordance with it, it is counted as belonging to the ultimate. Hence it is [also] called *proximate ultimate.*[35]

The figurative ultimate is the ultimate as it is understood at the conceptual level. Hence, it is not the actual ultimate but the mere concept of the ultimate. In Buddhist epistemological terms, it is the mere negation (*apoha,* lit., elimination) of the non-ultimate rather than the actual ultimate. For example, when we analyze production we discover that it does not exist ultimately. This nonproduction *(skye med),* however, is not the actual ultimate but just the polar opposite of conventional production. It is through the negation of the latter from an ultimate standpoint that one understands the former. Hence, an understanding of the figurative ultimate is still the prisoner of binary oppositions and has yet to reach the actual ultimate.

In view of this discussion, which is standard in much of non–dGe lugs scholarship, a question arises: if the figurative ultimate is the ultimate as understood by thought, does this mean that the actual ultimate can only be realized by primordial wisdom? Non–dGe lugs pa thinkers seem to be divided on this issue. Go rams pa holds that this is the case, that the actual ultimate is not accessible to thought and is thus utterly ineffable.[36] Mi pham disagrees, arguing that if this were so, ordinary beings would never understand such an ultimate since they could never develop the causes that lead to the generation of primordial wisdom. Thus, for Mi pham, the actual ultimate is accessible to thought, even though its access is different from that of wisdom. Whereas the latter realizes the ultimate by refuting all four extremes simultaneously (see above), thought proceeds in succession.[37] Accordingly, Mi pham defines the figurative ultimate less by its being conceptual than by its being a partial emptiness. It is the mere negation of the first extreme usually spelled out as absence of true existence *(bden stong),* nonproduction *(skye med),* and so on.

For Mi pham, this distinction between the two levels of the ultimate is central to the Svātantrika-Prāsaṅgika distinction. Mi pham defines the Svātantrika as the Madhyamaka who explains emptiness by emphasizing *(rtsal du bton)* the figurative ultimate, the use of theses, and formal reasonings in the search for the ultimate. The Prāsaṅgika rejects this approach, emphasizing the actual ultimate and thesislessness.[38] For Mi pham, this is the central difference between the two approaches. Other issues such as the use of autonomous formal arguments in the generation of the view, or the use of an operator such as *ultimately (don dam par)* or *inherently (rang bzhin du)* to modify Madhyamaka negations are mere secondary issues *(yan lag gi dbye ba tsam).*[39]

This characterization of the Svātantrika-Prāsaṅgika distinction is in certain ways idiosyncratic. It does not reflect directly what has usually been seen as the historical roots of the Svātantrika-Prāsaṅgika distinction, namely, Candrakīrti's response to Bhāvaviveka's criticism of Buddhapālita for not using autonomous arguments. From that point of view, the main question is the use of autonomous arguments and the issues that this raises, particularly the status of the subject of the debate as argued by Tsong kha pa, Go rams pa, and Shākya mchog ldan. Mi pham, however, is less interested in the texts relevant to this issue than in later texts, particularly Śāntarakṣita's approach to Madhyamaka via Yogācāra. From this point of view, the issue of autonomous arguments is merely symptomatic of a deeper pragmatic difference between the two attitudes concerning the way to approach emptiness.

This way of distinguishing Svātantrika and Prāsaṅgika makes it clear that for Mi pham the main difference is less substantive than pragmatic. Svātantrika and Prāsaṅgika do not disagree on the nature of the ultimate, since both agree that a full understanding of emptiness requires the refutation of all (two or four) extremes. Hence, they also do not disagree on the object of negation, contrary to Tsong kha pa's claim. It is true, Mi pham concedes, that Candrakīrti negates objective existence *(rang mtshan)* even on the conventional level, but this should not be thought to involve an ontological issue but only a pragmatic one.[40] It is not the case that the Svātantrika emptiness leaves out some object to be negated. Rather, objective existence is negated by the Prāsaṅgika, according to Mi pham, because it involves the provisional separation of the two truths and the assertion of the objective validity of the conventional as the subject within the context of a reasoning concerning the ultimate. There Svātantrika assumes the objective validity of the subject on which the absence of true existence is predicated. The assumption, however, is provisional and valid only inasmuch as the figurative ultimate is concerned, for when contrasted to the actual ultimate, conventional things are depicted as being illusion-like. By contrast, Prāsaṅgika refuses to separate the two truths even provisionally and emphasizes the inseparability of appearance and emptiness even in the context of debating on the ultimate with opponents. Right from the start, the Prāsaṅgika stresses that things should be viewed as empty and yet appearing and hence false, even within the context of a debate with non-Mādhyamikas.[41]

For Mi pham, Svātantrika and Prāsaṅgika disagree less on particular philosophical issues such as self-cognition or the store-consciousness than on the best approach to emptiness. Whereas the former emphasizes a gradual approach in which the first extreme is refuted at length before proceeding to the subsequent refutation of this initial refutation, the latter recommends a more direct approach in which all conceptual creations, even the ones closest to the ultimate, are undermined at once. Hence, Mi pham describes this latter view as *suddenist (cig car ba)* in opposition to the more gradualist *(rim gyis pa)* Svātantrika approach.[42]

This description of the Svātantrika-Prāsaṅgika distinction, however, raises further questions. Although it has some plausibility (Candrakīrti does seem to push further his undermining of philosophical categories), a more searching analysis reveals additional difficulties. For what does it mean for Prāsaṅgika to be suddenist, given its use of conceptual resources to understand emptiness? As discussed earlier, Mi pham argues that the main issue in the Svātantrika-Prāsaṅgika distinction is the place of the figurative ultimate. The Svātantrika stresses its importance, arguing that one should first refute the first extreme (existence) and prove its nonexistence. Only then can one proceed to the second step, the negation of this negation. The Prāsaṅgika argues that this gradual procedure is not true to the central Madhyamaka point, the elimination of all views. Madhyamaka arguments do not prove anything but merely refute views. Hence, rather than prove the figurative ultimate, one should focus from the beginning on undermining both extremes.

This difference, which is at the core of Mi pham's take on the Svātantrika-Prāsaṅgika distinction, is theoretically clear, but if we turn to the texts that are supposed to reflect this difference, we cannot but wonder whether they really differ so sharply. It may be true that many Svātantrika texts focus on the refutation of the first extreme and give only cursory mention to the refutation of the second. But are Candrakīrti's texts really so different from that? His MAv, for example, is a long refutation of production. In which way does it differ from the supposedly characteristic Svātantrika approach of emphasizing the negation of the first extreme (nonproduction, *skye med*)?

Mi pham does not deal extensively with this question, but his answer does appear to connect back to the question of autonomous reasoning. The Svātantrika position, according to Mi pham, is gradualist because it uses the language and tools of Buddhist logic to understand emptiness, seeking to prove the lack of true existence of the subject. This is, however, only a first stage, which is pragmatically emphasized only to be later sublated into a more radical negation of all extremes. The Prāsaṅgika position rejects this approach, stressing that the tools of Buddhist logic are ill-adapted to describe the Madhyamaka insight. One should not lose sight of the main point, which is not to prove any fact, even a negative one, but to refute any position by stepping on the opponent's ground and arguing on his own terms. Hence, instead of using autonomous arguments, one should use statements of consequence or other-intended arguments.

Is Mi pham a Prāsaṅgika?

Finally, in light of this discussion, a further question arises concerning Mi pham's own view. Does it fit his own description of what a Prāsaṅgika should be? Or, is Mi pham finally not a Svātantrika in his use of Buddhist logic to establish the absence of true existence *(bden stong)*, as some of his texts seem to suggest? To answer, let us come back to the *Nges shes sgron me,* which perhaps best represents Mi pham's own approach. As its name indicates, this text is devoted to the topic of the certainty *(nges shes)* or conviction regarding emptiness brought about by Madhyamaka arguments. In this text Mi pham stresses the importance of such a conviction, for without it most people cannot succeed in their higher tantric practices, particularly those of the Great Perfection. Mi pham also emphasizes the importance of studying and thinking to reach such a conviction before engaging in meditation on the nature of the mind. As Mi pham puts it, a small number of fortunate practitioners may be able to penetrate the nature of the mind merely on the basis of a few brief teachings, but most people require much more extensive study of Madhyamaka in order to gain the conviction without which it is difficult to penetrate fully the nature of the mind.[43]

In this text, Mi pham does not discuss the object of conviction in any detail. He seems to assume that such a conviction takes as its object the absence of true existence *(bden stong)*. If we remember the previous discussion, however, we realize that the mere absence of true existence does not constitute by itself the full extent of emptiness but merely the negation of the first extreme (existence). To realize fully emptiness one needs to negate the second negative extreme and understand freedom from all elaborations *(spros bral)*. The absence of true existence, unless it is assumed to be combined with the refutation of the second extreme, is in fact nothing but the figurative ultimate discussed above. Thus, it appears that when Mi pham urges the study of Madhyamaka as a preparation for the Great Perfection, he is recommending an approach that emphasizes understanding the figurative ultimate. But isn't this the hallmark of the Svātantrika approach according to Mi pham himself? And if it is, does it mean that Mi pham is actually a Svātantrika despite his claims of being a Prāsaṅgika?

The answer to this quandary reveals the complexities of Tibetan appropriations of Indian ideas. Mi pham is not deluded when he claims he is a Prāsaṅgika, but his Prāsaṅgika view is of a particular kind. It is in certain respects a *tantric Madhyamaka view,* based on the combination of an extensive investigation of the figurative ultimate with a vision of the luminosity of the mind. Mi pham puts it this way:

> To penetrate decisively primordial purity, one needs the Prāsaṅgika view. It is said that from the point of view of the freedom from elaborations, [tantra and Prāsaṅgika] are without difference. To eliminate the grasping to emptiness, the tantras teach great bliss.[44]

This important passage reveals the place of Prāsaṅgika and Svātantrika in Mi pham's system. For Mi pham, emptiness is the negation of all elaborations, that is, the negation of both positive and negative extremes. But what Mi pham also seems to suggest is that these two extremes do not need to be negated during the study of Madhyamaka texts. It is enough to understand the absence of true existence and negate the first extreme by the usual Madhyamaka reasonings, which are very helpful in weaning us away from reifying things. Once this comprehension has been achieved, one can leave aside the reasonings used in classical Indian Madhyamaka to negate the second (negative) extreme and one can enter the tantric domain. There the second extreme can be negated by a much more effective method, namely, focusing on the clarity of the mind. As the *Kālacakratantra* says, this focus on clarity or bliss is helpful in undermining the fixation on emptiness. It acts as an antidote to grasping to the negation of the first extreme, much like some Madhyamaka reasonings dereify the negation of the first extreme.[45]

This use of Madhyamaka as a preparation for tantric practice and the role of tantra in the completion of the view further explain why Mi pham is inclusive of and comfortable with approaches such as Śāntarakṣita's, despite their being classified as Svātantrika by Tibetan doxographers. As shown earlier, this view is useful for Mi pham in that it introduces an interpretation of Madhyamaka through the Yogācāra and is thus highly compatible with the view of the Great Perfection. Moreover, Śāntarakṣita's system also provides the kind of Madhyamaka approach that Mi pham requires, namely, an emphasis on comprehending the figurative ultimate, the mere absence of true existence. This is in fact the defining mark of the Svātantrika approach according to Mi pham's definition. Hence, inasmuch as Mi pham uses Madhyamaka as a preparation for the Great Perfection, his approach parallels what he understands to be the Svātantrika emphasis on absence of true existence, for this is all that he needs from Madhyamaka. The rest, the negation of the second extreme, can come from the practices of the Great Perfection involving other features of the mind such as clarity or bliss.

Again, Mi pham is not deluded when he claims to be a Prāsaṅgika, for it is only when the two elements in his view, classical Indian Madhyamaka reasonings refuting true existence and tantric practice, are combined that the full extent of his view emerges.[46] Seen in this way, his view may fit into what he understands to be the Prāsaṅgika inasmuch as it emphasizes the direct undermining of any conceptual elaboration in the context of the Great Perfection. Nevertheless, it remains true that in the exoteric context Mi pham has perhaps a certain inclination toward the views he himself understands to be Svātantrika, which he does not see as contradicting the Prāsaṅgika. The differences between the two views are small since they diverge merely on pragmatic issues. In fact, they are highly compatible and can be used more or less interchangeably.

Mi pham develops a similar inclusiveness toward other Tibetan schools including the dGe lugs pa. His focus on the absence of true existence *(bden stong)* allows him to provide an interpretation of Madhyamaka germane to his nonsectarian stance. Mi pham can show that his approach is not fundamentally different from Tsong kha pa's way of explaining emptiness, since both focus on the absence of true existence. Of course, Mi pham and Tsong kha pa do not mean exactly the same thing when they refer to *absence of true existence.* Whereas for Tsong kha pa this phrase is synonymous with *emptiness,* for Mi pham this is not necessarily the case. For, unless it is combined with a refutation of the second negative extreme, this term refers to the figurative ultimate of the Svātantrika, which is to be combined with a vision of the luminous character of the mind in order to reach an understanding of the actual ultimate. Nevertheless, Mi pham's own emphasis on certainty regarding the absence of true existence in his *Nges shes sgron me* is an attempt to incorporate Tsong kha pa's contributions into his system, particularly Tsong kha pa's stress on the importance of using Madhyamaka reasonings as an indispensable preparation to tantric practice.[47] By emphasizing the importance of the conviction regarding the absence of true existence, Mi pham can claim to accommodate Tsong kha pa's Madhyamaka explanations, and include the latter's contributions, particularly the emphasis on the inseparability of appearance, understood as dependent-arising and emptiness.

Conclusion

As the patient reader by now realizes, the Svātantrika-Prāsaṅgika distinction is far from obvious when examined closely. It is a highly involved and contested issue among Tibetan scholars, who created the distinction to bring some order to what they perceived to be different Indian Madhyamaka interpretations. This is not to say, however, that this distinction is irrelevant to or unhelpful in understanding the Indian tradition. Although the exact meaning and implications of this distinction are far from self-evident, the interpretations proposed by Tibetan thinkers such as Tsong kha pa, Go rams pa, Shākya mchog ldan, or Mi pham are valuable. Their views offer important resources for the interpreter interested in exploring central Madhyamaka issues and reaching a more fine-grained understanding. But the greatest strength of the Tibetan offerings comes less from a single author than from the tradition as a whole. Individual scholars offer philosophical discussions that may help the modern interpreter to prod further the Indian material, but it would be one-sided to rely exclusively on one tradition over the others. I believe that the preceding discussion illustrates this point quite clearly.

Consider, for example, Tsong kha pa's two key points concerning the Svātantrika-Prāsaṅgika distinction, namely, that there is a substantive difference in the view of emptiness between these two currents of thought and that there are other important philosophical differences separating them. To appraise fully these two points we would need a more detailed examination of the Indian sources, which has been started here and elsewhere but needs to be pursued further. What we have achieved in this paper is merely an overview of the range of opinions among some Tibetan scholars concerning these two points. By itself such an examination cannot decide the issue, but it can indicate directions for further research on the topic and caution against a premature adoption of one side.

My own feeling in this matter is that no side is completely right but each brings important insights. It is difficult to follow Tsong kha pa in his suggestion that the Svātantrika and Prāsaṅgika views of emptiness differ substantively. Tsong kha pa's analysis is extremely sharp but suffers from a real gap in credibility, which is well exposed by his critics when they argue that it is hard to believe that Candrakīrti, who was a relatively obscure figure until the tenth or eleventh century, is to be considered the main interpreter of Nāgārjuna, whereas the great Indian Mādhyamikas such as Bhāvaviveka and Śāntarakṣita, who are counted as Svātantrika by most Tibetan scholars, are dismissed as having only a partial understanding of Madhyamaka. This conclusion is unlikely, and Tsong kha pa's discussion does not seem to meet the high burden of proof it would require.

This does not mean, however, that we should go to the other extreme and reject his views altogether. In particular, his second suggestion that there are other substantial philosophical differences between the two traditions is important. Whether or not Tsong kha pa is right on all the "eight difficult points," it appears quite probable that he is onto something significant. His opponents deny this and downplay differences, but is their denial entirely credible? As traditional thinkers, Tsong kha pa and his critics overemphasize the unity of the Indian tradition, presenting it as the recipient of timeless truths rather than as the vehicle for historically situated and hence contingent interpretations. As modern scholars, we view the Indian tradition as constituted by individuals who disagreed and argued with each other. Inasmuch as Tsong kha pa helps to reveal these differences, his interpretation is important and valuable. Moreover, Tsong kha pa's critics appear overeager to reconcile Candrakīrti's views with that of other Mādhyamikas. Their assertion of the unity of the Madhyamaka tradition seems to be motivated by some particular agenda. This is also the case of Mi pham, who intends to present a Madhyamaka view well suited to the Great Perfection. Although this is in itself an interesting project, it is hard not to think that in doing so Mi pham is overreaching and glossing over important issues, such as self-cognition, that raise problems for his approach.

Finally, it is also clear that no tradition can claim a monopoly on delineating interesting differences between Svātantrika and Prāsaṅgika. Tsong kha pa's list is certainly important, but so is Go rams pa's, despite his reluctance to use it to the fullest extent. One of the sixteen features articulated by Go rams pa is particularly revealing of the complexities involved in the Svātantrika-Prāsaṅgika distinction. That feature is the Svātantrika use of an operator such as *ultimately (don dam par)* to modify Madhyamaka negations.[48] The Prāsaṅgika rejects such an operator, claiming that it overemphasizes and hence reifies the validity of the conventional. Mi pham mentions this issue but brushes it aside as a secondary problem.[49] But isn't it more important than most Tibetan scholars seem to think?

Considering the use of operators adds to the complexity of the Svātantrika-Prāsaṅgika distinction, for it suggests that most Tibetan authors make frequent use of an approach that is found in the texts that they themselves describe as Svātantrika. Tsong kha pa is a good example. He rejects the claim that the distinctive feature of Svātantrika is its use of a modal operator, arguing that the Prāsaṅgika also uses an operator, though a different one such as *inherently* existing *(rang bzhin du yod pa)* instead of the Svātantrika *ultimately* existing *(don dam par yod pa)*. But this difference in modal operators is predicated on Tsong kha pa's assertion that Svātantrika and Prāsaṅgika differ in their views of emptiness. If we do not follow his opinion on this point, we realize that his own use of an operator and his emphasis on the validity of the conventional put him in close proximity to the texts that he himself would classify as Svātantrika. This is also confirmed by Tsong kha pa's predilection for the use of Buddhist logic and epistemology in the Madhyamaka, perhaps Bhāvaviveka's main and most controversial contribution. Similarly, Mi pham's approach appears to borrow heavily from the texts he himself would describe as Svātantrika, with perhaps the advantage of being more open about it.

Thus, it appears that when we take the contributions of Tibetan philosophers seriously, we must face the complexities involved in the Svātantrika-Prāsaṅgika distinction. We understand that far from providing clear categories, this distinction is highly contested and that to speak of a *Prāsaṅgika philosophy* or a *Svātantrika view* without a detailed analysis of the sources involved is a crude simplification. We further realize that though it is problematic, such a label cannot just be dismissed, for it refers to interesting differences within the Madhyamaka tradition. Finally, we also understand the instability of such a categorization, for it appears that the most ardent proponents of a Prāsaṅgika view may belong to the other side *perhaps unbeknownst even to themselves*, at least according to some ways of drawing the distinction.

This is probably an unwanted conclusion for those who wish to hold onto clear distinctions. Madhyamaka is well known, however, for being an extremely slippery subject where an argument for a certain position turns out to favor its opposite. This shiftiness is a consequence of the Madhyamaka philosophy that reality is beyond any elaboration and hence, ultimately speaking, cannot be captured by any description. Any attempt to formulate a Madhyamaka view has to confront this difficulty and hence suffers from a certain gap between this basic insight and its necessarily limited discursive formulation. The shiftiness here, however, is due not just to this general characteristic of Madhyamaka but also to the fact that within Madhyamaka the Svātantrika-Prāsaṅgika distinction is particularly murky. It is, as we have shown at length, highly contested among Tibetan scholars and cannot be defined with any clarity without more or less arbitrarily adopting one view over another. It is always possible to do so and to declare that this or that is the meaning of the Svātantrika-Prāsaṅgika distinction. Such a move may even be useful within a limited scholarly context, but it remains in danger of forgetting the particularly opaque nature of this distinction and starting to talk about it as if it were well established. We need to realize, however, that when we do this, we are opting for one highly contested Tibetan interpretation among many and projecting it onto the Indian material. Unless we are able to gain a much better understanding of Indian sources and keep in mind the complexity of Tibetan interpretations, such a move is problematic and, perhaps, better avoided for the time being.

Notes

1 For a view of the history of Tibetan Madhyamaka, see Ruegg (2000): 41–72. For an overview of the early history of Madhyamaka in Tibet, see the contribution by Tauscher in the present volume: 207–255.

2 For discussions of Tsong kha pa's view, see the contributions by Cabezón, Eckel, Tillemans, and Yoshimizu in this volume. See also Hopkins (1983): 429–560 and (1989).

3 Tsong kha pa, *dGongs pa rab gsal* (Sarnath ed.) 130–136.

4 See Richardson and Snellgrove (1968).

5 See Pettit (1999): 134–136. Pettit argues that although Mi pham does not refer explicitly to Go rams pa, he is strongly influenced by the latter's ideas, which he probably encountered while studying with the Sa skya scholar Blo gter dbang po.

6 Trans. in Ruegg (1988): 1259. The last point refers to the distinction between two strands of Yogācāra thought, the True Aspectarian *(rnam bden pa, satyākāravādin),* who argues that the aspect of consciousness is real and true, and the False Aspectarian *(rnam rdzun pa, alīkākāravādin),* who holds that the aspect is false. This last view is sometimes described as *Madhyamaka,* but is not generally considered to be such by Tibetan doxographers.

7 Mi pham, *dBu ma rgyan rtsa 'grel* (1992): 97.

8 Idem.

9 For a discussion of the four extremes, see Ruegg (1977).

10 I use "probative argument" or "argument" to translate *prayoga (sbyor ba)* rather than "syllogism" to avoid the confusion between Indian or Tibetan systematized rhetorical arguments and Aristotelian syllogistic. As Tillemans (1984a) has shown, there is a fundamental difference between Indian and Tibetan arguments on the one hand and Aristotelian syllogisms on the other hand, for the former are not primarily deductive structures while the second indubitably are.

11 Tsong kha pa, *dGongs pa rab gsal* (Sarnath ed.) 226. This list of eight points differs slightly from a similar list found in *dKa' gnas brgyad kyi zin bris* by the same author. See also Pettit (1999): 129.

12 Although Bhāvaviveka accepts some of these points, particularly the first two, Tsong kha pa would argue that his reasons for doing so are different from those of Candrakīrti. Hence, Tsong kha pa adds the epithet "uncommon" *(thun mong ma yin pa)* to these first two points.

13 Shākya mchog ldan, *Lung rigs rgya mtsho* (1975) vol. 14: 559.

14 See Go rams pa, *Nges don rab gsal* (1968–69) vol. 5: 132a and 108a-117a; and *lTa ngan sel ba* (1968–69) vol. 5: 132a.

15 For a discussion of this episode, see Yotsuya (1999): 47–108.

16 Tsong kha pa, *Drang nges legs bshad snying po* (Sarnath ed.) 198.

17 See Hopkins (1983): 455–530, and Yotsuya (1999): 109–164.

18 Go rams pa, *lTa ba ngan sel,* 40a-42b; and Shākya mchog ldan, *Lung rigs rgya mtsho* (1975) vol. 14: 438–496.

19 Mi pham, *dBu ma rgyan rtsa 'grel* (1992): 99.

20 See Mi pham, *Nor bu ke ta ka* (1979) vol 13. This text is extensively discussed in Williams (1998).

21 Not all Tibetan scholars agree on this identification of the second and third turnings, which revolves around one of the most disputed topics in the Tibetan tradition. Following Tsong kha pa, dGe lugs scholars argue that the third turning is limited to the Yogācāra, which is identified with the Mind-Only view. Scholars from other schools dispute this, arguing that the third turning includes Madhyamaka texts and is thus not limited to Mind-Only. Some scholars also argue that Yogācāra and Mind-Only are not identical, though this point does not seem to be important for Mi pham. For a general discussion of these issues, see Ruegg (1969).

22 This is the core message of the work many consider as Tsong kha pa's masterpiece, the *Legs bshad snying po.*

23 Mi pham, *dBu ma rgyan rtsa 'grel* (1992): 60.

24 See, for example, Gyatso (1998): 200.

25 This view is rejected by nearly all dGe lugs pa scholars, who refuse the existence of a specifically tantric view in which the ultimate is not just emptiness but also includes the luminosity of the mind. For the dGe lugs pa tradition, the ultimate is limited to the empty aspect of the mind and its luminosity is seen as part of conventional truth; otherwise, the ultimate would exist really and would constitute the kind of absolute antithetical to Buddhist anti-substantialist commitment.

26 See, for instance, his *Theg pa chen po'i man ngag gi bstan bcos yid bzhin rin po che'i mdzod* (1983) vol. 1.

27 Email communication from David Germano, University of Virginia.

28 Pettit (1999): 90.

29 Ibid.: 94.

30 For a discussion of this distinction, see Dreyfus (1997): 60–72.

31 Mi pham, *dBu ma rgyan rtsa 'grel* (1992): 84–85: *de la dmigs mtshan spros pa thams cad dang bral ba'i gnas lugs kyi dbang du na / snang ba sems yin no zhes kyang mi dmigs mod / de ni tha snyad las 'das pa'i don dam yin la / tha snyad snang ba'i ngang tshul 'di la gnas na ni / phyi don yod pa la rigs pas gnod cing / sems tsam yin pa la rigs pa'i sgrub byed yod pas tshur mthong gi sa las ma brgal bar tha snyad zhig khas len na 'di las gong du gyur pa med de / rtog pa'i dbang gis bzhag pa tsam gyi chos rnams dpyad na gang du'ang ma grub kyang / rang ngor myong ba'i tshul gyis bslu med du snang pa (?ba) 'gog tu med pa 'di sems kyi snang ba'am rang snang tsam du dngos po'i tsobs kyis 'grub pa yin no /.*

32 Idem.

33 The nature of the relation between self-cognition and transcendent gnosis is a difficult topic. Some thinkers argue for a close connection. Shākya mchog ldan, for example, holds that gnosis is just the pure expression of ordinary reflexivity. In his study of yogic perception, he explains it as a state of pure apperception in which the flow of conceptualization has ceased through the power of meditation (see *Lung rigs rgya mtsho,* vol. 14, 548 and 556). Mi pham, on the other hand, is uncomfortable with this assimilation, which seems to compromise the distinction between ordinary consciousness *(rnam shes)* and transcendent wisdom *(ye shes).* Hence, for him, gnosis is not just self-cognition in a pure state. The relation between self-cognition and the self-awareness of the ground is indirect or analogical, as helpfully suggested by Matthew Kapstein in an oral communication. Ordinary self-cognition stands as an example suggesting gnosis, something akin to the exemplary clear light *(dpe'i 'od gsal)* described in the new tantras. See Mi pham's three texts on *gNyug sems,* in Collected Works, vol. 24.

34 Mi pham, *dBu ma rgyan rtsa 'grel* (1992): 88. The fifth feature also relates to this issue and concerns the compatibility between *prajñā (shes rab),* the wisdom that cognizes the figurative ultimate, and *jñāna (ye shes),* the transcendent gnosis that realizes the actual ultimate. Cf. also ibid.: 103–109.

35 Mi pham, *dBu ma rgyan rtsa 'grel,* 61–62: *de ltar dang po thos bsam gyi sgra rtog gi yul du gyur pa'i tha snyad du skye ba dang / don dam par mi skye ba lta bu tshul gnyis zung du bzhag pa'i ya gyal rnam grang pa'i don dam ni / kun rdzob yod pa'i zla la sbyar ba'i cig shos kyi zlas drangs pa'i phyir ram / don dam pa'i grangs su gtogs pas na rnam grangs te / bden pa gnyis zhes pa'i kun rdzob kyi zlar bgrang rgyu de yin la / de ni don dam mthar thug dang mthun pa'i sgo tsam mam / de goms pas thog med nas goms pa'i bag chags kyi mthu brtas pa'i dngos por 'zin pa gzhom nus pa'i phyir na don dam yang yin la / de'i ngo la ltos na skye ba med ces pa'i khas len yang yod par shes par bya'o / de'i dpyad pa tshad du phyin kyang rjes thob kyi*

nges pa skye tshul tsam yin no / yang dag pa'i gnas lugs mthar thug pa'i dbang du na / skye bas drang ba'i skye med ces pa'ang blos gzhan bsal ba'i rnam rtog gi gzugs brnyan tsam yin pas / skye ba yod med sogs mtha' thams cad las 'des shing sgra dang rtog pa'i spyod yul thams cad spangs pa'i 'phags pa'i mnyam bzhag ye shes shin tu dri ma med pa'i gzigs don ni rnam grangs ma yin pa'i don dam bla na med pa yin la / de'i ngo la ltos na khas len kun dang bral ba'ang yin no / rnam grangs pa'i don dam ni 'di dang nye zhing mthun pas na de'ang don dam gyi grangs su bgrang ste mthun pa'i don dam zhes bya ba yin no /.

36 Go rams pa, *Nges don rab gsal* (1968–69): 23b.

37 Mi pham, *Nor bu ke ta ka* (1979): 7–8.

38 Mi pham, *dBu ma rgyan rtsa 'grel* (1992): 99: *des na rnam grangs pa'i don dam khas len dang bcas pa de rtsal du bton nas 'chad pa rang rgyud pa'i mtshan nyid yin la / rnam grang ma yin pa'i don dam khas len kun bral rtsal du bton nas 'chad pa thal 'gyur ba yin par shes par bya'o //.* For a discussion of thesislessness, see Ruegg's two seminal articles (1983) and (1986).

39 Mi pham, *dBu ma rgyan rtsa 'grel* (1992): 99.

40 In conceding this point, Mi pham differs from Go rams pa and Shākya mchog ldan, who argue that there is no difference between Svātantrika and Prāsaṅgika concerning *rang mtshan*. When taken literally this term refers to the own characteristics of a thing as opposed to its general characteristics *(spyi'i mtshan nyid)* as found in Abhidharma texts. Such a defining characteristic exists in Candrakīrti's system as is clear in the MAv where Candrakīrti provides the definition of many phenomena. See Huntington (1989): 180–181.

41 See Mi pham, *dBu ma rgyan rtsa 'grel* (1992): 101 and 104. This discussion has been greatly helped by mKhan po rnam grol's explanations.

42 Mi pham, *dBu ma rgyan rtsa 'grel* (1992): 68.

43 Mi pham, *Nges shes sgron me* (1979): 9b. Mi pham does not explain any further why most people need study to penetrate fully the view.

44 Mi pham, *Nges shes sgron me* (1979): 9b-10a: *ka dag gdar sha chod pa la / thal gyur lta ba mthar phyin dgos / spros bral tsam gyi cha nas ni / de gnyis khyad par med do gsung / stong zhen pa bzlog phir du / sngags las bde ba chen po bstan /.*

45 Oral communication from mKhan po rnam grol.

46 It would also be a mistake to think that the Prāsaṅgika view is necessarily tantric. Mi pham denies this explicitly (see *Nor bu ke ta ka* [1979]: 7). It remains true, however, that it is in the tantric context that the Prāsaṅgika element of his view comes to the fore.

47 Mi pham, *dBu ma rgyan rtsa 'grel* (1992): 107–108. There Mi pham also quotes approvingly a key passage from Tsong kha pa's *Lam gtso rnam gsum.*

48 See Go rams pa, *Nges don rab gsal,* 132a. For a study of this issue in Bhāvaviveka's and Candrakīrti's works, see Yotsuya (1999): 80–92.

49 Mi pham, *dBu ma rgyan rtsa 'grel* (1992): 99.

Abbreviations

ACIP	Asian Classics Input Project
C	Co ne edition of the *bsTan 'gyur*
CŚ	*Catuḥśataka* of Āryadeva
D	sDe dge edition of the *bsTan 'gyur*. See Takasaki et al., eds. (1977)
MA	*Madhyamakālaṃkāra* of Śāntarakṣita
MAV	*Madhyamakālaṃkāravṛtti* of Śāntarakṣita
MĀ	*Madhyamakāloka* of Kamalaśīla
MAP	*Madhyamakālaṃkārapañjikā* of Kamalaśīla
MAv	*Madhyamakāvatāra* of Candrakīrti
MAvBh	*Madhyamakāvatārabhāṣya* of Candrakīrti
MAvṬ	*Madhyamakāvatāraṭīkā* of Jayānanda
MHK	*Madhyamakahṛdayakārikā* of Bhāvaviveka
MMK	*Mūlamadhyamakakārikā* of Nāgārjuna
N	sNar thang edition of the *bsTan 'gyur*
NB	*Nyāyabindu* of Dharmakīrti
P	Peking edition of the *bsTan 'gyur*. See Suzuki (1955–1961)
PrP	*Prajñāpradīpa* of Bhāvaviveka
PrPṬ	*Prajñāpradīpaṭīkā* of Avalokitavrata
PPMV	*Prasannapadā Mūlamadhyamakavṛtti* of Candrakīrti
PS	*Pramāṇasamuccaya* of Dignāga
PV	*Pramāṇavārttika* of Dharmakīrti
PVSV	*Pramāṇavārttikasvavṛtti* of Dharmakīrti
PVV	*Pramāṇavārttikavṛtti* of Manorathanandin
SDV	*Satyadvayavibhaṅga* of Jñānagarbha
SDVV	*Satyadvayavibhaṅgavṛtti* of Jñānagarbha
SNS	*Saṃdhinirmocanasūtra*. See Lamotte (1935)
T	Edition of Tashilunpo
TJ	*Tarkajvālā* of Bhāvaviveka

TS	*Tattvasaṃgraha* of Śāntarakṣita
TSP	*Tattvasaṃgrahapañjikā* of Kamalaśīla
VV	*Vigrahavyāvartanī* of Nāgārjuna
Zh	Edition of Zhol

Bibliography

N.B.: The locations of Tibetan texts in the sDe dge edition (D) of the Tibetan canon are given except in cases where a commonly used critical edition exists.

Ames, William L. (1982) "Bondage and Liberation According to the Mādhyamika School of Buddhism: A Study and Translation of Chapter Sixteen of the *Mūlamadhyamakakārikās* and Five of Its Commentaries." M.A. thesis, University of Washington.

Ames, William L. (1986) "Bhāvaviveka's *Prajñāpradīpa:* Six Chapters." Ph.D. dissertation, University of Washington. University Microfilms International, Ann Arbor, Michigan.

Ames, William L. (1988) "The Soteriological Purpose of Nāgārjuna's Philosophy: A Study of Chapter Twenty-Three of the *Mūla-madhyamaka-kārikās.*" *Journal of the International Association of Buddhist Studies* 11/2: 7–20.

Ames, William L. (1993) "Bhāvaviveka's *Prajñāpradīpa:* A Translation of Chapter One, 'Examination of Causal Conditions' *(Pratyaya),* Part One." *Journal of Indian Philosophy* 21: 209–259.

Ames, William L. (1995) "Bhāvaviveka's *Prajñāpradīpa:* A Translation of Chapter Two, 'Examination of the Traversed, the Untraversed, and That Which Is Being Traversed.'" *Journal of Indian Philosophy* 23: 295–365.

Ames, William L. (1999) "Bhāvaviveka's *Prajñāpradīpa:* A Translation of Chapter Three, Four and Five: Examining the Āyatanas, Aggregates and Elements." *Buddhist Literature* 1: 1–119.

Ames, William L. (2000) "Bhāvaviveka's *Prajñāpradīpa:* A Translation of Chapter Six, Examination of Desire and the One Who Desires, and Chapter Seven, Examination of Origination, Duration, and Cessation." *Buddhist Literature* 2: 1–91.

Āryadeva. (4th c.) *Catuḥśataka* (CŚ). Skt. and Tib. ed. and trans. in Lang (1986).

Atiśa. (11th c.) *Byang chub lam gyi sgron me dang de'i bka' 'grel.* Dharamsala: The Tibetan Publishing House, 1969.

Avalokitavrata. (7th or 8th c.) *Prajñāpradīpaṭīkā* (PrPṬ). D dBu ma, vols. *wa-za.* D 3859, P 5259.

Ba so chos kyi rgyal mtshan, sDe drug mkhan chen ngag dbang rab brtan, Jam dbyangs bzhad pa'i rdo rje and Bra sti dge bshes rin chen don grub. (1842) *mNyam med rje btsun Tsong kha pa chen pos mdzad pa'i Byang chub lam rim chen mo'i dka' gnad rnams mchan bu bzhi'i sgo nas legs par bshad pa theg chen lam gyi gsal sgron (= mChan bzhi).* Chos-'phel-legs-ldan, ed., *The Lam rim chen mo of the Incomparable Tsong-kha-pa.* With the interlinear notes of Ba so chos kyi rgyal mtshan *et al.* Reproduced from a print of the corrected Tshe-mchog-gling blocks of 1842. New Delhi, 1972.

Bateson, Gregory. (1979) *Mind and Nature: A Necessary Unity.* New York: Dutton Press.

Bhāvaviveka. (6th c.) *Prajñāpradīpamūlamadhyamakavṛtti* (PrP). D dBu ma, vol. *tsha,* 46a-259b. D 3853, P 5253.

Bhāvaviveka. (6th c.) *Madhyamakahṛdayakārikā* (MHK). D dBu ma, vol. *dza,* 1b-40b. D 3855, P 5255.

Bhāvaviveka. (6th c.) *Madhyamakahṛdayakārikā Tarkajvālā* (TJ). D dBu ma, vol. *dza,* 40b-329b. D 3856, P 5256.

Biardeau, Madeleine. (1964) *Théorie de la Connaissance et Philosophie de la Parole dans le Brahmanisme Classique.* Paris: Mouton.

Bod rgya tshig mdzod chen mo (Tshig mdzod chen mo). (1985) 3 vols. Repr. in 2 vols., 1993. Beijing: Mi rigs dpe sgrun khang.

Brandom, Robert. (1997) "Study Guide [to Wilfrid Sellars' *Empiricism and the Philosophy of Mind*]." In Sellars (1997).

Broido, Michael. (1989) "The Jo-nang-Pas on Madhyamaka: A Sketch." *The Tibet Journal* 14/1: 86–90.

Bronkhorst, Johannes. (1993) Review of *The Ideas and Meditative Practices of Early Buddhism* by Tilmann Vetter. *Indo-Iranian Journal* 36: 63–68.

bSod nams rgya mtsho, ed. (1968–69) *Sa skya pa'i bka' 'bum: The Complete Works of the Great Masters of the Sa skya Sect of Tibetan Buddhism.* 15 vols. Tokyo: The Toyo Bunko.

Buchler, Justus. (1940) *Philosophical Writings of Pierce.* Repr. 1958. New York: Dover Publications.

Buddhapālita. (ca. 500) *Buddhapālitamūlamadhyamakavṛtti.* D dBu ma, vol. *tsa,* 158b-281a. D 3842, P 5242. Also in Saito (1984).

Cabezón, José Ignacio. (1988) "The Prāsaṅgikas' Views on Logic: Tibetan dGe lugs pa Exegesis on the Question of Svatantras." *Journal of Indian Philosophy* 16: 217–224.

Cabezón, José Ignacio. (1990) "The Cannonization of Philosophy and the Rhetoric of Siddhānta in Tibetan Buddhism." In P. J. Griffiths and J. P. Keenan, eds., *Buddha Nature: A Festschrift in Honor of Minoru Kiyota.* San Francisco and Tokyo: Buddhist Books International, 7–26.

Cabezón, José Ignacio. (1992) *A Dose of Emptiness: An Annotated Translation of the* sTong thun chen mo *of mKhas grub dGe legs dpal bzang.* Albany: State University of New York Press.

Cabezón, José Ignacio. (1994) *Buddhism and Language: A Study of Indo-Tibetan Scholasticism.* Albany: State University of New York Press.

Cabezón, José Ignacio. (1995) "Buddhist Studies as a Discipline and the Role of Theory." *Journal of the International Association of Buddhist Studies* 18/2: 231–268.

Cabezón, José Ignacio. (1997) "Rong ston Shākya rgyal mtshan on Mādhyamika Thesislessness." In Krasser, *et al.*, vol. 1: 97–105.

Candrakīrti. (7th c.) *Catuḥśatakaṭīkā.* D dBu ma, vol. *ya.* D 3865, P 5266. Skt. fragments and Tib. of chapters 12 and 13 ed. and trans. in Tillemans (1990).

Candrakīrti. (7th c.) *Madhyamakāvatāra* (MAv) and *Madhyamakāvatārabhāṣya* (MAvBh). Tib. trans. in La Vallée Poussin (1907–1912).

Candrakīrti. (7th c.) *Prasannapadā* (PPMV). In La Vallée Poussin (1903–1913). Also in Vaidya (1960).

Chandra, Lokesh. (1963) *Materials for the History of Tibetan Literature.* New Delhi. Repr. ed. Kyoto: Rinsen Book Company, 1981.

Chatterjee, Satischandra and Dhirendramohan Datta. (1968) *An Introduction to Indian Philosophy.* Calcutta: University of Calcutta.

Chu, Junjie. (1997) "The Ontological Problem in Tsoṅ kha pa's Prasaṅga Theory: The Establishment or Unestablishment of the Subject *(dharmin)* of an Argument." In Krasser, *et al.*, vol. 1: 157–177.

Co ne ed. of the *bsTan 'gyur.* (1974) Microfiche. Stony Brook, NY: Institute for the Advanced Study of World Religions.

Conze, Edward. (1959) *Buddhism. Its Essence and Development.* New York: Harper Torchbooks.

Conze, Edward. (1967) *Buddhist Thought in India: Three Phases of Buddhist Thought.* Ann Arbor: University of Michigan Press.

Dancy, Jonathan. (1989) *An Introduction to Contemporary Epistemology.* 4th printing. Oxford: Blackwell.

Das, Sarat Chandra. (1902) *A Tibetan-English Dictionary.* Calcutta. Repr. ed. Kyoto: Rinsen Book Company, 1981.

dBus pa blo gsal byang chub ye shes. (14th c.) *Blo gsal grub mtha'.* Ed. and trans. in Mimaki (1982).

de Jong, J. W., ed. (1977) *Mūlamadhyamakakārikāḥ.* Madras: Adyar Library and Research Center.

de Jong, J. W. (1978) "Textcritical Notes on the *Prasannapadā.*" *Indo-Iranian Journal* 20: 25–59, 217–252.

de Jong, J. W. (1989) Review of *Perception, Knowledge, and Disbelief: A Study of Jayarāśi's Scepticism* by Eli Franco. *Indo-Iranian Journal* 32: 209–211.

dGe 'dun grub pa, Dalai Lama I. (1391–1474) *Tshad ma'i bstan bcos chen po rigs pa'i rgyan (= Rigs pa'i rgyan).* Dodrup Lama Sangye, ed., *The Collected Works of the First Dalai Lama dGe-'dun-grub-pa,* vol. 4: 97–519. Gangtok: Deorali Chorten, 1979.

Dharmakīrti. (7th c.) *Pramāṇavārttikasvavṛtti* (PVSV). In R. Gnoli, ed., *The Pramāṇavārttikam of Dharmakīrti. The First Chapter with the Autocommentary: Text and Critical Notes.* Rome: Serie Orientale Roma 23, 1960.

Dharmakīrti. (7th c.) *Hetubindu.* In E. Steinkellner, ed. and tr., *Dharmakīrti's Hetubinduḥ.* 2 vols. Vienna: Verlag der Österreichischen Akademie der Wissenschaften, 1967.

Dharmottara. (7th c.) *Nyāyabinduṭīkā.* In D. Malvania., ed., *Paṇḍita Durveka Miśra's Dharmottarapradīpa.* Tibetan Sanskrit Works Series, vol. 2. Patna, 1955.

Dignāga. (5th–6th c.) *Nyāyamukha.* In S. Katsura, ed., "Inmyō shōrimonron kenkyū" (A Study of the *Nyāyamukha*). *Hiroshima Daigaku Bungakubu Kiyō (Bulletin of the Faculty of Letters of Hiroshima University)* 37 (1977): 106–127; 38 (1978): 110–130; 39 (1979): 63–82; 41 (1981): 62–82; 42 (1982): 82–99; 44 (1984): 43–74; 46 (1987): 46–85.

Dignāga. (5th–6th c.) *Pramāṇasamuccaya* (PS). D Tshad ma, vol. *ce,* 1b–13b. D 4203, P 5700. Partial ed. in Kitagawa (1973).

dKon mchog 'jigs med dbang po. (1728–1791) *Grub pa'i mtha'i rnam par bzhag pa rin po che'i phreng ba.* Yongs dgon mtshan nyid grva tshang. N.d.

Dol po pa shes rab rgyal mtshan. (1292–1362) *bDen gnyis gsal ba'i nyi ma (= bDen gsal nyi ma).* In Lama Ngodrup and Sherpa Drimay, eds., *The Collected Works (gSuṅ 'bum) of Kun-mkhyen Dol-po-pa Śes-rab-rgyal-mtshan,* vol. 1: 1–45. Paro: Kyichu Temple, 1984.

Dol po pa shes rab rgyal mtshan. (1292–1362) *bKa' bsdu bzhi pa'i gtan tshigs chen mo (= bKa' bsdu gtan tshig).* In Lama Ngodrup and Sherpa Drimay, eds., *The Collected Works (gSuṅ 'bum) of Kun-mkhyen Dol-po-pa Śes-rab-rgyal-mtshan,* vol. 1: 363–417. Paro: Kyichu Temple, 1984.

Dreyfus, Georges B. J. (1996) "Can the Fool Lead the Blind? Perception and the Given in Dharmakīrti's Thought." *Journal of Indian Philosophy* 24: 209–229.

Dreyfus, Georges B. J. (1997) *Recognizing Reality: Dharmakīrti's Philosophy and Its Tibetan Interpretations.* Albany: State University of New York Press.

Dumont, Louis. (1964) *La Civilisation Indienne et Nous: Esquisse de Sociologie Comparée.* Paris: Librairie Armand Colin.

Dunne, John D. (1999) "Foundations of Dharmakīrti's Philosophy: A Study of the Central Issues in His Ontology, Logic and Epistemology with Special Attention to the *Svopajñavṛtti.*" Ph.D. dissertation, Harvard University. University Microfilms International, Ann Arbor, Michigan.

Eckel, Malcolm David. (1978) "Bhāvaviveka and the Early Mādhyamika Theories of Language." *Philosophy East and West* 28: 323–337.

Eckel, Malcolm David. (1980) "A Question of Nihilism: Bhāvaviveka's Response to the Fundamental Problems of Mādhyamika Philosophy." Ph.D. dissertation, Harvard University. University Microfilms International, Ann Arbor, Michigan.

Eckel, Malcolm David. (1985) "Bhāvaviveka's Critique of Yogācāra Philosophy in Chapter XXV of the *Prajñāpradīpa.*" In Chr. Lindtner, ed., *Miscellanea Buddhica.* Indiske Studien 5. Copenhagen.

Eckel, Malcolm David. (1986) "The Concept of Reason in Jñānagarbha's *Svātantrika Madhyamaka.*" In B.K. Matilal and R. D. Evans, eds., *Buddhist Logic and Epistemology: Studies in the Buddhist Analysis of Inference and Language.* Studies of Classical India 7. Dordrecht: Reidel Publishing, 265–290.

Eckel, Malcolm David. (1987) *Jñānagarbha's Commentary on the Distinction Between the Two Truths: An Eighth-Century Handbook of Madhyamaka Philosophy.* Albany: State University of New York Press.

Eckel, Malcolm David. (1992) *To See the Buddha: A Philosopher's Quest for the Meaning of Emptiness.* San Francisco: Harper San Francisco. Repr. ed., Princeton: Princeton University Press, 1994.

Ejima, Yasunori. (1980) *Chūgan shisō no tenkai Bhāvaviveka kenkyū (Development of Mādhyamika Philosophy in India—Studies on Bhāvaviveka).* Tokyo: Shunjūsha.

Ejima, Yasunori. (1990) "Bhāvaviveka / Bhavya / Bhāviveka." *Indogaku Bukkyōgaku Kenkyū (Journal of Indian and Buddhist Studies)* 38/2: 98–106.

Folkert, Kendall Wayne. (1993) *Scripture and Community: Collected Essays on the Jains.* Atlanta: Scholars Press.

Franco, Eli. (1994) *Perception, Knowledge, and Disbelief: A Study of Jayarāśi's Scepticism.* 2nd ed. Delhi: Motilal Banarsidass.

Frauwallner, Erich. (1959) "Dignāga, sein Werk und seine Entwicklung." *Wiener Zeitschrift für die Kunde Süd- und Ostasiens* 3: 83–164.

Frauwallner, Erich. (1961) "Landmarks in the History of Indian Logic." *Wiener Zeitschrift für die Kunde Süd- und Ostasiens* 5: 125–148.

Fukuda, Yūichi. (2000) "Jisō to rang gi mtshan nyid" [Japanese translation of *svalakṣaṇa* "jisō" and *rang gi mtshan nyid*] in *Kū to jitsuzai (Śūnyatā and Reality), Volume in Memory of Professor Ejima Yasunori.* Tokyo: Shunjūsha, 173–189.

Funayama, Tōru. (1991) "On *Āśrayāsiddha.*" *Indogaku Bukkyōgaku Kenkyū (Journal of Indian and Buddhist Studies)* 39: 1027–1021.

Funayama, Tōru. (1992) "A Study of *kalpanāpoḍha.* A Translation of the *Tattvasaṃgraha* vv. 1212–1263 by Śāntarakṣita and the Tattvasaṃgrahapañjikā by Kamalaśīla on the Definition of Direct Perception." Kyoto: *Zinbun (Annals of the Institute for Research in Humanities, Kyoto University)* 27: 33–128.

Gadamer, Hans-Georg. (1976) *Philosophical Hermeneutics.* Ed. and trans. by David E. Linge. Berkeley: University of California Press.

Gadamer, Hans-Georg. (1982) *Truth and Method.* New York: Crossroad.

Galloway, Brian. (1989) "Some Logical Issues in Madhyamaka Thought." *Journal of Indian Philosophy* 17: 1–35.

Gillon, Brendan. (1987) "Two Forms of Negation in Sanskrit: *Prasajyapratiṣedha* and *Paryudāsapratiṣedha.*" *Lokaprajñā* 1/1: 81–89.

Go rams pa bsod nams seng ge. (1429–1489) *dBu ma la 'jug pa'i dkyus kyi sa bcad dang gzhung so so'i dka' ba'i gnas la dpyad pa lta ba ngan sel (= lTa ba'i ngan sel).* In bSod nams rgya mtsho, ed. (1968–69), vol. 13.

Go rams pa bsod nams seng ge. (1429–1489) *lTa ba'i shan 'byed.* Varanasi: Sakya Students' Union (1988). Also in bSod nams rgya mtsho, ed. (1968–69), vol. 13.

Go rams pa bsod nams seng ge. (1429–1489) *rGyal ba thams cad kyi thugs kyi dgongs pa zab mo dbu ma'i de kho na nyid spyi'i ngag gis ston pa nges don rab gsal (= Nges don rab gsal).* In bSod nams rgya mtsho, ed. (1968–69), vol. 12.

Goodman, Nelson. (1968) *Languages of Art: An Approach to a Theory of Symbols.* New York: Bobbs-Merrill.

Grags pa rgyal mtshan. (1147–1216) *rGyud kyi mngon par rtogs pa rin po che'i ljon shing (= Rin che ljon shing).* In bSod nams rgya mtsho, ed. (1968–69), vol. 3.

Griffiths, Paul J. (1994) *On Being Buddha: The Classical Doctrine of Buddhahood.* Albany: State University of New York Press.

Gro lung pa blo gros 'byung gnas. (11th-12th c.) *bsTan rim chen mo* (1/2). ACIP, Release IV, SL0070–1/2.

Guyer, P., and A. W. Wood, trans. (1997) *Critique of Pure Reason* of Immanuel Kant. Cambridge: Cambridge University Press.

Gyatso, Janet. (1998) *Apparitions of the Self.* Princeton: Princeton University Press.

Haack, Susan. (1993) *Evidence and Inquiry: Towards Reconstruction in Epistemology.* Oxford: Blackwell.

Halbfass, Wilhelm. (1988) *India and Europe: An Essay in Understanding.* Albany: State University of New York Press.

Haldane, John, and Crispin Wright, eds. (1993) *Reality, Representation and Projection.* Oxford: Oxford University Press.

Hattori, Masaaki. (1968) *Dignāga on Perception: Being the Pratyakṣapariccheda of Dignāga's Pramāṇasamuccaya.* Harvard Oriental Series 47. Cambridge: Harvard University Press.

Hayes, Richard. (1986) Review of *The Heart of Buddhist Philosophy: Diṅnāga and Dharmakīrti* by Amar Singh. *Journal of the International Association of Buddhist Studies* 9/2: 166–172.

Heitmann, Annette L. (1998) *Textkritsher Beitrag zu Bhavyas Madhyamakahṛdayakārikā, Kapitel 1–3.* Copenhagen: Videnskabsbutikkens Forlag Københavns Universitet.

Hiriyanna, Mysore. (1932) *Outlines of Indian Philosophy.* London: Allen & Unwin.

Hoornaert, Paul. (1999) "An Annotated Translation of *Madhyamakahṛdaykārikā / Tarkajvālā* V.1–7." *Studies and Essays,* Behavioral Sciences and Philosophy Faculty of Letters, Kanazawa University 19: 127–159.

Hoornaert, Paul. (2000) "An Annotated Translation of *Madhyamakahṛdaykārikā / Tarkajvālā* V.8–26." *Studies and Essays,* Behavioral Sciences and Philosophy Faculty of Letters, Kanazawa University 20: 75–111.

Hoornaert, Paul. (2001a) "An Annotated Translation of *Madhyamakahṛdaykārikā / Tarkajvālā* V.27–54." *Studies and Essays,* Behavioral Sciences and Philosophy Faculty of Letters, Kanazawa University 21: 149–190.

Hoornaert, Paul. (2001b) "An Annotated Translation of *Madhyamakahṛdaykārikā / Tarkajvālā* V.55–68." *Religion and Culture,* Kanazawa University 13: 13–47.

Hopkins, Jeffrey, and Geshe L. Sopa. (1976) *Practice and Theory of Tibetan Buddhism.* London: Rider and Co., Ltd.

Hopkins, Jeffrey. (1983) *Meditation on Emptiness.* London/Boston: Wisdom Publications.

Hopkins, Jeffrey. (1987) *Emptiness Yoga. The Middle Way Consequence School.* Ithaca: Snow Lion Publications.

Hopkins, Jeffrey. (1989) "A Tibetan Delineation of Different Views of Emptiness in the Indian Middle Way School." *The Tibet Journal* 14/1: 10–43.

Hopkins, Jeffrey. (1996) "The Tibetan Genre of Doxography: Structuring a Worldview." In J. Cabezón and R. Jackson, eds., *Tibetan Literature: Studies in Genre.* Ithaca: Snow Lion Publications.

Hopkins, Jeffrey. (1999) *Emptiness in the Mind-Only School of Buddhism: Dynamic Responses to Dzong-ka-ba's* The Essence of Eloquence: I. Berkeley: University of California Press.

Humphries, Jeff. (1999) *Reading Emptiness.* The Margins of Literature, vol. 1. Albany: State University of New York Press.

Huntington, C. W. (1986) "The *Akutobhayā* and Early Indian Madhyamaka." Ph.D. dissertation, University of Michigan. University Microfilms International, Ann Arbor, Michigan.

Huntington, C. W. (1989) *The Emptiness of Emptiness: An Introduction to Early Indian Mādhyamika.* Honolulu: University of Hawai'i Press.

Huntington, C. W. (1995a) "A Way of Reading." *Journal of the International Association of Buddhist Studies* 18/2: 279–308.

Huntington, C. W. (1995b) "A Lost Text of Early Indian Madhyamaka." *Asiatische Studien / Études Asiatiques* 49/4: 693–768.

Ichigō, Masamichi. (1985) *Madhyamakālaṃkāra of Śāntarakṣita with his own Commentary or Vṛtti and with the Subcommentary or Pañjikā of Kamalaśīla.* Kyoto: Kyoto Sangyō University.

Ihara, Shōren, and Zuihō Yamaguchi, eds. (1992) *Tibetan Studies. Proceedings of the 5th Seminar of the International Association of Tibetan Studies.* 2 vols. Narita: Naritasan Shinshōji.

Iida, Shōtarū. (1980) *Reason and Emptiness: A Study in Logic and Mysticism.* Tokyo: Hokuseidō Press.

Iwata, Takashi. (1991) *Sahopalambhaniyama: Struktur und Entwicklung des Schlusses von der Tatsache, daß Erkenntnis und Gegenstand ausschliesslich zusammen wahrgenommen werden, auf deren Nichverschiedenheit.* Stuttgart: Franz Steiner Verlag.

Iwata, Takashi. (1993) *Prasaṅga und Prasaṅgaviparyaya bei Dharmakīrti und seinen*

Kommentatoren. Wiener Studien zur Tibetologie und Buddhismuskunde 31. Vienna: Arbeitskreis für Tibetische und Buddhistische Studien.

Jackson, David P. (1987) *The Entrance Gate for the Wise (Section III).* Wiener Studien zur Tibetologie und Buddhismuskunde. Vienna: Arbeitskreis für Tibetische und Buddhistische Studien.

Jackson, David P. and Shūnzō Onoda, eds. (1988) *Rong-ston on the Prajñāpāramitā Philosophy of the Abhisamayālaṃkāra: His Sub-commentary on Haribhadra's "Sphutārtha."* Biblia Tibetica Series, no. 2. Kyoto: Nagata Bunshodo.

'Jam dbyangs bzhad pa'i rdo rje ngag dbang brtson 'grus. (1648–1721) *dBu ma la 'jug pa'i mtha' dpyod lung rigs gter mdzod zab don kun gsal bzang 'jug ngogs (= dBu 'jug mtha' dpyod).* In Ngag dbang dge legs bde mo, ed. (1972–74): vol. 9.

'Jam dbyangs bzhad pa'i rdo rje ngag dbang brtson 'grus. (1648–1721) *Grub mtha' rnam bshad rang gzhan grub mtha' kun dang zab don mchog tu gsal ba kun bzang zhing gi nyi ma lung rigs rgya mtsho skye dgu'i re ba kun skyon (= Grub mtha' chen mo)* in Ngag dbang dge legs bde mo, ed. (1972–74), vol. 14: 33–1091.

'Jam dbyangs bzhad pa'i rdo rje ngag dbang brtson 'grus. (1648–1721) *Grub mtha' rnam par bzhag pa 'khrul spong dgong lnga'i sgra dbyangs kun mkhyen lam bzang gsal ba'i rin chen sgron me.* In Ngag dbang dge legs bde mo, ed. (1972–74), vol. 14: 1–31.

Jayānanda. (11th c.) *Madhyamakāvatāraṭīkā* (MavṬ). D dBu ma, vol. *ra.* D 3870, P 5271. Also in ACIP, release IV, TD3870-1/2.

Jñānagarbha. (8th c.) *Satyadvayavibhaṅga* (SDV) and *Satyadvayavibhaṅgavṛtti* (SDVV). D dBu ma, vol. *sa.* D 3881 and D 3882. Also in Eckel (1987).

Johnston, Mark. (1993) "Objectivity Refigured: Pragmatism without Verificationism." In J. Haldane and C. Wright, eds., *Reality, Representation and Projection.* Oxford: Oxford University Press, 85–130.

Johnston, Mark. (1997) "Human Concerns without Superlative Selves." In J. Dancy, ed., *Reading Parfit.* Oxford: Blackwell, 149–179.

Kajiyama, Yūichi. (1963) "Bhāvaviveka's *Prajñāpradīpaḥ* (1. Kapitel)." *Wiener Zeitschrift für die Kunde Süd- und Ostasiens* 7: 37–62.

Kajiyama, Yūichi. (1965) "Controversy between the Sākāra- and Nirākāra-vādins of the Yogācāra School—Some Materials." *Indogaku Bukkyōgaku Kenkyū (Journal of Indian and Buddhist Studies)* 14: 26–37.

Kajiyama, Yūichi. (1966) *An Introduction to Buddhist Philosophy. An Annotated Translation of the Tarkabhāṣā of Mokṣākaragupta.* Kyoto, Memoirs of the Faculty of Kyoto University, no. 10. Repr. ed. Vienna: Arbeitskreis für Tibetische und Buddhistische Studien, 1998.

Kajiyama, Yūichi, trans. (1967) "Chie no tomoshibi dai 18 shō" (*Prajñāpradīpa* chapter 18) in *Daijō butten (Mahāyāna Buddhist Texts).* Tokyo: Chūōkōronsha.

Kajiyama, Yūichi. (1968–69) "Bhāvaviveka, Sthiramati, and Dharmapāla." *Wiener Zeitschrift für die Kunde Süd- und Ostasiens* 12–13: 193–203.

Kajiyama, Yūichi. (1973) "Three Kinds of Affirmation and Two Kinds of Negation in Buddhist Philosophy." *Wiener Zeitschrift für die Kunde Südasiens* 17: 161–175.

Kajiyama, Yūichi. (1978) "Later Mādhyamikas on Epistemology and Meditation." In M. Kiyota, ed., *Mahāyāna Buddhist Meditation: Theory and Practice.* Honolulu: University of Hawai'i Press: 114–143.

Kamalaśīla. (8th c.) *Madhyamakālaṃkārapañjikā* (MAP). In Ichigō (1985).

Kamalaśīla. (8th c.) *Madhyamakāloka* (MĀ). D dBu ma, vol. *sa,* 133b-244a. D 3887, P 5287.

Kamalaśīla. (8th c.) *Sarvadharmaniḥsvabhāvasiddhi.* D dBu ma, vol. *sa,* 273a-291a. D 3889, P 5289.

Kamalaśīla. (8th c.) *Tattvāloka.* D dBu ma, vol. *sa,* 244b-273a. D 3888.

Kamalaśīla. (8th c.) *Tattvasaṃgrahapañjikā* (TSP). In Shastri (1981).

Kapstein, Matthew. (1988) "Mereological Considerations in Vasubandhu's 'Proof of Idealism.'" *Idealistic Studies* 18/1: 32–54.

Kapstein, Matthew. (1992) *The 'Dzam-thang Edition of the Collected Works of Kun-mkhyen Dol-po-pa Shes-rab rgyal mtshan: Introduction and Catalogue.* Delhi: Shedrup Books.

Katano, Michio, and Tsultrim Kelsang Khangkar. (1998) *Tsong khapa, Chūgan tetsugaku no kenkyū II, Legs bshad snying po, Chūgan shō wayaku (A Study of Tsong khapa's Mādhyamika Philosophy II, Annotated Japanese Translation of the Mādhyamika Section of Essence of the Good Explanations [Legs bśad sñiṅ po]).* Kyoto: Bun'eidō Shoten.

Katsura, Shōryū. (1977) "Inmyō shōrimonron kenkyū (1)" (A Study of the *Nyāyamukha* 1). *Hiroshima Daigaku Bungakubu Kiyō (Bulletin of the Faculty of Letters of Hitoshima University)* 37: 106–126.

Keenan, John P. (1989) "Asaṅga's Understanding of Mādhyamika: Notes on the *Shung-chung-lun.*" *Journal of the International Association of Buddhist Studies* 12/1: 93–107.

Kellner, Birgit. (1997) "Types of Incompatibility *('gal ba)* and Types of Non-cognition *(ma/ mi dmigs pa)* in Early Tibetan *tshad ma*-Literature." In Krasser, *et al.,* eds., vol. 1: 495–510.

Kelly, J. (1992) "Meaning and the Limits of Analysis: Bhartṛhari and the Buddhists, and Post-Structuralism." *Asiatische Studien / Études Asiatiques* 47/1: 171–194.

Kitagawa, Hidenori. (1973) *Indo koten ronrigaku no kenkyū—Jinna (Dignāga) no taikei (Study of Indian Classical Logic—System of Dignāga)*. Tokyo: Suzuki Gakujutsu Zaidan. Repr. Kyoto: Rinsen Shoten, 1985.

Klong chen rab 'byams pa. (1308–1363) *Theg pa chen po'i man ngag gi bstan bcos yid bzhin rin po che'i mdzod* in Sherab Gyaltsen, ed., *The Seven Treasures*, vol 1. Gangtok, 1983.

Klong rdol bla ma ngag dbang blo bzang. (b. 1719) *Theg chen gyi mngon pa'i sde snod las byung ba'i dbu ma'i skor gyi ming rnam grangs (= dBu ming rnam grangs)*. Lokesh Chandra, ed., *The Collected Works of Longdol Lama*. New Delhi: International Academy of Indian Culture, 1973: 408–448.

Krasser, Helmut, Micheal T. Much, Ernst Steinkellner and Helmut Tauscher, eds. (1997) *Tibetan Studies. Proceedings of the 7th Seminar of the International Association for Tibetan Studies, Graz 1995*. 2 vols. Vienna: Verlag der Österreichischen Akademie der Wissenschaften.

Lamotte, Étienne, éd. et trad. (1935) *Saṃdhinirmocanasūtra. L'Explication des Mystères*. Louvain/Paris.

Lamotte, Étienne, trans. (1976) *The Teaching of Vimalakīrti (Vimalakīrtinirdeśa)*. Rendered into English by Sara Boin. Sacred Books of the Buddhists 32. London: Pali Text Society.

Lang, Karen, ed. and trans. (1986) *Āryadeva's Catuḥśataka*. Copenhagen: Akademisk Forlag.

Lang, Karen. (1990) "Spa-tshab Nyi-ma-grags and the Introduction of Prāsaṅgika Madhyamaka into Tibet." In L. Epstein and R. F. Sherburne, eds., *Reflections on Tibetan Culture: Essays in Memory of Turrell V. Wylie*. Studies in Asian Thought and Religion, vol. 12. Lewiston/Queenston/Lampeter: The Edwin Mellen Press, 127–141.

Larson, Gerald James, and Ram Shankar Bhattacharya, eds. (1987) *Sāṃkhya: A Dualist Tradition in Indian Philosophy*. Vol. 4 of *The Encyclopedia of Indian Philosophies*. Princeton: Princeton University Press.

La Vallée Poussin, Louis de, ed. (1903–1913) *Mūlamadhyamakakārikās (Mādhyamikasūtras) de Nāgārjuna avec la Prasannapadā, Commentaire de Candrakīrti*. Bibliotheca Buddhica 4. St. Petersburg: Académie Impériale des Sciences. Repr. ed. Osnabrück: Biblio Verlag, 1970.

La Vallée Poussin, Louis de, ed. (1907–1912) *Madhyamakāvatāra par Candrakīrti, Traduction Tibétaine*. Bibliotheca Buddhica 9. St. Petersburg: Académie Impériale des Sciences. Repr. ed. Osnabrück: Biblio Verlag, 1970.

lCang skya rol pa'i rdo rje. (1717–1786) *Grub pa'i mtha'i rnam par bzhag pa gsal bar bshad pa thub bstan lhun po'i mdzes rgyan (= mDzes rgyan).* Sarnath: The Pleasure of Elegant Sayings Printing Press, 1970. Also published as *Grub mtha' thub bstan lhun po'i mdzes rgyan.* Lhasa: Krung go'i bod kyi shes rig dpe sgrun khang, 1989.

Lewis, Clarence I. (1929) *Mind and the World Order: Outline of a Theory of Knowledge.* 2nd ed. New York: Dover Publications, 1956.

Lindtner, Christian. (1980) "Apropos Dharmakīrti—Two New Works and a New Date." *Acta Orientalia* 41: 27–37.

Lindtner, Christian. (1981) "Atiśa's Introduction to the Two Truths, and Its Sources," *Journal of Indian Philosophy* 9: 161–214.

Lindtner, Christian. (1986) "Bhavya the Logician." *Adyar Library Bulletin* 50: 58–84.

Lindtner, Christian. (1987) *Nāgārjuniana: Studies in the Writings and Philosophy of Nāgārjuna.* Repr. ed. Delhi: Motilal Banarsidass.

Lindtner, Christian. (1993) "Linking up Bhartṛhari and the Bauddhas." *Asiatische Studien / Etudes Asiatiques* 47/1: 195–213.

Lindtner, Christian. (1995) "Bhavya's *Madhyamakahṛdaya (Pariccheda Five) Yogācāratattvaviniścayāvatāra.*" *Adyar Library Bulletin* 59: 37-65.

Lopez, Donald S. (1987) *A Study of Svātantrika.* Ithaca: Snow Lion Publications.

Lopez, Donald S. (1988) "Do *Śrāvakas* Understand Emptiness?" *Journal of Indian Philosophy* 16: 65–105.

MacDonald, Anne. (2000) "The *Prasannapadā:* More Manuscripts from Nepal." *Wiener Zeitschrift für die Kunde Südasiens* 44: 165–181.

Matilal, Bimal Krishna. (1971) *Epistemology, Logic, and Grammar in Indian Philosophical Analysis.* The Hague/Paris: Mouton.

Matilal, Bimal Krishna. (1986) *Perception: An Essay on Classical Indian Theories of Knowledge.* Oxford: Oxford University Press.

Matilal, Bimal Krishna. (1998) *The Character of Logic in India.* J.Ganeri and H. Tiwari, eds. Albany: State University of New York Press.

Matsumoto, Shirō. (1981) "Tsong kha pa no chūgan shisō" ("The Madhyamaka Philosophy of Tsong kha pa"). *Tōyō Gakuhō (The Journal of the Research Department of the Toyo Bunko)* 62/3 and 4: 174–211.

Matsumoto, Shirō. (1986) "Tsong kha pa no jiritsu ronshō hihan" ("Tsong kha pa's Criticism of the Independent Argument *[rang rgyud rjes dpag]*"). In Z. Yamaguchi, ed., *Chibetto no bukkyō to shakai (Buddhism and Society in Tibet).* Tokyo: Shunjūsha, 475–508.

Matsumoto, Shirō. (1997) "Tsong kha pa to rihen chūgan setsu" ("Tsong kha pa and the Theory of Freedom from Extremes as the Middle View"). In Sh. Matsumoto, *Chibetto bukkyō tetsugaku (Tibetan Buddhist Philosophy).* Tokyo: Daizō-shuppan, 321–401.

May, Jacques. (1959) *Candrakīrti Prasannapadā Madhyamakavṛtti.* Douze chapitres traduits du sanscrit et du tibétain, accompagnés d'une introduction, de notes et d'une édition critique de la version tibétaine. Paris: Adrien-Maissonneuve.

McClintock, Sara L. (2002) "Omniscience and the Rhetoric of Reason in the *Tattvasaṃgraha* and the *Tattvasaṃgrahapañjikā.*" Ph.D. dissertation, Harvard University. University Microfilms International, Ann Arbor, Michigan.

McDowell, John. (1998) *Mind and World.* 4th printing. Cambridge: Harvard University Press.

Mi pham. (1846–1912) *dBu ma rgyan rtsa 'grel.* Chengdu: Sichuan People's Press, 1992.

Mi pham. (1846–1912) *Nges shes rin po che sgron me (= Nges shes sgron me)* in Sonam Kazi, ed., *The Collected Works,* vol. 8. Gangtok, 1979.

Mi pham. (1846–1912) *Shes rab tshig don go sla bar rnam par bshad pa nor bu ke ta ka (= Nor bu ke ta ka)* in Sonam Kazi, ed., *The Collected Works,* vol. 13. Gangtok, 1979.

Mimaki, Katsumi. (1976) *La Réfutation bouddhique de la permanence des choses (sthirasiddhidūṣaṇa) et la preuve de la momentanétié des choses (kṣaṇabhaṅgasiddhi).* Paris: Publications de l'institut de civilisation indienne, fasc. 41.

Mimaki, Katsumi. (1977) "Le grub mtha' rnam bzhag rin chen phreng ba de dKon mchog 'jigs med dbang po (1728–1791)." Kyoto: *Zinbun (Memoirs of the Research Institute for Humanistic Studies, Kyoto University)* 14: 55–112.

Mimaki, Katsumi. (1982) *Blo gsal grub mtha': chapitres IX (Vaibhāṣika) et XI (Yogācāra) édités et chapitre XII (Mādhyamika) édité et traduit.* Kyoto: Zinbun Kagaku Kenkyūsho (Institute for Research in Humanities, Kyoto University).

Mimaki, Katsumi. (1994) "Doxographie tibétaine et classificationes indiennes." In F. Fumimasa and G. Fussman, eds., *Bouddhisme et culture locales: Quelques cas de réciproques adaptations.* Actes du colloque franco-japonais de septembre 1991. Paris: Études Thématiques 2: 115–136.

Mitchell, Donald W. (2001) *Buddhism: Introducing the Buddhist Experience.* New York/Oxford: Oxford University Press.

mKhas grub bstan pa dar rgyas. (1493–1568) *dBu ma la 'jug pa'i spyi don dGongs pa rab gsal gyi dgnos pa gsal bar byed pa'i blo gsal sgron me (= Blo gsal gron me).* In lHa-mkhar Yons-'dzin bstan-pa-rgyal mtshan, ed., *The Old and New Obligatory Texts (Yig-cha) for the Study of Madhyamaka of Se-ra smad,* vol. 2: 1–512. New Delhi, 1972.

mKhas grub dge legs dpal bzang. (1385–1438) *Zab mo stong pa nyid kyi de kho na nyid rab tu gsal bar byed pa'i bstan bcos skal bzang mig 'byed (= sTong thun chen mo).* In lHa-mkhar Yoṅs-dzin bStanpa rgyal mtshan, ed., *sTong thun chen mo of mKhas-grub Dge-legs-dpal-bzaṅ and other Texts on Madhyamika Philosophy.* Madhyamaka Text Series 1: 1–512. New Delhi, 1972.

Mookerjee, Satkari and Hojun Nagasaki. (1964) *The Pramāṇavārttika of Dharmakīrti.* Patna: Nava Nālandā Mahāvihāra.

Moriyama, Seitetsu. (1984) "The Yogācāra-Madhyamika Refutation of the Position of the Satyākāra and Alīkākāra-vādins of the Yogācāra School—A Translation of Portions of Haribhadra's *Abhisamayālaṃkārāloka Prajñāpāramitāvyākhyā.*" In *Bukkyō Daigaku Daigakuin Kenkyū Kiyō (Memoirs of the Postgraduate Research Institute, Bukkyō University).* Part I (Mar. 1984): 1–58; part II (Oct. 1984): 1–35; part III (Dec. 1984): 1–28.

Murti, T. R. V. (1960) *The Central Philosophy of Buddhism: A Study of the Mādhyamika System.* London: George Allen & Unwin.

Nāgārjuna. (ca. 2nd c.) *Mūlamadhyamakakārikā* (MMK) in de Jong (1977). Also in La Vallée Poussin (1903–1913).

Nāgārjuna. (ca. 2nd c.) *Vigrahavyāvartanī* (VV) in K. Bhattacharya, trans. / E. H. Johnston and A. Kunst, eds., *The Dialectical Method of Nāgārjuna. Vigrahavyāvartaniḥ.* Delhi: Motilal Banarsidass, 1978. 3rd ed., 1990.

Napper, Elizabeth. (1989) *Dependent Arising and Emptiness.* Boston/London: Wisdom Publications.

Newland, Guy. (1992) *The Two Truths in the Mādhyamika Philosophy of the Ge-luk-ba Order of Tibetan Buddhism.* Ithaca: Snow Lion Publications.

Ngag dbang dpal ldan. (b. 1779) *Grub mtha' bzhi'i lugs kyi kun rdzob dang don dam pa'i don rnam par bshad pa legs bshad dpyid kyi dpal mo'i glu dbyangs (= Grub mtha' legs bshad).* Modern blockprint, n.d.

Ngag dbang dge legs bde mo, ed. (1972–74) *The Collected Works of 'Jam-dbyaṅs-bz'ad-pa'i-rdo-rje.* New Delhi.

Onoda, Shunzō. (1986) "Phya pa Chos kyi seng ge's Classification of Thal 'gyur." *Berliner Indologische Studien* 2: 65–85.

Onoda, Shunzō. (1992) *Monastic Debate in Tibet.* Vienna: Arbeitskreis für Tibetische und Buddhistische Studien.

Oxford English Dictionary. (1971) New York: Oxford University Press.

Pagels, Elaine. (1988) *Adam, Eve, and the Serpent.* New York: Random House.

Pettit, John W. (1999) *Mipham's Beacon of Certainty: Illuminating the View of*

Dzogchen, the Great Perfection. Studies in Indian and Tibetan Buddhism. Boston: Wisdom Publications.

Phya pa chos kyi seng ge. (1109–1169) *dBu ma shar gsum gyi stong thun (= Shar gsum stong thun).* In H. Tauscher, ed., *dBu ma śar gsum gyi stoṅ thun.* Vienna: Arbeitskreis für Tibetische und Buddhistische Studien, Universität Wien, 1999.

Potter, Karl H., ed. (1977) *Indian Metaphysics and Epistemology.* Vol. 2 of *The Encyclopedia of Indian Philosophies.* Princeton: Princeton University Press.

Prajñākaragupta. (8th-9th c.) *Pramāṇavārttikabhāṣya.* In R. Sāṅkṛtyāyana, ed., *Pramāṇavārttikabhāshyam or Vārtikālaṅkāraḥ of Prajñākaragupta.* Patna, 1953.

Prajñākaramati. (8th c.) *Bodhicaryāvatārapañjikā.* In P.L. Vaidya, ed., *Bodhicaryāvatāra of Śāntideva with the Commentary Pañjikā of Prajñākaramati.* Darbhanga: Mithila Institute, 1960.

Price, Henry H. (1932) *Perception.* 2nd ed. (1950). London: Methuen & Co.

Putnam, Hilary. (1994) *Words and Life.* James Conant, ed. Cambridge: Harvard University Press.

Qvarnström, Olle. (1988) "Space and Substance: A Theme in Madhyamaka-Vedānta Polemics." *Journal of the Seminar for Buddhist Studies* 1: 3–34.

Qvarnström, Olle. (1989) *Hindu Philosophy in Buddhist Perspective: The Vedāntatattva-viniścaya Chapter of Bhavya's Madhyamakahṛdayakārikā.* Lund: Plus Ultra.

Randle, H. N. (1930) *Indian Logic in the Early Schools.* London: Oxford University Press.

Red mda' ba gzhon nu blo gros. (1349–1412) *dBu ma la 'jug pa'i rnam bshad de kho no nyid gsal ba'i sgron me (= De kho na nyid gsal sgron).* Varanasi: Sakyapa Students' Union, n.d.

rGyal tshab dar ma rin chen. (1364–1432) *dBu ma'i rtsa ba'i dka' gnas chen po brgyad kyi brjed byang (= dBu rtsa dka' gnas).* In Ngag dbang dge legs bde mo, ed., *The Collected Works (gsuṅ 'bum) of rGyal-tshab Rje Dar-ma Rin-chen,* vol. 1: 312-343. New Delhi, 1980.

Richardson, Hugh, and David Snellgrove. (1968) *A Cultural History of Tibet.* Boston: Shambala Press.

rMa bya byang chub brtson grus seng ge. (?-1185?) *dBu ma rtsa ba shes rab kyi 'grel pa 'thad pa'i rgyan.* Rumtek: Dharma Chakra Center, 1975.

Robinson, Richard H. (1972) "Did Nāgārjuna Really Refute All Philosophical Views?" *Philosophy East and West* 22/3: 325–331.

Roerich, George N. (1949) *The Blue Annals.* Calcutta. Repr. Delhi: Motilal Banarsidass, 1976.

Rong ston shes bya kun rig. (1367–1449) *dBu ma la 'jug pa'i rnam bshad nges don rnam nges (= Nges don rnam nges)* in *Two Controversial Madhyamaka Treatises.* Thimpu, Bhutan: n.d.

Rong ston shes bya kun rig. (1367–1449) *dBu ma rigs pa'i tshogs kyi dka' ba'i gnad bstan pa rigs lam kun gsal (= Rigs lam kun gsal).* Dehra Dun, 1985.

Rong ston shes bya kun rig. (1367–1449) *dBu ma rtsa ba'i rnam bshad zab mo'i de kho na nyid snang ba (= De kho na nyid snang ba).* Sarnath: Sakya Students' Union, 1988.

Rong zom chos kyi bzang po. (11th c.) *Dha rma bha dras mdzad pa'i lta ba'i brjed byang chen mo (= lTa ba'i brjed byang).* In 'Khor-gdoṅ Gter-sprul 'Chi-med-rig-'dzin, ed., *Selected Writings (gsung thor bu) of Roṅ-zom Chos-kyi-bzaṅ-po,* 187–246. Leh: S. W. Tashigangpa, 1974.

Rong zom chos kyi bzang po. (11th c.) *lTa ba dang grub mtha' sna tshogs pa brjed byang du bgyis pa (= Grub mtha' brjed byang).* In 'Khor-gdoṅ Gter-sprul 'Chi-med-rig-'dzin, ed., *Selected Writings (gsung thor bu) of Roṅ-zom Chos-kyi-bzaṅ-po,* 333–414. Leh: S. W. Tashigangpa, 1974.

Rorty, Richard. (1979) *Philosophy and the Mirror of Nature.* Princeton: Princeton University Press. 2nd ed., 1980.

Ruegg, David Seyfort. (1963) "The Jo-nang-pas: A School of Buddhist Ontologists According to the *grub-mtha' sel-gyi me-long.*" *Journal of the American Oriental Society* 8/2: 73–91.

Ruegg, David Seyfort. (1969) *La Théorie du tathāgatagarbha et du gotra.* Paris: Maisonneuve.

Ruegg, David Seyfort. (1977) "The Uses of the Four Positions of the *Catuṣkoṭi* and the Problem of the Description of Reality in Mahāyāna Buddhism." *Journal of Indian Philosophy* 5: 1–71.

Ruegg, David Seyfort. (1980) "On the Reception and Early History of the dBu-ma (Madhyamaka) in Tibet." In M. Aris and A. S. S. Kyi, eds., *Studies in Honour of Hugh Richardson.* Proceedings of the International Seminar on Tibetan Studies, Oxford, 1979. Warminster, England: Aris and Phillips, Ltd.

Ruegg, David Seyfort. (1981) *The Literature of the Madhyamaka School of Philosophy in India.* History of Indian Literature, vol. 7, fasc. 1. J. Gonda, ed. Wiesbaden: Otto Harrassowitz.

Ruegg, David Seyfort. (1982) "Towards a Chronology of the Madhyamaka School." In L.A. Hercus, F. B. J. Kuiper, T. Rajapatirana, and E. R. Skrzypczak, eds., *Indological and Buddhist Studies: Volume in Honor of Professor J. W. de Jong on his Sixtieth Birthday.* Canberra: Faculty of Asian Studies, 505–530.

Ruegg, David Seyfort. (1983) "On the Thesis and Assertion in the Madhyamaka/dBu ma." In E. Steinkellner and H. Tauscher, eds., *Contributions on Tibetan and Buddhist Religion and Philosophy.* Proceedings of the Csoma de Kőrös Symposium Held at Velm-Vienna, Austria, 13–19 September 1981. Vol. 2. Wiener Studien zur Tibetologie und Buddhismuskunde 11. Vienna: Arbeitskreis für Tibetische und Buddhistische Studien, 205–241.

Ruegg, David Seyfort. (1986) "Does the Mādhyamika Have a Thesis and Philosophical Position?" In B.K. Matilal and R. D. Evans, eds., *Buddhist Logic and Epistemology: Studies in the Buddhist Analysis of Inference and Language.* Studies of Classical India 7. Dordrecht: Reidel Publishing, 229–237.

Ruegg, David Seyfort. (1988) "A Kar Ma bKa' brGyud Work on the Lineages and Traditions of the Indo-Tibetan dBu ma (Madhyamaka)." In G. Gnoli, ed., Orientalia Iosephi Tucci memoriae dicata 3: 1254–1271.

Ruegg, David Seyfort. (1990) "On the Authorship of Some Works Ascribed to Bhāvaviveka/Bhavya." In D. S. Ruegg and L. Schmithausen, eds., *Earliest Buddhism and Madhyamaka.* Vol. 2 of Panels of the VIIth World Sanskrit Conference, Kern Institute, Leiden, August 23–29, 1987. J. Bronkhorst, ed. Leiden: E. J. Brill.

Ruegg, David Seyfort. (1991) "On *pramāṇa* Theory in Tsoṅ kha pa's Madhyamaka Philosophy." In E. Steinkellner, ed., *Studies in the Buddhist Epistemological Tradition.* Proceedings of the Second International Dharmakīrti Conference, Vienna, June 11–16, 1989. Vienna: Verlag der Österreichischen Akademie der Wissenschaften, Beiträge zur Kultur- und Geistesgeschichte Asiens 8: 281–310.

Ruegg, David Seyfort. (2000) *Three Studies in the History of Indian and Tibetan Madhyamaka Philosophy.* Studies in Indian and Tibetan Madhyamaka Thought, part 1. Wiener Studien zur Tibetologie und Buddhismuskunde 50. Vienna: Arbeitskreis für Tibetische und Buddhistische Studien.

Russell, Bertrand. (1912) *The Problems of Philosophy.* Repr. 1997. With a New Introduction by John Perry. Oxford: Oxford University Press.

Sa skya paṇḍita kun dga' rgyal mtshan. (1182–1251) *gZhung lugs legs par bshad pa.* In bSod nams rgya mtsho, ed., (1968–69): vol. 5, no. 3.

Sa skya paṇḍita kun dga' rgyal mtshan. (1182–1251) *mKhas pa rnams 'jug pa'i sgo.* In Jackson (1987).

Sa skya paṇḍita kun dga' rgyal mtshan. (1182–1251) *Thub pa'i dgongs pa rab tu gsal ba (= Thub dgongs rab gsal).* In bSod nams rgya mtsho, ed., (1968–69): vol. 5, no. 1.

Saitō, Akira. (1984) "A Study of the *Buddhapālita-mūlamadhyamaka-vṛtti.*" Ph.D. dissertation, Australian National University.

Śāntarakṣita. (8th c.) *Madhyamakālaṃkāra* (MA) and *Madhyamakālaṃkāravṛtti* (MAV). In Ichigō (1985).

Śāntarakṣita. (8th c.) *Tattvasaṃgraha* (TS). In Shastri (1981).

Sāyaṇa Mādhava. (14th c.) *Sarvadarśanasaṃgraha.* In V. S. Abhyankar, ed., *Sarvadarśanasaṃgraha of Sāyaṇa Mādhyava with an Original Commentary in Sanskrit and Exhaustive Indexes.* 3rd ed. Poona: Bhandarkar Oriental Research Institute, 1978.

Schmithausen, Lambert. (1981) "On Some Aspects of Descriptions of Theories of 'Liberating Insight' and 'Enlightenment.'" In K. Bruhn and A. Wezler, eds., *Studien zum Jainismus und Buddhismus: Gedenkschrift für L. Alsdorf.* Wiesbaden: Franz Steiner Verlag.

Schmithausen, Lambert. (2000) "On Three *Yogācārabhūmi* Passages Mentioning the Three *Svabhāva*s and *Lakṣaṇa*s." In J. A. Silk, ed., *Wisdom, Compassion, and the Search for Understanding: The Buddhist Studies Legacy of Gadjin M. Nagao.* Honolulu: University of Hawai'i Press, 245–263.

Schopen, Gregory. (1991) "Archaeology and Protestant Presuppositions in the Study of Indian Buddhism." *History of Religions* 3/1: 1–23.

Se ra rje btsun chos kyi rgyal mtshan. (1469–1546) *Zab mo stong pa nyid kyi lta ba log rtog 'gog par byed pa'i bstan bcos lta ba nga (sic) ngan pa'i mun sel (= lTa ba nga (sic) ngan pa'i mun sel).* Delhi: Champa Chogyal, 1969.

Searle, John R. (1995) *The Construction of Social Reality.* New York: The Free Press.

Sellars, Wilfrid. (1997) *Empiricism and the Philosophy of Mind.* With an Introduction by Richard Rorty and a Study Guide by Robert Brandom. Cambridge: Harvard University Press.

Sells, Michael A. (1994) *Mystical Languages of Unsaying.* Chicago: University of Chicago Press.

Shākya mchog ldan. (1428–1507) *dBu ma'i byung tshul rnam par bshad pa'i gtam yid bzhin lhun po (= dBu ma'i byung tshul).* In Kunzang Tobgey, ed., *The Complete Works (gsuṅ 'bum) of gSer-mdog Paṇ-chen Śākya-mchog-ldan,* vol. 4: 209–248. Thimphu, 1975.

Shākya mchog ldan. (1428–1507) *Theg pa chen po dbu ma rnam par nges pa'i mdzod lung dang rigs pa'i rgya mtsho (= Lung rigs rgya mtsho).* In Kunzang Tobgey, ed., *The Complete Works (gsuṅ 'bum) of gSer-mdog Paṇ-chen Śākya-mchog-ldan,* vol. 14. Thimphu, 1975.

Shākya mchog ldan. (1428–1507) *dBu ma rnam par nges pa'i chos kyi bang mdzod lung dang rigs pa'i rgya mtsho.* In Kunzang Tobgey, ed., *The Complete Works (gsuṅ 'bum) of gSer-mdog Paṇ-chen Śakya-mchog-ldan,* vols. 14–15. Thimphu, 1975.

Shastri, Swami Dwarkidas, ed. (1981) *Tattvasaṃgraha of Ācārya Śāntarakṣita with the Commentary 'Pañjikā' of Śrī Kamalaśīla.* Varanasi: Bauddha Bhāratī Series 1.

Siderits, Mark. (1980–81) "The Madhyamaka Critique of Epistemology." *Journal of Indian Philosophy* 8–9: [80:] 307–335; [81:] 121–160.

Siderits, Mark. (1988) "Nāgārjuna as Anti-realist." *Journal of Indian Philosophy* 16: 311–325.

Siderits, Mark. (1989) "Thinking on Empty: Madhyamaka Anti-realism and Canons of Rationality." In S. Biderman and B. Scharfstein, eds., *Rationality in Question: On Eastern and Western Views of Rationality.* Leiden: E. J. Brill, 231–249.

Sinha, Jadunath. (1956) *A History of Indian Philosophy,* Vol. 1. Calcutta: Sinha Publishing.

sNar thang edition of the Bstan 'gyur. Photocopy of the blockprint in the Royal Library, Copenhagen.

Solomon, Esther A. (1976) *Indian Dialectics: Methods of Philosophical Discussion.* Vol. 1. Sheth Bholabhai Jeshingbhai Institute of Learning and Research, Research Series no. 70. Ahmedabad: B. J. Institute of Learning and Research.

Sopa, Geshe Lhundub, and Jeffrey Hopkins. (1982) *Cutting through Appearances: Practice and Theory of Tibetan Buddhism.* Ithaca: Snow Lion Publications.

Stearns, Cyrus. (1999) *The Buddha from Dolpo: A Study of the Life and Thought of the Tibetan Master Dolpopa Sherab Gyaltsen.* Albany: State University of New York Press.

Steinkellner, Ernst. (1967) *Dharmakīrti's Hetubinduḥ.* 2 vol. Vienna: Verlag der Österreichischen Akademie der Wissenschaften.

Suzuki, D. T., ed. (1955–1961) *The Tibetan Tripiṭaka, Peking Edition.* Reprinted under the supervision of the Otani University, Kyoto, 168 vols. Tokyo and Kyoto: Tibetan Tripiṭaka Research Institute.

Takasaki, Jikidō, Z. Yamaguchi, Y. Ejima, and K. Hayashima, eds. (1977) *Sde Dge Tibetan Tripiṭaka Bstan Ḥgyur, Dbu Ma.* Preserved at the Faculty of Letters, University of Tokyo. Tokyo: Sekai Seiten Kankō Kyōkai.

Tani, Tadashi. (1992) "*Rang rgyud 'phen pa'i thal 'gyur* [Hypothetical Negative/Indirect Reasoning *(prasaṅga)* with the Implication of the Independent Direct Proof *(svatantra)*]." In Ihara and Yamaguchi, eds. (1992): vol. 1: 281–301.

Tanji, Teruyoshi. (1988) *Akirakana kotoba I* (Prasannapadā Madhyamakavṛtti I). Osaka: Kansai University Press.

Tanji, Teruyoshi. (1992) *Jitsuzai to ninshiki. Chūgan shisō kenkyū II (Reality and Cognition. Study of Mādhyamika Philosophy II).* Osaka: Kansai University Press.

Tauscher, Helmut. (1988) "*Paramārtha* as an object of cognition. *Paryāya* and *aparyāyaparamārtha* in Svātantrika-Madhyamaka." In H. Uebach and J. L. Panglung, ed., *Tibetan Studies. Proceedings of the 4th Seminar of the Interna-*

tional Association for Tibetan Studies, Schloß Hohenkammer Munich 1985. Munich: Bayerische Akademie der Wissenschaften, 483–490.

Tauscher, Helmut. (1990) "*Saṃvṛti* bei Tsoṅ kha pa" Part 1. *Wiener Zeitschrift für die Kunde Südasiens* 34: 227–254.

Tauscher, Helmut. (1995) *Die Lehre von den Zwei Wirklichkeiten in Tsoṅ kha pas Madhyamaka-Werken.* Wiener Studien zur Tibetologie und Buddhismuskunde 36. Vienna: Arbeitskreis für Tibetische und Buddhistische Studien.

Tauscher, Helmut. (1999) "Phya Pa Chos Kyi Seng Ge's Opinion on *prasaṅga.*" In Sh. Katsura, ed., *Dharmakīrti's Thought and Its Impact on Indian and Tibetan Philosophy. Proceedings of the Third International Dharmakīrti Conference, Hiroshima, November 4–6, 1997.* Vienna: Verlag der Österreichischen Akademie der Wissenschaften, 387–393.

Thurman, Robert A.F. (1984) *Tsong Khapa's Speech of Gold in the Essence of True Eloquence: Reason and Enlightenment in the Central Philosophy of Tibet.* Princeton: Princeton University Press.

Tillemans, Tom J. F. (1982) "The 'Neither One nor Many' Argument for *Śūnyata* and Its Tibetan Interpretations: Background Information and Source Materials." *Études de Lettres,* University of Lausanne, 3 (July–Sept.), 103–128.

Tillemans, Tom J. F. (1983) "The 'Neither One nor Many' Argument for *Śūnyatā* and Its Tibetan Interpretations." In E. Steinkellner and H. Tauscher, eds., *Contributions on Tibetan and Buddhist Religion and Philosophy.* Wiener Studien zur Tibetologie und Buddhismuskunde 11. Vienna: Arbeitskreis für Tibetische und Buddhistische Studien, 305–320.

Tillemans, Tom J. F. (1984a) "Sur le *parārthānumāna* en logique bouddhique." *Asiatische Studien / Études Asiatiques* 38/2: 73–99.

Tillemans, Tom J. F. (1984b) "Two Tibetan Texts on the 'Neither One Nor Many' Argument for *Śūnyatā.*" *Journal of Indian Philosophy* 12: 357–388.

Tillemans, Tom J. F. (1989a) "Appendix: Supplementary Notes on Tsong kha pa's Position on Opponent-Acknowledged Reasons *(gzhan grags kyi gtan tshigs)* and Similarly Appearing Subjects *(chos can mthun snang ba).*" Unpublished ms.

Tillemans, Tom J. F. (1989b) "Formal and Semantic Aspects of Tibetan Buddhist Debate Logic." *Journal of Indian Philosophy* 17: 265–297.

Tillemans, Tom J. F. (1990) *Materials for the Study of Āryadeva, Dharmapāla and Candrakīrti.* The *Catuḥśataka* of Āryadeva, chapters XII and XIII, with the commentaries of Dharmapāla and Candrakīrti: Introduction, translation, Sanskrit, Tibetan, and Chinese texts, notes. 2 vols. Wiener Studien zur Tibetologie und Buddhismuskunde 24.1 and 24.2. Vienna: Arbeitskreis für Tibetische und Buddhistische Studien.

Tillemans, Tom J. F. (1991) "More on *parārthānumāna*, theses and syllogisms." *Asiatische Studien / Études Asiatiques* 45/1: 133–148.

Tillemans, Tom J. F. (1992) "Tsong kha pa *et al.* on the Bhāvaviveka-Candrakīrti Debate." In Ihara and Yamaguchi, eds., (1992): vol. 1, 315–326.

Tillemans, Tom J. F. (1995) Introductory Remarks to *Asiatische Studien / Études Asiatiques* 49/4: 641–642.

Tillemans, Tom J. F. (1997) "Où va la philologie bouddhique?" *Études et Lettres: Revue de la Faculté des lettres de l'Université de Lausanne.* 1997/4: 3–18.

Tillemans, Tom J. F. (1998) "A Note on *Pramāṇavārttika, Pramāṇasamuccaya* and *Nyāyamukha.* What Is the *Svadharmin* in Buddhist Logic?" *Journal of the International Association of Buddhist Studies* 21/1: 111–124. Repr. in Tillemans (1999).

Tillemans, Tom J. F. (1999) *Scripture, Logic, Language: Essays on Dharmakīrti and His Tibetan Successors.* Studies in Indian and Tibetan Buddhism. Boston: Wisdom Publications.

Tillemans, Tom J. F. (2000) *Dharmakīrti's Pramāṇavārttika: An Annotated Translation of the Fourth Chapter (parārthānumāna).* Vol. 1 (k. 1–148). Österreichische Akademie der Wissenschaften, Philosophisch-Historische Klasse Sitzungberichte, vol. 675. Veröffentlichungen zu den Sprachen und Kulturen Südasiens, vol. 32. Vienna: Verlag der Österreichischen Akademie der Wissenschaften.

Tillemans, Tom J. F., and Donald S. Lopez, Jr. (1998) "What Can One Reasonably Say about Nonexistence? A Tibetan Work on the Problem of *Āśrayāsiddha.*" *Journal of Indian Philosophy* 26: 99–129. Repr. in Tillemans (1999).

Tillemans, Tom J. F., and Tōru Tomabechi. (1995) "Le *dBu ma'i byuṅ tshul* de Śākya mchog ldan." *Asiatische Studien / Études Asiatiques* 49/4: 891–918.

Tsong kha pa blo bzang grags pa. (1357–1419) *dKa' gnas brgyad kyi zin bris.* In *The Collected Works (gSung 'bum) of Rje Tsong-kha-pa Blo-bzang-grags-pa,* vol. *ba.* Delhi: Guru Deva, 1975.

Tsong kha pa blo bzang grags pa. (1357–1419) *Collected Works = Khams gsum chos kyi rgyal po Tsong kha pa chen po'i gsung 'bum.* Tashi lhunpo ed. dGe ldan gsung rab mi nyams rgyun phel series 79–105. Delhi: Ngag dbang dge legs bde mo, 1975–1979.

Tsong kha pa blo bzang grags pa. (1357–1419) *dBu ma la 'jug pa'i rgya cher bshad pa dgongs pa rab gsal = bsTan bcos chen po dbu ma la 'jug pa'i rnam bshad dgongs pa rab gsal = dGongs pa rab gsal.* Sarnath: Pleasure of Elegant Sayings Press, 1973. Also in *Collected Works = Khams gsum chos kyi rgyal po Tsong kha pa chen po'i gsung 'bum.* dGe ldan gsung rab mi nyams rgyun phel series 79–105. Vol. *ma.* Delhi: Ngag dbang dge legs bde mo, 1975–1979. Also in P 6143.

Tsong kha pa blo bzang grags pa. (1357–1419) *dBu ma rgyan gyi zin bris.* See Tillemans (1984b).

Tsong kha pa blo bzang grags pa. (1357–1419) *Drang ba dang nges pa'i don rnam par phye ba'i bstan bcos legs bshad snying po (= Legs bshad snying po).* Palden Drakpa and Damdul Namgyal, eds., Mungod, Karnataka: Drepung Loseling Library Society, 1990/1991. Also in Sarnath: Pleasure of Elegant Sayings Press, 1973. Also in *Collected Works = Khams gsum chos kyi rgyal po Tsong kha pa chen po'i gsung 'bum* (bKra shis lhun po ed.). dGe ldan gsung rab mi nyams rgyun phel series 79–105, vol. *pha:* 478–714. Delhi: Ngag dbang dge legs bde mo, 1975–1979. Also in P 6142.

Tsong kha pa blo bzang grags pa. (1357–1419) *Lam rim chen mo = sKyes bu gsum gyi nyams su blang ba'i rim pa thams cad tshang bar ston pa'i byang chub lam gyi rim pa* in *Collected Works = Khams gsum chos kyi rgyal po Tsong kha pa chen po'i gsung 'bum* (bKra shis lhun po ed.). dGe ldan gsung rab mi nyams rgyun phel series 79–105, vols. 19 and 20. Delhi: Ngag dbang dge legs bde mo, 1975–1979. Also in P 6001.

Tsong kha pa blo bzang grags pa. (1357–1419) *lHag mthong chen mo* in *Tsong kha pa'i gsung dbu ma'i lta ba'i skor.* Vol. 1. Sarnath: Pleasure of Elegant Sayings Press, 1975.

Tsong kha pa blo bzang grags pa. (1357–1419) *rTsa ba shes rab kyi dka' gnas chen po brgyad kyi bshad pa.* Sarnath: Pleasure of Elegant Sayings Press, 1973. Also in *Collected Works = Khams gsum chos kyi rgyal po Tsong kha pa chen po'i gsung 'bum* (bKra shis lhun po ed.). dGe ldan gsung rab mi nyams rgun phel series 79–105, vol. *ba.* Delhi: Ngag dbang dge legs bde mo, 1975–1979.

Tsong kha pa blo bzang grags pa. (1357–1419) *sKyes bu gsum gyi nyams su blang ba'i byang chub lam gyi rim pa (= Lam rim chung ba).* P 6002.

Ui, Hakuju. (1917) *The Vaiśeṣika Philosophy According to the Daśapadārthaśāstra.* Chinese text with introduction, translation, and notes. F. W. Thomas, ed. London: Royal Asiatic Society. Repr., Chowkhamba Sanskrit Studies, vol. 22. Varanasi: Chowkhamba Sanskrit Series Office, 1962.

Vaidya, P. L., ed. (1960) *Madhyamakaśāstra of Nāgārjuna with the Commentary Prasannapadā by Candrakīrti.* Darbhanga: Mithila Institute.

van der Kuijp, Leonard W. J. (1978) "Phya-pa Chos-kyi seng-ge's Impact on Tibetan Epistemological Theory." *Journal of Indian Philosophy* 5: 355–369.

van der Kuijp, Leonard W. J. (1983) *Contributions to the Development of Tibetan Buddhist Epistemology.* Wiesbaden: Franz Steiner Verlag.

Walser, Joseph. (1998) "On the Formal Arguments of the *Akutobhayā.*" *Journal of Indian Philosophy* 26: 189–232.

Wayman, Alex. (1978) *Calming the Mind and Discerning the Real.* New York: Columbia University Press. Repr. Delhi: Motilal Banarsidass, 1979.

Williams, Michael. (1999) *Groundless Belief: An Essay on the Possibility of Epistemology.* 2nd ed. (1st ed.: 1977). Princeton: Princeton University Press.

Williams, Paul W. (1980) "Tsong-kha-pa on *kun-rdzob-bden-pa.*" In M. Aris and A. S. S. Kyi, eds., *Tibetan Studies in Honour of Hugh Richardson.* Warminster, England: Aris and Phillips. 325–334.

Williams, Paul W. (1985) "rMa bya Byang chub brtson 'grus on Madhyamaka Method." *Journal of Indian Philosophy* 13: 205–225.

Williams, Paul W. (1989) *Mahāyāna Buddhism: The Doctrinal Foundations.* London and New York: Routledge Press.

Williams, Paul W. (1995) "Identifying the Object of Negation. On *Bodhicaryāvatāra* 9:140 (Tib. 139)." *Asiatische Studien / Études Asiatiques* 49/4: 969–985.

Williams, Paul W. (1998) *The Reflexive Nature of Awareness: A Tibetan Madhyamaka Defence.* Curzon Critical Studies in Buddhism. Richmond, Surrey: Curzon Press.

Wittgenstein, Ludwig. *Philosophical Investigations.* Trans. G. E. M. Anscombe. Oxford: Basil Blackwell, Ltd. 1st ed. 1953, 3rd ed. with alterations 1967, reprint 3rd ed. unaltered 1989.

Yamaguchi, Susumu. (1974) *Index to the Prasannapadā Madhyamaka-vṛtti.* Parts 1 and 2. Kyoto: Heirakuji Shoten.

Yonezawa, Yoshiyasu. (1999) "**Lakṣaṇaṭīkā,* A Sanskrit Manuscript of an Anonymous Commentary on the *Prasannapadā.*" *Indogaku Bukkyōgaku Kenkyū (Journal of Indian and Buddhist Studies)* 47/2: 1–3.

Yonezawa, Yoshiyasu. (2001a) "Introduction to the Facsimile Edition of a Collection of Sanskrit Palm-Leaf Manuscripts in Tibetan dBu med Script." In Y. Yonezawa et al., *Facsimile Edition of a Collection of Sanskrit Palm-Leaf Manuscripts in Tibetan dBu med Script.* The Institute for Comprehensive Studies of Buddhism, Taishō University, Tokyo.

Yonezawa, Yoshiyasu. (2001b) "Sanskrit Notes on the Madhyamakāvatārabhāṣya Chapter I in the *Lakṣaṇaṭīkā.*" *Indogaku Bukkyōgaku Kenkyū (Journal of Indian and Buddhist Studies)* 49/2: 47–49.

Yoshimizu, Chizuko. (1990) "Tsong kha pa no Nyūchūron chūshaku ni okeru nitai wo meguru giron I sezoku tai wo meguru giron" ("Tsong kha pa's Interpretation of the Two Kinds of Reality in His Commentary on the *Madhyamakāvatāra,* I *saṃvṛtisatya*"). *Naritasan Bukkyō Kenkyūsho Kiyō (Journal of Naritasan Institute for Buddhist Studies)* 13: 105–149.

Yoshimizu, Chizuko. (1992a) "*Rang gi mtshan nyid kyis grub pa* ni tsuite I" ("On *rang gi mtshan nyid kyis grub pa* I"). *Naritasan Bukkyō Kenyūsho Kiyō (Journal of Naritasan Institute for Buddhist Studies)* 15: 609–656.

Yoshimizu, Chizuko. (1992b) "The Distinction between Right and Wrong in the Conventional *(kun rdzob, saṃvṛti)* According to Tsong kha pa and mKhas grub rje." In Ihara and Yamaguchi, eds. (1992): vol. 1: 335–340.

Yoshimizu, Chizuko. (1993a) "The Madhyamaka Theories Regarded as False by the dGe lugs pas." *Wiener Zeitschrift für die Kunde Südasiens* 37: 201–227.

Yoshimizu, Chizuko. (1993b) "*Rang gi mtshan nyid kyis grub pa* ni tsuite II" ("On *rang gi mtshan nyid kyis grub pa* II") in *Indogaku Mikkyōgaku Kenkyū (Indian and Esoteric Buddhist Studies), Essays in Honor of Dr. Y. Miyasaka on His Seventieth Birthday.* Kyoto: Hōzōkan, 971–990.

Yoshimizu, Chizuko. (1993c) "On *raṅ gi mtshan ñid kyis grub pa* III. Introduction and Section I." *Naritasan Bukkyō Kenkyūsho Kiyō (Journal of Naritasan Institute for Buddhist Studies)* 16: 91–147.

Yoshimizu, Chizuko. (1994) "On *raṅ gi mtshan ñid kyis grub pa* III, Section II and III." *Naritasan Bukkyō Kenkyūsho Kiyō (Journal of Naritasan Institute for Buddhist Studies)* 17: 295–354.

Yoshimizu, Chizuko. (1996) *Die Erkenntnislehre des Prāsaṅgika-Madhyamaka nach dem Tshig gsal stoṅ thun gyi tshad ma'i rnam bśad des 'Jam dbyaṅs bźad pa'i rdo rje.* Vienna: Arbeitskreis für Tibetische und Buddhistische Studien.

Yotsuya, Kōdō. (1992) "An Introduction to the 'Svatantra-reasoning.'" *Sōtōshū Kenkūyin Kenkyū Kiyō (Journal of Sōtō Shū Research Fellows, Sōtōshū Shūmusho)* 22: 1–28.

Yotsuya, Kōdō. (1999) *The Critique of Svatantra Reasoning by Candrakīrti and Tsong kha pa. A Study of Philosophical Proof According to Two Prāsaṅgika Madhyamaka Traditions of India and Tibet.* Stuttgart: Franz Steiner Verlag.

Index

A Note on Technical Terms

Contributors to this volume employ a range of translations for technical terms from Sanskrit and Tibetan. All translations for technical terms are therefore cross-referenced to a single entry under Sanskrit or Tibetan, depending on the origin or standard usage of the term. For example, the entry under "inference" refers the reader to *anumāna,* where all passages that discuss inference are referenced. This system not only allows references to be grouped under a single entry, it also makes readers aware of the various translations for single terms. When subentries under main entries involve technical terms, those terms generally will be listed only in either Sanskrit or Tibetan if they have their own main entry. For example, under the main entry "Bhāvaviveka," all entries for "autonomous argument" are listed only as *svatantraprayoga,* since a main entry also exists under *svatantraprayoga.* To determine the various English translations for *svatantraprayoga,* one would consult its main entry.

A Note on Authors of Sanskrit and Tibetan Texts

In some cases, a contributor may cite a text in Sanskrit or Tibetan without referring explicitly to the author by name. In such cases, the entry will appear italicized under an author's name. For example, under the author Āryadeva, the italicized entry *99* refers to the *Catuḥśataka,* which is cited without mention of its author.

About the Authors

WILLIAM L. AMES is an independent scholar as well as a librarian at John F. Kennedy University in Orinda, California. His publications include translations of the first seven chapters of Bhāvaviveka's *Prajñāpradīpa,* with more to follow.

JOSÉ IGNACIO CABEZÓN is the Fourteenth Dalai Lama Professor of Tibetan Buddhism and Cultural Studies in the Religious Studies Department of at the University of California, Santa Barbara. He has translated mKhas grub rje's *sTong thun chen mo* in *A Dose of Emptiness* (1992), he is the author of *Buddhism and Language: A Study of Indo-Tibetan Scholasticism* (1994), and he has authored many articles in the field of Madhyamaka studies.

GEORGES B. J. DREYFUS trained for fifteen years in Tibetan monasteries, where he received the highest honor, the title of the Geshe Lharampa. He is presently Professor of Religion at Williams College, and is the author of *Recognizing Reality: Dharmakīrti's Philosophy and Its Tibetan Interpretations* (1997) and *The Sound of Two Hands Clapping: The Education of a Tibetan Buddhist Monk* (2002).

MALCOLM DAVID ECKEL is NEH Distinguished Teaching Professor of the Humanities at Boston University. His publications include *Jñānagarbha's Commentary on the Distinction Between the Two Truths* (1987) and *To See the Buddha: A Philosopher's Quest for the Meaning of Emptiness* (1992). He is also the editor of *India and The West: The Problem of Understanding* and *Selected Essays of J. L. Mehta.*

C. W. Huntington, Jr. is Associate Professor of Religious Studies at Hartwick College in Oneonta, NY. He is the author of *The Emptiness of Emptiness: An Introduction to Early Indian Mādhyamika* (1989) and a variety of articles on early Indian Madhyamaka.

Sara L. McClintock is a lecturer in the Department of Languages and Cultures of Asia at the University of Wisconsin, Madison. She recently completed her doctoral dissertation at Harvard University, entitled *Omniscience and the Rhetoric of Reason in the Tattvasaṃgraha and the Tattvasaṃgrahapañjikā* (2002).

Helmut Tauscher is a research scholar at the Institute for South Asian, Tibetan and Buddhist Studies in the Department of Tibetan and Buddhist Studies at Vienna University. He is a life-member of the Drepung Loseling Library Society in Mundgod, Karnataka, India and since 1991 has been engaged in a research project entitled "Western Tibetan Manuscripts, 11–14 c." He is the author of numerous articles and book-length works on Madhyamaka, including *Die Lehre von den Zwei Wirklichkeiten in Tsoṅ kha pas Madhyamaka-Werken* (1995) and an edition of Phya pa chos kyi seng ge's *dBu ma shar gsum gyi stong thun* (1999).

Tom J. F. Tillemans is professor of Buddhist Studies at the University of Lausanne in Switzerland. His publications on Madhyamaka philosophy include numerous articles and a two-volume work entitled *Materials for the Study of Āryadeva, Dharmapāla and Candrakīrti* (1990).

Chizuko Yoshimizu studied philosophy, Indology, Tibetology, and Buddhism in Tokyo and Vienna, and has been a research scholar and lecturer at several universities in Europe and Japan. In addition to various articles, she has published a book entitled *Die Erkenntnislehre des Prāsaṅgika-Madhyamaka nach dem Tshig gsal stoṅ thun gyi tshad ma'i rnam bśad des 'Jam dbyaṅs bźad pa'i rdo rje* (1996).

Studies in Indian and Tibetan Buddhism

THIS SERIES WAS CONCEIVED to provide a forum for publishing outstanding new contributions to scholarship on Indian and Tibetan Buddhism and also to make accessible seminal research not widely known outside a narrow specialist audience, including translations of appropriate monographs and collections of articles from other languages. The series strives to shed light on the Indic Buddhist traditions by exposing them to historical-critical inquiry, illuminating through contextualization and analysis these traditions' unique heritage and the significance of their contribution to the world's religious and philosophical achievements. We are pleased to make available to scholars and the intellectually curious some of the best contemporary research in the Indian and Tibetan traditions.

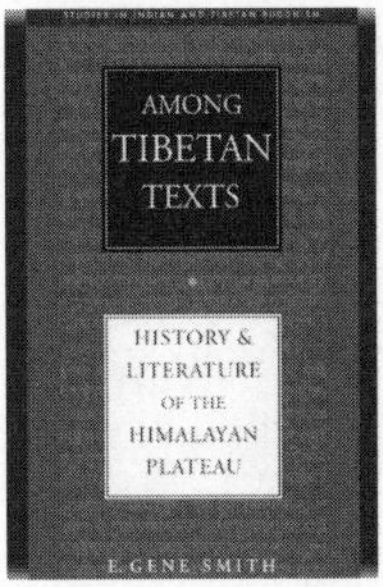

AMONG TIBETAN TEXTS
History and Literature of the Himalayan Plateau
E. Gene Smith
384 pages, 0-86171-179-3, cloth, $39.95

For three decades, E. Gene Smith ran the Tibetan Text Publication Project of the United States Public Law 480 (PL480)—an effort to salvage and reprint disappearing Tibetan literary works. In order to help clarify and contextualize these reprinted books, Smith wrote prefaces that quickly achieved an almost cult status. These legendary essays are collected here for the first time.

"Gene Smith opened more doors to Tibetan Buddhism than any scholar of the twentieth century. These essays are the keys." —Donald Lopez, University of Michigan, author of *Prisoners of Shangri-La: Tibetan Buddhism and the West*

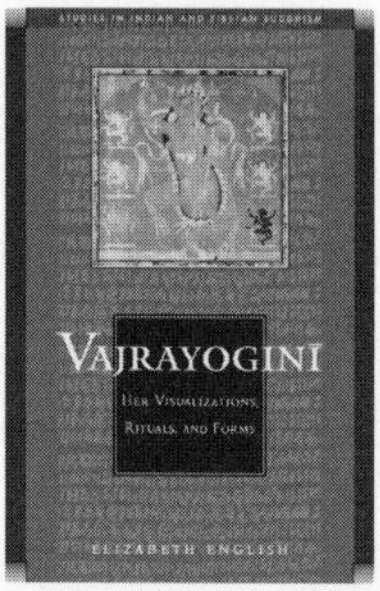

Vajrayoginī
Her Visualizations, Rituals, and Forms
Elizabeth English
598 pages, 0-86171-329-X, paper, $34.95

This in-depth look at the highest yoga tantra goddess includes a never-before-translated key text, the *Vajravārāhī Sādhana*, with commentaries, and a deluxe color section.

"A meticulously researched treasure trove for the scholar as well as the serious practitioner." —Judith Simmer-Brown, Naropa University, author of *Dakini's Warm Breath: The Feminine Principle in Tibetan Buddhism*

"A major landmark in the study of tantric Buddhism." —Geoffrey Samuel, University of Newcastle, author of *Civilized Shamans: Buddhism in Tibetan Societies*

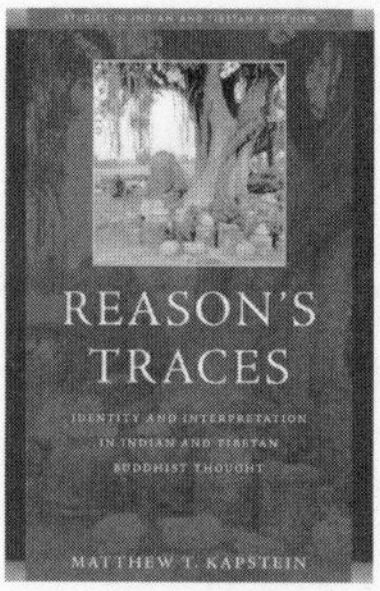

Reason's Traces
Identity and Interpretation in Indian and Tibetan Buddhist Thought
Matthew T. Kapstein
480 pages, 0-86171-239-0, paper, $34.95

"Kapstein brings his unmatched scholarly skills to bear in this set of linked essays that together explore with great precision, insight, and masterful scholarship a range of important issues in Indian and Tibetan philosophy, drawing on Western philosophical ideas, texts, and techniques where appropriate, and shedding light not only on these philosophical traditions and the problems they address, but also on the study of Buddhist philosophy itself, and the place of this project within philosophy as a whole." —Jay L. Garfield, Professor of Philosophy, Smith College

"Kapstein has given us a key to a deeper appreciation of reason as a valid tool for exploring reality." —Piet Hut, Professor of Astrophysics, Institute for Advanced Study, Princeton, NJ

MIPHAM'S BEACON OF CERTAINTY
Illuminating the View of Dzogchen, the Great Perfection
John Whitney Pettit
592 pages, 0-86171-157-2, paper, $28.95

"Dr. Pettit's perceptive exploration will be much appreciated by all serious readers in Buddhist studies and the Philosophy of Religion." —Matthew Kapstein, University of Chicago, author of *Reason's Traces*

"A thorough and clear study. A great source of understanding and inspiration." —Tulku Thondup Rinpoche, author of *Hidden Teachings of Tibet*

"A riveting and wonderful work." —Anne C. Klein, Rice University, author of *Meeting the Great Bliss Queen*

About Wisdom Publications

Wisdom Publications, a not-for-profit publisher, is dedicated to making available authentic Buddhist works. We publish translations of the sutras and tantras, commentaries and teachings of past and contemporary Buddhist masters, and original works by the world's leading Buddhist scholars. We publish our titles with the appreciation of Buddhism as a living philosophy and with the special commitment to preserve and transmit important works from all the major Buddhist traditions.

To learn more about Wisdom, or to browse books online, visit our website at wisdompubs.org.

You may request a copy of our mail-order catalog online or by writing to:

Wisdom Publications
199 Elm Street
Somerville, Massachusetts 02144 USA
Telephone: (617) 776-7416 • Fax: (617) 776-7841
Email: info@wisdompubs.org • www.wisdompubs.org

Wisdom Publications is a non-profit, charitable 501(c)(3) organization affilated with the Foundation for the Preservation of the Mahayana Tradition (FPMT).